# An Amazing Human Journey:

## Remembering from the Subconscious Mind

## Volume One

## SHAKUNTALA MODI, M.D.

Strategic Book Publishing and Rights Co.

Strategic Book Publishing and Rights Co.
12620 FM 1960, Suite A4-507
Houston TX 77065

www.sbpra.com

For information about special discounts for bulk purchases, please
contact Strategic Book Publishing and Rights Co. Special Sales, at
bookorder@sbpra.net.

ISBN: 978-1-61204-402-6

Design: Dedicated Book Services, (www.netdbs.com)

Humanity has an exciting potential. Out of the thousands of races in the galaxy, only few races in the universe are like ours, because of the fact that we have a unique emotional, intellectual and spiritual component in such proportion that if we develop spiritually, through the spiritual practices and power of positive thoughts and emotions, the spiritual field around us can be quite intense. If we can return to the original plan of spiritual merging and passing on our learned knowledge to the new incoming souls, making each individual of the race so much more developed due to whatever their ancestors had developed, the tides will sweep the planet and we will develop spiritually at the phenomenal rate. As we develop, those around us will develop and as more and more humans develop, the spiritual field around our planet will develop which can spread out from our planet to another and to another planet, and thus sweep the whole galaxy and the universe to God. Satan also realizes our potential and he puts extra efforts to keep us from developing but God is giving an equal and appropriate response by sending the extra masters and teachers to get our race moving, so that we can move all of the galaxies, universes and all of the creation back to God sooner. The desire for spiritual merging is built in the human race and it is possible for us to get back to the original plan of spiritual merging and become the most influential race in the galaxy.

Other books by Shakuntala Modi, M.D.

*Remarkable Healings: A Psychiatrist Discovers
Unsuspected Roots of Mental and Physical Illness*

*Memories of God and Creation: Remembering from
the Subconscious Mind*

*Prayers for Healing and Protection: A Gift From God*

# Dedication

*I humbly dedicate this book to God, and the whole of humanity*

# Acknowledgments

First, I acknowledge all my patients, through whom I was privileged to receive this amazing information. Their willingness to share this awesome knowledge is greatly appreciated

I am also thankful to Yvonne K. May and Barbara Hamric for the hours of typing and retyping. They are God-sent help for me.

Ultimately, I humbly acknowledge God, all the heavenly masters, archangels, angels, heavenly guides, my higher self, inner self, and all the other heavenly beings for their enthusiastic and consistent participation, assistance, education, guidance, protection, and the gift of this book. As always, I am eternally grateful for this amazing privilege and all the blessings.

# TABLE OF CONTENTS
## Volume One

# Introduction

I am a board certified psychiatrist, and have been practicing for about thirty-five years. I had hypnotherapy training in my residency and have used it successfully in my practice. Over the past twenty-five years, many of my patients have recalled past life traumas as a source of their physical, emotional, mental, spiritual, or relationship problems. After recalling, reliving, releasing, and resolving the traumas and issues from one or more past lives, patients were relieved of their symptoms.

Some patients under hypnosis described having human and demon spirits in their bodies and auras, causing them different physical, emotional, mental, spiritual, and relationship problems. After releasing these spirits from the patients, their symptoms were improved or completely relieved. Other patients described that their soul fragmented during different traumas, creating different symptoms for them. After resolving the trauma and retrieving the missing soul parts and integrating them back with the patients, they were healed.

After receiving similar information from a cross-section of my patients for many years, I felt compelled to write about this mind-bending knowledge. My first book, *Remarkable Healings*, was the result.

My patients, under hypnosis, also provided amazing information, resulting in my second book, *Memories of God and Creation*. It answers almost everything we always wanted to know about God and creation, such as who we are, why we are here, why are we going through these cycles of birth and death, and the whole history of creation and our soul.

During the sessions, while releasing human and demon sprits, patients often describe angels and other heavenly beings present to help us. These heavenly helpers also provided valuable information about these human and demon spirits, such as who they are, how they affected the patients, what I need to do to heal the patient, and what we all can do to heal and protect ourselves from these spirits. This was the subject of my third book, *Prayers for Healing and Protection*.

Over the years during the course of my work, some patients recalled that their first incarnation on Earth was in an ape body that would not be recognized as human, although they were definitely human because they had a human soul. They described what their purpose was during that first incarnation and how their divine plan derailed because of Satanic influences and how it slowed down human evolution.

Other patients under hypnosis recalled that many alien races interacted with the ape-like humans and did genetic modifications on them, bringing about evolutionary changes in humankind. Many of the apparent mysteries of anthropology and archeology concerning the appearance of humans in certain parts of the world are actually due to alien intervention. They moved a selected population from one place to another to isolate and see exactly what effects their genetic changes had on the population before permitting that change to spread through the entire population.

I was also surprised when many of my patients recalled living a life or lives in Atlantis and Lamuria, thousands of years ago, as a source of their problems for which they were seeking help. I had no knowledge about Atlantis and Lamuria before this. Patients often gave detailed accounts of lifestyles, culture, and the society they lived in. Some patients remembered being contacted by the aliens in Atlantis who gave them technology, or they remembered being given spiritual knowledge by the aliens in Lamuria. Some patients recalled being incarnated on different planets, while others remembered being abducted by the aliens, and the trauma of those experiences led to different symptoms for which they were seeking help.

So I began to inquire from the heavenly beings through my hypnotized patients about what my patients had revealed under hypnosis. They confirmed most of the information and also added information about the astounding past and future of humankind. This is the subject of this book, *An Amazing Human Journey*. This book is a compilation of information given by my hypnotized patients and by different heavenly beings through them. It is supported by a number of case histories, necessary to illustrate the consistency and derivation of the information, especially in this latest book, where the information is new knowledge, to some extent, regarding Atlantis, Lamuria, and aliens. The case histories are of critical importance, making it very clear that the information comes directly from the hypnotized patients with no editorializing on my part.

I realize there are gaps and disjunctions in the information. I can only publish information I get from my patients, and if I have only partial information on a topic, it is presented that way in the book. I have asked for clarifying details from heavenly beings when possible and it was appropriate for the medical treatment, but where it was not given, I did not make it up. The information is not one hundred percent complete because the information comes from patients who are seeking psychiatric and medical help. To detail the background of Atlantis or Lamuria is not the purpose of the writing. I have accomplished what is necessary while noting the interesting details of the circumstances. Always, the medical treatment was the important part, and the information that comes extraneous to that is fascinating but not the main purpose during treatment.

A word about terminology is important before we proceed. As in my other books, I use the word *Light* synonymously for God, heaven, and the Light that comes from heaven. The letter L in the word Light is capitalized to differentiate it from earthly light, and also because patients describe God and heaven as just pure white Light. I have addressed God as *He* or *It* because those are the ways my patients have addressed Him.

The information in this, as in my other books, is in no way a reflection of my own personal or religious beliefs, but is based solely on what hundreds of my patients have consistently reported under hypnosis. Their words may differ, the expression may vary, but the basic information is woven of common threads into the same essential themes.

# Chapter 1

## ORIGINAL PLAN FOR HUMANS

Here you will read about the incarnation of the first human couples, the so-called Adam and Eve, how they were selected to be the first couple in heaven, how they incarnated on Earth, what was their plan for spiritual development, and how it got derailed due to Satanic influences. To properly comprehend all this, we have to first understand the history and purpose of creation and the plan for development of individual souls and of God.

### History and Purpose of Creation

As described in my second book, *Memories of God and Creation*, my hypnotized patients state that God before creation was a ball of Light and had a black void all around It. There was no creation, only that ball of God. Inside God, there were little swirls or balls of energy that were individual consciousnesses that went into the making of the whole God, and all of them together were God. At this time, they described feeling pure love, peace, harmony, and content. There were no negative feelings. At some point, God, along with these little consciousnesses, came to the conclusion together that they should create. My patients, under hypnosis, recalled many reasons why God decided to create. They were as follows:

1. My hypnotized patients claimed that at some point, as God, the individual consciousnesses were beginning to feel lonely and empty, as if something was missing, but they did not know what. So I asked them to go back

1

in time to determine what had changed to create those feelings. What they recalled was that over millions of years, as the ball of God was growing and expanding, its vibrations became faster and its energy moved faster. As a result, pieces of God's energy began to splash out of the ball and then fall back into the ball of God again. However, as the ball of God began to spin even faster, the parts of God that were thrown out randomly were getting lost in the void, without any intent or control.

As a result, God and all Its parts began to experience loneliness, emptiness, and sadness. Some consciousnesses began to feel anxiety and fear, because they did not want to disappear in the void. When God as a whole became aware of losing parts in the void, a decision to create was made by every part of God. Some patients said the idea originated in the core of the big ball of God and spread instantly to all parts of God telepathically, while other patients said they did not know where the idea originated. It seems that all parts of God collectively decided to create by properly and purposefully releasing the ever-growing energy so that it did not disperse chaotically.

Also, over the course of billions of years, the energy of God built up inside the globe and there came a point when God, as a whole, knew that in order for the energy to grow, something had to go. As a consequence, God decided to let some energy out with protection. This way, the energy of God, released with protective shields, would continue to grow and expand, so that in time, God could spread out through the whole void and cover it in such a way that pieces of God would not be lost in the empty space.

2. People under hypnosis recalled that as different pieces of God began to break off and were thrown off into the empty void, the process created fear and anxiety in different parts of God; these parts began to vibrate

and grow at different rates. Before this, all the balls or pieces were of the same size, vibration, color, and brilliance. They were all white.

After a while, God realized that every consciousness in it was growing into a different size, color, and brilliance, and was no longer the same. Some parts were better developed than others. They all had the same powers, but not to the same degree. So, God desired to create, so that every part could grow to be equal in size and power and could evolve to perfection and have all the knowledge and awareness.

3.  Some patients recalled that it was very still, calm, and tight in the core of God. They felt wrapped up tightly in the core. As they moved away from the core, they shed some of this wrapping and calmness. Away from the core of God, they felt a little bit freer. The wavelengths were narrow near the core and wide toward the periphery, since God was not the same all over. It chose to create to achieve perfection and equilibrium.

4.  Other reasons for the creation surfaced in time after the decision to create was made. For one, when God as a whole began to lose pieces of Itself, It began to experience loneliness. The basic nature of God is love, which is ever expanding and growing. God wanted to experience its most wonderful attribute of love through the creation. It wanted to create partners to communicate and help one another grow through love. Love cannot be contained and must be experienced in various ways.

5.  Other reasons to create emerged later, after Lucifer and his rebellious followers left the globe of God. God wanted to send parts of Itself out to help bring back Lucifer and his followers, giving them another chance to return "Home." Without them God cannot be whole.

My hypnotized patients state that as different pieces of God began to break off and were thrown out into the void, it created anxiety and fear in different parts of God. They all began to vibrate and grow at different rates and display different colors and brilliance, whereas before, they had been all of the same size and color. Some people said that as all of the parts of God began to vibrate and grow, there was a kind of malfunctioning in one ball that, over time, became gray and black. Patients recognized this as Lucifer's ball. Then Lucifer began to influence other balls in God that were not in support of creation. After a while, these parts of God also began to change into gray and black balls. This happened in only a small part of the globe of God and not all over, according to my patients.

When the decision to create was made in the ball of God, most parts of God were in favor of the creation. Then, in descending scale, there were those who agreed to it but did not really want to, and those who were negative about the idea, until we came to a black ball called Lucifer and his followers, who were absolutely opposed to the idea.

According to the hypnotized subjects, Lucifer took with him as many parts as he could. As these little balls passed through the wall or the outer edge of the ball of God, they became the *demons*. They became the individual souls that were discrete, dark, and separate from the Light. They had gone through their own *forgetting* and did not remember where they came from or why. They were not created as angels, as some people believe, and they did not take any part in the creation. After they went outside the wall of God, Lucifer educated them, feeding them information or misinformation in his way. He told them he had created them, that they were his property and the Light (God) was their enemy. They should stay away from the Light because it would consume and kill them. He set up his whole scheme for fighting the Light—The God.

People under hypnosis stated that God did not begin to create until Lucifer and his followers left because He did not want them to influence His creation. So Satan and his demons were not created as angels and did not take any part in creation. After Lucifer and his demons left, God created masters and angels. He created them first so they could protect the universes and other beings from Lucifer and his demons. Then the universes and other dimensions were created; Dimensions ranging from those that are just energy areas to those that are almost entirely matter. The one we are in is the intermediary; part matter and part energy. Lucifer took his demons away to a dimension that had the lowest vibrations, far way from the globe of God, because they could not tolerate the higher vibrations near God. This dimension is known now as *hell*.

After the initial creation of all the universes was finished, God created the things to go into the universes, such as inanimate objects, plants, animals, and ending with the creation of the individual souls of the intelligent beings (humans and other souls for other planets) that would do most of the developmental work in the universe. As they go through their individual development, they will be developing that portion of God.

My hypnotized patients say that, after the creation of masters, angels, universes, plants, and animals, God began to create the intelligent or rational beings, that is, humans and other beings, to inhabit Earth and other planets. These beings would be responsible for most of the growth of God. Through incarnating again and again, they will learn and grow, and as they grow, God will grow. God wanted to create intelligent beings that would look different. They were to have more soul knowledge and superior communication skills and more wisdom. They would have a purpose, which would include the expression of free will, which is needed for spiritual growth. They would also procreate.

In creating human beings and beings for other planets, God took different things into consideration, such as function, beauty, the capability to adapt and survive in the environment they would be in, and the ability to communicate. He developed their forms according to the different universes souls would inhabit. He gave them denser bodies so they could function on the planet to which they would be sent. God gave them power to think and make decisions. God also created a silver connecting cord linking Him with all the souls, so He does not lose touch with them and they can have constant communication with Him when they are on a planet. Through the silver connecting cords, souls can travel to Heaven from the planet they live on, both while they are alive and after death. The souls' connection with God is eternal, and they will never be separated from God.

So, the proper order of the creation is: masters, angels, universes, inanimate objects, plants, animals, and the souls of intelligent beings, such as humans and beings for other planets.

Under hypnosis, my patients recalled that after the creation of their souls, they forgot almost everything about their existence before their creation. They forgot that they were one with God and what had happened before their creation. They call this "the first forgetting." Then after each subsequent incarnation, they forgot almost everything about their previous lifetimes. They called this "the second forgetting." After the creation, they report God spoke to every soul about their purpose and gifts. Then they were released to their respective godheads.

According to my hypnotized subjects, God created souls in groups that came into existence in long strings. As the souls were released into their respective godheads, there were differences between them, depending on how they *felt* about their creation. Some of them came out, drifted, and floated to the upper layers, while others went down a certain distance and stopped, and some went further down. Some of them seemed to sink to the bottom layers. As a result, there was a stratification of souls.

Under hypnosis, people recall that as the individual souls were created, they experienced a variety of feelings. Some felt fear, confusion, rejection, separation anxiety, and a belief that something had gone wrong. They felt they had done something bad and were being punished, but did not know why. They did not remember how things were before their creation and did not understand the creation process. They saw it as a negative, scary, upsetting, and traumatic event. These especially troubled souls got so self-involved that they contracted and folded in on themselves. If the godhead is divided into three layers, then these souls settled at the bottom layer.

Other souls also did not remember what happened but did not go through the agony described above. They seemed to be more positive and felt elation, even exaltation, as if saying, "I am separate, I am free, and I am ready to begin the work." Of course, at this instant, the soul did not know what it was talking about. It had the feeling but not the exact knowledge, because it had just undergone its "first forgetting." It did not remember that it is part of God, nor did it remember it made the decision to create with the rest of God, or that there was a plan. All it remembered was that it suddenly emerged into separate existence. These joyful souls remained on the top, or inner, layer of the godhead, near the core of God. They were expressive and outgoing, and they spread the Light everywhere.

The middle layer souls were happy but not joyful. They were a little dazed and confused. They spread some Light, but they were not sure what was happening. As we go down the layers, the souls were more inward, more confused, less giving of their Light, until at the bottom layer, all the Light of the souls was turned inward. They were folded in on themselves, self-conscious, and concerned with their survival. They had a misunderstanding of what had happened, along the lines of, "I have done something wrong. I am being punished. I have to be really careful. I cannot express myself. I cannot be outgoing. I cannot spread my Light outside."

The surprising thing was that when souls were created, even God did not know which would sink and which would rise. He had an idea how it would go, but He was not sure. So, as He created them, He watched what happened. Where the souls went did not depend on their size but on their feelings. Some of the larger souls sank down to the bottom because they were scared and confused, while some of the smaller souls floated to the top layers of the godhead because they felt joyful, happy, and excited after their creation.

So, when the souls were released to the godheads after their creation, they stratified themselves into layers, depending on how they felt about their creation. There are many, many layers of souls in the Light. But for practical purposes, we can say there are three main layers in a godhead, and each layer can be subdivided into literally hundreds of layers.

According to my hypnotized patients, after the creation of souls, God spoke to souls at every level, but He did not say the same thing to each level. For the bottom group, He gave a straightforward message, leaving little chance for confusion. "Pray, study, and try to develop spiritually." His message for the groups higher in the layering increasingly became more complex and more subtle.

For the top group, God's message was, in effect, "Remember to pray. You have access to my power through prayer, through your silver connecting cord to me. You can channel the Light through yourself and use it in your life. The dark beings, the demons, will have a difficult time trapping or confusing anyone who is filled with the Light. You have the ability to go beyond that which is normal by using the powers of the Light. While living on a planet, you can develop these powers through understanding and diligent practice. Love, compassion, sensitivity to the needs of others, fulfilling the needs of yourself and of others; these gifts you can take with you as you incarnate. They can also be acquired in any individual life if you do not bring them as gifts. In fact, much stronger spiritual development results if you develop them during a lifetime."

God also mentioned the possibility of souls developing into God-like beings. "If you live your human life well, you could develop into a God-like being," he said.

After the creation of souls, God told those in the top two or three layers to form groups. He told the next three or four layers, "Soon you will develop and join a group," to prepare them for the idea of developing and joining a group.

According to my hypnotized patients, God did not assign individual souls to a particular group, nor did He specify a group's purpose. He simply told them they were to form a group for spiritual development. He outlined the plan for the groups' development, for how the groups would work in the Light together, and how the souls within a group would co-operate on a planet. He told the souls to set up the main objectives, to pick out the steps, and to work within the group to achieve those goals.

When a soul determined what it was most interested in or needed to do, it broadcast a signal, and other souls that were reaching the same conclusion were receptive to that broadcast. They got together and went about creating groups, attracting others to the same location. They could be from different god-heads. All they had to be was an individually created soul.

Some of the groups that exist are: psychological, scientific, healing, religious, cultural, nutritional, educational, political, artistic, and humanistic. Different groups have different approaches to the spiritual development of human souls. Many groups work in each field, in Heaven and on Earth and on other planets, all with the same basic interests—that of cultivating a complete and thoroughly developed soul.

Satan and his demons did not take part in the creation, although they knew about it. They had all the powers of God among themselves, except they could not top God. These negative parts of God who are called Satan and his demons by my patients, set up their headquarters away from the globe of God in the dimension of the lowest vibrations, known as Hell, and set out to defeat God's plan. In fact, they planned to influence the positive parts of God to become part of the negative and work with them and take over the whole universe and all of God. Happily, this is not happening.

## Plan for the Development of God

The initial part of the plan of God was the creation of the universe and the individual souls and the refinement and the development of the individual parts of God, that is, the individual souls. After the universe was created, God created and separated individual souls apart from himself, so each individual soul in fact is a part of the substance of God, and all parts of the universe are actually the extension and expression of God. Then souls enter the universe in a body and play out their parts on the stage of the planets in the universe that God has created and the scenes are brought into existence.

As the universe came into existence and the process was going on, the individual souls who were going to play the major role in development of God were incarnated into the universe. As these first souls were infused into a body, Satan was there, trying to influence and prevent them from carrying out God's plan. There were a few planets where Satan did not succeed at all because their vibrations were very high and Satan and his demons could not tolerate the higher frequencies and could not get close to those planets. There are other planets where they have succeeded in greater or lesser degrees. The only universe in which Satan has succeeded in full scale in perverting is his own universe, which we call Hell, which has the lowest vibrations. Satan's followers, that is, the demons under his influence, have also totally rejected God's plan.

Very few races on different planets in the universe are carrying out God's plan fully. They are mostly the higher planets with higher vibrations. Then there are races who are carrying out less and less of God's plan and are more and more influenced by Satan. Intelligent beings everywhere in the universe, each have their own plan of carrying out God's purpose. When Satan succeeded in perverting the plan in different planets, it slowed down the development and perfection of the universe and thus the perfection of God.

According to heavenly beings, eventually the forces of good will win and the souls in the universe will realize completely that they are a part of God and can have full access to all the powers and knowledge of God. The field around them will spread, and more and more souls will come to enlightenment. When the whole creation comes to this realization and enlightenment, we no longer will need the universe. The universe will be taken down as if it was a stage and even Satan and his demons will be converted into the Light by the energy force field around every one else, and we all will be able to go back *home* to God and be one with Him. The whole creation will be de-created.

## Planning for the First Incarnation

Heavenly beings, through my hypnotized patients, state that about 3 ½ million years ago, human souls were first infused into the preformed bodies on the Earth. The soul groups, that is, the task groups, were already formed in the Light (heaven). At the beginning, only the group members from the top two to three layers of the souls were chosen and infused into bodies on Earth. The souls who did not join the groups in heaven were not allowed to be infused into the bodies at the beginning. Members of the top layers of human souls who were closest to God and were part of a group were chosen for the first incarnations because they appeared to have the best chance of successfully carrying out the plan for the development of mankind. They were part of a group, and their children were also group members. Those who were not part of the soul group were not to be the first incarnates.

According to my hypnotized patients, the first couples were chosen through a complex process, by other human souls, angels, masters, God, and others in heaven. The final decision was up to the souls who were going to incarnate as humans, as they determined, among themselves who had the best chance of success. It was a spiritual process and there was nothing in the way of self-aggrandizement or wanting to be the first, but selection depended on who had the best chance of carrying out the plan. The criteria were the apparent depth of spiritual development and the ability to communicate their plan on Earth. Perhaps it would have been better if they had chosen a stronger memory to carry out the plan on Earth, then maybe it would not have slipped so much.

## The First Humans Like Botticelli

My hypnotized patients state that the bodies of the first humans were prepared by the angels on Earth and then the souls were infused through their crown chakra. One of my patients recalled her life as the first human as follows:

- *"I open my eyes and I am in this body lying on grass. I feel a lot of energy, like sexual energy in my labia and my breasts feel heavy. It is startling to be in my skin. My soul is infused in a 16-year-old body which was already prepared by angel on Earth. It looks like Botticelli's painting. I have white skin. I am about 5 feet tall. It is kind of scary to be in my body. I have beautiful dark blond hair down to my hips, covering my whole body. I am feeling different parts of my body. I am feeling my legs and I realize that I can move them. First I have sensation of being inside the body, and then I notice what is out affecting my skin. When I open my eyes I see the sky but I do not know what it is. I feel like I am being dropped in a truly alien environment. I am lying on the grass and I can feel every blade. My senses are turning on one at a time. Touch is the first one, then vision and hearing. "I look like the current humans. It is like we have evolved again. If we did not have the fall, we would have started where we are right now during the current time. I fill my lungs by taking deep breaths. I look around and do not sense any animals, insects or birds around and do not sense anything like me in my environment. I am overwhelmed with everything. Then I do not know what happens to the sky. It is all dark here. I am trying to establish a sense of reality. I sleep a lot during the first 24 hours.*

  *"I know there was something before and I have consciousness of before as a Light being. After 24 hours, I*

*explore the environment and when I get too overwhelmed I go to sleep. When I wake up I feel dew on me and warmth of the sun on my skin. I am not hungry. I have no needs and I do not have to eliminate. I get more awareness when I sleep. I must be getting information and guidance from heaven during that time.*

*"I see a hill couple of miles away and I see something moving on the hill. I feel anxious about it. Then I feel that it is something safe and not to worry, so I calm down.*

*"The one on the hill is another one like me but looks different. He stops when he is about 100 feet away from me and looks at me and I look at him. He is about 5'6" tall. We can feel each other's energy. It is like there is some kind of psychic download and we know a lot about each other instantly. I know we are supposed to be with each other. When he comes close to me, he touches my shoulders. It is like a jolt. I feel as if my heart is being pulled out of my chest. It is as if our heart chakra is being connected. Then he gently touches my face, lifts my chin and kisses me and blows in my mouth. I feel like I am more awake, aware and grounded. We hug each other and then he takes me to the place where he came from the hill. Everything here is beautiful, vibrant and alive. Colors are more intense. When we reach the hill it is more lush. The weather is perfect. He picks a berry and gives it to me to eat. This is the first time I have eaten anything. It kind of electrifies my brain and I feel a rush in my brain. I feel safe with him. We basically stay under a tree. There is water close by. We can swim in it. There are no fish anywhere.*

*"We can manifest things like changing the temperature around us. If we are thirsty we can manifest water or if we are hungry we can find fruit trees. We communicate telepathically. We are always together but we do not have any sexual feelings. One day when I am 18 years old, I wake up early in the morning and go down to the water to get a drink. My friend is still sleeping. I sit out at the*

*bank of the river. I see a big python which is tall up to my knees. It communicates with me telepathically. It asks me where my partner is and I tell him he is sleeping. It goes all around me making a circle. It does not feel right, so I stand up to walk away and it follows me. He continues to talk in a kind of sing song voice. He is saying I can have anything I want. As I am walking, I see a tree with 24 golden apples hanging down. I never saw this tree before. I reach for the apple, not because I want it but because he tells me I should have it, but something in me tells me not to. So I begin to pull my hand away but he screams at me to take it. I am startled and scared and the apple gets jerked out of the tree.*

*"I take it to my friend. He wakes up and sees me coming. He is looking at me in a sexual way which never happened before. I am also feeling sexual stirrings which I never felt before. I notice that my hair is separating and my nipples are becoming hard. My lips are full and I am rolling my hips. It never happened before. He gets up and touches my breasts and kisses me. I think this is the snake's influence because we did not do this before. I feel Satan himself is watching us from a distance. I think when he was talking to me he downloaded some stuff in me. When my friend saw me walking in a different way, it activated sexual impulses in him. I get the thought that you have to eat the apple before you can have sex. I stretch my hand with the apple towards him. He takes the apple and takes a bite and then I take a bite. Then he drops the apple and we have sex. It was explosive.*

*"There is a deep shift in how we feel about everything after that. We feel afraid, anxious and self-conscious of being naked. We feel like we should cover ourselves. We see a man coming towards us. He is 6'4" with gray hair. He knows what happened. He looks upset. He puts his hands on my belly and tells me that I am pregnant but I do not know what that means. He tells us to leave the mountain because it is dangerous here. So we walk down. As we*

*turn around and look back we see a thorn fence there, so we cannot go back. We find another place to sleep.*

*"There is a change in my friend. He is upset with me a lot and less protective. So I sleep a lot. The snake is following us. It is hiding on the tree and looks different now and laughing at us. We lost the ability to transform our environment with our thoughts and to communicate telepathically. That was a big loss. Now we do not know what we are going to do. It is getting dark. We are angry and blaming each other which we never did before. There are no trees here so we do not know where we are going to sleep. We sleep in the bushes or at the base of the hill. Everything is hard now. It is hard to find food but we find it. I feel alone and antagonistic towards my friend and he feels the same toward me.*

*"I have a baby. The delivery is hard and painful. I have 2 children first. Then after a long gap I have 10 more children over the next 17 years. Children go to other places in search of mates. We are alone. It was a hard life. I die at the age of 132 years from fatigue. I fall into a coma and my soul comes out of my head. Satan comes and tells me to go with him. I tell him to leave me alone and he runs away. Then I am taken to heaven by the angels. I am still very tired. I get cleansed and healed.*

*"Then there is a review of my life with God and many other Light beings. They show me the movie of my life. I see that Satan possessed the snake. They are saying I should have told the snake to go away rather than talking to it. Now people on earth have to live harder lives. Then after a while my partner also dies and comes to heaven. He realizes that he should have not eaten the apple. He knew better because he was on earth for a longer time and had more knowledge and experience.*

*"From heaven as I look back, I see that my partner and I were somewhere on the east coast of Africa close to where Ethiopia is now. I see that before Satan influenced us we had the gift to manifest our environment such as: if*

*we were thirsty we see a river, if we are hungry we could manifest fruit trees, if we were hot we could create cooler environment around us and vice versa.*

*"I also see that the snake that was following me was possessed by Satan himself, trying to influence me. There were 24 apples on the tree because there were twenty four first couples who were infused at the same time in the body, including us, in different parts of earth. Unfortunately Satan succeeded in influencing all of us independently.*

*"As I look back in that life from heaven, I see that as that snake is circling around me, he grabbed my ankle bruising it and then sucking my Light energy (soul parts) through that bruise. I also see that I was more self-reliant taking care of my children and my husband. My husband did not help much and I was exhausted and lost many soul parts in that life which Satan captured. Since then he has caused more and more problems through those soul parts every lifetime including the current life.*

*"On Dr. Modi's request, angels took all the soul parts of my husband and children back to them from me and integrated them after cleansing and healing the soul parts and their bodies. Then they brought all my soul parts back from Satan, his demons, from my husband and children and from other people and places and integrated them with me after cleansing the soul parts and me.*

*"I see from heaven that many problems came for me from that life to the current life such as: problems with men, not being able to count on them, feeling tired and overwhelmed, feelings that I made a mistake, feeling fear and shame, ankle pain, feelings of abandonment and leaving the body under stress.*

*"From Heaven I see that the angels prepared the bodies of the first humans on Earth and then the souls were infused in the bodies through the crown chakra. All the souls were sparkly Light, similar to Tinkerbelle. There were 24 first couples whose soul was infused in an already*

*prepared body. All the males were infused in their bodies on the same day and time and all the females were infused in their bodies on the same day and time, about 5 years after their male partners. There was no one couple who was the first couple. They were all the same. All the first females were confronted by Satan who possessed a big python with legs and all of them were bitten or bruised in the ankle by it. At that time he took their soul energy in the form of blood and fed each of them sexual energy and their hips began to roll. They all pulled the apple not because they wanted to but because they were yelled at and intimidated by the python. All the men ate the apple first and then the women. After that all the couples were told to leave that area and were told that they will have to live a harder life.*

*"From the heaven I see that if the first humans chose not to eat the apple then the couples were supposed to go out of the body, merge together and pass all their learned knowledge to the soul who would be born as their child. These children would have been born with all our knowledge and would build upon that. This way we would have evolved very fast. Also the mothers would not have any pain during delivery. I see that each couple had two children within a couple of years and then when they were grown, they had ten more children. I am not sure why the gap after the first two children.*

*"From heaven I see that each area where the 24 couples were infused is a Garden of Eden. So there were 24 gardens. They all looked tropical. I am seeing a globe and the tropic of cancer and tropic of Capricorn with the equator in the middle. These are the lines that divide the globe. All 24 gardens were in the band of climate which is temperate. They are all not quite in the mountains but they are a little bit higher then everything around them except those in mountains. The one in India is in the mountains. They each are over an energy vortex and are called holy places because they are between the earth and heaven.*

*There are other holy places or vortexes which were not chosen to be Garden of Eden.*

*"I am getting a vision of tubes of glitter at each of these places. These are masters and angelic beings who are coming through the tube. I think I am seeing the future. I see that they are all going to come at the same time in those areas, which are like portals. I am getting the feeling that some of these are aliens. They are going to be helpful. They are all higher beings in the Light. I see these Light beings coming together. They are all holding hands literally or figuratively. They come vertically through these tubes. They have outstretched hands and are creating power grid between each of them. If the earth were a person, then it would be the section from under the breast bone to above the pubic bone. It is the waist of the earth. It looks like white Light and glitter. There is an energy field that goes around.*

*"All of them are coming together is some kind of a key. These Light beings who are enlightened and are masters, including the aliens, are the key. They are making a power grid. They are working on earth, the actual physical earth. It is an act of cleansing and healing of the earth. This has been predicted in the holy books of different religions. These will be different masters of the universe. From heaven, I see that the whole earth will be a Garden of Eden for the whole creation. These masters are coming down to heal the whole earth and everything and everybody on the planet. I see some of the healing is by fire to purify. This will happen in the vortexes.*

*"Underneath the masters create like a shell. They are spinning the glittery looking things and then there is all this energy inside this band of the earth focusing the energy in the center of the earth for healing. The effect will spread all over the earth. This is the healing and purification. I see fire and then purification. They are not showing everything right now. I see a thin curtain. I get the information that from the time we have been ejected from*

*the Garden of Eden and all the negative things we humans have done since then, has to be purified. Then the whole earth will become the Garden of Eden with perfect weather, not too hot or cold. It will be like a beautiful botanical garden and a perfectly balanced place. It is like there was a bubble over these areas. I get that you will be given detailed information later.*

*"I see that Satan possessed the snake and then influenced all the so called Eves by biting or bruising the ankle and sucking their soul parts and infusing negative dark energy into them. This happened with all the first couples. This was like a test. If they were not tested then they are just there, not choosing to be there. We were told to leave the Garden of Eden not as punishment but for character development.*

*"If the first couple did not get influenced then they would have been given the gift of knowledge of good and evil. But since they got influenced they have to learn and evolve because if they were just given that gift they would not understand because they would not be ready. It was a test. I feel God and the heavenly beings were very disappointed. Their hearts are heavy. I can feel it. They were disappointed that all of them failed. If even one couple had succeeded they could have evolved and they would have been the leader and could have helped the rest of them to evolve quickly. I also get the understanding that what happened on earth also happened on most of the other planets throughout the creation, except few higher planets closer to God who had higher vibrations.*

*"On Dr. Modi's request, angels cleansed and healed all the first humans and their children and brought back their soul parts from Satan, his demons, from people, places and from each other and integrated them with whom they belonged after cleansing and healing their bodies and the soul parts. The angels also cleansed, healed and filled all the Garden of Eden's and other energy vortexes with the Light on Dr. Modi's request. Before they were*

*looking darker because they had dark influences. Then they brought all the soul parts to those power places from Satan, his demons, people, places and darkness and integrated them where they belonged after cleansing and healing them. Then the violet flame was infused in those places and in all the first humans and their children, transforming and realigning their DNA's."*

The souls of first humans in heaven knew about Satan and his demons, but they did not know how strongly they would be influenced. They did not know how the "second forgetting," which they would have after the infusion of the soul in the body, would affect them. (The "first forgetting," which every soul experienced in different degrees, was after their soul was created by God and separated from him.) They also did not realize they would enter from a state of complete knowledge to a state of partial knowledge on Earth after their souls were infused into the body. Perhaps the analytical way would have been more suitable, where the beings could have contacted the subconscious memories by going into themselves. Also, the beings who were better protected, more spiritually inclined, more focused, more concentrated, and better rounded could have had the better chance in resisting Satan's temptations.

## First Ape Like Humans

According to heavenly beings, after all the first couples got influenced by Satan and his demons, they all had to leave their Garden of Eden and life was very hard. They lost the gift of manifesting what they needed. Also because of the harsher conditions and weather all the humans were wiped out from the Earth several times.

So God and heavenly beings decided to infuse human soul into young apes whose souls were pushed out and taken to heaven by the angels. And these apes became ape-humans because they had the human soul. One of my patients under hypnosis recalled a life when his soul was infused into an ape body and thus he became an ape-human.

- *"I am a 16 year old ape like female. My name is something like Ala. There are 13 people in our group. We are not very tall. I am about 4 feet tall and the males are about 4 ½ to 5 feet tall. We all stay together as a group. Most of the people are about 16 to 18 year old except one who is 10 year old. We do not have any special place to live. We just walk around from place to place. It is a flat area covered with tall grass. We have to stand very still together for a long time because wild animals are coming around. They pass by us and do not bother us. I think we are outsmarting them. We have a way of signaling each other when animals are close by.*

  *"We communicate with grunting sounds and sign language. After sometime, one of our group members dies and the wild animals smell the dead body and are coming around but are not able to see us. I think that collectively we can make ourselves invisible. As long as we are still, we can create an invisibility shield around us. We bury him and put a rock over him so animals cannot dig out the body. We also put flowers on the grave. We mostly stay together and search for food. We do not eat meat because there is no need. We are just living day to day.*

  *"I am 26 years old and I am pregnant with my first baby. Some of the other women died during the childbirth. I also lost my baby and die of bleeding. When my spirit comes out, I see an alien being that looks like the tall gray alien watching us from far away. I see a staircase made of golden Light and I go up the steps. There is a being that looks old but I keep on walking. I do not get cleansed or healed this time. I just get sucked in the Light.*

  *"As I look back from heaven I see that our spirits were infused into ape bodies which were between 16 to 18 year old and some a little older. As our souls went into ape*

*bodies, their souls were pushed out and gathered by the angels and taken to heaven. We were like walk-ins.*

*"There were several groups of souls which were infused in the ape bodies in different parts of the earth.*

*"From heaven, I see that we do not eat meat because there are lots of fruits and vegetables. We can feel the energy places on earth and those are the places we find food and water. We feel the tingling sensations as we walk and we know that it is the right place.*

*"As I look back from heaven, I also see that the aliens, who looked like the taller gray aliens, also influenced us. They put tracking devices in all the first humans so in the future they can track down the first humans. They gave them a lot of information such as: how to dig for water, how to find more food and water, how to think like a group, how to find things, how to build fire, how to make tools, etc. I think this gray being is a spirit being influenced by the darkness and looking old and wrinkly. We thought they were like gods. They put tracking devices in us while we were sleeping. After the alien influence we forgot about how to find the safe places through the feelings in our feet. I see that about a year after our soul was infused into the body, the aliens put the devices in us. After that the darkness came into us but we did not know it at that time.*

*"I see many problems and gifts came from that life to the current life, such as: issues in relationships, allowing myself to be dominated, wanting to save weaker people and ankle problems. I see that we could create an invisibility shield around us to protect ourselves from the animals. All we had to do was to think it and we had it around us. I also see that in the near future the first humans will be able to do that again. If we can raise our vibrations, we can create and use that shield to protect us. The whole world can pray and think of it around the earth.*

*"You were there too in our group Dr. Modi. Although we all had different gifts, you had more awareness and knew of things which most of us forgot after the aliens*

*influenced us. You were still able to manifest things and had healing powers. You were like a shaman.*

*"I see angels cleansing and healing all the first humans and removing all the alien devices. They brought soul parts of all the first ape humans, on your request, from Satan, his demons, aliens and each other and integrated them with whom they belong after cleansing and healing.*

*"As the soul parts come back to all the first humans and once they get cleared of darkness their powers will get activated and they can be used to do the higher things and be influential in the future.*

*"The gray alien beings who were observing us were ancestors of the short Grey aliens who are doing a lot of abductions currently. They had some dark influences. They were trying to observe the development of the first humans. Their planet was destroyed and they were looking for another planet where they can live. They were trying to manipulate the first humans. They wanted them to build the civilization and work for them. They gave them some tools through telepathic thoughts such as: how to build fire and make the weapons."*

**Dr. Modi:** *I request the angels to bring the gray aliens who were observing the first ape humans.*

**Patient:** *I see the tall, thin gray being in front. He is in a spirit form.*

**Dr. Modi:** *What were you trying to do to the first ape humans?*

**Gray Alien:** *We were trying to give them ideas about how to build a fire, make tools and weapons and how to cook on the fire so they could evolve and worship us and do what we ask.*

**Dr. Modi:** *You are in a spirit form for millions of years. You did not go to heaven after the death of your physical body?*

**Gray Alien:** *We wanted to stay here and control people. We wanted them to worship us and eventually we wanted to live on earth. We put probes in the first* *humans. These are tracking devices so we can track them. These devices read their medical condition, sociological history and everything that is to know about them. They are in the center of the brain at the joining of the center. They are still there.*

**Patient:** *I see he has a lot of dark influences but he does not know it.*

**Dr. Modi:** *I request the angels to bring all the gray aliens who worked with the first ape like humans and all the others.*

**Patient:** *The angels brought 8 of them and they are all tall gray aliens, in spirit form. They are all completely dark. I see that you already have transformed the whole gray alien race and their planet before except these beings.*

**Dr. Modi:** *Yes! (It is described later in this book) I request the angels to remove all the dark and other entities, dark devices and dark energy from these aliens. Lift them out, help them to the heaven or bind them in the space. Transform dark devices and energy into the Light and take it to the heaven. Take all the soul parts of other people from them and integrate them with whom they belong after cleansing and healing. Bring all the alien's soul parts back from Satan, his demons, people, places and darkness. Cleanse, heal and fill them with the Light and integrate them with whom they belong. Clamp the cords to the soul parts, which cannot be integrated at this time. Destroy the spaceships if they need to be destroyed, or cleanse, heal and shield them with the Light.*

**Patient:** *It is all done. I see the angels cleansed, healed and shielded their spaceships. The gray aliens are still looking tired for some reason.*

**Dr. Modi:** *I request the angels to lift out any soul parts of Satan and his demons out of these gray aliens and take them to whom they belong.*

**Patient:** *There were soul parts of Satan and his demons in them which angels lifted out and took them to whom they belonged. The soul parts of the aliens are brought* *back from Satan and his demons. Now the aliens are looking better and healed.*

**Dr. Modi:** *I request the angels to remove all the tracking devices which these gray aliens put in all the first humans and all the other humans. Dissolve and transform them in to the Light and take them to heaven. Scrub and scour everybody's brain where the devices were and take away any residue which is left over. Fill them with the Light. Bring everybody's soul parts back from Satan, his demons, from people, places and the gray aliens. Cleanse, heal and fill them with the Light and integrate them with whom they belonged. Store the soul parts in heaven which cannot be integrated at this time.*

**Patient:** *I see soul parts of all the first humans and other humans are brought back and integrated with them.*

**Dr. Modi:** *Gray alien beings do you all choose to go to heaven?*

**Gray Aliens:** *Yes, please!*

**Dr. Modi:** *All of you, we send you home to the Light with love. Go in peace. I request the angels to please help these beings into their section of heaven. We pray to God to please fill all the first humans and the whole creation and everything and everybody in the creation with the violet flame and heal and realign their DNA please. Thank you!"*

Beings experienced the second forgetting on every planet, but much less on the planets that have higher vibrations and are much closer to heavenly vibrations. When a heavenly soul is infused into the top universe, closer to the globe of God, just a little bit is forgotten. When they are infused in a middle universe like ours, whose vibrations are lower than the universe, which is on a higher level, much more is forgotten. The change in the vibration rate is what causes the forgetting. The universe that had the highest vibration rate were infused first, therefore, they are developing for a longer time. The vibration rates of the universe dictate when that universe was infused with souls. According to the heavenly beings, even now there are universes with very slow vibration rates that are being infused with the souls for the first time.

## Original Plan For Development of Humans

The purpose for creating the universe and for incarnating souls in the universe was to carry out the basic plan, which was to perfect and heighten those qualities that God desired and to change those qualities that were not desirable. The incarnation into the universe was designed to perfect those qualities and to give each soul the chance to develop compassion, understanding, caring, and loving attitudes, and to extinguish those qualities that are selfish, self-centered, and negative.

The original plan for the first couple was to pass on the knowledge to the incoming souls through spiritual joining of two souls while out of their bodies. While they were spiritually merged, their learned spiritual, physical, and emotional knowledge and qualities could be passed on to the incoming souls before entering the body. This way, the incoming souls would not have to start from scratch every time, but could continue where the previous generation had left off. This way their energy field would grow exponentially and everybody and everything it envelops would evolve too, first on their planet and then to other races on the other planets.

Following are examples of how human souls were supposed to do soul merging:

- *"I am seeing a man and a woman seated on the ground facing each other a distance apart, not touching each other. They are aligning their chakra (energy centers). They have very intense love for each other, for God, and for the universe. This is really an overflowing love and it does not matter who, what, and how. The first and strongest component of this love is an intense wish for the other person's spiritual development and a supportive, very uplifting, giving, encouraging love. Then a desire to pass this on to the spiritual child.*

*"Those two bodies are relaxed and facing each other. They meet in spirit outside the body and the energy is flowing into the body from the outside from the Light (heaven). The energy vibrates up and down the body, bouncing from one chakra to another, up and down. This energy is flowing through the entire body, all-pervasive. When the two spirits join, they have no doubts that it happened.*

*"Here there are two spirits united out of their bodies, out in the universe in the spiritual realm and another soul coming from the Light (heaven) to be newly born on Earth and approaching this field of love around two intertwined spirits. The incoming soul receives from them what spiritual development they both have made together. A desire to maintain physical and emotional health is passed on; the desire to pass on the knowledge is passed on to the incoming soul. The soul also gets the uplifting from every component of love. Then the incoming soul is ready to be infused in the body."*

- *"Man and woman who are on Earth have the natural tendency and inspiration from the Light (heaven) to do spiritual merging to pass on their development to the incoming soul. What I see is a man and a woman facing each other and their souls extending out of the body into the Light surrounding them. The two souls are moving into each other and occupying the same spiritual space. The spiritual knowledge they have learned is passed on like a package by the spiritual parents to a new incoming soul who is coming down from the heaven and is ready to go into a body.*

*"As the development would go up exponentially, there would also be a physical evolution occurring at a very rapid rate because the physical components would also be passed*

*on. This would be a very minor component, but whatever advances the two souls had made in their physical bodies get passed on to the soul, the spiritual child."*

The plan was and is to develop these positive qualities while living on the Earth so that they would be carried over and taken back to the Light (heaven) when the souls discarnate, leave the Earth and return to heaven. At the same time, had the plan been followed completely, those qualities would have been passed on to the next generation through spiritual merging of the souls of two people, which would pass on all the knowledge to the next generation, enabling the next generation to start where the previous generation left off. This would have resulted in a great leap and would have taken about thirty-seven human generations to reach perfection. Then humanity could have positively affected the races on other surrounding planets. The desire for spiritual merging is built into the human race and we can still go back to it.

Patients describe a mathematical graph showing the spiritual development of people. It is of linear growth. If each one develops into the universe as it is now, with some falling down, some going up a little higher, this leads to a very gradual slope to the development. What was intended in the original plan was like an exponential graph, where each step is built upon the other. It rises much, much faster and keeps getting steeper all the time, until it is going straight up. One graph is going up in a moderate slope while the other graph is going up in a dramatic curve, and in a matter of only a few generations, we would have had complete development and the whole of humanity would have been enlightened.

Currently, the incoming soul does start from zero. The only thing that has been developed is that the culture exists and it can pass on these values to some extent. Since the first couples failed to carry out the original plan, the progress of mankind was extremely slow, each soul having to relearn from scratch at every incarnation.

## Breakdown of the Original Plan Due to Satanic Influences

The first humans were never able to carry out the original plan of soul merging, that is, by the joining of two souls in the spiritual realm and passing on all their learned knowledge to the new, incoming souls. Instead, they got into physical sex and reproduction first, because they were influenced by Satan and his demons. Physical reproduction would have come naturally because it was part of the scheme to produce new bodies, but it was not supposed to be the primary focus. The primary focus was to have the spiritual development of the first couple, and then spiritual joining and passing on the knowledge to the incoming soul first, and then the two beings would have been ready to produce a physical body.

The breakdown of the original plan happened when Satan played on the first humans' emotions and convinced them that sexual intercourse, the lust and the physical pleasures, were important. These first humans failed to follow through the spiritual joining of the two souls and pass on their learned knowledge to an incoming soul from heaven, and act which should have come before physical sex. However, they did not achieve this. They were tempted by Satan and chose to have physical union first, making it the focus of their relationship and not the spiritual union.

The first step in the satanic influence was the observation. The first couple, the so-called Adam and Eve, were able to observe that the animals would physically unite in sex and create a new body. It was very natural for human bodies to do the same. They were observed and influenced by the Satan and his demons, who motivated them to indulge in physical sex. They decided to try the process, and liked it too much, since it provided physical pleasure and a partial substitute for spiritual union. They continued to use it and never entered into a true spiritual union.

At this point, according to a hypnotized patient, Archangel Michael, who was giving us this information, felt like crying because he felt so sad about it. He felt maybe he could have done more; perhaps he should have done something to keep this from happening. Most of the archangels and other heavenly beings expressed similar feelings of extreme sadness, through different patients. Normally they have a very matter-of-fact way and do not show much emotion, one way or the other.

According to the original plan, in about thirty or forty generations, human beings would evolve to the point where they would have been the saints, even though animal-like. Souls that came into human incarnation could become masters very quickly and would be ready to return to the main body of God very shortly after that. But Satan and his demons tricked the first humans, who had everything they needed to be successful, just not complete knowledge. They fell for Satan's trick and became firmly rooted in the physical body, which slowed down their spiritual development.

Before the first human couples came on Earth, they had the knowledge of Satan and his demons in heaven and knew what could happen while on Earth, but it was not thoroughly and completely figured out. There were the examples of incarnations in other universes, but the actual experience while in the body in the universe is something different in each case. Even though some of these souls had been incarnated before on other planets and had experienced Satan tempting them or influencing them in that body, it was a different experience in this body on Earth, because here those souls had a different vibration rate.

Human beings evolved painfully slowly after the first couple failed to carry out the original plan. During each reincarnation cycle, they tried to carry back and forth what they had learned and were very slowly perfecting themselves on Earth. They were doing a difficult job, and even though progress was extremely slow, they were making progress. Their understanding of the creation, of God, and of the mechanisms of the spiritual world has progressed very slowly since the first incarnation. The first task they had to work on was to get across the point that there is a part of us that lives after death, and death is not the end of life. It took many generations to acquire the idea of life after death and to infuse it into society. It seemed like a relatively simple idea, but there were people who did not believe it. The next area was understanding that God existed, who is the Supreme Being that created the universe and oversees it.

Heavenly beings, through my hypnotized patients, say that the plan for humankind was perfect. A lack of a language was a help. The initial ape-like humans had a vocal apparatus that was capable of sounds and simple words, but did not have the vocal apparatus for prolonged speech. They were not created for living their life in words. If the development of humanity had succeeded as it was intended, it would have been primarily complete spiritually, as the hairy ape models and language would not have developed as they have. Communication would have been simple but spiritual, and complete in terms of communicating feelings and understandings as opposed to verbal, auditory, and written, if the original plan had succeeded.

The development process takes place with every soul, but primarily with those who have a thinking ability, such as human beings and beings on other planets. According to the heavenly beings, on Earth, there are three different groups that have this ability: humans, whales, and dolphins. Humanity had to develop a culture as a way of doing things to survive and pass on that culture.

## Going Back to the Original Plan of Spiritual Merging in the Future

Heavenly beings, through my hypnotized patients, say that we need to reestablish the spiritual joining in humans, because this is really important. There is still considerable influence from the dark side, but it is possible to reestablish having spiritual children through the spiritual connection without physical sex. It does not have to be the couple creating the body that influences the soul. Those who are too old to create a body can mix, merge, combine, and influence somebody else's incoming soul. They can develop a spirit child who will be born into a physical body. It will have their spiritual knowledge and their spiritual characteristics and be someone else's physical child.

Heavenly beings state that the couple does not have to be husband and wife. It is impossible to commit adultery in the spirit world because there is no such thing. In the spiritual world, there is no homosexuality or adultery. These are human concepts. In heaven, it only means that the spirit is merging. The spiritual couple does not have to be a male and female. They can be two males or two females. Strictly speaking, it does not even have to be a pair. There can be three, four, five, six, or a dozen spiritual parents. There are no limits to the upper number. The more people involved in a spiritual merging, the more knowledge can be passed on to the incoming soul.

Spiritual merging can last for hours, and more than one soul can be infused on Earth during that time period. More advanced souls get preferential treatment, and they are more likely to gain that spiritual gift from the merging souls. Any child who is given knowledge this way, by a spiritual couple, the soul has to be infused into the body at conception and not later. Passing of knowledge is not just limited to a one-spirit child. The two souls can stay merged for hours and pass on their learned spiritual knowledge to many incoming souls. They do not have to be related physically but there is definitely a spiritual relationship. Currently, people do not know how and why they should.

Those past childbearing age can also pass on the knowledge through soul merging since it is not necessary that they create a physical body. There are others around creating the physical body, and if they can fuse in spirit, then any soul or souls who are incoming from heaven can come and get the gift of their knowledge. It can even be passed on to more than one child. It is not limited to the human soul; it is also possible for any soul, such as animal or plant souls that are coming down from heaven while that joining is occurring, to pick up the love, Light, and gifts and develop, too.

When a child is born after receiving the spiritual knowledge by the spiritually merged souls, he or she does not start at ground zero; the newborn child already has the knowledge infused into him or her. It is possible to get back to the original plan, because the desire for spiritual joining is built into us. As the graph develops, there will be spiritual joinings by tens of thousands or millions of couples. Even small groups can join together spiritually, and this can pervade the planet and even the entire universe. Everybody who is in their spiritual fields also gets evolved, including other humans, animals, and inanimate objects.

Here lies the importance of humanity. According to the heavenly beings, we are a unique race. We have the potential to transform the entire universe. There are only a few other races scattered around the universe that also have this capacity. We could be the end of creation. It is still possible for us to go back to the original plan of spiritual joining and passing knowledge to incoming souls. We can enlarge the spiritual field around us, and everybody and everything in it can get spiritually evolved. Gradually, it can spread all over the planet and even the whole universe. We can take everybody back to God with us.

We have a built-in capability to pass on knowledge to other souls and other races in the universe. According to the heavenly beings, even some of the highly evolved races in the universe do not have this capability. They are limited to developing within their own race. There is a little bit of spillover from them to their surroundings, but not spreading and covering others in their field.

# Chapter 2

## DNA: WHAT DO WE KNOW ABOUT IT?

### Karmic Imprints on DNA

Heavenly beings through my hypnotized patients state that our DNA has thirty two strands, but except for the two strands, the rest of them were blocked off from the beginning, including the self-healing strand of DNA. In this session we will only talk about two strands of the DNA which are active in humans at this time.

Heavenly beings speaking through my hypnotized patients state that DNA carries with it a basic genetic blueprint for life. Much of the basic blueprint is untouched by the life plan. Some of the necessities that have to come to the life require changes in the DNA of the life so that certain events become more likely, but they are not required. The tendencies can only be built in the DNA, not the requirement. As we are living the life plan in the universe, options present themselves to us and we can choose to follow the life plan or deviate from it. In following the life plan, the tendencies in the DNA are activated and the life plan proceeds as was intended.

In general, the basic physical information that is inherited from parents is unchanged. Physical appearance, blood type, and general psychological makeup are of direct inheritance and come with the parents' DNA. The fine points that are necessary to the life plan are the parts that are altered.

If we have determined in our life plan that a certain childhood illness should start at age thirteen to direct us toward a certain course of action in adult life, then a predisposing factor will be imprinted on the DNA, but not the requirement that it should be developed. There are many variables involved while living life. A certain childhood illness can predispose us to follow a course of action. As we are living a life, we make the choices and we can choose to go ahead and have that childhood illness or we could avoid it, even though the tendencies are imprinted in the DNA.

Not all events or structures are actually imprinted in the DNA. The attitudes, the psychological makeup that makes those tendencies possible, are imprinted in the DNA so that the life plan will go according to how we intended to structure it. The requirement that it should be that way is not actually imprinted on the DNA but the mechanism to make it possible is.

In the case of childhood illness previously mentioned, a certain tendency toward action builds into the psychological character of the person living the life. Once again, there is a decision point to follow that tendency or to go against it. To follow the tendency is to follow the life plan. To go against it is to deviate from the life plan. There are multiple decision points in each predetermination or tendency in the DNA. Even if there is an imprint on the DNA, it still has to be lived in the life. The tendencies can be there and the predisposing factors can be built into the life, but to actually make a decision when the DNA is imprinted is impossible. The entire life tendencies can be imprinted on the DNA but at each activation point and leading up to that activation point, there are decisions made in terms of following the life plan or going against it. There will be multiple decision chains, where each decision has to be made to follow the life plan in order to have everything come out as it was planned in the Light (heaven).

This does not mean that karma requires DNA to be in a certain way, or that DNA requires the person to live life in a certain way. This is not the true way to look at things; that would do away with free will in living life. Having karmic imprints on DNA does not mean that it compels the action during the lifetime. It just creates a tendency toward certain actions or outcomes. The DNA is not compelling it but increasing the probability of it happening. The person living the life still has to make a decision that leads it to actually happen. Imprints are still there; the tendencies will still develop, even if we choose not to follow them.

There are several different decision points possible here. First would be to allow that weakness to activate. Perhaps it will require a lack of self-care, or negative actions on our part as to how we care for ourselves. Perhaps it will require that we go to a certain place and be exposed to certain bacteria or viruses. In each of these cases, an opposite decision can be made so that the tendency is not put into the decision. If we choose not to activate a certain imprint, then it will still exist and can come into play later in life, but as far as following its proper place in the life plan, it would not happen.

There are many different types of karmic imprints which are made on the DNA, such as tendencies for physical illnesses; psychological illness; relationship problems; spiritual problems; basic intelligence and the possible range of intelligence; extrovert or introvert personality; violent tendencies; use of language; ability to handle quantitative concepts; physical manipulation; emotional content; etc. They are all chosen in heaven before coming into life. Of course, interaction with an adult does make a difference, but given the same interaction, there are many possible choices a child can make. The life path is determined actually in the life through the tendencies in the DNA.

When we talk about intelligence, we are talking about the range of intelligence, with the bottom limit and the top limit, and it can be fairly wide. Exactly where we end up in that range depends on how we choose to live the life. Language skill depends on early practice, and if the child chooses to do that practice, to play with the words in their own head, to treat them as fun things, then that child will develop a higher intelligence range. If the child chooses to find words boring and takes more pleasure in physical objects than in words, then the child will tend to lose the language skill, but develop more in the physical manipulation area. So, the general range of intelligence abilities is not only under our control in life, but also the specific distribution of them.

The body that is to be formed and the DNA for that body are programmed so that each individual characteristic that must be carried over such as, the positive to be fulfilled, the negative to be worked on, corrected, cured, or healed if possible in this life, are all placed on the DNA before the body begins to form. The ova and the sperm, which will meet and become the child, are both preprogrammed before they meet. Everything is included in both ova and the sperm. The hereditary parts, which are essential, are there. Those parts that are optional are actually random chance and you catch the luck of the draw.

When the first cells are formed and the body begins to grow, the imprints on the DNA for the lifetime are there. When the inactive part that contains the karma is put into the being, the pattern or the chemicals in it contain the information, just as the pattern of the active portion determines what chemicals will be made from it.

The life pattern is contained in the DNA in the inactive karmic portion. The tendency toward spiritual development can occur both in the karma portion and the active portion. It can be a matter of heredity. Psychic ability can be in both the karma and the active parts of the DNA. The genetic component of psychic ability is carried through, but the spiritual part is programmed in the karma section of the DNA. You don't just get the abilities from heredity; sometimes there has to be the corresponding spiritual portion in the inactive karma DNA for the ability to be expressed properly in life.

The positive karmas are the plans to come. It is a sort of *read only* memory, so we can consult back on the details when it comes time to put them into action spiritually or karmically. The negative karmas are those things from past lives that need to be cleared up, worked off, corrected, or healed. These are selected in the Light (heaven) to resolve before incarnation, based on the intentions of this life.

Negative karmas are not randomly assigned. We pick and choose which portions of karma would best be worked on in this life. It is not a matter of undefined burden. The burden is definitely there because we sometimes have to overcome it, and we in the Light (heaven) choose the portions this life is best suited for dealing with. We choose them on the basis of what we can do in this life. We should never feel that negative karma is a negative thing expressed in our current life. We are guaranteed by God to have all the resources we need to work through it. We will have the abilities, the spiritual bent, and whatever it takes to successfully resolve that issue.

Success is not guaranteed. The only part that is guaranteed is that the resources will be available. The resources can be external and internal. The external resources we can draw on include books, religion, our relationship with God, and the individuals who will be put into our life to help. These people are pre-chosen and are included on the karma DNA. When we meet a familiar person, very likely he or she is programmed in our DNA.

Then there are internal resources, such as our personality type, developmental influences as a child, our intelligence, our basic abilities, our emotional quotient, and our emotional, mental, physical, and spiritual problems. In making spiritual progress, we choose the difficult life more often than we have to so that we can progress faster.

Negative karma has to do with negative energy, but is not composed of the dark. It comes from the Light and it must be resolved to free ourselves from problems. Karmic imprints are of the Light and are composed of the Light, but deal with dark energy in some cases. Those things that are negative we must overcome so that we can make spiritual progress.

Karmic imprints are not a fatalistic things, but actually are positive. They are something that is decided by the person, by his or her judgment as to what is needed for spiritual growth, and are not imposed on by anyone else. We need to think of karma as always positive and always for the person's good and development. Simply because of the human value system, something that appears to be negative does not mean that it is negative karma. It means there may be a negative experience a person has to go through in their positive path forward. It may be perhaps a negative experience but not negative karma. Some things that are imprinted could be simply a carry-over from a past life and not a conscious part of a life plan in this life. Those things tend to be positive.

We can imagine the representation of karmic imprints in groups as a pyramidal form to illustrate what needs to be worked on. The imprint contains the whole of the pyramid, but in the DNA it is laid out in a linear structure and we cannot see that it is really interrelated and tied together. We are given this three-dimensional structure where the parts interrelate between below and above all the way up to the top. By removing different chunks from it, this huge pyramid will eventually collapse and the problems will be resolved. The karmic imprints are not removed but check out after they are deflated, collapsed, and resolved. There are many such pyramids on the inactive part of our DNA, representing different karmic issues we need to resolve.

Following are examples of how the karmas are imprinted on the DNA and what happens when they are resolved:

- *"I see DNA being healed. It appears like a straight comb with the lines out and the healing is taking place on the lines. The chemical bases which are there are being taken out and different ones are put in as if the DNA was together improperly and now they are correcting the flaws.*

*"I see that before the healing of my weight problems the DNA looked like they had dimples in them, kind of like a waffle surface. After finishing the healing, the dimples disappeared from the DNA and now they look smooth and flat.*

*"Before the healing of my eye problems my DNA looked kind of yellow and green for some reason and there was a crescent shaped irregularity with white streaks across it. It was removed after the healing."*

- *"The first theme that I worked on being psychic is fear of doing spiritual work and having skin sensitivity. The karmic imprint on DNA appears like a huge pyramid. On the top is the crux of the theme and underlying is this huge pyramid with lives and structure and the interrelationships between them. It is a four dimensional structure related in time with mutually supporting parts of different past lives. As those issues were resolved, one after the other, through the series of lives I relived, some seemingly inconsequential, some seemingly not-too-significant, yet each one was a portion of that pyramidal structure which was in a key position. Even when one significant life was resolved, the whole structure was dramatically weakened, making it easier to get in and make it loose to work it out. As we removed chunks from it by resolving the karmic problems from different past lives, the structure collapsed on its own and the problems are resolved."*

Parts that are not required are random. Whatever is required for this life, we have it. All the active parts come from the parents, and heaven guarantees that the characteristics we must have are there. The karmic imprints of physical problems are also on the active part of the DNA. Some symptoms that are not physical in nature are found in the inactive part of karmic DNA, such as emotional, mental, and spiritual symptoms. The imprints on the active DNA are also influenced by the heavenly beings. For the parts that are required, heaven makes sure they are inserted or preprogrammed in the DNA by the heavenly beings. Usually, new karmas created in the current life are not imprinted on the DNA, but occasionally there is potential that heavenly beings can add these karmas to be resolved.

Most commonly, when the life plan is fulfilled, the person dies, but not always. With most deaths, the life plans have been fulfilled, but this is not always the case. This is part of the reason why there are human spirits roaming the earth; they have not fulfilled the life plan. They are making an attempt to find out what and why. These are the people who die and have a feeling that they cannot go back because they have to finish something. Quite frequently, this unfinished business is, "I did not fulfill my life plan and I've got to get it done." This is not necessarily true, because they can go back to the Light (heaven) and pick it up in the next life, but they have an irrational determination, in the spirit form, after the death of the physical body.

## Planning the Karmas to Be Imprinted on DNA

The selection of which karmas should be imprinted on the DNA is made in heaven before incarnation, when we plan for our current life. This is done in small groups and in individual conferences following the general conference in heaven, when a series of two, three, or even four lives may be discussed and preplanned. As people die and return to the Light (heaven), they judge their life initially in the life review stage. As they go through the teaching and learning process in heaven, they also enhance that perception and look at it more completely, the extent of their success, and refine their planning for the future life in the light of what they have achieved.

The soul already has in its mind a series of lives. It is like a plot for a series of books; a general outline has been written with a particular goal at each stage. Of course, this is subject to modifications as lives are lived, and the person decides success or lack of success in living the life. The immediate upcoming life is planned in great detail. This follows the learning and teaching process in the Light (heaven). When the soul has determined the life plan to its own satisfaction, the steps it needs to take for its own advancement and development, then the soul knows at this point how it should go about attaining a particular goal it wants to achieve. In discussion with the other souls, in the small group meetings and with all of them being familiar with the human conditions, the specific outcomes that will be necessary are pretty well determined.

The heavenly beings, such as angels, guides, higher self, and masters, are there to help but they do not tell it what to do. They can counsel when asked, but they cannot make decisions for people. We have to make our own decisions. Heavenly beings cannot volunteer information. They cannot say, "Yes, that will work," or "That will not work." This has to be the human decision. Even in the Light (heaven), not everything that is planned is accurate, so not every decision made in heaven is for the very best of the individual, because conditions in the life may change. The plan has to be re-evaluated while in the life.

The souls of first humans in heaven knew about Satan and his demons, but they did not know how strongly they would be influenced. They did not know how the "second forgetting," which they would have after the infusion of the soul in the body, would affect them. (The "first forgetting," which every soul experienced in different degrees, was after their soul was created by God and separated from him.) They also did not realize they would enter from a state of complete knowledge to a state of partial knowledge on Earth after their souls were infused into the body. Perhaps the analytical way would have been more suitable, where the beings could have contacted the subconscious memories by going into themselves. Also, the beings who were better protected, more spiritually inclined, more focused, more concentrated, and better rounded could have had the better chance in resisting Satan's temptations.

According to heavenly beings, as far as God is concerned, he stays remote from the process. God does not impose his will, does not take an active part during the planning, but simply stays back and lets the mechanism that is set up play itself out to do its job. In heaven, the masters are easily approachable. Another way of looking at it is that God is intimately involved with every step of the process because every soul is part of God and always connected with God. Our plans go all the way back to when the soul was created and separated from God. That is when the original decision was made and that decision is affirmed again and again as we move down the chain of lives, and that is still the decision we are working under.

Decisions are made in small group meetings in heaven about how we achieve a particular goal. This is where errors creep into the process, because, sometimes, appropriate methods may not be chosen and, as a result, there will not be a perfect outcome. The best way to implement the overall goal is in part a large group decision, and also in part a personal decision. It follows a general outline laid out by God in his process of self-revelation to the universe. God has revealed himself again and again in varying degrees in different parts of the universe with the net result that many different people know of God in slightly different contexts.

## Process of Imprinting Karmas on DNA

According to the heavenly beings, after all the planning is done and the decision is made about how those goals will be achieved in life and what karmas will be imprinted on the DNA, then electromagnetic force is used and a particular gene pair is pushed out of its place and replaced by another gene pair that will match up in the DNA. So as the DNA is constructed, modifications are put into the DNA to match the person's life plan. This is accomplished through simple electromagnetic force. Since the other amino acids are present in the body guiding the right ones into position, It really requires no great effort.

After the plan is imprinted on the DNA, it does not compel us to follow it, but simply provides the tendencies. The guides and angels are there and are aware of the plan. The masters are also aware of the plan. Usually, but not always, the plan is optimum to achieve the goals desired in the lifetime. The other plans that will coordinate with it are set up in the same way. Then, when it is time to incarnate, to come to the universe and to assume the life role, the soul disembarks and incarnates into the body. The DNA is already there as the body is being prepared.

The imprinting of the karmic plan, or the life plan, on the DNA is an important step in a person's life. In general, the life plan is made in the Light (heaven), and the general parameters for the life are established about what the ends of the life shall be and toward what goals the person will be working. A general outline of the events of the life that will tend to move the person toward that goal is set up, and it is that plan which is imprinted into the DNA. It is not a rigid structure. It does not compel, but it makes possible and allows, rather than requiring, so that when the ova and sperm are merged and the DNA is constructed, those karmic imprints are included in the DNA.

The karmas are imprinted on the inactive portion of the DNA at the time of their formation, by the angels or the person's higher self. Generally, heavenly guides do not do that because it will be too involved for them, since they are there to guide and advise. They are not active participants and do not take action because this would be too active a role in creating a being.

The general mechanism by which this is accomplished is that an angel will exert a slight electromagnetic force upon the molecule that is going into the DNA. If it is not the proper molecule, then the angel will replace it with the proper one. It requires just a minute force on the molecular level to move one of the molecules out and put another in.

Of course, when the one element of the pair changes, the other element must change to match. In this way, the heredity is controlled to follow the life plan.

It indicates the tendency for that life to occur, but it does not compel it to happen. During the life itself, there are changes to be made which will permit the life plan to come into effect. There may be a series of four or five choices to get a certain result in the adult life. At each stage of the process, the proper choice, which is the choice in keeping with the life plan, must be made for the goals to be achieved.

If one step of the plan is not followed, it does not mean that the plan cannot come to be. It makes it more difficult and less likely, but it does not prevent it. The person can still follow through and complete that life plan even if the entire sequence can be short-circuited. The person at the proper age can still make that adult life choice that will lead him or her to the chosen path.

When the sperm and the ova join and the proper DNA is brought together, the individual is formed to fulfill the life path that is chosen in the Light (heaven). Again, it is not compelled but general tendencies are created and the choices in the life need to be made in the proper sequence to lead to a fairly sure completion of that life plan, as planned in heaven. Even if all the right choices are made down to the very last one, that does not guarantee that the life plan will be fulfilled successfully.

Following is an example of how the karmas, both negative and positive, are imprinted on the DNA during conception:

- *"I am in heaven just ready to come down to Earth. I have already prepared my blueprints or plans for my coming life on Earth. I have chosen certain physical, emotional, spiritual, mental, and relationship problems, my karmic issues from past lives, and I want to resolve them in the coming life. As I am ready to come down, I see a part of my soul like a beam of Light going down at the concep-tion, along with angels. I see angels as shafts of Light who have in their hands, beaded, beautiful, intertwined, brightly Lighted crystal, which they put in my DNA. I see the ova and sperm uniting, then dividing, going together and dividing again. I sense positive and negative karma imprinted as codes, which look to me like little beads, and there are comb-like teeth around the beads."*

Every person goes through the same process of planning, imprinting the karmas on the DNA, and carrying out the plans in life. If the person is less evolved, then the plans are simple; higher evolved people have extensive and more spe-cific plans.

# Chapter 3

## THE ALIENS ARRIVE: HISTORY OF ALIEN VISITORS ON EARTH

Most of the information in this chapter was given by different heavenly beings through different hypnotized patients, such as Angel Eichael, who claims to specialize in alien races; Archangels Michael, Gabriel, Raphael, and Uriel; different masters; patients' higher selves; guides; and other heavenly beings.

According to the heavenly beings, we are not the first-generation race in this universe. Actually we are a fourth-generation race. There are other races millions of years older and more advanced in the universe than we are. We were late bloomers because our planet was formed recently. The universe is about fourteen billion years old. The Earth and its sun are only about 4 ½ billion years old. It is a fourth-generation star.

Heavenly beings, through my hypnotized patients, explained that around every planet there is a spiritual energy field, and as the people on the planet evolve and become more spiritual, the field becomes bigger and stronger. It is always influencing everything else in the universe. Even when the spiritual field becomes weaker and we go further away, it still has effect. As more and more planets develop, the spiritual fields spreading through the universe get stronger and stronger, and they tend to pull the less developed planets along to help them develop faster.

Just like the Earth influences other planets, other planets can also help develop the Earth. The individual who does nothing on his or her own can also develop because there are other spiritually developed people in the society. Similarly, other spiritually evolved races in the universe and their energy fields can pull humans and the Earth with them, even if they do not do anything on their own.

According to Angel Eichael, there are different alien races that are on the side of God and the Light, and they are in a lot of different forms. Some of them are built like humans, some are like reptilians, some are bug-like, and some are like plants, while others are water dwelling beings like jellyfish. By their looks, it is hard to believe that they are spiritually advanced, but they are. These are all intelligent and spiritual beings with moral codes, and are aware of the existence of God and worship him. Their range is enormous. Over thousands of years, many alien races visited the Earth. Some just came and observed, while others studied the humans, made genetic modifications that changed them from the ape-like humans to current humans. Some alien races did spiritual teachings, while others gave different technologies to humans.

Heavenly beings stated that alien races came to Earth approximately a million years ago. Mankind was evolving painfully slowly after the first couple failed to carry out the original plan. By that time, mankind had advanced to where it could be recognized as an ape-like human but the aliens perceived them as an advanced ape. Multiple groups came to Earth over time but not all of them were interested in changing human beings. Some simply observed and studied but did not interfere with their development. The superadvanced races are not interested in Earth or its people. As spiritual beings, they preferred the much more direct experience of spirituality and growth than what mere humanity can give them.

## The Eight Alien Races Who Made an Impact on Humanity

Most alien races have multiple names, such as the names as they call themselves, the names as we know them by, and names depending on which star system they are in or close to. So each alien race and even the planets have multiple names. Some we know and others we do not.

The names of the eight alien races who did genetic modifications and taught humans as given by Angel Eichael are spelled as they sound when spoken by my hypnotized patients and are as follows.

## First Group of Aliens – Three Alien Races

There were three alien races in this group. Their names are spelled as they sound.

**First alien race:** They call themselves as Pharoni, a puffing sound and "roni." They are also called Vegans because they are from Planet Vega. We also know them as Pleideans. They came about one million years ago.

**Second alien race:** They call themselves Epsilon Eradante or X-Khuen or Ur-Ur-Hur. They look like gray aliens but have round eyes and are different than the gray alien race with big almond eyes that is currently doing the abductions. They came about 800,000 years ago.

**Third alien race:** They are known as Sirians from planet Sirius. They came about 770,000 years ago.

### First Alien Race of Group One – Pleideans or Vegans or Pharoni

**Name:** Beings of this alien race call themselves as Pharoni, a puffing sound and "roni," which is hard to pronounce, according to my patients. They also call themselves Vegans. Heavenly beings, through my hypnotized patients, state that the first alien race is from planet Vega, so they are also called as *Vegans*, but they are not connected to the star system Vega. They are also known on Earth as Pleideans, because planet Pleiades is very close to the planet Vega. The Vega is not part of the Pleiades, but close to the Pleiades. So for all practical purposes, Vegans and Pleideans are the same beings. Of course, they have political subdivisions, but they are a spiritual entity and they do not consider themselves as separate and apart from each other. Nor do they think of themselves in competition for the resources of the planet. As spirituality grows, competition disappears.

**Appearance:** The Pharaonis or Pleideans look like humans. They are built like a taller human being with a sloping chin. The following description is given by a hypnotized patient from the Akashic records:

- *"These aliens look like humans and are about six feet three inches to six feet four inches tall. They have a sloping chin. Their ears are small and the eyes are higher up. They have hair on the top of their head and down the back. Their skin is pinkish white. The eyes are set back in the head with no eyebrows above but there is something like eyelashes. The nose is kind of flat. They are slimmer than humans. They wear clothes like overalls. Their head does not look stronger and is slightly tilted on one or the other side as if they are ranging in on something or looking at it from one angle or another. Overall they appear slim and delicate."*

**Genetic modification:** This alien race came to Earth about a million years ago and was a spiritually developed race. Mankind by this time had already been on the Earth for about two and a half million years and looked like an ape but had a human soul. After the first human couple got influenced by Satan and forgot about their original plan of spiritual merging and passing on their knowledge to an incoming soul, they were developing spiritually very slowly and becoming human in behavior. This was not recognized by this alien race simply because they were fooled by their animal-like appearance. At this time, humans were living only on the northeast coast of Africa. There were no humans living anywhere else on Earth. Pleideans were the first alien race to interfere with the development of the human race. They worked with different families of the ape-like beings. They were trying to develop them into intelligent beings. They did not recognize that they had a human soul and would have developed over time. This alien race did genetic experiments with these ape-like humans.

Heavenly beings, through my hypnotized patients, say that the Pleideans did genetic manipulation after studying mankind intensively. They had studied the human brain. Having previously studied their own brains and those of other species, they determined that there is a center in the brain that can be developed that will make the human race more spiritual and more intelligent. They sought to enlarge the "divine," itself. They intended to make humans more spiritual but did not feel it necessary that they make them less ape-like.

The Pleideans did this by modifying the DNA and inserting it into newly developing human beings, at the single cell stage. Those beings then reproduced that DNA and passed on these traits to their descendants. The change was very rapid. The first child from the genetic manipulation was half ape-like. In the space of just a few generations, we changed from primitive ape-like beings to comparatively hairless, near-humans.

They did this with all the ape families they could identify. The pre-human apes were already group-living animals, so the aliens did not have to work to develop that. They considered living in groups and being social as an important part of development. According to heavenly beings, pygmy chimpanzees are very close to crossing over to being human. A regular chimpanzee is a little bit behind that, and then orangutans. Further back is great apes: the mandrills and gorillas.

According to the heavenly beings, Pharaonis or Pleideans were on this planet over an extended period of time, off and on, about 30,000 years at a time. They came back many times and made other modifications. With each subsequent visit, they spent less time working with other apes and more time worrying and wondering about the humans. They knew what genes they had tampered with and they tried to figure out just what changes occurred because of their tampering. They got fouled up because of natural evolution, and there were also other races coming and doing genetic modifications, which they did not know about. So there were changes also occurring on their own. They took things from this planet not as a form of payment but as an economic exploration.

One of my hypnotized patients, while watching from the Akashic library, gave the following account of how the Pleideans did genetic modifications with the ape-like humans:

• *"As I look back from the Akashic library, I can see that when the alien race one of group one first came on Earth about one million years ago, humans at that time looked like apes but had a human soul. The whole humanity was contained in one area of about one thousand miles long and five hundred miles wide, a strip along the northeast coast of Africa, which is underwater now. There were no humans living anywhere else on Earth at that time. Different groups of family units lived within that area, which ranged with each having ten to twenty-five individuals, consisting of a couple, their children, and other extended family members. The resources were not good enough to support them and life was hard, so after a while, they would break off and move to another area with resources. These ape-like humans were about three and a half to four feet tall and bent slightly forward. Their skin and hair color was black. They had straight hair all over the body except the face, and had protruding jaws. They communicated by grunting sounds."*

There was a predominance of women, who were traded from one place to another. This spread the genes and prevented inbreeding. Then a young male would go off with a female to establish their own group. The aliens recognized the spiritual nature of these primitive ape-like humans, who buried their dead because they believed in the continuity of the soul's existence. Their tools consisted of pointed shells and rocks.

This alien race had bases on mountains on the west coast of Africa, Asia, Europe, North, Central, and South America, and on other parts of the Earth. They were studying everything on the planet, including all life forms. One of the reasons was to see what plants, foods, and other resources they could take home and what effect these things would have on their planets. The humans were kind of a crusade for them.

These aliens studied humans for about a couple of hundred years and planned to do genetic modification on humans. They wanted to do it due to curiosity and partly due to the spiritual tendency they saw in humans, which they thought should be developed. They discussed this with their alien counsel and after a long discussion they decided to try to increase the physical size, enlarge the spiritual center, and increase the brain and skull size, with the objective of making humans more intelligent, better thinkers, and more spiritual. They also had a great deal of technical discussion about what parts to change in the DNA to achieve their goals.

These aliens had already studied the DNA of their race on their planet and had figured out what changes would produce what results. The discussion and decision about what changes to make took several hundred years, till every little detail was worked out about all the possible ramifications of everything that could happen.

Their requirement of the subjects for genetic modification was that the individuals had to be young and have a good chance of survival. They began the modification in the reproductive DNA when they were few years old. They chose a young male from one group and a female from the other group so that the individuals were coming from the different groups. The modifications were made in the aliens' spaceships and then the individuals were returned. The process was repeated several times with each person. When they became mature, the aliens transplanted these modified humans to another location in the south. A modified male and female were put together to start their own family and group. There were six of these pairs who were transplanted to a comparatively small area far away from their original groups but only about twenty miles apart from each other. They were allowed to develop near the coast so that the aliens could be sure about what changes occurred during the observation.

The children of these genetically modified humans looked slightly different. Their heads were larger, they had less hair, and their face did not protrude as much. They were slightly taller and straighter. They figured things out better, caught on quicker than the parents, but still like apes. They were not shockingly different because the changes were not made all at once. They lived like their parents did.

In two generations, the genetic modifications were in full effect and there was a pronounced difference between the grandparents and grandchildren. Within five generations, the aliens were sure how the changes were played out. Then they were returned to the original groups in the northeast and allowed to intermingle so that the modification could spread throughout the population. These newly evolved humans were guided to the northeast coast to rejoin the main body of humankind. Each group was like one big tribe, which moved to the coast, where they ran into the original groups of humans. They treated each other like humans, adopted each other's ways, and interbred, and all of mankind became the same but still ape-like. This is where archeologists get confused, as they find skulls that have partly ape and partly human features.

After another five generations, the genes had spread all the way north of the African east coast, and the changes were incorporated through all mankind. The aliens were still observing and seeing these changes play out, and among the results they had not foreseen was a greater survival rate of the young. They were hunting more efficiently, better at agriculture, and developed the idea of planting crops. They were thinking better, had better communication, and became more systematic. They were making better tools and developing specialized labor. The population was growing and the survival pressure was building with less food. So they continued to move north.

Around this time, about fifteen generations after the first genetic changes, the aliens did the second modification and transplanted them in Asia.

**Contributions made by the first alien race of group one:** Heavenly beings, through my hypnotized patients, stated that the changes made by the first alien race in the human race were the same all over. When they first came here, they studied humanity for hundreds of years and determined what changes needed to be made, and then they put their research into action. They followed the same pattern with all the different groups of mankind. They made changes in the brain to develop intelligence and spirituality, and as a consequence, there was a change in appearance of human beings, which was incidental and not planned.

These alien races understood the nature of genetic and the mechanism of how to transfer genetic information in the living being. According to my hypnotized patients, the first alien race of group one worked primarily in one area to change and refine the brain structure, increase the size of the brain, and improve its interconnections so that the brain could function more efficiently. They took the segment they thought controlled that characteristic out of the DNA and replaced it with the tailored segment, the one they had created.

They also made general changes in both sides of the cerebellum and cerebrum. The net result was an increase in the size of the human brain and improvement in its function, so the brain now has more memory capacity, more ability to interrelate the facts that humans have learned, to make corrections between them, to do deductive thinking, and an increase in spirituality of mankind.

Another result of their genetic manipulation was a change in the appearance of humanity. Due to the increase in the brain size, the size of the skull changed. Physical changes due to the genetic modifications made by the first race were a general increase in size of the body and the head, a more upright gait for walking, and a loss of body hair. These genetic modifications also caused an increase in intelligence and an increase in spirituality. Each individual became more aware of the effect of the spirit in his or her life. The perceptive areas of the brain, where sight, sound, smell, and taste are registered, also underwent a slight improvement. They made teeth more adapted to all sorts of food, contributed to an opposable thumb to grasp things, and gave them an upright posture.

Alien race one worked at developing spirituality with the view of promoting intelligence and communication. They enlarged the temporal lobes of the brain, the spiritual center that humanity already had, and made it better and more refined, and humans became more spiritual and developed better communication skills and abilities. Physically, humans were more refined and bigger. The brain size did grow and spirituality was enhanced. The spiritual center became larger and better developed.

**Negative outcome:** Some of the negative effects due to the genetic modifications made by the first race included the loss of some perceptive abilities. The increased brain size with a less corresponding increase in the skull size reduced some of the perceptive abilities of mankind. The skull size increased, but was not enough. Some of the physical changes that the mankind underwent could be considered negative outcomes, because humans were no longer as equipped to survive in the Earth climate as the ape-like humans were, because of the loss of body hair. Some of them were not as well adapted to the sun because of less body hair and lighter skin tone. Also, people became more touchy and more selfish, and developed more possessiveness because of the genetic manipulation.

**Spiritual understanding of the first alien race of group one:** This is a spiritual race. They have a deep understanding and a reverence for the Divine. They have attained the understanding that the physical world, while it has its own importance, is not the motivating power of the universe. The spiritual is the true existence of the universe. This race does tend to discount or overlook the existence of the dark side, or evil forces, because they are in a higher dimension and are not troubled by dark forces. As a result, it does not enter so completely in their thinking. It takes them away from the possibility of knowing the duality of God.

### Second Alien Race of Group One – Epsilon Eradante or X-Khuen

**Name:** The name of the second race is hard to pronounce. According to my patients, it sounds like a singing, trilling, and high-pitched sound that can be spelled roughly as "Ur-Ur-Hur." They also call themselves Epsilon Eradante and also X-Khuen. They can also be known as Grays because of their physical appearance, but they are a different gray race than the big almond eyes grays that are doing abductions currently. Epsilon Eradante aliens have the similar height, skin color, and physical appearance, but have round eyes and suction cups on their fingers and toes. Their feet are like pads.

**Appearance:** My patient under hypnosis gave the following physical description of this alien race from the Akashic records in heaven:

- *"These are comparatively short, about four feet to four feet ten inches tall and look humanoid, but the feeling is like an octopus because of their wiggly arms and legs and their motion. This is a being that has a basic spinal skeletal structure and has appendages with tentacles. They are undulating, as if waves are going down their arms. They are longer than they are wide. Their eyes are very prominent and round and they face forward. There are no external ears but only a hole. The mouth looks comparatively small and not well developed. The lips are very thin but can become quite hard and bite stuff off. They have no hair anywhere.*

*"Their necks do not appear to be very sturdy. It seems like a pole rather than a real neck. There is a feeling of no bones in the shoulders and arms. The fingers are more like tentacles. I do not know if there are any bones. When you look at this being there is a feeling of flexibility or lack of structure or bones. It seems as if they have a backbone with some ribs, maybe a pelvis or something where legs are hooked to a hinge. They feel at home under water. Their arms seem to curve rather than bend. They appear to have arms like tentacles, which flex, bend, and grab. Instead of fingers, they have little tentacle tips that can wrap around something and hold it, like an octopus. The skull seems to have bones in it.*

*"These gray aliens are more ethereal in nature because of a fundamental difference in biology. They are kind of unique in the way they get energy out of food. They eat the food, it goes down into the stomach and gets turned around, is digested, and the nutrients are extracted out of the food in the stomach. The residue comes back out by regurgitating or vomiting. They have a two-way digestive system, in and out the same way. They do not have a digestive tract, as such. This is their basic genetic pattern."*

This race came about 800,000 years ago, about 200,000 years after the first alien group came and found a considerably different ball game. These aliens found a mixed bag. Some of the beings they examined had developed brains, some did not, and some of them had an intermediate size brain. This group of aliens was intrigued and fascinated with the emotional nature of the mankind.

They set up their laboratory under water and on the mountains. They could fly their craft right into the ocean. No water could get into them and they were able to enter and leave, keeping the water out. When they moved from the lab into the ocean, they did not need anything to help breathe. Water pressure does not seem to bother them. Of course, they were only twenty to thirty feet below the surface of the ocean.

**Genetic modifications:** These aliens studied the brain of ape-like humans, and from what they had learned by studying themselves and other beings, they tried to locate the centers that handled spoken languages and understood language. These are the centers they tried to develop. They tried to refine certain areas of the brain to give spiritual and moral sense and the ability to communicate.

According to my hypnotized patients, they did not just work with primitive humans and apes on land; they also worked with sea creatures such as the killer whale, the bottle-nose dolphin, the blue porpoise, and other social members of the dolphin family they could find. Their criteria for choosing which ones to work with seems to have been brain size and social behavior. They were not interested in working on species that did not have a society of any sort.

After the time during which these aliens were working, two different things happened. The first alien race had already been here, worked, returned and examined the beings they worked with, trying to determine the results. They returned during wide time intervals. Of course, at the beginning they did not know that other groups were here, too. They did not know which changes were caused by their modifications and which changes were caused by other groups' modifications, plus those that occurred through natural evolution, so their results were not 100 percent accurate.

These were the aliens who were so taken by the emotional nature of humans that it puzzled them. They do not understand emotions. They left after about 7,000 years. They then made trips back and forth between their planet and Earth. When they departed, they left their labs and equipment behind, planning to come back.

From the Akashic record in heaven, one of my hypnotized patients tapped into the following information about how alien race two of group one worked with humanity:

- *"Looking back from the Akashic library, I see that alien race two of group one has greenish gray skin, is about five feet tall, and has large round eyes. The body resembles a loosely inflated balloon rather than having a rigid bony structure, loose flexible hands like an octopus with three fingers and one thumb with suction cups on the finger-tips to grasp. They are upright and humanoid. They came about 200,000 years after the first alien race came. Alien race one was not on Earth at this time. They had returned temporarily to their planet. Several hundred beings of alien race two arrived here on Earth. They also brought genetic materials with them and bred thousands of beings of their race while here on Earth. As a result they ended up with about 4,000 in their crew, all genetically differ-ent. Then they reproduced between themselves to keep the crew going. Eventually they ended up with about 6,000 individuals. They also brought a lot of training facilities for their young ones."*

Described and drawn by a hypnotized patients

Alien race two of group one

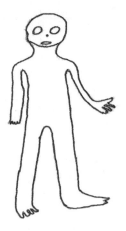 

Alien race two, the Epsilon Eradante, arrived on Earth about 800,000 BC. They also had bases all over Earth, including in the ocean. They began to examine the plants and different living things on the planet. When they found the humans in Africa, they also examined their DNA for a long time and found different anomalies for which they did not have any explanation, and which they did not find anywhere else on the planet. They also noticed that there were some genetic changes made in them. They saw some spirituality in these humans. By this time, there were considerable changes in mankind. Their social practices improved and they were planting for food. They were still moving from place to place.

When the first alien race did the modification, it was hard to detect a spiritual side in humans. By the time the second alien race arrived, it was easy to see that humans had thinking ability and a spiritual aspect. They still looked like apes, except their behavior was less ape-like. After humans started growing food themselves, the population exploded.

These aliens did genetic modifications in four groups and transplanted them all roughly in the same area that we now know as Thailand. Each group consisted of about fifty to seventy people, so a total of about two hundred and forty people had been transplanted to a forest, far away from each other so they cannot intermingle. These aliens did not think to transplant the food plants of these humans in the new land, so people were confused at first because the plants and foods they were used to were not there.

The babies who were born to the genetically modified people had less hair and there was a range of skin tone from dark to medium light. They were taller, the head was rounded and higher, and the brow was higher and more forward. The volume of the brain had increased and these humans were straighter, but still more like an ape than a human. After several generations, these modified humans were brought back to Africa to intermingle with the original human population, about a thousand years later.

Then the aliens did more genetic modification on other humans from central Africa and transplanted them where

China is now. They wanted to make people taller, stronger, spiritual, and intelligent. This time something went wrong in the modification. There was a defect that spread to all the children. They were seven feet tall, strong, more violent, aggressive, demanding, fought among themselves, and also struck out against the other humans. They did not seem to learn quickly, and even though they had a big brain, they did not seem to be particularly spiritual or intelligent. The aliens were very disappointed with this modification and decided not to take them back to the main population of mankind in Africa and Thailand, where modification was spreading well. The beings in China were allowed to die out naturally. By this time, mankind was spreading out of Africa to Asia Minor, Israel, Arabia, and ending up on the Mediterranean coast.

After the failure of this genetic modification in China, the aliens were discouraged. After a long time, they did minor genetic modifications, a little bit at a time, because they did not trust making major genetic changes at one time as they had in their first two modifications. The humans with minor genetic manipulation were transplanted to various parts of Asia. After the modification was established and the new generation was all right, they were returned to the general population. In Thailand, only part of the modified people were moved back to the general population in Africa, and the rest were allowed to stay where they were. They were expanding well. These aliens did not do any spiritual teachings but simply observed them.

When the second alien race arrived, the spiritual components were obvious and easy to detect. There was an island across the southeastern coast of Africa. They put people there after minor modification and let them develop. If the modifications were successful, they would integrate them with the general population in Africa. They also transplanted a genetically modified group in what is now Siberia, and when successful, they were transferred back to the general population in Africa because they wanted the change in DNA to be integrated in the entire human race.

Different genetic modifications were made with different groups and then after about five generations, they were allowed to intermingle with the general population in Africa. The spread of the population was first all over Africa and gradually through the northern route into Asia and Europe. Color and other physical characteristics began to change gradually in mankind. When people moved to different parts of the world, they changed more, depending on the climate of the region and sun exposure. As the brain became larger, the skull size increased, and the shape of the head changed and the eyes and the face moved forward. As a result, hearing and visual acuity lessened and, in a way, mankind became less apt to survive. However, with the increase in the brain and the increase in spiritual nature, they became cooperative and, along with the development of agriculture, the survival rate increased. By now, humans were planning for their lives and their families, cooperating, and living by rules. It made a tremendous difference in their survival rate.

The mother ship of the second alien race was not on Earth all the time. The bases on Earth remained occupied and functional, and even after most of them were withdrawn, the ones who were left on Earth to observe the program became old and died off. Those who were born on Earth died here and never saw their home planet. They stayed as long as 30,000 years at a time, on an occupied base set up to be self-sustaining. Then a ship would come back, trade some crew members, bring some equipment, and take information back. They kept three bases active in the mountains of Africa, Russia, and Asia, from where they could observe their experiments. They left about 200,000 years ago. Their bases are still there but they are not functional.

**Contributions made by second alien race of group one:** This second race of the first group basically had an intention to increase the overall size of the brain and to increase the size of the head. To their way of thinking, this would increase humans thinking capacity and change their perception, thought, foresight, and vision, and improve all the capabilities. Intention and fact are two different things. They did increase the overall size of the brain. The most significant change they brought about was the development of the concentration center, a center between the two hemispheres extending in both the hemispheres and shaped like a mushroom cap. They improved the functioning of humanity by increasing concentration and attention. They also improved their spirituality by enlarging the temporal lobes of the brain.

An animal requires a shifting attention. If the animal concentrates on eating grass, the animal becomes a lunch; it gets eaten. This is not the best way for human beings. They need to be able to focus on what they are doing. If humans had an attention span of an animal, they would not accomplish much and they would be known as hyperactive or having Attention Deficit Disorder, but due to genetic modification, the ape-like beings became better able to concentrate.

They did undertake the action to improve the size of the brain and the size of the skull and the supporting structure for the brain, so they would be in keeping with each other. Humans were improved in perceptiveness, thought process, interconnectivity within the brain, and interrelation of the thoughts within the brain. The change in the concentration center was not really their stated objective, but it was one of the most positive outcomes because it changed the fundamental thing about humanity. They were able to devote full attention for a longer period of time.

A negative outcome of their intervention is that it increased a sense of ego, such as "for me" and "myself." Humanity differentiated between the individual and the tribe more readily. Initially ape-like humans were the trooping-together type of beings; a being that was social and had to get along in groups. There was competition for food, but it was also the group that was defended. The group was the family to these individuals.

As the sense of ego, the sense of I, separated from the sense of group, which came with the increase in brain size, they lost connectedness with the group. Many people feel lonely and cannot pinpoint a reason. One of the reasons is because they are not functioning in a group. We still have some of this built-in trooping instinct, and if not satisfied by grouping, then the person is lonely. The ape-like heritage was a very strong part of humanity. When they began to think themselves as completely separate, the group instincts began to drop off. It was a positive gain in some sense and very negative in another sense. It did give humanity an ability to focus; it gave them individuality but it also took away their group support and group feelings.

Another outcome of the interventions of the second alien race was perceptiveness or the ability to perceive the spiritual. This had both good and bad effects. When we become more able to perceive the spiritual, we are able to perceive the Light and the help we receive. We are also able to contact our guides and other heavenly beings easily. On the negative side, Satan and his demons can also influence us easily. It is a real drawback in terms of Satan having much easier access to us. We have become a fair game for Satan. Of course, we were ever since the time of the first ape-like humans, but more so since much of our support structure that was with us as the ape-like-humans has been cut away.

This alien race worked at spirituality, and as a result, the spirituality of humans became more refined than before. But the drawback of this is that, combined with the possessive traits, it led to the development of the type of thoughts such as, "My religion is better than yours." It promoted a lot of conflicts in spiritual terms, and over the centuries, this was not a good thing. Also, since the spiritual center was developed through genetic manipulation, it is easily influenced by Satan and his demons. If it had been allowed to develop naturally, it would have been more stable, more secure, and less easily influenced by the dark side.

**Spiritual understanding of the second alien race of group one:** The second alien race of group one came to spirituality from an entirely different point of view. This is a race that evolved from a sea creature like a squid. Their understanding of right and wrong and their approach to life evolved differently than other alien races. Their way of spirituality may seem odd to a land-based race. They recognize universal good and have an understanding of love, but compassion is a foreign concept to them. They are kind of compartmentalized. If one of them gets hurt, it means nothing to them, but they will nurse the injured. They have appreciation for each other but do not have emotions like we do. They work together to accomplish things and have an appreciation for the common and universal good, and also know of evil. They can see the difference between good and evil, and prefer the good. Since they do not have much emotion, they instinctively do not recognize evil, although we who are very emotional often deny the role of evil in our lives, too.

These aliens depend upon each other so much that they see the sharing aspect of God more thoroughly than most. They know of a creator, but their conception is different. They understand that each being has a soul and that all souls are part of the same. It comes from their own shared nature. Their concept of sharing is that they have everything, therefore, they are perfectly willing to share their spiritual understanding. They do not need it just for themselves.

### Third Alien Race of Group One – Sirian

**Name:** The members of this alien race are called Sirians and are from the star system Sirius. There was a big time gap of about 200,000 year between the first and second groups of aliens. The third group arrived in about 770,000 years ago, relatively soon after the second group arrived (about 30,000 years after). The three alien races of the first group did not know about each other.

According to the heavenly beings, these beings are not from the star Sirus, but from a star that is close to it. They use that as a landmark because it is such a brilliant star. It overshadows their lives and is almost as bright as their own sun. They call their planet Sirus, but Sirus is a multiple star system and it is difficult for any planet to survive in its environment. Sirians are a much developed, highly intelligent, and evolved race. They spread beyond their planet of origin years before they came to our planet. This is a strange race by human standards. They seemed to be brutish and override you, despite their insect-like appearance, leading you to think they are not nice.

**Appearance:** According to my hypnotized patients, they look like they are a descendant of insects or lizards. They are humanoids and walk upright. They appear to have means for grasping. They look like an upright grasshopper or a praying mantis. They have fairly heavy bodies, walk on two legs, and have a short arm in front. They have triangular-shaped heads that remind one of a praying mantis. They talk in a high-pitched voice, so we do not even hear them. One hypnotized patient gave the following description of them from the Akashic record:

- *"Sirians are humanoid and are lizard or reptilian-type in looks. They are also bird-like because their face moves like a bird in jerky movements. They can also be thought of as insect-like because they have triangular, pointed heads like a praying mantis. They are upright, about five and a half feet to six feet tall. Their eye sockets appear kind of a holder and the eyes sit upright and out in the skull. There are no externally visible ears and there is a membrane with holes for the nostrils. They do not have hair. The face is triangular, with the eating part out front. The jaw gives an impression of being bird-like because the mouthpart protrudes like a beak. There is a suggestion of skin pattern, which indicates that there could be scales or it might be rough and have edges like plates, but the face is smooth and solid, almost like a mutant teenage ninja turtle. The neck is slightly narrower than the head and roughly circular, a little bit forward and front like ours. The body is rounded contributing to the insect-like feelings. What they remind me of more than anything else in terms of an insect is a praying mantis with shape of the head, the way the eyes look, and a little mouthpart sticking out in front.*

"These aliens have one pair of arms. I also see a second set. I guess you can call it a vestigial organ. They are at about mid-body and small and they do not look like they are good for much. These are used during sex. They have like hooking claws. The upper arms have more joints and are more flexible. The arms look like tubes and you do not see external changes when they move. You do not see the muscles swell or ripple. There are fingers, three opposed with the two. It is like you have two thumbs set on one side and three fingers set on the other side, opposite each other.

"Their second set of arms is good for manipulation and has sensitivity, better control and more precise

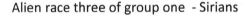

Alien race three of group one  - Sirians

*movements. So if the being wants to use fine muscle ma-
nipulations like threading a needle, it simply looks down
and its eyes will focus well at that range and it can manipulate whatever it wants to very precisely, but not with
the top arms. So they have three pairs of appendages, two
pairs of arms, one pair in the middle for sexual clasping
and fine maneuvering, and two legs for transportation."*

**Genetic modification:** Heavenly beings, through my hypnotized patients, stated that the primary concern of this alien
race was the spiritual development of mankind. They found
humans that were still primitive but already had a noticeable spiritual inclination. They believed this inclination was
a completely natural event, and it would have happened in
time without genetic manipulation. However, they did not
know that other alien races already had done genetic modifications to speed the process. They isolated an area of the
brain that they believed was responsible for spiritual development and where spiritual thoughts and feelings develop.
They genetically manipulated it to make it larger. After the
modification, this portion of the brain, the temporal lobe,
had enlarged on both sides and moved downward and forward, which enlarged the size of the skull and the face too.
The main difference between the two sides was the use of
the two halves of the brain.

This alien race also worked on development of the conscience center, a part of the brain on the top half of the forehead, slightly on the left of the center of the forehead. We
have not identified that center yet and do not have any name
for it. This center is responsible for the sense of right and
wrong. The Sirians, the third alien race of group one, genetically modified that center. As a result, altruism developed in
humanity, leading to an expanded sense of right and wrong
that includes a part of society, a town or country or all of
humanity, and not just individual. Before this, humanity was
not capable of stealing. If one person took what another person had, it was just fine, as in the idea, "It was good to eat

and I was hungry." After the development of the conscience center, people developed the sense of ownership and possession, and the concept of stealing and a sense of right and wrong was developed.

This alien race had interacted with mankind in the past with face-to-face contact, which had a devastating effect on humans. They came back at regular intervals to study the effects of what they had done. Of course, their work was not known to race one and two, which saw the effects of the experiments and thought maybe those effects were something they had done.

These beings are quite clever. They took samples back home to develop new food sources and to see if there was anything from our planet they could adapt to other planets, maybe to more than one planet, if they spread them around. Some of the unusual small beings, such as bacteria and small plants, were brought to Earth with these alien races. The bacteria on their shoes and clothing, which got left on Earth, reproduced and established a colony of these strange bacteria. So we have aliens bringing stuff to Earth and stuff taken out from the Earth. Someday when we get out in space, we will find that there are places in the universe with very familiar plants and animals because they are from Earth and were transplanted there.

A patient looking back from the Akashic library gave the following account of how this alien race worked with primitive humans and did genetic modifications there:

- *"From the Akashic library, I see that the Sirians came to the planet Earth around 770,000 BC. They established bases on the land of every continent, which they inhabited only part of the time. They did not form a large crew. They moved from place to place studying the local plants and animals on the planet. They found the developing humanity quite interesting and studied them for a long time. They were surprised to find much evidence that mankind had a spiritual nature even though they looked like apes. The Sirians also found evidence of intelligence in humans, who*

*had a sophisticated memory, were able to make connec-*
*tions from one event to another, were able to plan ahead,*
*and could recognize the existence of the soul and that it*
*continues on after death. They also realized that these be-*
*ings recognized the existence of God and were stunned by*
*that fact. They also detected cases of some psychic abilities*
*and foreknowledge."*

These aliens began to study humans and noticed some
anomalies in the DNA for which they could not find any precursor in the other micro-life of the planet. In their previous
experiences, any gene to show up and be expressed in an
advanced life form in the evolutionary chain, that gene had
to exist before and it had to have been used in a similar way
in a less sophisticated animal.

This led them to believe there might have been some genetic manipulation done with the humans. So, of the three
alien races that came to Earth, it was the third alien race
that first caught on that they were not the only ones looking
at human beings. This was because of their particular approach to genetic studies, which was to begin with the simplest creature and work your way up. Any gene expressed
in the advanced beings comes from the lesser beings. When
they found abnormalities in DNA, there was only one conclusion: somebody had tampered with the genes.

The Sirians took a look at the genes that did not naturally
come to the humans. They figured out what characteristics
had been contributed to the humans due to these genes. Then
they tried to puzzle out which gene had come to the humans
in an unnatural manner, even though they are natural on the
planet. They decided that several of these genes should not
have shown up in humans and must have been transferred in
by another intelligent source.

After they were convinced that there might be another
alien race on the planet, they began to look around for signs
and found the bases of alien races one and two, but found
no aliens other than themselves. They prepared signs and

information for other alien groups coming to Earth, to contact them. They prepared the analysis of DNA, particularly of the humans, along with the information they collected, making it obvious that they wanted to share their scientific findings.

The second half of their work, other than continuing the study of life on this planet, was deciding what they could do with the human beings. By this time, humanity was pretty well distributed all over Africa and in the south of Europe and Asia. They wanted to improve the quality of life and the quality of emotional nature, so they could have wider-ranging emotional responses. They did a series of planned changes and introduced them to the whole of mankind. This was accomplished in the space of thousands of years. Once the genetic mutation was established, they placed those humans in groups in various places where humans were, so it would spread evenly throughout mankind. Part of their thinking was that they wanted mankind to be a single species and not to diverge into different species.

Aliens chose a big island near the east coast of Africa to isolate the genetically modified humans. They selected it because the island was surrounded with water, so humans could not get out and leave the place and they could be sure of the experiment. This island is underwater now. The experiment was done in stages. A group of humans were brought to the island and a characteristic was established with genetic manipulation. Once it was stable and they were sure it was beneficial, then the group was put back into the human race. Part of the reason it took so long was because they waited for the changes to spread in several generations, which added a hundred and fifty years or so to each step of the experiment. The genes were placed strategically in very small individual groups in places in Africa where the local traffic would carry them up and down the continent. It was the same with the placement of the genes in Asia and in Europe, so that as people reproduced, the genes would spread. The third-generation descendants were taken back to the island after the genes had spread through three generations. This gave them a more accurate picture of just what was happening with the population on Earth.

The Sirians did similar modifications seven times, to establish one characteristic: an increase in human emotions. These changes occurred all over in mankind. The skin tone, eye color, hair type and color, and other variations were already developing because of the modifications and the local conditions. This was not planned but it was happening anyway. It was the plain old genetic drift, where things tended to be in a certain direction.

Each experiment took thousands of years. They were not about to make a mistake. They were also studying quite a few species on the planet. The main thrust of the expedition was still to survey everything on the planet. They were working on grasses, trees, just about every plant, insects, and animals to gather complete genetic data. They were searching for knowledge to understand how genes are expressed and what they could take back to the home planet. It was important to have a thorough understanding of genetics before anything went back with them and not to have a tragedy due to the unwanted genes.

They first looked at human spirituality and psychic ability. In the evaluation of spirituality, they went with what they observed in human behavior. The same observation was used in their evaluation of psychic ability. This resulted in a long debate and they decided to do the modification. Then they discussed which brain center they should help develop.

Another thing they began to develop was the concept of language, a communication concept within humans. It took repeated efforts to enhance the ability humans had and at the same time add more. In a series of steps, the centers that related to symbolic logic, universal ideas, and other such things related to communication, were developed in the brain. Part of the reason this process took so long was determining which part of the brain performed what function by putting the experiment in effect and then observing its success. This took thousands of years, and as each small phase was completed and pronounced a success, those individuals were integrated into humanity. Again there was the waiting period till those genes spread through the population. This was the first part of the experiment to develop enhanced communication.

When it was successful, no value judgment was placed on this type of communication or upon the quality of communication. Any sort of communication was considered to be a good thing. Communication was evaluated in terms of gesturing, speech (that is, grunts, sounds, and animal noises), significant eye movements, and body language. All these were recognized as forms of communication.

This alien group proceeded very cautiously and deliberately, taking small steps at a time. If at any time they decided the experiments were not beneficial, that phase of the experiment was terminated. The individuals who were involved in this would not be permitted to reproduce with the rest of humanity and were allowed to simply live out their rather sterile lives on the island, leaving no offspring. This happened a couple of times during all the experiments, but it was not the usual thing, not with their care and caution.

There were many changes which occurred in humanity as a result of these modifications. The psychic communication, which was already there, was improved and a greater variety of psychic talents were developed. The Sirians worked with language and went back to communication.

Then they had to start working on the physical structure of the body because the body could not perform as well as they wanted. This was when it really got touchy. They had to make the physical changes because they had already given humans more capacity than they could use. So they had to change the way the humans were built, otherwise they could not use the other changes that had been made.

For a while, it was a back and forth process. They worked on the communication center and developed a symbolic logic center and abstract thinking center; all this to help enhance communication.

Physically, they added more skull and permitted the brain to expand in the back. They included more nerves to the tongue and the lips for more dexterity. They also changed the shape of the mouth and domed the upper jaw so there was room for the tongue to flap.

They also did refinement in the hearing of sound, to better hear different tones. Originally, sound was important, to hear how loud and from what direction, whereas tone was not important, such as which note of the scale was being heard. One of the changes they made was to cut down on acuity, so they could not hear from far away and could not tell directions, but they could tell the difference between different frequencies. All these experiments took thousands of years each, and they were not continuous. There were time gaps in between, when they did not do anything, but allow these experiments to spread.

They also worked on the control of vocal chords and breath. All animals breathe when actively working, and less when resting. When they developed the concept of controlling the breath to suit communication, they had to change the perception of sound and then had to change breathing patterns and vocal chords.

This was where the aliens stopped, because they were all leaving the planet for a while. They had been on Earth for a long time, almost 45,000 years. So others replaced the original aliens after a while. This was when they bumped into alien race two, which turned out to be a good thing. They had left messages and the records, which race two really appreciated and enjoyed.

Races one and two did general modifications but not with the pinpoint accuracy that the third race did, because the third race had so much more genetic information about the whole planet than the others did. They started with microscopic creatures and worked their way up.

All three races had mingled with humanity, which had negative effects on humans. It was easy for mankind to recognize that these aliens had power to do things they were incapable of. They felt scared seeing something bigger and different than them, something they could not understand. In some cases they felt out-and-out panic. Since the alien races did not feel threatened, they saw no good reason for humans to feel threatened and did not realize till later how humans felt about them.

**Contributions made by the third alien race of group one:** According to the heavenly beings, the third alien race focused more on the temporal lobes, which had been developed by the first and second races earlier. In this case, they went specifically for spirituality and a more spiritual understanding of the universe. The primary result was an increase in spirituality, and the outcome was positive.

This race also worked toward refinement of the size and structure of the brain, and this improved the function of the brain. They made the cells smaller with more interconnections, more nerve connections, made the structures more complex and fine working, rather than just larger. The apparent positive outcome was that the brain functioned much better and had many more interconnections, leading to much better thinking.

They did give us a means through which we could develop a stronger telepathic bond by using the concentration center and developing spirituality and spiritually-based psychic ability. A drawback of these genetic modifications might be that some individuals became more interested in spiritual matters and less capable of taking care of the everyday business of surviving in the world.

Their genetic modifications were designed to get speech and thought communication and to promote spirituality and communication. The observed result was that humans became more intelligent and could communicate better. There were drawbacks in communication because they were not accurate; that is, "What I mean does not get said, and what you hear is not what I meant." This is a trait of communication out of this genetic manipulation.

Telepathic communication is much better because it gets across the exact nature of what we are saying. With telepathic communication, the feelings, the intent, and the information are all conveyed at once. We had also developed the skills of telepathic communication. This is what alien race four and five of the second group found so interesting about us; that we have telepathic abilities. This really intrigued them, because our race worked outside normal physics as they understood it.

Physical changes due to the genetic manipulation by the third alien race were that human beings became less strong and had much finer features. This second human was nowhere as strong and bulky as the great apes, just as the third human is nowhere as strong as the second human. They became taller after each modification. The original ape-type human was three and a half to four and a half feet tall.

**Spiritual understanding of the third alien race of group one:** Heavenly beings claimed that this race had difficulty expressing its understanding of the universe and had been developing spiritual understanding as it moved around in the universe. They had a fairly primitive religion and did not make the jump to a mature religion until they went into space. Since then they have grown and developed to the point that they do not have to have religion and spirituality connected in their mind. According to them, spirituality can exist without religion and religion can exist without being spiritual.

Heavenly beings, through my hypnotized patients, claim that this race seems to be cold and unemotional. They do have spirituality and they do have emotions, but they do not tend to be demonstrative. Emotions are not overriding in their life. They would be better off to be in touch with their emotions, since they are aware of them. They consider showing emotions and being emotional as a waste of time. They think they do not need it.

Emotion is the greatest motivating force. One of the fascinating things about us is that we have an intellectual, spiritual, and emotional aspect. We are making progress rapidly for many reasons: first, being emotional and the extent of our emotional development; second, the extent of our spiritual development and our wide potential; and third, the interaction between our emotions and the intellect, a great motivating force that keeps pushing us forward.

This alien race is learning spirituality from us. They see the interplay between emotions and spirituality, something they choke off. By observing us and really studying us, they get where they can connect with us. They think we are very lucky to have turned out the way we did because they can put us under the microscope, study us, and end up learning from us.

## Second Group of Aliens – Five Races

The second group of aliens includes five alien races. There was a big time gap between first group and the second group. Their names are spelled as they sound and are as follows:

> First alien race: **Chikanese:** came about 250,000 years ago.
> Second alien race: **N-hante:** came about 200,000 years ago.
> Third alien race: **Kicks** (in sounds and growls): –came about 150,000 years ago.
> Fourth alien race: **Zipson:** came about 70,000 years ago. Also known as **Capella.**
> Fifth alien race: **Meddac:** came around 50,000 years ago. Also known as **Kubold.**

These are five alien races that were significant because they interacted with the human race, studied it, provided teaching, did religious training, and provided technological advancement. They did not just come and observe; they actually got involved with humans. Of course the original group of three races was still making trips back and forth doing genetic engineering. It was the second alien race in the second group that transplanted the entire tribe to Lamuria, a place where they were isolated, so they could study them and be fairly sure there was nobody else coming in from outside the tribe. According to Angel Eichael, these races show up in various legends or narrative accounts in different parts of the world.

### First Alien Race of Group Two – Chikanse

**Name:** Their name is Chikanese. They came about 250,000 years ago.

**Appearance:** This alien race is also humanoid, bipedal, and walks upright. One of my patients gave the following physical description of this race:

- *"These are insect or bug-like. They are humanoid and walk upright. They have bulging eyes, which stick out of the head with a little bit of the external part showing. The ears appear to be like a membrane on both sides of the head with no external ears. They have knob-like projections on the top of the head. The body looks kind of hard as if it has an outside skeleton or outside shell. The limbs seem to be thin compared to the body size. Their fingers are like claws. There are two fingers like thumbs on one side, and three on the other side of the hand. They can grasp things quite tightly. Their feet are a duplicate of the hands except the feet are wider and the toes are shorter. Toes come to the side of the foot and point forward."*

**Contributions made by the first alien race of group two:** When the first alien race of the second group arrived, they found humans who were able to communicate, were spiritual, and were developing spiritual practices. These aliens worked with humans with the concept of God, developing rituals, and with the concepts of prayer – a way of communicating with God. They also educated them about the concept of Satan and his demons. A lot of this information came through them. Of course some of these things mankind had already figured out and the information was only confirmation.

This race arrived in different places on Earth and interacted with the local population. They were not well received. They worked on religious worship, giving mankind some framework to work with, leading to a better understanding of God. They also helped them organize a framework so there would be a way to pass down teachings from generation to generation. It was really group two that helped organize religion on Earth.

This race also did genetic modifications. They worked on spirituality and processing abilities. They figured that humanity had the brain size to be a really intelligent being. They were interested in improving processing skills so humanity could think more thoroughly and faster. But this was not their primary intention. They were more interested in passing on philosophy, spirituality, an understanding of life, and ways to live and be in harmony with the spirit. These were things about which they felt good. They also believed that humanity needed them and wanted to spread the teachings.

These aliens used to take humans up in their ships and let them see what the Earth looks like from above. They taught them astronomy, what the moon and other planets were like, and told them about the stars. They educated them in basic mechanics. They were technologically oriented, as any space race has to be, but they did not do a lot of technological teaching. Race one of group two did not really work with the people of Lamuria. They studied them after they became aware they were there. They also realized they had been transplanted there. They knew the continent had not been populated before, and they concluded that another alien race had made genetic changes and transplanted the population to Lamuria for research studies. So they simply observed the results, studied the genes, and noted the changes that occurred, but did not make any changes of their own. There were no significant drawbacks of what this race did.

**Spiritual understanding of the first alien race of the second group:** This race is aware of God and the Light (heaven). They do have people who serve as prophets, those who are in better contact with God and the heaven. They are very perceptive and psychically developed. One of the reasons they find us fascinating is that they see us developing and are aware that we are different than some other races in this regard. They feel as though they are getting a chance to watch their own development through us.

Even though physically very different, they relate to us because of their understanding of the soul. They relate to every other being in the universe. This is a group that taps into the spirit for technological inspiration. We happen to be a race that is developing psychically and they see the relationship between spirituality and psychic development, and form new theories and ideas concerning it.

### Second Alien Race of Group Two – N-hante

**Name:** Their name is N-Hante. They came about 200,000 years ago.

**Appearance:** My hypnotized patients described these aliens as reptilians and also like a lizard or an alligator. They are about five feet tall when they become adult and they continue to grow all through their adult life, up to seven or eight feet.

One of my patients gave the following physical description of this alien race:

- *"These aliens are humanoid and walk upright on two legs. They have a face like an alligator, broad and flat, with protruding jaws. The eyes are sticking out of the face and the skull doming up. They are about six feet tall when they are standing on their hind legs. The body is relatively large and legs are shorter. The front legs are like arms appearing to be longer for manipulation and handling things. The odd thing about this race is that the brain occupies the skull area and then extends down to the neck. There are holes for ears and a flap sticks out of the skull around it.*

*"The most dominant feature of the face is a long snout with the mouth in it. The nose is set into the top of the snout. When you look at the face from the side, with the long snout and the general shape of the skull, it looks like a collie dog, but from the front, the face really looks like an alligator. The skin is brownish gray, which depends on the individual and the sex. The female appears to be more brown and the male tends to be more gray. The aliens have a small tail, which is blunt and contains vertebrae for about half its length. The structure of the hip is modified and is actually four or five inches above where the body ends and then there is a tail.*

*"The front limbs are longer and legs are shorter, but are strong and have heavy muscles. The rest of the body continues between the legs and then the tail goes down in between the knees. They have pad-like feet with four toes. They prefer to walk on two legs, but they can also walk on all four limbs, which are used when they crawl into the water to catch fish. The hands also have four digits, which can fold, and the two center fingers are able to really wrap around things, and provide a strong grip. They have kind of lumps running from the skull down. Their bodies appear to be narrower than human bodies. Females are taller and bigger. The grown adults are about five feet tall and continue to grow up to seven feet."*

These alien beings really enjoyed life on Earth. It was a compatible planet. They loved to go fishing because they can actually jump in the water and catch the fish in their mouth. They had bases at the edge of the ocean because they enjoyed the water. Some lived on the spaceship and explored the planet and some had bases in concealed locations on a hill. The aliens could work and could live under water but usually they were surface dwelling beings. Some of their bases are still there.

This alien race was the one who transplanted the entire tribe from what is now Iraq to Lamuria, a place where they were isolated, so they could study them and be fairly sure there was nobody else coming in from outside the tribe. The technology the first and second race passed on was kind of accidental and it was not something they meant or had to do. This was about the technology of how to make things and how things worked in the world. All they were interested in was developing spirituality in mankind. Alien race two did genetic modifications in the tribe they transplanted in Lamuria, and dealt with spiritual interaction. They also did spiritual teachings in Lamuria.

**Contributions made by the second alien race of group two:** This race came around 200,000 years ago. They did genetic modifications on a tribe and transplanted the whole tribe to Lamuria for the experimental reasons. They identified the temporal lobes as the seat of spirituality through their studies. They did genetic modifications to develop spirituality by enlarging both temporal lobes. That was their specific focus and they were successful in it.

According to heavenly beings, both temporal lobes are connected with spirituality, but the right is more involved than the left. The left side tends towards local-reality and structured sensations, while the right side is concerned about contact with the spirit so as to become part of the spirit, which in fact is the true spirituality. Not as some religions would have it, sterile and meaningless by stressing on the intellectuality of the religion. One of the true purposes of religion is to put people emotionally in contact with the world of spirit.

N-Hante aliens did these modifications on the people of Lamuria and, as a result, Lamurians became more spiritual. The experiment was carried out under controlled conditions with the limited population. No other outside humans were involved, so the genetic changes spread through and stabilized within the population very quickly.

Physical changes occurred because the temporal lobes of the brain increased in size and protruded more downward and in front, which changed the face of mankind to look more like modern humans. The drawback of the genetic modifications is that they did not provide a sufficient support structure, so there was a re-shifting of the brain tissue.

Another outcome of their modification was a shifting in values, as to how you assign your time and what becomes important to you. This is not a drawback or a positive, but neutral, depending on your point of view about what you need and what you want. There were changes that happened which they did not intend and did not want. These were the refinement of the human features to present-day human form. They also did a lot of spiritual teachings with Lamurians.

**Spiritual understanding of the second alien race of group two:** This race is very spiritual. They have a strongly developed sense of right and wrong. There are some people who worry about the motivation of this race, believing they have to be evil because of their appearance. According to the heavenly beings, this is a waste of time because these beings have a very strongly developed sense of right and wrong in spiritual terms. They realized their conversion and change of approach to life before they came here to study us. In fact, a beneficial change.

This was a very predatory race; striking and eating like a komodo dragon, and was less developed for a long time before they came to Earth about 200,000 years ago. They could consume other creatures or us, but now they feel it is unethical to eat a being that is spiritually equal. It was before they were here that their great prophets arose, the ones who converted their ways. Before that, they were as interested in developing us as developing the food supply, but they were never intrinsically evil.

### Third Alien Race of Group Two – Kicks

**Name:** Their name is Kicks (in sounds and growls). They came about 150,000 years ago.

**Appearance:** Members of this race are humanoid and walk upright. Under hypnosis, a patient gave the following description of this alien race:

- *"This race is also upright, humanoid, and walks on two legs. They also resemble a lizard. They are about four to six feet tall with the average height about five feet tall. They are not very heavy beings. These aliens have a small tail, which bends at an almost right angle to the body. It does not hang down between the legs, but curves up gently. The face comes down and protrudes and there is bulging forward of the mouth. There is a soft rounded chin. The nose is set back and the eyes, just above that bulge out, and there are sliding skin patches that resemble eyelids. There is a heavy bony ridge above the eyes. The skin color has several shades of green with some gray in different parts of the body. Their heads have a collie dog look; the nose or mouth does not look like a collie snout but it does come forward. They have a very fine single strand of fuzzy hair around the eyes, upper lips, and around the ears. They have a stout neck, and the brain is contained in the neck. There are ear holes but there are no external flaps.*

  *"There is crisscrossing of the muscles going from one side of the body to the other rather than connecting to the centerline or side line. It makes them very strong. The shoulders are free floating and are not fastened to much of anything. Arms and legs have double bones in upper arms and thighs and single bone in the forearm and below the knees. There is a hump in the back because of the muscles crossing. Hands have five short fingers, almost like stubs sticking out, which are good for hanging on to stuff. There is a ring of bone around the lower part of the body like a hip but not firmly attached to the spine so it is very flexible. Legs are longer than the arms. Knees are also loosely attached and are kind of free floating. The feet are much bigger than hands.*

*"These beings are not particularly water loving. They do go in the water but they mostly prefer land. They are very intelligent, compassionate, and have spiritual concerns. They are independent beings and exert their free will. They also had bases on Earth in the forest when they were here for an extended period of time. They had multiple spaceships. The large one remained in space and many smaller ones were used for exploring the Earth from one place to another."*

**Contributions made by the third alien race of group two:** Heavenly beings, through my hypnotized patients, state that this race is very important because of the depth of its effect on humanity. This is a very perceptive race. The beings are highly spiritual, very evolved, with a very good understanding of genetics. Their intervention in the human race was intended to increase intelligence and to make humans more spiritually oriented. They have a deeper understanding of the unknown, invisible world that underlies this one and the fact that the invisible world is the real world.

When the second race was not on Earth in Lamuria, the third race arrived. They did not see any signs of presence of another alien race, so they also experimented with the Lamurians. They realized that this isolated population was an ideal test site for the experiments they wanted to do because this was a smaller population in a limited area, isolated from another population. They did their experiments with the intention that they could observe the results in Lamurians without contamination by the outside people. So, unknowingly, there were two races experimenting on the same group of humans in Lamuria.

This happened repeatedly on Earth at different times and at different places, but in the other areas where the humans were able to move and intermingle, the aliens could never be 100 percent sure of what was natural development and what was due to their genetic manipulation. The Lamuria population was supposed to get around that by having no possibilities of intermingling.

Although the first and second race of group one did genetic changes on the brain in general, their intention was simply to increase all the functions, but the second and third races of group two had their primary interest in the spirit. They had done this before. They actually intervened with populations on different planets and tried to teach them religious and spiritual values, morals, ethics, and even aesthetics, the appreciation of beauty.

They believed they had located the centers in the brain, which we know as the temporal lobes, that perceive spirituality, and by increasing the size of this area and increasing its functioning, they could make humankind a spiritual being. They introduced these genes into the human population and watched closely. They found no drawbacks in the procedure. They did witness what was taken to be in increase in human spirituality. Their analysis showed that this particular part of the brain (temporal lobes) had increased in size and had more nerves in them.

The other races did it before, and this race did it more, and all came to the same conclusion. The size of the temporal lobes increased even more. Where they really differed is that this race intervened directly. They lived among the people of Lamuria and taught them directly and indirectly by projecting a Lamurian image. The humans in Lamuria recognized them as people, although certainly as no other people they had ever seen, and accepted them peacefully, partially because Lamurians were more intelligent than average humans and much more spiritually developed. They recognized and accepted them as decent civilized beings, as humans, although they were not earthlings. This group found no indication that anyone had taught Lamurians before, so they worked with that population.

These aliens worked with Lamurians in developing spirituality. They helped them with general knowledge, made them aware of sacred writings, and introduced them to meditation and to channeling their own mind. This alien race helped in founding an individual religion, not a priestly religion. In this, they emphasized meditation, prayers, and rituals as ways to develop personal spirituality. They were there to explain the psychic phenomenon when it happened. As a result, Lamurians became far and above ordinary human beings in intelligence and spiritual development.

These benefits have not left the human race. Lamurians did expand and they did have contacts with North, South and Central America, and eventually across that, to include contact with Atlantis. Being humans, their genes were shared. At the end, when Lamuria was sinking into the ocean, Lamurians went west to Asia, to China, Japan, Southeast Asia, and India. This may seem like really a long way to go to be safe, but it was also the place where Lamurians felt more comfortable in resettling when they could not be in Lamuria. It was, then, their second choice. They primarily went into those areas because of the spiritual development of the people there. They also contributed greatly to the spiritual education of each of those people there. Those who went to North, Central, and South America founded various schools of shamanism.

The second race of group two, who transported people to Lamuria, also taught them, but the third alien race directly intervened. The second race studied them, made genetic changes, and observed what happened, but they were not a constant presence in Lamuria. They went back and forth.

Race three of group two also valued art. They worked with Lamurians in artistic expressions. They were not interested only in spiritual matters but also in the expression of spirituality in art, like music. Art is also an expression of mathematics and of physics. Music serves as a great way of expressing emotions and even as a way of conveying knowledge or information. They brought the beginnings of music, rhythm, and dancing. They worked with sketching and finding colors to add to paintings and to put on statues, and the arrangement of color.

The reason the aliens were inspired to come to Planet Earth and work with humanity was because there was a lot of dark influence on Earth, and God and the Light beings could not work directly with humans. In this case, Light could not work directly, but life could; that is, a living being in the universe could. So aliens in the universe were inspired by God to work with humans.

**Spiritual understanding of the third alien race of the second group:** This alien race came around 150,000 years ago. It worked on teaching spirituality to humans, especially after they detected what was present in mankind. This was the first race to become aware of the unique potential of humanity and the first one that tumbled into the combination of the sweeping power of their emotions, the strength of these emotions, and the depth of spirituality. In a way, they reaped the harvest that the second race of group two sowed. This race first found this special human capacity of intense emotions and spirituality in Lamurians and recognized them for what they were. They realized that these characteristics would become part of the entire human population.

They did not undertake any genetic manipulation worth mentioning. Humanity's gift, that extraordinary feeling for the spirit, was truly unique to them. There was a little at the beginning in the ape-like humans. So the aliens knew to look for it, but nothing like the sweeping emotions of humanity. It was as if human spirituality was connected to a power plant, a great driving force that was capable of pushing really far, very fast, and establishing a great depth of communication with the spirit.

The spirit is the end goal, which the third alien race had figured out. They had teachers and they had revelations. They had the idea that this is where humanity and the rest of the universe were going. When they found humanity with these unique characteristics, they were thrilled. In a way, it meant that humanity would supersede them as a spiritual group in the universe, but they were happy about it, simply because there was no other race that could do that.

This race is still in contact with humanity. They come and go, off and on, because we are of interest to them. Since they perceived it, they made other races in the galaxy aware of it. This is part of the structure that is building around Earth. All these groups of alien races are studying our interactions and us.

### Fourth Alien Race of Group Two – Zipson or Capella

**Name:** Their name is Zipson. They are also known as Capella. They came around 70,000 years ago.

**Appearance:** This alien race is tall, thin, and looks human. One of my hypnotized patients gave the following physical description of the race four from the Akashic records:

- *"The beings of this alien race look like humans. They are taller, about six feet four inches or more, and slim as compared to average humans. They look like Nordic people, blond, with a light complexion. The big toe is offset a little bit to the inside. The teeth are smaller and more numerous. Their face and nose are long, the mouth is small, and the eyes are not as prominent. They have smaller ears. Their hair is more pronounced at the back of the neck."*

**Contributions made by alien race four of the second group:** This race did very little religious or spiritual teaching. They had tremendous influence on human society. They taught science, metal work, and technology. They showed how to make tools, which was a very important step. They gave us different alloys to use. This race gave us the organized framework in technology and taught us about how to work with metals. The aliens' interest was in making useful articles. Their metalworking was quite advanced compared to what human beings knew. They also taught how to plan and build great structures like pyramids, plan and build cities, provide water supplies, and how to set up farms outside the cities.

The beings of this alien race were interested in teaching science and astrology. They took humans up in spaceships and showed them what Earth, moon, and planets were like and helped to get these concepts across. They also supplied some basic concepts of science. The result of their contributions was that humankind began to develop an organized body of knowledge and to appreciate its actual place in the universe.

The positive outcome was that they organized the framework for science and technological knowledge, both very valuable, while previous alien groups organized the spiritual framework. This group taught these concepts in Atlantis, Europe, and Asia.

On the negative side, without enough spiritual development, people misused and misapplied the technology. Instead of using metals for tools to make life better for everybody, humans made better weapons to kill people efficiently and to conquer and take over other people. Eventually human beings got atomic and hydrogen bombs. These aliens did not do any spiritual teachings.

The beings of this race considered themselves teachers, not researchers. They did some genetic experiments with embryo transplantation simply as an experiment, but it was not to improve the species or the Atlanteans. They did some hybridization experiments. But these were just experimental procedures. They were not intended to make improvements in humanity. They did genetic experiments, crossbreeding and embryo transplantation, resulting in some unhappy results. The beings that were lab-created were taken to another planet and are currently on observation as they develop and populate the planet. The name of the planet sounds like K'ohr, or Kkor.

One of my patients recalled a life in Atlantis when he was a technologist and was contacted by the fourth alien race of group two. These aliens gave technology to him and others with whom he worked.

- *"My name is Adel and I live in Cardi City in the north central section of Atlantis. It is 52,820 BC. I am twenty-five years old, married with two little girls, ages two and one. I live with my family in a high-rise apartment. This place is modern, spacious, and well designed. It has a kitchen, a living room, a dining room, a den/office, three bedrooms, and two bathrooms. We have a stove, a refrigerator, a freezer, a dishwasher, and other kitchen appliances. We have a television. We have radios, telephones, and a computer. I am a member of the wealthy class and we (myself, my family, and my co-workers) have no devices in our necks at this time.*

*"My mother is a nurse, and my father is a semi-retired medical doctor. My wife is a math professor and I am a scientist and I do research in a medical experimental complex. I work with animal and human cells and try to find ways to substitute animal cells for human cells and human cells for animal cells. My intent is to find ways to extend life, while making a stronger, healthier, and more durable human being. I also want to be able to replace a human's defective organ with a human or animal organ. My work is mostly trial and error. I do lab work and I also experiment on humans.*

*"I am on a team with six other researchers, where I am one of the two junior members. For the past five years (I'm now thirty), our team has been doing research on transplanting human or animal hearts into humans. We have also done a lot of research on how to put human or animal stomachs into humans. We work on real people. I don't do the transplants. The doctors do this, but I monitor, chart, and observe during the actual operation. I try to figure out what works and what doesn't work.*

*"At the age of thirty-seven, I am sitting at my desk where I am deeply engrossed in studying research about putting animal parts in humans. All of a sudden, this alien being appears before me. I am not alarmed. I feel very comfortable in his presence. He appears in person, saying that he has tuned into my thoughts because he has the same interests I have. He says he came to help me advance the work we are doing. He is very sociable, easy to be with,*

*and easy to talk to. Everything clicked and we hit it off. I am full of excitement. We sit and plan how he will return with a team of aliens to help our team of researchers with our future projects.*

*"The aliens are proportioned like humans, but they look more like a cartoon figure. The aliens have a stick-like body. They are tall and slender, going over six feet in height. Their body appears to be less than half the width of a normal sized human. They have little hairs on their heads that are thin and unkempt. They have large round eyes, a somewhat long pointed nose, tiny earlobes, and a slender mouth. Their hands and feet are of two kinds. Some have four fingers and a thumb and five toes on each foot, while others have arms and legs that end in somewhat rounded stubs. Their arms, legs, and torsos are very long and slender. Some are male and some are female. Later I discovered there are child aliens as well. The males wear light colored shirts and pants, and the females wear light colored blouses and skirts. The females are typically six to twelve inches shorter than the six feet to six feet six inch tall males.*

*"We decide that each member of our team will have his or her own personal alien. We do this so everyone will have a good level of comfort. Once the aliens' presence was established, then we all could become one large team with the same goal. As time went on, we became so harmonious that our thoughts became intermixed. As a result, we do not know who has the original thought. The aliens' team and our team worked together with the doctors. Lay people and our family members are not aware of the aliens. They have been living in spaceships and satellite stations hundreds of thousands of miles beyond the Earth.*

*"During my working lifetime, we had some modest successes. We were able to keep patients alive for several months using animal hearts. We had one patient who lived for fifteen months with an animal heart. We had*

some success in transplanting animal cells into human embryos. We feel that our subjects are more disease resistant, physically stronger, and more balanced individuals. Our goal here is to extend lives and increase the quality of lives. However, as researchers, we are aware that we need to observe several generations in order to accurately measure our efforts. All of us have good intent.

"I really enjoyed working with the aliens, and when I am invited to visit their spaceships, I am eager to go. I go there mentally, taking all my bodies except for my physical body. I visited the aliens' spaceship nine times during my lifetime, sometimes for social gatherings and sometimes for briefings on medical research. The aliens do not take their special reference manuals out of their libraries, so we have to go there to read them. I always travel with the personal assistance of my alien guide. As I sit in my office chair, he holds my hand and we travel up. I know that I am moving at a high rate of speed, but I do not feel the intensity. Shortly thereafter, we arrive at the spaceship.

"The outside of the ship is tall and it looks a lot like our spaceships today. It has a pointed nose as it sits vertically. There are fins or power source devices at its base. It is made of metal and it is gray in color. We walk up a series of around twelve steps into the large ship that carried fifty to a hundred aliens. Inside, the aliens are busy with their daily tasks. I am taken on a tour of the control room. I see pilots and co-pilots charting courses and studying graphs. I see the instrument panels, the knobs, the dials, the gadgets, and the buttons. The navigators are busy doing their own work. I visit their living quarters, which look like a nice home or hotel suite. After the tour, my alien guide takes me back to Earth.

"The last visit I make is on my sixty-fifth birthday celebration. My team of researchers and I go to their spaceship to celebrate my birthday. There are peanut flavored wafers, a variety of jelly-filled, bacon flavored, beef flavored, and fish flavored wafers. We drink a clear, tasteless beverage similar to water. We also have a fruity flavored *beverage that is light pink in color. My team gives me a beautiful wristwatch with diamond settings. The aliens present me with a gold plaque to commemorate our long-term partnership and years of service together. They thank me and my team for our contributions.*

*"At the age of seventy-two, I begin to experience health problems. Some of my arteries are becoming hard and are very narrow and blocked. I know I need to arrange surgery to correct my problems but I am in denial and I delay the surgery. In the meantime, I'm experiencing dizzy spells. Before I can complete medical arrangements, my spirit leaves my body, as I die of a sudden heart attack. My final thoughts are that I am disappointed and upset that I am unable to continue with more research. The angels who are searching for lost ones discover me and take me up into the Light (heaven). I get cleansed, and then I review my life with the assistance of five heavenly beings.*

*"Before going to the Light (heaven), I felt that my intent in that life was good and that the aliens didn't feel dark. But now, from the Light, I see that I lived a dark life because of all the human experimentation. I see that the aliens came to share their knowledge and also to learn. From heaven, I see how wrong it was to abuse other people in the name of research. There was a lack of ethics and a godless society in Atlantis. I see research and medical experiments were done without any guidance from the Light (heaven).*

*"From the Light (heaven), I can see how the aliens and I planned to come to Atlantis together to make positive changes. We knew in our planning that Atlantis was dark, but we planned to inject spirituality into this society. Sadly, the darkness blocked me and the aliens from carrying out our plans. I see that the aliens came from the planet Kyro. I also had several lifetimes on that planet thousands of years ago.*

*"I see that the aliens are still with us today working indirectly with people for positive changes. From heaven, I can see that these aliens have worked with many famous*

*inventors, such as Thomas A Edison (inventor of the incandescent lamp, phonograph etc.); Eli Whitney (inventor of the cotton gin); Henry Ford (inventor and automobile manufacturer); Jonas Salk (developed vaccine to prevent polio); and Alexander Graham Bell (inventor of the telephone). These aliens continue to live with humans (both the tall ones and the short ones). They stay in the background and keep a low profile, taking no credit for helping to make positive changes. Aliens have a strong desire to understand our spirituality.*

*"I see from heaven that I brought many problems from that life to the current life, such as being too comfortable with isolation from other people, having negative thoughts about some people, and not being open or receptive to others or wanting to get involved with others."*

**Spiritual understanding of the fourth alien race of the second group:** This race is particularly important to us because they are so human-like. They relate to us on a human level and we respond to them in the same way. We get along well together. Spiritually, they do not have as wide-ranging knowledge as us, but they certainly know about God. This race is not psychic. Race four has had more prophets, masters and spiritual teachers who were being sent to them. Other alien races also had more prophets, masters, and spiritual teachers being sent to them, but not as many as races four and five of group two, due to changeover in their history.

### Fifth Alien Race of Group Two – Meddac or Kubold

**Name:** Their name is Meddac. They are also known as Kubold on Earth. They came here around 50,000 years ago.

**Appearance:** This alien race looks like short, stocky humans. My hypnotized patient gave the following physical description:

- *"We know them as Kubold. These are human-like but look much shorter and stronger than humans, and appear like rectangular blocks stacked together. The shoulders are up higher, closer to the neck. Their neck is jointed differently. They do not move quite the same as humans, as if there are fewer bones with a better rotation system, but they cannot tilt their neck smoothly. When it comes to neck movement, we have an advantage in flexibility to the side. Their arms and legs are very human-like, but stronger and heavier. They are a little shorter, about four to five feet tall. They move different than humans. Their legs are not built the same. It looks like both their joints move forward, so that when they take a step first the leg raises then they go forward in two steps, come down and then the legs are pulled backward. As a result, they can take a longer stride. They look very powerful by simply how they are built. They remind you of great apes – short, blocky, and powerful-looking beings."*

**Contributions made by the fifth alien race of the second group:** The fifth alien race also made better metals; they developed the technology and helped humans work with higher temperature and melt tougher metals. They taught humans carpentry skills, metalworking, and planning, coordinating, designing, and actually building large projects. They also taught how to build temples and pyramids. Positive effects of what the fifth alien race did for us is that they made life easier, with concepts of planning, construction, and spreading out. They created the ideas of beauty and contributed to philosophy.

The metals they brought gave us the superior tools, which were used first positively, before weapons were created. This led to the modern world we see today. They also taught about food production by using iron tools. The hard metal tools made it easier to cut woods and to plow fields. The drawbacks of what the fifth alien race taught humans is that it led to efficient ways to kill large numbers of humans and the misuse of technology without applying spirituality.

They also benefited by studying mankind and they are also currently studying us. The psychic phenomenon in humans is part of what makes us unique. We are able to enter the world of spirit and we can have spiritual gifts and still be human. This alien race is very surprised that this exists. Overall, we are a unique combination. We have incredible violence and the capability to destroy others and ourselves, and we are also incredibly spiritual and have emotions. We stand out among the races of the galaxy. We are a latecomer, and others are interested in watching us develop.

**Spiritual understanding of fifth alien race of the second group:** This alien race is also human-like in looks. They related to us on the human level and we got along well. Like the fourth alien race, this race also had knowledge of God but did not have a wide-ranging spiritual knowledge. They are not a psychic race and do not understand the psychic nature of humanity. They intentionally chose to get rid of their emotions consciously. Race five has had a less turbulent history and not so much turmoil. They had a few teachers and prophets sent to them because they were less troubled and did not get messed up. They were more stable than the fourth race.

They have refined their understanding of spirituality after being in contact with Earth people. They believe now in their acceptance of spirituality. These were spiritual people but limited by their own experiences. They defined spirituality in their own terms, and after having been in contact with us, their definition of what could be a spiritual practice has evolved. This race and also the fourth race studied psychic phenomenon as they observed it happening. They are still doing it while searching for religious understanding. These last two races came pretty close together.

## An Overview of Genetic Modifications Done in Humans by the Alien Races

According to Angel Eichael, eight alien races had a great impact on the development of mankind. All these eight races are humanoid, and walk upright on two legs. This is not an exhaustive list of every alien race that has come to Earth. It is the list of the aliens who did major genetic modification on human beings. Other races have also done things on Earth and a few others have studied Earth, but they did not have any lasting effects on Earth.

These eight alien races are divided into two groups because there was a wide separation in time between the two groups and the extent of changes they made that affected the mankind. The first alien group includes the first three alien races, and the second alien group has the rest of the five alien races. The first set of changes, made by the first three alien races of group one, affected the entire human race. The second set of changes, done by the second group of five alien races, were close in time and did not pervade the whole of humanity. The changes these alien races instituted are still shaking down through humanity and still coming to fruition. Some of the alien races of the second group also did spiritual teachings and gave different technologies to human beings.

According to my hypnotized patients, these eight alien races contributed to significant changes in the human race. They were divinely inspired because they had the expertise but did not know it consciously. Three alien races helped with genetic engineering and the five alien races with teaching and the training, plus there were several other groups that just came and observed. These alien races slowly became aware of each other and realized that there were also other races here studying humans.

The first group of aliens arrived about a million years ago and their initial interest in mankind was simply to study them and to determine their capabilities. They thought of them as apes and did not detect their spiritual nature. They analyzed their DNA, along with studying their other physical attributes. These aliens thought they could make changes in the DNA and change the intelligence and the spiritual capacity of the humans, and they started a series of experiments to do that. This first group of alien races came to Earth many times and repeatedly intervened in human development, but they were not the only group interested in humanity.

A second alien race arrived about 800,000 years ago. The first group of aliens had already been to Earth and gone back to their planet several times, making changes in DNA and observing the results while trying to understand what they had done and what the outcome was. Of course, evolution also proceeded naturally in these ape-like humans. The second alien race found humans to have rudimentary intelligence, but no culture. They were very much taken by the idea of watching cultures develop. I guess you can call them anthropologists, as they were interested in how civilization, cultures, and evolution occur. This second alien race established more permanent bases on Earth than the first race. Some of them could maintain themselves on Earth for an extended period of time, while the rest of the group went on and explored other places. This was the first long-term alien settlement on Earth. They also made changes in the DNA, using slightly easier techniques in making their changes. They did not detect any substantial changes at once, not nearly as dramatic a change as they had hoped for.

The third alien race, which arrived about 770,000 years ago, was also interested in examining humanity. They found it to be a developing culture and wanted to study humanity and its civilization and the interaction between human beings and their nature. By the time the third alien race came, the first alien race had been already here many times. It was a major commitment of time and resources for the first two races to study human beings because of the distance. The third race lived much closer to the Earth and they had been back and forth repeatedly. For them to come to Earth was equivalent to a weekend trip, and it was practically like a joy ride.

Heavenly beings, through my hypnotized patients, state that the brain of today's human is not the same as the brain of the original ape-like humans. There were genetic modifications done by the aliens, plus the changes that came through natural evolution. Although alien genetic manipulations in humans brought about many positive changes, they caused some negative changes, too. Some of our chronic medical disorders are due to the tampering by the aliens. As advanced as they were in genetics, they did not completely understand what they were doing; therefore, not everything worked out for the better.

According to the heavenly beings, there were five major genetic modifications done on human beings by different alien races, as follows:

### First Modification

In trying to develop spirituality in ape-like humans, the aliens did genetic modifications in the brain. They changed the way the human brain functioned, the shape of it, and the parts of it. Their way of thinking was that these ape-like humans needed to have a specific brain part in order to be spiritually developed. The right side of the brain was considered to be more important for spirituality. So the first group of aliens modified the genes and increased the size of that lobe on both sides to make it more distinct from the rest of the brain and to make it stand out more. According to hypnotized patients, this was the temporal lobe of the brain. In the original brain, it was just a little more than a streak, a thin layer, and after the modification it became a distinctly bulging part of the brain. All three alien races of the first group and the first, second and third alien races of group two modified the temporal lobes of the brain.

The aliens hoped this modification would help humans with spirituality, not realizing that spirituality was already there in the ape-like human beings. These ape-like humans did become more spiritual due to the change in the temporal lobes of the brain. They related more completely to the existence of God and it helped to speed up their spiritual evolution.

That was one of the first modifications the aliens made. Since then, the temporal lobes on both sides of the brain have increased a great deal in size, but it was the lobe on the right that really interested them. They believed through their research with their race that this is where the spirituality was located.

## Second Modification

According to the patients' reports, there is a mushroom-shaped area in the center of the brain, almost in the center between the front and back. In that area is located a group of cells that help us focus and concentrate. The second alien race of group one recognized that this concentration center was necessary for development. They decided to improve that area to aid us in our spiritual development, and it did work. It became definitely bigger and, yes, people can pay attention and concentrate better.

According to the heavenly beings, these genetic manipulations were not needed. We already had these abilities and they would have developed naturally over time, but it did speed up the process. This intervention in the future could have some negative effects on us. As we continue to develop on our own and evolve, both spiritual center and concentration center may become too dominant and this could affect our daily functioning.

We can look at it from a slightly different viewpoint, which is the connection between spirituality, perception, and our relationship to the everyday world. The latter may be an illusion and it may be like living in a stage play, but we better take it seriously and do our best in the world because that is definitely a part of spiritual and human development. To live life to its fullest requires interacting with the real world, or what we perceive to be the real world. One of the drawbacks of the genetic modification is that when the centers for spirituality become overdeveloped, we may not pay attention to our relationship with the world, thus not really achieving the aims and ends of God because we are not living a fully human life. Spirituality and worldly life have to be balanced.

### Third Modification

According to heavenly beings, conscience center is a part of the brain on the top half of the forehead, slightly on the left of the center of the forehead. We have not identified that center yet and do not have any name for it. This center is responsible for the sense of right and wrong. The Sirians, the third alien race of group one genetically modified that center. As a result, altruism developed in humanity, leading to an expanded sense of right and wrong, which includes a part of society, a town or country or all of humanity, and not just the individual. Before this, humanity was not capable of stealing. If one person took what another person had, that was just fine, based on the idea, "It was good to eat and I was hungry." After the development of conscience center, people developed the sense of ownership and possession, and the concept of stealing and a sense of right and wrong was developed. The Sirians also did genetic modifications to develop emotions, communications, and hearing to improve humans' ability to hear different tones.

### Fourth Modification

The fourth and fifth modifications were refinements that made the spiritual centers more active. The fourth genetic modification was done about 250,000 years ago by the first alien race of group two. This was a telepathic race and they did this in an effort to improve our psychic abilities. The psychic abilities were already there and were previously increased and amplified, but in this change, they were trying to refine them. They also worked to develop the spiritual centers. They caused brain enlargement by enlarging the spiritual center, which also led to skull enlargement. They worked on enlarging the brain and skull both, and as a result, the spiritual center also became bigger. Although the first three alien races of group one worked on developing the spiritual center of the brain, which also led to overall enlargement of the brain and the skull, the gene this race modified was different but led to similar outcome.

### Fifth Modification

The fifth genetic modification was done on individuals about 10,000 years ago on an island on the Pacific Ocean, and they were allowed to mix with the general population about 2,000 years ago. This genetic manipulation was done by the short, stocky, human-looking alien race five of group two. They took people from the Middle East, Africa, Southern Europe, and Asia. They were isolated on a Pacific island, and when the modification was judged to be stable after 8,000 years of observation and study, then the people were transferred back to the general population. The aliens modified the right side of the temporal lobe of the brain to improve psychic ability.

It spread through the general population and is still spreading through the mainland. That is why we have such heavy alien activity right now. They are keeping tabs on us to see how this modification is spreading through the cultures of the Earth.

Through all these five modifications, humans have developed emotional, intellectual, and spiritual abilities that even surprised the alien races who did modifications on humankind. We can step outside the ordinary time and place and access power and information, which many of them cannot. These races are still observing and checking to see what happens to us.

A series of steps, both natural and imposed by others, caused changes in humanity. The effect on human beings while they were still ape-like was the increase in the brain part that deals with spirituality, and humans did become more spiritual. The next modification, on the concentration center, also worked. People were able to concentrate more and were able to pay attention over a long time span. This was not necessarily a beneficial adaptation to an animal, because animals have to be restless, have to be willing to move around to locate food sources and watch for predators. The animal whose attention is fixed on something is less likely to go out to explore and find more food sources. What we call hyperactivity now was of real benefit a million years ago as a survival mechanism, but not for the current humans.

Then, evolution was preceded by refining nerve structure, and the brain actually got a little smaller because it works better. The increase in intelligence and spirituality are not the results of the brain size but of the fineness of the nerve connections; that is, the interconnection within the brain. That is where evolution is currently working and improving the functioning of the brain, and not the size.

Finally, we wind up with the modern human, with the attention center developed with the expectation of the spiritual life. We have better developed attention span and are more spiritual than our predecessors due to the genetic modifications done by aliens, and also due to natural evolutionary changes. Over the last several thousand years, most of the changes in the spiritual nature of humans have been due to natural evolution. The first humans, the so-called Adam and Eve, were the closest to the functioning with the full consciousness, having been designed that way and sent for the special purpose from the Light (heaven), which changed after they got influenced by Satan and his demons.

### Gross Physical Changes

The first alien race, a million years ago, decided we should be bigger, according to their way of thinking. Since the apes appeared to be a crude model of a primitive animal resembling things that lived on their home planet, they decided we should evolve like they did and be relatively hairless and larger. So they tampered with genes to cause that to happen. Actually, the skin began to show through in quite a few places, although there were still a lot of hairs.

The second alien race made the second major physical change about 800,000 years ago. They amplified the same physical changes and made human beings even larger, increased the head and brain size, and also tried to go for less hair.

The third major change was primarily to the physical body and to the brain. They did some genetic modification that increased the size and weight of humans. Part of the reason for increasing our size was to make us less edible and to make animals think twice before attacking us. The physical change was to be bigger and more impressive. No longer 3 ½ to 4 feet tall, but over 5 feet tall, which makes predators think carefully about attacking.

## Summary

According to my hypnotized patients, eight alien races contributed to significant changes in the human race. All the eight alien races were divinely inspired and none of them meant any harm to humanity through their genetic modification. Their intent was to improve humans and that did occur, but there were also some unintended changes, which were both positive and negative. Most aliens look the same now as they looked when they first came on Earth. The first and last two alien races are human-like in appearance, while the rest are in humanoid forms; that is, they have a head, a body, arms and legs, and walk upright. There are as many differences between the alien races as between the individuals in each race. At the time, they were not worried about affecting humanity by being known and seen by humans, and they traveled freely among them. This had devastating effects on humans, so the aliens do not do this now.

All these races initially came to one location and spread to other parts of the world. At the time of the first encounter, the aliens did not understand that the ape-like beings had a human soul and were developing spirituality and they took steps to create more spirituality in them. The first three races of group one worked with humanity, which was only in Africa. Not with every human being and not with every group, but they did plant their changes wherever humanity had wandered. They hoped that changes would work pass a uniform manner through the entire human race. In the beginning, humanity was not dispersed as thoroughly as it is now. About a million years ago, when the first alien race arrived on Earth, human beings were found only on east coast of Africa. The rest of Earth did not have any humans at all. Each of the first three races went in groups to different areas, in different groups, at different times, and planted the same genetic changes in all the areas they visited. Then they allowed time for these changes to work their way through the general population.

Sometimes, in some races, their own stated intention to improve humanity was not clear. The intended outcomes and resulting outcomes were not exactly the same thing. Each of the alien races had an intention in every case to make a specified modification in the genetic structure of the human race. They planned, then, to study the results of that intervention to see what happened as a result of it, both as an understanding of the biochemistry and of the genetics, and to see the results of each particular change. It was also part of their scheme to better understand the overall structure of human DNA. The ape-like humans, whom the alien beings considered an inferior race, were not quite as inferior as they thought. They did have a spiritual sense, and intelligence.

The alien races stayed here for tens of thousands of years. Of course, there were trips back and forth. A single individual alien might spend thirty to fifty years here and would be replaced by another two or three beings. As they built up research facilities in different places, there were thousands of beings of one race on the planet at one time. They were scattered all over the Earth. The individual mission was the establishment of the base and its maintenance, even though it might be deserted for periods of time. Occasionally, all of the aliens from Earth would go to their home planet at the same time, and all the research stations in different parts of the world would be empty and the mankind would proceed on its own.

According to the heavenly beings, by the time these alien races got out in space, every group had come to the understanding that there is one universal God. One God who has created the entire universe, all that is, and all it can be. The primary difference between these alien groups is that some of them stress different aspects of God. Although some of these eight alien races are not as emotional and spiritual as we are, still some have some spirituality according to the norms of their races. Heavenly beings claimed that none of these eight alien races have as thorough an understanding of the duality of God, the purpose and intent of creation, the spiritual history of the universe, and the eventual de-creation of the creation that I have developed. Some have theory, some have intuition, but they do not have it solid.

All these eight alien races came to different parts of the Earth and during different time periods. Alien races one, two, and three of the first group and the first alien race of group two knew about Atlantis and Lamuria. The second race of group two transplanted the tribe in Lamuria, and race three came while Lamuria existed and while Atlantis was functioning well. Alien race four of group two just got in at the tail end of Lamuria and was also around Atlantis and worked with Atlanteans and gave them technology. Alien race five also worked with Atlanteans and taught them different technology.

Races four and five worked with Atlanteans extensively. This does not mean they did not work with other groups of humans in different parts of Earth, but not to the extent or with the purpose they did in Atlantis. They taught Atlanteans different technology. They were not responsible for misuse of the technology by Atlanteans, but they did give them the means. It was a fault of the Atlantean culture. They did it on their own. The fourth and fifth alien races were not very spiritual. They were more technologically oriented. They found Atlanteans to be better and easier to work with. Then the Atlanteans continued to develop on their own, they tried to imitate the Lamurian's spiritual gifts, using technology, and that is what led to their downfall.

According to the archangels, the situation back then was similar to the situation today. Not everybody in the Atlantean society understood how psychic abilities occurred. The popular myth among the common people was that the energy came from crystals. This was partly true, as the power was transmitted through the crystals and it came out the other end, and the common people assumed that the power came through the crystals. The big crystals transmitted power and the little crystals in the home received power and transmitted it to the devices in the homes.

Alien races four and five of group two were surprised at psychic ability in humanity. They saw it happen and they studied it, but humans saw it happen and denied it. The fourth and fifth alien races are still studying us and searching for spiritual and religious understanding.

Races two and three of group two worked mostly with Lamurians, and races four and five worked primarily with Atlanteans. Races two and three also worked with Atlanteans and the rest of the world's population. Race one of second group also observed Atlanteans but they worked primarily with the other populations of the Earth. Race two worked mainly with Lamurians and simply observed other areas.

Race three of group two did work with the Atlanteans when it was flourishing. They did not think much of the people of Atlantis and their culture. They considered Atlantean culture to be counterproductive regarding some of their spiritual beliefs and fragmentation of the worship, which ended up in worshiping different Gods. Also the belief that they should not discuss spiritual matters with other people was a real drawback of the Atlantean culture.

Races one, two, and three of group two dealt primarily in spiritual nature and religious teachings. Races four and five taught technology mostly to Atlanteans. They taught mankind metalworking and how to deal with different engineering problems. Race four taught humans about digging, ore mining, finding heat sources, and casting metals. Race five taught mankind how to work with hard and heavier metals, and dealt more with engineering, planning, and construction.

The experiments were not performed the very day they came on Earth. They studied humans and their DNA for many hundreds of years before a proposal for a research study was made. So, it was a long-term project and, in human time, it took thousands of years. It took quite a long time for the first alien race to determine what effects these genetic changes would cause on humans. They were trying to do a thorough job and they really wanted to understand the changes.

According to archangels, the so-called Garden of Eden was in the northeastern part of Africa, where the first humans were. It was not in Iraq, as believed by many, including the Bible. The first very large settlement or city was located in Iraq, but not the Garden of Eden. The first alien race of the first group worked with humans only on the northeast coast of Africa. The changes they attempted to make were uniform with each human group. The changes were predetermined, selected by a large group of their geneticists and scientists and were part of a combined decision. The same changes were put into effect everywhere in the human population on Earth. The first alien race lost interest when they perceived that there were changes being made in the humans that they did not include in the research project. This occurred when they finally realized other races were also experimenting on mankind.

A million years ago, ape-like humans had a limited distribution on Earth. They were only on the east coast of Africa. After the genetic modifications, the aliens transplanted humans into Asia, Siberia, and China. They were in scarce groups here and there, and the regions were not thickly populated.

According to heavenly beings, of the eight alien races that worked positively on Planet Earth, the home planets of only the fourth and fifth races were destroyed. The fifth alien race of the second group, the short stocky aliens, are very adaptable in colonizing new planets and they do have planets to live on now, but not their original planet. Because of their evolutionary background, they can inhabit many different planets and they are not even sure which planet was theirs originally. They also have bases on our planet. On our planet right now, these aliens number approximately 10,000. There are millions of them living on different planets, where they have colonized. It is just as natural for them to dig into the ground and create and live in tunnels as it is for them to walk on the surface.

Most of the races that have contacted Earth are evolved races but not fully enlightened when they came to Earth. Now they are very close to enlightenment. They are still evolving, and when they achieve the full realization of their nature, that is, when they are like God and they are part of God, then they can go back to God. At this time, they are still on their own planets. Even when these beings came to Earth the first time, they were much more evolved than we were. When we enlighten, some will choose to remain in the Light, some will choose to return to God, and some will choose to return to Earth and continue to work.

Of the races that came to Earth, some are more selfish than others. They were interested in what the Earth had to offer as they were studying us. Some things were stolen and some stuff was just left alone. There was one thing that was universally agreed; that it is immoral to take the natural resources of a planet where there is an intelligent race that will use them someday.

The alien races came back again and again to check and see what happened. After the eight alien races came in contact with each other, the word sort of spread all over the galaxy between all the races that there was a young race, a recently evolving race, undergoing spiritual development. This is a great experiment, because no race has ever watched another race develop that way. Generally, by the time a race was developed, it was not new anymore.

According to the heavenly beings, these eight alien races remained on Earth for extended periods, and even mixed with mankind and used human genes. The last two races are quite human in appearance and we could barely pick them from a crowd. Sometimes there were physical relationships between aliens and humans, between male and female, both ways; that is, male of alien race and a female of the human, or human male and an alien female. Direct offspring was not possible because the genetic differences were too dramatic.

In the laboratory, it was a different matter. There were genetic experiments where the genes were merged, and sometimes the embryo was implanted into a female host; sometimes into a human female and other times into an alien female. Pregnancy was carried to term to see what would happen. Not all these experiments ended happily. Human females had a hard time dealing with children who were not normal, while the alien female just dismissed it as a luck-of-the-draw experiment that did not work out. The offspring lived out their normal life spans. They were not cross-fertile. For them to have offspring, they had to have more lab work.

The more viable experiment done by alien race four was incorporating human genes with alien genes and growing the being to term in the lab so that it became viable without having a parent as such. Most of these beings worked out very well and it was in this experiment that they fine-tuned and did make a viable cross-breed race that was capable of reproduction. The aliens raised them here on earth, and when they were sure that the life was stable, they were taken from this world to colonize another planet. Alien race four did not want them here on Earth reproducing and creating a second race of human-like beings on Earth, so none were permitted to stay. They all were transplanted to another planet and are living happily there and going through their own developmental process. This is an experiment which alien race four is keeping a close eye on, to see just what happens with them. So those old stories are true.

Race Five also dabbled in the same thing, but did not go to the point of creating a new race. They did examine human genes and experimented in incorporating them with their own, with the idea of improving their own species.

But even the race which has done the fewest abductions has done hundreds of them. In the last 2000 years, there have been no genetic manipulations, but profound changes have occurred due to spiritual teachers who were sent to Earth. In that span of time, we had three great spiritual teachers who came to Earth: Jesus, Mohammed, and Druze. Druze was a teacher in Egypt and Lebanon.

## Modern Interaction Between Aliens and Humans

Heavenly beings, through my hypnotized patients, claim that strange things have always been seen in the sky. Most of them in the past were alien crafts. These days, much of what we see in the sky are U. S. government secret aircraft, which people think are alien spaceships; however, some of what we see are really alien crafts. There has always been an interaction between humans and aliens.

The treaty or protocol of understanding among the alien races, after they all became aware of each other's interest, insists that no alien race shall intervene any further with the genetics of humanity. This does not mean they cannot use human genes to manipulate their own genes. At the current time, some alien races are still doing genetic experiments, but they are experimenting upon themselves and not on the human race. For the most part, the alien races that come here simply observe, compare, and confer with other alien races.

Some alien races are still encouraging mankind in the development of science, technology, and the arts. Initially, the alien races four and five of group two handed the information to humans, which was detrimental to them because they were not able to conceive it and lacked a developmental background. Now aliens are helping humans with basic understanding and with individual breakthroughs that humans make, rather than aliens handing technology over to them. Aliens help by intervening in such a way that the humans do the work and aliens just guide and inspire them, often without their knowledge. This helps individuals to make an accumulative developmental process.

Even now, as sophisticated and developed as the human race has become, to contact an alien race would be a severe blow to humanity. The obvious fact that alien races are technologically so superior to us would be a tremendous jolt. For a human being to contact a truly spiritual alien and to perceive spirituality that seems to be so much more developed would be a serious setback to his or her spiritual development. Yet humanity has the potential to be a significant factor in the history of the universe.

Heavenly beings, through my hypnotized patients, state that there have been several intergalactic congresses concerning humanity and small groups of other discovered races that have the same potential as humanity. In these congresses, the results of the genetic modifications have been compared and analyzed on an overall basis. Where one race may have done a particular experiment and its own observation and analysis, this is now being done by all the races working together. They have developed a complete understanding of the human genome and the effects of the various modifications.

The eight alien races that have tampered with the human genetic component had been inspired by God to do so as a means of speeding up the spiritual, physical, and intellectual evolution of humanity. God inspired them because they were experts in genetics and had the technological expertise and spiritual knowledge. Through their genetic modifications and spiritual teachings, mankind became more spiritual, thus creating a larger spiritual field around them and the Earth. The larger the field becomes, the faster the general overall spiritual, emotional, and intellectual development of mankind will occur.

Heavenly beings, through my hypnotized patients, report that the alien beings that are studying us now have widely different views of how mankind exists. They are each partially accurate and partially wrong. They are seeing idealized pictures of what they want to see as compared to what is really there. We became something of an interest in the galaxy because we are the race that is entering the spiritual phase. Most of the alien races have never seen this happen. They have gone through their own evolution, through their own experience, but they did not have the science and the tools at the time, or the understanding, to really study it. Every other race they met had already been developed, so this is the first time anybody is having a chance to watch a race develop.

There are some of unique things about us humans. First; the depth of spirituality appears to be unusual as to how very spiritual some of us can be. This, in part, is due to the third race of the first group tampering with the spiritual center. Some feel that the genetic manipulation the third race did to enhance feelings is responsible for the emotions in humanity. They are surprised that we are such an emotional race and that it plays such an important part in us. We already had some spirituality and some emotions, but they did not know it. This is the main reason for all the interest in Earth. Not that there was anything that different about Earth, but because, before, nobody ever watched the development of a primitive race. That is an advantage of being a latecomer, to see the development of spirituality.

Some of them were startled to see psychic gifts popping up in humans. This gives aliens cause to rethink their understanding of the universe. That things can come in the spirit is a great surprise to them. It is safe to say that spirituality and psychic ability is not complete. We provoke quite a few discussions in a number of alien cultures, such as while these things are observed, how do we explain them? They do not have nearly as much trouble accepting what happens as some people here on Earth do.

There is no general overseeing alien counsel deciding who does what on Earth, nor regulating activity here. There is some cooperation between some alien groups. After they are aware of each other, they at least tell the other what they have been doing and what they found. But there is no organized plan of study. It is all just sort of freelance. The aliens are not united, but are not enemies, either. They do know of each other's presence now and they have been in communication. Some have exchanged ideas and knowledge.

Spiritual teachings have taken place to bring spirituality to us, and this process was aided by the alien races. Even though some of the aliens believe they were responsible for spirituality in us, it is not so, because the ape-like humans already had spirituality, which the aliens did not recognize. The aliens want to keep their presence here a secret because they do not want to affect the results of the observation and interfere with our progress and change what they are seeing. They fear that if we are aware of them, it will change our spiritual and technological perceptions. The various alien races that interact with us are also interacting with each other. Some of them have exchanged information and observations. But there is no overall spiritual research study plan for the study of mankind.

There is a common agreement now among most of the alien races that they will not interfere with humanity. They will not do any more religious or spiritual teachings and will not give more technology. They want us to catch up on our own, so they can study our development without wondering how it came about; that is, whether it was a result of outside interference or something that happened naturally. They want to leave the research field unmodified.

There are alien races that live on Earth in tunnels and caves, in particular the short and stocky fifth alien race of the group two called Kubold. This race is quite comfortable in the limited light. They do tend to live in natural caves and in tunnels developed in the caves. They are a natural-born mining race. Some of the aliens look like beings that dwell in earth, like earth spirits such as gnomes, fairies, and spirits, which are part of the earth system. They have developed here on Earth.

According to the heavenly beings, underground alien races do not affect us emotionally, mentally, physically, or any other way. They prefer to stay away from us and do not harm us. The existence of a race does not mean there is a UFO base. There are a few aliens who have come to Earth to explore. They do not want human contact. They are more interested in the structure and the history of the Earth.

It has been over 20,000 years since the positive alien races contacted humans in the open. Some of the positive alien abductions now relate to them checking on their experimental results. The stories of aliens, father-to-son reports to begin with, storytelling reports, got incorporated into religious literature and stories within their groups. But if we look at religious literature of different cultures, there are strong similarities.

According to the heavenly beings, we are not the first-generation race in this universe. Actually we are a fourth-generation race. There are other races, millions of years older and more advanced, in the universe. We were late bloomers because our planet was formed recently. The universe is about fourteen billion years old. The Earth and its sun are only about four and a half billion years old. It is a fourth-generation star.

Our sun contains materials from the three other stars. When a star is formed and lived out its life, it explodes and ejects its materials into the space. That material eventually gets incorporated into a second star. When it has lived out its life, the material is ejected into space and a third star was formed. When the third star lived out its life and material was ejected into space, then our solar system was formed. So we are the fourth-generation star in that line. Because our planet is around the fourth-generation star, we have lots of heavy metals. Here, the sun of the solar system is called star.

A planet that is around a first-generation star has just hydrogen and helium and there are no other heavy metals in that solar system. As the stars keep forming, exploding, and ejecting material, more and more heavy materials are formed. We have some wonderful benefits because of it. The Earth was not formed till after the materials had been processed. As a result, we have an abundance of metals. The original planets did not have metals, because they had not yet been made. The metals are made in the stars and are ejected in space when the stars explode. Among the advantages this gives us is a planet rich in heavy metals for building materials.

The archangels explained that initially the universe was all hydrogen. There were other elements that were created, but not in great abundance. A star is hydrogen gas, which, when compressed enough, some of it will fuse and turn into helium. This gives off an enormous amount of energy and this is what causes a star to be hot and to shine. Also, as the elements are being put together, stars build up larger and larger elements, and at the end of the star's life cycle, fairly large elements are built. Then, if the star blows apart, heavy elements get spread across the universe. Then they are available for the formation of the new stars and new planets. Stars are huge compared to a planet. They are extremely hot and give off tremendous amounts of energy because there is a nuclear fusion reaction going on. Stars are just gases and do not have any solid part, but at the center there is compressed gas.

There are two types of planets. One is a gas planet, and the other is a rocky, solid planet, such as Earth. Beings do live on gas planets, but they are not beings we are familiar with. They are made of matter, but it is very diffuse. They are like gas, or transparent like a ghost. They are simply a collection of molecules. They do have a soul. Gas planets in our solar system are Jupiter, Saturn, Uranus, and Neptune. Etheric is spiritual, like the heaven and the heavenly beings.

Heavenly beings state that there is the danger of doing genetic manipulation on your own race when you are not sure what the outcome will be. You can have an intended outcome; you may accomplish it. But you may make changes that you do not know about or do not understand and may terribly regret later. Gray aliens with big almond eyes who are currently doing most of the abductions for selfish reasons, had emotions at the beginning, but later, due to their genetic manipulation on themselves, they lost their emotions, an effect they did not intend.

According to the heavenly beings, the alien race called grays, with almond eyes, did genetic manipulation on themselves to make improvements in themselves and they accidentally eliminated their emotions and memories. The truly sad part is only the generation who was there at that time really understood what was happening, because those who came after the genetic modification, without emotions, never noticed it. Without the emotional component, God and the spiritual universe are not in the understanding of the grays. However, their unique lifestyle comes from their concept of the source and sameness. The source to them is a physical thing, and being telepathically in touch makes it easy for them to conceive of a community of souls. They are aware of soul as a spiritual part, but in genetic manipulation, they are not taking that into consideration and do not think of a soul as an important aspect of themselves. This has affected how they perceive the universe. Knowing God is an emotional experience, and not intellectual. The grays ignore the emotional aspect of the person.

My hypnotized patients state that because their females cannot have children because of a small pelvis, part of what they are currently doing is abducting humans and trying to get a complete bank of human genetic material from which they can grow mixed breeds. They already have techniques for doing it and have already created these hybrid babies.

One of the reasons they seem to be mistreating the people they abduct is because they do not understand emotions.

There are religions that have extinguished emotions through deliberate effort. Different meditations deal with different components. Some deal with intellectual, some with physical, and some with emotional. Different meditations develop different parts of a person and all end up in the same place.

There have been races that have made themselves extinct by manipulating their genes, and it may be that the grays are at the verge of doing that. Of course, people who make these changes are never there to reap the horrors that come. The genetic changes still rattle down through the race. Without observing, without recording, it takes about three generation to forget something completely because you do not experience it and know it.

Alien races are quite upset and quite leery of human efforts to tamper with genes without sufficient observation to know what a gene does or how it changes things. They are deathly afraid that negative characteristics may be introduced into the human race and may result in its destruction. They are shocked and dismayed that humans created genetically modified foods without a thorough understanding of how that particular gene interacts inside the human body, without having the full knowledge of their intended effects and the way to get those effects.

# Chapter 4

## LAMURIA: THE LOST CONTINENT

Most people have no clue or knowledge about an island or country called Lamuria, which existed in the Pacific Ocean a long time ago. Those who have heard about it believe it is a figment of peoples' imagination. Like many people, I did not know much about Lamuria either until some of my patients under hypnosis began to recall vivid memories about living a life or lives in Lamuria, which was a source of their physical, emotional, or mental problems.

So I began to inquire about Lamuria from heavenly beings through my hypnotized patients. Not only did they confirm the existence of Lamuria in the Pacific Ocean west of Central and North America, but gave detailed information about how it was populated, its amazing people, culture, and society, and the ultimate destruction of it. Some patients also tapped into similar information from the Akashic library.

The following is a compilation of the information given through different patients who, after recalling, reliving, releasing, and resolving the traumas from those lives experienced a great deal of relief from their symptoms.

### Geography and Location of Lamuria

According to my hypnotized patients, Lamuria was located in the Pacific Ocean and was a comma shaped island about three hundred miles wide. Its northern end was located off

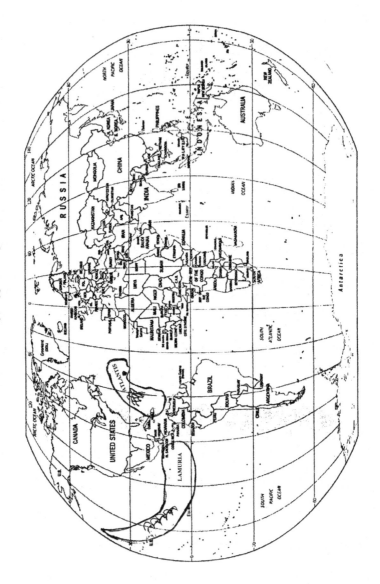

Lamuria and Atlantis as described and drawn by a hypnotized patient from the Akashic Library in Heaven

the coast of South America, and it stretched to just north of the equator, up to the Hawaiian Islands and north. Lamuria was mostly flat and near sea level. The highest part, with hills and mountains, was close to Central America. The land near the equator and near South America had sufficient water and was lush and green. There was an arid belt where there was less rain. North of that were grasslands and trees. Two different tectonic plates came in contact to create Lamuria. They later separated, causing the sinking of Lamuria.

At the beginning, around 200,000 years ago, before a tribe was transplanted in Lamuria by the aliens, my patients from the Akashic plane describe it as much smaller and roughly the same general shape. After that, it expanded in the northeast and southeast because of shifting of the plates. It grew over time, depending on how the earth plates moved together. As one pushed against the other, even though the one may get pushed down, the other can rise up and becoming prominent. The following is a description of Lamuria given by a patient under hypnosis:

- *"From the Akashic library, I see that most of Lamuria was in the northern hemisphere. The closest part of land was South America. Then it went north and west. It had a bulbous end down at the lower part and then most of it became straight and narrow going up into the northern Pacific Ocean. It went as far north as California. It was comma shaped, with the dot at the bottom near South America. The rest of it curved off up into the Pacific Ocean. The further west and north you went the further you were from North America. In the northwest corner of Lamuria, the original settlement was made where the aliens transplanted the tribe to begin their life in a new land. It was a rich, fertile land and seemed to have volcanic origin. As it moved down and curved toward the east, the farther you went, the warmer it became."*

## How Lamuria Was Populated

According to my hypnotized patients, about 200,000 years ago, N-hante, alien race two of group two, found the Earth. These aliens were spiritual and were divinely inspired to help humankind to speed their spiritual evolution, but did not know it consciously. They did not perceive these ape-like humans as having much in terms of spiritual development. They were unaware that these ape-like beings had a human soul. They were partially misled by their own idea of what was necessary for their spiritual development. The brain area they thought was responsible for spirituality was not as large as they thought was needed.

These aliens were interested in human spirituality and in studying its development. They researched to see if they could identify an area in the brain that contributed to spirituality. Having a pretty good idea from their study of themselves and of other races, and through their studies of lower creatures, they thought they had isolated a part of the brain that was responsible for spirituality in humans. By increasing it in both size and complexity, they thought they could contribute to mankind's spiritual development and study it in the isolation of Lamuria, away from everything.

First they located parts of Lamuria that would support life and be isolated from everything else, so there would not be any cross-contamination. There were no other humans living there at the time. They selected from the area where Iraq is now, a group of people of all ages that was cohesive and could survive together and provide support to each other. This was not a farming tribe. They had seen farming, had talked to farmers, and had the basic idea of farming, but they lived primarily off their sheep. The aliens took these people at night when they were asleep and when it was quiet. The aliens picked them up by a beam coming from a spaceship that changed people's gravity and transported this tribe physically to a carrying area on the ship. According to my hypnotized patients, there were about fifteen or twenty people taken in one spaceship. There were about five space-ships and each made three trips. They transported people, their livestock, tents, and all their equipment and supplies to the northwest part of Lamuria.

My hypnotized patients state that the alien race took the human tribe at night when they were asleep. They increased the tribe's sleep level by artificial means, so that they would not wake up. The next morning when they opened their eyes, things were changed all around. They were outside the tents, which were stacked up. The animals were there but the land was changed all around. They had gone to sleep in dry desert area and woke up on a low-lying flat land. The star positions were different and they knew they were not in the same place.

They had no idea where they were and how they got there. The land was green and lush, and the animals loved it. There were fruit trees and plants that were edible. They did not see any reason to complain. They were just confused and concerned how it all came about. In their exploration, they found they were surrounded by the ocean, except in the south.

According to my hypnotized patients, the aliens chose this particular tribe for several reasons. They were not essential to the society of that area and it made no difference to any-body else whether they were there or not. They were pretty much self-contained, and did not have property or land, as such. They already had a rudimentary spirituality that the aliens could recognize. The aliens considered it to be a good thing, because it would give them a measure of difference between how the humans were when they started and how they changed after the genetic manipulation.

The aliens also picked up humans from other areas who were of childbearing age. Just a few of them were brought in for genetic diversity, so that there would be a bigger gene pool, and they were also genetically changed. There were seven of them, five males and two females. The aliens did genetic manipulation on some of the members of the tribe, in particular the young and those of childbearing age. They were already mature and were ready to have children. From the tribe, they took both young and old. They took older people for their advice and their leadership. They took children, too. All together, they transported about 237 people, including the outsiders.

The abductions were not done with the people's permission; they just took them. The aliens did not see much spirituality in the tribe before the abductions. For them, the tribe members were like high-class animals that were just barely spiritual. It was like moving a herd of cattle; you know where the water is and you take them there without discussing it with the cattle.

Following is a description given by a patient from the Akashic library about how the Arabian tribe was transplanted to Lamuria:

- *"From the Akashic library, I see that an Arabian tribe was transplanted by the aliens in Lamuria. One morning they found themselves in a new place and they seemed to have a sudden, dramatic, and bewildering experience, which they could not make heads or tails of. This was a mystifying but delightful thing for them because the new land was lush. It made their lives much easier. Of course, they did have a difficult time learning how to adapt to and use this land. The food sources were new to them but there was abundant water.*

  *"I see that several genetic modifications were done before they were isolated and transplanted in Lamuria. Then further modifications were done after a period of time. In their initial contact while in Lamuria, the aliens observed the tribal people from a distance by electronic, optical, and auditory means. They did not move into the village to study them closely. On occasion, one of the persons of the tribe was taken to a spaceship examined in detail, usually while asleep, and also occasionally taken while wide-awake and actually communicated with. This*

*started Lamurian folk legends about the strange people in the forest.*

*"The Lamurians were under observation for an extended period of time. Their physical characteristics and psychological patterns were examined. Some observation was done on the spaceship, but most of it was done by electronic means from the spaceship or on the ground. The aliens tried to correlate the DNA with what they observed. When they found enough to convince them that they were dealing with beings similar to themselves, they felt fairly confidant in making decisions about what genes they should modify or change."*

They did their first genetic modification in the temporal lobe of the brain, which these aliens recognized as connected to spirituality. They worked on enlarging the temporal lobe of the brain on both sides and, as they grew and developed, these portions of the brain were pushed down and forward. As a result, the brain grew downward and moved brain tissue forward. This increased the skull size and, instead of being flat and back, the face was pushed forward to make room for growth of that part of the brain downward and forward.

The aliens studied how the genetic mutation was passed on through reproduction and observed the changes in spirituality, in terms of how wide-reaching and intense the spirituality was. The DNA, which was modified, was the DNA in the reproductive tissue, so the tribe itself stayed as it was but their children were different. Each individual's DNA was not modified because it was very difficult to get into each and every cell and change the DNA of all the cells one by one. These alien beings went into the reproductive tissue and changed the DNA pattern there, which was passed onto the embryo, and as it grew and developed, every cell received the new pattern. It was more efficient in terms of their time and energy to let it grow naturally, instead of changing everything.

In their second genetic modification, they again increased the size of the temporal lobe. They knew they had to make room in the skull for it, otherwise the brain would be crushed and there would be damage or death, or it would just not function very well. So the second manipulation was to make changes in the temporal lobe and to make more nerve connection in it, to refine it and to increase the size of the skull.

So, in the first modification, the aliens changed different genes to increase the size of the temporal lobes by increasing the cells. In the second manipulation, they modified the genes to cause more nerve connections in it. Then they learned by observation to see what kind of changes happened. My hypnotized patients report that there were also changes set in motion that caused a decrease in the size of the jaws and decreased the number of muscles and made them not as heavy as they had been. This was a side effect and was not intended. Following the changes, the aliens also wanted to see what they had changed without meaning to. So they recorded different changes: physical, emotional, mental, spiritual, and social.

The tribe members had children who were different. They accepted them, and by the time they were adults, people were used to them and they did not stand out as glaringly different. The tribe people lived out their normal lives. Each generation was different in appearance and more spiritual. It took about five generations until it was fully expressed in humans. Then came a time in which the gene had to spread sideways, as they married people with different genes. After a time, the DNA had pretty much spread throughout the whole population, with everybody having the gene, either active or inactive.

When the second set of genetic modifications was completed, there was a noticeable difference between parents and children in appearance. The most prominent aspect was the chin. Parents had one, but the children's chin was a triangular shape.

A patient recalled one of her past lives as a tribe member who was transplanted in Lamuria by the aliens:

- *"I am a ten-year-old girl. I have dark brown skin. I live in a tribe in a desert area which now is known as northern Iraq. My tribe lives in tents, pasturing sheep, living around the river, and wandering around from place to place. We have some horses, donkeys, and sheep. The whole tribe sleeps in a series of tents. There is a single tent that is larger than the others where most people are living during daytime and there are smaller tents for sleeping. People in our tribe are quite heavy.*

*"During one night, everyone has gone to sleep and when we wake up, it is full day light. We find ourselves in a different place. It is green all over and there are tall trees. The air is moist and it is not as hot. We are just astonished. Our sheep and animals are also here with us. We are afraid because no one can explain what has happened and why and how we all ended up in this place. There is much confusion. We are doing a lot of experimentation and exploring. Everybody takes a chance trying different foods and leaves, finding what food is good to eat and what is not. Men do the exploring and woman taste the foods.*

*"Two hundred and thirty seven people are brought here. Most of us are kind of bulky. We are more ape-like than human-like. Our faces are of larger proportion. Everything is exaggerated. The brows are bigger, cheeks are puffier, and the face is broader. We are more hairy than modern humans. Our legs are shorter in proportion to the rest of the body. Men are about five feet four inches and females about five feet tall. Our skin is brown. We have a language in which we communicate. We make cloth with wool from the sheep. We have a drape covering, like a robe, and a head covering from the wool.*

*"We cook and eat out of one clay bowl. We are assigned different jobs, such as exploring, planting grain, cooking, cleaning, taking care of children, etc. As the children grow older, elders choose who should be married with whom. We have a wedding ceremony in front of the whole tribe*

*during a worship service. The married couples live on one side, have children, and do the work, while the older women take care of the children. Kids are kids up until age six.*

*"I was the oldest child and the first to get married, at the age of fourteen. My husband and I have a child who does not seem to be as strong as the others. His skin is lighter and has less hair. His face is not as big and thick. This creates a concern over whether he is normal. The elders make a decision to wait and see how the child grows. We raise the baby in our tent for about two years. After the baby is weaned, he is sent to a family tent. There, the older couples and older kids help take care of the younger children. When they are seven, they go over to the workers' tent where they are trained to do different jobs with the older couples. This takes the place of school. I do other work such as cooking, cleaning, and weaving cloth.*

*"We are all surprised that our son seems to demonstrate adult understanding even though he is just about two years old. At the age of six, he seems to be much more interested in spiritual world, talking about God and spirits, and he shows great interest in the worship services. He sits with adults and discusses spiritual matters, like God and spirits. At twenty-two years of age, he is appointed for worship observance. He looks obviously different than us. His head is not as broad, face is not as lumpy, not as hairy, and his body is not as heavily built. However, he is not shockingly different from the others and is recognized as one of us.*

*"I have two more children, a boy and a girl. The middle son looks like the rest of the tribe, while the daughter is different, like her older brother. She also has a better sense of spirituality. Many other younger children in the tribe are also different looking. People think it has to do with the new place. When these different looking children have their own children, they look more like their parents than their grandparents. By the third generation, they are*

*marrying each other. Their children look totally differ-
ent than the great-grandparents, but only a little different
from their parents. The face and head are almost modern,
with no heavy jaw muscles and no prominent brow ridges.
The body does not resemble the great apes at all, but is
more like modern humans.*

*"I am dying of pneumonia at the age of thirty. My last
thoughts are about my children and about how different
they are. I go to the Light (heaven) with the angels. As I
look back from heaven, I see that our children were different because of the genetic modifications done by the
alien beings. They wanted to create spiritual beings. They
wanted to know several things and wanted to test their
study of genetics to see if they have properly picked out
the genes that will cause the changes they desire.*

*"I see that the aliens had a hospital type of setting in
their spaceships. They had taken people from our tribe to
examine them. I see that the aliens lifted me out while I
was sleeping, by a beam of light, and I went up in this
beam as if in an elevator. The beam changes my gravity
and I get pulled up right into the spaceship. It is a self-
regulating mechanism. If you get outside the beam, then
gravity pulls you right back into the beam. They put me
on a table and took some tissue samples, such as a piece
of skin off a leg, from inside my cheek, and other parts of
the body, but I did not remember or understand what happened.*

*"I now realize that the aliens chose our tribe to be
transplanted in Lamuria, because we were an isolated
tribe living in an isolated area with very little interactions with other tribes. We did not have any land or homes
as possessions. So if we were moved, we would not leave
anything behind and there would be no trace of us left
there and nobody would notice if we disappeared. Also
because we had some spirituality.*

*"As I look back from heaven, I can see that everybody
was asleep when the aliens lifted the whole tribe up in the*

spaceship. They made us inhale some chemicals, which kept us sleeping. They also lifted our tents, animals, and other stuff we had, and transported them with us to Lamuria. Aliens also brought different fruit trees, healing herbs, spices, shade trees, shrubs, flowers, and other plants from our homeland and planted them in Lamuria before they took us to Lamuria so they would be familiar to us.

"In Lamuria, before every pregnancy, they took me to the spaceship and injected a virus with the molecule added to it. The job of the virus is to get into a cell with the new genes added to the DNA. They hoped that it would go into the right spot. From heaven, I see that all the tribe members gave the alien beings permission in heaven, before being born into that life, to do genetic modifications on us.

"In my case, aliens only worked on me and I passed it on to my offspring. They did not work on my husband. They made modifications and changes in my DNA, and through me, my kids got them. They did it one time, and changes occurred in my ova. If the children do inherit the gene, then they have a recessive gene, with about a fifty-fifty chance of passing it on. If they do pass it on and they still do not see it expressed, then they have a fifty-fifty chance to pass it on in the next contact. If there is contact with someone who also has the same recessive gene, then there is a one hundred percent chance for them to pass it on because it is the only copy of the gene they have.

"From heaven, I see that the aliens were trying to change the spiritual nature of humankind, hoping it would produce a race of people that would be more spiritual and have a more direct impression in the world of spirit. The aliens did not plan to make the facial and other physical changes, but the segment that was carried by the virus could be attached in more than one place. It was a hit-and-miss proposition. This is part of the danger of DNA manipulation, getting the changes that you do not intend. The skull, facial, and general overall body changes turned out to be positive.

*"I see that from that life I learned a very positive trait of willingness to explore new things and a willingness to try and experiment. I see that my lung problems came from that life to the current life. I recognize my two sisters in my current life were my son and daughter in that life. My sister's schizophrenia in this life is a genetically induced problem due to damage to the genes. She was very sensitive when she had children because they were different from her in that life and she was different from her parents. That made her lonely and sensitive."*

The second intervention and the changes in the DNA took a bit longer to be activated, taking roughly eight generations before the gene was fully in effect. These children were quite different from the parents but still there was no question that these were their kids. They all survived and the gene spread sideways. This last generation was the one in which the aliens began to notice things they thought were impossible. They realized that these genetically modified humans had psychic abilities that could be observed. This then became the focus of the alien study, to examine these psychic phenomena in detail and figure out how they worked.

N-hante, alien race two of group two, studied the extent of the changes in terms of what changes occurred in the brain and what the aliens could see and understand of human spirituality. They were also interested in studying how the mutation was passed over the years. They believed that it would be dominant and that all humanity would change this way. In spirituality, there were many categories they wanted to look at, such as the extent of spirituality, how wide-ranging, the depth, and how intense it was. The aliens had no idea of spiritual communication, which was of psychic nature. They were not aware that it was possible to step outside the normal realm and communicate through the spirit.

After the second manipulation, they were hit by the strong evidence of psychic phenomena. This came as a real jolt to them because they did not have a tradition in their own race of psychic happenings. They were puzzled. They realized very quickly what the implications were. This human being they thought they had created was capable of entering fully into the spiritual realm and could effectively work and communicate in it and obtain information through it. The aliens were shocked, astonished, and really jolted. They thought they were working with these dumb animals when suddenly they were smacked in the face with the evidence that these beings were actually capable of spiritual abilities the aliens did not come close to. This was astonishing to them and they recorded it in their experimental results.

This alien group studied the who, what, when, why, and how this psychic phenomena came about and what happened. They were trying to determine how it could be that this relatively primitive race was able to slip into the world of spirit so easily. This alien race had seen psychic phenomena before, but not to this extent. One person was showing two, three, or four different aspects of psychic abilities, and the strength of it was unusual. When they met other alien races later, they talked about the extent and the strength of psychic phenomenon in a primitive race. They do come to visit and study us from time to time, just to observe, watch, and record.

According to the heavenly beings, this information spread around, as later they came into contact with the other alien races when they reached the information-sharing stage. The other alien races that came to Earth were also astonished. The information got to the other races in the universe with which they came in contact. As the alien races continued to study, they saw instances where suddenly there was a psychic insight and there was a great leap forward in human understanding. They kept track of all those new developments.

They could see where a situation was the same all the time, and suddenly one human looked at it differently and spread the word and the change occurred. They saw it in science, religion, politics, economics, and every aspect of life. A race that operated like that was beyond their comprehension.

They are used to progress being slow, deliberate, and accumulative, and here is a race that goes from point A to point D and completely misses points B and C. This was a great leap and they tried to figure out what must be in the middle.

The alien races that were studying us suddenly found that we are unique. First, due to the psychic phenomenon surrounding mankind and its spiritual development. Second, the intensity of the emotions with which we live set us apart from everybody else in the galaxy, as far as they knew. A human race who had everything; not too bright, not too big, but unique.

After different races in the universe found out how fast mankind was developing, there was a great deal of interest. Many different alien races came to visit. Some of the individuals in some of the races developed the idea that mankind may be the savior race of the universe because of its spiritual development and emotional capacity. The word spread in the universe about humanity and a lot of races are now coming to Earth to observe humanity.

Many of the alien races have spirituality, but very few have developed spirituality to the point where they became telepathic, clairaudient, clairvoyant, clairsentient, and had other psychic talents develop over a few hundred years. All of a sudden, the aliens are seeing fully developed psychic ability in humans beyond what these alien races have ever witnessed. The aliens have seriously begun to believe that humanity may be the savior race of the universe because of its spirituality and emotions. But there are some drawbacks. Humanity is also violent and has not made much progress in curbing that tendency.

Psychic ability is still spreading throughout humanity, according to the heavenly beings. It did not develop in all of humanity at once. These aliens were working with Lamurians and they helped only that group. The psychic ability developed only in Lamuria and not in the rest of humanity in different parts of the Earth. Of course, everybody on Earth had his or her own spirituality. So there was spiritual and psychic development going on all over the Earth, but it was intense in Lamuria. There were other people coming from South, Central, and North America, and Atlantis to Lamuria later, so the genes got mixed up and confused the aliens. It took them awhile to figure that out. It ended up with a substantial gene swap, which was unintended by the aliens.

The people of Lamuria were living there, growing and expanding. The aliens were experimenting on them, making changes in their DNA. The changes helped to intensify their spiritual nature. The humans became more apt and more likely to use their psychic abilities to reach out and contact each other. This indicates that genetic modifications may have a big role in human psychic abilities and spiritual development. However, according to the heavenly beings, anyone can develop psychic abilities, as it depends upon the individual's initiative as much as it depends upon DNA. If we have the right blend of genes in our DNA, it will make it much easier for us to be spiritual, but it does not guarantee it.

After Lamuria submerged into the ocean, the survivors spread out, and there was an intermingling with people of Atlantis, South, Central, and North America, Europe, Africa, and Asia and with other people all over the globe. The genetic material is still being spread around the Earth. It is not uniform among humans yet, but there is more spiritual development, more psychic ability, and more psychic improvement coming as this ability is refined and established in mankind.

The Lamurians began to spread and settle in different parts of the continent and crossed the dry region in about tens of thousands of years, to reproduce and spread. The few adventurous ones developed the means of sailing and transportation. They went about the country seeing the natural wonders, seeing different people, enjoying the benefits of different localities.

- *"My name is Honel and I am an eighteen-year-old male, traveling with a group toward the south of the dry area in*

*Lamuria. It is about 110,000 BC. I am about five feet tall with brown hair, and brown skin. I am wearing a robe and have sandals on my feet. We are wearing a head covering because the sun is very hot. We all are kind of young, and are bold adventurers who want to move to someplace new. My group and I found a place to settle where the land is good and there is plenty of water. We are starting ranches, raising animals and a few crops. It is located along a river. The river flows toward the northeast and we settle south of the river in the dry zone.*

*"We are telepathic beings and can communicate with our families back home. We meditate three times a day. As soon as we get up, we pray and meditate. Then we get together and discuss God and religion. We also meet once a week for spiritual practices. We are developing spiritually as a group because we have the same beliefs, the same shared background, and we all want to be spiritual.*

*"We went to the nearest settlement and brought women who were willing to marry us. I get married and have three children. We follow our spiritual path and communicate with others on the continent telepathically. Everybody feels connected through telepathy. Information is spread very rapidly this way and we are able to tune into the future, learning what is going to happen, and then arrange life accordingly. We very seldom have an unannounced weather disaster. Fishermen in the southeast made the first voyage to Central and South America, and people are beginning to explore those countries and are finding that they are already inhabited.*

*"At the age of forty-seven, I fall and break a leg above the ankle and get a severe infection and die. My last thoughts are, "It has been a great life and I am really glad I was able to live it." I die feeling very proud, although I am hurting physically. After I die, I do not even look around for the Light. I just go toward it and I am halfway in the Light by the time anybody comes to greet me from heaven.*

*"From heaven, I see that we had finer features than our parents, and our children had finer features than we did, and they were smarter and more spiritual because of the genetic modification. We are progressively changing, generation by generation. I do not see much demonic influence in Lamuria because of our spiritual practices and prayers. I see that when I broke my leg and had the infection, I lost many soul parts, but the demons did not bother to get them because they were of pure Light. My soul parts were like hot potatoes for the demons."*

## Sacred Garden in Lamuria

According to my hypnotized patients, the place from where the Lamurians originally came was near the border of Iraq and Syria, where it is dry and desert-like now. When the tribe from there was transplanted to Lamuria by the alien race called N-hante about 200,000 BC, there was not enough rainfall for trees but it was a grassland and fertile. There were trees around the water sources but not a forest. Wherever there was water, there were clusters of fruit trees, shade trees, bushes, shrubs, healing herbs, and flowering plants. It was essentially a prairie. These plants were brought and planted in Lamuria by the aliens before they brought the tribe. When people who were transplanted there by the aliens and saw those plants, they thought it was an act of God because they were different than the rest of plants in Lamuria. It was as if their homeland was transplanted with them.

From the thought of being touched by God, the concept of a sacred garden began. As the population grew and spread all over Lamuria, plants were planted and seeds were carried to wherever they moved, and thus they had a sacred garden in every town and city. Since they felt it was an act of God, they also made it more beautiful and artistic by planting those flowers, shrubs, and trees from their homeland. These sacred gardens were used as we today use churches and temples:

for worship, meditation, meetings, weddings, and other occasions. The original sacred garden was in the northwestern part of Lamuria, in the spot where the tribe was transplanted by the aliens and was considered to be sacred because of the vegetation there.

The area for the garden initially was pre-selected by the aliens where the tribe would be transplanted in the northwestern part of Lamuria. The aliens knew that the transplanted tribe in the strange land might not recognize the food plants, so they provided them with the food plants from their land that they could recognize and eat until they could learn about the new land and its plants. The garden was transplanted in that area with all the food plants, medical plants, and flowering plants, so that it would be familiar. The initial reseeding of the sacred garden to the new spot was really not a deliberate act, because when you take an apple with you, usually the seeds are also taken with it. As the people spread out in Lamuria, they carried their plants and seeds with them and created a sacred garden in the new area.

The aliens did not arrange for the concept of the sacred garden. Lamurians thought of it themselves. It was rather a human thing to take that which was familiar to them and to establish that homeland spot, wherever they settled. These plants were isolated, for the sacred garden only, and if one of those plants was found growing outside the garden, it was destroyed. The sacred plants grew only in the sacred garden and nowhere else. The plants from their homeland did not belong outside and nothing else belonged inside. These were trees, grass, weeds, shrubs, flowers, and plants that the aliens brought from the tribe's homeland in the Middle East and planted in Lamuria before they transplanted the whole tribe from Iraq to Lamuria.

Lamurians had an innate love of beauty in nature, in character, in spiritual development, and in humanity, and were constantly uplifted by it. They saw very little negative in their world. Diseases were literally not there till Atlanteans and outsiders came.

## Teachings by Aliens in Lamuria

In Lamuria, people who sat in the sacred garden to meditate found that they were inspired. When they entered the meditative trance state, information was passed to them so that their connection with the Divine would be strengthened and their understandings would be improved. Spiritual teaching was an ongoing process throughout the entire history of Lamuria, and because of this, the spiritual state of the people kept on rising.

The sacred garden concept was carried with the people when they moved to a new place in Lamuria. This turned out to be very helpful for the aliens to conduct their teachings since this place was treated with reverence. People prayed and meditated there. All Lamurians went there and all Lamurians were taught during their meditative trance by alien races two and three of group two. Alien race two took the form of tall, thin, old, wise-looking humans, wearing robes like the Lamurians, while the third alien race looked like ordinary human beings, generally a human male twenty-eight to thirty years old, five feet ten inches tall, and with an average build. When the Lamurians began to go on expeditions to other lands, they decided not to take the plants because they wanted to find them in another country, maybe their original country from where the original tribe came from, thinking if the plants were similar, perhaps it would be their original homeland, because they never found out about their homeland.

### Teachings by Alien Race Two of Group Two

Alien race two mechanized the teaching process by constructing a chamber in a convenient location in the sacred garden, placing the machinery inside with the power supply, and having it function whenever people were around so that a progression of impressions could be given to those who were meditating, even when the aliens were not there. They could even do the teaching from their spaceships. One of my patients recalled a past life in Lamuria when he had spiritual teachings by N-hante, alien race two of group two, as follows:

- *"My name is Ranel and it is my job to take care of the sheep. It is about 200,002 BC. One night when I am thirteen, our tribe goes to sleep in our tent, and the next morning when we wake up, we find ourselves in a new land. We have no idea how it happened and we are puzzled. Our sheep, tents, and other stuff are also here. Since we cannot change it, we accept it. The land is more lush and green than where we came from. We see some plants that are similar to what we had in our land, but also lots of plants, trees, fruits, and vegetables that are new for us. My parents and my mother's parents all live in a tent. Everybody in the tribe is doing different types of work. I decided to herd sheep because I do not want a hard and dirty job.*

  *"We are roughly human-like but our faces have rough and heavy features. The forehead slopes back and we have smaller skulls and brains. We are short, about five feet tall, heavily built, with big muscles and dark, curly, longer and thicker hair all over the body in both males and females, as compared to current humans. We are bent forward and are heavily tanned because we live outdoors most of the time.*

  *"One day at the age of eighteen, while pasturing the sheep in the valley, I see smoke. When I go to the source, I find an old man sitting. There is some cooked food and water. The old man invites me to eat, and then we sit and talk. He tells me his people have been here for quite a few years and he may be the last one still living. He asks many questions, such as: what makes the nature of human beings, what is a good way of living, what God do I worship, what happens after death, what do I do with my mind when I am wandering around the country side, what do I think about the idea of people spreading out*

*apart from each other and spreading out on the land, etc. He tells me that his people recognize and pray to God all the time. Our people also pray some and did occasional religious rituals at weddings, births, and deaths, but not every day. The old man invites me to come back and tells me to bring my friends too. The old man always has food for us but nobody has seen him cooking. I have never seen him eating or drinking, either. He is old with gray hair and looks like us. He dresses like us in a one-piece cloth robe. When I go back to our tribe, I tell my people about the old man.*

*"Next time, I take my friends with me. The old man fascinates us all. The word spreads and soon more and more people are going to visit him. He is not that far away from where we live. People like the idea of a priestly person devoted to them. He asks us about how we survive after death, what is the proper relationship with God and with people, how our souls came to be, and what happens before and after we live.*

*"My friends and I discuss these things sitting around the campfire and come up with some thoughts and then discuss them with the wise man, and he tells us his understanding about different things. He tells us that we are all from the Divine spirit and are here to learn, experience life, and that everything around us is part of the Divine spirit.*

*"We talk about what to do when we find out that the Divine spirit does exist. One of my friends comes up with the idea of talking to the Divine spirit like we talk to a friend or one of the elders. The wise man thinks it is a good idea so I try it that night. I talk to the Divine spirit about what I am thinking, what I am feeling, how life is going, and how we came to this new place. I talk to him about finding a wife.*

*"I am twenty-two years old now. I am preparing a ritual to worship the Divine in the garden. I have invited other people. I came up with an idea that it is a good thing*

*to speak with the Divine spirit in public in a group, as the wise man indicated before in one of the discussions. The worship was very successful. We all felt very joyful and happy. We made up songs about the Divine spirit working in us and about treating each other properly. Some of us sang out loud and others followed. Somebody came up with the idea of a concentration worship, where we would sit quietly and think of the joy of the Divine. We also practiced the proper balance between the regular life and the Divine.*

*"I am fifty-eight years old now. The wise man is still teaching. I am looking old like him but he still looks the same. I have two wives. One of our friends in the community died and I took his wife and children in, and she became my wife and his children became my children. It was only the right thing to do. Somebody had to take care of them and I could not afford to have two-households, so it makes lot more sense to have one. I go back to the wise man from time to time. Nobody ever saw him farming, cooking, or the wood in the fire, yet he always has fire burning and has food for everybody who comes to see him. It has to be a miracle. When we ask him about it, he smiles and says that the Divine spirit provides for him.*

*"I have moved to the south. I have big herds of sheep of my own and eight children, five from my first wife and three children of the friend's wife. One of the puzzling things I am noticing is that our children look different than people of our generation, and catch on to things real quick. Their faces are rounder and heads are bigger and rounder, and they are not as hairy as people of my generation, and our grandchildren are different than our children. I do not know how it is possible. Their faces are softer and features are smaller and finer. They are not as strong as we are. They are taller, thinner, and less muscular. They walk straight up, while we are short, hairy, muscular, and bent forward. They are smart and quicker in thinking. They don't seem to express as much joy while*

*praying as we do, but seem to be much more deeper and well saturated with the knowledge of God. They make up new words to describe what they are doing and thinking. We do not know whether these changes are good or bad and why and how they are occurring, but we accept and love them anyway. When they pray, it seems they are more in touch with the Divine. They are really attracted to the wise man on the mountain, who now has a constant stream of visitors, day and night.*

*"I am dying of cancer at the age of seventy-one. I expect to continue on to the Divine spirit, as the wise man explained. My heart stops and my spirit comes out of the body, feeling as alive as before, but with no pain. I see this huge Light, which seems to be calling me, and I go to heaven. After the cleansing and healing, I go for the life review with a few wise men who help me.*

*"As I look back in that life from heaven, I see that our tribe lived in the area where Iraq and Syria are now. We lived at the border. One day when I was twelve-years-old and attending the sheep, it seemed like a spaceship was hovering a short distance above me and they sent a beam at me, which jangled my brain and put me to sleep. Then they beamed me up to the spaceship. The beings resembled an alligator but were humanoid, upright and walking on two hind legs. They removed tissue from my testes and examined it. Then they put something like a computer chip in my neck, which was powered by my body, and later would completely dissolve. It sent out a signal to track me down on Earth.*

*"First they examined and did the tests to make sure I was a normal being, and that they were dealing with the right genes. Then a virus with a genetic modification was injected. After that, I was taken six more times to the spaceship, and each time they did a biopsy to see how completely the cells were changed. This virus actively targeted the reproductive cells and left the genetic material in the proper location in the genes. Each virus was*

*tailored to go to a specific gene for a specific gene modification. The gene was made partly of the virus and injected in the blood vessel close to the reproductive organ. It was a modified virus that, by getting into the cell, modified the DNA, and then fell apart as soon as the genetic portion was transferred. It self-destructed.*

*"They took me many times to check, because they wanted to make sure that the great majority of the reproductive cells were changed over to the new form. Some percent of them would still be of the old genetic stock. The aliens did this kind of genetic modification on every person in our tribe.*

*"From heaven, I see that one night all the tribe members were put to sleep and taken to the scout ships and then taken to the mother ship. There, we were put to sleep for a longer time with chemical anesthesia. They did not want to use the beams for a longer time because it could disrupt the brain. They checked our genetic modifications just to make sure that everything was all right. Meanwhile, the aliens took all the herds, tents, and other possessions to the new land, Lamuria, and got everything ready for the tribe to be placed there. I was thirteen-years-old when we were moved in the new place. When we woke up, we realized we were in a different place but did not know how.*

*"From heaven, I see that I was the first one who stumbled upon the alien teaching spot. The alien beings projected an image that looked like the local people, only older with gray hair and wiser-looking, because the tribe valued the human experience and allowed reverence for aging wisdom. The aliens projected the human type of image in the space by having two projectors, roughly at right angles, on each side, and where the beams intersected, the image was projected. It was like a holographic image.*

*"In heaven, I realize that my major group's purpose for that life was to intensify spirituality on Earth. I also see us planning with the beings that were going to incarnate as aliens, many lifetimes before. Genetic modifications and transplantation of the whole tribe in the new*

*land, Lamuria, was also part of the plan so that genetic experiments could be carried out in isolation.*

*"From heaven, as I look back in that lifetime, I see that it was alien race two of group two who did the genetic modification, transplantation, and spiritual teaching. I also see that the next generation looked different physically, and in three generations, humans were five inches taller, probably thirty pounds lighter, thinner, and not heavily built, and had less body hair. In about six generations, they looked more like current humans.*

*"I see that my skin rashes on my neck came from the tracking device that was put into my neck in that life. Also, beaming from the spaceship caused mental retardation in one of my past lives."*

### Teachings by Alien Race Three of Group Two

Before the Lamurians left the continent and before the Atlanteans arrived in Lamuria, the third alien race of group two, called Kicks, began to teach Lamurians. At this point, the Lamurians were completely self-contained because they had no outside contact and they had everything they needed, both externally and internally. They had no desire to leave their island-continent and explore. They did not have any way to go to other lands because they were not technologically oriented. They had what they needed without developing new technology. By now, the whole continent was sparsely populated. Alien race three of group two decided to educate and help Lamurians and prepare them for exploration outside Lamuria.

Kicks, alien race three of group two, told Lamurians that there were other inhabited lands to the east where they should go and teach about the Divine. Also they should learn a new way of trading, using money and making a profit. They gave them the whole plan, from boat building to instructions in trading and using money, to the plan of who should go and what to do. The aliens taught them how to build a boat, how to sail, gave them courses in capitalism, free enterprise, trade, and making a profit, which was a totally foreign concept for the Lamurians. They also taught Lamurians the different languages of people in various lands. They were told to spread the word of the Divine and teach them various spiritual practices. Aliens told Lamurians that they were different than the rest of the humans because they had special genes which made them so spiritual, and they should spread their genes for the benefit of the rest of humanity. Only people with high telepathic and psychic abilities were sent out as traders and spiritual teachers. When they went to South, Central, and North Americas, and Atlantis, they had affairs with different women and had children, who had superior Lamurian genes, which spread all over through the years.

Following is a life described by a patient when he and other Lamurians were taught by alien race three of group two:

- *"I am a thirty-year-old man living in Navula, on the southeast coast of Lamuria. My name is Phillius and this is 110,000 BC. We have a sacred grove on the higher ground so when we go there, we can look at the town and see the ocean. We all communicate telepathically with each other, and in our society, everything belongs to everybody. I take food inland and bring back food they raise, so there is exchange of food from area to area. Nobody makes a profit and everybody gets what they need to eat. We all share work and help each other.*

  *"I am in the sacred garden worshipping the Divine. It is about two miles long, with trees, shrubs, and flowers. In the center, there is beautiful rock, which is used as a speaker's platform, and other smaller rocks on which the listeners can sit. As I am worshipping the Divine, I get the feeling there is someone at the speaker's rock calling me and telling me to come over. He tells me he is a messenger from the Divine. He wants us to build boats and go out on the ocean to explore other lands. He is communicating*

*with me telepathically and mentally, showing me pictures of what the boat must look like, the kind of tools we need to build it, where it should be built, and how to go about it. He is explaining the whole plan.*

*"He is telling me that there are other inhabited lands to the east where we should go and teach about the Divine. We should learn a new way of trading, using money and making a profit. It is a foreign idea to me. As I am communicating with this being, I am also telepathically transmitting this conversation to other Lamurians, who can hear me all over the continent. They are not receiving information personally from the Divine messenger, but it is strained through me. He is giving me this whole plan from boat building to instructions in trading and using money, to the plan of who should go and what to do. The whole plan is presented in one package. He promises there will be help at every stage. He will send helpers like himself to guide us.*

*"A town called Hacksted is selected where the boats will be built. It is further up the southeast coast. There is a peninsula that breaks up the waves coming from the north, so as the boats are built, they are in calm and protected water. We will need skilled woodworkers to come to Hacksted to cut and prepare the timber, which might take about two years. Another two years will be needed to get the boat building yard set up, and then we can build a boat. After that, we can practice sailing and get used to going on water until we are capable of sailing to other lands where other humans live. He also promises us to help us learn the languages of different people.*

*"We gather timber cutters, woodworkers, and cloth workers to make the sails. Meanwhile, there are courses in capitalism, free enterprise, trading, and making a profit. These are all foreign ideas to us, so we have to start from scratch. As soon as one person catches on what we are doing, all the Lamurians also will understand by telepathic communication. Many people are training to be*

*crewmembers and many to be traders and teachers. We are not only being trained for trading but also to spread the word of the Divine and also to keep our mouths shut about our personal life. We are not to let other people know about our telepathic communication with other people in Lamuria from a distance because they will not understand it without the proper spiritual development.*

*"The master plan was handed to me and I was able to convey it immediately to all the other Lamurians all over the continent through telepathic communication. It contained all the components, such as the idea that we should become traders, build ships, set up the ship building factories, and get the produce for trading ready. The whole coordinated series of activities would require continent-wide cooperation. This is impossible without psychic connection. So there are all these different activities going on at the same time, all preplanned with messengers of the Divine coming and actually doing the instructions. They are teaching us about sailing, ship building, capitalism, trading courses, how to teach spirituality, and what to tell the outside world. At least seven of them show up every day from nowhere.*

*"I am chosen to be a trader and a spiritual teacher. Of course I will go on to make a good profit and become very rich in the land where I am going. This is not important to me, but in the other land, having money will bring prestige and power and make it easier for people to listen to me. It takes about four years to build the boats, and by that time, the crews and the traders are pretty well trained. One of the advantages is that we can share the experience, and if somebody is experienced in boat building, then that experience is transferred to other people telepathically, and when they start, they already have four years of experience. Not the actual feel of the job, with their own muscles, but they already know the job.*

*"At the age of thirty-five, I am ready to start the journey to the other land. There is a debate if we should take*

the sacred plants with us, but we decide not to take them because we do not want these plants to spread around the world by accident. If these plants get transferred to somewhere else, then we will never figure out from where we actually originated.

"When we are ready to sail, we have all cargo loaded and we are headed east and south. We come across some villages. One of the traders among us knows their language and chooses to stay here, and the rest of us move ahead. A couple of us decided to stay in a small city, where we trade our goods and get more goods to trade. I found a place to live and work and develop trade relationship with local people. We set up the trade route and maintain telepathic communication with people in Lamuria and other traders.

"After I settle down, I begin to teach local people about the Divine. We become good traders and make a lot of money, which we do not care for but find it is important to have money in this part of the world in order to be heard and respected. We start spiritual teachings in several different ways. We invite people to our houses to sit and talk, and we guide the conversation to spiritual topics, or encourage them to attend local religious services and to contribute to the congregation by discussing the religious understanding of these people. Another part of the ministry, which is not publicly broadcast, is to spread the genes as advised by the Divine messengers. When the opportunity presents itself, we have sexual relationships, and when the woman is pregnant she and her child are well supported, but they are never really the part of the household. The woman is comparatively well off, the child is well raised, and the genes are spread in this way. So our genes are spread to Central and South America, and later to Atlantis.

"There is no contact with the Divine messenger since we are out of Lamuria. They still conduct trading schools in Lamuria. Learning the other languages was difficult, *but after we learned them and practiced them for four or five years, the other Lamurians can draw on you. Then it is simply a matter of physical practice to get the accents right.*

*"When one of the traders is ready to return to Lamuria, another trader arrives to take his place. It seems to the people of the town that this is a new person moving in and he knows everything that the person before him knows, including what they look like and what to expect out of them. The new trader continues to support the children of the previous traders and the women. I have nine children from four different women.*

*"I go back to Lamuria when I am fifty years old. I am happy to settle back into my life. I never had a wife and family, and I know I could not take these women and my children to Lamuria because they would not fit in and would be unhappy.*

*"After my experiences as a trader, I am realizing that we need a foundation for the Lamurian society. I decide to devote myself to the structure of society and to learn about what is the right type of philosophy for us, starting with the institutions that the lower-ability Lamurians have come to despise because they do not understand them. They think of high-ability Lamurians as a kind of social controller, while actually they are a social liberator. We are working for a just society and if we are to infringe against one of the lower-ability Lamurians, then we will be damaging the whole society.*

*"We started out as herdsmen with a tribe leader. Then, as the psychic abilities developed and the groups spread out, we began to have different forms of society, until finally it evolved into one where everyone owned everything and everybody had an equal right to everything. Everybody worked and did what was necessary because it is the right thing to do.*

*"Now I am coming up with a formal alternative. We have to think of the establishment of the society and*

*decide how it works and why. Who has what responsibility and why, and how it must be in this unique society where people have varying degrees of telepathic abilities and everybody can hear but only the top ones are completely fluent in transmitting and receiving.*

*"One of my ideas is that we must not permit the society to stratify and have different layers based on the telepathic abilities. All the society has to be equal, not based on ability but on individual existence, which makes people valuable. The society establishes individual rights and prevents anybody from discriminating, particularly against the less adept, the people with lower telepathic ability.*

*"I have been out in the world. I have dealt with people who had no ability but were still human beings. To take advantage of them is to do them harm. I am transferring some of the lessons I have learned from the outside back to Lamurian society and creating a standard of conduct inside Lamuria. It is like establishing a sort of bill of rights, a declaration of independence and freedom, and a constitution, establishing the rights and responsibilities more formally. Others also get involved in this effort. This is when the decision is made to turn the government over to the middle- and the lower-ability Lamurians. So now there are only few high-ability people in government. This developed over time. I formalized the code and have taken the upper level out of the implementation of it.*

*"I am out on a training mission at the age of sixty-four. There is a severe storm and I drown. My spirit comes out and knows where to go. The belief of the Lamurians, when they were first brought to this continent, was that their life continued in an earthly manner. It was like the body died and the spirit continued living as if it were on earth and it still needed food and drink and still had to work, so there was little difference of being alive or dead except that it was on a different plane. As the Lamurians became more spiritual, the concept of the fate of the soul became popular;*

*not that souls will continue forming but they would go to the place where spirits live as spirit beings, not needing food, drink, shelter, or work. The idea evolved that there will be a growth and development process inside this spiritual existence. Eventually we came to believe that there are successions of the spiritual existences and successions of births in the universe, and developed the idea of reincarnation and karma. We carry different problems with us from one life to another to resolve them.*

*"I go directly to heaven and, after cleansing and healing, I go for the life review. In heaven I realize that my purpose for that life was to spread spirituality outside Lamuria and to elevate the general spiritual nature of mankind by spreading Lamurian genes in humanity. I also planned to work with aliens. I was chosen by the aliens to receive and pass on information to the rest of the Lamurians because of my open mindedness and being firmly rooted and not easily shaken by new and different knowledge and environment.*

*"From Heaven, I see that the aliens did not appear personally but were using three smaller spaceships that had projectors and video cameras in them. The space crafts stayed out of sight so they would not attract attention. An image was projected into the sacred garden where it appeared as real in three dimensions. This image, which they created, looked like a Lamurian. In reality they did not look like humans [as described in chapter three]. If they had appeared to humans as they are, it might scare the humans.*

*"From Heaven, I see that my lung problems in the current life came from that life because of death by drowning. I see that at this time, in 110,000 BC, Lamuria was not as big as it looks on the map because it stretches out on the outskirts of the map. So Lamuria appears to be larger than it was. Only the center of the map was of true scale. The further you go away from the center, the more distorted it gets. Atlantis is of true size because it was in the*

*flat part and in the center of the map. At this time, it was*
*whole and none of its parts submerged under water."*

Alien race three of group two came when Lamuria was already thinly settled. They did not appear in person because they did not look like humans. They projected an image of an average Lamurian. Once an idea was given to the Lamurians, they could transmit it telepathically to the other Lamurians. Those who taught class would teach only two or three Lamurians and then they left. They were seen for three or four hours at a time. The aliens emphasized the altruistic nature of this mission. They emphasized that it would be very altruistic for the Lamurians to share their genes with the outside world. It would be good for them to meet outside women and give them babies who would have Lamurian genes.

My hypnotized patients state that there were centers in cities of other countries where Lamurians were settled and had a succession of Lamurian travelers. They left children there who had Lamurian genes. Over time these genes spread throughout the population, and cities where the traders settled became spiritual centers. These spiritual centers became known on their continents as important places for spirituality. In modern records, these cities are scarcely known but at that time they became known as holy places. Also they were evolving physically. Lamurians were looking more like modern humans while the rest of the humanity was not as evolved physically, and they did not take a leap in physical change like Lamurians did due to genetic modification. Spreading the Lamurian genes into the general population caused the rest of the people to become more like modern humans, like Lamurians were.

The genes spread slowly in Asia, Europe, and Africa because Lamurians primarily headed east to the Americas and Atlantis, and from there, primarily to the Mediterranean. These places, such as Egypt, the coast of Asia-Minor and Greece, became significant spiritual centers. Then a great flood of Lamurians finally reached Asia during the dispersion of Lamurians, when most people chose to sail to the west to-ward Asia because they felt people were more spiritual there as compared to people in the Americas and Atlantis.

The second and third alien races of group two also did genetic modification and brought spiritual teaching to small groups of people in other parts of the Earth. At the time, the custom in Asia was that a woman would marry somebody from another village and move there and thus spread the genes and spiritual knowledge. The aliens also taught them agriculture, pottery, weaving, net making, etc.

## Society and Culture of Lamuria

My hypnotized patients state that the genetic adjustments the aliens made with the Lamurians were the enlargement of the brain, including the temporal lobes, and the development of more and finer neurons, providing more capacity for spir-ituality in that part of the brain. As a result, they were born with an intense interest in the spiritual nature of the world. To them, it was obvious that the spirit was the driving force behind the world. This really did not help their technological development because they did not feel the need to go after it. Instead, they felt a compelling need to develop spiritu-ally. Their houses were smaller because they did not need to own much. They felt more spiritually complete than we in current times do. Therefore, their need to own possessions lessened. A spiritually complete person would not need ex-tra things at all. They believed God would provide food and a place to live.

In Lamuria, there was not much competitiveness, because how can you compete with somebody when you know what he or she is thinking and doing? It is like, why play cards with somebody when you know what cards they are hold-ing. In Lamuria, there was an acceptance of human nature, a realization that human beings would not always measure up. Not everybody was expected to meet the highest standards every second.

Lamurians came close to reestablishing the divine plan of soul merging, but they just did not quite perceive it. Their observations of spiritual progress were based on the development of psychic abilities. As these developed, they figured that spiritual progress had been made. This was an observable phenomenon, something they could measure. Occasionally a few of the Lamurians could also use teleportation; that is, they could physically go from one place to another just with their psychic powers. But their teleportation was not reliable and they did not quite understand it.

Anything known to one Lamurian was eventually known to all Lamurians simply because they could communicate telepathically and the thoughts were picked up from mind to mind. Lamurians had a community closeness but with an awareness of their differences. They were all in contact, maybe not this second or this day, but eventually what was known in one place was in the awareness of everyone in the nation. They had a real understanding.

### Education in Lamuria

My hypnotized patients state that children were educated partly at home, partly in school buildings, and some in the sacred garden. Most of the education was spiritual. In school they were taught reading, writing, arithmetic, building, music, and dancing. Later on, they had libraries and books about spirituality, understanding about God, understanding of humanity, how to have contact with God, events that occur in the Light (Heaven), insights about what would help improve spirituality, and later, they studied geography, different cultures outside Lamuria, and map making. They did not have any romance or adventure novels because couples who were romantically involved were really in contact and did not need the escapism material. There was no pornography.

They did not act upon the original plan of spiritual joining and passing on the knowledge to the incoming souls as described in chapter one because it was not possible at this time and the timing was not right. They were not given the knowledge about it, and even the aliens who did the genetic modifications with them and did the spiritual teachings did not have any knowledge about it. Also, humanity was not ready at this time. Lamurian children were taught to read and write and they did have a language, which was needed to communicate verbally, because most of the time they did not develop telepathic communication till the age of twelve. They did have books and libraries. According to heavenly beings, there were some manuscripts in Central America in the Lamurian script. They will be found but will not be recognized as Lamurian. There will be unrecognizable symbols in rock, which will be badly eroded.

### Child Rearing in Lamuria

Child rearing practices were different in Lamuria. An adult was able to tap into the infant about what he or she was feeling or thinking through their psychic abilities, and did not have to guess or figure out what was wrong with the child. This reduced parents' frustrations and they raised much happier babies. Their psychological needs were met because the parents could see, hear, feel, and know what the baby was really concerned about. This made a tremendous difference in the way Lamurians grew into adulthood. They did not grow up angry or frustrated. They had appreciation for each other and each other's psychological, physical, and social needs.

### Priests in Lamuria

Those who were very good communicators of spiritual ideas became the primary religious teachers. They may not have been highly developed telepathic persons but could get the ideas across either by example, by practice, or by words. Their work was extremely important for the community and for the young. Only a small fraction of these spiritual teachers were highly developed. Most of them were moderately developed. The higher developed people, at whatever job they selected, did their jobs and stayed in touch with people. They communicated telepathically with a large number of people and made sure that society ran smoothly. It was recognized in society that this was their real job.

### Government in Lamuria

Each city in Lamuria had a functioning government for water and sewage and to make sure the food got in and trash got out, according to my hypnotized patients. They did not need much in a way of police because there was no crime. They did not need big houses, transportation, or energy. Each little town had its own set-up and they would cooperate with each other. If one town did not have a good well, then many people from the other towns would get together and dig a well in that town. People did whatever work they wanted to do and cooperated with each other. In their society, everybody took care of people around them. When one person was hurting, everybody else felt the pain psychically.

A few cities together would send a representative to the national group to be there physically and set up whatever was needed, but most things were taken care of by telepathy. They had a loose confederation of city-states and there was a central government that did not need power. It existed to provide structure. Any debates or discussions were done telepathically. The capital of Lamuria was in the north, close to the site where the original tribe was transplanted. Distance really did not make any difference to them because they could just telepathically know what was happening and could participate in discussions from anywhere. Written law was pretty rare because they could do it telepathically.

### Currency in Lamuria

By the time Lamuria was populated and settled, there was no currency. Each person worked according to his or her ability and interest, and results of that labor were freely available to all. Of course it worked in all directions. Everyone did their job and everyone's labor was available to all. Due to their telepathic ability, there was no hoarding and no selfishness. All things were shared equally and equitably. It was an anarchy that was equitable and impossible without real telepathy and a real understanding of humanity. Later on, people in different parts of Lamuria used different types of currency. In some places, local currency, such as certain stones, were used, while at other places they did not use any currency at all.

### Stratification of Psychic Ability in Lamuria

My hypnotized patients mention that there was a range of psychic abilities and telepathy among them, depending upon their age and natural talents. For a given age group, some were low, some medium, and others were very high in their psychic and telepathic abilities, and there was a complete range in between. Approximately 20 percent of Lamurians were highly developed, 20 percent were lower developed, and 60 percent were in the middle. Lamurians who were sent outside Lamuria were highly developed and very telepathic, so they were able to contact people in Lamuria and stay in touch. Not all Lamurians were that well developed.

Their schooling was completely different. It was based primarily on the ability to read and write and to communicate effectively, and they studied spirituality. When they made contacts with humans in other parts of the world, they definitely perceived the difference in spirituality.

The following is a past life in Lamuria recalled by a patient under hypnosis explaining in detail Lamurian society, culture, and lifestyle:

- *"I am a twenty-two-year-old male living in Zake City, located in northeastern Lamuria. My name is Enid and this is 87,931 BC. As a child, we communicate with our parents and others verbally. Around the age of twelve, we can communicate telepathically, just like all other Lamurians. We are in the school system from age seven to seventeen. From seven to ten, we are taught prayers, meditation techniques, and spiritual movements that are designed to open up the chakras (energy centers) and meridians. During our school career, we are also taught reading, writing, mathematics, and social studies. The schools have libraries with books on Lamurian history, spirituality, and prayers.*

*"Our people are small and they all look alike in a general way. The tallest ones are only five feet seven inches tall. We have copper colored skin, black hair, high cheekbones, deep-set eyes, a relatively long nose, and a wide, flat mouth. After graduating from school at seventeen, I maintained a small garden farm for myself for trading produce for other goods and services. I raised beans, squash, and maize. I follow a simple lifestyle, including three major prayer and meditation sessions daily.*

*"Our city is simple and clean, consisting of one-story houses with two to four rooms, constructed of stone and logs. Our roads are narrow and are more like paths. We require very little transportation, so we don't need finished roads. The city is very beautiful, with flowers, trees, and shrubbery around the homes and along the pathways. We don't go from one city to another, as a rule. We have telepathic skills so we know what is going on in other parts of the country by tuning in to other people's thoughts. We walk wherever we go. We do have a few carts, which are pulled by horses and donkeys. They are used to move the heavy loads.*

*"We have a special sacred garden in our city called the Garden of Light. All cities have these gardens. It is a special area set aside for prayer, meditation, and special events. The garden is approximately one hundred by one hundred feet. Gifted psychics tend it because they have a keen sense of knowing the Light. They nurture, maintain,*

*and care for it. The garden contains beautiful flowers, shrubbery, and trees. It has beautiful blue water ponds. It is special because it is a place for prayer and meditation. It would be like a temple in another society. The garden is surrounded by another park that is approximately two hundred yards by two hundred yards. The main difference is that the inside is for quiet meditation. Everyone is permitted in the Garden of Light. I go to the garden three to four times a week. There are meetings held in the park outside the garden and some important ceremonies, such as weddings and funerals, are held inside the garden.*

*"I marry at the age of twenty-four, and my wedding is held inside the garden. I have known my bride since elementary school. We always liked one another. We obtain consent from our parents and make plans for our wedding. At the wedding, my bride and I are wearing long, white, flowing robes made from a cotton type of cloth. I have no headgear but my wife is wearing a white headdress that matches her robe. The ceremony is conducted by a highly psychic priest, who is also a government official. He also is wearing a long, white, flowing robe. He provides guidance and clarity.*

*"The wedding is attended by both sets of parents other family members and friends. There are seventy-five in attendance. The ceremony is made up of prayers and meditation for half an hour. While the priest leads prayers and meditation, we all pray and meditate together about having a positive life and being able to serve the Divine. The others are also meditating for us, sending us blessings and wishing us a good life.*

*"Near the end, the priest asks the Divine to bless us and then he tells us we are husband and wife. We did not do any rituals during the ceremony. We simply prayed and meditated. During the prayers and meditation, I can see the Light coming down into me and my bride. I can see our souls joined by a connecting cord and blended into one Light. As others pray for us, I can see Light coming*

*into them and then, through them, into my bride and myself. We are receiving their blessings and well wishes. After the ceremony, we eat together and we sing songs to celebrate the event. We do the spiritual movements that we do during prayer and meditation times. After the ceremony, we return to our home, which was constructed by the community prior to our wedding. Everyone helped in building it. This is our custom.*

*"When I'm twenty-five, I'm appointed by our chief government official to head up the beautification committee for our city. I applied for this position, along with seventeen other persons. Three of us received appointments. There are thirty officials in our office. I am responsible to oversee all the beautification projects in the city. Everyone contributes to beautification because flowers, shrubbery, and trees are important parts of our lives.*

*"We have special stones for our currency in Lamuria, but we don't use them very often. Trading goods for services does most of our business. Most people choose to leave their body after their life's work is completed. We do not have crimes or diseases, and have healing places in Lamuria for the minor ailments. These are special places where people can go to be healed. The gifted healers heal by praying, meditating, and laying their hands on the person and letting God's Light flow through them into the person who is being healed. They also heal through visualization, where they visualize God's Light flowing to the patient and healing the patient.*

*"While some travel to other parts of Lamuria, I choose not to do this. Some even travel to other countries on ships, and we have a few people from Atlantis and South and Central America in our country. I know this by my telepathic communication with others in other parts of Lamuria. We do not have any Atlanteans in our city.*

*"We have a central government in Lamuria. It operates just like our city governments only on a larger scale. We have special days during the year when we pray together*

*(telepathically) as a country. Our capital city is located in the north-central part of the country. All government officials live in their own homes, but they work in a government office. The living standards in Lamuria are the same for all citizens.*

*"By the age of thirty-two, I have three children. When we get up in the morning, we pray and meditate individually, followed by family prayers and meditation. After breakfast, around nine a.m., I go off to work, the kids go off to school, and my volunteer wife either works around our garden or goes to a volunteer commitment. We always start our workday with prayers and meditation. We pray for others and ask for guidance in doing the day's work. Everyone returns home around three p.m. The family prays and meditates together for an hour. After this, we work around our home or in our garden for an hour. In the evening, we take walks, often visiting the Garden of Light. We pray and meditate again together as a family, and also individually, before sleeping.*

*"At sixty, I become the chief official of the city. I acquire this post through seniority. This is only my second position since I started doing government service. My new job requires me to oversee all programs in the city. For example, beautification programs, education, maintenance of the Garden of Light, libraries, volunteer programs, etc.*

*"At the age of seventy-four, I retire. I continue to volunteer for our beautification projects and other services. I feel physically fit but I am maturing and my hair is turning gray. At the age of ninety-nine, I have an inner knowing that I have completed my life's work. As a result, I decide to leave the body. I discuss this with my wife and three children. They understand my decision. My wife has decided that she will leave her body in about a year. She has a few more things to do before she leaves.*

*"I lie down on my bed and I pray and meditate, asking for my spirit to rise up out of my body and go to the Light (heaven). My last thoughts are that I had a good*

*life, I accomplished all of my work, and I have no regrets.
My wife, who is seated beside me, watches my spirit rise.
As my spirit leaves the body, I look for the Light, find it,
and go up into it. As I look back, I see a ceremony for me
headed by a priest. Family members, friends, and community people attend the ceremony. The psychic priest
leads prayers and everyone visualizes me going up into
the Light (heaven). Then the people pray and meditate
and visualize my presence in heaven. After that, my body
is taken to a special place to be cremated.*

*"From heaven, I see that this was a good life and I was
a good person. I see no demonic influences in Lamuria at
this time. I can see that there are heavenly beings working in the Garden of Light, and the Light is more intense
there. My plan for that life was to live in Lamuria and to
have the experience of living a Lighted spiritual life and
to be of service to others.*

*"I can see that I gave soul parts to my wife and children
that came back to me, as you, Dr. Modi, asked the angels to
bring them back and integrate with me, after cleansing and
healing them. I have a desire in the current life to be spiritual, even though I get blocked from this from time to time."*

In Lamuria, people had a united purpose. A town meeting was
going on all the time about what would be best for the country
and what would be best for a village. There was a continuous
interaction going on, which made them very efficient in whatever they undertook and in whatever social development they
did. It gave each of them a sense of belonging to that community. Pros and cons were discussed and a vote taken without anyone raising their voice or opening their mouth. After
a problem became apparent, such as a need for a clean water
supply, within a matter of weeks or months a solution would
be decided through consensus, and the people of the community would begin to work toward that goal. As children became about twelve years old and entered into what was called
an adult state, they too became aware of all these interactions.

Lamurians were simple people living a simple, peaceful, and happy life. They did not develop technology as the Atlanteans did because they did not need it. Usually economic necessity or shortage of resources is what pushes the development of technology. You have to have food, heat, profit, and trade. Here, the folks grew without these concepts in mind. In Lamuria, what was happening was that the people had sufficient food and other resources and they did not care for technology. They just wanted to be spiritual. They were being spiritual as they developed the psychic gifts coming to them. They were not seeking the gifts, but when they showed up, they used them and said thank you. They were spiritually very advanced and were using the psychic and spiritual abilities in place of technology. It short-circuited their technological development.

## Concept of Spiritual Development in Lamuria

As mentioned before, Lamurians had intense spirituality. It was a major aspect of their lives. A child grew up with prayers and different types of spiritual practices. All Lamurians worked extensively on their spiritual development, which included:

Spiritual awareness
Spirit in action or spiritual practice
Practice and study of meditation

### Spiritual Awareness

My hypnotized patients report that the Lamurians were born into spiritual awareness. In our culture, we are also born with a spiritual awareness, but it is not as intense as theirs. They perceived spirit as acting behind the physical world from the time they were little. They had the sense that the spirit was the driving force in the universe, but they did not have intimate knowledge of why or how. They knew it was there and had a purpose, a plan, and it was motivating things. Lamurians, with feeling for spirit in the universe, knew that the spirit functioned everywhere. Part of their spiritual practice included reading spiritual texts that others had written and creating ritual for being in touch with the spirit in the universe, that power of love.

Lamurians saw the existence of the spirit in many different things. They perceived each other as having a spiritual presence. They also saw the presence of spirit in the trees, animals, and cycles of life. They figured out the reincarnation process quickly. For them, it was not a hopeful, pious thought. They saw instances of it happening and these instances were documented and investigated. They found them to be supportive, that they were the details of true experiences.

As a result of their spiritual awareness, Lamurians developed different spiritual practices, such as prayers, meditation, and worship. To honor the presence of the spirit in humanity, they recognized the need for community rituals. To recognize the presence of the spirit in nature, they had nature rituals. To recognize the presence of the spirit in each other, they had holidays and special recognition days for each person. When they read spiritual texts, they were recognizing the spirit acting in the person who wrote the book and recognized their understanding. These were all honors for the spirit that were recognized by the Lamurians.

### Spiritual Practices

There is an apparent overlap of spiritual awareness and spiritual practice. For example, reading of a spiritual text can appear in both. As a result of spiritual awareness and the celebration of that awareness, we read spiritual texts. Also, we read spiritual texts as an actual spiritual practice, to develop our own spirituality even more. So the same thing appears in both categories. It is both a part of the spiritual awareness and a part of the spiritual practice.

According to the heavenly beings, in our culture, the idea of spiritual text is rather limited. Christians tend to think that the Bible is the only spiritual text; Muslims think that the Koran is the only spiritual text, and Hindus think that Vedas, Geeta, Ramayana, and Mahabharat are the only spiritual texts, but they are not. Anything that relates to spiritual knowledge becomes a spiritual text. Spiritual insights are found in all cultures, in all people, and in all religions. Heavenly beings strongly recommend that, for a complete, well-rounded understanding of God and his purpose, the spiritual texts of all the other groups should be studied, including all the current new age books which are being published. They definitely have spirituality in them and should be examined. They all contain spiritual awareness and spiritual insights. Lamurians followed many types of spiritual practices including prayers, worship, rituals, and meditation.

**Prayer**

Prayer is a communication with God. All communication goes both ways, because if it is not two-way, then it is not a communication. A true communication is give and take, an exchange, through which a defining and a mutual understanding develops. Many people pray and only tell God things. More often, they ask God, "God I need this, I want that, give me that." Often it is a shopping list. This is not a valid communication. Prayer should be where you speak and God answers. We can talk about many things and concerns, which is not exactly always about "what I want." Prayers that simply bombard God with a list of wants and needs are inadequate. There are many ways to approach God.

Lamurians were in constant communication with God. To them, prayers were a constant interchange with God. They were living in the Divine essence, constantly aware of the existence of God and constantly in prayer, communicating with God. To exist in this state of constant knowledge of being with God is also a spiritual awareness and when we practice that awareness it become a spiritual practice. It is a very high state of spirituality.

## Community Ritual

Community ritual is where the entire community cooperates in putting on an event or a spiritual happening for the benefit of all in the community. Basically, all rituals follow the same form. Ritual does not require that it be done the same way every time, but that it follows the same pattern set up for that particular event. Generally, a ritual involves a group turning attention to the Divine. Some patterns are being set up for everyone to follow.

Group communication with the creator of the universe is practiced in which the group prays together. There is a community involvement with each other and with the spirit at the same time. It is quite fulfilling and gives everybody a feeling of belonging to the human race and to the community, as well as being a part of God. Anyone who feels lonely should make an effort to get involved in community activities and in community rituals, and become a real part of the community.

This leads to another part of the community ritual, which involves spiritual discussions or discussions of spiritual perceptions. These are part of the communication between people and are a part of a spiritual practice. Perhaps in Lamuria it would be a matter of two people or a group talking about the different ways in which they saw God present in everything around them. It definitely drew their minds to the spiritual realm.

The concept of sharing is also included in the community ritual, where we give and receive in mutual benefit. We share our spiritual and physical gifts. We make sure that no one goes hungry and everyone has a decent place to sleep and be safe.

In Lamuria, community rituals were also applied on a national level, with the entire continent taking part in a day of spiritual ritual. Sections of government administrative for public purposes would hold a day of rituals. Organizations based on different interests would also have rituals, plus every person also set their own ritual time. There was spiritual ritual performed at every level in Lamuria.

## Individual Rituals

Rituals usually involve more than just one component of the person. There is a physical component, a visual component, an auditory component, a tactile component, and a movement component. Sometimes music or a song may be involved, on both the community level and the individual level; the more the person gets drawn into the ritual, the more powerful and satisfying the ritual is. If the person uses just one channel of communication, such as silent prayer, the ritual does not have as profound an effect, spiritually, for the person as it would when spiritual dancing, singing, spiritual reading, and spiritual prayers are involved together as part of the ritual.

Lamurians would set aside two time periods a day for some form of religious rituals above and beyond meditation and prayers or spiritual reading. During that time, they may set up a ceremony to honor the spirit of animals, or to honor the spirit of God in the construction of their dwelling. They could see the powers and the authority of the spirit, the God that caused the house to be built, even though it was made by natural materials and done by humans.

In Lamuria, the individual rituals were done first thing in the morning and just before bedtime, before a meal and work. But in general, Lamurians would do small individual rituals all day. In our culture in modern times, if you wish to develop spiritually, it is strongly encouraged by the heavenly beings to find those who are like-minded and spend time in their company. In Lamuria, they did not have to make that distinction because they were all like-minded people.

Writing and recording, what in our culture is commonly called journaling, was encouraged in Lamuria. To put down thoughts, feelings, events, and the perception of events in writing about what was going on in life was sort of a spiritual history that people kept as part of their spiritual practice in Lamuria. Children were encouraged to start keeping a diary at a very early age. This was part of their study of communication and was one of their main purposes for developing reading and writing. Due to spiritual journaling, children were quite aware of their feelings, motivations, and what they really wanted, and it kept these issues from being hidden from them. They were much more in touch with themselves and with reality, and also much more accepting of their own emotional state.

Lamurians were fully aware of the existence of demonic forces but completely rejected them. They also recognized that the dark forces served some purpose in God's creation, so they recognized them but did not accept them. They could tell the difference between good and evil and were very quick to make a choice. They were aware of the potentials of the dark; they were also just as aware of the potentials of the Light. It was very easy for them to make a choice for the Light and to reject the dark. They were so spiritually aware that they could feel and could know when there was a demonic presence, demonic attack, or demonic influence. It was really easy for them to reject those attacks. They used protection prayers and had a huge advantage of community support on a spiritual level. They were aware when another member of the community was under attack and could protect that person from the dark influences.

Occasionally, some Lamurians were mentally defective for one reason or another and were not able to develop telepathy or other psychic gifts. As a result, they could not participate fully in the spiritual life of the community. However, they were loved and cherished equally. These persons were relatively few, and due to genetic accidents, an occasional bad gene, or a developmental problem.

The planets with higher vibrations do not have demonic influences and do not live in duality like we do. As a result, they see only a limited part of the picture of creation. They only live in God. They do not see or have to face conflict; they do not have to strive, and as a result, they do not develop spiritually as much as we who live in duality.

## Practice and Study of Meditation

Meditation is the concept of the empty mind, where the mind has no thoughts and it is free and open and can receive impressions from the spirit easily. According to my hypnotized patients, Lamurians not only practiced meditation but also did research studies, such as comparing a mantra meditation with the movement meditation or contemplation meditation with the nothingness meditation, until they had a very good idea of the effect of each form of meditation. They came to the conclusion that they all led to the same place, but some meditation was more efficient and more effective in certain personality types.

For example, the meditation that is fairly effective with everyone is mantra meditation. Mantra meditation requires the repetition of a mantra out loud, moving to sub-vocalization, and then finally to a mental repetition. The meditation that is more intense and fastest developing for those who have an intellectual bent is contemplation meditation, in which you simply concentrate visually upon an object for an extended period of time.

The Lamurians studied the effects of various meditations and used this knowledge to prescribe meditation techniques for the young children so they could develop at a rapid rate. They did not have adolescent problems like we do. Usually by age twelve, the Lamurian children were considered to be adults because they were developed sufficiently and could perceive the thoughts around them. They were essentially immersed in an adult world to begin with. Then it was simply a matter of waiting for their physical maturity.

The research projects of the Lamurians dealt with spiritual problems rather than with technological or scientific problems. For example, a research study based upon a type of meditation defines the personality of the person using it, depending on how long and how vigorously it was applied and the amount of spiritual progress that could be observed. For example, mantra meditation may be the subject deciding which mantra is being used by each group, how long they meditated, and how often they meditated, and the degree of spiritual progress they made. They worked on different components of the meditation. Then they were all compared. This kind of research went on over a long period of time.

## Lamurians in Atlantis

They set out on sailing expeditions, primarily to Central and South America. There they found people whose spirituality was not as developed. It did not take Lamurians long to realize that these people were quite different from them and lacked spiritual development. As they expanded and learned to build ships with the help of aliens, they set up settlements on the coast of South America, Central America, and eventually in North America. Those in Central America eventually walked across the narrow countries and down the east coast of South America, coming in contact with the people of Atlantis.

Lamurians developed a few arts and crafts, and some technology and industry, but they never got into heavy industry or manufacturing. They mostly remained an agricultural society. As contact developed with Atlantis, Lamuria got some of the benefits of having Atlantean technology. Of course, the technology they gave to the Atlanteans was spiritual technology, which was misapplied and caused the downfall of Atlantis. The Atlanteans misused it because they applied technology to become psychic instead of developing spirituality. As a result, they controlled people and their minds, rather than doing things for the good of all. If you are developing from spirit, then you do not do those things. You do not take advantage of other people and hurt them.

One of my patients under hypnosis, recalled a past life as a Lumurian trader who went to Atlantis to trade and teach spirituality to Atlanteans as follows:

- *"I am a young boy. I was born in a town named Hurd-garn, near the city of Lama, at the southeastern tip of Lamuria. My mother, Hamite, tells me about a big continent to the east, with people who are different. As a child, I thought this was an absolutely wonderful, mysterious, exciting thing, which later made me decide to become a missionary. We know that these people do not have much spirituality. I grow up like a normal Lamurian child, running, playing, and working a little bit. I do spiritual practices such as praying, meditation, deep breathing, reading sacred books, and discussing spirit with my family and friends. By the time I am seven, I am following a regular pattern of schooling that includes spiritual practice of developing psychic abilities.*

  *"We work in a group. The first one to become psychic in the group makes it easier for the next one to become psychic, as he or she lends the energy to help the others become psychic. When there are two people who become psychic, it is even easier for the third, and when we have a large group of psychics, it makes it a lot easier for the next one. So when we practice at school, a group of adults also comes in and sits with us. All of us lend our energy to each other and the adults also help us with it.*

  *"At the age of twenty-five, I leave Lamuria for trade and a mission to spread spirituality. My first stop is in Central America, and I begin to explore the possibility of trading there. I find that the people here are pretty earth bound. Eventually, I cross the continent by a combination of boats, riding, and walking. On the east coast, I go by ship to South America, but my real desire is to get to Atlantis and work there. The name Atlantis always caused a magical twinge in me. I think if I can help them to become spiritual then they can carry it to the whole world.*

*"I go to Atlantis and settle there to do trading. I marry a Lamurian woman who lives in Atlantis and we have two sons and a daughter. I am frustrated and thwarted by Atlanteans not wanting to discuss spirituality. I enjoy their game of trade. I organize trading voyages, get the material to handle the selling of the contents, and divide the money with the investors. I am making good money by trading, which is my livelihood. I contract with ship captains and give them cargo to take out and they bring back valuable things such as furs, pottery, coral beads, and precious stones.*

*"I am living in a small shipping and trading port on the northwest coast of Atlantis. This city is an ideal place for trading. I also teach Atlanteans about spirituality. We Lamurians are quite plain and ordinary, but we are quite sophisticated in our spiritual understanding and techniques, much beyond what the Atlanteans are. In fact, I am here as a missionary trying to develop spirituality in Atlanteans. I am asking them to focus on One God and not on multitudes of gods.*

*"I am talking informally with people, trying to get them interested in spirituality, but they have their local gods and they are not really interested in listening to me. They do not even want to talk about religion. They feel that it is obscene for me to even mention it. I am teaching my own children about spiritual practices. I teach them about prayers, meditation, and reading the sacred writings.*

*"We Lamurians believe there is only One God and anything else that may have appeared to be God is simply an aspect of that One God. I am trying to develop that understanding in people and then get them to develop themselves spiritually by reading the sacred writings, praying, meditating, deep breathing, and recitation of a phrase or mantra over and over. Most Atlanteans are sort of put off by this. They do not even talk about God among themselves. I go to their religious priests to talk about religion, spirituality, and One God, but they*

*do not want to hear about it. I also talk to individuals and different groups, but nobody wants to listen. They are embarrassed by it.*

*"In Lamuria, we have a concept of mutual cooperation, mutual help, and working together with a common goal that is well ingrained in us. It is not an isolated thing, but something that we are used to and expect to do. It is this mutual cooperation that we find lacking in Atlantis. The only things the Atlanteans cooperate together on are trade, making money, and, to some extent, politics. They have no concept of helping each other spiritually. It is a totally foreign idea to them and I can hardly get through that barrier. It is hard to do group spiritual practices in Atlantis. We look for the areas where there are other Lamurians around, so that a group of us can sit with the kids when they are learning. There are a few adult Lamurians in this city.*

*"I am sending my children to Lamuria to get spiritual education and training, and to make sure they learn about the Lamurian culture. The few Atlanteans who travel to Lamuria are struck by the fact that it is such a poor appearing land and the people do not have much of anything. They do not realize that when you are spiritually developed you do not need much.*

*"Atlanteans here become suspicious of me because I can communicate telepathically from a distance without direct contact with people. They cannot understand how I know things before they happen. They think I have foreknowledge. Word gets to the ruler of the city and he begins to spy on me. He finds out that indeed I do know of events before they happen. So he sends his spies to talk to me and see if they can come up with some explanation. His men report that I just talk about spirituality. I am called to the palace. The king tells me that he is aware that I am psychic and have foreknowledge of events and he wants to know how I got that way. I tell him about prayers, meditation, worship, and other spiritual practices. The king tries*

*meditation for a few weeks but nothing happens, so he decides that it really does not work and that I am putting him on or lying to him.*

*"The king calls his advisors and science people and tells them that there is enough evidence that I am a psychic, and they are to invent something that can make him psychic too. He orders them to come up with technology that can make this possible so they can have communication from a distance and have foreknowledge of what is coming up. If the Lamurians can do it, then Atlanteans should be able to do it with technology, the king tells them.*

*"His spies realize that I use precious stones and crystals, so the king told his technologists to study these stones and crystals. The king wants it only for himself, because it is too valuable. He does not want the common people to know about it. The technologists look at the crystals and cannot see anything about them, and try to build their own special crystals. By this time, they are already growing some sophisticated crystals, which were already part of the technology they were using for electricity, conductivity, focusing, and for tuning their broadcast system.*

*"At the age of forty-eight, I decide to retire and go back to Lamuria after I have been in Atlantis for twenty-three years. I am disappointed because, even though I was successful in my business, my real mission in Atlantis was to do the spiritual teachings. I did not really succeed much because people did not want to hear about religion or spirituality. Since people found out I am a psychic, the king wants to get it, not by developing spirituality but by technology.*

*"I spend the rest of my life in Lamuria with my family and friends, leading a spiritual life. I die at the age of seventy-five, of a heart attack. I died feeling that I failed in my mission to get Atlanteans to believe in One God instead of the multi-gods, and to help them develop their spirituality. I die promising myself that I am going to be a better and more persuasive talker next time.*

*"After the death of my body, I see that they cremated it. I go to heaven right away and, after cleansing, I go for the life review with a Light being. I realize that my life plan was to spread spirituality and the understanding of One God. Even though Atlantis was the commercial capital of the world, it was the hardest place to spread spirituality. The culture in Atlantis was set up against it. I would have been better off going to another country for my mission. I needed to learn to apply my talents more judiciously.*

*"From heaven, I see that to some extent I was the instrument by which Atlanteans got turned to technology for psychic ability. I was careless and let them figure it out. This gave them the idea of mind-controlling technology, although it was absolutely not the intent at the time. The king was after a communication device, a way to communicate instantly over a great distance, to get knowledge from the past or future and what is happening this minute. My fault was that I let them know that I had psychic abilities and then I let them see me holding a crystal and slipping into a trance-like state while telling about the future. This turned them toward crystals, which gave them the idea to try and develop technology for psychic communication with crystals, and generations later, for some of the other uses for the crystals, such as the implants. The broadcast power through the crystals and the tiny little power generator were already in place. If you are spiritually developed, it is almost impossible to use psychic ability for an evil purpose. Atlanteans later used technology for psychic communication without spirituality. They did not have ethics behind it. It was a mechanical process and all types of evil followed.*

*"As I look back from heaven, even though there was no evil intent on my part and the rulers' part, at the end, technology was perverted and turned dark and evil and this had terrible consequences for future generations. I see that I had strong intentions to bring spirituality to the people in North, Central, and South America, and*

*Atlantis. I had planned to do it through trading but when I was on Earth living in Atlantis, I got into the Atlantean idea that the trading itself was more important. I became more interested in trading than in spreading spiritual knowledge. I see that my psychic blocks in the current life partly came from that life."*

## Traders in Lamuria

From time to time, people traveled to Lamuria. These were often traders from Europe, Egypt, Africa, the Americas, and Atlantis, who accidentally or intentionally came to Lamuria to trade. After a while, the Atlantean government also began to colonize in Lamuria. They brought technology to Lamuria and contaminated and corrupted the spiritual culture and the society of Lamuria, which then began to gradually change.

One of my patients recalled a past life in Egypt when he and a group of people who went to Africa, South, and Central America, and Lamuria on an expedition as follows:

- *"I am a twenty-five-year-old male living in Egypt. My name is Zeaus and it is 80,002 BC. My parents are merchants who sell jewelry and pottery. I have three older brothers and three older sisters. I have brown skin and black hair. I didn't attend school, but my parents trained me in languages, math, and social interaction. I married a merchant girl from the village when I was twenty-three. At twenty-five, I joined an expeditionary company of thirty-seven others and set sail for a new world. I leave my wife and a one-month old daughter to go off and seek riches.*

  *"We journey south down Africa's west coast and along the southern tip of Africa. We stop at regular intervals to trade, study the cultures, and replenish supplies. We leave Africa and travel west to the southern part of South America. It takes two and one half years to get this far. We sail up the west coast of South America until we come to the coastal city of Ord in southwestern Lamuria. We*

*stopped at various spots in South and Central America to trade, observe, and replenish supplies. We want to learn about other cultures along the coastline.*

*"By the time we arrive in Ord, we had lost eight people to disease and accidents. We lost five more within two days after our arrival in Ord. I am now twenty-nine and am immediately fascinated by this area. The weather is nice; the people are pleasant and easy going. I explore the city and the surrounding area with two comrades from the ship. We have an unexplainable attraction to the people of this area. They are friendly, balanced, and secure. They stay to themselves and do not bother others. They want only enough to sustain themselves.*

*"Their single-story houses are made from stone and wood. They are small, simple, and clean, and are modestly furnished. There is not much industry or technology in the city. There are only a few high-rise apartment buildings. The people here are tanned, and dressed mostly in simple robes. The taller ones are about five feet eight inches tall. They are friendly, helpful, and positive. They are passive and non-judgmental in personality. They live quietly, pray and meditate at frequent intervals. They are interested in becoming closer to God. They devote most of their lives to prayer and meditation. They are very spiritual people.*

*"I live in a rented one-story house with two other people from the ship. Four years later, when I'm thirty-three, a major storm with heavy rain and high wind strikes the city. It destroys our house, kills a fellow seaman, and severely injures another seaman, who later died from his injuries. I am also injured; my right foot is broken and I suffer a host of cuts and bruises. I am unable to care for myself and a Lamurian family takes me in. The family consists of a mother, father, and three children, a girl nine, a boy seven, another boy five, and two widowed elderly aunts. They nurse and feed me and pray for me.*

*"The father, a painter, and the mother, a sculptor, work at home and sell their creations. The aunts are*

*cheerful elderly people who help out with domestic is-*
*sues. The children attend school from nine to three daily.*
*Their home routine is made up of prayers and meditation*
*on a regular basis. The children are taught how to pray*
*and meditate. There is a great desire to become closer*
*and closer to higher-level Light Sources.*

*"This family prays for me and with me. They teach me*
*meditation techniques and try to heal me. I know they*
*have the ability because I've seen healing happen several*
*times during my four years in Lamuria.*

*"I am very unbalanced because of an infection in my*
*left leg and my right foot. Also, I'm developing an upper*
*respiratory tract infection. Six months after the storm, I*
*die of pneumonia. My spirit leaves my body and goes di-*
*rectly to the Light (heaven) at the request of the psychic*
*family that cared and prayed for me. I can see that the*
*Lamurian family gave my physical body back to the ex-*
*peditionary company. The company took my body a few*
*miles out to sea and buried it in the ocean.*

*"From the Light (heaven), I discovered that I didn't*
*heal because I would not allow it. I didn't believe enough*
*for it to happen. While in heaven, I see that I made a plan*
*to travel to Lamuria, learn spirituality, and take spiritual-*
*ity to other parts of the world and eventually return to our*
*homeland in Egypt. But I did not succeed. From heaven,*
*I see many problems coming for me from that life to my*
*current life, such as feelings of desperation, unfulfillment,*
*hopelessness, helplessness, and the foot problem that re-*
*sulted in gout in the current life."*

Another patient under hypnosis recalled a life in Atlantis in
76,002 BC, when he was a trader who went to Lamuria to
trade as follows:

• *"I Am a twenty-seven-year-old male living in Zain City*
  *located in the northwestern part of Atlantis. My name is*
  *Artz, and this is 76,002 BC. I am married and have two*

*sons, ages one and two. We live in a rather attractive high-rise apartment building. I am about six feet tall with light tan skin and brownish hair. I am very charismatic, handsome, sophisticated, and well spoken. I look very close to the current humans. I am an international trader. I trade technology such as radios, televisions, and other electronic products for gold, silver, and other precious metals. I also trade some paintings and sculptures. I go to South, Central, and North Americas, Europe, and Africa and now, at the age of thirty, I am planning to go to Lamuria, to see if we can trade or develop a market there.*

*"I have a fairly big ship and have many people in my crew, and also passengers who want to go to Central America or to Lamuria. It takes about seven months to reach Lamuria. We land in a city called Jerr in the southeast of Lamuria. I investigate about trading possibility but there are very few who are interested in trading. Some are interested in our paintings and sculpture, but they don't care for any electric or electronic equipment. They also do not have much to trade with. I travel in different parts of Lamuria. I brought my solar powered car so I can go from one place to another, since Lamurians do not have any vehicles to go from one place to another. During my travels, I have sexual relationships with many Lamurian women, since I was good looking and sophisticated. I also realize how spiritual the Lamurians were, which I did not understand and was not interested in it. I returned to Atlantis after staying there for about two months.*

*"I travel to Lamuria three more times in the next thirty years. My promiscuity continues and I find out that I have many children with different women in Lamuria and other countries where I went for trading.*

*"At the age of eighty-nine, I die of pneumonia, feeling guilty about being unfaithful to my wife and forsaking my children in Lamuria and in other countries. My spirit went to heaven after a few years. From heaven, I realize that I planned to do spiritual paintings. I was to go to Lamuria,*

*where I was supposed to learn about spiritual practices and put my spiritual feelings into paintings, which I would channel from the Light. But I completely failed to do it."*

## Atlantean Colonies in Lamuria

My hypnotized patients say that the tip of Lamuria closest to the Americas was where the initial Atlantean colonies were established. Atlantis was still young, strong, and vigorous, and was in the expansionary phase. Atlanteans were aggressive and had a war-like attitude. As they established trading outposts in Lamuria, they were not well received by the Lamurians. By this time, the Lamurians had been to Atlantis. Atlanteans, in their first expansionary phase, went south and east, because in going west they were pushed north by ocean currents. So it took them a lot longer to go to Central America and across to get to Lamuria.

Heavenly beings, through my hypnotized patients, state that about 90,000 BC, Lamurians first became aware of Atlantis. This knowledge spread among the Lamurians almost instantaneously through telepathic communication. After some debate and with the help of alien race three of group two, it was determined that contact should be established with Atlanteans. So about 83,000 BC, they tried the first tentative attempt, but the sea currents were not conducive to a direct trip to Atlantis because Lamurians were not the greatest sea travelers. About 82,000 BC, they finally figured out a way to do it and reached Atlantis and began to establish there. The Atlanteans, being diverse, traveled freely at this time. Lamurians, with care, did not stand out in Atlantean society. They lived in Atlantis for a considerable period of time before revealing themselves to Atlanteans as being separate and apart.

It was after this, around 80,000 BC, that the Atlanteans reached Central and North America and established trading outposts in Lamuria. Being aggressive people, they tended to move inland, away from the ports, and tried to establish more inland colonies. In the beginning, they did not have access to the main body of the continent, so rather than calling them colonies, it is more appropriate to call them trading outposts, which is a more accurate description.

For the most part, Lamurians, recognizing the fundamental difference between themselves and Atlanteans, and stayed away from the Atlanteans who came to Lamuria. When Atlanteans occupied certain territories, the Lamurians would automatically leave. Lamurians were not interested in the Atlantean technology and their material wealth. By using their telepathic abilities, they were able to stay away from Atlanteans, who were violent, pushy, and aggressive. Atlanteans never understood the game. They thought they were actually taking away the land, not realizing that Lamurians were simply stepping out of their way, but still through telepathy, knowing what Atlanteans were thinking and planning, so they could either thwart or encourage them. While Atlanteans thought it was a conquest, Lamurians did not see it that way.

Atlanteans colonized primarily in the southeast coast of Lamuria, but individual Atlanteans had been almost everywhere in Lamuria. After a while, a large portion of the southeastern tip of Lamuria became Atlantean land. They felt that had driven the Lamurians out, not realizing that they had left on their own, leaving behind the small number of trade representative groups of the lower-level Lamurians who intermingled with the Atlanteans. They were strongly tempted by technology and material wealth, which were literally meaningless to a highly developed Lamurian.

As the traders went to Lamuria, some married Lamurian girls and settled there. Over time, there were people from Atlantis, South, Central, and North Americas, Europe, and also some from Asia. The Atlantean government began to send people to Lamuria to colonize it. The Lamurians did not want anything to do with Atlantean technology and wanted to keep their society and culture pure. They did not have any crime and did not care for materialistic possessions. As more and more Atlantean began to settle in Lamuria, they brought more technology and Atlantean culture. They contaminated and corrupted the spiritual culture of the Lamurians. Coastal cities where Atlantean colonies were became more modern, with high-rise buildings, electricity, electrical and electronic appliances, and solar powered cars and trains.

Following are some reports by my patients, recalling how the gradual changes occurred in Lamuria as more and more Atlanteans settled there:

- *"I am a twenty-nine-year-old male living in Gear City in southwest Atlantis near the coastal area. My name is Edd and it is 75,509 BC. I am married and have three children. I am a medical lab technician. I read x-rays and analyze blood work. My wife is the director of a large food service organization. We live on the twentieth floor of a high-rise apartment house. It is well furnished, with a full range of cooking and refrigeration equipment in the kitchen. We have a TV for news, movies, and listening to our ruler's speeches. We also have computers.*

  *"I am attending meetings to discuss plans for an upcoming trip to Lamuria. I have been selected to go on the trip because I have been recognized as an excellent lab technician. I'm also a political person. I have regular social contacts with the chief sub-rulers of the city. I don't know much about Lamuria, which is to our west. The distance is too far to take an airplane, so we have to go by ship. There are a few Lamurians in Atlantis but I don't know them personally. I understand they are a little odd. They don't seem to want to take advantage of our constantly improving technology. They seem as though they don't want anything to do with the ways of our society.*

  *"We have assembled a team of eighteen people, including sub-rulers (in charge), physicians, lab technicians, business people, nurses, architects, geologists, and scientific researchers who are dedicated to improving the technology of our country. There are eleven males and*

*seven females in our party. While families are permitted to go to Lamuria, they are not going on this government-sponsored fact-finding trip. We sought and were granted permission to visit Lamuria by the Lamurian government.*

*"We head west on our ship and sail to Central America. We depart the ship and travel overland a short distance, using crystal powered cars. We board another ship that takes us up to the city of Ero, which is located on the southeast coast of Lamuria. Our trip is uneventful and we stop and observe other places in Central and Northern America. It takes us about seven months to get to Lamuria.*

*"There are ten Lamurian officials waiting to assist us upon our arrival. We find them to be friendly and courteous. They take us to a place where we can eat and then show us our hotel. It is a clean but unimpressive place with almost no technology and limited electricity. There is no electricity in the rooms. There is some electricity where we eat and gather for meetings. Some kind of gas-powered lamps are used in the hotel rooms. We find later that many Lamurians use torches (fire on a stick) for night-lights.*

*"The Lamurian people all look alike in a general sense. They have tan skin, dark black hair, thin lips and wide mouths, and small eyes that look excessively recessed into their heads. The taller ones stood five feet six inches to five feet seven inches in height. We are larger physically (some over six feet tall) and have more refined facial features. We have many skin colors, from black to white and all other colors in between, and have many hair colors in Atlantis.*

*"The next day, we tour a garment factory. The city officials conducting the tour did not seem to be concerned by the extremely long walks. We find the lack of transportation to be very backward. We are astounded by the lack of technology. We find Lamuria to be a very primitive society. We see one of only four high-rise buildings in the city. These five-story buildings are without elevators and other*

technology. Most of the buildings in the city are one-story structures made from wood and stone. Most of the buildings are much more primitive than our most ordinary buildings in Atlantis. We see very rich plant life and beautiful flowers. There are a lot of paths but little to no roads in the city.

"We do not find any hospitals or medical doctors in the city or anywhere in the country. We discovered only small clinics and spiritual healers. These healers are recognized as highly gifted individuals who have the power to heal people and to keep disease from manifesting in people. We find no appreciable evidence of disease in Lamuria.

"We visited an elementary school. We observed the children in prayer sessions. We see them doing various meditation techniques. The guide explains that most of their day is taken up with prayer, meditation, and celebration of higher-level Light beings. They spend a little time on writing, reading, and math.

"We go on guided tours and also go out on our own. The hotel is our base. We hold regularly scheduled meetings to discuss our findings. The purpose of our trip is to find other trading partners, find resources we can take back to Atlantis, and find new markets for our goods. We have radios, TVs, cars, and other goods that we can trade, but we are disappointed by the Lamurians' lack of interest in our technology. We find it difficult to understand why the Lamurians would reject improvements in their lifestyles. We are in Lamuria for just under two months and our people do not see much potential for Lamuria. However, we do include in our research report that we could import many people from Atlantis to Lamuria in an attempt to get Lamurians to open up to our thinking.

"We took our ship back to Central America and took the crystal-powered cars east across the land mass and got on another commuter ship that shuttled us back to Atlantis. Our ship is comfortable. We have electricity, cooking, and refrigeration equipment, and have a TV-like device with which we can watch movies.

*"Upon returning to Atlantis, we file our reports that Lamuria is not favorable for business. Interviews with Lamurians reveal that they have another calling and they are not interested in changing their lifestyle to have conveniences of technological advances.*

*"I go back to Lamuria with another government-sponsored party when I am fifty-five. By this time, more Atlanteans have gone to Lamuria. Some have stayed, married, and raised families. We wanted to see if the country had opened up a little to technological progress. To our pleasant surprise, it has but on a very limited basis, and as a result of Atlantean influence, a select few have radios, TVs, cooking and refrigeration equipment, and small computers.*

*"Plans are being made by the Atlantean government to build more roads, to open up other kinds of schools, build hospitals, and import medical doctors and staff to run them. We Atlanteans continue to find the spirituality in Lamuria fascinating but we don't understand it. We are especially interested in spiritual healing, but we are not spiritually advanced enough to believe in it. We stay in Lamuria for five months before returning to Atlantis.*

*"At ninety-nine, I am dying of heart failure. My last thoughts are that I'd like to see Atlantis grow and continue to advance the way it has during my lifetime. After my spirit leaves my body, it stays around for over one hundred years because I had no spiritual or religious beliefs when I lived in Atlantis and I prayed very little. My transition to the Light (heaven) is made as a result of prayers from Lamurian psychics. They not only prayed for all lost ones to be taken up but they also prayed for Atlantis, because they knew it lacked in spirituality.*

*"From heaven, I see that Atlanteans lived in darkness because they had no spirituality. I continued to stay blocked from spirituality, even when I visited Lamuria and missed chances to open up to the Light. From heaven I see that I planned to bring spirituality to Atlantis by going to Lamuria, learn about spirituality from Lamurians and*

*bring back healing and spiritual practices to Atlantis but I did not fulfill my plan."*

- *"I am a thirty-six year old male living in the city called Karn, located on the west coast of Atlantis. My name is Cid and this is 74,931 BC. I am married and have two children. I am a city planner and I develop real state, coordinate building sites with architects and government officials. I live in the upper-class area of the society. My wife is a librarian. I work with business officials, government officials, land developers, and the rulers to find ways to develop the city and expand it. I have been involved in creating some high-rise buildings on the outskirts of the city and expand it.*

  *"I am asked to go to Lamuria with a team of fifty-one other people by the central and city rulers because they want to develop parts of Lamuria. I go to Lamuria with other people who represent different branches of society, such as medical, business, architects, developers, and others. We go to Central America by ship, then cross the land by solar powered cars and then rent another commuter ship owned by the Atlantean government and go to Lamuria. It takes about eight months to reach Lamuria. We land in Tari City, located on the southwest coast of Lamuria.*

  *"We have a series of meetings and do planning. There are Atlanteans who have already settled there. They make up about 5 percent of the population. Lamurians do not like the modernization of the city but do not say anything and do not refuse us entrance to their country. We expand our colonies with more and more Atlanteans coming to settle here. There is also some intermarriage.*

  *"We build a small three-story hospital and few ten-story apartment buildings with electricity, elevators, and electrical appliances. The roads are improved. There are other teams of Atlanteans who are sent from Atlantis to colonize the different cities of Lamuria. I think Lamurians are backwards*

*and I do not understand their spiritual practices. We settled
in Lamuria but visit Atlantis from time to time. My daughter
went back to Atlantis and my son became a city planner. He
married a mixed Lamurian-Atlantean girl.*

*"I am appointed as a chief administrator of the Atlan-
tean section of the city at the age of fifty. I insist on technological progress of the city and expand the city. Now we
have about 35 percent Atlanteans in this city. Every city
in Lamuria has a beautiful garden where people go for
prayer and meditation, or on special occasions such as
weddings or other group meetings. Lamurians consider
it a holy place. We go there just to visit from time to time.*

*"I die at the age of eighty-nine of kidney failure. I am
very pleased with how I have expanded the Atlantean colony in our city over the last twenty years. I feel I have done
a good job. I stay around my family for about a month and
then I am taken to heaven by the angels. From heaven, I
see that I planned to open up to spirituality in Lamuria
but I did not succeed."*

- *"I am a thirty-seven-year-old male living in Skete City,
located in the southwestern part of Atlantis. My name is
Bard and this is 74,819 BC. I am a physician living in
an apartment. I am single. It is common knowledge that
many Atlanteans have gone to Lamuria. Initially it was
for trade and to possibly open new markets, exchanging
products, and maybe for colonizing. By now, there are Atlantean colonies in different cities in Lamuria. So there
is an increasing need for doctors in Lamuria because
there are many Atlanteans who have lived in Lamuria for
a long time. There are intermarriages between Atlanteans
and Lamurians and a great deal of people move back and
forth from Atlantis to Lamuria. There is some evidence
of disease coming to Lamuria. A few hundred years ago,
there was no disease in Lamuria.*

  *"There is a need to establish conventional institutions
in Lamuria for medical treatment. As a result, Atlantean*

*central government is planning to send a team of city planners, engineers, builders, business people, government officials, medical doctors, nurses, and other people to build and work in a hospital there. I am one of the fourteen physicians who have been chosen. I was in Lamuria seven years ago on a government assignment with a team of people to tour, explore, and map out what was needed. We concluded that there was a great need of commercial products because there are great numbers of Atlanteans settling in Lamuria. We go by a commuter ship to Central America, cross the land mass with solar powered cars, then take another commuter ship to go to Lamuria. We land in a city, called Jetty, on the southeastern coast in Lamuria. It is heavily populated and has a large concentration of Atlanteans. It takes about seven months to reach there.*

*"In Lamuria, there are three Atlantean people who receive us and take us to a hotel. After resting, there are a series of meetings for a week about planning and executing the plans. The hotel is a five-story building with Atlantean architecture. It is a miniature version of the twenty-five story buildings in Atlantis. It has electricity, an elevator, a device to communicate, and dining facilities. We are planning to build a hospital. Right now there are a few clinics with Atlantean doctors working in them but there is no hospital.*

*"In the city, there is a section where Atlanteans have settled. This area is much more modern. There is electricity and electrical appliances and solar powered vehicles. Buildings are much more sophisticated, designed by Atlanteans. The rest of the city, where Lamurians live, is comparatively humble. Their buildings are simple, with no electricity except in some government buildings. They do not have good roads because they do not feel a need for them. By now about 20 percent of the population in this city is Atlantean, and the number continues to increase.*

*"We build the hospital within a year. It is a modern ten-story building. The first three floors are used for patients. Then next four floors are used as living apartments for hospital workers, and the top three floors are used for research. I live in one of the apartments in that building.*

*"I marry a Lamurian girl at the age of forty. She works with one of the city planners and lives in the Lamurian section. I am fairly open minded, inquisitive, and interested in Lamurian civilization. I do not understand her spiritual practices but do not object to them. We get married in a downtown government building by an Atlantean priest. We live in a two-bedroom apartment. My wife continues her routine of prayers and meditation. I also join her sometimes but I am not very comfortable. We get along and tolerate each other's lifestyle. By the age of fifty-seven, I have two children. As time passes, they follow Atlantean culture, but my wife also teaches them about prayers and meditation routine.*

*"There is a beautiful garden in the central part of the city in the Lamurian section where people go to pray and meditate. They use it as a sacred place or a temple where people can go for spiritual practices. They call it a sacred Light garden. It is also used for special occasions such as weddings and meetings. Every Lamurian city has one such garden and everybody makes an effort to take care of it. Atlanteans also go there for recreation, but not to pray or meditate. I also go there sometimes with my family. I do not have much appreciation of it from a spiritual point of view. I do pray and meditate sometimes, but not with the same intensity as my wife.*

*"By the time I am seventy-five years old, Atlanteans are elected to the council and are involved in Lamurian politics, and at times they get a majority of the representation. I am semi-retired and work only a couple of days a week. One of my sons became a high-ranking government official in another city and my girl is teaching in school.*

*"At the age of eighty-six, I am dying of a heart condition. I am wondering about what will happen to me after death. I am surprised to realize that even though my body is dead, but I do not feel dead. I stay around my body until it is cremated after a short Atlantean ceremony with friends and family, where a priest recognizes me for my service. My wife prays for angels to take my spirit to heaven and they do.*

*"During my review in heaven, I realize that I planned to be a physician and go to Lamuria and open up to spirituality. But even though I was exposed to it, I did not become spiritual."*

## Atlanteans Drilling in the Mountain in Lamuria

The Atlanteans in Lamuria needed heat for energy. They already had their crystals and their energy supplies. They also knew that if they could find sources of heat, they could increase the energy output and expand the technology base of their outpost in Lamuria. There was an area along the mountainous section where there were volcanoes, and the Atlanteans came up with the idea of drilling there. They had the hard metals and technology to operate the drills to get to the source of heat under the volcano so they could extract the heat to use it to produce electricity. Atlanteans decided to drill a hole on the sides of a volcano in the mountain and tap into heat that could be used to generate electricity. This was the beginning of the Lamurian destruction. They drilled into the fault-line where two tectonic plates pushed against each other, slipped, and went under the other. This was the beginning of a chain reaction of earthquakes and volcanoes, and the cataclysmic destruction of Lamuria. It was spotty at the beginning. For the most part, Atlantean influence remained on the coastlines, which were the first to go under water.

One of my patients recalled under hypnosis a past life in Lamuria as an engineer who was in charge of the drilling project as follows:

• *"I am a thirty-four-year-old male living in Lamuria. My parents came from Atlantis but I was born in Lamuria. My name is Lamener. I am married and have two children, ages seven and five years. I live in a town called Menhap, named after a mountain god in Atlantis, outside a port on the east coast of Lamuria. It is 73,789 BC. I am an engineer but I think of myself as a military man. Here an engineer is considered a military man because we build things for war, even though there is no war.*

*"In my town, most of us are Atlanteans and very few are Lamurians. Most of the Lamurians moved away from here. Local Lamurians mostly trade, but they have little to trade. They do not mine; they have some timber, rocks, wool, and food, but nothing of real value. These Lamurians are simple people. They hardly know how to make anything or grow anything and do not have any technology at all. We Atlanteans have electricity, devices to communicate with, a broadcast system, and devices for cooking. We are really very advanced. Our homes are one story because there is a lot of space here.*

*"We Atlanteans have doctors here but these primitive Lamurians do not even have any doctors. They say they do not need them because they do not have any diseases, but I don't believe them. They are the simplest, dopiest people I have ever known. We Atlanteans have schools here. I am in the military, where I was educated and trained as an engineer. I can lead men in combat but can also lead a town in peacetime. Right now, since we do not have any wars, my job is to provide water, power, and sewage services to this town.*

*"I am a field engineer. I am in charge of a drilling project to get heat. We want to drill a hole on the side of a volcano in the mountains and tap into the heat, which can then be used to generate electricity. The electricity will come through wires and we will put it into a crystal. This crystal will broadcast energy, which will be picked*

*up by the other crystals in the city and the electricity will be distributed to everybody.*

*"The drill we are using is small and weighs very little. It is made of crystals. As the drill rotates and the crystals wear out, we pull out the drill and put a new drill head with a new crystal on it. The drilling is an intermittent process because the drill is battery-powered, and as we use up the electricity, we stop for a while and let the battery recharge.*

*"We are drilling a hole on the side of the volcano up in the mountain. It is a relatively small hole, no more than five inches across. The crystals will convert the heat into electricity, which will come up to the wires. Then it will go to the sending crystal, which will send it down to the city. Electricity then will get picked up by the city and will be sent around to everybody who needs it. It will work even at night. We will get energy all night long and it will not depend on the sun. There are no volcanoes in Atlantis, so we are lucky to have them in Lamuria.*

*"Right now, I am working on this project to gain more power because we do not have enough crystals and batteries to keep a town of this size supplied with power all night long. Our power project is completed successfully. The good part is that we are putting out so much electricity that the city does not need it during the night. So we are sending part of it to the city and part of it up to the crystals and the battery setup, which can be stored overnight and then sent to the city during the daytime.*

*"At the age of forty-two, I am appointed to govern a smaller town nearby and I am determined to make it as good as the other town. At the age of forty-nine, there is a skirmish. The guards ran into some people who are hostile Atlanteans from the other town. They withdrew right away.*

*"I am struck by a sword in the back at the age of fifty-six. My spirit comes out wanting revenge. I stay earthbound in my town for a long time. After about four hundred years,*

*my town goes underwater due to an earthquake caused by the drilling of a series of power holes. I am confused. I do not know what to do anymore.*

*"I see some Lamurians coming to see me. They can see me. They tell me they are a rescue party, rescuing spirits who are lost. They say that I am supposed to go to the Light. I see what they are pointing at. It is a big Light up above. They say that all I have to do is let go of my hold on the city and I will be able to go there. I ask them, "How do you Lamurians know this and we Atlanteans do not? We are so much smarter than you." They say that we are smarter technologically, but they know more about spiritual matters, which is more important right now. What is needed for me is to go to the Light. Finally, I go to the Light where there are people I know who come and take me inside the Light.*

*"After cleansing and healing, I go for my life review with Leathia, a goddess of the forest, Murduk, god of the sea, and Menham, a god of mountains. From heaven, I see that I needed to learn that the human being is a complete physical, spiritual, emotional, and mental being. Not just mono-dimensional, as Atlanteans think. Also, I became too attached to the physical world and was not able to leave when I died.*

*"I see my problem of chest pain, chronic weakness of my left lung, depression, and sense of hopelessness came from that life to my current life. I also hate to see the water coming to the shore.*

*"From heaven, I see that this was the beginning of the Lamurian destruction. We drilled into the fault-line and lubricated it. So the fault-line, where two tectonic plates pushed against each other, gave way, and when the fault-line slipped and went under, that section of the east coast went down. It was the beginning of a chain reaction of earthquakes and volcanoes. With all that stuff going under, when it melts, it all comes out through the volcanoes. I see from heaven that it set off a chain reaction and*

*caused the geological changes all over Lamuria and also in Atlantis. Mountains got pushed up and more volcanoes erupted. Similar drilling was also done on the west coast of Lamuria and part of it went under too. It was not pleasant to live in Lamuria at this time because of the volcanic dust and destruction."*

## Lamurians Using Crystals to Control High-Ability Lamurians

Those Lamurians who were least developed and had the least psychic abilities were tempted by Atlantean technology and their material wealth, which did not interest the well-developed Lamurians. As a result, some conflicts developed in the Lamurian society. The higher developed Lamurians recognized the equal worth of all beings, but those who were less developed, or even moderately developed, often were more interested in a strong contact with Atlanteans and the use of their technology. They saw this as a shortcut to what they did not have internally or had not developed: the highly developed psychic ability.

In some places where there were Atlantean outposts, there was a social dislocation among the Lamurians, with low and some medium ability Lamurians wanting to mingle with and move into Atlantean outposts to be more like the Atlanteans. In its most severe form, this caused a downfall of Lamurian society and a breakdown in Lamurian social structures. On the east coast of Lamuria, there was a revolt among the lower and some moderately developed Lamurians against what they felt was the control of the more highly developed Lamurians.

When Atlanteans went to Lamuria, they brought a great deal of demonic influence with them. This affected low and some moderately developed Lamurians who chose not to follow the example of those who were better developed. As a result, they ended up giving in to the material wealth, technological advancement, and perhaps even the promise of becoming equal to the highly developed Lamurians by transmitting thoughts through the Atlantean crystal in the power plant.

In time there were intermarriages between Atlanteans and lower-level Lamurians whose offspring degraded even more in their attitudes and psychic abilities. The Atlanteans took the stories of Lamurian psychic abilities as religious nonsense, superstition, and for many years did not believe it. It was only after they had seen enough evidence that they began to believe the Lamurians were really telepathic.

Having Atlanteans in Lamuria made it difficult to train young Lamurians. Atlantean culture was new and exciting to Lamurian children and education about how to develop spiritually was old-fashioned to them. It became a serious matter of contention because the young ones were not following the proper spiritual path for their development. Instead they were seduced by the Atlantean culture.

There were sporadic attempts off and on where low-ability Lamurians used Atlantean crystal technology to influence and control other mid- and low-level Lamurians and turn them against the high-ability Lamurians, till one person perfected it as follows:

- *"I am a forty-five-year-old male living in Lamuria in charge of overseeing an Atlantean power plant. Atlanteans have figured out that Lamurians who are experienced in city administration are actually very good administrators, and even the low-level ones are much better suited to manage anything than Atlanteans. We are much more aware of what other people are thinking and feeling, so we can deal with a problem before it develops.*

  *"In the highland, the Atlanteans are using geothermal energy from the volcanic heat under the hills to create electricity through a crystal. I am aware that some Lamurians have tried to use the crystal to influence others but they did not make much progress. I am trying to figure out how to do it. First I focus my thoughts on the crystal in the*

*Atlantean power plant in the mountains and then extend my thoughts through the crystal to reach a person. I have medium-level telepathic ability and I am able to establish communication through the crystal. First I practice communication as I think the upper-level Lamurians do. Even though I am not a good transmitter because my transmission of thoughts is erratic, spotty, and weak, I am able to communicate successfully with another person through the crystal amplification. I practice this by communicating with Lamurians I know.*

*"Then I try communicating with groups of Lamurians. I begin with three and work my way up to twelve. When I increase the number up to fifteen, the communication does not work as well. At first I just practice to send information and am careful not to send the information about how I am doing it. I am curious about how I am getting the answers back. I realize it was through the channel I established through the crystal. I know this does not match the telepathic communication abilities of the high-level Lamurians, but it is better than what the mid-level Lamurians can do. I am just excited that I am able to communicate with so many people accurately for such a long time.*

*"Gradually, I begin to build on the idea of influencing others and controlling what they do. I began to practice this on mid- and low-level Lamurians on the highlands. I try to duplicate what I think the high-level Lamurians do to control people. In order to judge success, I want to first practice on people who are here in the city, so I can observe what happens. First, I start to influence the low-level Lamurians one at a time. I find I cannot take over their thoughts or minds but I can prompt them to do things, or I can prompt them not to do things they were intending to do. I find it a very significant achievement because I think this is how the high-level Lamurians are controlling us.*

*"I continue to practice on low-ability Lamurians and work up to a group of three people who I could control. I give exactly the same message to each person. Then I*

*begin to influence them in their attitude toward the control by the higher-level Lamurians. This is when I attract the attention of high-level Lamurians. They are concerned because they see a Lamurian interfering with another Lamurian. It is as close as you get to a crime in Lamuria. They do not do anything to me because it will interfere with my free will.*

*"I find that there is an important factor: that is how close I must be to the crystal. If I am too far away from the crystal, my energy is so dispersed that I cannot effectively focus on the crystal. I have to be right beside it to focus my energy, and not many Lamurians are allowed that close. It is an Atlantean power plant. There are Lamurians who administer it but the Atlanteans are the ones who guard it. So the Lamurians cannot use the power plant crystals. We have to be inside the plant near the crystal before we can focus the energy enough so it can be transmitted to amplify it. I also find out that how I am functioning that day affects my transmission through the crystal. If I am weak, I have to be real near to the crystal. So it is limited to those who can get into the power plant.*

*"I try to focus my controlling ability on the Atlanteans too. I am also able to influence the guards and, unlike the Lamurians, they have no idea they are being influenced. Eventually, I set up a group of people who think as I do about controlling and taking over Lamuria. We decide on some objectives, such as trying to influence low-level and some of the mid-level Lamurians to come and work for Atlanteans. We focus our energy as a group and contact individuals psychically with the help of crystals. We create dissatisfaction in them about the high-level Lamurians controlling them, and motivate them to move to the Atlantean-dominated cities. We are successful in many cases, and finally there is a stream of people moving to the coastal cities that are ruled by the Atlanteans.*

*"One of the drawbacks about this type of mind control is that if we do not use these methods every day, the*

*influence on other people wears off. The person will go back to his or her original thinking. The result of what we are doing is taking away the strength of the administrative social structure of the Lamurian cities. The Lamurians who came to the Atlantean-dominated cities are often used for cheap labor.*

*"We organize multiple groups of Lamurians in the power plant, which then exert control over other Lamurians to turn them against the controllers, the high-ability Lamurians, and create a war climate against them. This is something totally foreign to Lamurians. The so-called controllers, the high-ability Lamurians, are aware of what we are doing but they do not feel they should interfere with our free will. I pass these skills to other mid-ability and low-ability Lamurians who also come into the power plant. The Atlanteans do not find out about what we are doing because they do not understand what we are doing and because they also are controlled.*

*"As the technique is perfected, groups are organized by Lamurians for every power plant in every Atlantean-dominated city. All of them were broadcasting their thoughts around the clock as long as the power plant is turned on. There are five Atlantean-dominated cities on the east coast right now.*

*"There were times when power plants were shut down awaiting crystal replacement arriving from Atlantis. The crystals were grown in Atlantis and, not knowing which power plant would need one, they were manufactured and stockpiled in Atlantis. Not all the power plants ran on heat energy. In some of them, current was generated by the temperature difference in water and in some they wanted to see how they worked using wind power.*

*"This is about fifty years before the end of Lamuria. This influencing continued till Lamuria was completely destroyed. Thousands of Lamurians moved to the Atlantean-dominated cities. We primarily went after men and*

*not women, because women are focused on many different things and we could not influence them.*

*"Since the crystal is not designed to handle that much psychic energy along with generating electricity, it damages the crystal, which eventually develops cracks. Atlanteans have to eventually replace it. Also the crystals take so much heat out of the earth that it develops hot and cold pockets, which create stress in the earth's crust and makes the breaking of it more pronounced. This caused the motive power for some of the earthquakes.*

*"When we are using the crystal to amplify and transmit psychic energy, it uses a fair amount of electricity for that amplifying process. The crystal was not designed to handle psychic energy that way. This added stress and caused the crystal to develop hairline cracks, requiring crystal replacement, because if we try to use crystals in that condition they can shatter and kill everybody around. These crystals are about one hundred and one feet long, four to five feet in circumference, and have to be grown in Atlantis. Each Atlantean city has at least three power plants, each of which is capable of supplying all the energy needs for the city. In case one or two go bad, we can still keep the city functioning.*

*"When the psychic energy goes through the crystal, it amplifies it by using a lot of electricity, so there is a great current draw, and the current disappears without going to the outside world. The psychic energy goes to the outside world and a lot of the electricity is used up. To keep the power supply up, we have to bring more heat from the piping system that goes down into the cave, resulting in cold spots developing in the earth layers with hot spots all around them. Eventually, the energy has to move, and when earthquakes start, the temperature difference provides a lot of energy for these earthquakes, which are more intense than usual. It is the same when cold and hot air masses run into each other causing a great deal of*

*wind as the energy is transferred from one to the other,*
*bringing on earthquakes and volcanic eruption. All of this*
*was caused by the misuse of psychic energy."*

Toward the end of Lamuria, some Lamurians told the Atlanteans about using the crystal to transmit psychic energy. Even though Atlanteans did not understand it, they sent the information to Atlantis, where Atlanteans tried to understand psychic abilities by observing the Lamurians when they came to trade. Lamurians who went to Atlantis were all high-level Lamurians. The concept of control through electricity and through technology was acceptable for Atlanteans because they were into technology, not into spirituality. This later led to the total control of the Atlantean society by Atlantean rulers and the devastating downfall of Atlantis.

## Low-Ability Lamurians Joining the Atlanteans

Those Lamurians who were less apt in the use of the telepathic skills were coming to the Atlanteans and aligning with them, thinking that Lamurians with higher abilities were their enemies and wanted to control them. Lamurians who had higher telepathic gifts were so well developed that it was impossible for them to think that way. For them, the welfare of the less-developed Lamurians was as important as it was to the higher group, and if any action in the society damaged one group then it should not be done. In terms of power struggles, the highly spiritual Lamurians did not even want to be a part of the government and left that for the middle- and lower-ability Lamurians.

In Lamuria, to begin with, there were natural earth changes on the east coast where the Atlanteans primarily settled. The southern tip and much of the southeast coast up to the hilly area had already submerged into water and the Atlantean settlement moved inland. The lower-ability Lamurians were fighting in their minds against the highest-level Lamurians. They were joined by some of the middle-ability Lamurians and were trying to attack the highly-developed Lamurians through mind power and also physically. So there was gradual destruction of Lamuria due to earth changes and also due to all this psychic energy being generated on the continent through the conflict between the higher- and lower-ability Lamurians. A tremendous amount of energy was unleashed, leading to earthquakes and volcanoes causing a massive destruction.

Some of the lower-ability Lamurians were focusing their psychic energy on the Atlantean crystal in the power plant in the mountain, and then used it against the higher-ability Lamurians. They were using that geothermal energy along with the crystals and their own amplified psychic power through crystals to attack the upper-level Lamurians and getting a psychic backlash, damaging the society. The whole continent cracked in half first, and then in time went under the ocean, leaving less than half of what the continent used to be.

The following account demonstrates the power struggle between the upper, mid- and low-ability Lamurians that literally shook up the fabric of the earth and caused the destruction of Lamuria:

- *"I am a forty-six-year-old Lamurian male, living in a town called Ballmon. Atlanteans named it after the bull god of the sea who tosses storms with his horns. My name is Rasteniese, and this is 70, 983 BC. I am leading the Lamurians who are fighting for their rights against the injustice perpetuated by these so-called social Lamurian leaders. They are oppressing us, keeping us from realizing our full potential. They refuse to share their special power and they structure the Lamurian society. We are as good as they are and we have all the values they do. We do all the work and they set up the structure and control the society. They do nothing worth mentioning. They do not take their fair share of responsibility and work. They just sit back and reap the profits of our work.*

*"I used to run the city of Teknamon, which is under the control of the Lamurian power elite. I was the chief administrator of that city. There we provided the food and water supply and took care of the entire city, but they are the ones who set up the social structure and how things ran. They can contact everybody telepathically. We cannot do that as well as they can. I can hear what they are saying but not everybody can hear me. I feel they do not teach us their secrets. I left the job because I did not want to work as their servant.*

*"The high-ability Lamurians do not do anything. They just concern themselves with truth and beauty. They design parks, set up educational experiences for children, teach them spiritual practices, and set up worship services, but never the real work. They, not us, decide how society should be organized. Through their mind power, they control people. They say they are working for the good of all and are not promoting injustice. They do not share their secrets with others. As a child, I took those classes and I feel that they did not teach me as much as they taught others. I felt second-rate. They did not make me feel that way; I just felt it. They say everybody is equal but they do not act like that because they do not do any real work. They tell you to do spiritual practices and you can do it, too, but it is just their cover-up. I do not let my children attend those worship services. We do not believe in it.*

*"I move to Ballmon, which is ruled by Atlanteans, to get away from the controllers and to work with Atlanteans. Here there are 90 percent Atlanteans and 10 percent Lamurians living on the outskirts. Atlanteans have a nice social structure. There is a chief boss and his subordinates. When the chief found out that I ran Teknamon, he gave me an important job. I told him what is happening with Lamurians and he got the idea of taking over the country. I am a high-ranking person in this Atlantean community and in the power structure. I am trying to get*

*Atlanteans to get rid of Lamurian controllers, the high-ability Lamurians. I spread the word out that we right-thinking Lamurians are gathering here on the Atlantean coast, and people began to arrive in large numbers.*

*"At the age of fifty, about four years after I moved to Ballmon City, I helped Atlantean to set up an Atlantean army to take over Teknamon and then maybe the whole of Lamuria. I am a technical advisor. I provide the Atlanteans with the names of high-ability Lamurians who are the social controllers of every city and of those who follow their path and believe in their teachings. Once we get rid of them, then we can have a free Lamuria.*

*"These Atlanteans are very ignorant. They cannot conceive anything about mind power. They are expert in technology but totally ignorant about mind power. Now they are trying to figure out how the mind works. I hear Atlantis is a lot different than Lamuria.*

*"About 20,000 people in the army are from Ballmon. The plan is that the ones from the north will collect into three main bodies. One group will come down the coast and follow us inland and two groups will cross the highlands and come down the plains. There will be seven main military bodies moving, but not as a single unit.*

*"We Lamurians who are cooperating with the Atlanteans are with the army but not a part of it. We will help them but will not fight or kill anybody. We are riding the supply train making sure the food is there and the shelters are set up so Atlanteans are free to fight. As the army is moving through the villages, it continues to win and takes over the villages. Lots of killing is going on.*

*"There is a lot of ground rumbling and shaking as we are crossing the hills. The coastal land, including Ballmon, is going under the ocean. There are four columns of smoke rising from the mountains, which are far away, and the earthquakes continue. We consolidate our forces from the north and south as we are coming close to Teknamon. I am feeling sick about the upcoming deaths but realize that*

*it is necessary to break their grip over the country. I also get the thought that maybe I am wrong but I dismiss it as a thought transplanted by the controllers, although they deny it. They all know telepathically what we are planning. The Atlanteans attack and kill all those high-ability Lamurians on the isle and anyone else who shows resistance. They are doing nothing to defend themselves. At the same time, the land is violently shaking and rocking like a boat on the ocean, volcanoes are erupting, and the air is polluted with smoke. Land is splitting; Ballmon and other coastal cities are underwater and Teknamon is flooded. We move to the highland because water is coming closer. Even though we took over Teknamon and even though all the controllers are killed, I do not feel any freedom.*

*"I am sixty-four years old now. We live on the hills because most of the land around is under water. The ground is still shaking and splitting and volcanoes are still erupting. There is fire and smoke in the sky, ashes are falling on us, and life is a living hell. Air is all polluted and it is hard to breathe. We who survived are isolated on the hills and cannot travel anywhere. We do not know what is happening in the rest of Lamuria. I am dying of some wasting disease and losing weight. I am thinking that, in the earlier days, I would have gone to a sacred garden and asked for a high-ability Lamurian to heal me. It was kind of short-sighted to kill the healers. I am also wondering if I was mistaken about those Lamurian social controllers. My body dies and the spirit comes out. I do not feel dead. I see the Light as I was told when I was a child, and I head toward it. I wonder if there is any truth in what they told me.*

*"In heaven, I see my parents and son. During the cleansing, I see many demons coming out from my body. After cleansing and healing, I go for my life review. From heaven, as I look back in that life, I see how wrong I was about those Lamurians who I thought were controlling us, and the destruction and killing that I set in motion. Even*

*though I did not kill anybody, I did set it all in motion and was responsible for it.*

*"In heaven, I realize that I planned to make it possible for people to live better by improving the water supply. I also planned to improve my spirituality and advance to mid-level communication but I did not succeed. I did not have enough belief and faith. It really damaged me, and other people, and the whole of Lamuria. I can see now that when I set up the plans with Atlanteans to get rid of those upper-level Lamurians, it literally shook the foundations and the fabric of the Earth. It caused the collapse of the land of Lamuria. The spiritual energy that supports the universe and keeps it intact was suddenly knocked out from under Lamuria and it submerged under water. Part of this was a natural disaster, but the killing off of the elite really hastened it because it damaged the spiritual support. Physics and chemistry are not the only foundations of the universe; spirit is the underlying source of it and that supersedes the physical. When the spirit is shaken, the physical cannot stand. I can see it now very clearly.*

*"I realize that I needed to learn to have faith, belief, and trust in the Divine and the saints whom I thought as controllers. All this comes naturally when we take care of ourselves and do our job. In an honest and spiritual society like Lamuria, things just come to you.*

*"As I look back from heaven, I see that in that life I had a lot of demonic influence, around the head, heart, intestines, and throughout the body. Other Lamurians who were unhappy and dissatisfied were also like me; while the higher-level Lamurians whom I thought were controlling were mostly filled with the Light. I also see that the people of the Atlantean-dominated city Ballmon were totally covered and controlled by the demons and there was very little Light.*

*"From heaven, I see that the high-level Lamurians, if they chose, could have destroyed the Atlantean army*

*through their mind power. They could have turned the individuals against each other, but they chose not to because it was not the right thing to do. They made the decision that some of them would survive to teach and should go to the hill and continue to do the right thing. They could have freed other people from the demonic influence through prayers, but they did not want to interfere with people's free will. They believed in everybody's free will and also lived it too. They went overboard to protect the rights, status, and the free will of the mid-and lower-level Lamurians. They absolutely did nothing to make themselves above anyone else. They tried to keep the highlands from going under through their prayers, but not much was done in actions.*

*"I see that many of my problems are coming from that life to the current life, such as stomach problems, and lack of faith and trust in God."*

## Destruction of Lamuria

The destruction of Lamuria began around 80,000 BC and gradually escalated, and by 70,000 BC, almost all of it was gone except a few mountain peaks which are now found in the Hawaiian Islands, the Fiji Island, and Easter Island. Lamurians had known that the continent would be destroyed in a few thousand years and had a choice to leave and settle in other parts of the world. Some of them migrated to the east, and to South, Central, and North Americas, Atlantis, Europe, and Africa. Most of them chose to go west, although it was farther away, because people in Asia were more spiritual than in the Americas, Atlantis, Europe, or Africa.

People under hypnosis claim that Lamuria gradually sank about 70,000 years ago. By this time, the Lamurians had achieved a high level of spiritual development and had started with technology. There was feedback to Atlantis that some of the people in Lamuria were using technology to control their neighbors. When the low- and mid-ability

Lamurians disagreed with the high-ability Lamurians, they tried to stop them and were trying to take over by way of spiritual power through crystal technology. Maybe not to the same degree, but they definitely had it, and they ended up with a tremendous battle.

According to the heavenly beings, there was an intercession by Satan. He influenced people in Lamuria. Lamurians did not have any flaws except for a few selfish people. They were peaceful and happy. A few selected Lamurians, aided with Atlantean technology, were trying to take over the rest of the Lamurians and the Atlanteans were there helping them.

So there was this battle going on and tremendous mind forces were being unleashed, literally shaking the fabric of the earth. There were many spiritually powerful people using their mind powers to destroy people. It seemed that as this was happening and the psychic fabric of the universe was torn, the natural forces came welling up. The land rose and fell, there were tremendous earthquakes, and volcanoes were popping up. By the time Lamuria sank, there was not much left. The political power, social power, and economic power were already transferred to Atlantis. Most people of Atlantean origin chose to go back to Atlantis. Most Lamurians chose to go to Asia, because people there were more spiritual. Some Lamurians went to South, Central, or North America, but still quite a few people were left, who died when the continent sank. Now only some of the remaining mountain peaks from Lamuria are above water. Hypnotized patients claim that these are now known as the Hawaiian Islands, Fiji Island, and Easter Island.

One of my patients recalled the following life who chose to go to Asia because they felt that people in Asia were more spiritual then Americas and Atlantis:

- *"I am a twenty-three-year-old male living in Lir City on the southeastern coast of Lamuria. My name is Dere and this is 71,151 BC. I am married and have three children. I am a priest-type government official. We have many people who are of Atlantean decent, almost 50 percent of the total population in our city, and about 50 percent of the government officials are of Atlantean origin. I am a Lamurian and we live in the Lamurian section of the city. There is Atlantean architecture in the section where Atlanteans live. The Lamurian section is more modest but buildings are more modern compared to those of several hundred years ago, because of Atlantean influence. By now our city has many high-rise buildings and there are solar powered cars and trains. There is electricity everywhere in the Atlantean section and some in the Lamurian section.*

*"My wife works in a library and also teaches spiritual songs and dances that are designed to open up meridians and energy centers. We have a one-story, five-room home. We have electricity, a stove for cooking, and a basic refrigerator. We have a radio but no television. Our kids are grown and are on their own. I had eleven years of basic school and three years of advanced education to become a priest. We are taught courses in psychology, sociology, history, and spirituality. I am appointed as a priest of one of the sections of the city on the Lamurian side. A priest is also considered a government official. I conduct weddings and funeral ceremonies, and I am in charge of taking care and supervising the Garden of Light, which is in the center of the city. This garden is a place for prayers and meditation and is like a temple or a holy place for us. I am very bothered that most Atlanteans who go to the garden do not treat it with the same reverence as we do. It is not as blessed a place as it was before and we are very sad about that. We like to keep our culture and spiritual practices pure, but more and more people are leaning toward the Atlantean life style.*

*"I also work in the healing clinics on the Lamurian side, where we do spiritual healing such as hands-on-healing, healing through visualization, and remote healing; that is, visualizing the Light energy healing a person who is*

*not present there. I am psychic and am able to communicate telepathically with others who are also psychic. Only a few of us can do it now. Before the Atlanteans began to come to Lamuria and settle, our culture was pure and every Lamurian after the age of twelve could communicate with each other telepathically regardless of the distance, and everybody was spiritual. Now things have changed and people are turning to the Atlantean lifestyle and are less spiritual.*

*"After seven years, at the age of thirty, I am promoted as a chief priest and a government official. I am in charge of supervising all the other priests. My office is in the government building on the Atlantean side. It is a high-rise building with electricity and all the other modern facilities. I am a liaison between the government officials and the priests. My job is to communicate the government directives that have to do with religion to the priests in charge of the different sections of the city, and to oversee and advise the priests.*

*"The Garden of Light is in the center of the city on the Lamurian side. The focal point is in the center, a cylindrical mound about fifteen feet in diameter, slightly higher than the other ground. It is like a stone based area which has a dome-shaped ceiling supported by four pillars. There are benches all around which can seat about one hundred people. A park-like area surrounds that center garden, which is about two hundred square yards. There are ponds, waterfalls, trees, shrubbery, and beautiful flowers all over. The central garden area is used for weddings and other spiritual ceremonies. The rest of the area is used for meetings and parties. Unfortunately, many people are going to the garden for recreation and are not keeping it sacred and spiritual.*

*"I am promoted as a senior priest of the city at the age of fifty, and I need to relocate to another government building. I am in charge of all the Lamurian priests and my duties are mostly administrative.*

*"We have had a series of natural disasters, such as earthquakes, storms, and floods. Parts of our country are breaking off and sliding into the ocean. We have fore-knowledge that, in a few hundred years, all of Lamuria will be under the ocean. Many people are choosing to leave the country. Many Atlanteans and Atlantean descendants are going back to Atlantis, while most of the Lamurians are choosing to go west to Asia because we feel they have some spirituality. We find that people in the South, Central, and North Americas do not have much spirituality and we do not think much about Atlanteans, because they are not spiritual at all.*

*"At the age of fifty-two, my family and I, including my children and their families, along with other people, decide to leave Lamuria and go to Asia. There is a ship leaving which belongs to oriental people who came here to trade. We sell our homes and pay the traders to take us to Asia. Our currency at this time is made up of metal coins. Thirty of us board the ship and leave for Asia. The facilities on the ship are basic. It is not as advanced and luxurious as Atlantean ships. The ship stops in different ports to replenish food and other supplies. After a few months, we are caught up in a storm and five people are killed. Three of them are ship workers and two are Lamurians. Life on ship is hard and it takes us about two years to reach the western coast of India, where the ship makes a stop. We decide to settle there. We trade some stuff we have for supplies. We camp in an area slightly outside the city. We continue our spiritual routine there.*

*"In time, we build our homes with wood and rocks that we find in the forest. We live off the land and sea. I get guidance from heaven to start the healing services here. A child falls and has a broken leg bone. I put a splint and bandage on and do the hands-on healing and visualization of Light coming to him and healing him. I do this for two or three weeks, three times a day, and his leg is completely healed. Eventually, I set up a healing center with two other*

*Lamurian priests, where people can be brought in for healing. We also teach local people about prayers and meditation. All the Lamurians volunteer in the healing center.*

*"By the age of seventy-five, we have done a lot of healing work. It started out with one healing room and now there are many rooms where we do healing. One time a person died due to drowning, but after I did some hands-on healing, the person started coughing and breathing.*

*"I am dying at the age of seventy-nine of lung infection. By now, I have done thousands of healings, taught and trained many about how to pray and meditate, and contributed to the enlightenment of the society by organizing and expanding the healing center. We also beautified the area by planting trees, flowers, and shrubbery, and made it a brighter and more positive place. I am happy and contented about what we have done here. I am sorry about what is going to happen to Lamuria, but I made the best of the situation.*

*"My spirit stays around for a day or two. There is a large ceremony celebrating my life and achievements by participating family members and local people. There are short speeches. They pray and meditate, giving thanks for my contributions, and visualize me going to the Light, ensuring that I find my path to the Light. Then they take my body to a specific burial place and cremate it.*

*"I see the Light and angels who take me to heaven. From heaven, I see how Lamuria over time continued to change and became less spiritual due to the Atlantean influences. I can see the gradual evaporation of the Light and spirituality in Lamuria. The Gardens of Light in every city in Lamuria were not as pure as they used to be. From heaven, I also see that from the community in India where we lived, spiritual practices spread to surrounding areas, and more and more people are using them and the healing techniques. I see my dust allergy and lung problem are partly coming from that life."*

According to my hypnotized patients, the earth trembled, volcanoes started to rise, and things in Lamuria got pretty nasty. Those who could leave climbed on boats and got out. Those who could not make it were stuck right where they were and died. Few who were spiritually powerful enough transported themselves by mind control, telepathically. Not everyone in the population could do that. To transport one-self telepathically is a special ability. You have to be able to remain centered and grounded while you are flying in the air without support. This is not an easy thing to do.

- *"I am a twenty-one-year-old female living in Ortiz City on the west central coast of Lamuria. My name is Cero and this is 70,123 BC. I live with my parents and I am working part-time as a garment maker while I prepare to become a teacher of young children. I have two older brothers but they are married and no longer live at home. My daily routine consists of prayer and meditation as soon as I get up. I have a small prayer and meditation session before and after each meal, a prayer and meditation session in the late afternoon, and another one prior to going to bed. I pray and meditate before and after each class when I am at school. The school has special rooms set aside for any-one who chooses to go there to pray and meditate.*

  *"I have been able to communicate telepathically since the age of twelve. A lot of classes at school are taught on the telepathic level. Typically children here go to school for ten years. While in school, they learn the basics, such as reading, language, writing, math, history, geography, and spiritual studies. I have a fiancée and we plan to get married in a couple of years. I wanted to wait until I fin-ish preparing for my teaching career. I want to teach one year and then I'll be ready to get married. I decided to marry my fiancée with guidance from the Light. I have known him since I was fourteen years old. He is now a city manager. When we are too busy, we tune in to each other telepathically.*

"*Everyone in our society has the general knowledge that our country will not exist by the next fifty to three hundred years. I have a lingering anxiety about this. I am aware of my choices because hundreds have left our country over the past several years, although there are still several thousand people remaining. I know that the Americas, Atlantis, and other continents can be reached by ship. My parents and my fiancé's parents have chosen to stay in Lamuria. They are middle aged and they feel that they'll be able to live out their lives before the end of Lamuria. My fiancée and I have decided to stay and help out if there are disasters of great magnitude.*

"*I am twenty-three and it is two months before my wedding. I have taught for one year. I teach young children spiritual prayers that they can recite. We do physical exercises that are spiritual in nature. Actually, these exercises are basic dance steps that can later be put together into a classical spiritual dance. I teach beginning meditation techniques and I also teach basic reading, writing and arithmetic.*

"*One day as I am walking home from school in the late afternoon, the sky suddenly darkens and high winds begin to spray mists over the city. This storm is expected, but not with much strength. Suddenly, as I go into our house, the sky opens up and heavy rains and high winds engulf the city. Water is coming so hard and fast that in a matter of hours buildings and people are being washed away into the sea. I feel very unsettled. I am upset, uptight, anxious, and in severe panic. I can also feel other people's feelings. I have a knowing that this is going to be a storm of mass destruction and before it ends our city will be gone. I know that my parents and brothers have been swept away by this storm. I see this clairvoyantly.*

"*I climb to the roof for protection from the rising water. Few houses remain. My fiancée is trapped in a downtown office building. I know through telepathic means that thousands have already been consumed by the storm. I feel sad, upset, frightened, and alone. I see only a few rooftops. I see parts of buildings, home furnishings, and human bodies passing past my rooftop. I am on the roof for three days before the water starts to subside. There are big problems on the ground. Mud is everywhere and there are lots of harmful bacteria everywhere. I am aware of only two other living humans at this time.*

*"I am weak, tired, and thirsty. I climb down at the end of the third day. By the seventh day, I am dizzy and disoriented as I sit on a grassy slope. I see no way out of this. I lie down, close my eyes, and pray that I will be taken to the Light. I relax and will my spirit out of my physical body and go to the Light. I choose for this to happen.*

*"In heaven, when reviewing my life, I can see where negativity came in me when I became anxious about the destruction of the civilization. I realize that I planned to leave Lamuria so that I could spread spirituality to other parts of the world, but I got off-track by choosing not to leave the country. I see from heaven, that the Hawaiian, Fiji, and Ester Islands are actually parts of the Lamurian mountain peaks remaining above water.*

*"From heaven, I am aware of many people who were there in that life who are also here in my current life. I also see many problems that came from that life to my current life, such as anxiety, feelings of panic and fear, feelings of not being on the right track, feelings of isolation and despair, and feelings of helplessness."*

## Altruistic Nature of High-Ability Lamurians

One of my patients recalled a past life that explains the altruistic nature of the high-ability Lamurians, and how, at the end of Lamuria, they felt that all Lamurians had to be saved and not just the top-level Lamurians. At this time, low- and mid-level Lamurians were kind of cooperating with the Atlanteans. The Atlanteans believed they were in charge and running the show, not knowing that by this time, the low- and mid-level Lamurians were taking control of them psychically, particularly the military leaders. The Lamurians were already running the city administration and growing most of the food. Atlanteans were almost completely dependent on Lamurians, yet thought of themselves as the bosses.

- *"I am a fifty-one-year-old living in Teknomon City. My name is Onn and this is 67,788 BC. Most of Lamuria is submerged under water due to the ongoing earthquakes and volcanoes. Only the tops of the mountains and some hills are above the water. One of the Atlantean power plants still exists because it was built in the highland. Atlanteans still have electricity. We are in a crisis situation now due to the earthquakes and the floods. We are trying to grow food and ship it to other villages where there is not enough food. The villages are separated by water. I am a Lamurian spiritual teacher. I teach knowledge of the Divine and proper life for Lamurians.*

   *"Most of the low-ability Lamurians have moved away to the Atlantean towns. In our town, only high- and medium-ability Lamurians are left. Other Lamurians who do not have good telepathic abilities are upset with us who do have good telepathic abilities. They think they are not able to have these abilities because we teach only a few selected ones, but it is not true. They did not learn because they did not put time and effort into practicing it. Some of them moved to other Atlantean-dominated cities because they think we are controlling them, but this also is not true. We want every Lamurian to have an equal opportunity and we work for the good of all.*

   *"Some of the unhappy Lamurians who moved to an Atlantean-dominated city are using the crystal in Atlantean power plants to transmit their thoughts to other Lamurians and manipulate and control them, and are turning them against us. They helped Atlanteans attack the Lamurian cities, which killed many Lamurians.*

*"The low-level Lamurians are controlling Atlanteans and other low- and mid-level Lamurians by broadcasting their thoughts to them through the crystal in the Atlantean power plant. They are broadcasting their control thoughts toward us too. They feel as if we are oppressing them or forcing them to live a certain way, and that we have created a society that controls them and have created a slave system. They feel somehow we picked and chose those who would be high-, mid-or low-level. They do not understand that society is set up to make them more spiritual, to improve their telepathic ability, and to make it easier to pass on spirituality to the next generation and to realize the fruits of it now and later. The same teachings are shared with all, but they tend to reject the system. No one receives a preference. Sometimes there is a basic difference in natural ability, difference in application, how long and hard one tries and applies it. So everybody develops to a different level. We set up society in such a way that no individual is more important than the other, and the whole of society has to be cared for. The low-ability Lamurians continue to broadcast their thoughts and feelings into us through the crystal in the power plant. To us higher-level Lamurians, these attempts are very transparent. We can tune into their thoughts and resist them without any difficulty.*

*"The earthquakes are more severe. We have called every ship within range to come, and have sent out calls to all Lamurians, including those who rebelled and went to the Atlantean cities. We are making preparation to leave, collecting food and water. It is inevitable. Ships are coming in and are being loaded. People are loaded and sent out with instructions to follow the currents and sail along the south of Lamuria till they find land.*

*"I am trying to convince the low-ability Lamurians to come with us, but they do not want to. We are living on the ships now because the tremors are not as intense as they are on land. This way we will avoid drowning if the land*

*goes down. After all the people have left, we also board on the ship to leave. The wind is blowing toward the east and we are moving forward. We reach land to the south of Columbia. There are fishing towns here. I am fifty-two-years-old now and we are setting up the outpost system here. We are spreading spirituality and genes here. We do have our families, but we are also planting children across the land.*

*"Some Lamurians went to Atlantis with the Atlanteans. They feel like outsiders there. Many of them moved to the east coast of Atlantis to avoid the other Lamurians, and others moved to Europe and Africa. Most of the other Lamurians settled on the west coast of Central and South America. Many went west to Asia. So the Lamurian genes and spirituality spread all over the world. The divine messengers told us that we are different than rest of the world. We have spiritual gifts that other people do not have. These are in our genes and we have to spread them for the benefit of the rest of humanity. This made great sense to us.*

*"At the age of sixty-three, I am dying of tuberculosis. I know that after death I will return to the source, will re-enter the source, and eventually come back and re-enter the universe. My glands are swollen, my lungs are bad, and I have itching. Finally my heart stops and I die. I see a bright Light and go to it.*

*"After cleaning and healing in heaven, I go for the life review. I realize one of my purposes for that life in Lamuria was holding true to the principal and not giving it up during trying times. We lived by altruistic principles to do the best for all, and we held true to that. Even when the low-level Lamurians rebelled, we continued to live by those principles and continued to incorporate them in our prayers, whether they stayed with us or not. We did not think of them as enemies. We did not distinguish between them and us. Another purpose was to develop spirituality to do good for all.*

*"We knew the Atlanteans would be suffering through their selfish actions, so you have to have the tempering balance and the altruistic nature to keep humanity in balance and keep the earth from fracturing. Atlantis was already becoming a nation of conquest, way before the destruction of Lamuria.*

*"We could not impose on the free will of other Lamurians. To keep the land stable, we would have to overcome low-level Lamurians and we could not do that. Even though the end was known, the exact mechanism was not clear. There was no way to preplan, and even after it became apparent, it was not possible for us because our policy was "Best for all," but not if it means imposing on the free will of even one person. We could not damage other persons by going against their will by forcing them to take a course of action they did not want. We tried teaching, explaining, and demonstrating, and they rejected all.*

*"We had very little experience with demonic influence because it was not a prevalent problem in Lamuria. We never considered that these angry Lamurians and Atlanteans might be influenced by demons because we do not really have any experience with that. Traders had some experience with people who had demonic influence. We were aware telepathically but did not have first-hand experience.*

*"Even later, if some of the Lamurians welcomed the demonic influence, then for us to force the influence away from them is infringement of their free will, and it is better to live by our principles than to go against them for a temporary gain. Even if we prayed to God, He would not reach out and take demons out of them. God's working would be to give them the grace and motivation to throw the evil entity out.*

*"I needed to learn the lesson that, even though you are doing your very best and doing the best thing for all, not everybody will be happy about it. Even if you act altruistically and balanced, by being fair and honest, your*

*motives will be questioned and you will be accused of doing the wrong things.*

*"From heaven, I see that many problems came from that life to my current life, such as my lung problem, low immune system, and blunted sense of smell. I also carried over the altruistic attitude."*

## Genetic Changes

According to the heavenly beings, the genetic changes that were made in the Lamurians did spread among the whole human race and pass on to people who are alive today. Almost all humans now have the capacity to develop spiritually; and to make themselves more like the Lamurians. They can devote themselves to spiritual practices and to spiritual development in order to attain some of the benefits Lamurians had.

Gene-spreading by the Lamurians was a deliberate act, premeditated and preplanned. It may appear to be immoral and questionable, but from their point of view, it was a deliberate attempt to spread their genes to improve the general mass of humanity. The independent Lamurian traders fell into casual affairs with women, occasionally impregnating one and leaving behind the child who would bear their genes, which would spread from generation to generation. More and more Lamurian genes appeared in humans. Since only the highly developed Lamurians were sent out of Lamuria to go to other lands, they spread the very best of the Lamurian genes.

Some traders were quite conscientious about it, and had affair after affair and left behind many children. This was not always a happy state for a mother and child, but it definitely left behind a superior child who was more apt to be spiritually developed. One of the effects of this was to give rise to the very strong strain of spirituality in the Native Americans, who have deep spirituality, and also in the Central and South American Indians. Of course spirituality was expressed differently in different locations.

Lamurian genes also spread to Africa and Europe, in a backward way. After Lamuria sank and the great westward exodus happened, those who lived and escaped generally headed to the west. They felt people in Asia were more spiritual than those in Americas and Atlantis, so the genes got to Asia and spread from there to Africa. Some Atlanteans, by then, were going to Europe and Africa and also carried Lamurian genes, but not in any great numbers. Thus the Lamurian genes spread to humanity all over the world.

After many thousands of years, there is a pretty good distribution and most humans carry some Lamurian genes. Occasionally there will be an individual who has both parents carrying a fair proportion of the Lamurian genes, with the result that the person becomes very spiritual. These individuals are capable of passing on these traits and are recognized as very spiritually developed.

Psychic people are individuals with a fair proportion of Lamurian genes, and they can make an effort to develop the Lamurian heritage. The individual who wishes to develop the Lamurian genes they possess can be pretty sure that they have those genes by their interest in spirituality. If they have absolutely no interest in spirituality, such as not believing in God and religion, or find no value in spirituality and think of it as a religious superstition, then the odds are that they either have no Lamurian genes or very few. Those who know that God exists, that there is truth in religion, and who feel a calling toward spirituality probably have a fair proportion of Lamurian genes and they should be taking active steps to develop their spirituality through prayers, meditation, breathing, and formal worship. All these should be part of their lives. According to heavenly beings, most of humanity has some Lamurian genes and approximately 5 percent lack them.

Heavenly beings, through my hypnotized patients, mention that there is one spiritual practice that focuses on the gene pool that encourages members to marry in the same religion. The true intent behind this is that if these people are in this religion, they must have Lamurian genes and by marrying another one with Lamurian genes, maybe the proportion will increase. So it is a hidden reason for encouraging marriage within the same religion in the hope that this will focus on the gene pool and develop a stronger strain of Lamurian genes. It is not a conscious effort, since most people do not even know that Lamuria existed or that these events occurred.

Psychic ability is still spreading throughout humanity, according to the heavenly beings. It did not develop in all of humanity at once. These aliens were working with Lamurians and they helped only that group. The psychic ability developed only in Lamuria and not in the rest of humanity in different parts of the Earth. Of course, everybody on Earth had his or her own spirituality. So there was spiritual and psychic development going on all over the Earth but it was intense in Lamuria.

Humans became more apt and more likely to use their psychic abilities to reach out and contact each other. This indicates that genetics may play a big role in psychic abilities and spiritual development. However, according to the heavenly beings, anyone can develop psychic abilities, depending upon the individual's initiative as much as upon DNA. If we have the right blend of genes in our DNA, it will make it much easier for us to be spiritual, but it does not guarantee it.

According to heavenly beings, the genetic material is still being spread around the Earth. It is not uniform among humans yet, but there is more spiritual development, more psychic ability, and more psychic improvement coming as this ability is refined and established in mankind.

# Chapter 5

## ATLANTIS: FACT OR FICTION

Since the time of Plato, people have debated about Atlantis, whether it is a legend or a fact. People either believe in it or discredit it. For the past twenty-five years, many of my patients, under hypnosis, regressed to a past life in Atlantis that was the source of the problems for which they were seeking treatment. According to my hypnotized patients, during the golden age in Atlantis, technology was far superior than we have now, but Atlanteans were not spiritual at all. Their use of technology without spirituality led to the downfall of Atlantis. They gave vivid and coherent accounts of the place, the living conditions, and the lifestyle in Atlantis. Read and decide for yourself.

### Location and Geography of Atlantis

Looking back from the Akashic record in heaven, my hypnotized patients described Atlantis as being so big that it deserved to be called a continent. It was not nearly as large as Europe and slightly smaller than Australia. It could be called a continent primarily because it was independent of other lands and it was so large that no other island could approach its size. It could also be called a country, and it is also appropriate to call it an Island-Continent.

The size of Atlantis varied because sometimes more land was above water than at other times. It tended to be larger at the beginning. It was almost as if there would be a period of retraction and re-expansion, but in general, each contraction was larger than the expansion which followed. So Atlantis, in time, continued to reduce in size. From the Akashic library, people see that Atlantis, at the beginning of its civilization, about 130,000 BC, was much longer at the north end, crossing over the center of the Atlantic Ocean. The southern and southwestern edges were swampy. The long narrow continent had highlands and lowlands that eventually turned into fairly high grounds. As the continent began to slide out, it became wider at the south end and the north end disappeared. Part of it broke off and went to Greenland, Iceland, Scandinavia, and Northern Europe, and part of it submerged.

My hypnotized patients claim that, just before destruction, Atlantis stretched up a couple of hundred miles from Venezuela to the north into the Atlantic Ocean. Atlantis did not extend as far west as Florida. It was south and east of Florida, less than a hundred miles off the coast of southern Florida. In the north, it went up to hundreds of miles off the coast of North Carolina. In the west, it was less than halfway across the ocean, between Europe and America. The biggest bulging part of Atlantis was in the south and it was narrower up on the top. It stretched toward Europe from one-third of the way of Spain and south, and it ended across from where the African continent starts to bulge.

My hypnotized patients state that there were mountains in the middle, extending from east to west, thus separating the north and the south of Atlantis. There were lowlands all around the seacoast, so people could walk around either west or east of the mountains. It was easier than climbing over the mountains. The traffic of Atlantis followed around the highland areas. North and south sections of Atlantis were flat lands. Atlantis had a river, which ran from the mountain, through the plains, and by the time it got to the sea, it was pretty big, although not extremely long. It went from the middle of the continent to the east, along the south edge of the mountains. The northern part of Atlantis was industrial, with manufacturing and technological areas, while the southern section was agricultural.

Atlantis had many big cities, with the majority on the northeast coast where they could take part in commercial trade with Europe, Africa, and the Near East. Atlantis was never more than moderately populated because the government would not permit crowding. There was a limitation of immigration due to Atlantean's suspicions of outsiders. They did not even like to work with the sailing ships. They were stay-at-home folks. After they had their establishments going on the other coasts, it was quite frequent for these establishments to be visited only by foreign sailing vessels. Very few Atlantean ships went out for trading, leaving the dangerous ocean travels for the other races of the world.

According to my hypnotized patients, the capitol of Atlantis changed from time to time, and the area where the capitol ended up was more in a neutral territory. It was isolated from the outside. The central capitol was in the north-central area, north of the mountains, and at one time was called Atlantis. Another time the area where the capitol was located was called Mesodon. It was the name of a small city that occupied one side of a large flat area that ended up being the capitol.

Part of the contention that caused the shifting of the capitol was competition between the cities. It was as if the group that ruled that area wanted the capitol in its area, and with the competition between the groups and individuals, the capitol shifted several times. Finally it was decided that rather than have the capitol on the coast and have it be a bone of contention, they should put it in a more neutral area, where it did not belong to anyone's city-state. The area that was least controlled by the city-states was a site toward the center of the continent and north of the mountains, and this became the capitol of Atlantis. That settled most of the conflict about the capitol and which city actually owned it or was using it for political or financial gain.

We have seen the same thing in the United States, where the capitol shifted from place to place, from Philadelphia to New York, until it finally was decided that the capitol would be in a neutral territory. Even different state capitols were moved around until they were put in a neutral place.

Heavenly beings, through my hypnotized patients, state that the part of Atlantis that is near the surface can be found, but some of it is deep under and some of it can never be seen because it has gone under the crust plate. There are parts of Atlantis that are seen above the surface of the Atlantic Ocean, which we know as the Caribbean Islands. These were the former high mountain areas and had relatively little in the way of structures on them. Back then, people did not live in really high places. The parts of the northeast coast of Atlantis are under shallow water and can still be reached comparatively easily because they are not very deep.

Following is a description of Atlantis before its destruction, given by a patient from the Akashic records:

• *"I am at the Akashic library looking at the different shapes of Atlantis as it changed over the years. I am seeing an outline of the map of earth as it is now, overlaid on a map of the earth as it was then. There were chain of islands that is Florida now and up north there were glaciers. When the glaciers were here, the sea level was maybe two or three hundred feet lower and that exposed a lot more land of Atlantis. As the glaciers melted and the sea level rose, the swampy part of Atlantis went under the sea and Atlantis became much smaller. Since it was bigger than an island by itself, I guess you can call it a continent. The island of Cuba and all the islands of the Caribbean combined together were smaller than Atlantis by far.*

*"In the south, Atlantis came down near Venezuela. On the left side, the west coast of Atlantis bulged out to the left and started north past Florida, missing Florida by not too many miles. Of course, Florida then was not Florida as it is now. It was more separated, as an island, with less solid land. Then Atlantis went north until maybe five hundred miles from the coast of North Carolina. The north tip of it was not very wide. It started south again and as*

*it came down it got bigger so that the major part of the continent was pretty far south. In the eastern side, it did not go as far as the mid-ocean. On the east coast, about a third of the way down, the continent went further south and there was a real bulge of Atlantis in the south. It had fertile land and a good growing season. The north end was a couple of thousand miles off Europe at the level where Spain is and then it went down to northwest of Africa. The northern part is still visible under water and can be found. The Caribbean Islands are the high mountainous parts of Atlantis."*

## How Atlantis was Populated

My hypnotized patients state that about 130,000 BC, people came from different parts of the world to populate Atlantis. Before that, there were no humans there, only plants, animals, and birds. It would seem that the first settlers would be people from South America because it was so much closer than Europe, but sailing winds were very difficult. So there was less impulse for South Americans to travel the relatively short distance to Atlantis, whereas the conditions were just right for people to come from Europe and Africa, as they had larger sailing ships, plus the prevailing wind currents, to take them to Atlantis. People from South, Central, and North Americas settled in the south and central part of the west coast of Atlantis, while people who came from Africa and Mediterranean countries settled along the southeastern coast, and people from Europe settled in the northeast of Atlantis.

People who originally came to settle in Atlantis from Europe, Africa, South, North, and Central America brought their own religion and culture with them. So, in Atlantis, the religions varied from region to region, and eventually got all mixed up, depending on which tribe you were dealing with. Culture also differed from place to place, till it all became unified in time. Artwork varied from place to place, with a lot based in the old culture of the tribe. These various forms spread all over the continent and merged till over time it was all one mixture. The northern part of Atlantis, which was richer, was remade more often. The poorer part, the agricultural south, was less blessed. Much older buildings were found in south Atlantis than in north Atlantis. Atlantis flourished more than any of the surrounding countries because it was self-contained. Also it was almost impossible to attack Atlantis with any force at all.

## Appearance of Atlanteans

According to my hypnotized patients, an adult Atlantean male was about five feet eight inches in height but there were also taller and shorter people. They were taller during the golden age because there was better nutrition. There were variations in complexion, lighter in the north and darker in the south. There was a full range of hair and skin colors, because originally, people came there from different countries. There were some who had an Irish look, pale skin, blue eyes and blond hair; some looked like Scandinavians; some like central Europeans; some black, brown, and red. Very few came from eastern countries because of the distance.

## Development of Atlantean Culture

My hypnotized patients state that initially, about 130,000 years ago, people from North Africa and southern Europe and later from South, Central, and North America, came to Atlantis by ship. They looked like current humans. They came for adventure and settlement. Before this, there were no people in Atlantis, only plants, animals, and birds. It took about 10,000 years to populate the whole country. In Atlantis, the agriculture was around the cities in the south. Manufacturing occurred primarily in and around the cities, which tended to be on the seacoast and on the river. The islands in the middle of Atlantis served as a water source for the southern part, which was irrigated. This was where most of the crops were grown, with cotton being the main crop.

Atlantis started out primarily as two kingdoms, divided by the hilly mountainous region in the middle. This did not quite cut the island in two. People could walk around the east and west ends of the mountain on the coastal plains. Other than that, the mountain range was a barrier to transportation and communication between the two parts. This was at the beginning of Atlantis, when technology was not very advanced. Transportation was usually by canals and riverboats. On the road, they traveled by wagons and draft animals. A lot of shipping was coastal, so a boat could move agriculture products to the cities. In early history, Atlantis was mostly isolated. People did not sail to the surrounding areas of South American and the North American coast. Europe and Africa were pretty much beyond thought.

The concentration of the population was mainly toward the north. Most of the cities and most of the manufacturing were further north. The main products were crafts, cloth, and pottery. To begin with, there was a lot of wood cutting and hauling and there were clay mines in the northwest. Then they discovered charcoal and began to use it as a fuel. It was lighter and easier to haul. They developed an understanding of the renewable sources quickly as they began to burn up the wood about 100,000 BC. This is when the study of biology really started in Atlantis.

Initially the land was divided into two kingdoms, with each kingdom divided up into areas of provinces with ruling lords and king. Then they united and became one territory – one country. The land was flatter and they used water because there was plenty of canal transportation. The Atlanteans used mostly manpower to start with. As the fuel supply got short, this started the beginnings of physics and chemistry as they looked for other ways to get heat. As the population grew, biology started early because of the crops and the animals, and the primary source of energy, burning wood. When people in Atlantis started to run out of resources, primarily food, this sparked an increased interest in biology and ecology. They discovered solar power and solar heat, and developed magnifying glasses and reflectors. They also started the study of light.

Meanwhile, as physical science was developing, human science was also developing out of religion. Initially people were nature worshipers and had developed a hodgepodge religion of ancestor worship, animal spirits, and of the nature spirits, which they personalized into gods. In different locations, different gods were considered to be dominant. Near the seacoast, the sea god was considered to be the most important. Inland, gods of other things were considered to be more important. So they had different priestly groups developing. It was the priestly groups who began to study people; that is, psychology and philosophy. Then motivated by several different things, including profit and control over people, different priestly groups began to share knowledge and integrate it. Thus psychology and psychiatry began to develop.

Three things made Atlantis great and then caused its downfall. They were:

- Agriculture promoting the growth of biology
- Lack of fuel promoting ecology and biology, leading to the development of physical sciences
- Development of religion, spiritual sciences, and human studies

According to my hypnotized patients, cooperation in the priestly groups and the need for the technical knowledge sparked the beginning of the university system, as a way to study, do research, and spread knowledge, while the lords ruled a city or an area of the country. There was an oddly mixed system where a priestly group, which functioned pretty much independently, and a political structure made up of lords and smaller rulers. But on the local level, the people were appointing and electing their own leaders.

So there was a combination of a hereditary system of rulers mixed in with the democratic system, and the religious systems that operated beside it independently. Out of this conglomeration, an educational system was developing. The written language was being spread and books being written, material being produced, spreading from one religious group to another. The rulers seemed to apply the talents of the educated groups to the development of technology and industry. This was around 90,000 BC.

The university system and educational system brought some great advances. The ruling class thinking to apply to the university system for development of manufacturing and technology was a real spurt to progress. They organized efforts to have research laboratories very early on. Groups of people worked on a common goal, with the result that there was a lot more understanding, growth, and development as this evolved. At this time, they did not have a resource like coal or oil, so they were developing solar power, electricity and its use, but without wasting heat. The heat went to run factories and the people were responsible for staying warm. The Atlantean's developed alternative power sources after the Lamurians came.

By this time, Lamurians, who were colonizing the west coast of South and Central America, were able to come and settle in Atlantis. Contact between the two cultures started about 80,000 BC. By the time the Lamurians first came, the priestly groups already had a pretty good understanding of humankind. Lamurians came to Atlantis by the dozens instead of by one or two. The priests found out that the Lamurians had their own spiritual development. In Atlantis at that time, folks were mostly practical and the development of religious systems was based on practicality. They were developing the concept of business and finance.

As the Lamurians came, the culture shifted. While Atlanteans had their independent priests for each god, the Lamurians brought the concept of One God, with all gods subservient to Him as different aspects of One God. So when one group is worshipping a god, they are actually worshipping the One God, just focused on god from a different viewpoint. Lamurians brought in this concept of a single overall God where all the different gods and paths are pointing to Him. These ideas spread in Atlantis and after a while they were pretty universally accepted. The further south you went, the more likely they were to stick with the system at the beginning. There was an interchange driven by sports, such as physical exercise, and by economics, such as trade. There was cross-fertilization between the cultures where Atlanteans learned from Lamurians and Lamurians learned from Atlanteans.

The first idea Lamurians brought to the Atlanteans was of personal spiritual development. Up to this time, Atlanteans had their priest groups for each of their many gods. The Lamurians helped the Atlanteans understand that true spirituality does not come from religion, but it comes from their own personal relationship with God. And it is up to them to develop that relationship. They stressed the idea of meditation, prayers, and of right living. The Atlanteans had no idea that you had to live a good life. They thought the priests were responsible for dealings with the gods and it was not their responsibility.

People of Atlantis perceived that people of Lamuria were not exactly like them. They came to understand that these people from Lamuria were using senses that they did not have or had not developed and were communicating in a way that the Atlanteans did not understand. Lamurians were obtaining and sharing information with each other mentally through telepathy. They could be trading with people of Atlantis and at the same time they were discussing trade privately between themselves, and the Atlanteans did not even know that it was happening.

Eventually they perceived that there was something going on that they did not understand and could not explain. This was when they really got interested in what the Lamurians were teaching them about religion and about personal spiritual development. Lamurians got the idea across to them that these things happen naturally when you are developed spiritually through prayers, meditation, personal connection with God, and right living. The negative side of it was that some of the Atlanteans started to feel less than the Lamurians. Some of them felt that they had been slighted or shortchanged by the universe. Some of them did not really feel that Lamurian psychic abilities had much to do with the real world and ignored those abilities. But most of them wanted to develop those psychic abilities.

When the opportunity came, the people of Atlantis were much more ready for the psychic abilities than they had been two years before. Lamurians taught Atlanteans about prayers, meditation, personal connection with God, and responsibility to live a decent human life. According to heavenly beings, this is a lesson that needs to be retaught today. This is one of the messages that all the masters, including Jesus, brought, but organized religions have twisted it to where the church stands as an intermediary between people and God, and people hardly have any responsibility. Masters told all to develop a personal spiritual relationship with God, but very few religions teach that. It is more of a power play; like you need the church and that is the only way you can contact God or go to heaven.

Lamurians were more advanced spiritually and mentally. They were able to use their telepathic senses; they could do psycho kinesis, that is, actually move something with their minds. These abilities were developed because of two things: first, their personal spiritual development, and second, their society accepted them. If society rejected them, they would have been considered strange. As different segments of Lamurian society in Lamuria used the same talents, it created a spiritual field around them, and the spiritual development built on itself. So, when the first person used psychic perception, it made it easy for the other people to follow. When they all used it, the spiritual field around them increased and that added to their own abilities and made it easier for the folks around them to be able to do it. The spiritual field became a part of the life and was not an odd thing.

One of the things the Atlanteans learned how to do was to measure the spiritual field around the body. Once they had that concept down, they could find out how to go about amplifying it without being able to measure it. Measurement is basic to science, and in this case, they were dealing with the measurement of the electromagnetic energy field around the body. Like a radio amplifier, you cannot see radio waves yet you can build a device that can make them stronger. They used a device, placed outside the helmet, that amplified psychic abilities. This device detected and measured the strength and wavelength of the waves that were within the brain. Then electronic circuits making more and more powerful vibrations were created and it put them out with the quartz crystal.

When the Atlanteans learned to use technology to amplify their brain waves, they realized it was possible to amplify their psychic power with technology, and they went to work on it full force, but without spirituality. They short-circuited the steps. They were developing psychic abilities without developing the underlying spirit, and all the evil that became Atlantis sprang into being. Since Lamurians were spiritually developed, they could not use technology to harm each other. It was always used for the good, working with the Light and trying to make society better, to make life easier.

In Atlantis, they applied technology to have the psychic ability but they did not have spirituality to control it and use it for the good of everybody. That is where the abuse started to come in and all the evil that became Atlantis sprang into a being. "If I develop a bigger power station, I can control the brains of people around me, and then I can become more powerful myself." They had artificial means to develop spirituality and for abusing others because spirituality was not based on spirit but on technology. That took only a few thousand years. Atlanteans got their technology rolling since they could communicate through technology easily.

Technology became more and more improved through the crystals, which were relatively small. To do telepathy, the crystals were supposed to be smaller because the smaller ones had the proper vibrations. Big crystals (as big as a thumb) are not good for this purpose because they have too high vibrations. The smaller crystal (not quite as thick as a pencil and maybe one and a half inches long) is closer to the needed vibrations. In Atlantis, the energy waves were broadcast through the air by a large quartz crystal that was hooked on top of the palace in a dome. This put out its light and benefited people in the palace and in all of society.

The rulers who used and controlled technology developed control over society. By now they had gone through the kingdom type of government to an elected type of government and over the years they did away with the lords and kings, and there was a democratic government for the whole subcontinent. But as the less fortunate were shoved aside, it ended up with people taking advantage of other people for personal (power) gain and to get people to do what they wanted them to do. This is where abuse came into the system.

## Ruling Class

As described before, about 130,000 years ago, people from North Africa and Europe, and later from South, North, and Central America, sailed to Atlantis in primitive boats for adventure and settlement. Before this, there were no humans on Atlantis, only plants and animals. Atlantis started with a separated tribal organization. My hypnotized patients state that as the population grew, the groups came in contact with each other. There was an intermingling of people and there were little wars in which one group took over the other, and rulers would extend their grasp over more territory and more people. There were intermarriages between the ruling groups of each tribe and they formed alliances and incorporated other tribes, sometimes by marriages, until there were fairly large territories. Alliances formed and a single overall king selected himself with the help of the army. The land then became unified.

It took about 1000 years after people migrated to Atlantis for the beginnings of consolidation to take place. The initial consolidation was simply among the small groups of one tribe, which took place in different parts of the island at different times. It was common for one group to take over another, making a bigger and growing government. Originally, there were kings in different groups and eventually there was one king for the whole area. In the space of 1000 years, the government was pretty much consolidated and had one king for the whole Atlantis in about fifteen hundred years. It was a very rapid human process.

Initially, in some tribes, kings and rulers were voted on, to pick the best ruler available. In some tribes, the positions were hereditary. Later, kings were chosen by birth. Of course, this meant that over time, the family kept expanding and expanding until it had thirty or forty different generations of cousins. They all became part of the ruling class. The way they dealt with this was by having intermarriages between the families. Occasionally someone would drop out of the ruling class and would get shoved into the general population.

Trade passed freely from one section to another. There was a ruling class structure equivalent to a king, earls, barons, high lords, and under them, lesser lords and the local rulers. Sometimes, local rulers were elected, depending upon the custom of the people. As the population grew, the ruling structure expanded and a civil service developed. There was communication, and police and an educational system were set up. Things were pretty good all across Atlantis. Of course, there was the inevitable tax system to pay to the government.

- *"I am a seventeen-year-old woman living in a desert area in Atlantis on the west side of the mountains. This is 84,240 BC. Here, the winds come primarily from the east, so they blow across the mountains, and when they get here, they are pretty dry. There are storms that come in when the seasons shift and we get seasonal rains. Most of the air is dry and dusty. I am wearing a blue veil and a long outfit, with the veil down. My skin is white and my eyes are blue. I am not wearing this outfit for modesty but to stay out of the dust. I am allergic to dust.*

*"We have small villages because no area here can possibly support a large number of people because it is too dry. We have our water and food supplies. Each village has four to six hundred people, and the way they govern themselves is that they form a tribe and all of the tribes live by the same set of laws. The ruler is determined by election and also hereditary. The people choose who they want from a pool of candidates and then they choose their council people. Each village will have a delegate from four or five villages who will get together and pick one person for council.*

*"In my society being chubby is beautiful, but I am thin. I wear that long robe so people will not know I am thin. I am about to get married. My father is on a tribal council and has arranged my marriage. Tribal laws are very strict about any intimate contact before marriage, so my husband was not aware that I did not fill those robes. He was very upset and disappointed that I was not chubby and doesn't want anything to do with me. As a result, I cannot have children. He had affairs with other women.*

*"I die at the age of sixty-eight, promising myself that I will never be skinny again. I have to eat a lot and be voluptuous.*

*"From heaven, I see that this life was partly responsible for my weight problem and dust allergies in the current life."*

My hypnotized patients state that kings or the masters were selected by birth and by merit, so it was not necessarily the oldest child who was selected as the king, but the one who was best suited. Generally the parent would decide who should be the future king. The wealthy people would build their dynasty and the family would keep expanding until they realized that the only way to stop diminishing their wealth was to marry other family members, so families began to interlock and the total number of the people became roughly the same. Each retained about the same proportion of the wealth.

The only way to get into the ruling class without being born into it was through the religious structure. Since the priests did not have a hereditary class, the leaders of the priestly class had to be selected. So from the various levels of the temples, priests were selected and moved into the ruling class. They were selected by the hierarchy of the priests with the approval of the rulers. In the priestly class, the upper hierarchy was included in the ruling class and were not controlled. The top technology class was also part of the ruling class.

## Trade in Atlantis

In the expansionary phase, the Atlanteans had big ships, sent armies to conquer other lands, and had superior weapons and superior technology. They set up colonies in Europe, Africa, Asia Minor, the Mediterranean area, and South, Central, and North America, and later also in Lamuria. They were already settled in Africa, Europe, partly in England and Ireland, Mediterranean areas such as Egypt, Spain, Turkey, Italy, some in Greece and South and Central America. The east coast of North America was still hard for them because of the constant flow of the water streaming north, so if they launched from southern Atlantis, they could land on the east coast of North America but they could not get back.

Atlanteans became more proficient at sailing and navigation and they went on to dominate the world through trade and colonization. Eventually it led the Atlanteans to wars of conquest rather than trade and cooperation. They were trying to take over and dominate other people and the people of Atlantis were generally successful. They extended their physical presence and their control into the other lands.

Atlanteans were a stay-at-home people, but there were a few who had a sense of adventure for sailing and went on trading missions. They went to South and Central America, Europe, and Africa. Later they controlled people generally through political and economical means but sometimes they did it by force. They did not share their power and technology with others. They wanted exclusive control of knowledge. They refused to train people of other countries. They did not put big power stations in other countries because they did not want other countries to have that much access to energy and knowledge. It was a way to control other people. If an installation went, let us say to Spain, it was forbidden for the Spanish people to know how it worked, how it was built, and how it was operated. That was reserved for the people of Atlantis. They were controlling people all over the world, and where they could not do so by trade and economics, they did it by force.

After all of Atlantis was put together and tied into a single government about one thousand years after people settled there, there were no wars in Atlantis, but the country did make wars on other nations. Of course, this meant moving the army overseas, which was not the easy thing to do. Even though Atlantis had superior weapons and superior technology, they preferred to conquer through the trade and economics rather than by force. Though sometimes they did use force.

One of the patients who was having back pain off and on for several months recalled the following past life as the source of her back pain:

- *"I am a thirty-eight-year-old female, living in Atlantis. This is about 80,000 BC. At this time, Atlantis is a young*

*culture, still growing, sailing ships and trading back and
forth during the seasons. During the trips to Europe, we
sail in the winter and for trips back to Atlantis, we sail in
the summer when the wind belts move. I moved to Spain
to develop a trade route with my husband, and we are
living in a coastal city on the south coast of Spain. The
trade goods are shipped to me from Atlantis and I sell
them in Spain. I run a bank. I handle the financing and the
accounting. I lend money to the natives and collect. I am
funding a trading network so that the goods that come in
get spread all over the place and not just sold at my trading store and warehouse. In Spain, my name is Condalita.*

*"My husband handles the warehouse, packing the
goods for shipping back to Atlantis. I take the profit in
cash and gold and keep track of what is lent to traders and
collect interest from them. We have two teenage boys who
live with us. My trading routes are pretty well established.
My trading partners in Atlantis are rich people. They pick
out the stuff they hope will sell in Spain, load it on the
ship, and send it to me.*

*"One of our trading partners brings back his load of
goods, the stuff he has taken in trade, and brings it to me,
along with whatever he has accumulated. When I took out
the cash, he stabbed me on the left side of my back and
took all the money. He stole money and a load of goods,
too, and loaded them on his donkeys and packed the
money under it. When he was done, he closed the place
and left me lying there. I am bleeding. He also hit me on
my head. I am feeling angry with him.*

*"My last thoughts are: "It is not worth it. All this hard
work, all this accumulating, and he kills me. Money is not
worth my life. I treated him well and made him rich and
this is the reward I get. He betrayed me." I die in a couple
of hours. My spirit is confused, wandering around as if I
am still alive. I finally find my body. I don't know what to
do and feel panicky. After several hours, I see the bright*

*Light coming from above and my mother in it. She tells me that she has come to take me to the next place. I go with her to the heaven.*

"*After cleansing and resting, I review my life with a few wise beings. As I look back into that life, from heaven, I can see that I was born in the northern part of Atlantis in a city called Hilrand. It was one of the inland cities. It was further north of the capitol on a flat low-lying land. We had good education in reading, writing, and arithmetic so we could communicate over distances. I lived with my parents in a home. My father was a trading merchant, so I was trained in the trading business.*

"*I met a trader in the coastal city who brought goods to us and we ended up getting married in a temple at the age of eighteen. Our family gathered at the temple. Everybody was wearing a white robe, including the groom and me. The priest also had a white robe, with a golden band around the bottom. During the marriage ceremony, we light a fire in the metal bowl in a stand. The priests give us vows to make to each other and then we were married. I was given a sash to put on my left shoulder, which signified that I am a married woman. It could be in the form of a ribbon or a thread worn anywhere on the body.*

"*The temple was made of sandstone. It was rectangular from the outside. The roof sat on pillars and the walls went only part way up and there was an opening between the roof and the walls from where the light comes. Inside there were two statues of a goddess, which looked like a slim human body with a cat's head. They called that goddess Hus.*

"*As I look from the Light, I see that some houses were made of baked bricks, some were made of wooden logs, and others were made of finer bricks. I see people traveling in small, light hand-pulled carts. After the wedding, my husband and I moved to a coastal city called Mardula. It was a deep-water port, so the ships can sail right up in. There was a manufacturing plant in Mardula. It made good glazed pottery. They also made wool, fabric, and leather. It was a prosperous city. The roads were built of stone.*

*"Few years after the marriage, when I was twenty-six-years-old, traders offered us the chance to go to Spain and set up a trading post there, so that goods from Atlantis would be sent to us in Spain. We set up our own trading network in Spain and shipped Spanish goods to sell in Atlantis. I had two children in Spain.*

*"From heaven, I see that I had to learn the lesson of non-attachment because money and material things meant too much to me. I see that my back pain in current life came from that life due to stabbing. My dislike of handling money also came from that life because it got me killed."*

After bringing the soul parts that she lost in that life from people, places, and hell, her back pain and other problems were healed.

- *"I am a twenty-two-year-old man living in Spain in a low land, not too far from the seashore. This is 72,800 BC. I am building an irrigation system and I have to get the local farmers lined up to work. My job is to build an irrigation system, get the farmers to work, and raise food to ship back to Atlantis. It is not enough to just raise grain; I also have to raise food for which people will pay higher prices. So I raise delicacy items. This area is considered ideal for that because it is sunny and there is water available. I am raising a bulbous plant like an artichoke.*

  *"I am sent here by the city ruler and the food company, just south of the mountains on the east coast of Atlantis. They did a series of surveys to see what the climate is like, what the land is like, what the people are like, what their land customs are, and how we can own land in the society. This information was taken back to Atlantis. They planned where to go, what to plant, and whom to send.*

*Then somebody goes there and sets up for the land and water. An engineer will come and set up the irrigation system. Then the person that runs the farm comes. We go out of Atlantis to other countries because of cheap labor.*

*"I am getting the workers to work on the farm. I get my planting stock from Atlantis. Ordinary crops that do not bring a good price can be raised in Atlantis. We grow the food that they eat daily right in Atlantis, but for the really expensive, fancy stuff, which only a few can afford, we do not have enough land left over to do that in Atlantis. It is in the ruler's best interest to keep the people happy. If they do not have food, they become unhappy.*

*"The food we grow overseas is sold at higher prices, which only the noble people can afford. The middle class and the poor cannot touch it. So Atlantis has established outposts around Europe, South, Central, and North America, and Africa for raising special crops for special purposes.*

*"I am in the southern part of Spain, living on the plains. The engineers got water on the property and recruited the workers, and now we are planting the crops. I have been trained pretty well in such things as local language, farming techniques, and engineering. I never go to Atlantis. I have a conflict with the local people over the land and somebody stabs me in the back. I die at the age of sixty, feeling that I will not be so far away from home again. I never had a family because I really did not fit in with people so I never married.*

*"I can see that my allergies to dust, my sense of not belonging, and my feeling like an outsider came from that life to the current life."*

## Religion and Spirituality in Atlantis

As explained before, originally people came to Atlantis from different parts of the world and settled there. With them, they brought their religious belief systems. So some religions and gods were imported. The vast majority were homegrown. In the beginning, there were multiple gods and each of these gods was generally worshiped in a particular area. Originally, they had a tribal god and they would generally have one head of that temple, with the priest under that person. If the areas were large, there would be one head, like a bishop, who would control many local temples.

As the people spread across Atlantis under different conditions, different ideas started and different concepts of God came into being. Usually they were nature gods, such as: forest god, wind god, sun god, rain god, fertility god, animal gods, etc. There was also a powerful war god in charge of war who was worshiped by some people. As people moved and spread around the continent, they would take their beliefs in their gods with them, until there were pockets of worship of each god in all parts of the island.

Atlanteans originally had tribal gods, and when the different tribes merged into one nation, different groups of people kept worshiping their tribal gods. Of course, as people moved about in Atlantis, the different gods were scattered from place to place rather than remaining in one isolated location. Over the thousands of years that Atlantis existed, different religions were scattered pretty uniformly throughout Atlantis. My hypnotized patients mentioned the names of several different gods and goddesses which they believed in, in different past lives, in different parts of Atlantis, such as: Magan, god of sea; Lanhem, god of woods; Naimini, goddess of forest; Yolanda, goddess of cooking; Umulei, goddess of compassion; Borus, god of wind; Ishta, cow goddess; Diti, love goddess; Appoe; god of healing; Bathous, god of swamps; Naxous, god of mountains; Melson, a coastal god; Hus, cat goddess; Dagan, livestock god; Erdos, the goddess of growing things; Garnish, god of swamp creatures; Monistra, a sun god; etc.

My hypnotized patients claim that in Atlantis there was a very strange spiritual culture. There was a hallmark characteristic that it was impolite to speak of religion, spirituality, and of your own spiritual development. This did not mean that priests did not preach a need for spiritual development. They did mention that it was important. They simply did not specify how to go about it. As individuals tried to apply spirituality and develop it, they were essentially leaderless and had no idea of what they were doing and where they were going or how to go about it.

They had a twisted sense of the word "spiritual" because it was not open for discussion, and when something is not discussed or traded back and forth, it becomes undefined and not refined. In temples, a priest would talk vaguely about spirituality; they would tell about a specific practice but would not talk about how it would help develop spiritually. They talked about "It is a good thing to resolve your quarrels" or "It is a good thing for the community to take care of the poor," but not about how to develop spirituality.

Contact between Atlanteans and Lamurians was first made in Central and South America. Lamurians were there trading and spreading their own view of spirituality. They ran into the Atlanteans, who were also there for trading, and they found out about the existence of each other's culture. Atlanteans were usually stay-home people. There were few people who had the sense of adventure to go sailing, or on trading missions. Lamurians initially did not venture outside, either, but when a few people went by ships to Central and South America, they realized that other people were quite different than themselves in spirituality. Their original trading missions were exploration to see if there were other people anywhere. Later on they traveled to different areas as missionaries to carry Lamurians' view of spirituality. They realized that people in different parts of the world were not very spiritual and did not understand it.

As described before, when Lamurians went to Atlantis, they realized there was no sharing of spirituality among Atlanteans and that different religious groups were worshipping different gods. So they began to teach Atlanteans that they were actually worshiping different aspects of One

God and they began to spread this message all over Atlantis. Some of the Atlanteans were surprised to see Lamurians talking dirty all the time when they talked about spirituality, because in Atlantean culture, they were not supposed to speak about it to others. Each was thinking that their culture was the only culture, and was not making any allowance for each other.

Lamurians got across the idea to the Atlanteans that all their gods were valid, that they were worshiping different aspects of One God, and they began to promote a one-God religion. Lamurians taught them about One God and how all the other gods that the Atlanteans were worshiping were the different aspects of the same One God. This caused confusion and problems for Atlanteans. But Lamurians were very persistent and very gentle about it and Atlanteans ultimately did accept the concept of One God and that their individual god is part of that One God. It improved religious tolerance, but still they did not feel any special connection to God.

One thing Lamurians were not able to overcome was the Atlanteans' reluctance to talk about spirituality. It was supposed to be bad manners in Atlantis to discuss religion or spiritual beliefs with others from the very beginning. This was a very strong cultural prohibition. They did not discuss spiritual matters so as to avoid conflicts because there were so many different religions.

Lamurians encouraged the Atlanteans to impose a structure over all religions and universally recognize the value of every religion. This proved fairly easy to do. The end result was that, in addition to all the other religions, they added another one and said this one was in control of all the rest. Now they had a temple that worshiped One God with some adherence and the head of this temple was nominally in charge of all the temples.

There was a single overseer for all the temples and all the religions. That person was known to be the supreme head of the religious structures. Under him were regional directors, each of whom oversaw certain regions. Then under them were sub-commanders and then the individual churches and the priests. Religion was a part of the life, but not as meaningful. It seemed to satisfy the inclination of the people while absolutely failing to teach spirituality. The effort to be spiritual without being spiritual was what led to the Atlanteans' downfall. They saw the spiritual part of the Lamurians and tried to duplicate it with technology, and that was what caused the real downfall of Atlantis.

Patients under hypnosis claimed that in Atlantis, they did have ministerial schools, apprenticeship programs where things were taught very privately to the coming priests. Even though it was necessary to share the knowledge, they did not. The problem became worse as time went on and spiritual privacy became a more essential part of the culture. Priests did preach to the general public and they did preach things that were of essence to the spirit. They would say it was a good thing to do good works and to be charitable, but they did not say it was part of spiritual development. The priests would teach about spirituality, but would not say, "You develop your spirituality this way," but they would preach essential parts of it. Although the people would be in the temple paying attention with good intentions, still they could not overcome that cultural bias about not discussing spiritual matters.

The culture of Atlanteans held that spirituality was important but they considered it to be an individual, private matter. Just as people do not discuss their toilet and bathroom functions and habits in public, spirituality was also considered a private matter to Atlanteans. It was very impolite to discuss it publicly or even mention it to other people. This was one of their cultural hallmarks, and was accepted by everyone. The priest did not have to tell people not to talk about spirituality; it was a culture in their society, and children were told by parents not to talk about it. If a child would ask parents something about the spirit, parents would give them an open-ended answer and tell the child not to talk about things like that in public. In the temples, priests would not face the listeners or have eye contact with them. They felt embarrassed about talking about religious or spiritual matters and the listeners also felt uncomfortable about it. Of course, there were socially deviant people who did talk about spirituality, and everyone called them perverted or crazy.

Following are examples of how preachers preached at a temple and the attitude of society toward religion and spirituality:

- *"The preacher has a holy book and he is reading out of it to the congregation. The preacher is not facing the congregation but stands off to the side, generally on the audience's right, and faces the opposite wall, and not the congregation. This is to help the priest not to be so embarrassed and to try and ease social discontent that the audience might otherwise feel from someone talking about what might be considered spiritual. The preacher talked to the opposite wall and the audience would overhear. There was no eye contact and no emotional connection.*

   *"I am a twelve-year-old girl living on a farm in the northern part of Atlantis. My name is Mani and this is 62,122 BC. I go to the temple of the god Monistra. I am curious as to why the priest never looks at the people and how the people never look at the priest. All of them are studiously doing something else while they are trying to pay attention to what the priest is saying. I feel it is very odd but I also see how it is right, because it can be very embarrassing if we have to pay attention to him directly. Everybody will die of shame.*

   *"I tell my parents that I want to become a priestess of Monistra. My parents are very embarrassed, as if I had told them that I want to be a sexual pervert. I myself have reached a reconciliation in my mind about it. I can see how silly it is and yet I know how intensely embarrassing it is for people, because this is how people grew up. I feel more mature and grown up than they are but I can*

*appreciate their feelings. There is a family discussion. They feel honor and also embarrassment.*

*"The primary duty and responsibility of the priestesses in Monistra is teaching young children, sometimes teaching adult women, and they do talk about the spirituality. Everybody knows that but it really embarrasses my mother, as if I told her that I want to work in a whorehouse. When I am fourteen, my father takes me to the temple of Monistra and I am enrolled. I feel excited and homesick at the same time. There in school, I learn what kids in the village need to learn, such as how to read, write, how to do simple arithmetic, handicrafts, learn to sew, knit, crochet, needle work, preparing food, preserving food, how to garden, etc. I am told that the priestesses' role has expanded to teaching all this for the last ten years. The chief priest got the direct message from Monistra, the god of the sun himself, instructing that this material be added.*

*"I am on my first assignment at the age of seventeen. I am sent to a temple in a nearby medium-sized city. There are two priests and two other priestesses. On the right side of the temple as you face it, is the school with several rooms. Then there is the main body of the temple where the people come in to worship. On the left side of the temple are the rooms where the priests and priestesses live. There is a living area, a kitchen, and bedrooms for the priests and priestesses. In the center part of the temple there is an open space. On the walls there are paintings of signs of the zodiac. There is a statue of the god Monistra and some candleholders and candles. There are also painted scenes of Monistra's life.*

*"I realize that the other priestesses disappear at bedtime and come back in the morning. I ask the two priestesses where they go every night and they told me that they go and sleep with the priests. One of the priests will ask one of the priestesses to come to the room and she sleeps with the priest that night. The two priestesses instruct me to how to behave, what to expect, and how not to get*

*pregnant when a priest calls for me. They give me a tin of grease that is very thick and heavy, and kind of brownish in color. They instruct me to take a big glob on my finger and put my finger inside of me until I find the hard part that sticks out and rub the grease over the end of it and around it. This will keep me from becoming pregnant. I have to do this every day. I practice and am able to do it. One afternoon, the younger priest asks me to come to his room in the night and when I go, he makes love to me and I am not a virgin anymore.*

"I am teaching women sewing, knitting, crocheting, needlework, etc., and the other two priestesses teach the little kids and the two priests prepare the sermon and preach. Sometimes they go to the villages and talk to people about the sun god Monistra. Priestesses rarely preach because it is very embarrassing for the priest to talk about religion, but it is even more embarrassing for the priestesses. Later, I teach women how to dry and preserve food. I also go out in different parts of the city and countryside to teach women. Sometimes men in the villages and city will ask me to go in their bedrooms and sleep with them and I do. I found out that the priests do the same thing with women.

"I got pregnant by a priest at the age of twenty-nine. We are all appalled. It is just absolutely unheard of. Now this is a real problem. There are several choices, such as abortion or hiding in the king's palace with his permission, which has been done before because such a scandal will not do anybody any good. I will remain there until the baby is born. The baby will be accepted in his household and I will go back to the temple and no one will know about it. It has been done before. So I go to live in the palace.

"I am free to walk around in the palace. I am watching and analyzing everything. I am realizing that the king's position is not as strong as it seems. I watch the flow of money and the taxes. I become suspicious of things that* *are going on behind the back of the king and I tell him about it and as a result some officials were fired.*

*"The king realizes that I am very sharp and have better views of what is real than many of his lords do. He offers me a job in his court and my job is just to walk around and watch. My son is growing up in the palace. I get to see him and play with him, but he does not know that I am his mother. After a while, I also have a child with the king, and he also grows up in the palace. The weather changes to where it gets colder in the winter and hotter and drier in the summer. So it is hard to grow food. I tell the king to try food preservation techniques by salting and spicing them. It was because of me that food preservation techniques spread all over the country.*

*"At the age of seventy, I am dying from a growth in my throat and it is pushing on the blood vessels and the arteries, closing the windpipe. I am still living in the palace and kind of forgot about being a priestess. Women and the society benefited from my teachings. I feel that I have lived a good life, except that my children do not know that I am their mother. I decided that I would never let that happen again. I feel I damaged them because they did not know their mother.*

*"After the death of my body, my spirit goes to the heaven right away. After the cleansing, I go for my life review. There I see god Monistra glowing like a sun and wearing a crown. I learn that he is one of the masters in the Light (heaven). I am confronted with the fact that my primary plan for that life was to teach spirituality and change their embarrassment about discussing religion and spirituality. My accurate seeing and understanding was supposed to convince people that there is nothing wrong in practicing and discussing religion and spirituality. But I got sidetracked. I used my talents for the king's court and there were good things that came out of it, including the food preservation process, but still I did not follow my life's purpose. I could have changed the religious perception*

*of these people and also all over Atlantis, and maybe the whole future of Atlantis, but I failed to do it.*

*"I also see that because of my food preservation techniques, the soldiers and people can survive for a long time away from home, making wars easier for them. It was not intended to be that way but it was a side effect.*

*"I needed to learn the lesson to deal with the separation from the family. To see your kids every day but not being able to tell them you are their mother and cannot just reach out and hug them was hard. From heaven, I see that in the past in another life, I was responsible for splitting up many families. I had at least fourteen lives, including the current lifetime, when I was separated from my family one way or another to make up for my negative actions.*

*"From heaven, I also see many problems coming from that life to the current life, such as high blood pressure, throat problems, and separation from my family."*

Lamurians were very spiritual and as a result they were very psychic and were able to communicate telepathically and could predict future. Lamurians were perceived as strange people because they were talking about spirituality, and Atlanteans would make fun of them as if they were talking dirty. This cultural hallmark was part of what kept the Atlanteans from understanding that the Lamurians developed their psychic ability, and their powers through the application of spirituality. The Lamurians prompted the Atlanteans to look at psychology, medicine, the study of the brain, and technology, all together.

Atlanteans needed to see only once that Lamurians had psychic powers to believe it. They did not have to observe it dozens of times to believe it was real. In our modern culture, we see the example of psychic phenomenon again and again, but we dismiss it. We feel, since it is impossible to scientifically prove it, it does not happen.

The person who experiences psychic phenomenon knows that it happens, but objective proof is very hard to provide. It is not at the control of very many people. Usually, for ordinary people, the occurrence is spontaneous and non-repeatable. To prove something scientifically, the experience must be consistent; it has to happen the same way every time and it must be repeatable and occur on demand. These are not the ordinary characteristics of psychic abilities. Most Atlanteans did not have psychic ability and when they saw examples of it occurring among the Lamurians, they did not question whether it was real or not. They saw it happen, therefore it must be real. In their analysis of psychic ability, Atlanteans were trying to figure out how it worked with technology. They wanted to achieve it with technology without developing their spirituality. They did not want to invest the time and effort that was needed to do it. This led to the downfall of Atlantean culture and, ultimately, to destruction of Atlantis.

## Drug Use in Atlantis

Heavenly beings, through my hypnotized patients, state that drugs were used all over Atlantis, particularly in the northern third of the continent. Their traders brought back the opium poppy from the Mediterranean along with other hallucinogenic plants. Cocaine reached southern Atlantis through trade with South America, while the coca bush was grown in Atlantis. They also had hallucinogenic mushrooms, which naturally occurred in Atlantis and were well known in Atlantean culture, being used for religious experiences. By the time Atlantis had real chemists, they were able to fractionate opium and intensify its effect. This was around 95,000 BC. They were also able to modify coca leaves chemically and extract cocaine. They did not tamper with the mushroom because it was believed to be a spiritual substance, and they ate them in private to get religious experiences.

At first, drug use in Atlantis was frowned on and was believed to cut into the productivity of society's members. The government did not want people of Atlantis to lose their edge and be nonproductive. As time went on and the illegal trade of drugs began, drugs were bootlegged and sold secretly against the law. Really serious use of drugs began as the central government was collapsing and the nation was going back to the city-state culture, which was resuming its importance. This was around 50,000 BC.

Stories about Lamurian psychic abilities had reached mythic proportions in Atlantis. Lamurians had been to Atlantis, and stories of their psychic abilities were vastly exaggerated and made quite mysterious. The Lamurians originally tried to teach the Atlanteans how to develop psychic skills and spiritual abilities by using spiritual practices, but the Atlanteans did not believe them. They regarded Lamurians as strange people because they talked about God and spirituality all the time. Atlanteans wanted to duplicate those mythic psychic abilities through other ways than by developing spirituality. So they began to experiment with drugs.

It did not happen all at once. In the north, where the city-states formed, the aristocracy got into using drugs in an effort to develop spiritually, until they were controlled by demons. Ordinary people were doing it, as well. There was a thriving trade in the drugs. In the city-states, drugs were not really illegal. There were other hallucinogenic plants that had been brought from other parts of the Mediterranean and the primary means of using these plants was to smoke them and breathe in the fumes. Only toward the very end did they inject any of these substances into the bloodstream, usually with the fatal results.

When the Atlanteans perceived that the Lamurians had spiritual gifts, they saw relationships between spiritual gifts and agriculture. They had trance-inducing drugs, which they considered to be spiritual drugs. People considered a drug-induced trance to be a spiritual experience, a way to leap into spiritual development and to enter the altered state without having to develop themselves first. Atlanteans began to grow more drug plants and used them, hoping there would be a shortcut in developing spirituality rather than develop it through prayer, meditation, and worship. They mistook these trance states that were induced by drugs as true religious experiences.

Atlanteans knew of opium, marijuana, and other hallucinogenic drugs. They already knew that drugs can alter consciousness. After they got the concept of spiritual and psychic experiences from observing the Lamurians, they realized there were other benefits in the altered states of consciousness. They assumed without practical experience that the drug-induced trance was a religious state, identical, or at least very similar, to what the Lamurians had. So they began to use drugs that way, thinking that they were experiencing spiritual and psychic experiences similar to the Lamurians.

They had this concept of a quick and easy way, and it seemed to be very attractive to them to be spiritual without having to actually be spiritual. In Atlantis, spirituality was considered to be a waste of time and very silly. Rather than go through the developmental process of prayers, meditation, worship, etc., they tried to speed up the process and short-circuit it by using drugs, believing that they were experiencing the same thing as the Lamurians were.

Atlanteans did not realize that spiritual trances are vibration-raising, positive experiences, while drug-induced trances lower the person's vibrations and are negative experiences. Drugs actually slow vibration rates and result in an altered state, but not one that is beneficial. They certainly do not bring you closer to the Light or closer to the creator. Drug-induced states have a dampening effect. By lowering the vibration rate, they put people into a lower state of being and cut down on the flow of the higher vibrations from the Light. People are less easily influenced by the Light and more easily influenced by the demons. Drugs also weaken the protective electromagnetic energy field around people, allowing the demons and other spirits to come in and control them.

Another problem with drugs is that they actually lead you to believe that you have improved yourself or gone into a state in which you have a higher form of consciousness. You can be thinking that you are getting spiritual guidance but you are not getting the kind you really want to have. This is not from heavenly beings, but from demons. Both spiritual and drug-induced trances are altered states of consciousness. The spiritual trance is an elevating state of higher vibrations, while the drug-induced trance is a depressing state and lowers the vibrations. One improves communications with God, while the other dampens it. The higher elevated spiritual state dampens influences from the demons, while the drug-induced trance opens influences from the dark side.

In Atlantis, some of the religious groups bought into the idea of drug-induced trances as religious experiences and it became the fashionable thing to go to the spiritual centers and experience these drug-induced trances. As a result, people opened themselves for demonic possessions and influences and the population regressed spiritually. They actually went backward, becoming less and less able to contact the Light, God, and heaven, and more and more influenced by the demons. This made it easier for the population to be violent, to create wars, and have the desire to conquer and control other people.

## Technologists in Atlantis

Heavenly beings, through my hypnotized patients, said that in Atlantis, a technological class developed through science. Primarily it began as agricultural science, biology, metallurgy, and crystal growing. Then from these, they developed biology, genetics, chemistry, and then physics. Their development of science was different than that of our modern culture. The very basics of technology began with selecting the best grain to grow: which seed do you pick, breeding animals, irrigation developing machines, etc. The technological people were there in every branch of science.

Technologists were individuals to begin with. At the very beginning, they were simply interested in improving their regular jobs and would experiment and make new discoveries. Eventually they became proficient and a group developed who did this for a living, where they would work at developing the technology and answering questions for others. This was the true beginning of the technology class.

Atlantis had developed a great deal of technologically and was very prosperous between 70,000 to 50,000 BC. Then the rulers developed loss of respect for workers and humanity about 50,000 BC.

One patient recalled a life in Atlantis when he was appointed as a chief technologist:

- *"I am a thirty-four-year-old female living in Ward City, located in north central Atlantis. My name is Jer and this is 70,851 BC. I grew up in an upper class family living in a rich neighborhood. My father was an electrical engineer and my mother was a research scientist with a specialty in mathematics. Both my parents were technologists. I have a sister and two brothers. We believe somewhat in certain animal gods and some nature gods. We do not talk about religion or spirituality in Atlantis. I go to the temple for special occasions, such as weddings, funerals, etc., but not on a regular basis.*

  *"I went to school for seventeen years, twelve years of regular school and five years at the university. While at the university, I studied engineering, math, sciences, and courses in computer technology. I have a degree in engineering, a degree in math, and a minor in advanced chemistry. I graduated from college and now I am working for a computer manufacturing company. I like my work in research. I developed technology to expand computer memory and make it faster long before other companies caught up with this technology. I helped make our company the number one computer company in all of Atlantis.*

  *"At the age of thirty-one, I received a phone call from a representative of our ruler asking me to join him and two others for lunch. There was a technologist from the ruler's palace, a priest, and the sub-ruler. They asked me*

*to come to work for our ruler at his palace. They told me of the biggest benefit, that I would become a member of the ruling class by appointment from our ruler. I accepted the offer! From now on, my family and I will be members of the ruling class, with all the privileges. I will be working with six other technologists in the palace compound.*

*"We moved within a month into a two-story house with an attached lab and office. This beautiful home, located on the palace compound, has solar (crystal) electricity, a complete kitchen, refrigeration, air conditioning, computers, TV, radio, phones, etc. This is a good set-up because my husband is an "in-house" physician for the ruler.*

*"I am an attractive, dark-haired woman with greenish-brown eyes. I am five feet seven and a half inches tall and weigh a hundred and twenty-five pounds. But I didn't get this position on my looks. During the eight years I spent in private industry I increased the memory and speed of our manufactured computers. I also redesigned the physical size of our computers, making them more appealing to the consumer. As I mentioned previously, I was instrumental in making our company number one in the country.*

*"My new job puts me in charge of all computer maintenance. I'm also responsible for updating hardware and software for all our computers. I also teach college-level computer courses, do research, and work with the priests to develop the curriculum for computer technology. But my main job is the maintenance of the whole technical group. I go to my office around nine a.m. each day and get a briefing concerning the issues and problems of the day. Sometimes I can solve these problems over the phone. Other times I use a computer to correct problems, and sometimes I must go out in the field to analyze and work toward a problem solution.*

*"When I'm in, I have a daily briefing with the ruler and other staff members from ten thirty to eleven thirty a.m. After this we have lunch with the ruler and/or members of his staff. Sometimes my husband joins us for lunch when*

*his schedule permits. At one thirty p.m., I go back to the office and check inventories, making sure that sufficient parts are available for our updates and other maintenance projects. I also do research at this time. I am currently working on a networking system that will bring uniformity to all air travel, anywhere in the country. Our ruler is well respected by the ruling class and all other citizens. He is unselfish and works hard to bring a better way of life for all of his subjects.*

Described and drawn by the different hypnotized patients

This alien being appeared in Atlantis during the Golden Age. He was tall and slender with a 15 inch waist. He stood 6 feet 7 inches tall. His light gray body was smooth surfaced and his initial appearance was without any clothes.

This alien with clothes is a stick figure being. This intelligent being was seen in the city of Cardi in the North Central section of Atlantis in 52,000 BC by Adel, the lab technician.

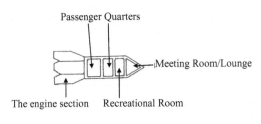

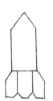

This space ship was designed, built, and used by stick like aliens from the planet Krypto.

"At forty-nine, I am promoted to the position of chief technologist. This appointment puts me in charge of all technology in the city. We move into an apartment in the palace and I become the highest ranking technical person in the city. There are fourteen technologists working in the palace now. This number has doubled from the time when I came here. Four of these technologists, plus me and my husband, live in the palace. In the evenings, we attend a lot of events that include our kids; for example, movies, carnivals, etc. We either go out to parties, movies, plays, dances, etc. or we stay in the palace and attend them. We are invited to all the events that take place in the palace.

"One day, a naked alien made contact with the ruler of our city, telling him he could help our society advance technologically. In return he would like to have fuel for his spaceship, food to be stored on the spaceship to be used during space travel, and the right to land his ship in Atlantis without fear of being injured, captured, or killed. The ruler listened intently to the naked male alien who appeared "out of nowhere." Having no aptitude for technology, the ruler sent the alien to see me, the chief technologist.

"Even though I knew the alien was coming, I was startled when the alien appeared before me. I quickly settled down. The alien had the ability to put me at ease. This alien stood six feet seven inches tall. He was very slender. His waist appeared to be under fifteen inches. He stood upright, had two arms and two legs, with respective fingers and toes. He had large, round eyes and a large, long nose. His nose and eyes were out of proportion to the size of his long, narrow face. He was white in color, with a smooth-surfaced body; that is, there were no marks of any kind on his body, such as navel, breasts, or sexual organ(s). His round, nearly-bald head featured little sprouts of unruly hair. He told me he had advanced technology that would beneficial our society. I was interested in hearing more so I arranged for the alien and his fellow aliens to meet with our committee the following morning.

"The first time we spoke, it was done through telepathic communication. That is probably why I became at ease so quickly. We tuned in to one another's thoughts. One of my first thoughts was that it was pretty unconventional for the alien to "just appear," as opposed to knocking and entering the room through the doorway. I also thought, Where are your clothes? While I saw nothing offensive, I found his naked appearance to be highly unusual. After our telepathic conversation started, we communicated verbally. And I know that he tuned in to my thoughts, because he exited through the doorway when he departed.

"The next morning, we assembled for the meeting with the aliens. The ruler, three of his top sub-rulers, the high priest and two other ranking priests, and four of my top senior technologists were present. Right on time, the alien and two of his fellow aliens walked through the door, dressed in white trousers and white shirts buttoned down in the front. The alien had picked up on my thoughts yesterday about entering rooms and dressing for public appearance. He wanted to make a good impression on us. All these aliens looked very much alike; one was six feet four inches tall and another one was six feet nine inches.

"The alien, assisted by his two fellow aliens, explained how he would provide us with ideas and suggestions on how to improve certain medical technology that would reduce the aging process. He went on to explain how the aliens could show us how to use our crystal technology in more efficient ways.

"Near the end of the meeting, we decide on a two-year agreement that would be considered a trial period. We agree to provide the aliens with food, fuel, and landing rights in exchange for improved technology. We agree that I would hold monthly meetings with the aliens during this two-year trial period. I would have the right to refer the aliens to other technologists when this became necessary. After the meeting, the three aliens walked out through the doorway.

*"After this, the aliens contact me and other ruling class technologists. Over time, they gave us suggestions on how to create medicines that reduce the effects of disease. They advised us on how to create machines that can be used to reduce aging, thus enabling us to live longer lives, and they showed us ways to improve our crystals. We are able to build better, more efficient engines for our transportation system and factories. They showed us ways to reduce the size of our crystals without losing their effectiveness, and as a result, we have excellent phone systems and our computers have more capacity, memory, and speed. The aliens also showed us ways to use crystals to improve healing. I maintained alien contact almost all my working life, and the contact stopped when I retired.*

*"In addition to being in charge of all technology, and reporting to and advising our ruler, I teach an advanced technology course to college graduates. I have also written two books, Computers - The Key to the Future and An Introduction to Computer Science. Staying active and contributing has been rather easy for me. I am gifted in computer technology. I was recognized as "very special" when I was five years old.*

*"At the age of seventy-three, I have retired. I have relocated with my retired husband to the retirement section for nobility, located on the palace compound. At ninety-eight, I am dying of old age. Pneumonia is the actual cause of my death. My last thoughts are that I had a good life and I hope others living after me will have as good a life as I did. My spirit leaves my body and watches while people have a small ceremony for me before my body is cremated. I stay around for many years before Light Beings find me and take me to the Light.*

*"From heaven, I see that I had a good life. Atlantis at this time was not a dark place, but it was without spirituality and without God. I did not have any dark influences. I see that my giftedness was really guidance from the Light. I see that I planned to make contributions to*

*society through inventions and creations, and in doing this, I would be guided by the Light. These creations would make people's lives easier and better.*

*"From heaven, I see nothing negative (control/implants) in Atlantis at this time."*

## Technology in Atlantis

As described before, Atlantis started to populate about 130,000 BC. First agriculture technology began and then others by 100,000 BC. They were making progress and had a solid biological background and their food supply was good. They were doing selective breeding on food crops and animals. That was the extent of technology at this time. They had developed an education system and it was becoming common that the study of science and mathematics would be part of the education.

From there on, it was a building process. There were great advances in mathematics, they became interested in study of crystals, and from that developed chemistry and physics. They discovered solar power and developed solar cells and electricity. From solar-generated electricity and having sophisticated knowledge of crystals, they were able to go into solid state electronics immediately and control the flow of electric current. All these flourished by 80,000 BC. When Lamurians came to Atlantis about 80,000 BC, electronics was really starting and Atlanteans thought of developing the spirituality and psychic abilities that Lamurians had, by using electronics.

### Electricity

My hypnotized patients state that, in our current culture, we have primarily fossil-fuel-driven electricity generating plants. Atlantis did not get to electrical power by mechanical means. The initial development of electricity in Atlantis came through chemical means. The initial mass generation of electricity was based on solar power and solar cells, so that electricity was available in fairly large quantities, but locally only. Electricity was generated from sun power at each location where it was needed. Atlanteans never developed an electrical distribution system from building to building, all the way back to a power plant as we have. Instead, electricity was wired locally, used locally, and generated in the vicinity, using non-polluting means.

When larger amounts of electricity were needed in all locations, Atlanteans developed their electrical transmitting capabilities through crystals, to transmit the electrical field, which was then picked up by other crystals. So, even though they were using a large amount of electricity, there still was no electrical distribution network in terms of wires. They used multiple sources of energy and really never did get into generating electricity from fossil fuels. They used solar-generated electrical energy, through solar cells.

In Atlantis, electricity was transferred without wires and without electrical discharge. Electricity was electronically transformed into an electromagnetic wave that passed through a crystal that regulated the vibrational rate and was broadcast to anyone who had a receiver. The antenna setup would absorb the energy, pass it back to crystals, and convert it back to the electrical power that could be used at the site. For a large amount of electricity, it was necessary that Atlanteans have a larger setup, but for small amounts, a very tiny setup was sufficient. It was like a battery-operated device and they did not have to see the antenna in order to use the electricity.

Generating power by electrical means led to the development of solar cells, which led to the development of nuclear power in Atlantis. The sequence was perfectly logical as they developed their understanding of the atom. They did not use fossil fuel and build large plants to convert heat energy and electrical energy. Instead, they went through a chemical and then physical pathway. As their understanding of the atom grew, they discovered radioactivity, created nuclear power plants, and then were able to shift to alternating current so they could transmit it. But their means of transmission was different.

Some of their breakthroughs were aided by alien race four of group two. The aliens at the time were very enthusiastic about giving technology to Atlanteans, which they misused later on. Now, in current time, those aliens are taking a stand-back-and-wait attitude. Heavenly beings, through my hypnotized patients, state that a little bit of technology has been fed to us by the aliens in the current time, such as solid state electronics and the concept of multiple-use circuits.

## Genetics

The discovery of DNA, the understanding of how genetics worked, led Atlantean scientists to try to substitute things on the DNA strands. The first studies of genetics were done on the basis of agriculture, trying to find better crops to raise, better varieties of plants, ones that were more productive, more disease-free. They also used genetics to improve the hardiness of the crop, to get better yields under more severe growth conditions. In short, they tried to do several things to get better food production, improving varieties, and even creating new fruits and vegetables. Atlantean scientists also found they could modify animals as easily as they could modify plants. So they modified cows to give more milk with more butterfat, or better meat, more of it and faster, and chickens that laid more eggs.

Initially, there was proper use of technology. After the Atlantean scientists became really bent or twisted, it made sense to them to try and change people to make them better slaves. They also genetically manipulated people to control them. They lowered their intelligence level because nobody wanted a smart slave. They did it by changing the DNA. Sometimes it was a simple procedure; just simply adding a chemical agent. Then they changed the DNA of people by adding animal DNA to them.

Initially, this was for scientific curiosity. Later, it was just for fun and taking control over different beings. The scientists in Atlantis were still working by trial and error. They had a lack of understanding of what they were doing, so it led to a lot of experiments just to see what would happen. When they mastered the techniques of genetic manipulation, they were able to make different organisms for different purposes. The first and most basic form was to manipulate the genes to create a new and different species and new and different organisms.

For example, they began to take a gene from a horse's head and putting it into a different kind of animal, so that the animal's head would be the head of a horse, and they mixed and matched different body parts. Of course, there were quite a few failures due to leaving out something essential and putting in something that fouled up the living organism. They did surgical experiments by hooking different parts onto people surgically, like transplants. Some of the changes were due to genetic manipulations and some due to the surgical transplant.

### The State of Biology and Genetics

My hypnotized patients claim that Atlanteans really jump-started in these fields with the help of the alien races. They had the understanding of the chemical process in the cell and how chemistry related to biological activity, and also the existence of DNA and the DNA functions in the cell. This led to some very interesting experiments, in which they changed, adapted, and modified the DNA. These people in Atlantis were dealing with the inner workings of the cells. They already had a good understanding of the physiological process that happens and they began to tamper with the DNA. The scientists of Atlantis started to make changes, integrating DNA from other beings into humans.

Atlanteans started to make genetic modifications in plants, then in animals, and then in human beings. In some cases they took animal genes and put them into humans, thinking that would transfer certain abilities to people, such as improve their eyesight, improve their circulation, mental acuity, etc., all with good intentions, but not always with good results. At the same time, they transmitted human genes to some of their pets, primarily house pets. This was not successful. Their hybrid animals did not thrive. They did not develop the characteristics the scientists hoped for. Instead they became less apt in terms of survival.

They tried to improve the switching speed of the human brain in the nervous system. They felt that if humans had faster reflexes like animals, they could think faster. What they were after was to make the switching network in the brain more efficient and quicker. Not that they really wanted to give humans a better reaction capability, but they wanted to take the same ability and stick it into the thinking process. This did not work out well.

They wanted to make animals more human, in particular the primates, so they would relate better with people and be more emotionally useful to people. That worked in part, but the animals already had these capabilities. The Atlanteans were trying to amplify these abilities, to really make the animals empathetic to people. They did succeed to some extent, but this had, in general, negative effects. Some of those characteristics carry over with them now.

Some of the modifications initially appeared to be very successful, but one of the things that Atlanteans did not know was that genes have multiple uses; a portion of DNA may be for making certain protein. But it may be also partially used in creating another protein for another gene in another place. So it creates the building blocks for other proteins, and without those fragments being available you cannot make some of the more complicated things. Even DNA, with all of its millions and billions of combinations, is not big enough to do everything. So parts of the genes double over.

Genetic experiments such as placing animal genes into humans and human genes into animals sometimes produced good results, but mostly they had bad side effects. These experiments did manage to improve human acuity, but they also produced a brain problem, because there was increase in the number of neurons going from the eyes, which created switching problems where the optic nerve goes back into the brain, thus creating an imbalance situation.

The Atlanteans did manage to improve human reaction time, but in doing so, they did damage to the thinking process of the individuals who received the genes. In terms of neurons being fired too quickly, the logical sequence of nerve impulses was interfered with, so that people who had these genes, even though they could think faster, did not think in a coherent manner. They were not able to sequence information or instruction as well. Even though they could move quicker, they were not as coordinated, and even though they could think quicker, the thoughts were not coherent.

One of my patients recalled a past life in Atlantis, when genetic modification was done with devastating results:

- *"I am a six-year-old boy living in the north of Atlantis in about 60,000 BC. I look like a cross between an ape, a cat, and a human. My face is misshapen. My jaw is thrust in front and I have heavy teeth, like fangs. My arms are suitable for walking like a cat, but I still seem to have hands. I stand upright in a squatting position. My arms are long. I have a part-human and part-animal mind. I am big, strong, and can be mean if picked on. I have dark hair all over. It is like fur."*

  *"The other kids in the daycare pick on me a lot because I am different. As a result, I get upset and, being stronger than the other kids, I grab them and throw them around. At the age of seven, I am very wild, so they isolate me in an outside enclosure, just to keep the other kids safe. What they do not anticipate is that I can climb like an ape.*

*As soon as I get a chance, I climb the twelve-foot fence and run away into the woods and live there. I learn to protect myself from the cold, find food, and survive. I fit neither with the apes nor with the humans.*

Described and drawn by the different hypnotized patients

This buffalo like man has the head and facial features of a buffalo. The arms are similar to a human's, but the hands feature the hooves of a buffalo. The legs are human like, however, the knee on the left is on the backside similar to that of a buffalo. Excessive thick wooly hair covers the body.

This wild dog like human baby has the face of a wild hunting dog. It has a stub for a right arm and a left arm and hand that resembles a human's. The dog has stubs for legs.

This ape like human baby has a stub for a left arm and a stub for a right leg. The right arm and left leg resem-ble human appendages.

This goat like human has the arms and body of a human, the legs of a goat, and the hands and feet (hooves) of a goat.

*"I stay away from people in the woods. I die of pneumonia at the age of thirty-two. After the death, I do not have the slightest idea about what to do and I do not relate to the messengers of heaven. I move from people to people, possessing them, making them violent and insane. They eventually are killed or kill themselves. I do not stay with anybody for a long time. Finally, I am helped into heaven by angels.*

*"After the cleansing and healing, I review my life with the heavenly counselors. From heaven, I see that I am a creation of a genetic experiment. They cut a part of a chromosome and inserted part of an ape chromosome. They took out a chunk of chromosome from the arms and replaced it with a chunk of chromosome of a gorilla, which made my arms like gorilla arms. They had the chromosomes all mapped out, so they knew what part is where. They modified the skeleton, particularly from the waist down, making it more like an ape. They changed my teeth, mouth, and general shape. They did in-vitro fertilization and implanted the fertilized egg in a female. Once she gave birth, they took the baby away and my mother was sent off. They raised me in a nursery. They did not allow any close contact. When I grew a little older, I could not connect or socialize at all. They put me with the children of the people who worked there, in the daycare center at the laboratory.*

*"I was allowed to mingle with normal children because the researchers wanted to see how I interact with normal children and if I could grow up normal. What they wanted was to create good workers, somebody who is very strong but not very smart, and can do heavy labor. There were about six experimental children. A couple of them looked like ape crosses and the rest were like dog crosses. They wanted to use dog humans because of their sense of smell.*

*"From heaven, I see many of my problems came from that life to this current life, such as uncoordination, aches and pain all over the body and feelings being disconnected to the experience and the words."*

Atlanteans were guided by the aliens to study DNA, and they encouraged them to do some experiments. Some of the experiments were done because the scientists of Atlantis were very anxious to know the results themselves. They never did get feedback about what the aliens thought about the unsuccessful experiments. They were not quite aware of aliens helping them. It was kind of how when we think they are there but nobody has hard evidence. That is, the scientists did not meet with aliens regularly, to sit down and discuss things. Aliens were behind the scenes and were known for sure to a very few.

## Physics

My hypnotized patients report that physics in Atlantis developed in dual pathways. First, the traditional methods, the way we use physics through mechanics and the very beginnings to understand momentum and other properties. But a large portion of the Atlantean physics came through chemistry. They found the chemical processes that dealt with physics. It was as if our physics started with mechanics and grew out in all directions. Meanwhile, it was as if the Atlanteans' physics started with mechanics and stayed there. A second growth area came down from chemistry and spread into physics, dealing with electricity, electromagnetism, the nature of matter, nuclear physics, quantum theory; all of that came not from mechanics, but from chemistry. Mechanical law, which we all know is as the Newtonian law, and quantum mechanical laws seem to differ from these. Here in Atlantis, they did not even connect them as being similar. They found no relationship between the two for quite a while. It was as if they had two different sets of physical laws in the universe.

## Combined Physics and Chemistry

According to my hypnotized patients, in Atlantis they had a very good understanding of the fundamental properties of nature. They had a much more thorough understanding of crystal structures and how to use crystals for various tasks. In our culture, we have rudimentary knowledge of crystals and know very little about their unique properties and how to use them. We are just beginning to get an understanding of the nature of matter as thoroughly as Atlanteans knew it. Scientifically, we are still behind Atlantis in chemistry, physics, and biology.

In Atlantis, when the scientists became aware that the Lamurians were having psychic experiences, it was beyond the scope of what they could explain and what they could experiment with. Since they observed it, they accepted it as being true. They did not pretend that these experiences did not exist. They said, "I saw it, therefore it exists. Now let us study it and figure out what, when, and how it is happening." So they began to study the human brain, trying to determine how it was that some people could be psychic or could have psychic experiences. At the same time, this overlapped in the field of biology, psychology, physics, and chemistry, and they began to come up with scientific explanations for psychic phenomenon. The Atlanteans always thought in technological terms, and spirituality for them did not exist as such. They primarily understood the technology and did not really want to spend time to comprehend it spiritually.

### Crystals and Physics

According to my hypnotized patients, the discovery of the properties of the crystals came about as the result of the Atlanteans' entry into physics. They did not begin to study physics from the same basis as our current society did. It gave them a different viewpoint. Our scientists started with the study of mechanics and light, and eventually discovered electromagnetic radiation.

In Atlantis, they had crystal mines in the interior hills and mountains. The Atlanteans' first experience with crystals came when they found crystals that were naturally eroded out of the rock, broken off by the previous new cycle. They picked up the crystals from the shore and examined them. Their first interest in the crystals came from their beauty. They had a definite geometric shape and Atlanteans found this interesting. They used the crystals first for decorations. Both men and women wore them as jewelry. They did learn to use crystals for metaphysical healings, something they learned from the Lamurians.

By now they had already gotten into material sciences, chemistry, and ceramics, and they were into biology because of agriculture, but physics started with investigations of the properties of the crystals. They found unusual characteristics in crystals. This interested them greatly. They began to study physics from that interest. They found the science of electronics by studying the crystals and finding the electricity that they generated and the field that was around them. Lamurians could sense the spiritual field around the crystals, but they did not have scientific knowledge of that fact. They were aware of metaphysical knowledge about the crystals, but not of the physical properties that the Atlanteans developed so well. Lamurians did not need it.

There were quite a few experiments, and the Atlanteans developed the science of crystal growing. They also learned how to tailor the size and the shape of the crystals, even to put impurities in them to alter how they worked and to control their properties. They used the vibrational rate of the crystals as a control mechanism for broadcasting electric power and receiving it. They controlled the vibrational rate of electricity. Crystals were used to tune in to the vibrations and to change the vibrations. The crystals had to be tuned to each other in order to pick up what was being broadcast. So the two crystals had to operate on the same frequency. Later, they began to grow crystals that were like small computers in the lab to their specifications.

One of my patients gave the following description of how they grew crystals on a mass scale:

• *"I see a chamber with clear sides and a clear, flat lid. Next to this chamber is another chamber in which a crystal is growing and it is the same shape and size as the other crystal. The work starts with the entire chamber filled with a solution, and there is a skin-like surface over the entire outside area of that solution. A beam is shining down through it from above, piercing the membrane-like surface. In that fraction of a second, the membrane is separated; a molecule is attracted to that spot, and is deposited. First they start with the very beginning of a crystal. This is a quartz crystal, which is calcium carbonate, I believe. The membrane can be seen through, but it has a bluish tint. It appears that if you touched it, it would be slimy and jelly-like.*

*"The container in which the crystal is grown is very small, about the same size as the crystal. It is about a half inch in width and two inches long. The little chamber is contained inside a bigger chamber. There is a flat lid and this is optically perfect so nothing interferes with the laser beam. It can be directed precisely. There is also a system for adding more of the solution into the membrane and then into the enclosed bubble. The membrane is between the solution and the tube, between the solution and the atmosphere above the tube, between the solution and the crystal surface itself. As the beam comes through it, the beam pierces the top and pierces the bottom of the membrane so the molecule will deposit there.*

*"So they are growing these crystals with the circuitry in three dimensions. The process is controlled by a computer, where the pattern is imprinted and it is hop-scotching all over the crystal's surface, moving at a high speed, making contact, allowing an instant for the molecule to deposit, and then moving somewhere else. The pattern begins when the electron beam pierces the membrane and the very first molecule is deposited, then another and another. When they have the platform, they start to implant the circuitry molecules. They grow the crystals and at the same time,*

*they are adding the impurities or inclusions that will be the electrical circuitry. The very first molecules deposited are the crystals themselves.*

*"When the crystal is grown, the solution and the tube are removed and a new tube is put in place. The solution is put back on the top and they start again. The tube containing the new crystal is split and the new crystal is removed.*

*"I am shown a device that will control electro-potential by emitting a beam that will strike a surface. It shines into a crystal-growing chamber from above. There is a crystal-growing apparatus in that chamber. From the top, there is a solution containing all the molecules that will be used in the crystal. To this is added a gel-like substance that will create a skin around the solution and keep the molecules from actually touching the crystals, except for where they need to go. The electron beam fires through the solution and through the semi-permeable skin, disrupting it and establishing an electron potential on the surface of the crystal. Molecules that are wanted at that location are attracted to that potential and deposited there so the electron beam skips over the surface, allowing the charge of the other place to dissipate after the molecule is deposited, then moving to another place where a second molecule is deposited, then the third and fourth and so on. The process does take days, sometimes, before the process is perfected.*

*"Many crystals are grown in a lab with one person attending the machinery and supplying the solution. There is only one crystal in each set-up. There are many of these set-ups in one work area with a number of machines that emit the beam. The technician's job is to keep the machines functioning. The operation is controlled by computers that tell what potential is to be put to grow the crystal, with the included electrical circuits, transistors, resisters, and everything needed to make it a functioning device.*

*"The workers determine what molecule will deposit in which place. It is for growing the proper inclusions in the*

crystals. These crystals are about one-quarter inch across and one and a half to two inches long. They are designed for neck implants. Later, as they become more advanced, they were about as thick as a safety pin and about one half to three-quarters of an inch long. Initially they were implanted on both sides of the neck, but later on one side only.

"The crystals, after they were better developed, could be implanted only by a hypodermic needle. The needles were slid in below the skin and the crystal was pushed out. The earliest ones required surgery, where a cut had to be made in the skin, the crystal placed inside, and the wound closed. The people who had them would have had six scars on the back of their necks where the crystals were implanted.

"Archangels are saying that what I have described will not enable anyone to duplicate this device because heavenly beings do not want these devices duplicated. They have disguised the information. What they have shown me is not wrong, but it is incomplete and disguised so that anyone who tried to follow these directions will not be able to do it. It will be possible to duplicate it many years from now, but by then humankind will hopefully be developed spiritually to the point where they will not have a desire to use them for negative purposes. One of the secrets the angels do not want to share is the gel itself and how you make the layer that keeps the solution away from the crystal except at the spot where the beam pierces it. These are not complete details. The general process is accurate, but other information is being withheld by the Light for a purpose. The information provided gives current mankind nothing more than a starting point."

### Electronics

Probably the most significant change that occurred in Atlantis was the development of electronic circuitry. Atlanteans had a very good understanding of solid state physics of semiconductors, all derived from their initial studies of crystal structures. Their developmental path was quite different from our culture. The Atlanteans, working with crystals and crystal structures, found the importance of semiconductors from their low-voltage electricity. It was intuitively obvious to them that the powers lay in the proper utilization of transistors, micro capacitors and other semi-conductors. They were able to build miniaturized circuits from the beginning. The concept of the large, powered vacuum tube amplifiers set-up was just beyond them because they were not used to thinking in those terms. They were much more efficient in their use of electricity and their use of materials than we are and have been.

There was a marriage between psychology and electronics; that is building the electronic circuitry that taps into the flow of the current into the brain and influences thoughts, intentions, and conduct. It was a breakthrough for Atlanteans and was quite logical to them. Their approach to the study of psychology was based upon the Lamurians' spirituality. As described before, what attracted the attention of the Atlanteans to the Lamurians' spirituality was the obvious fact that the Lamurians were aware of the things they could not know. They were also able to communicate from a distance with no direct means of communication and they exhibited other psychic talents. Things would appear and disappear, and time could be distorted around them. Sometimes these effects were purposeful and at other times they simply happened at random. From time to time, Atlanteans had the feelings that the Lamurians were actually reading their minds and were aware of their thoughts when they said things. Atlanteans' initial interest was in duplicating the states achieved by the Lamurian mystics, and even the common Lamurians who walked around in a spiritual state. They wanted to duplicate that state by technical means.

These Atlanteans could not see or feel or know the interaction. They could only see it as a fact that a group of Lamurians who are not in contact with each other would suddenly start acting as a unit. All of them were working toward the same goal. This bewildered the Atlanteans; they knew these people had not been in contact. How could they have possibly arrived at this goal, which they could not have known in advance, and start working toward it, unless there was communication. One outstanding difference between us and Atlanteans was their thinking. When they observed a fact, they believed it. They did not say, "This is impossible." We in modern times do not believe in psychic abilities, therefore, we think it cannot be, so we ignore the evidence. It is difficult to prove or repeat the phenomenon, but it exists on an individual basis and cannot be denied.

In the initial investigation, when those who were able to get the Lamurians to reveal something, the Lamurians were perfectly willing to teach them, but Atlanteans could not bring themselves to believe that the Lamurians were being open and honest, although they were. Lamurians were showing them how to develop a spiritual attitude, knowledge of God, to immerse oneself into the spiritual field, and to raise the vibrations to enter the spiritual field more fully with a higher rate of vibrations, realizing that, with this, psychic abilities will come naturally. This was beyond the Atlanteans. Most did not believe it and those who did realized it would take an extended time to develop these abilities.

So their development of the field of psychology came out of that study of trying to duplicate the spirituality of Lamurians without doing the spiritual practices or exercises the Lamurians followed. Their intention was to short-circuit the process and achieve the benefits and results, without really having to do the work. It seemed like a wonderful idea because they were too lazy to do the spiritual practices. However the benefits were not there. So they began to place a crystal implant in the back of the neck so rulers could control their people's thoughts and emotions.

Once Atlanteans had computers and radio-transmitting capacity, superimposing the electronic signal on the radio signal was a simple task. They could implant a little device containing a microcircuit in a crystal in a child when he or she was small,. It could be inserted anywhere in the back of the head and neck area and it would transmit something that could interact with the brain. These devices were biologically powered; that is, they were able to use the nutrients in the blood to power their little power plant. They generated their own electricity, and the waste products were carried out by the blood. It caused no particular strain on the body.

- *"I am a thirty-one-year-old soldier living in a coastal city of Atlantis called Illicun, in 60,132 BC. I am wearing a short skirt type of outfit and a shield with a wooden frame and two layers of leather. I am a commander. I have been in the force since I was sixteen. I am a heavily-built man with brownish white skin, brown hair, and brown eyes. This is an army and police force. We keep the law and peace in the city, and when we are needed, we can be mobilized to be an army force. Right now there is civil unrest and the ruler tells me to stop it.*

  *"People are objecting to the neck implants. They found out that implants are being put in by hospital employees from stories that are floating around. They are putting the implants in babies, but they are big and can be felt under the skin. People think it will give the rulers too much power. They will be able to track people and control them. People want to burn the hospital and kill the doctors who are putting in the implants. It is our job to break up the riots and catch the ones who are doing it. This goes against our own city's people.*

  *"I am also wondering if the ruler really knows what he is doing, but it is not our job to ask questions. Our job is to follow orders. We are in front of the hospital. I have the whole city guard around the place. I am wondering if these people could be right; perhaps the ruler made a mistake. Maybe we should not be doing this. I am really vacillating and wondering if these folks know something I do not. Defending our city against our own people seems odd.*

*"We attack and kill the first group of people who protest. It makes me sick to kill my own people. How can they be enemies? All of a sudden, I realize that if we are being given such radical orders to kill our own people, maybe there is something radically wrong. But the protest is broken off and the ones who are living are running for their lives. I am pretty sure that the ringleaders are among the dead. I have these really nagging feelings that the ruler is mistaken or lying to us. Could these folks know something I don't about what is really going on? It seems to be pretty sickening to kill our own people. These thoughts are going through my mind as I am cleaning up after the riot. The more I think about it, the more I worry.*

*"There is a lot of protest about what the army police did. The situation is getting worse. The king is recruiting people to be palace guards and I have to assign some of my men to train them. He is training a fighting force that has to answer to him directly rather than to me. I can see where this is dangerous. It is a danger to me personally, to the police guard, and it is a danger to the city. If a king has an army around him, what makes him answerable to the people? He did not ask me to join his army because he knows that I believe in the rights of the people.*

*"There is another uprising and it is in the better part of town. I am really confused. I am just trying to contain the problem but not telling my people to kill. The new unit of palace guards gets there and kills people right and left. All of a sudden I see great danger to the city and to the people because the king will have too much power and he will not be answerable to the people. I want to send my men to kill the palace guards and get that danger stopped, and then we will go to the king and demand answers to these things. But it still does not seem right to kill all those palace guards, either. In the end, nothing is done. I end up not taking any action and doing nothing.*

*"As the situation worsens, I begin to believe that I have failed in my duty to the citizens. I can see that the freedom*

*of the people is slipping away and I am sick about it. We do not get new recruits anymore. At the age of forty-two, I see the ruler's guards marching in the city and taking adults for implants, killing those who resist, and I am powerless to stop them. I kill myself with my sword, driving it into my heart thinking, "What a failure I am. I could not decide, did not act, and could not make things work. I let down my wife, family, the people, and myself. If I ever get another chance I will strike right away. I will not wait and I will not let the evil grow and develop."*

*"My spirit is bitter and angry. I go to the palace and try to damage the king, but I realize that there is not a thing I can do now. I cannot affect matter and cannot make things happen. I try attacking the king in various ways and try entering his body, but I cannot. I end up entering one of his wives. I feed thoughts and ideas to her to discuss with the king, such as, "If it is a good idea, don't you have a responsibility to the people and not just to yourself and the nobles." The king gets irritated with her but listens anyway. Soon the king dies of an infection. After his wife dies at the age of eighty-four, I follow her to the Light.*

*"First I go through the debriefing stage, where I talk to a Light being about my feelings of frustration, anger, self-resentment, and remorse about taking my own life. Then, after cleansing, I go to the life review. The sea god Marduk is there. From heaven, I see that I planned to defend the rights of the people and expand them and to give power to the people. I needed to learn never to commit suicide, no matter how bad things get. It is the greatest damage we can do to our soul. Also, I needed to learn the lesson to act rapidly when I have the chance.*

*"From heaven, I see that my life plan was to join the army police, where I would have the power and the means to make changes and protect the rights of the people. And as one city became independent, other cities would follow. The word would get around to the other cities that would be inspired and follow the example to keep the freedom. It was a chance to change the system of government. It*

*could have been the first real democracy in Atlantis but I did not succeed."*

## Alien Races Four and Five of Group Two in Atlantis

According to my hypnotized patients, alien races four and five of group two provided Atlanteans information about different technologies, including electronics, and how to use it. The Atlanteans received technology in particular from race two, four, and five of group two, as described in chapter three. Race two got them started. Race four gave them knowledge of nuclear power and helped them with electricity and electronics, and race five helped them with electronics, medicine, psychology, and radio all across the board, but the hard science primarily came from race four. Nuclear fission formed the basis for the power plant; that is, breaking uranium and generating electricity in the process.

Although alien races four and five of group two inspired technology in Atlantis, they did not inspire all the technology. Atlanteans already had a good deal of technology in place from their own knowledge of crystals, and beginnings of an electrical revolution, where they figured out on their own how to generate electricity from the crystal pattern and solar batteries. They already had semi-conductors and individual semi-conductor devices. By this time, the Atlanteans had made transformers, so they were generating large amounts of power by steam energy. They still had not built any fossil fuel engines to use heat energy to convert it to mechanical energy. They developed a fuel cell from the basis of their understanding of crystals, not on the basis of their understanding of the rest of chemistry.

After they developed nuclear power with the aid of aliens, Atlanteans realized that the stars shine by the same process. They never thought of where all the energy of the stars came from. They did not even realize that stars have nuclear energy. For some reason or other, they were not interested in looking up and studying astronomy. In some ways, the Atlanteans were very practical people and studied things that were of immediate interest and that they could use immediately. They did very little basic research to open new fields to make important new discoveries. Instead they just let the progress or progression of science sort of evolve, step by step.

When the aliens helped Atlanteans understand DNA, they cut many years off the developmental process by showing them how particular groups of bases on DNA would produce a particular change in an organism. The Atlanteans had already begun to experiment on plants and animals by making DNA changes. This small understanding gave them the courage to try big experiments on humans. They began to modify human DNA and injecting the modified DNA into live people. When they made a mistake with the strand of DNA not viable; that is, when it could not continue living, the cell into which it was injected would die. When the DNA was viable and could have its effect, the cells in which it was inserted would reproduce it and spread it.

Alien races four and five of group two gave different technology to Atlantis, but they did not inspire all the technology. Atlanteans came up with much of it on their own, especially the technology to control people; Also, they figured out the beginnings of the electrical revolution where they sorted out on their own how to generate electricity from the crystal pattern and the solar batteries.

None of the alien races intended or taught Atlanteans to use these technologies negatively. They intended them to be a cheap and easy source of electric power. They did not intend them to be used as a weapon of destruction or as a means of controlling other people. This was negative to them; something they did not indulge in and did not approve of the Atlantean's indulging in it. They could have stopped the Atlanteans, but they chose not to.

### Alien Race Four of Group Two

Heavenly beings, through my hypnotized patients, state that alien race four of group two came to Atlantis around 70,000

BC. This group had a tremendous influence on mankind. They taught humans metal work, science, and technology. They gave Atlanteans an organized framework in technology and gave them different alloys of metals to use and taught them how to work with metals, which were used later to make the weapons of war. They also taught Atlanteans astrology. They gave Atlanteans the concept of the multi-use circuit where they could pile together in one chip a whole series of functions, just like computer chips. It is not a new concept.

With a multi-use circuit, a single wire can be a part of two or three circuits, where a single transistor can serve multiple functions in different circuits at the same time. This requires very advanced mathematics and a very advanced electrical knowledge. The Atlanteans had not developed those skills yet. Race four brought that concept to Atlantis and showed them how to apply it. The size of their electrical and electronic components was drastically reduced because they were able to use the same device in two or three circuits at the same time. It was a fantastically powerful tool.

When race four first arrived in Atlantis, the Atlanteans had already found the gene and were beginning their experiments of removing gene fragments, modifying them, and reinserting them into a living cell. After the aliens arrived, Atlanteans were able to work with the genes much more efficiently and were able to have better and more direct means of changing a gene, knowing what changes were made, and then observing the results. Through precision measuring and precision cutting, they were able to work molecule by molecule, making the process very accurate. This was where aliens were able to get to the molecular level, and they passed on this technology to Atlanteans.

One more thing which alien race four brought to the Atlanteans that was important was the study of the brain and it's functioning with electronic circuits. This was not possible in detail before they brought the electronic circuits. The electronics themselves did not cause their negative actions, but the intent with which they were used did.

According to heavenly beings, in terms of the role of dark influence, Satan already had a plan for Atlantis and was behind every negative action in Atlantis. He knew the potential. Satan even helped the Atlanteans develop their psychological and mind-control capabilities. When alien race four arrived, they were influenced by Satan to provide other parts of the puzzle for the complete domination of the population of Atlantis. They led to the computer, which led to the enslavement of the Atlanteans. They provided the electronics to do it. The intentions of aliens were all right but they were not aware of demonic influences. They were providing exactly what was needed for the domination of the culture, for the rich and the powerful to take over completely, to literally own the people. But the aliens did not realize it.

The aliens thought of themselves altruistically and provided the Atlanteans with the technology they needed. It was true that they were providing them with good technology and they did not legislate Atlanteans to use it improperly. Atlanteans did that on their own, with the help of Satan and his demons. It was possible, so they chose to do it. Alien race four found Atlanteans more interesting because they were the most advanced on Earth and it made sense to give the advanced technology to the most advanced race on the Earth. They also worked in other parts of Earth but not to the same extent or the same depth that they worked with Atlanteans.

Alien race four made significant contributions to the Atlanteans knowledge. They gave Atlanteans metals and taught them how to work with them; that is, solid state circuit, the multi-use concept, and the mathematics and electrical theory to make solid state work. They also gave them the impetus to develop computers utilizing circuitry and electrical and electronic knowledge. Atlantis had sophisticated computers after race four came and introduced the technology. Their computers were more advanced because they had the multi-use circuit concept and the mathematics to figure out the theory behind it.

There were many, many contributions by race four. The most pronounced and profound are the things mentioned above. Alien race four also contributed the theory of light; what it is and how it functions. The Atlanteans already had an understanding of radiation and saw radiation as a wave phenomenon, just as our people in modern times do. Alien race four made it possible for them to understand the particle phenomenon of radiation. In chemistry and physics, also they helped Atlanteans understand natural radioactivity and artificially amplified radioactivity. They gave them information that eventually led to the development of the nuclear power.

The Atlanteans always had enough electricity because they used small quantities and had very efficient appliances. They were able to get enough electricity from the solar cells and hydroelectric power. They used geothermal power by utilizing the temperature difference of the Earth from the inner crust to the outer crust. They were able to develop atomic power and nuclear power with the information the aliens provided them. What they had was accumulative knowledge. We are talking a long time span during which they developed and compiled scientific knowledge. With each stage, they were a bit more advanced. Other contributions were relatively minor compared to these and were passed on in all the sciences, technology, and mathematics.

The aliens used several different methods of transferring knowledge. In some cases, there was a direct transfer of knowledge, where a member of alien race four worked directly with an Atlantean scientist, usually at a time and place of the alien's choosing. They would take the scientist in a kind of abduction. The second way was for the information to be fed covertly to the Atlantean scientists. They arranged for different material to find its way into the scientist's hands, or a disguised alien would work in their lab and feed them small discoveries that would lead to a major thing.

Aliens did make themselves known to some individuals. Small groups of Atlanteans were aware that there were beings from other planets. It was not a common knowledge but it was talked about and suspected. Those who worked in sciences and technology and the rulers knew about the aliens. It was a secret, but a widely known one. Of course, there were rumors in the general population, but they really did not know for sure.

By this time, the Atlanteans had made transformers, so that they were generating large amounts of power by steam energy. They still had not built any fossil fuel engines to use heat energy to convert to mechanical energy. They developed a fuel cell, again from their understanding of crystals, not on their understanding of the rest of the chemistry.

None of the alien races intended or taught Atlanteans to use these technologies negatively. They intended them to be a cheap and easy source of electric power. They did not intend this to be used as a weapon of destruction or as a means of controlling other people. This was negative to them, something they did not indulge in, and they did not approve of the Atlanteans indulging in it. They could have stopped the Atlanteans but they chose not to.

The following two examples are very interesting. Here, two different people separately recalled a past life in which they interacted with each other. One patient had a past life as a technologist in Atlantis and another patient had a past life as a tall, thin alien of race four who was in Atlantis and was in contact with the technologist mentioned above. They describe the events from their own point of view. The following is a past life of one patient as a technologist in Atlantis who recalled torturing an alien family and demanding that the alien being hand over certain technology to them.

- *"I am a thirty-year-old female living on the east coast of Atlantis in 70,300 BC. My name is Laran Akpick. I am married to another technologist and we have two daughters. I outrank my husband, which becomes a problem in the family. My family came from a farming area and moved into the town. I went to school there for eleven years and then went to technology school for three years. It was my choice and it was free and open. Nobody else decided what I could or could not do.*

*"We live in a two-story house in the city. It has a sloped roof and three bedrooms. We have an electrical heater, which is unusual because electricity is not supposed to be used for heating. We have a receiving unit mounted at the corner of the house. It looks like a cabinet with a metal box and there is a crystal on top. The whole thing is a receiving unit. It takes what is coming into the crystal, modifies it, and sends it out to do the work. We have electric lights, a cooling unit, a refrigerator, which does not have the freezing part, and a stove. My husband and I created a house heater. We have calculators, a broadcast receiver, and a telephone.*

*"I am an upper ranking technologist serving under the chief technologist who serves the ruler. I am primarily involved with the generation and transmission of electricity. There are many sources of generation for the electricity we use. First is geothermal and solar, where we use the difference between the heat in the atmosphere and the temperature of the earth. We also use the solar power directly to generate electricity. The third source is the rising and falling of ocean waves, coupled with the wind action of the waves as they go up and down. We also use tidal forces when the tide comes in and fills a small bay. We close the doors and use the returning water to generate electricity.*

*"Each of these sources generates a relatively small amount, but when added together it is sufficient for the city. We also use the coastal winds, putting windmills up along the shore to be driven day and night by the interchange of the air between the land and the sea. Depending upon the tides, the time of the day, and the time of the year, sometimes there is more wind than there is need for*

Described and drawn by the different hypnotized patients

A solar powered (through crystals) car with 4 seats was used for transportation in Atlantis. A crystal located inside the horizontal hood ornament to insure good radio reception.

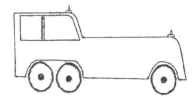

The subway solar powered (through crystals) engine can pull 30 passenger cars containing 900 to 1,000 passengers. The duel rear wheels provide ample traction and safety. The engine features antennae containing crystals for communication with the passenger cars and the station house.

The subway passenger car can seat 30 people comfortably. It features antennae (containing crystals) on the front and rear and double doors which open on each side for easy loading and unloading. These antennae provide for clear communica-tion with each passenger car.

*the electricity. At those times, when other conditions are right, we take extra water and pump it into the bay for generating tidal electricity. So we have water supply in reserve to drain out. This occurs in spring and fall for a period of weeks, when there is not too much demand for electricity during the day.*

Described and drawn by the different hypnotized patients

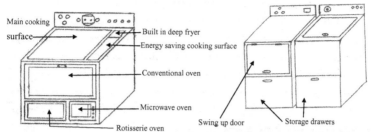

The solar powered stove with crystal inserts (for energy) features a rotisserie oven, a microwave oven, and a conventional oven. It has a built in deep fryer and an energy saving cooking surface. All ovens are equipped with self cleaning devices and a glass front for easy visibility.

The solar powered washer and dryer with crystal inserts (for energy) feature storage drawers in the bottom area. The versatile washer, loaded from the top, can wash everything from industrial to the finest articles of clothing. The versatile dryer is loaded from the front and is equipped to dry all forms of clothing. Its door swings up so that it can be locked in a horizontal position. This provides the user with additional space to manage the clothing.

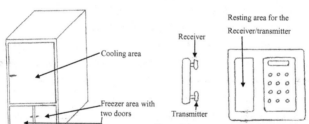

The solar powered refrigerator with crystal inserts (for energy) features a spacious freezer and cooling area. It contains an ice maker in the cooling area and a dry ice maker in the freezer area.

Crystal inserts are built in to the wireless tele-phone which is equipped with a receiver and a transmitter. The phone can be mounted on a wall or placed horizontally on a desk or table. A similar (sometimes smaller) version was used in cars, subway trains, and airplanes.

*"I am very good at my job. I am very organized and pushy enough to get others to work. I also flirt and use my feminine charm to get what I want, primarily with the chief technologist. My husband and I were in the same position but I was promoted and he was transferred to another department, to a dead-end job of maintenance technologist.*

*"I am suspicious that the chief technologist has an alien contact and believe some of the things we are working on are alien-inspired. I notice that he disappears from time to time. One time, I was called by my chief into his office. I saw three people sitting there. They were odd and looked very much alike, and suddenly I perceived that this unusual information we are working on is not native, but alien-inspired. These beings look like tall, thin humans, but their faces are different. They have longer faces, lighter hair, a longer nose, and human-like eyes and lips. Their whole face is elongated or stretched out. They sit high in the chairs.*

*"The chief confirms my suspicions that these beings are aliens and that the project we are working on, which provides better forms of power transmission with crystals, is given by them. This means modifying the crystals so they are more efficient and can handle bigger power loads. The chief calls me into his office another time and tells me he has captured some of the aliens because he wants more information from them, which they are not willing to give. The chief wants the crystal-making technology to control how the crystals are made. The way we build the crystals controls the vibrations that go through them. By making little modifications in the way the crystal is built, it will handle more power, more energy, and will be more efficient. A natural crystal has a power limit, and if we push more power into it, it will fracture. Of course, we cannot get more power out of it when it vibrates into sympathy because it will fracture. So we are limited to a low power exchange. It is not until we start to modify them that the crystals can handle a larger amount of electricity and be more useful.*

*"Human ears can hear about fifty to about twenty thousand cycles per second. Past twenty thousand and below fifty, we cannot hear those sounds. The vibrations that Atlanteans are sending out are affecting sea creatures. It is like a continuous noise and interferes with their feeding, communication, and reproduction. It had a profound effect on sea creatures.*

*"The chief wants more of the technology and wants it now by force. The chief thinks that these aliens do not appear to have any violence in them because they do not have any weapons with them. He wants the technology of heavy-duty power transmission. Then he wants the crystal-growing technology. He also realized that the aliens have technology that they have not shared, such as some of their calculators, and he would like to have things like that to work with and to understand.*

*"It is an alien family; a male, female, and two children. The female looks just like her husband but is shorter. She just gives an impression of being female. There are no feminine characteristics such as big breasts or anything like that. They each wear a robe, and there is clothing underneath. The chief has strapped them to a board, which can be moved from place to place. The male alien seems to have information and the chief wants me to torture the female and the children to make the male break down and give the information. He wants me to bring the electrical unit and give the male alien a couple of shocks, first to experience what it feels like. Then he wants me to give shocks to the female, like sticking the probes in two different spots on her neck, which causes spasms in the neck and a twisting of the head. Then I give shocks to the kids.*

*"I put headphones on the male and hit him with a couple of sound blasts and then do the same to the wife and kids. The intensity of the sound vibration is extreme and unbearable. This is when he wants to talk and the chief wants me to stop. As the male alien and the chief are speaking, I continue to give shocks to the female every now and then, so when she screams, it is like a warning to the male not to fool around.*

*"The alien agrees to give the technology but he does not have it here. The chief is in a dilemma. If he lets them go they might come back with weapons or bring more aliens. The alien writes the message to the other aliens on the spaceship. The other aliens decide to give some of the stuff the chief asked for and they will take steps*

*to get their people back. Four alien beings are sent with the technological information. They also have protective devices and weapons, in case they have to use them. They handed over written information on the technology but did not explain it, and take their people back to the spaceship.*

*"The aliens complained to the ruler and other people they were in contact with and it has repercussions for the chief and me. We both lose our jobs. The aliens become a lot more careful with the information they share and do not trust people as much anymore. We both get jobs in an electrical industry whose people want the information the chief received from the aliens. We have the backing of the industry now. The chief tells the head of the company all about the aliens and the contacts in the past. It is the industry that actually causes the biggest problems.*

*"The aliens were dealing with a very limited number of people. Before, the industry got its information from the government but now the alien technology goes from the chief to the labs of the industry. The industry people figure out where the spaceship is, in the mountainous area of Atlantis. They send a military force to the spaceship and capture the alien and bring him to our headquarters. The alien is tortured to get more information about these devices, how they work, what they do, and how they are made. We torture him with electrical sounds and shocks. This goes on for about five days and then we end up strangling him.*

*"A group of seven adult male aliens, two females, and two children come to rescue him but he has already been murdered. This time they are not as nice. The last time they did not do anything about the kidnapping and torture except control the information flow. This time, they fire their weapons, which are like electric convulsion devices, so the people get a very heavy shock. It is like a stun gun, only you do not even have to hit with the ray. It is a transmitted ray. They find the dead alien's body and take it back to their spaceship. They are absolutely furious. They*

*move their ship a couple of mountains away and hide it better. There is no more alien contact with this city.*

*"I get divorced and my kids pull away from me. I die at the age of sixty-eight from cancer of the brain, which was caused by the lower powered radiation. I have delusions, hallucinations, an inability to communicate, poor vision, and pain. I die thinking that nothing worked out too well in this life. There are not too many thoughts. My spirit comes out of the body and is feeling very bitter and angry with my ex-husband and the children. I try to attack my daughters for rejecting me. One of my granddaughters is aware that I am there and tells her mother, but she does not believe it. The daughter does the blessing and the clearing ceremony on the house and I get forced out. I go to the other daughter's house and attack her. I enter inside her body and try to affect her. I come out of her body after her death and follow her to the heaven.*

*"I am taken to a debriefing table, where I ventilate my anger with a couple of heavenly beings. As I talk, I begin to calm down. Then after cleansing, I am sent to review my life. There is Marduk the sea god, who helps me with the review. I am seeing the instances of cruelty, anger, the pain and suffering I caused to the other people. I see that my life was like a canoe trying to fight the current and paddle upstream, and did not make much progress. Now I am realizing that I was moving in the opposite direction. If I had gone a slightly different route, I could have been carried along with the current and by my own efforts.*

*"From heaven, I see that this was the lifetime to overcome the childhood physical, emotional, and sexual abuse by both parents. I was supposed to forgive my parents and move on in spite of that negative childhood. I was supposed to develop self-confidence by overcoming the childhood abuse. I had to learn to be self-loving, self-activating, and to have compassion for others and myself. I could have grown to do creative work in technology. I planned to contribute to the original technology given by*

*the aliens and come up with further discoveries myself. I was supposed to discover a way of strengthening the crystals so they could handle much larger power loads and make them a lot more useful. But I failed because I did not grow out of the childhood abuse and did not develop self-compassion.*

*"Marduk is saying that I planned to extend the alien research. They handed me a way to improve the crystals by a factor of ten. I was supposed to take this and be able to double up with the ideas and extend the power-handling capability of the crystals by a factor of one hundred. Ten times more than what the aliens gave me, which would have been a shock to the aliens too. It could have been a great benefit to the people of Atlantis, if I had lived the life as I had planned. Also part of the development I was supposed to make after overcoming the childhood trauma was through religion and personal spiritual development, which did not happen because I did not overcome the childhood trauma.*

*"From heaven, I see the problems that came from that life to this life are neck spasms and pain because of what I did to the aliens, and memory problems due to brain tumors.*

*"Another patient recalled a past life as a tall, thin alien being whose friend was tortured and killed by a technologist who wanted the alien being to hand over technological information to his associates."*

• *"I am an alien male about two hundred and eighteen earth years old, living in about 70,307 BC. I am about six feet five inches tall as you measure. I have blondish white hair, a long face, elongated ears, a long nose, and my eyes are watery bluish green with sparse eyebrows and light colored eyelashes. I have two hands, two legs, one head, and a single backbone. I have a thumb and three fingers. I am wearing a white robe. I am living on a spaceship based on the mountains on Atlantis, for about forty-five years. Before this we lived in an exploration base on another planet in buildings, and not just on the ship. It was a planet we were exploring, hoping to find a place for ourselves.*

*"Our planet was destroyed by another alien race a long time ago. We were essentially peaceful but they attacked us. The ones who were on the spaceships exploring other planets survived. We try not to be bitter and blame the alien race that destroyed our planet. We wish them no ill will. I have been told that they were shorter than we are, about five to five and a half feet tall. They had advanced technology, even beyond ours, and they were able to set up a vibration field on our planet, which eventually caused the explosion of our planet.*

*"I was born on the spaceship. I was trained as a specialist in crystals, chemistry, and physics. We can communicate with other people of our race, on spaceships and elsewhere. We can travel and also transfer small objects from one spaceship to another, or even to another planet, with a device we have. At long range, it requires that the beam be very focused. Over a huge, long distance, you can only send a small object that will fit inside the beam. But if you are only a few thousand miles apart, you can have a large, diffuse beam, and you can put very large objects into the beam and have them emerge at another place.*

*"There are several reasons why we are on your planet in Atlantis. First, we have to re-equip our ship. We are taking on food and processing it into storable units in large quantities. We are also storing water. We want to make all necessary repairs and get our ship's stores back to standard. We are searching for fuel or materials we can use to fuel the spacecraft. When all this is done, we could leave, but it is taking quite a while to find fuel. We found deposits of the radioactive materials here that we need for fuel. We are on this planet to re-supply the ship. You cannot run a spaceship in space forever. Every now and then, we*

*have to restock our food, water, air, and fuel supplies. We have just about enough air compressed and frozen to last awhile. We have to mine the fuel, which takes a long time.*

*"We land our spaceship on the top of the mountain because there are very few people who come here. Also this is the area where the fuel is, and since digging the fuel is the hardest part, it is best that we be here for a while. Of course, collecting enough food to re-supply the ship takes a while too.*

*"There are about ten adult males, five females, one adolescent boy, one girl, and eight children, three boys and five girls. Our ship resembles a tube, pointed at one end and tapered at the other, with the fins located at the bottom and halfway up at the waist of the spacecraft like a rocket. The food storage area takes up the major part of the spaceship. The water and fuel storage areas take up a large part of what is left. The actual living quarters are not all big and there is not much room for controls. The cargo area will be packed with food and water. The spaceship is almost four hundred feet long and forty feet in diameter.*

*"We watch and examine people in Atlantis. We resemble them enough, depending on the population you mix with, so that we can pass for one of them. We choose to land in Atlantis because it has mountains handy, has plenty of food, an organized culture and government, and fuel. It is the first time our ship has been to Earth. For the quantities of food we need to store, we have to make contact with people and arrange for the food to be placed where we can obtain it.*

*"We do this by trade. We are not thieves. We have things that can be of value to these people. They know very little, but they raise good food successfully. Technologically, they do not know much, so we can upgrade their technology just a little bit, which can make a great improvement in their lives, and get everything we need in return. The culture here is good for dealing in crystals and ceramics.*

*We make improvements to their crystal-growing and their ceramic technology. It is a fair trade; otherwise it will take them generations to perfect. We can give them the technology much earlier and at the same time pay for the food we have to have.*

*"We deal with the rulers and the ruling classes directly. We avoid the common people and make our deals with those who actually run the government. They collect the food for us and we transport it to our ship. We are all happy. We have dealings with many of the government individuals scattered around this island. Inevitably, we know that technology will spread, and in a matter of time, every technologist on the planet will end up with the same information, but for a while they have the exclusive franchise on the information in their territories.*

*"They are using crystals for power transmission. We can give them methods of growing crystals that will improve the quality of their crystals. Their use of crystals is quite limited. They are quite used to growing them but do not have much in the way of sophistication. So we can show them how to add impurities or variations in the crystal structure that will change the electrical properties of the crystal and make it possible for the crystal to transmit greater power loads. After they accumulate that information and make it part of their continent-wide technology, we can teach them another simple device, and thus we pay as we go. We feed them technology a little bit at a time, and as it works through their culture, we give them a little bit more.*

*"We pay for the ore we mine. Sometimes we actually pay for workers who help in mining the ore. We need it for fuel for the spaceship. It has to be purified, extracted, and put into a form we can handle easily, and then transported to the ship and put in our fuel bins. The ones who provide the food get the franchise in that area. We give out the same information on the north, south, west, and*

east, and the central cities. The city we give information
to can make the devices, which they can sell to make more
money. It costs us practically nothing and benefits them
greatly.

"We are continuing with our metal working, ore mining, and food storing. We have enough water. We have almost enough metals accumulated, because this planet is
rich in metals. Ore mining is the slowest and most difficult
job. It turns out that the natives are quite susceptible to
the radiation, so they cannot work for long periods.

"We have mechanical helpers on the ship that are like
tireless robots. They can repeat the same task innumer-
able times with high accuracy. They can perform more
precise movements than we can, and there are some jobs
they are much better suited to carry out than we are. We
have about forty of them on our spaceship.

"When we first came, we tried to take simple technology and distribute it in various places on Earth, such as
Europe, Africa, the Middle East, Southeast Asia, India,
China, Australia, and other places, but it did not spread;
instead, it disappeared. We started with a little bit of electricity and the people we introduced it to were fascinated
by it but they did not understand it and, in time, it died
down.

"We found we were not welcome when we tried to give
technology to Lamuria because they had no use for it and
did not want it. They did not laugh at us, but we noticed
there was something different about them. In Lamuria,
when we tried to introduce electricity, they rejected it.
They were not operating as everyone else. They had a different sense of the world and a different understanding
and, as a result, did not seem to need radios and electricity. It is a shame we no longer have them here to study.
Those who survived have dispersed all over the world and
merged into the local culture. They passed everything
down to their children. They were an interesting culture
to study. I wish we had understood them better.

*"We cannot just give the technology. Sometimes we have to go there and demonstrate. We discovered that humans are not rational beings. Sometimes they want more than they can handle and want it immediately. Some of them act rashly and foolishly. If it comes down to it, we have the capability to destroy a city, to remove it from the face of Atlantis, but it is something we would not do. Our representatives have been attacked and forced to hand over more technology and completed devices that they will never understand and we had to have more than one rescue operation to free our people.*

*"We had an instance where one of our persons was killed before we got to him. We did not know where he was when we were attempting a rescue. They kidnapped my friend Uhrar and his family. He was dealing with a chief technologist in the city of Katar. They captured him and his family and tortured them in an effort to force us to give them more technology immediately. We made arrangements to deliver more technology, making sure that they cannot understand it. Our heavily armed rescue team went out and brought him back, along with his whole family. Then we got into contact with the ruler of this city, and the chief technologist and his associates were removed from their jobs. Then we reestablished contact with the ruler. We are much more valuable to the rulers than the chief technologist.*

*"After a while, there is an armed attack on our metalworking operation near the ship, and my friend Uhrar is there at the time. Several of our people are killed and Uhrar was captured. They took him with them. We are not exactly sure who has attacked us, which slowed the process down. When we finally figured out from which city the attack came, the ruler and the people there profess absolute ignorance and it did seem to be true that they had no idea where the attack came from and they had not authorized the attack. We finally figured it out that it was the chief technologist and his assistant who have gotten*

*jobs in an industry. They talked their bosses into attacking us in an effort to get more technology. By the time we managed to figure all this out, five days later, the rescue team finally located him but it was too late. My friend had been severely tortured and killed by strangulation. We were very despondent, and even felt responsible. If we had figured it out sooner, he might still be alive.*

*"We do believe in a Supreme Being and we believe in forces of evil. We have seen both at work but we do not think of evil in our day-to-day life. When we gave technology to Atlanteans, we did not think they could use it for evil purposes. It was a perfectly straightforward business deal.*

*"At this time, as far as we know, there are no other beings of our race on the planet Earth. We are the only ones and have been there for almost forty-five years. When we move, we leave markings and maps so others of our race can find the mines easily when they come. We also inform the other people of our race about the bargaining tactics we have used with the rulers and what we have traded with them.*

*"I am dying when I am eight hundred and thirty years old. I am dying of accumulated metal poisoning from too many mining operations over the years. The metals accumulate in the cells. We have good masks and good techniques, but eventually over the years, we do accumulate metal. We had moved to a new site closer to a mine on the other side of Atlantis. As I am dying, we are in space moving from one planet to another. I am feeling tremors all over and am in poor control of my limbs. There is interference in my nerve impulses, an irregular heartbeat, and eventually my heart stops.*

*"My last thoughts are that it is best to meet a well-controlled race, one that is well-organized, well-disciplined, and safer to deal with. That relieves us of worry about them attacking us. We lost quite a few people on different planets with unprovoked attacks. It made us pretty leery*

*of having personal contacts with those people. We have now established a policy of bringing people to us one at a time; that way we are not put in so much danger.*

*"When my spirit comes out of the physical body, I am no longer shaking. My family remains with my body for a while. Friends come by and speak to my family and pray. They disassemble my body and the elements in it are restored in the ship for future purposes as organic chemicals. I see my deceased family members in the Light and they take me to the Light (heaven). After cleansing, I am sent for the life review. There is a council of five people. I see that many people who were there in that life are also here in this current life.*

*"I see my lung problems, digestive problems, and the generalized fine tremors are coming from that life to the current life. I also see that I lived many lives on these aliens' planet before it was destroyed.*

*"From heaven, I see that we provided Atlanteans technology that was valuable to them. From our point of view, it cost us nothing and we got everything we needed. It was a legitimate business deal. We were kind of surprised by how inventive these humans were. Some of the things they came up with, there was no logical precursor to it. It was just a leap out of the blue. Something beyond our comprehension as to how, they figured it out. We told other people of our race about this.*

*"We have also seen that humans do not think like us. They do not act in sensible or logical ways, which we have known for a long time. We gave them technology we thought was harmless, and they found a way to do harm with it. This is another example of their ingenuity and inventiveness although it is a pretty negative one."*

### *Mystery of the Bermuda Triangle*

The Bermuda Triangle is an area in the Atlantic Ocean between Florida, Bermuda, and the Sargasso Sea where many ships and planes, along with people, have vanished without a trace. The patient in the case above described how, in that past life as the tall, thin alien being in Atlantis, the aliens had devices on their bases in the mountains of Atlantis through which they could travel or transfer objects from one place to another, one spaceship to another, or from one planet to another. I wondered if what is happening in the Bermuda Triangle was a similar phenomenon. I asked the heavenly beings who were helping us during the session.

According to heavenly beings, the falling through the space-time continuum to another dimension or another part of space does happen in this universe. In their mountain bases, which were hidden from the Atlanteans, they used these devices for travel or to ship materials to places on Earth, in the same continent, from continent to continent, from their ships in space, and even from one planet to another planet. One of these devices is still operating. It is a device in one of their headquarters, not too far under the water, on the side of an Atlantean mountain. It was a place the Atlanteans never thought of climbing, so they never knew what was there. They knew the tall, skinny aliens were there and they knew they just showed up, but they did not know how it was that they managed to appear out of nowhere or how they disappeared into nowhere. This was the transportation and the communication device. They had several in Atlantis. This one is still working.

When anything enters the field of that device, it creates an inter-dimensional pathway and it is capable of projecting itself. The transfer point can appear in the middle of the sky or in the ocean or even on an island, and if the plane, boat, or even water or air moves into this point, it is transferred to another planet or another spot in space, depending on where the device is sending at that time. Depending on where the machine is projecting, people or things can be sucked in. It can happen to anyone and at any time. All of a sudden, the air around persons or objects is transferred to another place and all one can hope is that when you come out to the other side, it will be a place that can support life. Sometimes they come out on an earthlike planet; other times they can come out on another planet or in space. According to heavenly beings, we cannot remove these devices spiritually because they are physical devices.

### Alien Race Five of Group Two

According to my hypnotized patients, alien race five of group two came to the Earth about 50,000 BC, well before the destruction of Atlantis. They are about four to five feet tall, human-like, short, muscular, and stocky. This race provided refinement and made the Atlantean system more efficient. There were quite a few ideas and thoughts in Atlanteans that had not been correlated. Alien race five provided the idea and technology so that the information could be used in a better way. They refined most of the technology to make it more energy efficient, faster, and more accurate. They made metals better and taught the skills of carpentry, metal working, planning, co-coordinating, designing, and actually building large projects such as temples and pyramids. They also found Atlanteans to be the most advanced race on Earth. So they spent most of their time with them.

Heavenly beings, through my hypnotized patients, say that one of the genetic modifications done by this race was that they took two different plants, mixed them together and created a new seed, which we know as wheat. Since wheat was not a natural grain on Earth because it was genetically modified, many people developed allergies to it, leading to abdominal bloating, cramping, water retention, weight gain, high blood pressure, etc. It has a high percentage of carbohydrates and is a hunger-creating grain. Those who are allergic to it tend to retain water and add fat easily because the body gets twisted and cannot turn food into energy. So the food gets converted into fat and is stored. Parts of the plant are not good for people; as a result, their body reacts to it. Initially large numbers of people developed severe allergies to wheat and died in childhood. Many people in current life are allergic to wheat, suffering with bloating, cramps, high blood pressure, water retention, and weight gain. It is one of the common reasons for obesity currently.

These aliens first went to countries that had large populations, such as India, Japan, and China. Compared to Atlantis, very little technology was given to them and other parts of the world. This is part of the reason why, when the fall of Atlantis came, it came so completely. The other countries did not have the vested interest in technology that the Atlanteans had. In fact, the other areas on Earth had very little technology. They used simple machines, simple physics, chemistry, and mathematics, but not the sophisticated stuff the Atlanteans were using.

The Atlanteans had already developed and were using control devices when alien race five arrived on Earth. This race should have been warned, should have been aware, and should have seen, but they were also influenced by the demons and did not recognize the dark influences. They ignored what was happening; not that they consciously would have approved Atlanteans' mind control activities, but in a way, they gave passive approval by continuing to work with them.

The drawback to this side of the story was that, when the Atlanteans went to other parts of the world and settled in as refugees after the destruction of Atlantis, the natives of those other countries did not have mechanisms to keep them out of the cities. They did not have the technology needed. After the destruction of Atlantis, the Atlanteans, who had superior weapons and superior organization, decided not to use any technology. They made their policy to destroy what they found and to renounce its use for themselves.

Alien race five saw the Atlanteans controlling the general population but did nothing about it. They were also influenced by Satan and his demons and did not recognize this. The people of their planet had a good deal of influence. They were loving, generous, kind, and were connected with God, but did not have knowledge of the dark side and did not recognize the dark influence in themselves and in Atlantis.

Heavenly beings, through my hypnotized patients, state that alien races four and five are still working with us today and are careful not to make the same mistakes. They recognized the bad effects they had on Atlantis when the culture collapsed and fell apart. It came as a shock to both alien races four and five. They thought that all those technological advancements were positive things and did not realize how Atlanteans were misusing them. Alien races four and five were aware of Satan and his demons to some extent, but they did not recognize the dark influence in Atlanteans or in themselves. They might have figured it out when they saw the patterns emerging and saw the result, but not before. They were not very spiritual races like race three of group two.

This was a being of the fifth race of group two, as described in chapter three. At this point, I decided to heal that race on different planets wherever they were living at this time. I prayed to God and requested the angels of Light to collect and remove all the foreign spirits, including the dark entities, dark energies, dark devices, and dark connections from each and every being of that alien race. Cleanse their bodies, auras, souls, connecting cords to God, energy centers, kundalini, meridians, psychic antennae, their surroundings and spaceships, and all the planets where they are living or have bases, including the Earth; lift them up, help them to the Light or bind them in space. Scrub and scour; take away any residue that is left over. Bring all their missing soul parts back to them, including the ones for their emotions and spirituality, cleanse them, heal them, fill them with Light and integrate them with whom they belong. Create a shield of Light around them and their connecting cords to God. Cover the shields, with a triple net of Light, a violet shield, with reflective mirrors and rays of white Light around each and every one of them, their dwellings, work places, spaceships, and the planets. Open their connecting cords to God. I pray to God to please fill them with love, Light, emotions, and spirituality, and guide them in the right direction. I request each and every being's higher self, guides, and angels to please connect with them and guide them in the right direction.

The patient described, "I see the healings being done and soul parts are brought back to all their chakras and the DNA, as if rebuilding them all over differently. I see reactions in these beings, such as annoyance at having these silly thoughts. Some are intrigued by a unique and different way to think of it and are playing with the ideas and thoughts in their minds, extending them and what they might mean. I see a whole gamut of reactions in these beings, starting from instant and absolute acceptance to wondering why they were having such a silly thought, which may get questioned and incorporated sooner or later. The archangels are also saying that the whole race is cleansed and healed, and in time, they will heal. They are telling it is part of your job, Dr. Modi, to help with the healing of multiple races in the universe, upon multiple levels. This is in keeping with your purposes."

## Golden Age in Atlantis

The Golden Age in Atlantis was from 70,000 to 50,000 BC. During this time, Atlantis had a strong organized government and people were cooperating with each other all over the country. It was the most powerful nation on Earth, with trade and information flowing back and forth with explorations, settlements, and colonies. This was the time period when there was rapid technological, medical, and architectural advancement and many things came into being. They learned to build small airplanes, to get electrical power on ships, and they had enough electricity to live well. They were able to communicate long distances. They had ways of communicating over wires or through space, where they could get messages from one place to another, via mechanical devices and through crystals. The crystal, of course, is a natural tuning mechanism as well as a natural transmitter.

Crystals tuned to each other could be used to exchange messages over a long distance, like sending a telegraph early on. Eventually, there was voice transmission, image transmission, and radio transmission, which was developed after the aliens arrived around 70,000 BC.

It was a positive, happy, highly functioning, and fairly balanced society at this time. Everybody seemed to have plenty from the economic perspective. It was a good society from a cultural, social, environmental, and medical perspective. There were lots of theaters and fine music. Even average and lower class people had a comfortable lifestyle. Everybody had education and a chance to go to college if they chose. There was a lot of harmony in the society and rulers cared for their people. It was a pretty happy, productive, positive, and contented society. They had more emphasis on science and technology but little emphasis on spirituality.

### Technologists in the Golden Age

Technologists during the Golden Age were actively doing research and inventing different technologies, which added to the prosperity of the country. Top technologists were selected by the rulers to oversee technology programs in the whole city. They were given a place to live in the palace or in the palace compound, and they became a member of the ruling class and were provided all facilities and luxuries of the royalties. One of my patients, under hypnosis, recalled a past life when he was a technologist in Atlantis as follows:

- *"I am a forty-five-year-old male living in Sire City, located in the south of Atlantis. My name is Runi and this is 71,432 BC. I am married and have three children, a boy twenty, a girl seventeen, and another boy fifteen. I am a technologist working with crystals. I am living in a lavish house near the palace for the past five years. My mother is an engineer and my father a physician. I grew up in an upper-class neighborhood. I had twelve years of school equivalent to our high school, and then five years of college. I had courses in mathematics, chemistry, physics, and courses relating to general and crystal technology. I chose to become a crystal engineer.*

*"We are growing crystals in the laboratory and use them as a power source for different machinery, including for cars, trains, airplanes, for electricity, and different electrical and electronic appliances. After finishing college, I worked for a private company that designed computers. Then I worked for a government electrical power plant. I was also doing research in the advance use of crystals, where they can be used in medical technology for pacemakers. I am also doing research to see if crystals can be used to cure or heal, where they somehow alter the cell mechanism and cause it to possibly heal a cancer. I also developed advanced crystal computers.*

*"I am selected to be a technologist to work with the other technologists for the ruler of the city. I was appointed to live and work in the palace because I had seventeen years of experience in different technologies. I am recognized as a top expert in crystal technology. I moved into a beautiful house in the palace compound. Normally a priest and a technologist are born in the general population, but when they are appointed by the ruler to work in the palace, they move to live either in a section of the palace or in the compound of the palace. When this happens, they become a member of the ruling class. There are twelve technologists appointed by the ruler at this time.*

*"My job is to advise the ruler about what we can do to better educate and train our technologists and how we can develop new technology to improve our society. I am also responsible to prepare the educational curriculum, along with the priests who also live in the palace. High priests are actually responsible for all education in different fields in our city and in all the other cities in Atlantis. They consult directors of all the different educational fields and then set up the curriculum.*

*"There is a research laboratory where I do research. We grow crystals in the lab to suit our needs. They are like tiny computers that are used for certain purposes. We use crystals for everything as a power source. They can be as small as a head of a pin, while others can be as big as a dime or a quarter. Some are round and flat while others are elongated like the usual crystals, from a very small to a very large size, depending on the purpose. I also teach in the colleges.*

*"Our society is very advanced and people are happy and live in harmony with each other. Everybody has freedom to live the way they want to live. Everyone has plenty and nobody is poor. Our ruler is bright, positive, progressive, and cares about his people. He tries to do right by the people. We have solar powered electricity, electrical appliances, computers, telephones, and television. We also have different solar powered vehicles such as cars, trains, airplanes, boats, and ships.*

*"We have various forms of entertainment places in our city, such as movie theaters and the theater for performances. We also watch movies and other programs on our televisions at home. We, being a ruling class, are invited to the palace for different parties. Sometimes dancers and entertainers are brought in for a performance in the palace from all over Atlantis.*

*"My wife is a high ranking government employee, like a secretary of state or a cabinet member. She has a lot of power and a lot of prestige, and can represent the ruler at different events in and outside the city. Our youngest son also became a technologist, the daughter married a sub-ruler, and the eldest son is working his way up in the government.*

*"At the age of sixty, I am appointed as the director, or chief technologist, for the whole city by the ruler and I am given a lavish apartment in the palace. I am in charge of all the technologists in the city. I plan and monitor all the education and research programs in technology.*

*"At the age of sixty-one, while living in the palace, I am contacted by three tall, thin, human-like aliens who are about six feet to six feet eight inches tall. I am sitting in my office and thinking about the computer chip when they just appear from nowhere. They are about one half or one third the size of a human in width. They have long faces, bigger eyes, long noses, and a little bit of dark and unmanageable straight hair growing wild. They have an ear on each side, like humans. The hands have four fingers and one thumb, with five toes on each foot. They are wearing white lab coats and white trousers.*

*"They tell me they can provide more efficient ways of designing a computer chip. We are communicating mentally. They met with the ruler and made a deal to give us technology and we will give them large quantities of grains and other food to store in their spaceship. They also mine the fuel for their spaceship. I meet them several times over the years. It is with their help that I develop the new computer chip, and they show me how to develop better crystals in a short time. They also work with other government technologists.*

*"I retire at the age of seventy-six. By this time, I have invented very small computer chips that hold a large amount of information. I have improved different technologies, making them more efficient and user-friendly. I am happy with my life and accomplishments. After I retire, I move to a well provided home in the section for retired rulers, with all the conveniences and all the domestic services I had in the palace. At the age of ninety-two, I have a mild heart attack and am taken to the hospital. There I had another heart attack and I die.*

*"I stay around for several years because I did not know where to go till some angels help me to heaven. In my life review in heaven, I see that I planned to develop and refine different technologies to make people's life easier and I succeeded in achieving these goals."*

## Medical Technology During the Golden Age

Atlanteans, in their prime time before the control, on average, lived a long life. They had excellent medical care, and a very good understanding of biology and pharmacology. They were much superior than the current time. They were working with technology. They did not think of cutting with a knife for surgery. With them, by the time they got around to surgery, it was laser-based. They started from that.

They had advanced technology. They were doing microsurgery from outside the body, using technology to reach inside the body through a tiny opening. They did complex surgery at the very beginning, like we do now. We still do not have microminiaturization and the ability to actually use a tiny device to do the work at a remote location as they did. They had remote viewing; that is, they could see what was going on in the sinus cavity and used a little device that could go in the sinuses and do the surgery. They also did organ transplants. My patients recalled the following past lives when they were physicians in Atlantis.

- *"I am a thirty-three-year-old male living in the north-eastern city of Atlantis called Gaar. This is 64,620 BC. I have dark brown skin, black hair, and black eyes. My wife works in a library and I have three children, ages six, four, and two. I live in a beautiful house that has two stories. The upper story contains four bedrooms, bathrooms, and a sitting room and office. Downstairs, there is a kitchen, a living room, and a recreation room. We have a stove, refrigerator, TV, computer, VCR, and a radio.*

  *"I came from a middle class family. I wanted to become a doctor and because I scored well on my tests, I was allowed to go to medical school. I am a surgeon working in a hospital in the city. I have an office in the hospital and another office for consulting work. I do different organ transplants, including heart transplants. I see patients in the hospital before and after the surgery and also in my*

*office outside the hospital. The hospital looks like an industrial building made of stone blocks. It has five stories and has about five hundred-bed capacity.*

*I have been doing kidney and heart transplants and also laser surgery. I am also involved in teaching and consulting. I work very conscientiously and care for my patients a great deal.*

*"I die of heart failure at 360 years of age of their time, or 90 years of our time. It was a full and satisfying life. After my death, they cremate my body after the priest gives thanks to different animal gods. Angels help my spirit to heaven.*

*"In heaven, I review my life after cleansing and resting. I see that this life was a good life overall. Although we did not have much belief in One God and did not pray, Atlantis was not all dark or evil at this time. There was a lot of Light and people were living a very advanced and prosperous life. Everybody had a choice about how he or she wanted to live and what he or she wanted to do. It was a great society and there was no control by rulers and other hierarchy. They were fair and caring."*

- *"I am a fifty-six-year-old doctor in Atlantis. I am married and have two children. My wife is a plant chemist. I have a home by the lake. It looks like a mixing bowl turned upside down. There is a pregnant woman who is sitting in what looks like a dentist chair, and the lower part of the chair goes into water in a tub. She doesn't look like she is in pain at all. She has a smile on her face and looks like she is in bliss. She has not been given any drugs. She has headphones, not on her ears, but on her temples. There is a sound in the room like the ocean. The vibrations from the sound are conducted through her temple bones to her whole body. All the women in the room have earplugs, because they are not supposed to hear the sound since they might respond to the vibration. That sound makes the body so relaxed that there is no resistance with dilatation or birth, but it affects other women, too. They would also feel too relaxed so they have to use earplugs to avoid it.*

*"I am holding a crystal pyramid in my hand. The crystal pyramid is heavy and as big as the palm of my hand. The lower part of her body is under water and her legs are spread apart. My hand and crystal are also under water and I am pointing the crystal toward her perineum. The vibrations of the crystal have a soothing effect. It disperses the energy to the other areas. The crystal acts as a diffuser. The sound vibrations are doing all the work. The sound is coming from a frequency box. It has dials that can be set at different frequencies. We put a drop of blood of the person from a finger prick. We also put the swirls of the person's fingertips on the box with a drop of blood. The blood and the pattern of the fingertips help us find the right frequencies. I discovered this machine and technique when I was thirty-two. I train other doctors in how to use it. It is just wonderful. There are no downside or pain, and it is very effective.*

*"Every person has his or her own healing vibrations and there are ways to find that vibration. When you find the vibration and play the sound, it will heal them without any pain. It is also used during surgery. It is like an ultrasound.*

*"The device or the sound box looks black and is about three or four inches in diameter. On the top, there is an indentation where you put your index finger. Then a lens comes from the bottom and causes a very tiny pin prick. A drop of blood is analyzed. They also measure the swirls on the index finger. It analyzes the precise individual sounds. The sound comes through the headphones, which are connected to the box, and spreads all over the body through bone conduction. The box has an electrical source.*

*"This device can be used for all ages, both male and female, and for many different conditions and diseases, such as purifying the blood from parasites by stimulating the immune system, fighting infections, and removing*

*"tumors or gallstones. Patients do not need anesthesia because there is no pain."*

- *"I am a forty-two-year-old male living on the east coast of Atlantis. This is about 60,000 BC. I was an engineer and then later I became a physician. I am working with a team of seven members from three fields: medicine to do surgery, physics to create lasers, and psychics. We brought people from these three fields together so we can work on a hologram that has all the sections of the whole body. Everything that was in the big body was also in this little hologram. It looks like an MRI machine. It takes three lasers at each point, in each direction, to get the image. It has depth and thickness. It makes a perfect image. The reason it works is because there is an energy connection between the holographic model and the actual person. The holographic model and the person are very close when they do the work, so that their consciousness and emotional and mental electrical energy will not affect what we are doing.*

  *"We can do most surgery except on older people, bleeding problems, and births, like caesarean sections, because you cannot take live things out. You can take parts, dead tissue, or tumors out with psychic energy, but our first choice is to dissolve them if we can, with chemicals that we inject into the holographic model. Then we do not have to do anything. There is no incision or pain; it is all energy. I was forty-two when we had the working model.*

  *"To remove a tumor from the body, we first use the red laser to make an incision, and then we use the green laser, which stops the bleeding. Usually we try to dissolve the tumor if possible. If we have to cut it, we cut it out with red and blue lasers. Then, with psychic surgery, we put the hand on the top of the body, gently scoop the tumor out or lift it out, just by mind control or energy healing. People usually recover completely within three to five days.*

  *"I retired when I was sixty-four-years-old. I died when I was eighty-three years of age. I had a pretty good life.*

*I regret that I did not spend much time with my family. I worked hard. Since I retired, they have improved the technique a lot. The psychic abilities were not understood at this time but the technique was accepted.*

*"As I review my life in heaven, I see that some of the ideas were given to us during our sleep or, sometimes, while working with tall, thin aliens. I see the technique we invented to help people positively will be used negatively in the future by 40,000 BC. I see in future people in one large room that has the same electromagnetic field. The technologists put an implant in one hologram and it will affect everyone. Thus they will not have to physically put the implants in one at a time. They can put the implant in one hologram and it will be done for everybody. They also give them impulses to do things the rulers want, such as to be loyal to the rulers, not to be rebellious against the rulers, not feel tired no matter how hard they work, etc.*

*"There will be time-released chemicals and electrical messages sent to them and they will follow those automatically, like robots. They have models for different functions, such as: to be an explorer, to do farm work, or be a soldier, to be stronger so they do not wear out, etc. They put implants in joints for strength or put rods in the bones. It is more like the movie Terminator. If they are going to be runners, they will fix their legs so they can run really fast, and their hip joints will not wear out. If they are going to be lifters, they will put things in them so they will be strong and their wrist, elbow, shoulder, and back joints will not wear out. If they are going to work under water, they put some kind of canister system in their lungs to give them increased capacity so they do not require as much oxygen. They insert different devices in people to enhance their functioning."*

• *"I am a thirty-five-year-old man with a wife and two children. Our daughter is seven and our son is five. My name is Arvis Shakel and I live in the city of Roar, which is located in the north central part of Atlantis. It is 65,000 BC. I am five feet seven inches tall and I have dark tan skin. My wife is a lab technician and I am an orthopedic surgeon. We have lived in the same high-rise apartment during our seven years of marriage. Our lavishly furnished apartment is located on the twentieth floor. We have a large kitchen, a dining room, a recreation room, a living room, two bathrooms, and four bedrooms. We have a television, a VCR for movies, a radio, a computer, and a variety of kitchen appliances. We have hardwood floors, fine carpets, beautiful wall hangings, and our own car.*

*"I had four years of undergraduate education, five years of medical school and two years of residency before becoming an orthopedic surgeon. I am becoming well known and respected for my work. I work in a hospital and I have my own office. I have been successful in substituting animal bones into humans. I am becoming known for taking impossible cases and making them successful. I have done numerous screw and pin operations with good success. Our hospital has an excellent physical therapy program. We use a good deal of water therapy in our hospital. We all care about the welfare of our patients.*

*"Our operating rooms are well lighted with state of the art technology. We do laser surgery for certain operations on the eyes. We use laser technology to remove nodules and other growths, to break up kidney stones, and to stop bleeding.*

*"I typically do my surgeries from six to ten a.m. I see patients from two to six p.m. in the hospital and in my office. I also do consulting work and I will start teaching in the immediate future. We (other physicians and I) treat everyone, rich or poor. There is no discrimination. I am paid by the hospital, and privately by my patients. Ours is a government-operated hospital. The concept of insurance exists and some of our patients carry medical insurance. I continue my studies in orthopedics and I am involved in doing research on animals.*

*"We are a close family, and my wife and I are greatly involved in our children's affairs. We go to movies, visit our parks, eat out, and enjoy each other's company. We have maidservants for our apartment. These folks cook our meals, clean our apartment, and do other chores. We pay them well and have a good relationship with them.*

*"I stop doing major surgery when I am sixty-four, but I stay on to teach and consult until I am seventy, and then I retire. While there is no forced retirement, most retire between the ages of seventy to seventy-five. When I am eighty-four, I discover that I have cancer of the intestinal tract. I become weaker and more helpless as the disease intensifies. When I am eighty-five, I die of pneumonia. My wife, family, friends, plus two priests, gather to pay tribute to me. The priests recognize and honor certain animal gods. My wife is sad because of the loss of companionship. After the short ceremony, my body is burned.*

*"My spirit stays around for a short time. The Lamurian descendants continue to pray for lost souls. As a result, the angels find me and take me to the Light (heaven). From heaven, I see that I had guidance from the Light, even though I wasn't aware of it. I saw that there was not much darkness in the society at this time. However, there was some darkness, because we did not pray or have communication with God. Overall, life was good and I did not see any special problems coming from that life."*

### Architecture During the Golden Age

According to my hypnotized patients, Atlanteans had individual dwelling units, individual houses, and, sometimes, clustered housing units like apartments. They were very economical in the use of space, in keeping with the small amount of electricity they used. It was as if they took their thinking and concentrated all the beauty together, instead of using large, rambling designs. They condensed them and developed very beautiful styles. Cities were well planned. There was a nice flow from one building to another, and the skyline of the buildings was harmonious. The Atlantean culture was very old. When we look back at Egypt, it has a recorded history of about 10,000 years. Consider the changes that occurred in Egypt during those years. There is not a single building other than the pyramids, that date back to the beginning, that is still in use. They have been torn down, reconstructed and the new things built, or just blocked away and covered with sand.

The Atlanteans had a much longer time period than that. In that time span, the country was made again and again. There were periods of time where there was a lot of construction and a lot of design. Cities were remodeled, sometimes constructively, sometimes haphazardly. It was known in Atlantis that an entire city would be reconstructed; that is, they would change the street patterns and the functions of different parts of the city and thus, progressively, over a span of years, a city would be totally rebuilt. The northern parts of the Atlantis, which were richer, were remade more often. The poorer part, which was the agricultural south, was comparatively less blessed. Many older buildings were found in the south of Atlantis. In the Golden Age, life was very good for the people.

One person recalled a past life as an architect in Atlantis as follows:

- *"I am a twenty-nine-year-old male with dark tan skin. My name is Samo. I live in Gord City in the south central part of Atlantis. It is 69,880 BC. I live with my wife and three children, a boy and two girls. I am a construction architect. My wife is a manager of a grocery store. I belong to the rich, upper class of society. I live in a very large spacious apartment in a high rise building on the nineteenth floor. It has four bedrooms, two and a half bathrooms, a kitchen, living room, dining room, an office, and a recreation room. We have many kitchen appliances, which are powered through sun energy through the crystals. We have a computer, TV, radio, and a telephone. We have many nice wall hangings, beautiful carpet on the floor, and beautiful hardwood furniture. The apartment is well decorated.*

*"We have different classes of society. There is a ruling class that rules the city. People are born into the ruling class. Every city has a ruler, and then there is a central ruler for the whole country who is above all the city rulers. Then there is the wealthy class, who live in a high-class section of the city. There is a working class, which today would be the blue-collar workers. Then there is a small portion of society that lives in mission houses or welfare-type facilities. These are the ones who cannot take care of themselves.*

*"Working class people live in a segregated section of the city. They live comfortable lives. Most of them have their own little cottages and homes. They are not as large and not as well appointed. Most of them have different appliances, but they are not as elaborate because they cannot afford them. They do live comfortable lives.*

*"Sometimes I travel in my own car or co-workers' cars. Other times, I take rapid transit, like a subway train. Compared with today's cars, my car is smaller. It can seat about four people, a driver and companion in the front seats, and two people in the rear seat. It works on solar power via crystals. The subway trains are also solar powered via crystals. They have a larger engine that pulls about twenty-five or thirty passenger cars. The concept is the same as today's subway, with seats and vertical poles in places for support if people have to stand.*

*"I went to college for a total of five years of what would be equivalent to today's bachelor program, and then the advanced study what would be equivalent to today's master's degree. I did advanced studies in architecture. We have free choice as to what profession we choose, but the rulers have to stamp approval on our choice and we do have to qualify academically.*

*"We believe in nature gods and animal gods, but we do not know about One God. We have temples where we*

*go from time to time for weddings and other special social occasions, to celebrate Nature Day or Harvest Day, but not regularly for any religious services. We worship many different gods, such as nature god, sun god, sea god, star god, animal gods, etc. Some people, who came from Lamuria, brought the concept of One God to Atlantis, but most of us believe in multiple gods, depending on what part of Atlantis we live in. Occasionally we have some religious services, but mostly for information, and there is often one-way communication. The priest does not show us, preach to us, or help us in learning about One God or how we can connect to that One God through prayers.*

*"I also go to the temple occasionally. Last time I went was several months ago, to celebrate Nature Day. The temple has some very high, pointed steeples on it. It is made out of stone blocks. There are rich hardwood doors in the entryway. Inside, there are busts of different animal gods. The priest speaks to us from a high podium about ten to twelve feet above floor level. The priest gives thanks for the harvest, thanks to the different gods for the bounty that comes from the ocean, and for the fruit that come from different trees.*

*"We were told stories concerning the continent Lamuria, which came apart and went under the sea. Many of those people fled and came to Atlantis to settle. They believe in one creator God, who is the God of the whole creation. I am kind of indifferent to their philosophy. We rarely discuss religion or spirituality.*

*"I am working as an architect for two and a half years, for a firm that bids for projects. Sometimes the contract comes from the government and sometimes from a private company that is expanding its business. We have built major high-rise buildings, finer houses, some bridges, and commercial buildings that will house business operations. People own their own houses and businesses.*

*"At this time, I am working on a high-rise building. The buildings we are constructing look very modern.*

*In commercial buildings, there are glass doors, and the structures are good looking and brightly lighted and spacious. They are well planned for the movement of people. There are long-range plans where the buildings are harmonious with one another, so that you do not see one style and then another to detract from the other. There is a nice flow from one building to another, and the skyline of the buildings is harmonious in that area of the city. The whole city is very well planned, clean, with lots of land with trees, flowers, parks, and water fountains. It is a nice, warm, receptive, and people-friendly city.*

*"Currently we are working on a building that is twenty stories high. It has a basement area below the ground where heating and cooling facilities, general maintenance operations, plumbing, sewage, and the water facilities are hidden. There are solar powered elevators in different sections of the building. Some of the rooms on the first floors are used for office space. From the eighth floor up, it will be used for residential apartments. Some of the buildings are designed as hotels. There is more creativity in buildings when compared to the current time. There are deeper, free-flowing thoughts that go into creating these buildings. The color schemes are more personality friendly and they naturally put people at ease. There is music played through intercoms all over, which is stimulating and soul touching.*

*"We are also designing a project that would include an array of shops, restaurants, high-rise buildings, hotels, and a park, all in one area. It will take between two or three years to put together before we actually start. There are business people and government involved in it. It took close to four years to finish this project. We are very pleased. Buildings seem to be more sturdy than our current buildings because of stone block construction and strong foundations. We also constructed a bridge over a river.*

*"I am about 380 years old, or about 95 years in today's time. It is their years divided by four. I am dying of old age.*

*My spirit is confused because it does not feel dead and does not know what to do. I stayed around for a while. Several Lamurians prayed for the lost souls and as a result angels came and helped me to the heaven. After cleansing and resting, I review my life with four Light beings.*

*"I see that I was a person with good intentions and did not want to harm anybody but I did not have any spirituality. I needed to learn the lesson that it is necessary to pray and be connected with God and the Light. I was happy and it was a good life because I was doing what I wanted to do. I see that my desire to build things in current life is partly coming from that life."*

### Art During the Golden Age

In Atlantis, the arts were very advanced and beautiful, especially during the Golden Age from 70,000 to 50,000 BC. Probably their most unique and most beautiful art was the technique of painting in Light where colored chips would be suspended in a plastic medium. As the plastic was added and chips were put in place, the Light would shine through, perhaps from the bottom or from the top. The patterns and the designs that came from the superimposition of the colored chips were one of the most exquisite creative art forms.

Following is an example given by a patient under hypnosis:

- *"This is really a unique art form because the chips are in the three-dimensional medium. From one direction they form one pattern, then when you walk around to the side, there would be another pattern formed, until you have covered all six sides: left, right, front, back, up, and down. It is almost like the changing patterns of a kaleidoscope. You can see the work of art from every direction and from each direction, it becomes a different pattern. This is a very creative art form that requires a very highly sophisticated capacity to visualize the emotional impact*

*of patterns and colors. The arrangements in space are so*
*beautiful that from one direction they may look like a se-*
*ries of pleasing patterns of geometric shapes while from*
*another direction they may form a ship."*

According to the heavenly beings, we do not have that art
form anywhere now. There were attempts along these lines,
but not to the extent of the Atlanteans. This art was Atlantean's own and was not inspired by the alien races. We might
have similar art forms here in the future.

They also had the usual arts such as poetry, music, painting, sculpture, and carving, which were different from the
current times. Later, their art at times became very ritual-
ized, stilted, and lost its reality. During some periods, the
Atlanteans' formal patterns were followed by others. This
was a characteristic of the people, which went with them to
other lands when Atlantis broke apart and sank. My hypnotized patients report the artwork that shows this is in some of
the artwork in Egypt, where art followed formal convention.
The head is shown in profile, but the shoulders and chest are
shown square to the viewer. The hips and legs are pointing
the same direction as the face. It's a physical impossibility
and not practical, but this was the formal convention of the
art. This is the way you show a person. They did it this way
because sometimes they considered it a challenge to show
the creativity and the reality within a rigid framework. It
was an art style that came and went. It was before, during,
and after the Golden Age. During the Dark Ages in Atlantis,
art was considered a waste of time and was abolished.

The rapid, formal style of art also showed up in music and
poetry. They had to follow the formal rules in writing poems.
Of course, this is not too different than modern techniques,
where you have the rhyming lines with so many syllables per
line. They did very much the same thing. Poetry contained
deep and important thoughts in a relatively small space.

During the golden time, music and paintings also
flourished. Perhaps their strongest area of talent was in

architectural design. They created beautiful objects from ordinary things. Rather than a chair just being a chair, it became a work of art, or a building became a work of art. The materials, the decorations, the all-over design of the building became a piece of artwork. Function-wise, it served the same purpose as in modern times, but as far as beauty, Atlanteans were superior to us. Their work was much more beautiful than ours.

According to heavenly beings, buildings of the modern world are functional without much beauty. The Atlanteans mixed the two. They had the same function to fulfill, but they put extra effort into it to make it more beautiful and pleasing to the eyes and the senses. They integrated music with the building's architecture, so as they entered from one place to another, each place would have its own music, contributing to the overall effect.

The following is an example given by a patient:

- *"Private offices as such are not musically tuned; that is the music is not provided for them, but the large public areas and the hallways definitely have their own music. As they walk through the door, people would become visually immersed in the entryway or the lobby area, while at the same time, they would start to hear this beautiful music that could change from whatever direction they were facing, to help contribute to the overall impact of the building. As they walk through the door and look to the right, they get a certain music, depending on what the visual scene is; and if they turn to the back that is opposite to the door, there is a third type of music."*

It shows the complexity in Atlantean thinking. Just like in the light sculptures in which from whatever direction you looked, there was a different design with a different impact. In this case, they used the same type of idea with music.

In Atlantis, just as religion varied from region to region and eventually got all mixed together depending on which tribe you were dealing with, the culture also varied from place to place, till all was unified in time. Artwork varied from place to place, with a lot based on the old culture of the tribe. These various forms spread all over the continent. Then different forms merged till they were one mixture, but the individual components were not the same.

People had freedom. They worked where they chose and could do what they wanted. There was, of course, economic control; that is, if you could not do the job, you could not serve. Music, art, and literature flourished during these times.

One of my patients recalled a past life as a singer and a dancer as follows:

- *"I am a twenty-three-year-old female living in Gardi City, in the northwestern part of Atlantis. It is about seventy-five miles inland. This is 69,160 BC. I do a lot of traveling because I am a very popular singer and dancer. I had special training in singing and dancing. I perform in theaters, nightclubs, and in resort areas. I enjoy my profession. I do dances that look something like ballet and tap.*

  *"At the age of twenty-nine, I meet and fall in love with a person who is a movie actor, and we get married a year later in a temple. The priest gives thanks to different animal gods and then we are given blessings as a married couple. My husband is a very versatile actor. He can do drama, comedy, or adventure movies. We have two children a boy and a girl. Later on, I also act in the movies and become very famous. We were both invited to perform at the royal palace, which was very successful, and that propels me into more prominence because only the top artists are invited to perform in the royal palace.*

  *"Movie scenes are more realistic, as if viewers are really there. They are extremely well done and well received. Movies are shown in the movie theater and also there are videos. We live a very good life. Society is very positive and prosperous. I died at one hundred years of age of pneumonia. It was a happy and productive life.*

*"From heaven, during the review of life, I see that it was a positive, liberal, happy, and productive society. People who wished to work hard and advance themselves had the opportunity, no matter what class they came from. People were able to own properties and had total freedom of movement without questions or restrictions. Atlantis was a good place to live at that time. Although I came from a lower middle class family, I was able to move up into the rich class because of my talent. We owned some of the resort areas and had all the available comforts. Even people in lower middle class society were able to own their own house. I see that I was recognized as a major public entertainment figure in the country. We also helped many underprivileged talented people."*

### Transportation During the Golden Age

According to my hypnotized patients, at the beginning, Atlanteans had draft animals and wagons and carts. There were something like a horse and buggy, but the animal looked more like a llama than a horse. Later they had a cart six feet by six feet square and six feet high, and there was a cab where the driver sat on the left front. These were hooked together like railroad cars, only they had regular tiers on them and each had its own crystal for bringing in power and the electronics for electricity. Each ran by its own low-voltage electric motors. It was train-like transportation, with fifteen little cars hooked together. These were set up for passengers, and people would ride from place to place. These were the public transportation. They were electrical, and the electricity got to them through the broadcast transmission through the crystals. This was around 80,000 BC.

They had water transportation, which was larger than the cars, and more stuff was hauled by water transportation than by mechanical means. They developed a canal system from north to south, connecting the river. The canals ran from north to south naturally because the river ran away from the center of the island. They would connect a canal across a narrow part where the land was not too steep. There were mountains in the center, extending from the east to west, dividing Atlantis between north and south sections. There were some highlands in the south, a flat level plain that happened to be several hundred feet above sea level.

They also had airplanes that were very low flying planes. They were not the primary means of transportation. It was difficult to power them as they went farther away from land. They were most effective close to land where power was strongest. They did not have a portable source of power. They could not load a gas tank and fly across the Atlantic Ocean. That is why boats were more successful, because they could use the transmitted power that came from crystals and sail.

The Atlanteans were very reluctant to leave home, so people tended to use ships, where they could have a more home-like atmosphere. They were kind of stay-home people. Airplanes had to have several receivers to get electricity to power an airplane engine, and even then had to be small and light. Atlanteans usually had electrical-powered glider planes. They did not have an internal combustion engine, but they did not need it because since they had their power needs met, so why bother to develop it. The internal combustion engine was ignored after it was built.

Their airplanes were very small, a bit bigger than our model airplanes, with five power receiving stations. All the power in each went to one segment of the motor. The engine was divided into five parts, and each part got its power from a different receiver. Working together, they could provide enough energy to get a small airplane off the ground. They could fly with these airplanes from one end of Atlantis to another, but when you got off the continent, the power supply dropped off so they could not fly. According to my hypnotized patients, some Atlanteans used body suits to fly individually. These body suits had a device at the lower end to lift the body in the air.

Atlantis had ships, boats, and multiple means of water transportation; that is, barges for hauling goods through the canals and up and down the river, coast-hopping small ships that held a lot of cargo, which sailed around Atlantis taking things from one coast to another, from south to north and vice versa through these small ships. Atlantis' power supply was not sufficient. They could get electricity from multiple sources, but to do huge amounts of work with it, they did not have enough electricity at any one time. That was why they had multiple receiving stations for an airplane or a boat. Their boats had ten receiving generators.

One of my patients gave the following description of the subway trains in Atlantis:

- *"There are many subway systems in Atlantis. The subway train is solar powered and pulls twenty-five passenger cars which run on a track. It is bigger and heavier than the passenger cars. It contains a seat for a co-driver. Its instrument panel features a series of dials and gauges, some of which are used to adjust speed and power. The cars have a metal exterior. They are boxes on wheels, in many ways similar to today's subway cars. We have a variety of means of transportation. There is water transportation, such as mechanical ships, and submarine-types of transportation. We also have flying machines, but we do not use lift as we use in the current times. We have vehicles for traveling on the ground. They have wheels and are very similar to cars and trucks, but are slightly higher."*

One of my patients under hypnosis described some Atlanteans using a body suit to fly individually. The body suit had a device at the lower end to lift the body in the air:

- *"I am a twenty-six-year-old male living in Paris, France. My name is Hydra and this is 57060 BC. I am a strong person, six feet two inches tall, with a well-built body. I live alone. My parents and a sister live in another city. I*

*am a journalist. Here, everybody is talking about a place
called Atlantis. A person who is a trader has come from
there and is describing it as a totally different world. I am
told to go to Atlantis to find out more about Atlantis. I go
with a trader on a ship. He told me that Atlantis is like a
magic kingdom, where people are prosperous and happy
and they live an effortless life.*

*"I travel by a ship with other travelers and traders from
different places. It takes about three months to reach there.
It is just a beautiful place, well planned and well mani-
cured. The buildings are very beautiful. Many buildings
are made with glass. They use solar energy everywhere. I
am in awe of everything. I see some people are flying individually, with a body suit. Some people are traveling in
a car type vehicle. I also rent a body suit, put it on, and I
can also fly like a bird. After some practice, I get the hang
of it. The body suit for flying has a rocket type of device at
the lower end, which lifts the body in the air. I hear that
people have been using this body suit to fly for about ten
years. It is almost like a superman.*

*"They have robots doing work for them in the homes or
office. They have a human form, are about five feet tall, and
are made of metal. They walk, talk, and do different chores,
but in a very mechanical way. They have a dishwasher and
many other appliances. It uses steam to clean instead of
water. Most of the appliances here work with solar energy.
In Paris we do not have any of these appliances.*

*"People here live in family units. They have a device
that has everything, like television, computers, and phone.
They also have pen-type devices that they can convert into
computer, television, or telephone any time they choose.
All they have to do is activate them and they can project
images on a screen, or use it as a phone where they can
also see the person on the other side like a video phone.
They are also using crystals as power sources.*

*"I stay there only for a few days because the ship is
returning. When I reach Paris, I write an article about*

*Atlantis and it becomes very popular. I get a promotion after that. I get married and have children. In the back of my mind, I always wanted to go back to Atlantis to visit, but did not go because after a few years I heard bad things happening in Atlantis and people who go there sometimes disappear and never come back. So people were afraid to go there.*

*"I died at the age of seventy-five. I was run over by a wagon and I died instantly. After a while, I see angels and they take me to the Light. There I get cleansed with a shower of Light. I see lot of murky stuff coming out of me. Also a lot of attachments are coming out of me. They are soul parts of my wife and children.*

*"Then I am taken for my life review. There are about seven Light beings who are waiting for me. They are kind and not judging me. I see my life being projected on a movie screen. I am still wondering if I should have gone to Atlantis again and they are giving me a comforting look, saying it was okay either way.*

*"From heaven, I see that there was a large vortex under the whole of Atlantis; as a result, it was a very high-energy place. That is the reason it was way ahead of the rest of the world in technology. I see that they discovered those flying suites about ten years before I went to Atlantis. I see that people were disappearing because they were used for some kind of experiments.*

*"I see I had a good life and the only problems that came from that life to the current life were aches and pain all over the body because I was crushed by a wagon cart.*

*"Dr. Modi prayed for me and everybody who was there with me in that life and also for everybody whoever lived in Atlantis and the whole Atlantis and the vortex under it to be cleansed and healed with the brilliant, white Light. Then all the soul parts which we lost in that life and all the other lifetimes from the beginning of our existence are brought back from Satan, his demons, from each other, and from other places, and integrated with us after cleansing*

*and healing the soul parts and us. Everybody's past life personalities were integrated with whom they belonged after cleaning and healing. Also I see that the whole vortex which was under Atlantis was also cleansed, healed, and shielded with the crystal shield, metallic shield, mirror shield, and rays of blinding white Light."*

## Priests During the Golden Age

The priest class was also a part of the ruling class. Since the priests did not have a hereditary class, the leaders of the priest class had to be selected by the high priests and were moved into the ruling class with the approval of the ruler. Besides preaching to and counseling the general population, the high-level priests were also responsible for the educational system in the society. They talked to the heads of different educational fields and prepared the curriculum for all the schools and colleges. Typically, to become a priest, a person has to go through twelve years of education and then four years of college and take courses in psychology, sociology, history, and how to be a priest. Once included in the ruling class, they were provided luxurious places to live within the compound, or in a section of a palace itself. After retirement, they were provided luxurious living arrangements in the section of the city where the ruling class lived.

One of my patients under hypnosis recalled living the life in Atlantis as follows:

- *"I am an eighteen-year-old-male living in Key City on the northwest coast of Atlantis. My name is Simon and this is 76,541 BC. After eleven years of regular school, I am entering college to become a priest. I am studying language, history, philosophy of the priesthood, courses on the nature gods, basic healing, sociology, and psychology. All of us are required to take a comprehensive final exam after all the coursework in this four-year program. Part of the final exam is written and part of it is oral.*

*After passing everything and receiving an approval from our ruler, I am now a priest. The basic philosophy of the priest is to serve people by helping them with their personal and health problems, through counsel and advice, and to insure that a quality education exists for all our citizens. This includes kindergarten all the way through college. The priests are responsible for all the educational programs in Atlantis.*

*"My father is a priest and my mother has a college degree in teaching, although she never worked. I live with them in a luxurious house in a section of the palace because my father, being a priest, was also a member of the ruling class. Upon becoming a priest at twenty-three, I am also given an apartment in a section of our ruler's palace. I have tan skin, black hair, and I look like humans appear today. I am wearing black pants and a long flowing purple and yellow top that falls below my knees. I work in a temple in the city. I am a member of the priest class, which is included in the ruling class.*

*"There are nine priests living in a section of the palace. There are nine temples in the city and one is located here in the palace. Since I am in the ruling class, I am involved in all of the policy meetings conducted by the rulers. These meetings are not religion based, but they are about business, political, educational, and social issues. One of our priests is the high priest. He is the senior-most member of the priests, and is the administrator in charge of the priests.*

*"I am very excited now because I get to go to my first convention for priests. I am going with four other priests by plane to another city some hundred miles away, to a convention that is held at a large downtown hotel. I'm finding this to be a social event, and religion is not discussed here. I am taking a class on basic healing. The two presenting priests discuss how some in Atlantis can connect to a higher-level god for the purpose of healing, and they have the ability to heal through these gods. I*

*am taking another class titled, "Becoming a Successful Priest." This session is available to all new priests. The class offers practical suggestions about interacting with the people of the community the priest is serving. This three-day event concludes and we return to our city.*

*"I go to my temple every day. It has bright ornamental objects on the outside. The building is made of cut gray stone. There are twelve steps leading to a large double door main entrance. There are cat faces representing animal gods on either side of the entry doors. They are carved from stone and are considered gods. Inside there are other animal god faces, such as bear, wolf, and cat around the walls. There is a waterfall inside the temple and benches for people. There is a large pulpit some six to seven feet above floor level. There are a variety of brightly colored cloths (red, blue, silver, gold, green, purple, yellow, and white) hanging down from the pulpit. The temple also has meeting rooms and classrooms and a small apartment with a kitchen, living room, and bedroom, for the convenience of the priest.*

*"My daily routine consists of getting up around seven a.m. and going to breakfast with the other priests. We sometimes take a moment and give thanks to the animal gods before we eat. Around eight, we have a one-hour meeting with the high priest. He is very busy and has two regular clerks to assist him. Our discussions usually center around new polices made by our rulers. We discuss these policies and how we should implement them.*

*"Around nine a.m., the other priests and I go to a meeting with the ruler(s). We discuss our subjects, topics of speeches, and ways to help improve our ruler's image. Sometimes we give reports on our respective temples, but we rarely discuss religion or spirituality.*

*"Around ten a.m., all priests go to their respective temples. Attendees of these temples all believe in the same gods. The temples are located in various parts of the city for the convenience of the people. While at the temple,*

*I counsel people about personal problems and self-improvement. Sometimes I meet with business people and act as a spokesman on behalf of our ruler. My other duties are administrative paperwork relating to the temple. During my counseling, I sometimes mention the animal gods, but I don't mention spirituality, religion, or God, because I'm not aware of Him.*

*"I go back to the palace at noon to have lunch. This process takes about an hour and a half. By two p.m., I'm back at the temple, counseling and doing administrative chores. Our main god is the god of water. His name is Oceanus. We have other gods for wind, rain, sun, crops, and one for each animal.*

*"I return to my palace apartment around five p.m. each day. I freshen up and do a little reading. At six p.m., I join my fellow priests for dinner. We eat fruits, grains, breads, and animal meats from ones we do not worship. After dinner, for entertainment, we watch movies on our TV, play cards, go to dances or to plays. We can do all of these things in or outside the palace. We can bring women in anytime we choose for sexual favors. These are "willing" women and they are not abused. After entertainment, I retire to my room and read histories and biographies of former Atlanteans. I have several books, including some books on the animal gods.*

*"Our ruler is a good person. We have mutual respect. He is approachable and easy going. We like him, and the people of the city like him. The city is free and there is no control anywhere in Atlantis. We use crystals now, but only for positive technology. Atlantis has cars, trains, and planes that are solar powered. The ruler and some subrulers have their own planes. Our high priest also has his own plane.*

*"I preach twice a month. I wear a colorful red and white striped robe. It has a golden cord around the waist. I wear a headpiece that is gold in color. The temple has a gold theme to it. The pulpit is six to seven feet higher than*

*the floor level where people are sitting. This design puts me at a distance from them. This helps all of us, because none of us are comfortable talking about anything with a religious or spiritual connotation. We have no eye contact. I spend a small amount of time telling people about family harmony, self-improvement, and health care. There is no mention of god, religion, or spirituality. When I speak, I look down or around the temple. The people are generally looking at the floor or walls, and not looking at me. There is a feeling that everyone will be relieved when this is over, which is always less than an hour. Occasionally I talk about our rulers, which is always favorable, and I always stress all the good things they are doing for us. After this ceremony is over, people socialize and talk about their lives. They do not mention religion. Even when we are together as priests, we do not openly talk about religion or spirituality.*

*"I'm going to marry a woman, at the age of thirty-six, who is the daughter of a ruler of another city. I met her two years ago at a social function. I see her at frequent intervals before we decide to marry. We get permission from each of our rulers and set a wedding date. This marriage is welcomed by our rulers because it helps to form an alliance between our cities. We also have a central ruler by this time.*

*"The wedding is held at the temple in the palace. Our families, friends, and the rulers are there. The ceremony is conducted by the high priest, with three other priests participating. I am wearing a white linen outfit. The jacket has golden buttons and designs on it. My wife to be is wearing a white, full-length, flowing gown. The priest speaks about the importance of family and continuing the Atlantean race. Before he pronounces us man and wife, he looks at the ruler, who stands and nods in approval, and we are pronounced man and wife.*

*"The high priest makes a toast to us. Everyone raises their glasses and drinks to our success. After the*

*ceremony, there is dancing, feasting, and drinking. The party continues for two days. We go to another city for our honeymoon. We travel by train to our chosen spot. We arrive and are privately chauffeured to our hotel. In a month's time, we return to my city. We resume the same living arrangements in the palace.*

*"My father and mother are retired and living in a high-rise building for the nobility. We have sections in Atlantis that are exclusively set aside for nobility. All these buildings are lavishly furnished. They are larger and taller than any other buildings. We have several twenty-five-story apartment buildings, all of which have elevators. All the ruling class buildings are more colorful, have more glass, and are built by our best craftsmen, who use the latest technology and the finest building materials.*

*"There are also healing priests in Atlantis. They are trained by medical doctors and work in cooperation to heal the sick. We have two priests in our palace who are healers. Their temples have healing rooms where people can go for healing. These two priests went to a medical facility for a year to work with medical doctors. These healing priests have a psychic ability and are respected by the medical doctors. They are an important part of the Atlantean society. Unfortunately, I do not have psychic ability.*

*"I retire at seventy-three, and was a high priest for the last seventeen years of my working life. I am now living in a retirement village exclusively for nobility. At the age of ninety-seven, I have been moved to a hospital because I'm dying of heart disease. The medical doctors and the healing priests attend to me but I do not respond. My last thoughts are that I hope my descendants enjoy the same good life that I did and I hope things continue the way they did during my life. I believe that when I die I'll be gone forever and I will not exist. As a result, I'm apprehensive and frightened.*

*"I am fading into an unconscious state and my spirit leaves my body. I stay around and watch over my body.*

*There is a ceremony after my death, which my family, friends and many others in the ruling class attend. The high priest conducts the affair. He praises me for my outstanding service as a priest. After this, my body is cremated. My spirit stays around for seventy years before finding the Light because I did not know where to go.*

*"From heaven, I see that Atlantis was without God, and as a result I was blocked from the Light. I also see many people who were there are also here in the current life. The problems which came from that life to the currant life are: feeling that I am blocked from the Light, and having a lack of interest in religion."*

### *Priests With Psychic and Healing Ability*

Some of the priests who had intuition, psychic ability, and/ or healing hands could take special training in healing people by the laying on of hands or visualization techniques. They were trained for about one and a half years in schools where doctors were educated and trained. These priests took many of those courses. They learned about different medical conditions and how to diagnose and treat some of the ailments, not with medicine or surgery but with other healing techniques, such as visualization and the laying on of hands. They worked in cooperation and harmony with the physicians.

One patient under hypnosis recalled the following life as a healing priest:

- *"I am a thirty-four-year-old male living in Mitz City, located in the southwest of Atlantis. My name is Jarvis and this is 79,903 BC. I am married and have two children, a girl eleven years old and a girl nine. I have been a priest for sixteen years. We priests have luxurious living quarters for our families in a section of the palace. There are seven other priests who live in this section of the palace and there are seven temples in the city. The high priest, who is the oldest, does not go to the temples in the city but takes care of the administrative work and the smaller version of the temple in the palace. Each of us has a temple where we go and work, and for which we are responsible.*

*"The temple I am in charge of is one and a half stories tall. It is made of stone and has a lot of gold and copper colors inside. There are figureheads of different animal gods, such as bear, cat, lion, etc. There are also the exaggerated faces of people that represent different nature gods, such as the sun god, rain god, sea god, and wind god. There is a high pulpit from where the priest speaks, and there are benches below for people to sit. Also there are counseling rooms, healing rooms, and there are also rooms for patients to stay overnight or for several days. There are about ten such rooms with beds.*

*"My father was a priest so I also decided to become a priest. We don't automatically become a priest by inheritance. We have to go through four years of special education to become a priest. Anybody in the general population who wants to become a priest can go through the special college and become a priest, with the ruler's approval. Similarly, a priest's son does not have to be a priest. Only males are allowed in the priesthood in our city. I hear there are female priestesses in other cities.*

*"To become a priest, I went through the four years of college after finishing school equivalent to the high school. In college, we have courses that deal with history, sociology, psychology, language, healing, and how to be a priest. Some priests and I have special healing gifts, such as healing hands, intuition, and clairvoyance, and on request, I go for special training. We are trained for one and a half years in schools where doctors are educated and trained, and we take many of those classes. We learn about different medical conditions and how to diagnose and treat some of the ailments, not with medicine or surgery but with other healing techniques such as laying on of hands and visualization. We work in harmony with*

*the doctors. There are two of us who do the healing work. We priests are considered to be part of the ruling class. My son becomes a priest and my daughter marries a sub-ruler.*

*"In the mornings, I go to the temple of which I am in charge. I counsel people and do healing of people who are sick and have minor ailments. Sometimes I do hands-on healing to heal a problem or enhance the healing so it takes less time. Sometimes I use a visualization technique where I focus and visualize them being healed by a healing god when I am with the sick person, or even if it's from a distance from my office. I pray to the healing gods daily, more than the other priests, because psychically I am more aware that the gods are real. I ask for guidance from these gods but I do not talk about this with others, because in our culture, religion, gods, or spirituality are not discussed openly. It is considered bad manners.*

*"Even when we preach two or three times a month from the pulpit, we do not look at people who are there, because everybody is feeling embarrassed by it. Listeners also tend to look at the floor or walls or somewhere else to avoid embarrassment. We talk about how people can improve, different ways they can better themselves, ways to stay healthy, and other general advice, but we do not talk about One God, prayers, spirituality, or how to connect with gods.*

*"We priests also have meetings with the rulers. We are advisers for them about education and other matters. The priestly group is also in charge of all the education, and we set up the curriculum for colleges. We work in harmony.*

*"Our ruler is very fair and caring and always thinking of ways to improve the lives of his people. Everybody in the society has freedom to live the way they want to live and do what they want to do. Nobody is poor and everybody is well taken care of, including those who are sick or mentally ill. We have three classes in our society. The ruling class includes rulers, sub-rulers; priests and*

*technologists who are appointed in the palace are also included in the ruling class. They live in a special section of the city with their families. Then there are the rich and business classes and then the average class, each living in a separate section of the city. Anybody can advance from the average class to the rich class. Life in general is good and peaceful.*

*"I retire at the age of one hundred and five. I die of pneumonia and kidney failure, hoping more people open up to spirituality. I remain around for a couple of days till my body is cremated after a small ceremony. Then I see angels, who escort me to the heaven. During the review of my life in heaven, I see that I planned to introduce spirituality in the society and do healing work."*

### Healing Temples During the Golden Age

My hypnotized patients state that during the Golden Age, there were healing temples where patients were treated by the priests who had psychic abilities. They were trained with medical doctors, about medical diagnosis and the treatment. They also used other healing methods, such as prayers, visualization, and hands-on healing. They were often guided by the healing god Appoe how to heal.

Following is a past life recalled by a patient under hypnosis when he was treated in a healing temple:

- *"I am a forty-two-year-old male living in a ship-building city called Woston, on the east coast of Atlantis, on the right of the mountains. My name is Nextor and this is 58,627 BC. I am a craftsman. I am married and have seven children. We build the ships in a shipyard. I was pegging the deck and a metal worker dropped some tools and I got hit on the head. I am knocked unconscious. I wake up with the healers in the healing temple. It is believed that God Appoe, a healing god, comes in your dream and he may give you specific instruction, or heal you right there by touching you, or he may show you things you may or may not understand. When you tell your dream to the chief priest, he will tell you what it means. Usually, Appoe tells the priest and the priest tells you. I have heard stories about some of the dreams people had here. How they have been healed, just like that.*

*"When I wake up, the chief priest tells me that he has been getting directions from Appoe on how to treat me and what to do. I am very thirsty. First thing, they have me do is urinate in a can. Then they give me a little bit of water. They tell me that I was unconscious for four days. Then they give me some juice, which is sweet and bitter, and some broth. They tell me to lie still and not to move and they will check on me from time to time. I kind of drowse back off. After a while, they wake me up, give me some water and that bitter-sweet juice, and some thin, boiled grain. Then I doze off again. This goes on every hour until dark.*

*"When I sleep again, I dream about Appoe, who looks huge about a hundred feet tall and maybe twenty-five feet wide, big and strong, and radiating like a sun. He is just walking down the hall. When I wake up, I see black spots in front of my eyes like flies. When the priest comes, I tell him about my dream and he says that Appoe is aware that I am here but he has not decided about what to do. The very fact that I dreamed about him shows that I have his attention.*

*"My wife comes to see me. We live on the other side of the city. It takes hours for her to come here. I remind her to make a donation for the priest, because they do not charge for their services but they do need the money. Next day, the priest comes to talk to me. He asks me questions about me falling asleep off and on, something I cannot help. He is concerned about that. I pray to Appoe for healing but I do not tell anybody about it. I keep it to myself.*

*"I have been here for about two weeks. The swelling on my head is gone down and the pain is much relieved but*

*I am still falling asleep. The chief priest comes to see me and tells me that he has received a message from Appoe that the priest is supposed to tell the king who owns the shipyard that I cannot continue with the work. I can teach other craftsmen but I cannot go back to that work. I am to receive full salary and the same considerations of any of the king's workers, and a reminder that this is the order of Appoe. The king agrees to it because the king is responsible for his people. One of the king's people talks to me to set up the training program.*

"I am sent home after two months. I am to do physical therapy at home. I never recover from my sleeping problem, the black spots are gone, vomiting and staggering is gone. I teach how to build ships but I never go back to work in the shipyard.

"At the age of eighty-seven, one day I go to sleep and never get up. I die of a heart attack thinking that it was inconvenient to fall asleep. You do not get rested; it does not make it better. I am just walking around, and couple of figures who are glowing show up. One is the master craftsman who trained me. I have not seen them for a long time. They take me to heaven.

"I am taken to a table where I talk to beings about my life, about being hungry growing up because my father left and how hard it was. Then after cleansing, I am directed to another table. I see Marduc and Parsudon, both worshiped as sea gods. They explain to me that they are here to help me review my life. From heaven, I see that I had five brothers. My father went to another country and never came back. My mom worked for rich people, cleaning. I worked around the docks as a helper. I only went to three years of school. I could read, write, and do calculation. I kept pestering the master craftsman to teach me. He taught me for many years and then I worked as his apprentice for four or five years. By the age of thirty, I was a certified master craftsman and got a job in king's shipyard.

*"I also see that Appoe is a Light being who was helping the priests who saw him in dreams, so people would not feel embarrassed about seeing him.*

*"From heaven, I see that there were hospitals in Atlantis at that time, but there were also healing temples where priests were medically trained. They are the priests with spiritual and psychic gifts and also have medical training.*

*"I was supposed to experiment with different woods to find the best wood to make pegs that will swell and be strong to hold the ship together the best. It was a group goal to make sea travel safer, which I succeeded. Passing on the technical knowledge to make the strongest ships was also a personal goal. Another goal I planned for that life was to be a healer, particularly for self healing by working in the healing temple after the accident, and also to pass it on in everyday life. I did not achieve that at all.*

*"I see that I did not accept that healing can occur psychically or through Appoe, and I did not follow through in life at home. I was supposed to learn the techniques to heal and pass it on. These are internal and external techniques, using the breath to direct the energy to the place that needs the healing and to use visualization in the healing. External techniques to bring in the energy and direct it to the proper spot for healing. I learned those techniques, used them while in the temple, but did not believe in it and did not follow through at home.*

*"There are many people who were there in that life and are also here in the current life. I see that my sleeping problems, weight problems, and forgetfulness came from that life to the current life. Also, the head injury affected the right side of my brain and made spirituality easier in that life. That is why I was able to perceive Appoe in the dreams.*

*"I see angels cleansing, healing, bringing and integrating the soul parts back to my head, brain, eyes, finger, my GI tract, and all over the body.*

*"I see that I needed to learn the lesson of faith and confidence in God.*

*"There were natural psychic abilities in some people. It was considered spiritual but it was not talked about. These persons might communicate information, and the information only, but there was no understanding of its source or how you get it. Even though natural psychics existed, they did not tell others about it."*

### Rulers During the Golden Age

The rulers during the golden years were very fair and just. They cared about their people. There was no class discrimination. Everyone was permitted to advance. People lived well and enjoyed a quality life.

One of the persons recalled a past life as a ruler in Atlantis during the golden years as follows:

- *"My name is Zar Rolli and I am a thirty-two-year-old, tan skinned male who lives in Dial, Atlantis. It is 67,000 BC. I have a wife, a five-year-old boy, a three-year-old boy and a one-year-old girl. I am the ruler of Dial, a city of several hundred thousand. Our country has one central ruler, and all of our cities have regional rulers. I started my reign when I was twenty-five. I became a ruler by birthright, as my father ruled Dial before me. I live in a large palace. From the outside, it looks similar to an eighteenth century European castle. It contains a section for living quarters. It has a section for my office, plus offices for many of my support staff. There are living quarters for our servants in this lavishly furnished palace.*

  *"I start the day by rising around seven a.m. I go to the exercise room where I do stretching exercises and calisthenics. After this, I walk and jog on a walking/running track that I had built for this purpose. Next I shower and take a light breakfast of fresh fruit, a variety of fruit juices, and an assortment of fresh bread. I go to my office around nine to sign papers and listen to my staff reports and the issues of the day. Around eleven a.m., I frequently*

*tour the city and mingle with the people. I tour in my solar powered car with an entourage of staffers. Sometimes I go to dedicate a park, to open a school, or to take part in the grand opening of a new business. Sometimes I just go out to mingle with the people.*

*"I return to the palace around noon to have lunch with my staff and/or family, depending on my schedule. Lunch usually lasts until two p.m. because we hold lively discussions on the business of the city or the social topics of the day. After that, I go back to my office to sign more official documents and meet with department heads of our city.*

*"I usually spend about five hours a day at the office. I have a fine staff of lieutenants who handle the details of the day-to-day problems. I live more like a king than a high-ranking government official. I love what I do. My duties consist of mostly positive issues. We have a lot of harmony and contentment in Atlantis.*

*"After four p.m., I go back to the family quarters and spend time with my family and/or my mistresses, who live in separate quarters in the palace. We have dinner from six to eight p.m. After this we watch movies, attend plays, listen to comedians perform, or watch a variety of magic shows. We bring all these acts in, and we enjoy their performances, which they enjoy doing.*

*"We enjoy a very fine lifestyle. Our subjects live very well too. Everyone is paid well for their work. Our people have their own homes and live with their families. These homes typically have a variety of modern appliances. There are televisions, movie screens (which are often part of the televisions), VCRs, and radios. The televisions are frequently built in the walls. They have buttons and dials for channel selection, tuning, volume, and on/off. Our VCRs are loaded from the top (like some modern day toasters). Our kitchens have stoves with many options, refrigerators, and other kitchen appliances. We have washers and dryers that are designed to wash and dry all types of clothing. All our appliances are solar powered through*

*crystals. We have telephones in Atlantis. The phone sys-
tem is wireless. These phones are made of transmitters
and receivers. They contain crystals, which enable them
to work efficiently. We have phones mounted on walls and
we also have portable phones.*

*"I have my own airplane. It is a small plane containing
two seats. I can fly but I prefer not to pilot my own plane.
When I fly, my pilot sits at the controls and I sit behind
him. I fly only in Atlantis. We do not fly outside the country
because our solar powered planes will carry a charge for
only a short period of time. As a result, we have concerns
that our plane might come down if we go out of the country.*

*"Our society has no real class discrimination. Some
in our society have more than others but that is a function of their ability and work effort. Everyone is permitted to advance. If they have the ability and willingness
to work hard, they can become high-level professional
people. There are no really poor people in Dial. People
live well and enjoy a good quality of life. All people can
enjoy a variety of cultural events, movies, the theater, and
recreational areas. There are sections of the city that have
bigger homes, but that is a function of the marketplace as
opposed to any discrimination.*

*"Our city is laid out in sections. There is a government
section for the business of government. There are many
residential sections, with individual homes and high-rise
apartments. There are industrial sections that contain factories that produce home appliances and building products. We have shopping sections with large department
stores. We have several public parks, wide paved roads,
and hard surfaced sidewalks. Parking space is ample. We
have water fountains, tree lined streets, and lots of flowers
and shrubbery in our city.*

*"We do not have religious beliefs. We don't believe in
One God. We worship and honor animal and nature gods.
These gods represent crops, the ocean, nature, etc. We*

*have priests, which are members of the ruling class. They support our philosophies as rulers. We are basically a scientific and technological society.*

*"There are several educational programs in Atlantis. Our children start school at five or six years of age and continue their education up through high school. We have universities that offer four- and five-year programs and a variety of professional programs such as medicine, law, the arts, etc. There is no student discrimination. Anyone who has the ability and a work ethic can attend our universities.*

*"I have helped our city advance by encouraging free enterprise. We have lots of business investments, which include shopping centers, apartment buildings, factories, universities, and hospitals. Our city is alive with bright, progressive people. Our business people travel to other countries to trade and market their products. I do not travel outside the country. I'm content to be in Atlantis. Our city continues to grow. People enjoy living here and they are happy and content.*

*"About ten percent of our society is made up of the Lamurian population. And there are outsiders from other places who come to settle in our city. The Lamurians are different than we are. They believe in One God and they worship One God. Many are psychic and they have a special communication with God. They have a perception or special understanding of God and other higher-level Light beings. We do not thoroughly understand the Lamurians, but we do not dislike them. We provide for them the same rights and privileges as all our other citizens. We find the Lamurians to be productive members of our society.*

*"I have the equivalent of a bachelor's degree in economics and management. This, along with special leadership training, helps me to be an able ruler. I have a very good relationship with my subjects. I live to be seventy-nine. My oldest son replaces me as the next ruler of Dial. Like me, my son has taken special training in leadership.*

*He has a college degree in sociology and history. I feel he will be an able ruler.*

*"Before I die, I become very weak and experience difficulty in breathing. I have a defective heart. I'm losing control of my ability to move. I fade in and out of a coma. Just before I die, my spirit leaves my body. My spirit doesn't know what to do or where to go. I had no concept of God and I believed that once I died that would be the end of me. I stayed around for less than a year before going to heaven. Our Lamurians prayed that all lost souls would find their way to the heaven. As a result, the angels found me and escorted me into the Light (heaven).*

*"After going to heaven, I renewed my knowledge of God. I saw that while I was generally guided by the Light, our society as a whole was not guided by the Light. As a result, I could see that there would come a time when darkness would overtake our society. The main lesson of that life was to know the importance of the Light and One God for individuals and society.*

*"Things began to change at the end of the Golden Age, with economic pressure, such as controlling wages, work hours, and loss of respect for the working people. Crystals were already there in the houses as part of the electrical transmission system, then used for the communication system, television, and radio. Crystals were used in the houses and everyone had them. They later used these crystals to control people."*

## Precursor Lives

Precursor lives are the original lives where different ideas began at different times and in different cities in Atlantis, ultimately leading to its downfall. It all began at the tail end of the Golden Age, around 50,000 BC. In all these following lives, we can see clearly how in each life the individuals in heaven, before coming to Earth, planned different purposes and goals to make a difference in Atlantis. After incarnating in the body and living that life, good intentions and life goals became twisted and subverted and turned into something bad and evil due to demonic influences. All these events compiled together led to the collapse of Atlantean culture and ultimately to the downfall of Atlantis.

Atlantis was still a functioning unit. There was communication from one part to another. There were ideas going back and forth from city to city. An idea that originated in the South would be heard in the North. Many different minds were in these things. The growing selfishness of the ruling class caused a growing disregard and dehumanizing of humanity. People were developing new ideas in different cities of Atlantis and gradually testing them. This began around 65,000 BC.

By then, the idea had come from Atlanteans living in Lamuria about utilizing Lamurian technology to enhance psychic abilities and for control. Around 70,000 BC, the low-ability Lamurians were using Atlantean crystals in the power plants in Lamuria, to control other low- and medium-level Lamurians and to turn them against the high-level Lamurians. When Atlanteans in Lamuria found out about it, they did not understand it, but sent the idea to Atlantis to work on and to develop the technology for control. The idea spread around the continent. That life, described in chapter four, became one of the most important precursor lives.

As the mind work was being developed, they were able to understand how the mind worked and how the brain was related to it. By controlling certain parts of the brain, they could control what the mind was thinking. This whole batch of ideas fit together, and this is the cluster that evolved into the hellhole that was Atlantis.

This began because of the ambition, arrogance, and selfishness of the Atlantean ruling class; their desire to make their way through the world by force. They would conquer other countries and become rich. They would send a great army by boats and take over another country and strip it of its wealth and make the people slaves so they could continue to send wealth back to Atlantis. This was happening before the end of the Golden Age. They had great ocean vessels and could send the army across the ocean, supply it, equip it, and launch it so that they could coordinate and take a kingdom with no trouble. They did this in Lamuria but here they were not active as a nation encouraging this conquest. Here it was independent action by the local commanders.

After that, different people at different times and in different parts of Atlantis came up with different ideas, such as ideas to break up the family, breeding special kids for the rulers, using crystal to develop psychic abilities, and implanting crystal device that started initially as a communication devices into the neck to control others. These ideas converged as they spread across Atlantis. This led to the abject, grinding misery that went on for more than 30,000 years. Finally, God had mercy, and the whole continent was destroyed and this got the human race back on track and moving forward again.

These lifetimes are important to examine. Many different decisions were made in different places and led to different problems. All those good intentions and purposes which were planned in heaven before coming to this Earth got slightly twisted and subverted, and turned into something bad and evil in the end. All taken together, it led to the collapse of Atlantean culture. It is a warning to humans in the present time. How many decisions are being made today that can lead to something similar? Innocuous little things that government officials or scientists decide to do could eventually lead to something like this. We should be cautious. In Atlantis, as the Golden Age was coming to an end and the Dark Age was beginning, all these events, compiled together, led to the collapse as things got perverted and twisted.

### Origin of the Idea to Use Crystals for Telepathic Communication

One of my patients recalled a past life in which he was a king of a city. He was told that there were a few Lamurian traders in the city who could communicate with others at a distance and had foreknowledge of future events. The king became intrigued by this and asked a Lamurian how he could do it. The Lamurian explained that, through prayers, meditation, and spiritual development, everybody could do the same. The king did not believe it, and since some people found the Lamurians holding crystals in their hands, he ordered his technologists to create crystals through which he could do the same. This was where the idea of using a crystal to communicate with others from a distance began, which ultimately led to the idea of implants to control people, leading to slavery. From heaven, the king realized that he planned to learn spirituality from the Lamurians and spread it in Atlantis, but it got twisted and he became obsessed with developing spirituality with crystal technology.

- *"I am a forty-four-year-old king of a coastal city called Hammerschmit, on the northwest coast of Atlantis. This is 77,201 BC. My name is Charl. I became king when I was thirty-three years old, after my father died. He was very clever. He had just one official wife and he did not even marry her right away because he did not know which son he would select as his successor. He had many women, and many children from them. Another advantage was that he did not have to worry about being murdered, because there was no definite heir to the throne. He selected me to be the future king when I was nineteen-years-old. Then he married my mother and made me his legitimate son. He chose me because of my judgment and being closed mouth and not chattering about anything. This way, people do not know what I am thinking and feeling. This is a good quality in a king.*

  *"Following my father's example, I also have many women and have children from them but am not married to anybody. I am a good king. I have a man in charge of each section of the city and I have men in charge of each specific task. Several of them are siblings of mine, but I have someone watching them. In my palace and in*

*the city, we have electricity, light, and a small amount of heat. We can make concentrated heat with electricity for a small area. That is all we have, technology-wise. In my city, for the most part, education is a private thing. Parents educate and train their children as they want to. I was educated in communication, learning how to be a king and run a kingdom, judging, passing laws, and how to know who is your friend and who is not.*

*"We have three Lamurian families in this city and all of them seem to be different than we are. They seem to communicate with people at a distance and have a foreknowledge of what is going to happen. When I asked one of the Lamurians about how he knows, he said that it could be done through spiritual development with prayers, meditation, and other spiritual practices. I tried to meditate for a couple of weeks but nothing happened, and I realized that he must have been putting me off. I am sure they have something they use which makes them psychic. My men saw him holding a crystal while trying to communicate with somebody at a distance. My men could not figure out how they do it either.*

*"At the age of forty-five, I gave orders to my technologist to take the clues they have and figure out how those Lamurians get their psychic abilities and foreknowledge, and then make a technological device. I am not fool enough to believe that rubbish about psychic development through spiritual practices. They are just trying to fool us and throw us off track. We suspect that they have some secret device about which we do not know that makes psychic communication at a distance possible. We do not know what it is or how it works.*

*"I told my technologists they should watch these Lamurians and reach their own conclusions. Their job is to figure out how and build me a similar technological device that will help me to do it. They are sworn to official state secrecy. They cannot mention this to anyone. I want that technology. I want it for my city and me. I told them to*

*keep their mouths shut and work diligently to figure out how to make it. At first they spy on Lamurians, trying to find out what is happening and how it is happening and, in particular, how the crystals are used. Of course, you cannot look at a crystal and see the inclusions or impurities so easily, especially when they are done atom by atom.*

*"I am dying at the age of sixty-eight of some lung disease. My technologists could not figure out how the Lamurians communicate with the crystals. They did not succeed. My successor has been picked and he knows what is going on, so this work will continue. I have a terrible cough and am very sick. I lost a lot of weight. I die feeling frustrated about not being able to accomplish everything I wanted to accomplish, such as creating the technology for distance communication and foreknowledge. We still have not figured it out, but someday we will. I will not be here but my son will carry it on. I have done well in other areas. We regulated commerce very well and we made it easy for the citizens to make money. Of course, if they make money, they pay taxes. We took care of tax and self-defense problems. There is a beautiful harbor and we made sure that citizens could trade.*

*"I die thinking I am going to get that technology. I really want it so I can know what is happening, who is doing what, and who is plotting against me. I can make my city the richest city on Earth. I feel remorse because I did not let anybody become close to me, so I did not experience real love. I had plenty of people around, plenty of women and kids, but never allowed any closeness with them. As my body dies, my spirit comes out of my body and I am just shocked to find that I still feel alive. I can see my dead body lying there but I am not dead. I do not feel sick anymore. I always thought that when you die, that is the end of you, but it is not true. I see this big ball of beautiful Light above me. As I am looking at it, I am traveling through it and I see my mother waiting for me. She takes my hand and leads me into the Light (heaven).*

*"After cleansing, I go to a place where I see the god of the sea, Marduk, who helps me to review my life. I see that one part of my life plan was to learn and develop spirituality in Atlantis with the help of Lamurians, but it got twisted and I became obsessed with trying to develop spirituality with technology without developing personal spirituality. I feel chagrin because I missed the opportunity I was given to bring spirituality to Atlantis and to accept and talk about it.*

*"From heaven, I see that I needed to learn the lesson about not getting so tied to the traditions and to not get so fastened onto the old solutions that you cannot see a new one that is better. Just because technology has always been the answer in Atlantis does not mean that technology is still the answer. And just because spirituality has never been the answer in Atlantis does not mean it cannot be now. I need to learn to be flexible to see around the problem.*

*"I see from heaven that I was very responsible for getting technology for spirituality started, which later led to the crystal implants in people to control them. It just kept on building and led to total slavery and ultimate destruction of Atlantis. I see now that I had many series of lives after that life where I was given many chances to make it better in each of those lives but it didn't happen because the demonic influences kept building upon themselves. I see a whole long chain of lives with lots of tiny dots, meaning that those lives bear on it but are not very important. I see that I have to look at least six lives, and resolve them to resolve my karmas.*

*"From heaven, I see that the constant queasiness in my stomach in my current life came partly from this life in Atlantis, where, as a king, I was always on guard and always worried about somebody trying to kill me. Being closed mouthed and non-communicative back then was a virtue, but is a big drawback for me in the current lifetime."*

### *Origin of the Idea of Crystal Implants*

Following is an example of a patient who recalled a past life in Atlantis in which he was a crystal engineer, where they used crystals originally to counteract abnormal behavior and to reduce the violence in the mentally ill and also in criminals. Subsequently, there was a desire to use crystal devices in the military to cause violent behavior in their soldiers so they could brutalize their enemies. Crystals were already being used as receivers above every home and building for all types of communication devices, such as television, telephones, computers, and different electrical appliances. They were also used as locating devices and for locating things that were lost, and the rulers had the ability to broadcast from their crystals to the rest of the community. Then they began to develop crystal technology to enslave people for hard work and to reduce rebellion by implanting crystal devices in their necks. It was the beginning of the misuse of crystal devices for slavery, which led to the ultimate downfall of the Atlantean culture.

- *"I am a sixty-two-year-old male living in Hethopollis City in 75,003 BC. My name is Niran. I am a crystal engineer. I designed the crystal-growing process. I grow the crystals as computers. It has the matrix, which is the circuitry pattern. Crystals are drawn up with an electromagnetic current and they grow. There is a messaging system that is used to address. You can send a message to anyone with these devices or you can send the message to a group or you can broadcast based on the pattern and the message. Each device reports its location and a variety of information that it gets from the body and can influence thoughts. It was designed originally to help counteract abnormal behavior. The implanted device senses those abnormal patterns occurring in the brain and sends stimuli to counteract those patterns, particularly violent behavior, and to reduce the violence and pacify it.*

*"Since the age of twenty-five, I have researched the nature of circuitry and have created a variety of different programs. I worked with neuroscientists, understanding and mapping the impact on different areas of the brain, and how the signals can be sent out wherever they have to be stimulated. I basically developed that crystal device to control an abnormal behavior, and subsequently, there was interest in using this crystal device for other purposes, such as by the military for defense purposes, basically causing violent behavior in our own soldiers; controlling violent behavior in criminals; and also in mental illness. Basically, I supported the development of that technology and continued to work on and evolve it for additional purposes as needs came along.*

*"The crystal device was fairly small when it started, about an inch long, which was sufficient for what we were using it for. They have grown in size for other purposes. Originally it was done with external stimuli and then we developed ways for individuals to stimulate themselves when they felt behavioral problems coming on, with the individual having some control over the device. It is effective. We are also using the crystal devices to stimulate different organs, or the implants could have different substances, which could correct biological imbalances in certain organs or lack of production of certain chemicals, and things of that nature. We really have not perfected it at this time but there is research going on in that direction.*

*"I am the top technologist and belong to the ruling class, and I am working closely with the rulers. Crystals are also used as receivers above every house. They are used for all types of communication devices, such as television, videos, video telephones, computers, etc. We have digital technology and we have the ability to tune into an identifier like a video phone just like you have phone numbers and you can communicate with people from place to place or from the broadcast or to send messages and information to a small group of people. The communication*

*can be stored so you can still pick up the communication like an e-mail or voice mail in the current time.*

*"The technology used in this crystal device was built upon other technology, such as putting crystal receivers above the houses for communication. It has similar circuitry; it is just that there is another part of it that was specifically designed for the brain. Crystals are also used for locating different devices and locating something that is lost. Rulers have the ability to broadcast from their crystals to the rest of the community. We also have the ability to communicate with other computing devices for tabulations and polls.*

*"We also use the crystals for storing knowledge. Basically, our libraries are in the crystals. We have the ability to access knowledge that is needed via the same mechanism as you would use to think of devices in a particular home. Each area of knowledge is indexed in certain ways so you can search through or look for a particular kind of information, like we do on the Internet, but it is more advanced in Atlantis. We have something equivalent to video in the homes as well as in the theaters for entertainment. We have theaters and amphitheaters and there are a variety of cultural events.*

*"Computers are crystal in nature, but in modern technology, they are built on silicon crystals. Computers in Atlantis were designed differently, but they had very similar functions because today's computers are crystals also, but they have different types of circuitry. Atlanteans did not get the circuitry the way we do now. They were not necessarily linear, the way we have it in the current life. In Atlantis, our computers have primarily the ability to store things and identify and filter indexes. They are primarily involved with storing, searching, and retrieving information.*

*"Crystals in Atlantis are also used for healing, music, and decorative purposes, but I do not have much knowledge about that. I focus only on its electro-dynamic*

*properties to carry signals. My involvement and discoveries with crystals are mostly about technology connected with behavioral modification. I built upon the work of others who have already used crystals for communication. My specialty is in the circuitry itself and the programming of it and how it would be organized.*

*"In my city, we already have enslaved people with my crystal technology. We have a lot of manual labor to be done in agriculture, construction, and other menial labor jobs. I basically created crystal devices and the doctors implanted them in people. We have done research on whether they can be used to create slaves for doing hard work and reducing their reactions to hard work. We basically assist people by having the strength to work in this way and stop them from rebelling. It is more effective. We do not have to force or beat up people, and no violence involved. We do not have to be concerned about an uprising. In our city, we are using this technology in a large scale in the labor class, which is about ten percent of the total population. About five or six cities in Atlantis have controlled slaves. We are fairly early in the adoption of this technology. There are about six hundred large cities and several thousand smaller cities in Atlantis.*

*"We belong to the ruling class or nobility class. There is a merchant class that provides for the needs of society. They are also represented in the legislature. Then we have a technological class. There is a religious class, and the higher priests also belong to the ruling class and are very rich. Then we have state labor class, which lives in a different section of the town. We do not have street people. Everybody is provided for and taken care of. We do not have a feeling of division. Everybody plays an important role in society and everybody lives in harmony.*

*"I have a team of people working with me. We are invited to another city by the king to train their technologists to see if this will work. In the new city, we first present and demonstrate the use of our technology and then*

*manage, coordinate, and work with their technologists. We lay out our plans about how and where it will be done, the production facilities that need to be built, and help coordinate the construction and the whole process until they are self sufficient to use it on their own.*

*"After training people in that city, I go back to my own city. I die of a brain aneurysm at the age of eighty-four, thinking about how wrong it was to control people and that I will find a way to stop it. I was concerned about technology developing without love and spirituality. My spirit goes to heaven with angels and gets cleansed.*

*"I review my life in a garden with a couple of masters, looking at the implications of the decisions I made about using technology without love and spirituality, and the implications of controlling people. I am shown what could happen to society in the future and the potential for misuse of technology and the need to safeguard against that. I feel a sense of tremendous responsibility in developing and using the technology. If the worst did happen, then I would have great karma to suffer and to experience what those people suffered. I need to be more humble and need to balance technology with spirituality. From heaven, I see that my head and neck problems in the current life came from that life."*

### Program To Grow Crystals to Enslave People

In a past life, one patient recalled being a princess in Atlantis, where she and her father adopted a program to grow crystals in the lab, to be implanted in people to enslave them. Although she did not put the implants in people directly, she was responsible for planning and overseeing that the program was successful.

* *"I am a young woman living in a city in the northeast part of Atlantis in about 75,000 BC. My father is a ruler, a king. We live in a big palace. Being royalty, I had one-on-one*

*interaction with knowledgeable people. I could pretty well adhere to whatever I want to learn. I study about the history of Atlantis, the history of our city, and the history of how the society was formed. I also learn how to be royalty and of our role in society.*

*"We are beginning the experiments on a few people in a scientific lab in a big building where they are growing crystals. The crystals are grown in a tank, almost like an aquarium. There are matrixes at the bottom and they grow in the tanks. Each crystal has the same matrix and each part has the same pattern, which we will be able to influence by a remote device. Every single crystal that they implant into a person will have something that distinguishes it. If we want to, we can do broadcasts to everybody, which is like a generic message, but we can also single out a certain person. We have doctors come and implant crystals in people. I am not responsible for doing this but I am responsible for planning and overseeing, because my father does not trust anybody else.*

*"We want to control people and make them do what we want by making adjustments to the crystal implants. We implant two two-inch crystals in each person on each side of the neck. We do this to many people. We tell them that it is good for them and they will thank us for it. It will make their lives easier. They will not have to think and make decisions and they will be happier. Initially we have to make adjustments, but eventually the process became very successful. We have some kind of device outside through which we can control and monitor people. We make them do different things to see what happens and see if they can follow commands. We are successful in making them our slaves. It is new and my father decided to do it. It has been done in only a few other cities.*

*"My job is to oversee the whole experiment. I am excited about this project because, for the people who are basically controlled slaves, this will make them want to do better and be happy. We will have no risk of uprising or*

*rebellion. They will be more motivated to do the work and we will know of any potential problems before they arrive. The whole city will become rich and prosperous.*

*"I fall in love with the surgeon who puts the implants into the slaves, and at the age of twenty-two, I marry him. During the marriage ceremony, I am wearing a long velvet dress. I have a crown. The groom is wearing white pants, a jacket, and boots. The ceremony takes place in a temple. Behind the priest, there is a symbol of the sun. The top of the temple can be opened. There is a lot of light. When closed, there is a glass ceiling of different colors, so the light shines through. The floors are made of marble. The seats go up. I do not see any statues of gods or goddesses. The priest calls certain heavenly beings to come before and during the marriage ceremony. We are kneeling at one point, and the priest blesses us. Then there is a big celebration.*

*"By the age of thirty-five, we are very successful with the program. Besides the laborers, we also began to put crystal devices in the people who are working with the basic tasks of the project. We have two children, a boy and a girl. My husband has trained other physicians how to put the implants in people. My father died of old age and my brother became the ruler.*

*"At the age of fifty-two, I die of cancer of the reproductive organs. My spirit goes to heaven and gets cleansed. I review my life with twelve beings. I have a sense of dread about what will happen in the future because of what we began; that is, control of people. I see that it was a manipulation of the laws of nature, not realizing the full consequences of controlling people. It is always wrong, even if it seems like it might make their lives better. I see that my father and I had a lot of darkness. Heavenly beings are showing different things that can happen in the future, and I am realizing that I will have to suffer similar symptoms in future lives to make up for what we began. Control can be stopped in the future or it can get worse with total control of society. It depends on our free will.*

*"I see my headaches came partly from that life because the implants caused pain in those people's heads, which I chose to suffer as a karmic problem."*

### Origin of the Idea of Breeding Superior Children for the Ruling Class

A patient recalled the following past life as a source of relationship problems, a fear of being in a powerful position, and a fear of making a wrong decision. In that past life in Atlantis as a ruler, he decided to create a breed of people for the ruling class because he realized that the ruling class people are just as ordinary as regular people except that they are in a powerful position. So he started the idea of a developmental academy and selecting the top students to breed superior kids for the ruling class.

After his death, when he went to heaven, he realized his divine plan was to encourage the royal ranks to intermarry with the best and the brightest people from the general population. This would have improved the ruling stock and integrated ordinary people into the ruling class openly to make society more equal. This way, those in the ruling houses would know what it was like to be poor and what it was like to work for a living instead of isolating themselves, thinking of themselves as gods and goddesses to the lower class. It would have given power to the general population and would have had great support from the general public, too. Instead, the idea got twisted and misapplied due to Satanic influences, setting up a system where people would be misused and abused for generations to come.

- *"I am a ruler of the city called Nemity, a coastal city in southern Atlantis. This is 64,807 BC. I became the king at thirty-one, after my father died of a sudden heart attack. In the ruling class, there is a structure. The king and the nobles control the city. There is a noble in charge of each section of the city, and they all answer to me. Part of my concern is to keep the nobles from ganging up against me. I play a continuous game of power politics. I have several wives and many children from them.*

*"I am setting up a plan for improving children of the ruling class, because the real difference between the nobles (the rulers) and the common people is that the noble people have swords and people do what the nobles say, but you can also see that they are just ordinary people. I want to improve the ruling class. I want to make sure that we are better than the ordinary people. At first, it is a topic of conversation only among the kings as they make their courtesy visits to each other and send their messengers back and forth. The other kings of neighboring cities also think it is a good idea.*

*"This idea is born among kings and they begin to decide what it is they want to do. We begin to hammer out a plan to improve our breed and we decide to base it on physical, emotional, psychological, and intellectual levels. We come up with the idea of a developmental academy and taking the top students from it to breed our kids. I insist on the school being in my kingdom, under my control, and with my contributing money and people to help.*

*"First I get the school set up and the mechanism to get the kids in the school. The recruiters go out to a different city every year. We start out with five and end up with seven cities contributing to the school, helping out with its upkeep and providing the money to run it. Every year the recruiters start out, first going to one city and recruiting kids from in and around the city. We move between the cities once every five years, collecting the kids who are in the right age range for these schools. There is only one school for seven cities because it is not economical to have one school in each city, since there are not that many superior kids.*

*"We put them through the educational plans. We teach them all the things that are very important, such as how to read, write, do arithmetic, how to run a business, and*

*how to run a kingdom. Then only a couple of the kids are chosen from these. They must be good-looking, intelligent, and have emotional stability. The rest are educated and sent home. Those who are selected for further training continue and become the technicians and chief people for the rulers, being the ones the kingdoms cannot function without.*

*"Meanwhile, one of my sons tries to kill me so he can become the king, but he does not succeed. I send my oldest son to another ruling family, so he does not end up killing me. He can learn how to run a kingdom there. Then I send my other sons, the ones who might inherit the throne, to other cities that are widely separated. It is like apprenticing them out. At the same time, other kings send their kids to me to be trained. I first train them how to be chief functionaries and how to run things. Then I teach them about the particulars of ruling. This is another of my innovations, so we, the kings, do not get killed by our children and also they get the training in how to be a good king by other kings.*

*"Right now, the superior kid breeding program is developing slowly, but there are plans for the institutions where the genetic experiments eventually begin. The kids who are chosen for it and their parents are never notified. Eventually, the parents are told that their child died of a disease or was killed in a fall or something else happened to him or her. In reality, they are inside the walls going through the breeding program.*

*"The institute for breeding is set up and is developing slowly. There are kids in the school who are trained, and then begin running the institute. The medical people have become better because of the school. The technical workers who are becoming scientists get better and better. Accidentally, it is having a very beneficial effect on my kingdom because each stage is causing an improvement in the technical and biological areas. I was not planning this at all. My city is becoming a technical center for the*

*whole country. We already have technical people, medical people, and scientists, but this is the first real, organized system for getting these people created and for concentrating them in one area at a research center.*

*"At the age of sixty-seven, I die of a stroke. My spirit wanders around the palace and after a while, the spirit of my mother, who died many years before, takes me to the Light (heaven). After cleansing, I go to the review of my life. I see that Megan, the god of the sea, is a master in heaven. He is telling me that it is just a life review and there is no judgment from God or him. He is telling me that basically I was a good king. One of the divine inspirations I brought from heaven was that, as people prosper, so does the kingdom and the king. If a king manages to set up a system where the people are happy and prosperous, then the king gets richer than ever. I wanted people to prosper so the kingdom could prosper. I brought the gift of being innovative and coming up with new ideas from heaven. Those ideas were divinely inspired. I see that I first brought the gift of innovation of being able to analyze the situation and second to see what possible solutions were there and to come up with innovations that would provide for what my analysis showed is needed. This was a unique gift and yet it was twisted and misapplied because of the demonic influences.*

*"From the heaven, I can see that I took that gift of being innovative a little further. Instead of encouraging the royal ranks to intermarry with the bright people from the general population, which was a path I could have chosen, I chose to keep the royal ranks exclusive and set up this school scheme to get new higher quality genes into the royal houses. This was not necessarily the way it should have been done. It was effective but not the one blessed by the Light. As far as the Light (heaven) is concerned, the more effective way was that I would have seen the problem, just as I did, but I would have come to a different conclusion on how to solve it.*

*"If I kept the program hidden, I kept my purposes from the people. Even some of the kings and lords did not figure it out, but they were not too bright in the first place. I could have developed the same results without this horrendous program, but demonic influences twisted my original divine plan.*

*"My divine plan was to encourage the nobles, the rulers, and the lords to get the sons- and daughters-in-laws from the general public who were superior, using them to improve the ruling stock through breeding, and integrate the ordinary people into the ruling class openly, to make the ruling class more equal. Those in the ruling houses would know what it was like to be poor, to work for a living, instead of isolating themselves as a strongly insulated group thinking themselves as gods and goddesses to the lower class. This would have had great popular support from the general public and would have given power to the general population with the knowledge that the lords and ladies were not super-people and were not gods.*

*"From heaven, I see that Atlantis could have been a good place if we had more spirituality, which was lacking in society, and that made it easy for the evil to permeate the whole of society. It ultimately led to slavery, total control of the society by the rulers, and the ultimate destruction of Atlantis. I am feeling shame and intense sadness about starting the idea of a breeding program, leading to abuse and misuse of people for generations in Atlantis.*

*"I see from the Light (heaven), that many of my problems came from that life to the current life, such as not wanting to be in a powerful position, not wanting to take responsibility, fear of making a wrong choice, and relationships problems with different people.*

*"Although I did not hurt anybody personally in that lifetime, because the program was not developed completely, I did set up the plan for it to develop and trained my son to follow the plan. It was my brain child and thus*

*I was responsible for all the damage caused to the individuals and the society for future generations."*

## Origin of the Idea of Separating Children From Parents

A patient recalled a past life in Atlantis where he was a physician and a research director. He was doing research to change the gene in people making it easier to control them. He was also doing research on breeding into people a selfless desire to work, and breed out the instinct to form a family and raise children, because his parents were very abusive toward him. He came to the conclusion that kids should not be raised by their parents. So he began to experiment with ways children should be raised and began the idea of separating children from their parents at the age of six months to one year of age, and bringing them up in a childcare facility. He also started the idea of eating the slaves after they were dead instead of wasting them, and also grinding their bodies into fertilizer.

After his death, when he went to heaven, during his life review, he realized that he had planned to have a traumatic childhood so later on he could work on improving family life and gain better parenting skills. But his parents went too far with abuse and trauma and opened him up for the demonic possession, which altered his plans. He began to destroy family life by taking kids out of the family. Also, his parents accused him of being out of control; that is where he got the idea that he had to put control into the genes of the children who were being born.

Following is the account of that past life:

- *"I am a thirty-four-year-old man living on the eastern coast, north of the mountains of Atlantis, in a city called Urrill, in 62,935 BC. I have light hair, light skin, and blue eyes. I am wearing a white toga and sandals. I am a physician and the director of a research laboratory. I am involved with genetics and human behavior research. I am working on changing a gene in people that will make it easy to control them. I am trying to breed a control gene into people so that the masters can manipulate them and control them. This way they can follow orders without questioning and be more economically productive, and the rulers can make more money from their work. I am ordered to do it by the rulers and I am excited about it. Some people on whom we are doing research have implants in them and my work is involved with making these implants more effective so we can control these people more effectively.*

*"Some of the things I am doing in research concern breeding into people the selfless desire to work, and yet I want them to be healthy so we do not have to take care of them and they can work practically for nothing, just for food and shelter. I am trying to figure out how to change the genes so the children who are born will have these characteristics. I am also trying to remove the instinct to form a family and to come together to raise children.*

*"Basically I know it is unethical to do this, but I do it because I am asked by the rulers, and also for the prestige, power, and money. If I do not do the job, I will be disgraced, replaced, and I do not want to have to give up all of what I have achieved. I believe that what I am doing to people does not matter, as compared to what benefits me.*

*"We treat people like animals by doing needle biopsies or small surgeries without any anesthesia. We are trying to harvest ova mechanically from women by making a cut and putting some apparatus inside, next to the ovaries, and trying to flush the developed eggs into the suction device. They have been given hormones to cause eggs to ripen and to be ready so, as they are released, we pick them up. We do these experiments on people who are specially selected for their genetic characteristics, from the farms outside the city, but once they are in the research center, they are pretty much treated as slaves. They work*

*in the fields here and have to raise the food. They are kept and fed, and when we need the genetic material, we give them hormones and harvest the ovum. Ninety percent of those here are women, because it is harder to harvest the ova than it is the sperm.*

*"Before the egg is fertilized we tamper with the DNA, trying to change characteristics to diminish judgment, make them able to be controlled, make them more willing to take orders blindly and to follow what they are told, make them more interested in producing and fulfilling their commitment to the master than they are in taking care of their own survival, create a crazy altruism, and diminish an urge to take care of their own children and form a family unit based around the children. We make the changes we want in the ova, fertilize it, and put it back in a woman. When the baby is born, we take the baby away from the mother and watch its development.*

*"Some of these research subjects have neck implants but not everybody, because we are still experimenting about how to get it right. My genetic modifications are the other half of the equation. Here is this device for control, but at the same time, I am trying to change the genetic makeup so that people will be more like what the masters want in the beginning. The thought is that if you can get these characteristics put into the human race genetically, the control device in the neck will be ten times more effective.*

*"Most of the younger workers in the research institute who we get from the schools are educated and come here to learn about our research. Once they come, they stay. They all have neck implants. The older researchers, like me, do not have them. Some of the people outside the research center, especially the young ones near the rulers, the source of power, have devices, but most do not.*

*"Most of the genetic experimental babies do not survive, and very few of those experiments are successful. We kill most of the misfits or mal-developed babies, such*

*as babies with no brains or other organs, or with de-
formed body parts, or anything that is not perfect. After
being killed, we grind them up and use them as fertilizer,
because it is a shame to waste the calcium, nitrogen, and
phosphorus. We should put it back in the dirt and grow
stuff with it.*

*"I am also experimenting with the ways the children
are raised. This is the precursor to breaking up the family unit. Another thing I am interested in is controlling
the children's education, their upbringing, so that we can
make them more prone to be controlled or more suitable
to being controlled. Once in a while, I will get together
with the researchers from other cities to discuss what I
have discovered, and how to spread the idea and have
other people duplicate my work to make sure it can be
done consistently.*

*"I live in an apartment in the institute. I have been liv-
ing here since I started, at the age of eighteen. I was selected to work here to become a doctor and do research. I
am pretty vicious. I even killed two competitors to become
the director of this program, and the rulers found out and
they wanted somebody like me who is totally unscrupu-
lous and is not bothered by moral character.*

*"I met my wife when she came here to the research cen-
ter to work as a technician and I married her. I have two
children, but rather than keeping them with us, since it is
one of my objectives, I put them in a child-rearing facility
in the research center. My wife goes to see the kids sometimes. I try telling her not to, but she does not have good
sense and she does not listen. It is important that these
children be raised properly, in a childcare center by somebody else. I want to destroy the family impulses so parents
do not care about their own children, and I want to get rid
of their survival instincts.*

*"Our research facility is very large and it encloses its
farm. There is a fence all around so nobody can leave
the place except the few high-ranking officials. This way,*

*nobody can get into the city and nobody outside will know what we are doing. The people who live here (the slaves) raise the food and do the farm's work. It has its own independent water supply so we are not dependent on the outside world. We do have to import some things, but not in large quantities.*

*"By the age of sixty-one, it has become an obsession with me that these research subjects are less than people and should be treated as lab animals, so I work at developing the control techniques with my own staff. They have to stop thinking of these research subjects as human beings, and become immune to their suffering, because they don't count for anything. Later, when the research subjects die, we grind up their bodies to use them as fertilizer, too. I encourage the research workers to think of them as pre-used fertilizer and as a reservoir of genetic material. I have a strong desire to eliminate, by genetic modification, the instinct to have a family.*

*"We are still studying the effect of genetic modifications. We cannot try it on the general public until we know what we are doing. We are making changes inside the gene. When we have the strain perfected and we know what we are doing, we will start planting the children out in the general population so they will grow up and their genes will spread throughout the general population. Even if we only get five or six babies a year who live, that is enough over time to spread the genetic changes throughout the whole population.*

*"We chose these people for experiments in different ways. Generally, they are picked up from the rural areas with the excuse that they are going to school or that they are hired by the research institute or some other place. After we get them, and after a period of time, letters are sent to the parents on their behalf, but they do not get to communicate. After awhile, the parents are told their child got a job overseas and is planning to be there for several years, so the parents don't expect to get any*

*communication. Sometimes, parents are told that they died accidentally or from a disease, so they stop expecting to see them.*

*"In this facility, the husband and wife live in an apartment and the children are taken away when they are six months to one year old, to be raised in a child care facility. It is healthier for the children. Some of the mothers get very upset. I will be pleased when the instinct for family and raising children is totally eliminated from the race. It is just silly.*

*"I die at the age of seventy-three of cancer of the spinal cord. I have appointed a younger man as the director. I have established some of the traits in people. As I am dying, I wish I had more time. After death, my spirit is feeling rage. I go to the young man who is going to be the new director and go inside his body. I want to make sure he continues what I started and I want to make sure he does exactly what I want. I whisper in his ears, talk to him, and push him to make the experiments go faster. But it takes time for children to grow and you barely get a chance to influence three generations in a lifetime through genetic modification. I am also motivating him to use dead people's bodies as meat; that way people can stop thinking of them as humans and turn them completely into farm animals. Their treatment inside the institute became like that of animals.*

*"After this doctor dies, I go inside the next lab director, pushing him to continue the experiments. After this one dies, I go inside the next director. One day he went to visit the child-rearing center, and through this director, I am able to see that the children are very unhappy and sad. I realized that being raised there is not a good thing and I was wrong about it. It shook my confidence, the first quivering in the wall of my indifference. After the death of this third director, in whom I have remained, I pay attention to his spirit, which is looking up. I follow where he is looking and I see the Light and then his relative comes*

*and takes him to the Light. Then I also see my mother inside the Light and she takes me up in heaven too.*

*"In heaven after cleansing, I review my life with the heavenly guides. I see that, while growing up, I had an indifferent mother who did not care for me, and a mean and punitive father. They were very cruel and abusive to me. I was beaten, burned, starved, and chained. I hated them and one time I tried to poison them, but I did not succeed. They did not know it. At the age of fourteen, I was sent to another school, and at the age of eighteen, I was selected to go to the institute. I can see that my abusive childhood led my drive to eliminate the urge to have a family and children, with the whole race. I also see that my parents were very dark and my early childhood traumas also opened me for the demons to come into me.*

*"I also realize from heaven that I did plan to have a traumatic childhood so I would work on improving family life and gain better parenting skills. But that got twisted by the demons who came into me during the childhood traumas because my parents went to the extreme with abuse. Instead of improving family life, I ended up destroying it by taking kids out of the family. Now I am realizing that my impulse to save the children, to get myself saved in childhood, led to the conclusion that twisted my original plan to improve parents. What I intended to do became lost, and I was driven to get kids out of the home, assuming that all parents were brutal.*

*"My early mistreatment at home with all its negative consequences was supposed to help me develop tolerance for humanity and acceptance that people could do bad things and still rise above. Instead, I immersed myself in evil and lost that wonderful opportunity. At this time, Atlantis was very dark in the north and then it tapered off. The central mountainous region was relatively clean.*

*"From heaven, I also see that I planned to work with genetics. I was to discover three useful chemicals that could*

*be used in genetics. Again, because of the demonic influences, I went overboard and tried to change the genes. My parents always accused me of being out of control and that is where I got the idea that I had to put control into the genes of children being born and, I was not just doing what the rulers wanted. This was built into me.*

*"From heaven, I see that my problems that came from that life to the current life are empty feelings due to a lack of close relationships and lower back pain.*

*"I asked for forgiveness from all the people I hurt directly or indirectly in that life, and all the other lifetimes from then on, because of what I started in that life, such as breaking up family units, which continued for generations, until Atlantis submerged under water. When Dr. Modi prayed to God and requested the angels to heal me and every human being whoever lived in Atlantis, I saw a tornado type of Light coming from God and lifting out all the demons from Atlantis and humans from all over Earth, because almost everybody had lived many lives in Atlantis.*

*Then Dr. Modi requested the angels bring all the soul parts I lost in that life and for everybody who was hurt because of my actions and for all the human beings who ever lived in Atlantis, cleanse them, heal them, and integrate them with whom they belong. I saw it happening. That was a massive karma I had incurred. I also asked God to forgive me for my evil actions and not following my plan, and I heard God say, "Do not think of it as not following your plan but think of it as doing the best that you could under the circumstances. There was extreme darkness in Atlantis to interfere with everybody, so do not feel guilty; you did you best. Just learn your lesson and move on."*

### Origin Of the Dorm System

Following is another example where a patient recalled a past life in Atlantis, where he began the idea of implanting crystals to enslave people in his city and of separating them from the general population and putting them in a dorm.

- *"I am a forty-nine-year-old man living in Justin City, on the southeast coast of Atlantis. My name is Sardand and this is 49,519 BC. I am married and have two children: a girl, twenty and a boy, eighteen. I am a physician, surgeon, and a researcher who works with organ transplants. I live with my wife in a nice apartment house in the upper-class section of the city. My children are in college. We continue to enjoy the amenities that life in Atlantis provides us. We have the full range of cooking appliances, refrigeration, etc. in our kitchen. We use phones, computers, TVs, radios etc. We have elevators and air conditioning. Our apartment is well appointed.*

*"We have a ruling class, an upper class (of which I am a member), a middle and a lower-middle class, and a low class. The low class is made up of genetically altered people, mentally unbalanced people, and poor people. Our society has undergone change for the last few hundred years. Everyone here no longer has free will. Before, everyone was free. The low classes are the least free and most abused at this time.*

*"I am involved in doing experimental research on lower class people. I have begun to install implants in these experimental subjects. I have been working on this project for twenty years and finally it is gaining attention and producing results. These implant devices are made from oblong shaped crystals and were initially about two inches long and three-quarters of an inch wide. They were installed on both sides of the neck. Incisions were made about the length of the crystal, which is inserted under the skin, and the incision is sewed up. I have also done implant installations in the arms just below the shoulders. These were not successful and this approach was ruled out.*

*"The purpose of these experiments is to see how people will react with the implants. We want to see if people can be controlled using these implants and to what degree. But there are still a lot of problems in getting the implants to work effectively. We have created other sizes of implants and we hope to put them into practice sometime in the future. We have an implant that is about one and a quarter inch long and five-eighths inch wide. We have another one that is a half inch long and a quarter inch wide.*

*"I am in charge of this research unit and I work with other staff members. To date, I've done over seventy implants. All my initial research and my current implant projects have been approved by our rulers. Now that we know that implants can be done on a practical level, our goal is to produce a small, efficient crystal implant that is easy to install on masses of people. Our leaders continue to see the need for people who will be programmed to do hard physical labor.*

*"As the demand for more experimental subjects increases, government officials go out and gather up poor people against their will and bring them to me for experimentation. Our findings show that the implant program can be a success. There is a long way to go before it becomes efficient but it is a doable program. I summarize my findings in a report that goes up the chain of command all the way to the national technologists and the central government ruler. Meanwhile, we have run several controlled experiments with subjects involved in practical work situations with a hundred percent success rate.*

*"After the report goes through all the channels, I am ordered by the technologists to go on a country-wide tour to share my findings with others. I am well received and there is a great demand for my presentations. As I mentioned before, I've had this program from its infancy some twenty years ago. We continue to improve with smaller, more efficient crystals. By now we've reduced the size of the crystal from two inches long and three-quarters of an*

*inch wide to one and a quarter inch long and half an inch wide.*

*"By the time I am seventy years old, our technology has continued to advance. We are using only one crystal as opposed to two crystals. The crystal's size has been reduced to less than one inch long and three-eighths inch wide. We have implanted five thousand in our city alone, with thousands of others receiving implants in other parts of the country.*

*"Some of our subjects are at home, some are kept in the lab, and some are in special housing dorms for experimentation. These dorms were constructed at my request. I wanted to expand the experiments to a broader scale. We keep families as well as individuals in those dorms. Some families remain together and others are separated.*

*"We tried isolating certain children from their families to see how these children would respond under control. This project was done at the suggestion of our psychological staff. We gave up this program because the children did not respond well and we saw more physical and mental symptoms in isolated children. They appeared to be less bright and were more underdeveloped physically and mentally than non-isolated children of their age. Sometimes, we would implant an entire family of dorm people. But mostly we didn't implant until people were in their late teens or older.*

*"We are using our subjects to do common labor, domestic work, and physically demanding labor. The government decides where our subjects are needed. My current research is concerned with reducing the size of the crystal implant. The government is becoming more involved in mind control. They have special computers that allow them to communicate with implanted subjects via the implants.*

*"My wife, a college professor of social science, suspects something, but really doesn't know what I am doing, and the general public is not aware either. Some others at*

*the hospital do not approve of what we are doing but they
don't say anything to anyone.*

*"At seventy-seven, I retire from my job. I continue to
teach a course at the university for the next five years. At
the age of eighty-three, I totally retire from all public life.
I have time to reflect on my life and I have some reserva-
tions about my program. Initially, my idea was to create a
means to have a more efficient work force. But now I see
the implant program as something out of control. Implants
are increasing all over the country but the program is still
secret. Now over 11,000 people in our city of 200,000
have been implanted. I understand that the program could
branch out to other classes. I have anxious thoughts about
the abusive nature of the program.*

*"At the age of eighty-eight, I am in the hospital dying of
a weak heart and lungs. I have difficulty breathing. I slip
into an unconscious state. To my surprise, my spirit leaves
my body. My last thoughts are that I enjoyed the success
and notoriety of my life. But my enthusiasm is tempered
by the lingering doubt that remains with me. I am concerned about the excesses and the abuses in the implant
program. I have promised myself to never be involved in
anything like this again.*

*"My spirit stays around until my funeral ceremony is
complete. I watch as a priest, family members, friends,
and some rulers attend the ceremony. After this, my body
is cremated. I don't know where to go, so I stay around
and observe the implant program. I can see that the program is growing more rapidly than I ever imagined. After
several hundred years, I am found by Light beings and
taken to the Light (heaven).*

*"In reviewing the life from heaven, I see that Atlantis
had lot of demonic influences at this time. I see that I also
had demonic influences. Many people are influenced and
even controlled by demons. I see demons in the labs and
where the implants are taking place. When I started my
project, there was not nearly as much darkness. I can see*

*that Atlantis will continue to become darker and become a terrible place to live, partly because of my implant and dorm programs.*

*"I realize the magnitude and scope of this life. I see that the seeds I planted will grow and eventually affect all of humanity. I am horrified as I experience feelings of shame, guilt, and sadness for my actions. From heaven, I realize that my plan for this life was to become a medical doctor and do research to reduce the aging process and prevent disease, but my plan got sidetracked because of demonic influences.*

*"From the Light (heaven), I see many of the emotional, mental, and physical problems in humans are caused due to implants, such as serious mental disorders leading to feelings that somebody is taking thoughts out or inserting thoughts; feelings of being controlled; and the feeling that somebody is watching them. Also, mental retardation, speech disorders, serious physical diseases such as Parkinson disease and multiple sclerosis. The implant procedures reduced people to robots or to the animal level, and stripped people's spirit, dignity, and humanity.*

*"From heaven, I can see that I've had many lives in Atlantis after this life, where implants and other tortures were done on me and was forced to live in the dorms. I also see many of my problems coming from that life to the current life, such as feeling guilty about hurting others, feelings of carrying heavy burdens, feeling that I was undeserving of God and the Light, and having the soul parts of those people in whom I put implants, resulting in taking on symptoms of panic and lack of emotions. By keeping these soul parts, I planned (in this life) to be emotionally isolated and to shield myself from the pain and guilt of that Atlantis life. I did this by placing a layering of dark shields around my emotional and physical body, my brain, and my soul. These shields have blocked my emotions and disconnected me from God and the Light. As a result, I have felt undeserving of being connected to the Light.*

*"I asked forgiveness from all the people who were damaged due to the crystal implants and being put in dorms in that life and all the other lifetimes after that life, which includes almost all the human beings who lived in Atlantis during the existence of Atlantis over the last 30,000 years. Then, as Doctor Modi requested the angels to bring all the soul parts which I lost in that life and all the other lives after that, and also the soul parts of all the human beings who were affected due to my implant and dorm programs, and integrate them with whom they belong after cleansing and healing, I saw it all happening, healing me and all the other human beings who were affected.*

*"As I see the size and scope of my implant and dorm programs and the far-reaching negative effect it had on all of humanity, I asked God to forgive me and free me from guilt and take down the walls and shields around my emotional and physical body, my physical brain, and my soul, and to connect me with the Light. I saw that all of the walls and shields were removed and protective Light was inserted in their place. I felt God's forgiveness by experiencing natural, comfortable feelings of freedom from my burdens.*

*"I felt a new-found freedom and I have a better emotional connection to the Light. I feel that I experienced spiritual growth. I know that I can function more positively in this life because of the negativity from that life was cleared away during this session."*

### Origin of Optical Technology Given By the Aliens and its Misuse

A person recalled a life as an alien from race five of group two, as described in chapter three, on her planet and came to planet Earth on an expedition. While on Earth, she worked with people in Atlantis and gave them optical technology, which led Atlanteans to develop crystal technology, leading to the control of people and ultimately the collapse of the whole culture.

- *"I am a twelve-year-old female about two feet tall with a wide, thick body, which looks very compact and muscular. I have two arms and two legs, which appear stiff. I look like a human but am shorter and blocky. My head appears square or cubic. There are two eyes with heavy bones surrounding them. There are ear openings and flaps as external ears that resemble human ears. The back of my head looks flat, so that most of the face and head are forward. The hair is black and coarse, mostly back away from my face. My eyebrows are thick. My nose is small and very close. My mouth is wide and the teeth resemble human teeth. My skin is brownish. I am not full-grown physically and I am not sexually mature yet. On the average, a full-grown male is about four feet tall and a female about thirty-two inches tall. My name is Langehrithen and I live on a planet called Hockvieaier. It is the year 932 of our new government. That is when our calendar started. Our years are longer than Earth years. Our planet is larger than Earth and the gravity is stronger.*

  *"Our grown adults appear very strong because they have heavy bones, heavy muscles, and with their short movement, a lot of force is applied to the bones, so they can lift heavy weights. They are not fast but are very powerful. Our hands have four fingers and a thumb. Our feet also have five toes, and a wider space between the big toe and the little toes. The foot is flatter, and instead of walking off the big toe as humans do, we walk off all the toes. The foot rolls directly forward. We have short necks, fewer vertebra, fewer connectors, and less flexible backs. There is hair on our shoulders and upper backs and on our lower bodies in both front and back. We usually use very plain and dark clothing; straight cut jackets and pants. It is a unisex outfit. Our sense of smell is strong.*

*"I am living with my parents in a little farming town where we raise food for the city and chickens for eggs. Our house is wide and blocky, made up of a material that is compacted and fused together of stone and dirt. On this planet, women can have a child roughly every six years. After I was born, my parents did not have a second child right away. A female is fertile periodically close together. Then the conception time widens out. The woman has an ovulation cycle every six years after the first child.*

*"My mother is going to have another baby when I am twelve, and I will be pushed out of my baby status and into adult status very quickly. Physically, I still have six years to grow into the adult size and be capable of childbirth. As soon as the baby is born, I am expected to behave like an adult with more adult responsibility.*

*"My mother went to a birthing place, which is like a city facility. Hospitals are only for the sick. My mother has a baby boy. At birth, he looks like a rock, blocky and solid, and about eight inches long. The baby is not as hard as grown-ups are. It looks like his ribs and shoulders are more flexible and they can bend down. Later on, in adulthood, the flexing point is in front of the rib cage where the ribs connect, and in the back where the backbone is, so when a child is born, the ribs tilt down at these connecting points in the front and rear. It is like having a collapsible baby. One of the first things an attendant does is to hold the pelvis, and with her hands, she pops the ribs and shoulders into place.*

*"As the child grows, the cartilages that collapsed will harden and, in young adulthood, become solid. The legs are set differently than human legs, which are mounted on the side, while ours are mounted straight under the pelvis. Our anatomy is slightly different than humans. In the female, the vaginal opening is above the pubic bone toward the front of the body, and the same is true of the male penis.*

*"At the age of twenty, I am about to get married. As I mature, my teeth grow longer, like fangs. It is a sign of sexual*

*maturity. We are very proud of those teeth. I had just a basic education in reading, writing, and math in school. My primary work is digging underground and making tunnels. All of us use our digging skills as a sexual desirability gauge. Both males and females dig tunnels, which they use as transportation pathways, as cultural connections, and also as living quarters. Underground living is as natural to us as living on the surface. I am marrying a man who is a trader. He is six years older than I am, which is accepted as an ideal age. It is a civil service, like a court marriage. We go to a building equivalent to a courthouse and we enter into the marriage contract literally like a business deal, signing the papers and making a formal commitment. The writing kind of resembles Chinese writing. After a celebration, we start our life together.*

*"According to the marriage contract, the marriage is renewable every six years following the fertile period. We have the option to separate if we choose, if the couple has no child. If there is a child, then we have to wait for twelve years if we want to separate. The child must be twelve years old. If there is no child, then after each fertile period, if we do not get pregnant, we can divorce. We have to stay together to raise the child for twelve years.*

*"The land we live on is provided to us by our parents, and it is permitted by the government. We dig a hole underground and live there. We start out by digging a small hole for two, and enlarge it as the family develops and grows. As we have more children, we build a home above ground and leave the starter home for somebody else. The place underground has ventilation shafts going above ground to ventilate the entire house. All the beginners live underground in those hole-like dwellings, which have openings but no doors.*

*"At the age of twenty-two, I give birth to a baby girl. I decide I do not want a second child. I want to go to school to learn about science and technology, and I tell my husband about it. We can choose to go to college after we turn*

*eighteen, and the government pays for it. Some go after they have children. After twelve years, I am not pregnant and I decide to go to college. We get a divorce. I live close to school with my daughter. First I study general science for a year. Then two years in other sciences, such as biology, chemistry, physics, geology, anthropology, botany, and everything else which is considered science. I study two or three sciences together. Then I pick two or three subjects to study in more detail. It takes me six years to cover the general courses. Then I study physics, chemistry, and biology in depth for two more years. After that, I study and become a genetic engineer when I am fifty. I begin my work in a plant genetics lab and also study how DNA is implemented in the body.*

*"I marry one of my colleagues at the lab at the age of sixty. My daughter is married and has children of her own, so she is not concerned with me. We have no real emotional attachments or connections with our children after they are grown and on their own. My husband and I join one of the space expeditions. After we get some more experience, we are accepted for a space expedition when I am seventy-three years old. Our seventy-three is like thirty years of Earth time.*

*"We go on a mother ship type of craft, which is perhaps ten miles across and is expected to be out for maybe thirty years. The mother ship looks like a conglomeration of plumbing from the outside. It is a boxy structure that is arranged roughly as sphere with pipes, plumbing, and all types of appendages on the outside. It is a relatively short-range mother ship. It can make journeys of up to about one hundred light years, taking a small scientific crew of up to about thirty thousand people. Our mission is to go to a nearby solar system simply to catalog and genetically analyze the plants and animals.*

*"There are about one hundred and fifty each plant biologists, animal biologists, and human geneticists. Then there are farmers, electronic prospectors, medical staff,*

*police keepers, etc. There is everything we need to set up our culture on another planet for a period of thirty to forty years. We already have our bases there and know this planet well. After we land on the planet, the mother ship returns to our home planet with the people who have been there for the last thirty years. It seems to take about a year to make the journey to that planet, but as we travel fast, time compresses, so not as much time passes inside the ship as passes outside the ship.*

*"We build a new city with all the supplies we bring and what is already there from before. There are only plants and animals, and there is no other life on this planet. It is dry and dusty where we are. Here we study geology and plant and animal science, so maybe sometime we can colonize and inhabit the planet after we understand the plants thoroughly.*

*"With our expedition, we have a huge amount of supplies and construction people to build the cities. As we do the scientific research, they are building the city with part of our time put into the construction. The other plant engineers and I examine plant after plant and catalog them, classifying the growing conditions and analyzing everything else. Our people are all over in different parts of the planet. After thirty years, we go back to our home planet.*

*"After several years, we go on another expedition to another planet that is further away. This is what is known now as planet Earth. Here, we just study the plant life and observe different things. It is about 50,021 BC in Earth years. We realize there have been genetic modifications done on Earth people because there is a big difference between the original humans and the current humans. We also see the same thing in the plant life. During my time on these expeditions, I have learned about other sciences and different technology. We all have to learn about everything else and help each other, wherever we are needed. We were cross-trained from the beginning. So we are helpful in other fields too.*

*"We set up our bases in lowlands surrounded by jungles in what is now known as Indonesia. Over time, five of our ships have landed here. First, we start to clear paths between the highlands and the low lands. We have smaller spaceships that remain on Earth, such as one-person ships, unmanned scout crafts, and other types. The command structure is two-fold. We have a ship commander whose primary responsibility is safety of the ship and his crew, which does not include the rest of us. The expedition commander is responsible only for his people and the success of the mission.*

*"From the main base in Indonesia, the groups go out to explore and study in different areas of the planet. We set up the first structure, stone quarries at the base of the mountain here in the jungle. This is part of the headquarters. It is pyramid shaped and it is big. No humans are seen in this area. The genetic scientists go somewhere else to study them. I am classifying, categorizing the plants and their properties, their genetics, their growth habits, and everything for thousands of plants. The human genetic engineers are mapping the population. They want to know about how many humans there are. They are studying their current genetics and coming to the realization that there has been tampering with the human race. They have genes that came from nowhere.*

*"We have smaller spaceships we use to go from one place to another on Earth. When the colony is set up and self-supporting, the mother ship goes off to explore for a period of time before coming back. It does not go back to the home planet. Then there is a reestablishment of contact and then the mother ship goes off to explore again. It comes back again and the expedition is ready to switch the crews. The mother ship then returns to the planet. We never know what decisions will be made in the home world. It may be that another ship will show up any day or another crew will be arriving to replace us or another crew may arrive to set up another research crew.*

*The only thing the ship captain and the expedition leader knows is that after thirty years our people can return to our home planet on the mother ship. It is expected that most of the crew will return to the home planet. Some may choose to stay here. If the decision is made about no more colonization on that planet, then they will be picked up by some ship that is going by.*

*"During the thirty years on this planet, I learned about different technology, human genetics, and other things. We meet and interact with the Earth people on different parts of Earth. They cannot seem to understand what we are. Although we look human we are still different than they are. We also go to Atlantis, which is by far the most technically developed civilization. In fact, they can teach us a thing or two about crystal growing. We have never met a race that knows so much about that. It is not a one-way exchange, though. We learn from them about crystals and ceramics, while at the same time they learn from us about physics, electronics, biology, and technology such as matter duplication devices that can reproduce what is put in them.*

*"I gave Atlanteans optical technology. I showed them how to build crystals as lenses and prisms and how to use light for different purposes, such as for message carrying and information storage. The Atlanteans were able to use that for technology that I could never imagine. They used it for focusing, transmitting the light, and for digital encoding systems using light. They were able to take things they did not understand and just make fantastic leaps. But they ended up misusing that technology for things we did not foresee. They compressed information into packets of light so they could transmit huge quantities of information and directions in one little flicker of light. Something that required an electrical current ten miles long could be sent as one little packet and a million more times the information could be sent in the time it would take to transmit one bit by electricity, simply because light is more compact and able to hold more.*

*"After thirty years, we go back to our home planet. Some people stay there to take care of the base. I die at the age of two hundred and twelve years in a bus accident. I am struck on the left shoulder, which collapses, damaging my lungs and heart. My eyeballs are jolted and pop out. I die thinking that I wish I could go back to Earth and study more. My spirit comes out of my body. I feel confused because I do not feel dead. When they cremate my body, I realize that I am dead. It does not seem to be a religious or emotional occasion on this planet. Only my husband comes to my funeral. My colleagues at work talk about missing me but that is it. I see a bright Light and am drawn to it, and enter into a reception area. After cleansing, I am sent for a life review. I see not a religious figure, but a council of six people, a civil government counsel like we had on our planet. They explain to me that they are there to help me and not to judge me.*

*"From heaven, I see I had group plans and individual plans for that life. There is a group meeting of about five hundred beings in heaven. As a group in heaven, we were concerned about spirituality in Atlantis. The feeling was that Atlantis had to have a more spiritual nature to prevent problems from arising. When we say "spiritual nature," what we mean is a feeling of right and wrong based in spirit in the Light (heaven), a sense of ethics, and a sense of morals. This was one of the downfalls of Atlantis. The people are basing their sense of right and wrong on their own self-interests. As things are going down in Atlantis for the last 20,000 years, our group is trying to develop spirituality in Atlantis to get them over the hurdles that have been erected by not speaking of spiritual things.*

*"Originally the group was trying to aid the Lamurians in establishing the sense of spirit in the Atlanteans. Then we decide in small groups who is going to incarnate where and do what. I am first meeting with about a dozen souls. I am choosing to work as an alien to modify the perception of emotions. I believe in some lives in the past*

*I was too emotional and I am planning a life now without many emotions, to restore the balance. Also I will have that great scientific knowledge, but at the same time, a kind of lack of feelings and innovation and moral sense. My life plan was to learn about the importance of emotions, in an attempt to bring some innovation into my own life. Any change or forward development I accomplish as an alien being will count ten times as much as if I did it as a human.*

*"From heaven, I see that the optical technology I gave to Atlanteans was used to transmit the desires of the rulers to the transmitting station to send it out to the people and control them. That was what made communication efficient enough to be able to control many people; otherwise, they would not be able to transmit all that information. I realized that we did not have any bad intentions when we gave the technology but we were kind of short-sighted and did not think of the consequences. Even though we did not do anything wrong and did not create that harmful technology, I feel responsible in some way. We did not anticipate what might happen and did not set up any safeguards. I also realized that we were not a very spiritual race and did not recognize the dark influences in Atlantis.*

*"I see that we interacted with the scientific group and the rulers, but not the average person. I was on duty and I gave them the technology. I pointed out that they could create lenses by growing them and they could create control devices for the light, mirrors and one-way mirrors, by modifying the light beam. I also gave them a little bit of information about the nature of light. The Atlanteans built on that information and created a means of transmitting huge amounts of information quickly. They also created laser weapons and laser cutters.*

*"From heaven, I see that I planned to incarnate on that planet to experience life without emotions and spirituality, and to make a comparison within myself between a life*

*filled with emotions and spirit and life without emotions and spirit. I needed to compare and contrast what I saw in that life with what I see in this life and learn the value of spirit and emotions.*

*"I need to learn the lesson of my quest for independence. I need to be careful with technology. I had a lack of spirituality. As I look back from heaven, I realize that the few people who had spirituality on our planet were considered aberrant and strange and socially deviant. There was no religion or spirituality. We did not have any temples or churches. We tended to function around a civil government. We were not emotional people to begin with. We considered emotions a drawback and worked to strain the emotions out. It was more of a selective breeding program. The society pushed out the folks who had emotions and those genes were left out. Males and females were separated out and they were not permitted to marry and the gene disappeared. As far as they were concerned, an undesirable trait was eliminated.*

*"From heaven, I see that I had about three lives on that planet and twenty-nine lifetimes among that race on many other planets they colonized. I see that my eye problem came from that life to this one. It was the symbolic darkness. It is a reaction to the damage that was done with the optical technology I gave to the Atlanteans that caused the damage to my eyes and damage to the whole Atlantean culture. I did not do the negative work or make the negative decisions, but I did provide the technology for it and somehow this gives me a measure of responsibility for it. I provided the information; they made the decision as to what to do with it, and I got caught up with part of the responsibility. It produced a systemic reaction in me, causing the dimming of my sight, in part because of not seeing it and also because of the cataract interfering with the transmission of the light to the eyeball and to the retina. The structure of the cataract upon which it is building is larger than the cataract itself, the darkening of the*

*cataract appearing on that framework and now the light-diminishing part is being formed suddenly. Also because of that technology, many people were damaged. I really did not do it so I am not really going blind but I am being reminded to be careful.*

*"The emotional lack in that life was natural. In this life, I was losing all emotional ties with everybody, and in that life we weren't supposed to have any. My whole emotional system was affected and some other lymph system in the current body is blocked and the lymphatic fluid does not flow freely because of the lack of emotions in that life on that planet. These are like emotional blockages in the lymphatic system, which also cause aches and pains in my legs. The primary blockage is in the groin area, and when that is cleared, the legs will drain properly. The next blockage is much higher, at about the third chakra level. Also my lung problems came from that life.*

*"There are three levels of healing: experiencing and resolving the past life, seeing the spiritual content of the life, and seeing how it affects this life. There are past life incidents that carry over, such as unresolved past life emotions and decisions. At the same time, we have the individual and the group purposes that may or may not have been carried through. More often, it has not been carried through and will affect future lives. These are three different levels of healing that occur during a past-life regression therapy. They can all come from a past life: the physical incidents, the emotional trauma, spiritual healing or a lack of spiritual healing.*

*"From heaven, I see that this is alien race five of group two. This is one of the alien races that are observing us and they come back and contact humanity at regular intervals to study the effect of the technology they gave. They see how emotional and spiritual we have become and they see the great leap we have made in our development, and they would like to have one too. It is not a case of jealousy but a case of feeling that we have some characteristics they*

*do not own, and if they can incorporate these traits into their lives, then maybe they could make these great intuitive leaps forward. They are already in contact with some human spiritual teachers to learn from them. This race, in the past, made a conscious decision to sever and strain emotions out by excluding from their society those who had emotions, and eliminating them completely. Now they are beginning to realize that it is not totally undesirable. It has some drawbacks and some difficulty involved, but it also has great benefits in terms of spirituality, innovation, intuition, sudden inspiration, and great leaps forward.*

*"These beings tend to like mountainous regions like the Alps, and can often be found in rough, hilly land, high lands such as the Himalayas or wherever the highest, roughest ground is. They can also be found in caves, mines, and underground tunnels.*

*"From heaven, I see that I chose to have lymphatic blockage and eye problems to resolve my karma. The justification I imposed upon myself is not a complete cut-off of the communication (transportation?) or whatever the analogy would be. In this case, I have chosen the analogy of the lymph system, where the lymph passes through the body, through the connecting tubes to the field, and part of the field is constricted to reduce the flow of the lymphatic fluid. As a result, drainage from the lower part of the body is impaired, so that the fluid tends to collect and debris are not removed readily. Cellular debris, living and dead bacteria, intercellular blood cells that died outside the blood vessels, intercellular fluids, and things that leak out of the cells are not removed fast enough. This leads to weakness, tiredness, and a susceptibility to infections, where I cannot deal with the bacteria as effectively. This lymphatic blockage is only in the lower part of my body, roughly from the third chakra down. To remove the effect without resolving the karma does not permit the healing to go forward. Once we understand what has happened in the past and why, then we can change it.*

*"With Earth people, I gave them a little bit of technology, and in a short time, they innovated many different things from it. While on that planet, we worked for a long time before we could invent anything new. It was because of a lack of emotions on that planet. Emotions have some drawbacks but they also carry some great benefits. That is why this and the fourth alien race of group two, the tall thin aliens, feed us a little bit of technology and wait and watch, not knowing what we will find.*

*"Similarly, in that past life, I passed on that technology not knowing that they would invent such negative and damaging technology with it. Within fifty years, they learned all about the light and were leaping past us. We only showed them how to grow crystals, to manipulate light, to make them grow in a lens shape so the light would be focused, diverged, or bent with the prism.*

*"In this life, karma resolution was made. I had that burden of karma and I divided it up in two ways to work off the karma, the communication and transportation component, and the component for the use of the light, the optics part. The interference with the light is part of the price for that karma; that is, the blocking of the light leading to vision problems. So this barrier was constructed. To resolve it, I first had to recognize the life and the nature of the karma, how it came about, and why it existed. When I have that, I can let go of the payment of that karma. The structure or the cataract was erected, which did not make the cataract inevitable. It made it much more likely but not inevitable. When the structure is removed, the cataract will fall apart without it.*

*"The healing will be complete when the positive action takes place. So the first part of the healing has occurred here. Comparatively, the healing of the lymphatic system and communication problem were simple. I have to understand and resolve it and allow it to be healed. The eye problem is more complicated and is the fundamental problem. I gave them the optical technology. Now I understand what*

*happened and what the problem is and I am now making up for it with understanding and the resolution. But to remove the entire thing – the black floaters, vision distortion and all of the cataract – there has to be a positive action which can be substituted, such as works of charity, working with the blind, aiding the guide dog foundation for the blind, audio books; anything that can comfort, cure, and help the blind. This way the karma can be worked off consciously. Without conscious knowledge of where the problem came from, we continue to pay with the cataract. Part of the problem can be resolved just with the understanding, but the rest of the problem has to be worked off in some positive fashion. We get four goods and three bads; that is, for one good action you earn four times the benefit, while one bad action earns three times the negative. So good is always rewarded more than bad is punished."*

### Origin of Organ Transplant From A Healthy Living Person

One of my patients under hypnosis recalled living a life in Atlantis as a physician. He was forced to do heart transplants on subrulers, using the hearts of healthy living humans from the lower class who died in the process.

- *"I am a forty-five-year-old physician living in Galt City, in the northwestern part of Atlantis. My name is Reid and this is 44,382 BC. I am married and have two boys, twenty-one and nineteen. We live in an apartment in the hospital building where I work. I am a physician. At this time, society is not totally free. About 20 percent of the people have implants inserted in them. Most of them are from the labor class. Energy is not devoted to improve technology now as much as it was few thousand years ago.*

  *"I have been a physician for about eighteen years and I work in the research facility in the hospital. There are twenty-five floors in the hospital and the top ten floors are used for the living apartments. I am doing research about*

*transplanting ape hearts into humans. I am the first one to try it but there was not much success. I am successful in transplanting a human heart to another human. For over twenty years, I have tried human kidney transplants and also transplanting ape kidneys in humans successfully.*

*"At the age of sixty-five, since I am an expert and a pioneer in doing heart transplants, I am ordered to do heart transplants in two sub-rulers, using the hearts of healthy humans. I was horrified with the idea and refused to do it. They threaten me that if I didn't do it they would use my children's hearts. It was emotional blackmail as I was forced to transplant the hearts of healthy humans from the lower class, who in the process, died. I believed it was very unethical. I felt anger, guilt, remorse, shame, and anguish. From then on, it became common practice to use healthy human hearts or other organs, transplanting them in the rulers.*

*"I stopped doing surgery but continued the research to find some other ways to help and heal people. We found new drugs, which reduce the organ rejection. I retire at the age of seventy-five and die of pneumonia at the age of eighty-seven, feeling angry with the ruler. I stay earthbound for a long time. I hang around rulers and give them thoughts to stop the program but they cannot receive it. After about two hundred years, I am taken to the Light (heaven) by the angels.*

*"From heaven, I see that I planned to be a physician and do research and organ transplants in sick people and find ways to help people. I was one of the pioneers who started the heart transplant program. I see that after I was forced to transplant the hearts of healthy humans to rulers, it became common practice to use organs from healthy humans for the rulers, and although I was forced into it, I became indirectly responsible for that idea. It became a precursor life where I created negative karma. From heaven, I see that after that life, I had several lives where similar things were done to me in order to balance my negative actions in that life.*

# Chapter 6

## FALL OF ATLANTIS:
## THE DARK AGES

As described before in chapter five, life was initially very easy in Atlantis when people arrived there. The land was fertile, there was plenty of food to eat, weather patterns were good, and there were abundant natural resources. The population grew rapidly. People were free and independent, to begin with. That is, each person was doing what he or she thought was best, regulated by small-group regulations. Later, as tribes consolidated and rulers developed, laws were established and means of enforcing the laws were set up like the court system. They had all the freedom to do what they wanted to do. This continued for thousands of years till electronics were developed in Atlantis, around 80,000 BC, around the time Lamurians came to Atlantis.

According to my hypnotized patients, Atlanteans perceived that people of Lamuria were not exactly like them. They came to understand that these people from Lamuria were using senses they did not have or had not developed, and were communicating in a way that the Atlanteans did not understand. Lamurians were obtaining and sharing information with each other mentally through telepathy. They could be trading with people of Atlantis and at the same time discussing trade privately between themselves, and the Atlanteans did not even know it was happening.

Lamurians were more advanced spiritually and mentally. They were able to use their telepathic senses; they could do psychokinesis; that is, actually move something with their minds. These abilities were developed because of two things: first, their personal spiritual development, and second, the society accepted those abilities. If society rejected them, they would not be so common and they would be considered strange. As different segments of Lamurian society in Lamuria used the same talents, it created the spiritual field around them, and the spiritual development built on itself. So, when the first person used psychic perception, it made it easier for other people to follow. When they all used it, the spiritual field around them increased and that added to their own abilities and made it easier for the folks around them to be able to do it. The spiritual field became a part of life and was not an odd thing.

Lamurians got the idea across to them that these things happen naturally when you develop spiritually through prayers, meditation, personal connection with God, and right living. The negative side of it was that some of the Atlanteans started to feel less than the Lamurians. Some of them felt they have been slighted or short-changed by the universe. Some of them did not really feel that the Lamurians' psychic abilities had much to do with the real world and ignored those abilities. But most of them wanted to develop those psychic abilities.

When the Atlanteans perceived that the Lamurians had spiritual gifts, they saw relationships between the spiritual gifts and agriculture. They had trance-inducing drugs that they considered to be spiritual drugs. People considered a drug-induced trance to be a spiritual experience, a way to leap into spiritual development and to enter into the altered state without having to spiritually develop themselves first. Atlanteans began to grow more drug plants and use them, hoping they would be a shortcut in developing spirituality, rather than developing it through prayer, meditation, and worship. They mistook these trance states induced by drugs as true religious experiences.

Atlanteans also developed the idea that it was possible to reach these elevated trance states by other means, without developing spiritually. This led them to experiment with electronics to see if they could develop spirituality. Since they were unsure of what the Lamurians did and said, they developed the concept of electronically-aided spirituality and developed electronic devices for it. Since the owners of the society, the rulers and the ultra-rich, controlled the technology, they were the ones who got to use the so-called spiritual devices to dominate and control other individuals.

When they found out that they could project and control the thoughts of other people, no way was the technology going to the poorer classes. The first ones to be controlled were those nearest to the rulers, those who worked in their buildings and those who worked around their people. After that, they began to expand and control other people as well. The rulers did not know the technology themselves, but had priests who had technologists working under them. Some of the important priests were on the same level as the rulers, like the pope and the king.

The Lamurians were upset by the problems they saw Atlanteans getting into. They did try to warn them that their beliefs were not correct and that they were not going to succeed. Their warnings were not very popular with the people of Atlantis. They took it as jealousy on the part of Lamurians because they had found better ways to develop spirituality faster. They were able to intellectualize and come up with reasons for the Lamurians to be jealous, and dismissed their warnings. The spirituality of the Lamurians got pushed further and further away from Atlantean thought. This attitude led to a partial withdrawal of the Lamurians from Atlantis.

Until about 70,000 BC, Atlantis was a functioning unit and people were prosperous and happy. Things began to change gradually when different people developed various ideas, such as putting neck implants in people, first to communicate with them and later to control them; breeding special kids; breaking up the family units by separating children from parents; etc. These ideas gradually spread all over the country. This began around 65,000 BC. By this time, the situation had been set up where the rich and powerful were in solid control of society. The rulers began to regulate the family by putting economic pressure on the family and controlling their wages and income so the family could not have an easy life.

During the Dark Ages, which began around 50,000 BC, there were shifts going on: more people were needed in the technology section, fewer people were needed in agriculture, and fewer people were needed in transportation. They had new energy sources. They had better power supplies for moving freight on water. This was an increase in the living standard. Things were better than they had been. Only they were not really better, because yesterday they were free and today they were not. Early in the period of control, people were still fairly independent and economics and political factors were being brought to bear on them to insure their vote for the favorite candidate. This changed later on.

Atlantean rulers during the Dark Ages also used economics as a control mechanism, making it almost impossible to survive in a culture without using money. They regulated the amount of money that people could get. By regulating wage rates, sometimes by law and also by incentives—such as, if you would do this, you would live a better life—but it was always an empty promise and things did not get better.

As time went on, the system in Atlantis got more and more rigid. The ruling group separated more from the common people, until they were thinking of themselves as different or better, and the common people as being more like beasts of burden who were to serve them. The growing selfishness in the ruling class caused a growing disregard and dehumanizing of humanity. They were selfish and stingy and wanted everything for themselves. The rulers and ultra-rich owned everything and reaped the benefits of society. Their only contribution to society was to keep everybody and everything under control, to serve them. This was possible because the ruling class and the whole society were lacking in spirituality. They did not have the necessary respect for other human beings and for inanimate nature. At the beginning of the Dark Ages in Atlantis, about 50,000 BC, the real decline began in the Atlantean culture and people were made slaves. Control of people was there for a long period of time from 50,000 to about 20,000 BC, until a series of accidents made it possible for the people to break free.

The bridges, roads, and other means of transportation, and the cities eventually disintegrated. The essential services were still there, but if the people did not have to go very far, if their dormitories were right near their work, then you did not need the roads and the bridges. Of course, eventually the masters noticed that they had trouble getting their products to the market to trade. Also, the internal market dried up because the controlled population did not buy stuff. They simply lived at subsistence level, with bare necessities. The only new money that was coming in came from their outside trades, and this was entirely at the mercy of the foreign sailors. So in attaining their dream, the masters destroyed their dreams.

I have included many case histories because they give a detailed and realistic account of the events, lifestyle, and culture. They also give glimpses of the unbelievable, gut wrenching, heinous tortures and crimes committed against the human beings.

## Atlantean Spirituality During the Dark Ages

As explained before, people originally came to Atlantis from different parts of the world, such as Europe, Mediterranean countries, North Africa, South, Central, and North Americas, and settled there. They brought their religious belief systems, with various religions and gods. The vast majority of the religions were homegrown. In the beginning, there were the multiple gods and each was generally worshiped in a particular area. Originally, they had a tribal god and, in general, had one head of a church, with a priest under that person. If the area was large enough, there would be one head, like a bishop, who would control many local churches.

As the people spread across Atlantis under varying conditions, different ideas started and different concepts of God came into being. Usually these gods were nature gods, such as sun god, rain god, sea god, wind god, mountain god, forest god, swamp god, etc. Also, there were gods of love and compassion, fertility, animals, etc. There was also a powerful war god in charge of war, who was worshiped by some people. Many of these gods were carried over to Egyptian mythology, where we see animal figures worshiped as gods. Also some of the Atlantean medical experiments showed up in Egyptian mythology, such as a god with a human body and the head of an animal, or a mixed animal with the characteristics of several different animals. As the people moved and spread around the continent, they would take their beliefs in their gods with them, until there were pockets of worship of each god in all parts of the island.

The folks in Atlantis were not particularly spiritual. They did have their religion and it developed in the gods of each area. They had no concept of One God or of their developing to be closer to God. As far as the formal religion was concerned, there was no stress on personal spirituality. It was not until people came from Lamuria that they started to conceive of God as a whole. Lamurians taught them that the different gods they were worshiping were actually different aspects of the same God. Lamurians were very spiritual, and due to different spiritual practices all their lives, they became very psychic. They were able to communicate with each other telepathically and could predict future events.

When Lamurians came to Atlantis, they began to promote a One-God religion and recognizing the value in each of the religions. One thing Lamurians were not able to overcome was the Atlanteans' reluctance to talk about spirituality. It was supposed to be bad manners in Atlantis to discuss religion or spiritual beliefs with others from the very beginning. This was a very strong cultural prohibition. They did it to avoid religious conflicts, because there were so many different religions.

Lamurians encouraged the Atlanteans to impose a structure over all religions and universally recognize the value of every religion. This proved fairly easy to do. The end result was that, in addition to all the other religions, they added another one and just nominally said that this one was in control of all the rest. Now they had a church that worshiped One God with some adherence, and the head of this church was nominally in charge of all the churches. This person ended up among the rich and powerful rulers during the Dark Ages.

There was a single overseer for all the churches and all the religions. That person was known to be the supreme head of the religious structures. Under him were regional directors, each of whom oversaw certain regions. Then under them were sub-commanders and then the individual churches and the priests. Religion was a part of life, but not as meaningful. It seemed to satisfy the inclination of the people while absolutely failing to teach spirituality. The effort to be spiritual without being spiritual was what led to Atlanteans' downfall. They saw the spiritual aspect of Lamurians and tried to duplicate it with drugs and technology, and that was what led to the technological advances that caused the real downfall of Atlantis.

Of course by the time of the Dark Ages in Atlantis (about 50,000 BC to 20,000 BC), religion was practically only a memory. The ruling class completely got away from worshiping. Anyone in the ruling class who did worship God was considered to be abnormal. The priests and other religious subordinates became figureheads to be there in front of the people to calm whatever spiritual or supernatural urges people had. Just as homosexuality was encouraged to thwart heterosexuality, spirituality was thwarted while appearing to be satisfied by twisting the spiritual urges. The priestly class preached very sterile things and did normal religious practices without any intent or thought by simply going through the motions. Still, some got more than they bargained for when God would answer a formal request, and when they received it, they were shocked.

Following descriptions were given by my hypnotized patients about their religious and spiritual practices while reliving their past lives in Atlantis:

- *"There are many temples in Atlantis but not much spirituality. I didn't attend the temple very often. I saw the priests on occasion but they never talked about One God or how one should go about getting connected to One God. These temples are large stone block structures with high steeples and high-pitched roofs. Inside there are a variety of busts representing different gods. Some are busts of animals (rams, cats, dogs, birds, and wolves). People worship these gods.*

   *"I was married in a temple when I was twenty-three. My marriage was arranged by my parents, with permission from the rulers. I wore black shoes and an all-white garment. My bride wore an all-white floor-length dress with a headpiece and a veil that covered her face. People attended in formal clothes of many colors. The ceremony lasted over two hours and consisted of pledges to many different gods, all of which was orchestrated by the priest. The marriage ceremony was followed by a huge banquet with dancing and good fellowship.*

   *"While people didn't talk much about religion, God, or spirituality, there were temples in Atlantis. These temples were constructed of stone blocks, had high steeples and high-pitched roofs. The priests wore robes with a variety of colors, such as white, red, green, etc. I see stations inside the temples which feature busts of spiritual beings and busts of animals. All of these busts represent a god. The priests' message to working class people was to mind your own business and to always respect rulers and those of a higher class. There was never a mention of God, religion, personal growth, or how to connect with God."*

During the Dark Ages, people really had no religion. It existed just to keep the population a little bit quieter. None of the ruling class believed in God or spirituality, and even the priestly class just went through the motions. It was simply a formal arrangement, a memory of something that used to be. They did not talk about God and religion, just maintained the empty, formal practices of church services. They prayed for peace and prosperity of the masters primarily, and to keep themselves healthy and working. Their prayers became empty.

## Drug Use During the Dark Ages

When the Atlanteans perceived that the Lamurians had spiritual gifts, they saw relationships between the spiritual gifts and agriculture. They had trance-inducing drugs that they considered to be spiritual drugs. People considered a drug-induced trance to be a spiritual experience, a way to leap into spiritual development and to enter into the altered state without having to spiritually develop themselves first. Atlanteans began to grow more drug plants and used them, hoping that they would be a shortcut in developing spirituality, rather than to develop it through prayer, meditation, and worship. They mistook these trance states that were induced by the drugs as true religious experiences.

They knew of opium, marijuana, and other hallucinogenic drugs. They already knew that drugs could alter the consciousness. After they got the concept of spiritual and psychic experiences from observing the Lamurians, they realized there were other benefits in the altered states of consciousness. They assumed, without practical experience, that the drug-induced trance was a religious state identical or at least very similar to what the Lamurians had. So they began to use drugs that way, thinking they were having spiritual and psychic experiences similar to that of the Lamurians.

My hypnotized patients state that Atlanteans had this concept of a quick and easy way, and it seemed to be very attractive to them to be spiritual without having to be spiritual. In Atlantis, spirituality was considered to be a waste of time and very silly. Rather than go through the spiritual developmental process of prayers, meditation, worship, and right living, they tried to speed up the process and short-circuit it by using drugs, believing that they were experiencing the same thing as the Lamurians were.

Atlanteans did not realize that spiritual trances are vibration-raising, positive experiences, while drug-induced trances lower the person's vibrations and are negative experiences. Drugs actually slow the vibration rates and result in an altered state, but not one which is beneficial. It certainly does not bring you closer to the Light or closer to the Creator. Drug-induced states have a dampening effect. First, by lowering the vibration rate, it puts people into a lower state of being and cuts down the flow of the higher vibrations from the Light. As a result, they are less easily influenced by the Light and more easily influenced by the demons.

Drugs also weaken the protective electromagnetic energy field around people, allowing the demons and other spirits to come in and control them. The second problem with drugs is that they actually lead you to believe that you have improved yourself or gone into a state in which you have a higher form of consciousness. You can be thinking you are receiving spiritual guidance but it is not the kind you really want to have because it is not from heavenly beings but from demons. The spiritual and drug-induced trances are both altered states of consciousness. The spiritual trance is an elevating state of higher vibrations, while the drug-induced trance is a depressing state and lowers the vibrations. The higher elevated spiritual states allow communication with God and dampen influences from the demons, while the drug-induced trance opens influences from the dark side and blocks communications with God and heavenly beings.

In Atlantis, some religious groups bought into the idea of drug-induced trances and it became the fashionable thing to go to the spiritual centers and experience them. As a result, people opened themselves to demonic possessions and influences, and the population regressed spiritually. They actually moved backward, becoming less and less able to contact the Light, God, and heaven, and more and more influenced by the demons. This made it easier for the population to be influenced and controlled by demons and to be violent, create wars, and have the desire to control and conquer other people.

Also, in Atlantis there were places known as spiritual places. Volcanic gases would accumulate in a cave and people would go and sit just inside the entrance where the hot springs would bubble up and fumes would come out. They would tie a rope around a person's waist so, in case they passed out, they could be pulled out. This was methane gas. They had asphyxia due to lack of oxygen, which caused alteration in the sensation of time, space, color, and sound, which they misunderstood as a spiritual experience.

The following is a case history of a patient who, in a past life in Atlantis, used and did experiments with the drugs in groups with devastating results:

- *"I am a sixteen-year-old female, a member of the upper aristocracy, living in Goper City, in the north central part of Atlantis. It is about 43, 123 BC. My name is Hepbed and I am a niece of the ruler. I began to use drugs for pleasure at the age of eight, because everybody in the royal family was using them. Priestly groups, royalty, and common people had used mushrooms for religious experiences for centuries. I heard stories about these marvelous abilities Lamurians had and I got the idea that if we take the drugs in certain doses and combinations, it would free our mind to have similar psychic abilities. So I tried different doses in different combination and discover that it is possible to have psychic experiences.*

  *"I did these experiments on different members of the royal family, who actually had some success in developing some psychic abilities, but nobody was able to communicate telepathically. We also found different ways of using drugs; by ingesting, injecting, or by inhaling. The word*

spread about my experiments all over the city and other cities, but was exaggerated. People in the northern part of the country also began experimenting with drugs in groups, trying to develop psychic abilities. Ordinary people who still lived as families were also free to try these drugs for psychic ability.

"When I am eighteen years old, I go to the caves where people describe having unusual experiences. The safety people tie the rope around me so that if something goes wrong they can pull me out. In the cave, as I sit in a chair, I see a burst of bright light in my mind's eye and several spiritual beings surrounding it. It seems to me that they are telling me secrets about something very important and spiritual. I am also having other experiences as if I am expanding and shrinking.

"At the age of twenty-six, I am married to my father's half brother. In the royal family, we marry other members of the family. I am still doing experiments with different doses and combinations. By the age of thirty-four, I have four children. After awhile, I become detached, spacey, and have lost reality.

"I die at the age of forty-three of kidney and liver failure. My brain and other organs are damaged because of the life-long use of drugs. After death, my spirit remains confused and spacey for a long time. After about sixty years, I am taken to heaven by the angels and taken to a place where two beings are sitting. They want me to talk about my life. I am still very confused and cannot understand the conversation till I realize that my brain was damaged due to drug abuse. The more I talk, the better I feel. Then I am sent for cleansing.

"As I clean in a bathtub, black globs come out from all over my body. These are the demons that came into me due to drug abuse. The biggest one was in my head, which expands tenfold when it comes out and breaks up into many individual blobs. After cleansing, I go for the life review.

*"From heaven, I realize that I planned to be confronted with drug use in that life, which was common in the royal families. I had two options, to either experience the negative problems or not give in to the drugs. I had to make those choices when I was on Earth and I chose to immerse in it and have this negative life experience, as a counterbalance to some other lives I had. To fully develop, we have to experience both good and bad lives and experiences. In this life, I did not achieve or overcome anything, but instead totally immersed in the negative experiences. If I managed to overcome the negative experiences, this life would have been an exceptionally good life and a positive growth experience. But due to the heavy demonic influences in Atlantis at that time, I did not succeed.*

*"I realized in heaven that I needed to learn the lesson of moderation, and that drugs and alcohol create an opening in the human aura leading to possession by lowering our vibrations and immune system. Another lesson is that there is no shortcut in spiritual development. Drugs cause an illusion of leading to psychic abilities, but they do not, and do not lead to increased spirituality.*

*"From heaven, I see that many of my problems came from that life to the current life, such as eye pain and memory problems".*

## Trade and Colonization During the Dark Ages

My hypnotized patients mention that Atlanteans became more proficient at sailing and navigation, and they went on to dominate the world through trade and colonization. Eventually it led the Atlanteans to wars of conquest rather than trade and cooperation. They were trying to take over and dominate other people and extended their physical presence and their control into the other lands.

At the beginning, Atlantis was a progressive, building nation, up until the initial visit of the fourth alien race, which was about 70,000 BC. At that time, they became atomically oriented and had huge amounts of electricity to draw upon. They had atomic power, which they could use for powering the boats or they could use it as a weapon. So they began conquest. Instead of going somewhere to settle and live as people there, they went out to take over as bosses of the world or to bring people back to use them as slaves.

When Atlanteans went to other countries to trade or colonize, they took some of their technology with them, and it did exist on other lands before Atlantis was destroyed; lands like Spain, Italy, Greece, the islands in the Mediterranean, Israel, Lebanon, Egypt, and along the north coast of Africa, Nigeria, Libya, Morocco, etc. Technology did not go to the European coast except only to France. On the other side, it was found in South and Central America and some even went to what is now the United States of America, and also to Lamuria. Technology existed in these countries to some extent, but not as extensively as in Atlantis.

They controlled the people through political and economical means, but sometimes they did it by force. They did not share their knowledge and technology with others. They wanted exclusive control of knowledge. They refused to train people from other countries. They did not put big power stations in other countries because they did not want other countries to have that much access to energy and knowledge. It was a way to control other people. If an installation went, let us say to Spain, it was forbidden for the Spanish people to know how it worked, how it was built, and how it was operated. That was reserved for the people of Atlantis. They were controlling people all over the world, and where they could not do so by trade and economics, they did it by force.

They did this very successfully right up to the time when the rulers decided they wanted complete control of their own people. There was approximately a 20,000-year span when most of the world was effectively under the Atlantean domination through trade and economics. The only part they did not bother and did not touch was Asia. Technology was used in these countries to some extent until the destruction of Atlantis, and then there was the total rejection of technology by the whole world.

Following is a past life recalled by my patient under hypnosis when he and others went to Spain to colonize there:

- *"I am a twenty-eight-year-old soldier living in a military barracks in Atlantis, just outside the city called Marducai, which is a big seaport with a network of manufacturing towns around it. It is 60,650 BC. I am a soldier equivalent to a sergeant. I am training young men who are sixteen or seventeen years old who are just coming into the army. I train them to follow orders, how to use weapons, how to fight, and how to live in the woods, on the plains, and in swamps. So anywhere they end up, they will be able to cope. After they are trained, they are sent out to a hill camp where they have to survive on their own in the hills and wooded areas.*

  *"We are loaded on the boat to go to Spain to colonize. The soldiers are there to make sure the natives are friendly. We leave in late spring. It takes several weeks before we begin to pass land. We stop in an area to resupply the boat and then head south into the Mediterranean and land in Spain along the coast. The army gets off and starts to build fortifications on the high ground and settlers begin to build a town in front of that. There are three ships that came. One ship has soldiers on it; and on the next two ships, there are settlers with more women than men. There are about two hundred soldiers and about two hundred and twenty-five people all together on the other two ships. Among the regular people are farmers, traders, hand workers, and others.*

  *"The military starts to explore and the colonists go with them looking for various things. In a few days, they are plowing the fields and sowing the seeds. The army moves north about fifty miles and builds another fort, and half of the colonists go there and build rough dwellings and begin*

*plowing and seeding. Here it is much greener. The local people got upset, so I suggested that we train the colonists to fight. Some of the soldiers marry the women who came on the ships and more houses are built. The pottery makers find decent clay and they are making their pots. The sand is not good here so people cannot make good glass. I marry one of the women and I live in the village with her. We are planning to move into the forest and cut timber, which can be shipped to Atlantis for making more ships.*

"The natives attack the northern colony and most of the soldiers survive in the fort. The settlers also moved into the fort to defend it, so their training paid off. At the age of thirty-six, my senior officer is killed by the natives and, as a result, I end up in command of the army. I have a bad temper and I lead with a fury. I am also mean to my wife and kids. We get more settlers from Atlantis. More soldiers get married. They are going into farming and trading and not acting like soldiers anymore. I am still training colonists so they know how to handle a spear, a shield, and a knife. There are no priests here because we did not bring any religious leaders with us. The colonies have expanded. We are shipping the wood to Atlantis regularly. The rulers in Atlantis are sending people to start a shipyard in Spain. We have our own little country set up. Two small towns are already established and we are starting the third town. We have three military posts.

"At the age of fifty-two, I am stabbed in the back by a native. I die thinking that I wish I had had a better relationship with my wife and children. My spirit is very angry. I try to attack the natives but cannot. Some of them are aware that my spirit is there. They have their spirit people, the shamans, go into trances and try to drive me away. As my spirit is trying to attack the natives, these shamans thwart it. Eventually, I notice the Light, and my parents and my captain are in it. They take me to heaven.

"I go through a debriefing or ventilation stage, because I am furious about being killed. I talk to two heavenly *beings about it and they patiently listen to me. As I talk, I begin to feel relieved. Then I am taken for cleansing and then to the life review table. I review my life with the sea god Marduk. My city was named after him, as Marducai.*

*"From heaven, I can see that I had to learn the lesson of humility, respecting women and humans, in general. This colonization could have been peaceful and people did not have to die for it. I also see that after the first two shiploads, more Atlanteans did not come to Spain. It shows their reluctance to leave their homeland. I see that in this life I was bold, adventurous, and forward-looking. I planned to go with this expedition, establish a thriving colony, which did happen, and it is doing well in its third year and the building of the seaport already started. If it was not for my temper, I could still be alive, and would have returned to Atlantis on a ship along with a shipment of boats and some pottery the settlers made.*

*"I was supposed to go back to Atlantis to inspire people to leave by making the change look attractive, and getting them out of that isolated state. They were ingrown, inbred, not wanting to leave, and as a result they only fed on themselves. This sets up a climate where the rulers eventually lose all respect for their subjects and turn them into animals. I underwent the same thing in Spain. Instead of learning compassion and dealing properly with people, I went into killing. As a result, I died without going back to Atlantis to fulfill a valuable purpose of motivating Atlanteans to come out of their shells and to venture outside of Atlantis. Also, I was to help prevent the loss of lives by the ruling class in the future, and prevent the tragedy by keeping new ideas and new products coming in. By this time, more and more people were stopped from achieving their life goals because of demonic influences.*

*"On the other hand, I see that it was a good thing that Atlanteans did not want to venture out; otherwise, they would have been shipping their technology out and spreading it into the colonies and then into the foreign*

*lands. I also get the understanding that the colonies out-*
*side of Atlantis were so independent that they would have*
*rather fought than to allow negative technology to come*
*in.*
   *"From heaven, I see that some of my feet pain came*
*from this life because I had to march a lot."*

Sometimes Atlanteans attacked people in other countries,
captured them, and brought them to Atlantis. They used
them as slaves for heavy labor. Following is a past life recalled by one of my patients under hypnosis:

- *"I am a thirty-year-old man living on the east coast of*
  *South America. It is about 63,000 BC. People from At-*
  *lantis come and raid our area and take my people and*
  *me to Atlantis as slaves for cheap labor. We were put to*
  *heavy farm work, such as pulling plows and wagons. We*
  *work cheaper than horses and I am being used as a draft*
  *animal. When my legs get weak and cannot do the heavy*
  *hauling anymore, they switch me over to working in the*
  *mines in the mountains. My knees and hips are damaged*
  *and hurt a lot.*
     *"We are regularly whipped. The rock dust and other*
  *stuff from the mine really irritates me inside. At the age*
  *of forty-six, I die of a lung infection, resenting being torn*
  *away from the family that was left behind in South Amer-*
  *ica. I had promised not to be separated or partitioned off*
  *from the family. They keep telling me that I am better off*
  *as a slave because I do not have to think for myself and do*
  *not have to go out to hunt for food. In order to live well,*
  *you have to have your freedom.*
     *"From heaven, I see that my lung problems, joint pain,*
  *allergies to dust, and pain of separation from loved ones*
  *came from that life to the current life."*

Another patient under hypnosis recalled a past life in which
her parents were from Atlantis but she was born and raised

in Italy. Traders who went to Atlantis to trade told the settlers how things had changed in Atlantis and how people were made slaves by putting in a crystal neck implant. She told people that they are free and independent people and they should be free from Atlantis.

- *"I am a nine-year-old girl living in a city on the west coast of Italy. This is 42,728 BC. We are Atlanteans settling in Italy. We are farmers and my father has planted some grapes. My father is an Atlantean born in Italy, but my mother came from Atlantis. We grow food and send it to Atlantis, and most of the colony is engaged in that. We also send wood and some local fruits. The local people are learning organized farming from us and they teach us what they know.*

   *"The people of the colony initially came from one city or area of Atlantis and they brought their religious beliefs with them. Later, people also came from other areas and brought their religious beliefs. So we have several different gods who are worshipped in this area. We had a small understanding of the concept of One God, which was taught to us by Lamurians in Atlantis, but this disappeared and we went back to worshiping different individual gods.*

   *"I marry an Atlantean boy at the age of seventeen. We have a small piece of land where we plant grapes, olives, and other things. There are stories coming from Atlantis about what life is like there now. They are really scary. We hear about the implants and the rulers controlling the people. The stories are told by people who go to Atlantis to trade. They are free to roam around Atlantis. Not many ships come from Atlantis but our ships go to them. When the ship shows up in Atlantis, it is a big event. A lot of trade goes on and we bring back a lot of goods from Atlantis. They make beautiful leather pieces and woodcarvings.*

   *"There is a meeting of all the Atlanteans in the colony when I am forty-one years old. I am speaking to my fellow*

*Atlanteans and telling them that we are a free people and we are not subject to Atlantean rules anymore. We are perfectly capable of taking care of ourselves and it is time for us to stop thinking that we are part of Atlantis. Atlantis is no longer good for us because of the terrible things that are happening there. We are free and independent people and we must keep the real Atlantean culture alive, free from Atlantis. I propose that we colonize with the native people on both sides of the river, going upstream. We establish a city, or the beginnings of a city, further up the river. We develop this city as a port and the other city will be developed as a main living area and the folks in this area should concentrate on making themselves strong and free. I am afraid that Atlantis will make an effort to take over this colony to take over the people and to make us like the people in Atlantis.*

*"People agree with what I am saying, that we are in danger, not from the local people but from Atlantis. We make the decision to keep trading with Atlantis but not to let them know where the boats are coming from. We decide that we should think of ourselves as Atlanteans in exile and our colony as the new Atlantis. We are settling on both sides of the river. We establish towns and villages as we go, and when we get to the good area, we start to establish the outlines of a city.*

*"I suggest that we give up thinking in Atlantean ways. We have plenty of room and we can create a new Atlantis right here. I advise that we make the streets wide and straight, organize the housing areas and shopping areas, cut down on the intermingling, and make multifamily dwellings. I become a city planner and a revolutionary. I have been thinking about it for a long time. Since there is no special leader or a ruler here, and since I was providing people with a new crystal-clear view of this colony's purpose, they seem to agree with me.*

*"In time, we bridge the river at several spots with stone supports, with wooden bridges from support to support. It*

*is like making stone columns. The city is established. This idea spreads over the Mediterranean and into the other Atlantean colonies. They all stop thinking of themselves as Atlantean colonies and begin thinking of themselves as free Atlanteans. We are still shipping stuff to Atlantis and getting things from there. So trading is still going on. The ship will collect stuff from all the Atlantean colonies to take to Atlantis and trade those things for fine crafts, such as ceramics, pottery, and other things that are just superb.*

*"I die at the age of sixty-six of what we now know is malaria. My last thoughts are that I wish I could have done more. I wish I had been able to organize the colony better. We need a central government. We are never, ever going to live like the Atlanteans; we will never accept that or tolerate it. I can see my dead body out there, but I do not feel dead. My spirit still feels as alive as it was in my body. I see my parents, who died a long time ago, in the bright Light and they take me to heaven. There, after the cleansing, I go for the life review.*

*"I review my life purposes with the god Marduk, the sea god, who I believed in. From heaven, I see that my life purpose, which I planned before incarnating in that life, was to salvage what was good in Atlantean culture, to let go of the part that was bad, to be strong enough to withstand Atlantis, and to make all the colonies stronger. At the same time, I was supposed to establish the idea of individual and community freedom. I feel satisfied that I was able to accomplish everything I had planned for that life and more.*

*"From heaven, I am surprised to see how widely my ideas spread later. I see that God inspired me through my heavenly guides. I planned to be open to inspiration from heaven and be in contact with God and my heavenly guides.*

*"From heaven, I see that there were Atlantean colonies scattered all around the Mediterranean, up to the coast of Europe into England and Ireland, but not too*

*much further north in England and down along the coast of Africa. The South American colonies and the Central American colonies were too close to Atlantis and it had too much influence on them. The North American colonies were further away and not so easy to reach, and they escaped much of the negativity of Atlantis. I see the city in Italy that I helped plan is now called Rome.*

"*From heaven, I see that my allergy to grape mold came from that life.*"

## Ruling Class at the Beginning of the Dark Ages

In the Golden Age, Atlantis had a strong and organized central government. It was still the most powerful nation on Earth, with trade and information flowing back and forth and the exploration, settlements, and colonies still going out. People were cooperating all over the island. It stayed that way for many thousands of years, and then as technology developed and the local rulers began to control their own populations more and more, the central government gradually became extinct. This started around 50,000 BC, and was completely broken down by 40,000 BC. The central government was not really abolished; it died from lack of use. As the city-states became more isolated, more contracted into themselves, fewer resources were devoted to the central government. As the central government simply occupied the capitol city, it became a city-state itself. The nation became more and more a city-state country, with each local city ruler drawing the city to him. As the population became more controlled, there were fewer people going from city to city, until at the very end, Atlantis was completely a city-state. People were living in dorms and were not permitted to go outside the dorms and the city.

Each city and the villages close to it were under control, and there would be a band of territory that was a no man's land. If any political power collected there or if it became a threat to the city, the city would launch an attack and destroy that power. Occasionally a couple of cities would end up co-operating with each other to destroy a threat, so the cities were still capable of reaching out into the land, but they were never able to really control that territory. They could go out and launch an expedition and control it for a while, but then the troops had to go back to their home city because the rulers were afraid of losing control.

My hypnotized patients say that before the control was made possible about 50,000 BC, people of Atlantis were happy and prosperous, but problems were gradually occurring before that. One serious thing that the Atlantean power structure overlooked was that their wealth was based on what the people consumed, and the people were the important part of their economy. The consumer and the producer are what make a wealthy class wealthy. When you interfere with them and restrict and destroy their purchasing power, who is going to buy the merchandise the rich sell? So in the end, the rich made themselves poor and had to depend on the overseas trade, which they did not want to do. When they got the trading network of other people set up in Atlantis and the products of Atlantis were carried to other lands, some money could come to Atlantis. Of course, this allowed many, many uncontrolled human beings from other countries who came to trade to see the actual conditions in Atlantis, with the horror stories spreading through the world.

Masters and other rulers during the Dark Ages abused people physically, emotionally, mentally, and sexually. They would use conditioning through electronics so the person would seem to be madly in love with the masters. After using them as sex slaves, masters threw them back into the dormitory or killed them. There were alternative sexual practices and different types of sadistic sexual acts promoted by the rulers and their families, such as sexual torture, whipping, beating, or whatever would cause pain.

Control of people was there for a long period of time from 50,000 BC to about 20,000 BC, until the series of accidents made it possible for the people to break free. Before that, people were prosperous and happy. At the beginning of the dark period in Atlantis, about 50,000 BC, the real decline began in the Atlantean culture and people became slaves. By this time, the situation had been set up where the rich and powerful were in solid control of society. The rulers began to regulate the family by putting economic pressure on the family, controlling their wages and income so the family could not have an easy life. They were selfish and stingy and wanted everything for themselves.

Following is a description of a past-life in Atlantis given by my patient who was a ruler at the beginning of the Dark Ages:

- *"I am a seventeen-year-old tan skinned male named Argus Scarzan. It is 47,000 BC and I live in the north central city of Gara in Atlantis. I have two younger brothers and two younger sisters. My father is the chairman (president) of the entire central government, making him in charge of the whole country.*

  *"I am attending a large banquet to celebrate my taking over a regional area to govern. Rulers from all over the country are in attendance to pay tribute to me. I am excited about my new role as a ruler. I have had special guidance from my father as I was growing up, plus I've received private tutoring in leadership training. The party is being held for me at my father's palace in the north central part of the country. Leaders from all over have brought me gifts, such as horses, paintings, saddles, money, land, etc. My father's palace is a spacious, multi-storied palace. My father and mother live in a lavishly furnished section of the palace. From outside, the building looks like an old English castle. Inside, there are many apartments. Each family member has his or her own private quarters, complete with servants.*

  *"The weekend, following the celebration, I arrive in Hebris, the city that my father assigned me to govern. I*

*take a tour of the city. I see parts of the working class section, parts of the wealthy class section, and parts of the ruling class section where many of the nobility live and work. I see the working class homes as small and under-maintained when compared to the fine large homes of the wealthy class. After my tour, I return to my new palace and appoint my chief of staff and several of my cabinet members. All of these people are from the ruling class.*

*"At this time, the region is experiencing a shortage of working class people. These people are needed to do the work that keeps the country going and to keep the doctors supplied with experimental subjects in our medical experiment complexes. To solve the problem, I bring in working class people from other, more heavily populated areas. I also start to use some of the lower level wealthy class people as subjects in our medical experiments. To ensure that we have a totally controlled community, I have insured that everyone but the nobility has a neck implant at this time. The neck implant is used as a mind control device. We routinely install it in all citizens, except the nobility.*

*"When I am twenty, I become engaged to a fourth cousin in our family. I knew her from childhood. While the marriage is arranged, I have my choice of five women to marry but I have chosen Leah for my bride. At twenty-three, I get married in a huge ceremony in a large temple. Nobility from all over the country attend. The large stone block temple has high steeples and a high-pitched roof. There are many busts of gods and goddesses inside the temple. Some busts have the facial likeness of a human, male and female, but most of the busts have the likeness of animals, such as goats, birds, lions, tigers, wolves, cats, dogs, and rams. We worship them as gods. We have no special religion, no spirituality, and we do not have One God with which to connect. I have come to the temple before, but mostly for the purpose of social gatherings.*

*"I am wearing a white uniform with black boots. My coat features gold buttons and a gold braid, which I wear*

over my right shoulder. I am wearing a wide red sash around my waist. My cloth hat has diamonds and fine jewels attached to it. My bride is wearing an all-white floor-length dress. She wears a headpiece and a veil that covers her face. Her hands and arms are covered with long white gloves.

"My dad is wearing a uniform. He has white pants and a navy coat that has gold buttons. Gold braids hang from each of his shoulders. He has many ribbons on his coat to show his accomplishments as a ruler. My mother is wearing a full-length yellow dress. She is holding a bouquet of fresh-cut flowers. Other men are in their uniforms. The women are wearing floor-length dresses in colors of blue, yellow, peach, green, etc.

"During the ceremony, certain priests talk to me and other priests talk to my wife as thanks are offered to different gods. My father gives a speech honoring me and my new bride. Other priests speak, and finally we are pronounced man and wife. After this, we attend a large banquet that features food, drink, music, and dancing. This party, and other parties, extend over several miles of the city.

"I live in a large palace that looks like an English castle. I get up between seven and seven thirty a.m. With the help of servants, I take a hot bath and then I go to breakfast. This meal consists of fruits, tea, breads, and juices. All members of our family live in separate quarters; sometimes we take breakfast together and sometimes I eat alone or with my wife, or with our children without my wife. Sometimes I have breakfast with a mistress. I am currently keeping nine mistresses.

"After breakfast, I go to the country for a pleasure ride on one of my horses. I am taken to the country in my solar powered car. I ride through the countryside with five to ten security guards. After my ride, I return to my office for reports and briefings from my cabinet members. I respond to questions and problems. I resolve any problem *pertaining to my city, but if they involve the whole country, they are noted for the next countrywide meeting with the other rulers. I rule other rulers in my region.*

*"I have a computer in my office. It is used for scheduling my appointments, planning meals and events, updating medical experiments, etc. The computer is connected to a movie screen so that people can be watched. I use the computer to control people's minds. There is a built-in receiver in people's neck implants. I send mind-control messages from the computer to a transmitter located in my office. These messages are received by the receiver in the neck implants. The transmitter in the neck implants transmits the message into the brain as though it was the person's thought. All people except the nobility are controlled by the rulers.*

*"After meeting with my cabinet, I take lunch from noon to approximately one thirty p.m. From one thirty to approximately three p.m., I meet with visitors. I see the secondary rulers under me. I meet with special friends and sometimes members of my extended family. From three to four p.m., I retire to my chambers to rest. At four p.m., I have a light snack consisting of wine, tea, and juice with a cake or crackers. Rulers from other regions, rulers under my command, and special guests frequent this hour-long, afternoon event. From five to seven p.m., I work in my office. I listen to cabinet briefings and updates, sign policy papers, and make policy decisions. I check in with the computer technicians for updates about medical experiments and the conduct of the people.*

*"After seven p.m., I return to my chambers to prepare for dinner, which is held from eight to nine thirty p.m. I dine with family, special guests, and other rulers. Sometimes some of my mistresses attend. After dinner, I watch plays performed by live actors and actresses. Sometimes I watch video movies. Sometimes we sit around and drink wine. Quite frequently, I bring in wealthy class and working class women and we have orgies that last for several hours.*

*I have a staff that selects the women for me according to my tastes. I usually bring in women ages fifteen to twenty-two. After the evening events, I retire to my chambers.*

"At twenty-five, I am touring my city and there is a breakdown of security. A disgruntled man charges the podium where I am standing and throws a knife into my left shoulder. My muscles are cut and I am badly injured. This wealthy class man was very upset because I had previously ordered some of his family to a medical experiment station. The man was immediately captured and I had the man beheaded the next day in the city's largest public square. I wanted to make this man an example. I wanted to show to the people what would happen to anyone who tried to bother the nobility. While I had the best doctors at my disposal, my shoulder was never quite right after it healed.*

"After ruling for only a few years, I have accomplished many things. I have built buildings and parks, paved roads and increased the medical experiments. I have improved the subways by streamlining the cars and improving the engines. I have rounded up all the people in the poorest section of the city and sent them to a medical experimentation station to be used in medical experiments. I have intensified the research of using animal parts in people.*

"When I am forty-three, I begin to experience stomach problems. I have bouts of nausea and difficulty in digesting my food. I am sluggish, weak, and experiencing pain in my stomach. After initially attributing the stomach difficulty to bad food, I was treated by my personal physician. But in a few days, I started experiencing the same symptoms. My doctor this time used stronger medicine. In about ten days, I started to vomit blood. I could no longer eat so I was put on intravenous support and fed through my veins. This wasn't helping and I started to fade away. My spirit left my body and my physical body died.*

"I was sad about dying at such an early age because I did not have enough time to rule. I stayed around the city* *for a time to watch over my wife, children, and others. Finally, I discovered the Light because some psychic people prayed regularly for every soul to find the Light. Their prayers opened me up enough to find the Light and I was taken to heaven by two angels. In heaven, I'm cleansed and I'm given time to rest.*

*"Then I am taken to a place where I review my life with five heavenly beings. From heaven, I see the abuse of people at the medical experiment stations. I see the wrong in keeping mistresses while having a regular family unit. I see that I used my power wrongly. I personally hurt people for my own sadistic pleasure. I beheaded four people when I ruled. I had servants whipped for small infractions. I physically assaulted rulers under my command. I see how wrong it was to put implants in people to control them. I was without compassion and was a very dark being. From heaven, I see that most of the ruling class was dark and the main rulers were totally dark. The physicians were also dark and were also controlled by the rulers. The priests, who were part of the ruling class, represented the rulers. I see that all of Atlantis and everybody in it was possessed and controlled by demons.*

*"From the Light, I see that I died because I was poisoned by a woman from the wealthy class. She passed security as a working class woman and worked in my kitchen for a few months. She was upset with me because I ordered several of her family members to be sent to the medical experimental stations. Some were killed, some were deformed, and some became deranged as a result of the medical experiments. Her deed was not discovered until six months after my death and she was executed at a public square.*

*"I brought certain problems from that life to the current life. In this life, I show arrogance by being too judgmental and critical toward some authority figures. I am impatient and sometimes I am callous and unforgiving.*

*"I recognize my wife in the current life. She was my mistress in that life. I treated her well until she became*

*demanding and disagreeable. As a result, I sent her off to a medical experimentation station. The doctors did surgery on her brain and also did a kidney transplant. They also did surgery on her joints, removing knee joints and replacing them with other human joints. As a result, in the current life, she experiences a lack of focus and concentration, and has difficulty in communicating with me and with others. She has pain in her joints, particularly in her knees. She also has experienced a minor kidney problem in the current life. I see two of my brothers-in-law who were rulers under my command. I did not treat them well. I physically assaulted one and verbally abused the other. In this life, they have verbally abused me and I have had some hard feelings toward them. In that life, there was a ruler under my command who I threatened to kill. In this life, he threatened my life by pulling a pistol on me."*

## Technology During the Dark Ages

As described before, Atlantis started to populate about 130,000 BC. First agriculture technology began, and then others. By 100,000 BC, they were making progress and had a solid biological background and their food supply was good. They were doing selective breeding on food crops and animals. That was the extent of technology at that time. They had developed an educational system and it was becoming common that the study of science and arithmetic would be part of the education.

They got into the study of electricity and electronics through their knowledge of crystals. Their engineers, miners, and beginning scientists became experts in creating crystals and examining their properties. When they found that these crystals would actually give off electricity, this led them into the study of electricity. The culture we are in now got into electricity through chemical reaction batteries and then the mechanical generation of electricity. The Atlanteans found out that there are crystals that have electrical properties, and properly made crystals would even put out electrical currents from sunshine through the solar cells.

From there on, it was a building process. There were great advances in mathematics; they became interested in study of crystals, and from that developed chemistry and physics. They discovered solar power and developed solar cells and electricity. From solar-generated electricity and having so much sophisticated knowledge of crystals, they were able to go into solid state electronics immediately, and control the flow of electric current. All these advances flourished by 80,000 BC. When Lamurians came to Atlantis, about 80,000 BC, electronics were really starting and Atlanteans thought of developing spirituality and psychic abilities, which Lamurians had, through the electronics.

It is interesting that most of the Atlantean science developed independent of the alien culture. When the aliens arrived, Atlanteans already had an understanding of electricity and electronics. What the aliens helped with was in the transmittal of large quantities of power developing alternative energy sources.

The original Atlanteans' energy source was solar, powered through crystals, and they used the electricity that was produced on the spot. The storage of electricity came about with batteries and their applications, with very little voltage to start with. The Atlanteans were quite used to working in the range of electronic equipment with very low voltages. They were aware of all this and had the talent and the knowledge of semiconductors from the very beginning from their intensive study of crystals.

When the aliens arrived in Atlantis about 70,000 BC, they helped in developing geothermal energy, which is using the heat of the earth to produce electricity. They also helped with mechanical energy generation, using mechanical means like waterfalls to make large quantities. Of course by now, Atlantis, compared with our current culture, used very little electricity to do a job, as if they were conservative in its use. They started with high efficiency and with immediate local capacity.

The rulers were unable to tax the use of the electricity, so they taxed the means of production; that is, when you buy an electrical generator, you pay a tax on it. The electrical generator was simply a solar cell, and the more solar cells they bought, the bigger their yearly taxes were. It was very difficult to hide these from tax collectors, since they had to be out to collect the solar energy.

One of the most important advances in Atlantis was that they were able to put together precision machinery with the advanced electronics. They could actually see what they were doing with gene manipulation rather than depend on chemical means. It was dealing with a high-powered electron microscope, so that they could actually distinguish the genes with a precision machine to physically enter the cell, remove the genes, and modify them directly. This was not necessarily by chemical means but by physical means, and reinserting them with electronically-controlled equipment and with very precise measurement.

Lamurians came to Atlantis about 80,000 BC, before the aliens came. They taught Atlanteans spirituality, which they misunderstood, and began to apply science to develop spirituality. They did it on their own before the aliens came. When alien race four of group two came, around 70,000 BC, they were also interested in genetics and bio-control, so to them it was an intellectual exercise. Alien technology did help Atlanteans in the development of control mechanisms.

Initially, it was the proper use of technology. After the Atlantean scientists became really bent and twisted, it made sense to them to try and change people to make them better slaves. They also genetically manipulated people to control them. They lowered their intelligence level to make them less rebellious, because nobody wanted a smart slave. They did it by changing their DNA. Sometimes it was a simple procedure; simply adding a chemical agent. Then they changed the DNA of the people by adding animal DNA to them.

## Relationship Between Psychology and Electronics

My hypnotized patients state that the Atlanteans' interest in psychology was in studying what they saw in Lamurians, the ability to communicate with each other mentally. They were trying to figure out how the Lamurians could do those things that they obviously could not. So they studied the processes of the brain and the mind. In studying the mind, they used electronic means. They were already aware of the electric currents and different cycles in the brain and they were able to pinpoint different activity centers in the brain. By the time they began to study the functioning of the mind, they were already fairly advanced in medicine and knew the anatomy and physiology of the brain. They were able to isolate areas and measure the nerve currents. This was the basis of their knowledge and application of electronics to the brain and to psychology.

Initially, electronics were used to study the psychology of the mind and the interplay of the brain, as certain ideas were formulated and transmitted. Atlanteans were also trying to duplicate the spiritual state of the Lamurians. After they were able to precisely measure a particular psychological state, they attempted to duplicate it by the transmission of the electrical currents to the brain in the same location as the sensors. It was a backward approach. They wondered if a particular feeling generates a pattern of the brain waves and if they duplicate that pattern of brain waves, would they get the same feelings. They found there was a great association between the brain waves and the feelings, so they were able to induce in someone a feeling of being happy, angry, jealous, and loving by feeding the proper currents into the sensors that would feed the brain and the mind. According to my hypnotized patients, this is what led them to the breakthrough that ultimately helped them in controlling people.

According to my hypnotized patients, the biggest scientific breakthrough the Atlanteans made was learning how to pick up the psychic impressions from the brain, amplify them, and broadcast them to other people. The amplification was done with electronics. The detection of the psychic waves in the brain was the important part. They did it by first isolating the brain waves by difference, and then learning to pick up those impressions and take them to an electronic amplifier.

They used small, separate, short induction coils that had a solid core, like an iron nail wrapped with many layers of very fine wires. This was placed on the head, then as the electromagnetic waves from the brain go out, they passed through the wire and made a very tiny electric current in that wire. That electric current was picked up and taken to the amplifier. The psychic waves that were generated had a certain frequency, and the electricity that came out of the induction coil had the same frequency. They picked the waves at many different locations on the head. These waves traveled with the speed of light because they were electromagnetic.

The computer-controlled device was able to isolate the waves that came from the psychic center in the brain. The brain was constantly putting off brain waves from its own activities, plus minor electric currents and minor electromagnetic waves from the tiny little electric currents within the brain. When this device was used, the brain could have the sense of hearing and seeing, but it was not occurring outside the head. It was occurring only in the brain. Even though it would seem that this was a real life experience as it was happening that seemed to be from outside, but it was actually occurring within the brain. At the receiver end, it had a receiving antenna, a quartz crystal that converted the energy that had been received into an electromagnetic wave. Then all the little induction coils, working backward, caused an electric current in the brain.

The initial sensors were only good while hooked to their machine and while a device was worn on the head, with all the electrodes on it. Later, they made advances in electronics that helped them do away with this. The electrical current that contained the signals was transmitted by the crystals.

Eventually, they actually inserted the crystal into the back of the head and neck near the brain.

Initially, it was a crystal carried on the body. Then it was a crystal placed in the home, so all those in a home could be controlled with one crystal. Then it became a device implanted in the body so that a person could be controlled directly. Practically everywhere in Atlantis the reception of the power crystal was sharp and clear except up in the high mountains. Once a crystal was implanted in the body, the person had no chance of getting out of its range. As long as the person was within the range of a power-sending crystal, that person was subject to control.

This is one of the main reasons Atlanteans did not do extensive colonization during the Dark Ages. In the early days, they sent out ships and traded with the other lands. The ships were not huge, but they could carry cargo. A crew of several people was able to make ocean voyages. They had navigational skills. Once the Atlanteans had to stay within the range of the crystals to control, the masters (rulers) were very leery about allowing anybody to be out of that control. It became a situation where those colonies of Atlanteans were left on their own. These Atlanteans in other continents had little technology to begin with, and soon, for all practical purposes, they were just like their neighbors and not really Atlanteans like those at home, although they still thought of themselves as Atlanteans. For the most part, it was the outsiders who sailed to Atlantis to trade and the Atlanteans stopped going out.

Once Atlanteans had computers and the radio-transmitting capacity, superimposing the electronic signal on the radio signal was a simple task. They could implant a little device in a child when he or she was small, containing a microcircuit in a crystal. It could be inserted anywhere in the back of the head and neck area and transmit something that could interact with the brain. These devices were biologically powered; that is, they were able to use the nutrients in the blood to power their little power plant. They generated their own electricity, and the waste products were carried out by the blood. It caused no particular strain on the body.

## Alien Races Four and Five of Group Two in Atlantis

According to my hypnotized patients, alien races four and five of group two provided Atlanteans information about different technologies, including electronics, and how to use it. The Atlanteans received technology in particular from races two, four, and five of group two as described in chapter three. Race two got them started. Race four gave them knowledge of nuclear power and helped them with electricity and electronics, and race five helped them with electronics, medicine, psychology, and radio all across the board, but the hard science primarily came from race four. Nuclear fission formed the basis for that power plant; that is, elements breaking the uranium, and generating a lot of electricity in the process.

Although alien races four and five of group two inspired technology in Atlantis, they did not inspire all the technology. Atlanteans already had a good deal of technology in place from their own knowledge of crystals and the beginnings of an electrical revolution, where they figured out on their own how to generate electricity from the crystal pattern and solar batteries. They already had semi-conductors and individual semi-conductor devices. By this time, the Atlanteans had made transformers, so they were generating large amounts of power by steam energy. They still had not built any fossil fuel engines to use heat energy to convert it to mechanical energy. They developed a fuel cell from the basis of their understanding of crystals, not on the basis of their understanding of the rest of chemistry.

After they developed nuclear power with the aid of aliens, Atlanteans realized that the stars shine by the same process. They never thought of where all the energy of the stars came from. They did not even realize that the stars had nuclear energy. For some reason, they were not interested in looking up and studying astrometry. In some ways, the Atlanteans were very practical people and studied things that were of immediate interest and that they could use immediately. They did very little basic research to open new fields to make important new discoveries. Instead, they just let the progress or progression of science sort of evolve step-by-step.

When the aliens helped Atlanteans understand DNA, they cut many years off the developmental process by showing them how particular groups of bases on the DNA would produce a particular change in the organism. The Atlanteans had already begun to experiment on plants and animals by making DNA changes. This small understanding gave them the courage to try big experiments on humans. They began to modify human DNA and injected the modified DNA into live people. When they made a mistake with a nonviable strand of DNA, that is when it could not continue living, the cell into which it was injected would die. When the DNA was viable and could have its effect, the cells into which it was inserted would reproduce it and spread it.

Alien races four and five of group two gave different technology in Atlantis, but they did not inspire all the technology. Atlanteans came up with much technology on their own, especially the technology to control people and the beginnings of the electrical revolution, where they figured out on their own how to generate electricity from the crystal pattern and the solar batteries.

None of the alien races intended or taught Atlanteans to use these technologies negatively. They intended them to be a cheap and easy source of electric power. They did not intend them to be used as a weapon of destruction or as a means of controlling other people. This was negative to them, something they did not indulge in and did not approve of the Atlantean's indulging in it. They could have stopped the Atlanteans but they chose not to.

### Alien Race Four of Group Two

Heavenly beings, through my hypnotized patients, state that alien race four of group two came to Atlantis around 70,000 BC. This group had a tremendous influence on mankind. They taught humans metal work, science, and technology. They gave Atlanteans an organized framework in technology and gave them different alloys of metals to use and taught them how to work with metals, which were used later to make the weapons of war. They also taught Atlanteans astrology. They gave Atlanteans the concept of the multi-use circuit, where they could pile together in one chip a whole series of functions, just as computer chips. It is not a new concept.

With the idea of a multi-use circuit, a single wire can be a part of two or three circuits, where a single transistor can serve multiple functions in different circuits at the same time. This requires very advanced mathematics and a very advanced electrical knowledge. The Atlanteans had not developed them yet. Race four brought that concept to Atlantis and showed them how to apply it. The size of their electrical and electronic components was drastically reduced because they were able to use the same device in two or three circuits at the same time. It was a fantastically powerful tool.

When race four first arrived in Atlantis, the Atlanteans had already found the gene and were beginning their experiments of removing gene fragments, modifying them, and reinserting them into a living cell. After the aliens arrived, Atlanteans were able to work with the genes much more efficiently and were able to have better and more direct means of changing a gene, knowing what changes were made, and then observing the results. Through precision measuring and precision cutting, they were able to work molecule by molecule, making the process very accurate. This was where the aliens were able to get to the molecular level, and they passed on this technology to Atlanteans.

One more thing that alien race four brought to the Atlanteans that was important was the study of the brain and its functioning with electronic circuits. This was not possible in detail before they brought the electronic circuits. The electronics themselves did not cause their negative actions, but the intent with which they were used did.

According to heavenly beings, in terms of the role of dark influence, Satan already had a plan for Atlantis and was behind every negative action in Atlantis. He knew the potential. Satan even helped the Atlanteans develop their psychological and mind-control capabilities. When alien race four arrived, they were influenced by Satan to provide other parts of the puzzle for the complete domination of the population of Atlantis. They led to the computer, which led to the enslavement of the Atlanteans. They provided the electronics to do it. The intentions of the aliens were all right but they were not aware of demonic influences. They were providing exactly what was needed for the domination of the culture, for the rich and the powerful to take over completely, to literally own the people. But the aliens did not realize it.

The aliens thought of themselves altruistically and provided them the technology that they needed. It was true that they were providing them with good technology and they did not legislate Atlanteans to use it improperly. This, Atlanteans did on their own, with the help of Satan and his demons. It was possible, so they chose to do it. Alien race four found Atlanteans more interesting because they were most advanced on Earth and it made sense to give advanced technology to the most advanced race on the Earth. They also worked in other parts of Earth but not to the same extent or the same depth that they worked with Atlanteans.

Alien race four made significant contributions to the Atlanteans knowledge. They gave Atlanteans metals and taught them how to work with them; that is, the solid state circuit, the multi-use concept, and the mathematics and electrical theory to make solid state work, the impetus to develop computers utilizing the circuitry and electrical and electronic knowledge. Atlantis had sophisticated computers after race four came and introduced the technology. Their computers were more advanced than the current time because they had the multi-use circuit concept and the mathematics to figure out the theory behind it.

There were many, many contributions by race four. The most pronounced and profound were the things mentioned above. Another contribution of alien race four was the theory of light: what it is and how it functions. The Atlanteans already had an understanding of radiation and saw radiation as a wave phenomenon, just as our people in modern times do. Alien race four made it possible for them to understand the particle phenomenon of radiation. In chemistry and physics, also, they helped Atlanteans understand natural radioactivity and artificially amplified radioactivity. They gave them information that eventually led to the development of the nuclear power.

The Atlanteans always had enough electricity because they used small quantities and had very efficient appliances. They were able to get enough electricity from the solar cells and hydroelectric power. They used geothermal power by utilizing the temperature difference of the Earth from the inner crust to the outer crust. They were able to develop atomic power and nuclear power with the information the aliens provided them. What they had was accumulative knowledge. We are talking over a long time span during which they developed and compiled scientific knowledge. With each stage, they were a bit more advanced. Other contributions were relatively minor compared to these and were passed on in all of the sciences, technology, and mathematics.

The aliens used several different methods of transferring knowledge. In some cases, there was a direct transfer of knowledge, where a member of alien race four worked directly with an Atlantean scientist, usually at a time and place of the alien's choosing. They would take the scientist in a kind of abduction. The second way was for the information to be fed covertly to Atlantean scientists. They arranged for different material to find its way into the scientist's hands, or a disguised alien would work in their lab and feed them small discoveries that would lead to a major thing.

Aliens did make themselves known to some individuals. Small groups of Atlanteans were aware that there were beings from other planets. It was not common knowledge, but it was talked about and suspected. Those who worked in sciences and technology and the rulers knew about the aliens. It was a secret, but a widely held one. Of course, there were rumors in the general population, but they really did not know.

By this time, the Atlanteans had made transformers, so that they were generating large amounts of power by steam energy. They still had not built any fossil fuel engines to use heat energy to convert to mechanical energy. They developed a fuel cell, again from the basis of their understanding of crystals, not on the basis of their understanding of the rest of the chemistry.

None of the alien races intended or taught Atlanteans to use these technologies negatively. They intended them to be a cheap and easy source of electric power. They did not intend this to be used as a weapon of destruction or as a means of controlling other people. This was negative to them, something they did not indulge in and did not approve of the Atlanteans indulging in it. They could have stopped the Atlanteans but they chose not to.

Following is an example of how alien race four of group two interacted and gave different technologies to physicians and technologists:

- *"I am a twenty-nine-year-old female, married with two children. I live in Reldo City in the southeast part of Atlantis. This is 55,220 BC. I am a surgeon working in a medical research lab. I have been working here since the age of twenty-seven. I am doing a variety of experimental surgeries on patients, such as attaching arms and legs to amputated people, attaching animal limbs onto a human, or inserting human or animal joints into human joints. Later on, I also do organ transplants, such as lung, kidney, liver and other organs, using human or animal organs.*

  *"At the age of thirty-one, I am sitting at the desk making notes on some of the surgeries I have done. I am wondering what else we can do to better the outcome of these surgeries. All of a sudden, an alien being appears in the room from out of nowhere. He claims to have special knowledge*

*and ideas that can help me with my research. I feel comfortable in the presence of this being. I am not afraid.*

"This being appears to be tall, thin, like a long stick-figure, almost half the normal human body width. He looks like a human, but the facial features look more like a drawing in a comic strip or on a TV cartoon. His face is long and thin, with a big long nose and big eyes. He is wearing a white lab coat and white pants. His skin is black, but his face, feet, and hands are lighter. He has black hair, which is thin and sparse. He is communicating telepathically, which I seem to clearly understand, but I talk to him verbally.

"Later, he brings a team of his physicians and scientists, who will be working with our group of eleven surgeons and other scientists. As we work on research together, their thoughts and our thoughts intermix and we cannot tell who is doing the original thinking. These aliens help from their spaceships and also in person. They are assisting in surgeries and in the maintenance of patients after the surgeries, and also in the preparation research of the surgery. They are showing ways that are more cosmetically appealing, and better ways to store the organs before they are used. They are also like cheerleaders, encouraging us to do more research.

"We are also taken to their spaceships for medical updates, and sometimes just for socialization and relaxation. The first time I was taken to their spaceships I was thirty-one years old. One of the alien beings invited five of us for lunch. We went mentally; that is, all our other bodies went except the physical body, which remained in the lab. The aliens escorted and assisted us in going to their spaceship. We feel comfortable going there. There is no anxiety or fear. The spaceship is missile-shaped, pointing up, and slender on the top. There are fin-type designs at the bottom of it. It sits vertically. It does not look like a flying saucer. It is made up of light gray metal.*

*"We are greeted by a group of aliens. They let us take a tour of the spaceship. There are instrument rooms with the control panels where navigators, pilots, and co-pilots are working together, charting and designing the travel route. They have a lab area. Then there is a kitchen area, although they do not need to eat. They have living quarters with bedrooms, living rooms, and recreational rooms, which are very similar to what we have in Atlantis. There are alien beings of different ages; that is, children, teenagers, young adults, and older beings. After the tour is complete, they serve us lunch, which contains foods of different flavors that they prepared just for us. Then we are escorted back to earth to our labs, where our physical bodies are resting. I visited the spaceship a total of sixteen times during my lifetime.*

*"I die of old age when I am eighty-five years old. I stay around for a while and then am taken to heaven by angels. During the review of my life, I can clearly see that using healthy, normal human beings for the experiments was wrong, and I was inspired by the demons because I had no spirituality and no concept of One God and did not ask for protection and guidance through prayers. I also see that my intentions were not bad. I did those experiments on normal human beings because that is the way we were told to do the experiments.*

*"From heaven, I can see that because of lack of prayers, there was less Light and more darkness all over Atlantis and the society. Even the aliens were influenced by the dark beings but they were not aware of it. Their desire to help was genuine and they had the knowledge, but they were misguided. From heaven, I see that their planet was destroyed thousands of years ago and, as a result, these beings are living in the spaceships.*

*"A series of events led to the destruction of their planet. They were invaded and driven off their planet by many alien beings from other planets. Eventually, the planet just disintegrated and exploded in space. I see from heaven*

*that I also had a few lives on that planet and that is why I felt comfortable with them when they contacted me in Atlantis, although I did not remember it at that time. I see from heaven that many different alien beings from different planets are living on spaceships at this time because their planets were destroyed a long time ago.*

*"The lesson I needed to learn from that life was to treat all humans with respect. I see that my joint problems and lung problems came from that life, which are karmic because I damaged many people's joints and other organs through my experiments. Also, these people's soul parts are in me and all their symptoms are transferred to me. They were removed from me and integrated with whom they belong after cleansing and healing by the angels, when Dr. Modi requested them to do that. My parts were brought back and integrated with me after cleansing and healing."*

### Alien Race Five of Group Two

According to my hypnotized patients, alien race five of group two came to the Earth about 50,000 BC, well before the destruction of Atlantis. They are about four to five feet tall, human-like, short, muscular, and stocky. This race also provided refinement and made the Atlantean system more efficient. There were quite a few ideas and thoughts in Atlanteans that had not been correlated. Alien race five provided the ideas and technology so that the information could be used in a better way. They refined most of the technology to make it more energy efficient, faster, and more accurate. They made metals better and taught the skills of carpentry, metal working, planning, co-coordinating, designing, and actually building large projects such as temples and pyramids. They also found Atlanteans to be the most advanced race on Earth. So they spent most of their time with them.

Heavenly beings, through my hypnotized patients, say that one of the genetic modifications done by this race was that they took two different plants, mixed them together and created a new seed, which we know as wheat. Since wheat was not a natural grain on Earth, because it was genetically modified, many people developed an allergy to it, leading to abdominal bloating, cramping, water retention, weight gain, high blood pressure, etc. It has a high percentage of carbohydrates and is a hunger-creating grain. Those who are allergic to it tend to retain water and add fat easily because body gets twisted and cannot turn food into energy. So the food gets converted into fat and is stored. Parts of the plant are not good for people; as a result, their body reacts to it. Initially, large numbers of people developed severe allergies to wheat and died in childhood. Many people in current life are allergic to wheat and have bloating, cramps, high blood pressure, water retention, and weight gain. It is one of the common reasons for obesity currently.

The rest of the time, they spent in cities and countries that had a large population, such as India, Japan, and China. Compared to Atlantis, very little technology was given to them and other parts of the world. This was part of the reason that, when the fall of Atlantis came, it came so completely. The other countries did not have the vested interest in technology that the Atlanteans had. In fact, the other areas on Earth had very little technology. They used simple machines, simple physics, chemistry, and mathematics, but not the sophisticated stuff that Atlanteans were using.

The Atlanteans had already developed and were using control devices when alien race five arrived on Earth. This race should have been warned, should have been aware, and should have seen, but they were also influenced by the demons and consciously did not recognize the dark influences. They ignored what was happening, not that they consciously would have approved Atlanteans' mind control activities, but in a way, they gave passive approval by continuing to work with them.

The drawback to this side of the story was that when the Atlanteans went to other parts of the world and settled in as refugees after the destruction of Atlantis, the natives of those other countries did not have the mechanisms to keep them out of the cities. They did not have the technology needed. After the destruction of Atlantis, the Atlanteans, who had superior weapons and superior organization, decided not to use any technology. They made their policy to destroy what they found and to renounce its use for themselves.

Alien race five saw the Atlanteans controlling the general population but did nothing about it. They were also influenced by Satan and his demons and did not recognize this. The people of their planet had a good deal of influence. They were loving, generous, kind, and were connected with God, but did not have knowledge of the dark side and did not recognize the dark influence in themselves and in Atlantis.

Heavenly beings, through my hypnotized patients, state that alien races four and five are still working with us today and are careful not to make the same mistakes. They recognized the bad effects that they had on Atlantis when the culture collapsed and fell apart. It came as a shock to both alien races four and five. They thought that all those technological advancements were positive things and did not realize how Atlanteans were misusing it. These alien races four and five were aware of Satan and his demons to some extent, but they did not recognize the dark influence in Atlanteans or in themselves. They might have figured it out when they saw the patterns emerging and saw the result, but not before. They were not very spiritual races like race three of group two.

One of my patients recalled a past life where she incarnated on another planet as an alien from race five, who came to Earth to replace other technologists so they could go back to their home planet. She recalled how, while on Earth, they took genes from two different plants, mixed them up, and created new seeds of the plant we call wheat. It is not a natural grain on Earth because it was genetically modified. It is causing allergic reactions, leading to hunger, bloating, and weight gain.

- *"I am a ninety-two-year-old middle-aged alien male living in Atlantis. My name is Maron Habeal and it is 28,918 BC according to Earth time. I am about four feet eight inches tall, have wide shoulders, and we are built like blocks. My body is longer than my legs and my arms are as long as my body. My face is a blackish leather-like color but my hands are dark brown. My hair is coarse and black. I am from the planet Marfan. I have been on planet Earth for about forty-five years. I am a chief scientist living in Atlantis inside a mountain, underground in a tunnel. The tunnel is large enough for three or four people to walk side by side. We have living quarters on both sides of the tunnel, holes in the rock with several rectangular rooms in a line for each family. There are ventilation and emergency shafts in each room. There are lighting and heating systems. We also have work and research areas. The living quarters for the families have a living room, a kitchen, and bedrooms all in one line.*

*"We cut the furniture in the rock walls of the rooms, and spots to sit or sleep. Here on earth we are also learning to make furniture with wood and to make softer sleeping surfaces, such as mattresses. We set up a chemical manufacturing device, using petroleum we found, and are making artificial fabrics. We wear button-down tunics that are hip length, and pants. Men and women wear similar clothes. We have about fifty-three people in our group, and seventy-nine individuals all together on planet Earth at this time. There are twenty-seven families, including ten boys and eight girls who were born on Earth. I have a wife, one son, and one daughter. She is twenty-three. The children learn from the adults, from computers, and books.*

*"We are evaluating the effects of technology that was given by our race to Atlantis and what happened to the society because of it. We are not happy with what we have found. We see that technology had a bad effect on society, which we did not intend. The technology and the material we supplied are being used negatively. We gave them*

*little ideas for technology and they came up with new techniques, new ideas, and new technology in no time. They are very inventive and clever, but so emotional. They get carried away with their emotions, which seem to spark them. We gave them the science of optics and growing lenses and prisms out of crystals, and they made extremely fine-quality lenses that the Atlanteans then misused to control people. They had a rudimentary electronic system. They already knew the properties of crystals and they invented high frequency electricity and radio waves from these. We helped with the theoretic understanding of radio waves, and when they were pretty well established, we broadened their knowledge of electronics.*

*"Now they are using crystals as control devices and not just to broadcast electricity to the homes. The devices are used for broadcasting signals to control people. Atlanteans have taken the little science of electronics and have built tiny little computers to fit into people. They are using these control devices to control their thoughts, feelings, emotions, and actions. We have found that the technology we gave to the Atlanteans is not used to make people prosperous and better, but to control them.*

*"As the local rulers control people, productivity drops off and weakens the central government because each of the city-states is withdrawing into itself. The national government is shrinking and dying out. Another thing we are seeing is that Atlanteans are not going overseas in great numbers anymore. They did a lot of trading when we first came. They were always making ocean voyages. Now you cannot get them to step out of their cities anymore, much less climb aboard a boat and sail away.*

*"We send unmanned scout crafts to watch people, and larger crafts that will stay farther away, take pictures and do sensor scans. We have cameras and sound devices in them. Very seldom do we actually go into cities.*

*"I am one hundred and ten years old and our evaluation is complete. We have been studying other things*

about these people and we see that no one else on Earth has progressed as the Atlanteans have. Every technology we gave them was adopted and they created many different things. This has been beneficial to us because they created new things with little bits of the technology we give them and they come up with new techniques and technology that we can use too. Unfortunately, we see them applying it for negative purposes and destroying themselves. This distresses us.

"We have been evaluating the factors that made Atlantis different from other countries. First, they had the concept of cooperative research in laboratories, and they had a concept of class or groups of people who are paid and are dedicated to do this kind of work. We have not found another society like that. The Atlanteans are clutching the technology to themselves and refusing to even share it with us. This also means that no other people on Earth can be enslaved. We can see their industrial production is dropping off and their raw materials are decreasing. It is not a good situation.

"We are concluding that if things do not change in Atlantis, we may have to intervene with this culture. We are recommending to stop the repressive use of technology. It is not our decision alone. We will have to consult with our home planet and see if those in charge approve. In the meantime, this culture is getting worse. Our research results have to be sent to the home planet.

"We are also looking at the genetic modifications that were done on humans by other alien races. We can clearly see the evidence of the genetic modifications that have been done with the different groups on Earth. The group that settled in southeast Asia had one group of modifications; the group that settled in China had another. It is quite clear that there have been multiple interventions with humans all over the Earth by multiple alien races. As a result, we find that these alien races have modified humankind in more than one way for the better. We found modifications on the

*people in Lamuria, Atlantis, and all over Earth. We know
this by comparing the DNA of one group against another.*

*"Sometimes our race intermingled with humans and
had sexual relationships. We are genetically quite different but our genitals can fit together and we can have sex,
but no children resulted. We created some babies by mixing the genes of the two races, like test tube babies. Most
of them did not survive and those who did are sick. They
live near our base. They look like a mixture of humans
and us. There are about nine of these created beings and
they are allowed to mix with our people.*

*"I am one hundred and forty two years old when my
replacement arrives. The ship will be leaving for my home
planet in a couple of years. That gives me two years to
train my replacement. My wife and I will return to the
home world and back to civilization. Our children have
chosen to stay. This is the place where they grew up and
where their work is. I am surprised to find that I am feeling sadness. Our race usually does not have any emotions.
Our son is working in physics, looking at the adaptations
the Atlanteans have made in their crystal-growing techniques. We find it intriguing that they can put an entire
computer in a tiny crystal. Our daughter is working on the
genetics of various groups around the world.*

*"The new group knows the planet Earth and has a
good idea of what our research is, and on the other side
of the coin, they are retraining our staff in various things
concerning our science, politics, and everything that has
gone on since we have been on Earth. I was a young man
when I came here. I stayed here for three terms because
I found it fascinating. Also, I progressed fast and became
a chief scientist at a rather young age and I could not see
any reason to walk away from that. I am warning the new
group about how violent these people can get.*

*"About eight years later, after we returned to our home-
land, I am called back to Earth to evaluate the situation
and make recommendations. When I come back to Earth,*

*I find that the people of Atlantis are more thoroughly en-
slaved, and the new chief is worried about it. My advice
to him is to do nothing. Then I go back to my home planet.*

*"When I come back to my home planet, I double check all
the research through the centuries and disseminate the results to the politicians, scientists, groups of military people,
technologists, and builders so they could be familiar with
what the Earth people are like. I had many meetings with
the geneticists and then I develop plans for future studies.*

*"I am trying to get the point across to people on my
planet that we have to be careful. We already have given
the technology to the Earth people, in particular the technology that humans are misapplying to control the population. What little we gave them about computers they
ran through the whole gamut, until they got little needle-
sized computers that they could just slide under the skin.
They grow into the nerves and the surrounding tissue to
get energy and become a perpetual operating device. We
are benefiting from them with what they create from the
technology we gave them, but at the same time we have
some responsibility for what has happened to the people
on Earth.*

*"I present the case before the counsel. I have to convince
eight different councils, showing the evidence that I have.
Eventually a decision will be made as to what to do. My wife
and I go back to school to study what has happened here.
We lecture to demonstrate what we learned from the Atlanteans. What the next generation will bring should be significant, such as when my son figures out the crystal technology. Imagine having spaceship computers that are only an
inch long and are fast, accurate, and have fabulous memories. I have been teaching Atlantean science on our planet
and telling them about Lamuria and what we found. We are
also studying the advancements in science made here on our
home planet while we were gone.*

*"At one hundred and ninety eight years of age, I have a
hormonal problem that affects the men of our planet, due*

*to exposure to chemicals in our labs. I am dying, thinking that we sure screwed up in our self-interest by not being more careful with the Atlanteans. We gave them technology, not realizing what they would do with it. I do not want to live in a culture where emotion is not part of life. Emotions spark you to work hard and be tremendously creative. I guess I was jealous of them. I do not know what will happen after death. There are some beliefs that are picked up by different races in the solar system that suggest there is meaning to life and about God. I think that is crazy. I think when you are dead, you are dead, and that is the end. I am feeling a good deal of pain and sickness. I have infection all over.*

*"After the death of my body, my head clears up. I can see my dead body but I do not feel dead. Maybe it is part of that eternal life people talk about. My body is burned. My wife and one senior colleague are there. It is not a big emotional time on our planet. People die and that is it. My wife does nothing embarrassing, such as crying or sobbing. Some of my old friends who are dead come to me and point to the Light, saying that is where I belong, and they take me to heaven. After cleansing, I am sent to a cave room where I review my life with a couple of men who look like me and are sitting on rock, like we did on our planet. They invite me to sit down and talk. As I look back into my life, I can see that the beliefs we had on our planet were not correct about the afterlife. Now I can see that there is an afterlife and this is it.*

*"The beings ask me to look back to the time before I was born. First it sounded ridiculous but then here I am. I am dead but still exist, so maybe I better take this seriously. It seems to me that I existed before I was born. It was all Light, just like where I am now. I planned to be very judicious and have good judgment about analyzing situations, knowing who I am dealing with before I begin to hand out technology. I should know the Earth people, understand them thoroughly, and have a good idea about what they are*

*going to do with it. But in the life, I did not follow that plan completely; some of it, but not enough. I also planned a group goal to try and establish some concept of the afterlife in this race. I failed in achieving that too.*

*"One thing I succeeded in was to contribute in assessing the effects of technology our race gave to the Atlanteans and other cultures, and what they did with it. I realize that giving technology to people on other parts of the Earth died down because people were not ready for it. So just handing over technology to people before they are ready to comprehend it is not right.*

*"From heaven, I see that my race did genetic modifications on two plants, mixed them and created a wheat plant, made the kernels bigger and thicker, with more grains per plant. This was done in Asia Minor. This grain is very productive, pretty hardy, and does not need the best conditions to grow. It was a good act with negative results. It made it easier for them to grow and store food that can be kept for several years with no problem. In Atlantis, it made it possible to raise more food with fewer people and they were able to enslave the rest of the people with it. The wheat grain was cheaper.*

*"Since wheat is not a natural grain on Earth because it was developed genetically, a lot of people developed an allergy to it, with symptoms such as bloating, high blood pressure, and weight problems. It has a high percentage of carbohydrates and is a hunger-creating food. It came from our modifying the plants. Also, those who are allergic to its structure tend to retain water and add fat easily because the body would get twisted and could not turn food into energy. So the food gets converted into fat and gets stored.*

*"Wheat began to spread around the world by taking it to Atlantis and elsewhere. Initially, wheat existed in Asia Minor and through trade it spread over the Earth. Wheat did not reach Europe until recent times. Before that, the primary crop of Europe was millet.*

*"Wheat was readily available and was inexpensive. So the ruler could devote the people's time to other things and not have to have them tied up raising crops. This meant that more people could be moved into cities and fewer people remained free outside the city raising crops. After the Atlanteans understood what we had been doing, they began genetic modifications on grain before understanding anything about it. Most of the modifications the Atlanteans began were disastrous. Sometimes these booby traps were not expressed in the first generation and spread to other seeds. In some of the modifications, they made wheat even more toxic. They were trying to put in insecticides to keep pests away from the plants, and the insect killer grew in the seeds too, poisoning people. Wheat is not a natural grain to Earth, and as a result, humans have always had a reaction to wheat. We have wheat allergies due to the toxins it produces in some people.*

*"I did not do the genetic modifications and create wheat; other people from our race did. I did not mean any harm by encouraging trade and transporting wheat grains to Atlantis and other parts of the world. However, by not being careful enough and not knowing the effect that genetic modifications would have, I was partly responsible for the problems in humans due to wheat. Then the Atlanteans made it worse by doing more genetic modifications, and I am the one who helped them figure out the modifications.*

*"From heaven, I am realizing that coming to the planet Earth and examining the genetic modifications and occasionally giving a little nudge ourselves, just to see what effect it was going to have on the Earth people, was not exactly the ethical and spiritual thing to do. We were experimenting on humans to keep our race safe, rather than experimenting on our own people and taking the chance of hurting them. That was the evil part of it.*

*"Also, feeding the technology on Earth that humans were not ready for, just to see what they would develop out*

of it for our benefit, was selfish. At that time, we did not care what use they made of it. We did not take responsibility for the outcome of our involvement. We were taking a chance with another race to benefit our race, which we did intentionally. It was not right and was evil.

"Our race was doing an experiment by jacking up the number of genes to see if we could get the wheat plants to continue living. Then we planted in just one area and watched it so we could control it. We found that it made a good food source. We allowed it to happen. It did produce a good carbohydrate source and a lot of nutrition, but also a lot of allergies because of the abnormal nature of the genes. The plants produced chemicals that we do not want to consume. Parts of the plant that are not necessarily good for people, and their body reacts against it.

"What I see from heaven is that it was Turkey where we put the seeds in the ground for the first time. When this was successful, people transported the wheat to Atlantis and to other parts of the world for trade. It created karma for me because I had created those seeds in the lab and planted them, and they were sold to people all over.

"Even though our race had limited imagination and practically no intuition, I could foresee that when people control others completely it will have disastrous results. Due to my propaganda, I was setting up the expectation in my home planet that they would get involved and bear some responsibility for what happened in Atlantis.

"One of my personal goals for incarnating on that planet was to bring some emotional life to people. By seeing the emotional life in humans, I did develop a small amount of emotions by caring for my kids and wife and really caring for my work, and also worrying about the Atlanteans and thinking of right and wrong. I succeeded to some extent.

"We also planned a group goal to try and develop some spirituality in that alien race. They were spiritually sterile on that planet and had practically no understanding of

*God. Part of my purpose was to bring them cultures from Earth that do believe in God and divinity, and infect the culture on that planet with those beliefs. I showed them pictures and videos that I brought from Earth to explain their spiritual beliefs, so that they would be germinated with that idea and it would sprout in them. I also planned to develop personal emotions.*

*"Those of us who actually live on Earth and are constantly exposed to emotions are realizing that there are things in the universe of which we have no concept and have absolutely no control over because our ancestors made a conscious decision to get rid of emotions in their race.*

*"I needed to learn the lesson that it is wrong to experiment on another race to benefit your own, and also learn the joy of spirituality. I see that because of the modified wheat, people suffered with bloated bellies, cramps, pain, weight gain, an increase in blood pressure, etc. In the beginning, a larger number of people suffered with these allergies. Some people died in childhood and did not pass their genes on. The ones who had the worst problems were weeded out of the gene pool and there were a substantial number of deaths in the population at that time.*

*"From heaven, I see many problems coming from that life to my current life, including a dislike for technology, wheat allergies, weight gain, chronic fatigue, GI tract problems, high blood pressure, and low metabolism."*

This was a being of the fifth race of group two, as described in chapter three. At this point I decided to heal that race on different planets wherever they were living at this time. I prayed to God and requested the angels of Light collect and remove all the foreign spirits, including the dark entities, dark energies, dark devices, and dark connections, from each and every being of that alien race. Cleanse their bodies, auras, souls, connecting cords to God, energy centers, kundalini, meridians, psychic antennae, their surroundings and spaceships and all the planets where they are living or have bases, including the Earth, lift them up, help them to the Light or bind them in space. Scrub and scour, take away any residue that is left over. Bring all their missing soul parts back to them, including the ones for their emotions and spirituality, cleanse them, heal them, fill them with Light, and integrate them with whom they belong. Create a shield of Light around them and their connecting cords to God. Cover the shields, with a triple net of Light, a violet shield, reflective mirrors and rays of white Light around each and every one of them, their dwellings, work places, spaceships, and the planets. Open their connecting cords to God. I pray to God to please fill them with love, Light, emotions, and spirituality, and guide them in the right direction. I request each and every being's higher self, heavenly guides, and angels to please connect with them and guide them in the right direction.

The patient described, "I see the healings being done and soul parts are brought back to all their chakras and the DNA as if rebuilding them all over differently. I see reactions in these beings, such as annoyance at having these silly thoughts. Some are intrigued by a unique and different way to think of it and playing with the ideas and thoughts in their minds, extending them and what it might mean. I see a whole gamut of reactions in these beings, starting from instant and absolute acceptance to questioning why such a silly thought may get questioned and incorporated sooner or later."

The heavenly beings also confirmed that the whole race is cleansed and healed and in time they will heal. They claimed it is part of my job to help with the healing of multiple alien races in the universe, upon multiple levels. This is in keeping with my purposes.

### Creating Robots in Atlantis

One of my patients recalled a past life in Atlantis where he was given technology by the tall, thin alien race to create the robots in an assembly line to do heavy labor.

- *"I am a thirty-seven-year-old male technologist living in Novair Town in Atlantis in 37,032 BC. I am in charge of creating human-like robots in an assembly line. It is my invention. The tall, thin aliens gave me the technology and I developed them. These robots will be the workers. Everybody who works in that factory lives close to it in an isolated area. We work and live in that area and are not allowed to leave. I have an apartment overlooking the factory. I am allowed to get married and live with my wife, but others are not allowed to marry. They live with other people of the same sex in a room. I do not have any children.*

*"We are making robots on the assembly line. The base is all the same and then they will be put in different outer bodies, depending on what their job will be. They all look like real humans and their skin is warm. The machine is going in from the back of the head to the eyes and then they are going to put the eyeballs in front of the head. They are stitched like big dolls, and then on the top, the outer shell of the body is being put on. From a distance, it looks like real skin, and feels real and warm. They put in the white eyeballs and then they are going to put the lens on them. I see that it is computer-based. They are like robots but more than a robot; they look like young adult males and females of different ages. I feel they are mechanical with different circuits, computer, and pathways. Just like in the movie Terminator, Arnold Schwarzenegger is like a machine but he has a light in him, and when he dies, his light goes out. These robots are like that.*

*"Some of these robotic beings we are keeping in Atlantis for heavy labor, and we are also sending them to other worlds. The government is selling these robots as a commodity to other planets. We just create the basic universal model and send it to other worlds, where they put on the outer body, depending on how they need to look on that planet. They can carry out an order and do hard work mechanically. As I look back now, I can see that, as*

*they are being created, I am very proud of my invention and a tiny piece of my soul goes to each of them. They are programmed for a certain job and are sent to do it in Atlantis.*

*"When they get stamped and imprinted by an external identity, they take on the characteristics and personality of that imprint. When I am fifty years old, one of the robots does not want to be like the others, so somehow it picks up a towel and wraps it around its neck because it does not want to be stamped like the others. This is a rebellious action. People think it is defective and destroy it. Most of the robots are sent off to train to do different jobs. I see it as a creative birthing process and I am very proud of my work.*

*"These robots are not creative or problem solvers because I did not want them to be able to figure out how to revolt. They do not have ambition, free will, or leadership qualities. They do what they are told, over and over, until they are told to do something different. When they are not useful, they are dismantled.*

*"I continue to work until eighty years of age. Then the ruler had me killed by poisoning me with mushrooms because I was old and not functioning well. My spirit stays around the factory for a long time. I am able to see the broader picture. I was shocked that these are not as non-sentient as they appear. They are aware of their existence. I am feeling guilty that they were used as slaves. After a long time, I see angels, who take me to heaven. Then I go for cleansing. I stand under a waterfall and all the dark entities and energies are washed out of me. Then I go to review my life with many Light beings. I am ashamed of what I did, although I was forced to do it. Occasionally during my life, I had feelings that those beings had some awareness. One of them was working as my secretary and she was so human-like that I even began to have some feelings for her, so I sent her somewhere else so I did not have to deal with her.*

*"I see that at first I programmed the computers with robotic speech and pathways of thinking. It is not really*

*thinking but a flowchart, such as: if you encounter a symbol like a stop sign, put your foot on the brake. Lots of things these robots did were like that. They were like critical pathways. They were programmed basically like a procedure manual for running a nuclear power plant and they would always do it the same way. It feels and looks like a thinking being but it is not. Aliens taught me the biological aspects of how to make the outer shell look real, such as skin, eyes, face, and voice, how to use the circuitry to make fluid, how to change the temperature of the skin, how people react when they move, when they sweat, or how many times their eyes blink. They made better servants because that is all they knew. Their only job was to do their job and they did not have distractions. They made much better workers and they did their jobs with precision and consistency.*

*"I was not empathetic to those created robots. I got the idea from the aliens during my sleep, channeling the information from the aliens, although consciously I was not aware of that. First I created dolls that had computers, and then the outer shell, which had very sophisticated sensors. You put different magnetic cards in the computer for different circuits for different functions of the body.*

*"From heaven, I see that many problems came from that life to my current life because my soul parts went to each robot because I felt so proud of creating them. Symptoms like feeling empty because of losing millions of my soul parts, joint pains because they were dismantled joint by joint, no strength in my body, total dislike of computers and technology, eye and memory problems, bloating, irritation of throat and larynx due to poisoning.*

*"On Dr. Modi's request, angels brought back all the soul parts of me and all the other people who were there in that life, from Satan, his demons, from people, places, and darkness, and integrated them after cleansing and healing them and our bodies. Many soul parts came back to me from every robot that was created. Many soul parts*

*came to my reproductive organs because it was like a creative birthing process to me."*

## Programming of the Computers by the Masters

Atlanteans eventually came to use crystals in the control mechanisms. The broadcast mechanism of the devices was amplified to broadcast their psychic abilities, amplifying to the point where they could control others. The rulers controlled people by inserting or dampening thoughts, substituting the ruler's own information or commands. They also took away thoughts. They also tried to control people's emotions, and definitely had some success in this, and substituting other emotions.

The rulers would put on a positive memory device and positive mind device. They would think their control thoughts, which would be transmitted to a computer-like device to be impressed on the brain waves of another person and reproduce the state in them that the ruler was asking for. Then those waves would be transmitted to the population in that master's area. Sometimes they would transmit a desire to build a certain project and people in their area would have that desire. They would go to work on the master's project, achieving it in a very short time. Anytime you control a population that completely, it is always wrong. All people have free will, and to violate that free will, especially in such a complete manner where you take away their feelings, was the ultimate crime.

Those Lamurians who were no longer able to live in Lamuria after its destruction were still in a high state of physical and spiritual development. People of Atlantis hesitated to tamper or interfere with them. Lamurians could still read minds and they had not lost the genes, but it was of a lesser power because they did not have the support of a large community around them. They had support from their small community.

One of my patients recalled a past life as a computer programmer in Atlantis during the Dark Ages as follows:

- *"I am a twenty-five-year-old male living in a northern city in Atlantis in about 37,655 BC. I am a computer programmer and also keep the computers running. I had four years of college in computer technology and then one year on the job training. I have been married for a year and my wife works at a university library. I become very popular and in demand because of my problem-solving abilities with computers. I also continued to discover new ways of programming computers*

  *"I created many mind control programs by entering the messages into the major transmitter of a centralized computer area and sending the messages out to the individuals who have had implants in their necks since an early age. These messages are received by their implants and then transmitted to their brains. I send messages to the doctors and nurses to carry the experiments to the extreme. By this time, devices are put in most people's necks when they are infants, including doctors and nurses, who also had neck implants and were controlled by the rulers. My computer programming for mind control caused a lack of emotions, feelings of thought insertion or removal of thoughts, and paranoia.*

  *"At the age of forty, I begin to brag about what I am doing and the rulers become suspicious. They suspect that I am jamming the signal for my own purposes. As a result, I am sent for medical experiments, where they do brain surgery on me to do studies on my memory center and metabolism center. Before that, they substituted my knee and ankle joints with animal joints. After the brain surgery, I slip into a coma and die.*

  *"When I go to heaven and review my life, I can see that it was wrong to control people through devices and computer messages. I see that the whole of Atlantis and*

*everybody in it, including me, were influenced by the de-*
*mons and were very dark.*

*"Many of my problems came from that life to the cur-*
*rent life, such as joint problems, metabolism problems,*
*and memory problems because of what was done to me.*
*Also, I have no desire to learn about the computer and use*
*it because I misused my knowledge about it."*

### Chemical Weapons

My patients under hypnosis state that, in Atlantis, they created weapons of mass destruction such as chemical gases
that can disable or kill masses of people. One of my patients
recalled a past life in Atlantis when he was an engineer and
he and his associates were ordered to create different gases
to hurt people.

- *"I am a thirty-year-old male wearing a plastic chemical*
  *protection suit that covers my head and face, and I also*
  *have goggles. I live in Tartoon City in the west part of*
  *Atlantis in a mountainous area. It is 26,000 BC. I am an*
  *engineer doing research about chemical weapons. We are*
  *creating gases to immobilize people. We are working on*
  *how to make chemical gases that will disable people and*
  *then dissipate fast. The people remain immobilized and*
  *our forces can capture them and not have to wear protec-*
  *tive suits. These are like nerve gases that disable the brain*
  *but do not kill. We have internal uprisings and revolts, and*
  *sometimes problems with neighboring cities over territory*
  *and trade. Our militia is a national reserve. In the past,*
  *we have gone to South America, Africa, and Europe to*
  *look for resources and attacked those areas. We have not*
  *gone anywhere for a long time and nobody has attacked*
  *us. But this is in preparation just in case something hap-*
  *pens. The military is now mostly used for local uprisings.*

  *"I live in an apartment adjacent to the military facility*
  *in the mountains, with other men who work with me. I am*

*not married because we are not allowed to marry. There are females in this military research facility, but they live in a separate section. We do not see women except in pictures. We usually satisfy sexual desires with other males or through masturbation.*

*"I do not have any memories about my family. I lived in a dorm in a training facility until I was fifteen years old, and then I was brought to this military facility. I went for a total of ten years of education. It was decided by the rulers what I should do.*

*"We are researching a variety of gases. Initially, the gases we produced had lethal and long-lasting effects. Right now, I am working on a particular compound, a particular type of nerve gas that has short-term effects. Then we test it on human slaves made available to us. They are put into a facility where people are sitting and working normally and do not know about anything that might happen. We put gas in that room, which is sealed, and we monitor the effects. Basically, we keep track of how long they are unconscious and how quickly they come out of it.*

*"At age of thirty-eight, there is a leak of gas in the facility and many people, researchers and subjects, died. There was an attempt to mix compounds and it exploded. At the age of forty-three, we are asked by the military hierarchy to produce gas that dissipates in a short time and kills people. We create this designer gas, and when it is tested on the slaves, it kills them in a few minutes. We block our feelings because we are doing a job.*

*"I retire at fifty-seven. We know a lot of secrets, so we are not given freedom to go elsewhere. We are given a place to live, adjacent to the research facility, in a dorm-like place. We sit around and play games and reminisce. Some people disappear and never come back. We do not know what happens to them. At age sixty-five, I am taken to another area in the facility. I am given a liquid to drink. I have burning all over, feel paralyzed, and die in a few minutes, thinking, "What a waste." I am angry. I have to find a way to stop it.*

"I step out of the body. I feel betrayed. I wander around the facility. I go to the leader to find out why I was killed, but he does not hear me. I find out that they are planning to kill masses of people. I am angry. I feel I am trapped in the darkness, and then I am inside somebody. I am inside the leader. I punch him in the stomach and cause him pain and curse him. Every pain I felt, he is feeling. As I look around, I see many spirits of researchers and the slaves who were killed are also in him.

"A psychic healer was praying for the lost souls, and as a result, all of us were pulled out of this person by the angels and are taken to heaven. After cleansing and healing, I go for a review of my life. From heaven, I see that my parents were researchers at another facility. My parents were not married, but were ordered to produce children. I was taken away from them when I was very young and raised in a school-type of facility with other boys. I had a device put in my neck when I was a toddler. The device is about an inch long and one-fourth inch in diameter. They were inserted in both sides of the neck, then they unfold and, in time, grow. Then I was moved to another place where I lived until I was fifteen. Then I was taken to the research facility.

"From heaven, I can see that you, Dr. Modi, were the psychic healer whose prayers freed me and other human spirits from the darkness and sent us to heaven. I see my gastrointestinal tract problems, throat problems, and stuffy nose problems came from that life.

"From heaven, I see that I had six karmic lives after this life where similar research was done on me. I see now that they were creating those gases to use on their own. I see that it is inhumane by its very nature, and we should not engage in it. I also needed to learn the lesson of respecting human life.

"I see in hell there is a whole city that has storage of Atlantean records, patterns, and soul parts of people who were there during those 130,000 or more years. There are

*different dark centers from where they are using differ-
ent ways of introducing genetic engineering in individuals of our current day society through their soul parts.
The demons are trying to influence our scientists to do
similar damaging experiments, such as creating chemical, biological, and nuclear weapons, and different types
of genetic experiments like cloning and others. They are
influencing humans in all areas of science and technology, and basically motivating them to reinvent different
technology that was used in Atlantis. Biologically-based
computers could be precursors to the implants for control
purposes. The demons are trying to promote the researchers whenever they can to invent damaging technology."*

I requested the angels to dissolve and transform the whole
city or area in hell that is connected with Atlantis, and bring
back everybody's soul parts from there, cleanse them, heal
them, and integrate them with whom they belong. For those
who are not ready to receive them, store them in heaven until
people are ready to receive them. Everybody and the whole
area in hell connected with Atlantis was cleansed, healed,
filled and shielded by the Light. The patient saw it all happening as requested.

### Biology, Psychology, and Medical Care in Atlantis During the Dark Ages

Atlanteans had many, many years to learn about DNA and
develop an understanding of genetics and how they worked.
When they had contact with the alien races around 70,000
years ago, they helped with the technology for studying DNA
and also provided insights for the Atlanteans as to how to
use DNA. The Atlanteans started their experiments shortly
before the fourth alien race arrived around 70,000 BC. They
contributed greatly to the understanding of the broadcast
power. The aliens were amazed at the sophistication of the
Atlanteans in dealing with crystals. They themselves had

not achieved the Atlanteans' expertise until they were able to literally see a crystal.

They helped the Atlanteans apply scientific discoveries to medical care so that when there was a better understanding of chemistry and biology it could be put into effect in medicine. Atlanteans had discovered DNA and the basis of genetics not long before the aliens came. They were in the process of finding out how DNA worked when the aliens arrived. After contact was established, the alien scientists helped the Atlantean scientists to see the effects of different parts of DNA. This was beyond the Atlanteans' understanding at that time. They took the information without having a fully rounded, encompassing picture, taking the aliens at their words. They began to do genetic modification in plants and animals.

### Genetic Modifications on Plants and Animals

According to my hypnotized patients, Atlanteans did genetic modifications on fishes, different animals and plants they would eat, by making them bigger and fatter, and made plants more productive. Here is another heinous crime they did not understand. When they modified different plants, they changed the seed that was produced, and that seed is no longer in keeping with the karmic plan for this plant. Plants have karmic imprints too. Everything has DNA, and when you make a modification in DNA, you change the plan. By making changes in the plant DNA, they changed the plan for that plant. The contact with the spirit that infuses the food with life, above and beyond the simple chemistry, is missing. It provides substance to the body, sustains the body but does not sustain the spirit. You can eat this food to satisfy the body's hunger and still be spiritually hungry.

These were relatively harmless modifications, trying to make them more disease and insect resistant, and to provide better quality food, which did not always mean "better quality food." This could mean food that would ship better and last longer. It may not taste as good and may not be as healthy.

One patient had allergies to different grains, which caused her to feel tired and nauseated, and to have pain and swelling in her legs. She recalled the following life as the source of her grain allergies:

- *"I am a twenty-three-year-old female. My name is Anna and I live in Lemar City in Atlantis. I live with my parents and one younger sister. I am almost finished with my education in sculpting and the arts. The buildings here look like they are units stacked one on top of the other in pyramidal shaped, high-rise buildings. There are large, covered tunnels made of translucent material supported by the half hoops. These are like walkways from one place to another, and they are temperature controlled. I live in one of those buildings. You can acquire as many units as you choose. We have something like television, but it is interactive, and we can also communicate through it. It also functions as a computer.*

  *"I have had a boyfriend for a couple of years. He is studying biological science. His name is Brin. He is learning the techniques of genetic engineering on small birds and animals, like chickens. We get married in a huge tent-like thing. It is kind of pretty. I am wearing a cream colored long dress and I see other women also wearing long gowns of different colors. The groom is wearing some type of tights. I see us joining hands and then putting a hand on each other's hearts. It is a secular ceremony. There is no priest. A government official is marrying us. He is wearing a dark colored robe. After the ceremony there is food, drinks, and celebration.*

  *"I am pursuing my artistic pursuits. The building at which I go to work is beautiful. It is free form, and the light comes in from an angle to give good lighting. After marriage, my husband, Brin, is doing further research. I beg him to take me to his work and show me what he*

*is doing. He cannot take me there during the day, but he takes me in the night to the institute. I see huge birds they created that are much larger than normal. They are working on having birds that can hatch an egg cheaper and faster. I am appalled. I think it is unnatural. My bent is toward beauty. I do not recognize some of the birds there. There is something that looks like a friendly vulture. I am upset. I tell him that he has to quit working there, but he refuses because they will not let him. It becomes a constant problem between us. My husband is not as open and talkative as he was before.*

*"I seek out people who think as I do. We have small underground meetings and I bring literature and information to show what has been done to try to convince them. I am noticed going to these meetings by some government official. As a result, my husband comes under suspicion and they watch him very closely. One of the created creatures gets loose and attacks people. This triggers underground discussion about what is going on.*

*"There is an uprising and an attack on the institute by underground groups. They try to destroy equipment and any unnatural animals. People are caught. I am implicated by some of the people who are caught. My husband decides to leave the institute and we move to the countryside. We try to blend in with a group of workers who are working on a farm. We also do farm work. It has a certain positive aspect, because my husband is not doing genetic modification anymore. Later, we find out that what we are harvesting was also modified by other scientists. It was supposed to make it better. It grows better in a shorter time span, is resistant to diseases, looks nice and plump, and it delivers different nutrients, such as a more complex mix of amino acids. We grow barley, corn, and other grains.*

*"I start to get sick. I am losing weight and have diarrhea and intestinal cramps. Doctors do not know what is wrong. We find out that there is a certain sub-section of the population that cannot tolerate and absorb the*

*genetically modified food. To the government, it is not a concern because that part of the unhealthy population will be weeded out. They are considered genetically inferior. I get sicker and weaker and cannot work anymore, and wither away. I get nauseated and get swelling of the legs and sometimes of the hands. I die at the age of thirty. My last thoughts are, "I do not like this type of control. I am going to pay attention and be more knowledgeable about this type of thing."*

*"My spirit is curious. I look around to see what they are doing on other farms. It is worse than I thought. What I see is that they are doing experimentation for the sake of experimentation and not for any good reason. I see a grown creature with a cow's body and a human face, and other combinations of animals and humans. I feel disgusted and sick in my stomach. I go inside my husband, Brin, as a spirit, and inspire him to do something to destroy all those research areas. He becomes more militant in his underground work. He gathers more information about where things are located, where the equipment is, and where the knowledge is stored. He was able to formulate how to destroy some key areas.*

*"He and his group attack the research center. They stun the guards, gain entry, scramble all the data, and kill all those created beings. They get caught, but the center is totally destroyed. As a punishment, they use him and the others as experimental subjects. They try to graft different parts of him on animals. They graft his arms on a cow because it will be handy to have a cow that could grab its own food. They put his head and shoulders on another animal just to see if it becomes more intelligent and productive. They use different drugs and things to keep the animal alive for a few days, but then it dies. They also try to harvest his sperm to do genetic modification. They use all his parts to graft onto different animals. He dies and we both come out of his body. I think my husband goes to the heaven.*

*"Even though I would like to be done with all this, I cannot. I try to find another person who is open for possession. This time, I am looking for someone who is higher up and open. Someone who can change things. I enter into a person who is researching. He is doing more of the genetic engineering. I feed him doubts about what he is doing. I keep working on him and get him to a point where he destroys the research and the knowledge. He is taken away and put to work on one of the farms, thinking he just snapped and had a breakdown. When you are new, nobody trusts you, and then people on the farm found out what he did. He still does not know why he did it.*

*"He starts to talk to some of the underground people. They plot to destroy the research facility and the knowledge. After destroying the center where he worked, they formulate another plot with outside sympathizers and gain access to a sister facility in another town and destroy it. He and his followers were caught and sent for experimentation. They transplant every part of him on animals. There is some interest in how a head can exist on its own so they amputated his head above the shoulders. He was given all types of nutrients to produce the brain chemicals to keep the head alive. They are able to keep it alive for days with the nutrients and the fluid they invented. They have a re-pumping mechanism so it can survive without heart and lungs.*

*"My spirit comes out of him when they begin to cut him up. I feel that now it is time to go to heaven, where I get a loving, warm acceptance. After cleansing and resting, I go to review my life with several wise heavenly beings. They are pleased with me and about how I lived my life. From heaven, I see that we should not trade physical comfort and complacency for not paying attention to the core values of society. What was happening in Atlantis was very wrong. Because I felt about it so strongly, I also felt power to affect it.*

*"From heaven, I see that my allergies to grains came from that life. Also the pains of being cut when my spirit was in Brin and the other person, such as shoulder and arm pain, and other aches and pains. I am just terrified when our scientists talk about doing genetic experimentation with grains and dairy products. I feel it can be dangerous. From heaven, I see a lot of darkness in Atlantis at that time. That is why they were doing such evil things."*

### Genetic Modifications on Humans and Animals

When the aliens helped Atlanteans to understand DNA, they cut many years of developmental process by showing them how particular groups of bases on DNA would produce a particular change in the organism. The Atlanteans had already begun to experiment on plants and animals by making DNA changes. This small understanding gave them the courage to try big experiments on humans. They began to modify the human DNA and injecting the modified DNA into live people. When they made a mistake and made the strand of DNA not viable, that is when it could not continue living, the cell into which it was injected would die. When the DNA was viable and could have its effect, the cells in which it was inserted would reproduce and spread it.

At the beginning, the changes they were making in the DNA were beneficial medical ones and they were trying to cure genetic diseases. It was not very long before someone got the idea to try it on a living baby. They made genetic changes in the baby and then watched the baby grow. This was a heinous act, to actually interfere in the reproduction of a human being, to change its genetic codes without really knowing what was going to happen. They would take several children and modify the DNA slightly. Then as the child grew, they would watch to see how that gene was expressed and what changes they could detect in the body.

Described and drawn by the different hypnotized patients

This dog like human has a face and head that resembles a domestic dog. Its body, arms, legs, and hands resemble a human, but the feet resemble a dog's paws.

This wolf like human has the head, neck, and face of a wolf. Its other body parts resemble that of a human being.

This bird like human has the physical fea-tures of a chicken. Its arms and left leg are similar to a human, but its body, fingers, toes, right leg, and head are similar to a chicken. Even the hairline resembles a chicken's comb.

As a result of genetic experimentation, many ape like human being like this one lived in Atlantis. This adult human being has the physical features of a gorilla.

In medical DNA, they worked with genetic diseases first, such as the conditions that were inherited through genetics. They tried to create a DNA that would duplicate the original,

Described and drawn by the different hypnotized patients

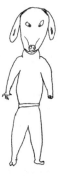

This young goat like baby has the upright body of a human.  Its left leg and right arm are similar to a human's.  Its right leg and left hand have hooves similar to a goat.

This man has a normal left leg, but his arms have hooves instead of hands and his right leg has a hoof instead of a normal foot.

This snake like human has the face and neck of a snake.  The arms, hands, legs, and feet closely resemble those of a human.  The round shape body becomes a little larger as it extends downward.  Scales and different shades of skin pigmentation cover the body.

except for what they thought was the damaged string. They would take that damaged string out and insert a string they thought would cure that inherited condition. They would reproduce the cells, then reinsert them in the body. Their hope was that the bad effects would be overcome and that would be enough to produce whatever chemicals were needed to make the body function properly.

They also tried to modify human beings through DNA substitution. They tried to improve eyesight, and tried to get rid of diabetes and other genetically inherited disease. With humans, they changed eye color, skin color, hair color; any kind of modifications they could make, they tried. They tried changing the size of the muscles to make people stronger, tampered with color and black and white vision, and tried to create larger macula to avoid macular disease.

In making their genetic changes, sometimes wild changes, they were interfering with that being's spiritual patterns and with his development, even obliterating positive karmas by changing the wrong parts of the DNA. This was a severe problem, and, strictly speaking, this was a heinous crime against humanity done completely unintentionally by unwitting people who thought they were only dealing with the physical. It was one of the worst things ever done in the history of the universe, to obliterate karmic patterns and remove those positive imprints. Without the positive spiritual karmic imprints, organisms did not even quite know how to grow, because their purpose was obliterated and their spiritual destiny was changed.

They attempted to modify the DNA of various animals and of humans so they would be compatible with each other. This way, an organ of a pig or other animal could be transplanted into human beings. They also genetically modified human beings to accept the transplanted organs of other human beings and animals. They were quite proud of this ability and showed it off by grafting limbs from animals onto humans, or human parts to the animals by modifying certain provisions of the DNA in the animal and in the human. This way, the organs or the parts were not rejected.

They also did stem cell research and grew different organs to use in people whose organs were failing, but during the Dark Ages, they introduced genetic defects and diseases in the organs and transplanted them in people they wanted to punish, as described in the following past life recalled by a patient:

- *"I am a thirty-five-year-old male living in Ventu City in Atlantis. My name is Verylan and this is 22,000 BC. I work in a research institute. We are doing genetic modifications. We are growing organs. It is stem cell research. We take the stem cells and stimulate them with crystals in a culture outside the body. When they begin to grow in a particular organ, at a certain stage, we transplant them into human subjects because they need a human medium. When the organ has grown to a certain stage, we cut the person again to harvest the organ. We use some of these organs in people who have organ failures. Others we use to cause sickness in people as a punishment. We introduce genetic defects or diseases in the stem cells so the organs grow with it, and then we transplant these organs into people we want to punish. We have created hearts, pancreas, livers, stomachs, colons, kidneys, etc.*

    *"I live in a research institute in an apartment with other men. At the age of fifty, I begin to question what we are doing. So they did the same thing to me, by opening my abdomen and replacing my liver, colon, and pancreas with diseased ones. I get diabetes, diarrhea, cramps, and bleeding. My incision gets infected and is very painful. I die within a month. My spirit is feeling angry. I go into the physician who implanted the organs in me and scream and curse at him, but he does not hear me. I squeeze his organs and cause him pain. I see there are many other people inside him on whom he did experiments. They are also angry with him.*

    *"I feel like I am trapped in a demon and then I am sucked down into hell. It is like a tar pit and I and the demon around me are stuck in the tar. I hear howling and screaming. All the demons there are waiting for an assignment. I am scared; I do not know what is happening. I*

*see this pit of fire burning all around me. It is like being in a steel mill and you see sparks, red fire, and lava all over. It smells bad, like something burned. I sense evil, anger, and violence there.*

*"The demon gets another assignment from another large demon and suddenly we are out of there and go into someone else in Atlantis. This time, it is a ruler who has control over all the genetic experiments. The demon and all the human spirits in it are trying to make his life miserable. When he dies, we are taken into another person, and then another and another, and this goes on for hundreds of years. We are taken back to hell and are waiting for the next appointment. I am sick and tired of it.*

*"I can hear some music and I focus my attention on it. It gets louder and louder and suddenly I am out of the demon. It was due to prayers and singing. I think some Buddhist monks were chanting in the Himalayas. They must have focused their prayers and chants on hell to free souls from there. The reason my soul can hear the chants is because I had done that kind of chanting in other lives and, as a result, my soul was able to tune into it. I am out of the demon and hell and lifted up by angels and going up in this multicolored tunnel.*

*"In the heaven two luminous beings are healing me. First there is singing going on which heals me. I am bathing in a pool of liquid Light which takes all the darkness out of me. Then they are placing herbs on my body. They also put something like gauze with herbs and liquid over my eyes, ears, throat and third eye. They put a wrap of some type over my brain. It is like being in a spa. They heal my organs by putting their hands over my heart, abdomen, and back and the Light comes out of their hands.*

*"I rest for a while and then I go for a review of my life. I am in a room, seated at a table that is made of Light. There are two masters standing next to me on either side. The table becomes like a movie screen and I begin to see my life. I am actually looking back at several lives tying*

*to this life. I see my birth. My parents were two physicians who were put together by the rulers to produce children, but they did not know each other before. After they had six children, they were separated and never saw each other again. I was taken away immediately and was brought up in a male dorm. They also put a device in my neck just after birth.*

*"I stayed in that dorm till I was six years old. Then they moved me to another dorm. I lived there till I was fifteen. I was beaten, poked with a rod, and shocked. They had all types of torture devices to punish us. They had an ankle and wrist iron to chain me to the desk or clamp it tight. As I grow, I become cruel, too, being rough and abusive with people. Most people in my dorm go to college and have a professional education. I went to eight years of college to become a physician.*

*"From heaven, I realized that I needed to learn the lesson about the sanctity of life. Each human life is precious and needs to be respected. There are dangers in genetic engineering and how far it can go. How could a potentially positive idea of creating organs for organ replacement lead to manipulation and control? You can use stem cells to create organs. The intent can be positive to create organs for organ replacement when people are ill, but it can also be used for evil purposes like introducing diseases into organs. It can be profoundly dangerous in the wrong hands.*

*"Genetic modification is an open door to an introduction of new viruses and new diseases. We are only utilizing a small portion of the DNA and we do not know what is in the rest of the DNA and what it is doing to people's souls, spirituality, and their mission. It opens the door to some good, but without a complete understanding of DNA and spirituality, we are opening the door to the worst. In evil hands, we are opening the door to the depths of hell.*

*"From heaven, I see that my shingles, diabetes, GI tract problems, stuffy nose, and joint problems came from that*

*life to the current life. I also see that I lived three lives after this life, where similar types of research was done on me.*

*"Atlanteans got into designing a being by taking DNA, modifying it, inserting it into a fertilized egg, and allowing that to grow into a living being. They made changes as to how many limbs the being can have and changed its characteristics effectively, either speeding up evolution, if you choose to look at it that way, or violating the intentions of God. He intended every being to have certain distinctive characteristics, and anyone who interferes with that is interfering with God's plan.*

*"They would take a being that had certain characteristics and change them around, so that as the fertilized egg grew, the developing being would be different than anything that had been born before. The DNA would spread throughout the body, even in the reproductive cells, so that the children would have these characteristics, as well. Some examples would be putting hands on animals that did not have them so the animal would have fingers and could hold things, or literally putting monkeys' hands on a cat, etc."*

Atlanteans did two different types of modifications:

- Internal modifications
- External modifications

**Internal modifications:** The first thing that had to be genetically modified was the receptivity of the beings. So the immune system and other bodily systems had to be changed. This interfered severely with the karma of that human and the animal. When they modified the DNA, it changed the spiritual patterns on the DNA. This was a severe crime.

**External modifications:** These would show up externally, like a change in the eye color, multiple pupils in the eye, different number of fingers, different number of limbs, human bodies with animal heads or bird heads, etc. In general, if it basically had a human appearance, they thought of it as human. If it had a basic animal appearance, it was thought of as an animal.

Following are some of the past lives recalled by hypnotized patients of such modification:

- *"I am a seven-month-old male, a lion baby, in 27,000 BC. I have the facial features of a male lion. I have kind of a large head, a flat nose, and eyes that resemble a big cat. My hairline resembles that of a lion's mane. I also have a very small tail. My hands and feet are rounded like paws and have claws coming out of them. The rest of my body is more human looking than animal, but my stomach area looks a little softer and a little lighter in color than my back area. I die at one year of age because my organs were not functioning properly.*

   *"From heaven, I see I was a genetic engineer in a couple of lifetimes, where I also created the genetically altered babies, and this life, as a lion baby, was a karmic payback for what I did to others."*


- *"I have a life as a little girl in the west central city of Eroc in about 45,000 BC. I am currently four years old and I have the facial features of an eagle. I have a sharp, curved nose, deep set eyes, a rounded head that resembles a bird, and tiny ears that are flush with my head. Both of my hands have sharp talons extending from where my fingernails would have been. One foot is similar to my hands and the other foot has only one toe. I have bony legs that resemble bird legs. I have an arch in my back and my rear end protrudes like a bird's behind. I walk upright but I waddle as opposed to walking normally.*

   *"I'm in and out of medical clinics. I am very self-conscious about my looks. I cry a lot. I can be very aggressive and mean if I'm teased. I function like a human. I sleep in a human bed, but sometimes I like to stand to rest. I*

possess some birdlike tendencies. My family tries to pamper me. I feel like a bridge between my family and me. We seem to be uncomfortable with each other. I cannot attend normal school because of my looks, my behavior, and my health. I am ill quite frequently and I must stay in and rest.

"For the next three years, I'm very antisocial and aggressive. Once, when a person from a medical research clinic stopped at my parents' home, I became frightened of him. I attacked him and took out his right eye with my sharp talons. I am also becoming weaker and weaker. When I'm seven, I have a lot of difficulty breathing. I don't eat much, so I'm a little undernourished. My lungs start to shut down and I can't breathe. Other organs also shut down and I fade into death. Shortly after my physical body dies, I am taken to the Light. I am cleansed of all darkness. I rest and relax. Then I go and review my life with four spirit guides. I see that I was a bird girl because of a genetic experiment that went bad and my birdlike tendencies resulted from a genetic predisposition.

"I see that the Light was provided for my immediate ascension because I was an innocent child. The problems that came from that life to the current life were over-aggression, impatience, and social isolation. That life was a karmic lifetime. In an earlier time in Atlantis, I was a genetic engineer who was responsible for over one hundred genetically defective babies. As a result, I came back to balance out karma."

- "I am a two-year-old girl living in a special dorm for deformed children in Aris, Atlantis. It is about 29,000 BC. I am a cat child because of the genetic modification they did with my mother. I have the facial features of a cat. My eyes are glassy like a cat's eyes, my ears are pointed out a little bit, and my nose is small and flat. One hand looks like a cat's paw and the other hand has only three fingers. My feet are like cats' paws. The rest of my body looks human. I make sounds but cannot speak. There are many *different types of children here. There are bird babies, monkey babies, lion babies, goat babies, etc. The caretakers in the dorm are indifferent. They do not show any affection. If we get sick, they let us die or kill us. They do not treat or help us.*

*"They also do experiments with us, such as putting us in extreme dark or cold and starving or depriving us of certain foods or water. I die at the age of four because of heart and kidney failure. From heaven, I see my lung and memory problems coming from that life to my current life.*

*"These Atlanteans created miserable beings who lived miserable lives. People who were different and did not fit into society, were terribly unhappy, especially when they knew that they had been designed before they were born. They knew that they were genetically modified, and if they did not know, then other people around them certainly told them. For a while, the scientists were stuck in a mode of putting different limbs on people so, for example, they might have legs of deer, or a deer might have human legs. One patient recalled the following life when he was a victim of genetic engineering and lived a miserable life.*

• *"My name is Felixx and I live in the city of Adeil, which is located in south central Atlantis. It is 44,800 BC. I am three years old and I live with my parents, two older brothers, one older sister, and one younger sister. My brothers and sisters are all normal but I am not because I am the victim of a genetic engineering experiment. I am an animal baby. I spend a good deal of my time being shuttled from home to a medical research complex. I am currently being evaluated because I am too aggressive. I bathroom on the floor, I destroy property, and I'm very antisocial.*

*"I have facial features that resemble an ape. My head is shaped like an ape's head. I have deep set eyes and a flat nose. My mouth is very wide and I have a severe overbite. I have the body physique of an ape. My arms seem*

unusually long and my legs are bowed. All of this makes me sad. I sit and cry because I do not look like my brothers and sisters. When I'm seen in public, people tease me and make fun of me.

"When I'm five, my parents enroll me in school. I'm only there for a few hours when other children begin to tease me and call me names like "ape-boy." I sit and cry. I'm not the only different looking child in my class, but I'm the most extreme looking. There is a girl who has webbing between her fingers and thumbs. And there is a boy who has some facial characteristics of a wolf. He has a human face but he has a long nose and pointed ears. The other children do not stop teasing me, so I become very angry. I scratch two children's faces and run around the classroom, throwing books and school supplies, running from the teacher who is unable to control me. I run out the door into the street and I am able to find my way home. I am taken out of school because I cannot get along with others and I cause too many disturbances.

"I stay at home for the next few years and receive private tutoring in basic reading, writing, and arithmetic. I am constantly angry and frustrated because people continue to make fun of me. When I am thirteen, I am in a big market area of the city with my parents. A group of normal teenagers start to tease and make fun of me. I become angry and throw fruit at them. Then I grab a broom that I found in the store and strike one of the teens, rendering him unconscious. The police come and try to take me to jail. I break free from the police by kicking and biting them. I find that I'm stronger than most humans and very fast on my feet. As a result, I run away and hide in the innermost depths of the city.

"I take refuge with a community of street people. This group of people includes animal people like me, the mentally ill, and a few criminals and escapees from various medical research centers. I live in hiding for the next *twenty-eight years. During this time, I lead a life of petty crime, robbery, burglary, and assaults on others. Several times, I was almost caught but I always found a way to escape. I live in alleys and under the city. I have a neck implant but I no longer live at home or anywhere else where there is a receiver. As a result, the authorities cannot find me. I live with other animal people in the deepest caverns of the city. Most of the animal people's faces and limbs resemble an animal. There are bird people, goat people, cat people, wolf people, and dog people. They are still humans and they stand and walk on two feet. They are different because of the genetic modification. All of us are fugitives and we live from day to day.*

*"I eat by stealing items of food from marketplaces. Sometimes I rob people, then I have someone else, who looks physically normal, go and purchase food for me. Sometimes I go to my parent's home when they are away so that I can steal from them. Our community is like most other communities. Some of the people get along with others and some do not. Sometimes there are fights and someone gets killed. We run in gangs for our own protection. I live in the rubble, in alleys, under buildings, and underground in a network of sewer lines and pipes. Normal people know of our existence but they are frightened of us. They know we will kill them if they come into our territory. The police do not make a sustained attempt to capture us unless there is a major disturbance. We hide during the day and come out at night.*

*"When I'm thirty-nine, I begin to have health problems. I tire easily, get headaches, and have trouble digesting my food. I 'm becoming increasingly irritable because I do not feel well. I continue this pattern for two years. At forty-one, I'm very weak. I can't eat. I have a fever and I lie down on some leaves and garbage. Someone puts an old rag cloth over me and I fade into death. I die of malnutrition, but I have an assortment of other problems. I*

have abscessed teeth and many of my organs are shutting down because of the genetic modification.

"My spirit leaves my body but it doesn't know what to do or where to go. I'm angry because I do not know why I look like I do. I'm in the dark and I cannot find the Light. I am taken to hell and put inside a demon. The demon instructs me to enter other animal people. I cause them to have the problems I had. I increase their fear, aggression, and outlaw behavior. I possess twenty-five people in one hundred and fifty years. A group of psychic people pray for everyone who has not gone to the Light. Their prayers bring enough Light. I find the Light and go with angels into heaven.

"In heaven, I cleanse myself and I rest. Then I go with three spirit guides who help me review this life. From heaven, I am able to see that doctors transplanted animal cells in my mother's embryo. I see why I was always aggressive and antisocial. I had a genetic predisposition to act like an ape. I understand why my parents and siblings felt limited sorrow about my condition. They were basically without emotion because of their "concentration camp" lifestyle. I see the darkness in the people and all over Atlantis. There is very little Light from heaven.

"I brought several problems from that life to the current life. Sometimes I have over-aggressive thoughts that I'd like to physically hurt someone. I'm basically a loner. I sometimes feel I'm not as good as other people. I've had a desire to "go off" and live by myself in the mountains. And I feel in some ways that society has abused me.

"My wife and a sister-in-law were in that life. They were two of the teenagers I assaulted in the marketplace when I was thirteen. I continue to have unresolved issues with my wife and my sister-in-law. A high-ranking person in my place of employment was in that life. He was one of the doctors who transplanted the animal cells into my mother's embryo. I have unresolved issues with this *person. From the Light (heaven), I see that I've had one other life in Atlantis as an animal person."*

- *"I had a life in about 37,000 BC, in the city of Idol, which was located in the northwest section of the country. In that life, I was a goat child. I had the facial features of a goat. My eyes, ears, and nose looked like they belonged to a goat. My left hand had two fingers and a thumb, and my right hand looked like a goat's hoof. My left foot looked like a goat's hoof and my right foot was normal. I had a one-inch tail coming out of my tailbone. I had the chest and back of a human but I had excessive brownish hair on my back and lots of light colored hair on my chest and stomach. I ate like a human and my body functioned like a human. I was almost two years old but I was underdeveloped socially. I acted as though I was only nine or ten months old. My mom and dad and my two brothers were normal. They felt bad for me because I was different.*

  *"At two years of age, my organs began to stop functioning. My kidneys and lungs were failing badly. My spirit left me, and my physical body died. I was taken to heaven soon after the death of my physical body."*

Another patient recalled the following past life when geneticians created her by mixing different genes in a test tube.

- *"I am a thirteen-year-old girl living in Antrak City in Atlantis. My name is Asson. I have a hard time believing what I am seeing. I look different. My hands look like turkey claws. I have human legs and feet, but they are turned inward. I have very strange eyes, which are big and dark. My nose is like a beak and my mouth opens under the beak. The ears are tiny and there is a small chin. I have a very strange, bulbous-shaped head, which almost looks like a light bulb, and I have feathers. I have two hands and two legs. I walk upright but I am bowed down. My head and face look like a turkey's but I have a human mouth.*

*"We live in a group in huts. There are different types of beings of different ages in the group. There is a cat person who has a catlike head and ears, fur on the back, and a little tail. It has beady eyes and can smile. It is kind of hunched down. It can walk on four legs but usually walks on its hind legs. The hands and rest of its body are mostly human. There are also beings who look like pigs, birds, apes, etc.*

*"I have lived here all my life. I have aches and pains all over, all the time. I have a hard time walking due to the pain. I do not sense a whole lot of intellect. I just feel deadness. We just work, eat, and sleep. Our animal characteristics come out from time to time. We are living like outcasts. I get the sense that we can be taken anytime and nobody will really know what happens to us when we are taken away.*

*"At the age of thirteen, I am on an operating table and I feel sick to my stomach and have a headache. They want to see if I can reproduce, so they are having a male turkey person have sex with me and it feels real gross. They put a tube in me so the penis can go in. I become pregnant and am feeling nauseous and having headaches. At full term, they cut my abdomen and take the baby out and sew my abdomen back together. I never see my baby.*

*"At the age of fourteen, they just come and take us, put us in single file, and chain us to each other. We walk for a long time, and then we go in this boat to a pit. We are still in single file, being chained together, and are told to jump in the pit. When the first one jumps in, the second one and all the others are pulled in. In the pit, it smells horrible. They are pouring something like hot tar on us, which is painful and burns. I am suffocating and cannot breathe.*

*"As I am dying, I am thinking, "Who is doing this and why? Please make it stop." My spirit comes out and I see angels. They take all of us out and take us to heaven. We are all kind of twisted, so they straighten us up. After cleansing, my memories are coming back. We are all shiny*

*and glowing. They take turkey soul parts out of me, which do not belong in me, and my soul is integrated with the rest of my soul because only part of my soul went into my body. I feel happy and a lot smarter.*

*"I am taken to a room where I review my life with many masters and my higher self. I see scientists in a lab who are mixing the cells and growing these babies in jars. It seems that they have storage of human cells that are taken from different people in society. They mix the gene of a big turkey with a human cell. It divides and grows into a being in liquid. Then they transfer it into different containers as it grows. When it is a fully formed baby, there is a place where it is taken. It is like a factory where they are creating these different types of babies. After we are grown, we are sent to the farm where we lived in huts. They showed us how to work and left us there with people who oversee us. They do all types of tests on us.*

*"The heavenly beings are asking me if I remember why I decided to incarnate in that life. I needed to experience this because I have done these things to others before and it could happen again, and we need to know so we can try to prevent it. This should not be allowed to continue.*

*"From heaven, I see that when people do these things, anything is possible. When we go along with it, we also become responsible. I think in the other life I was also responsible for some of the technology, but I actually did not do it and never thought that anyone would do it for these kinds of purposes. There is a lesson for the scientists in the current life now who are working on cloning and stem cell research. They probably do not think that anybody will clone people or use this technology in a hideous way, but people with demonic influences might do it again. So we all need to take responsibility and pay attention to what is happening in our society.*

*"I see that my headaches, pain in the neck and back, and not feeling like an upright, graceful human being came from this life. When you, Dr. Modi, asked the soul*

*parts of me and others to be brought back, I saw soul parts
of all of us coming from people, places, darkness, the pit,
and also from the turkey and other animals. Demons are
pressing, pounding, and jumping on my soul part to my
head in hell, which creates headaches in me here. After
bringing the soul parts back and integrating them with
me, my headaches were not so severe but still continued.*

*"As I look from heaven for the other reasons, I see an-
other lifetime in Atlantis in 37,000 BC when I was a female. I was a cold scientist who was using the technology of being able to put different types of cells together
with different DNA and making other cells. I created such
things as: mice with human eyes, legs, hands, and mixed
facial features; a snake with a human head but no hair,
scales that go up to the forehead, and a human face. The
rest of the body is a snake body. I also created a combination of duck and human, bird and human, etc. I also performed the experiments on these mixed genetic humans,
cutting them open to see what they look like, how they
metabolize food, and how that is different from normal humans and the animals they are crossed with.*

*"From heaven, I see that I had many lifetimes when I
was a scientist doing genetic and other types of experiments. After bringing my soul parts from all those lifetimes, my headaches were relieved."*

"Heavenly beings, through my hypnotized patients, state
there was a remarkable thing that happened after the dispersion from Atlantis, after its destruction. All the modified genes were in the population that dispersed. The people
carried those modified genes around the world where, in
time, the genes became extinct. The child would have normal genes and the modified gene, and in almost every case,
the normal genes were expressed. The modified gene was
not expressed and did not show up in the child when it was
time to reproduce. The normal DNA was reproduced selec-
tively more often than the abnormal. So over generations,

the number of modified genes dropped and the number of normal genes went up, until humanity was back to normal and in touch with the karma.

"Even beings from Atlantis who had been subject to severe genetic manipulation, after enough generations, the abnormal genes disappeared and the people went back to being normal. Now there are very few abnormal genes from Atlantis carried over in the entire population. A few of the genetic problems we have could be from Atlantis, such as few cases of endocrine disorders, multiple sclerosis, muscular dystrophy, etc. There are few of those modifications still drifting through in isolated individuals and over the next thousand years, they will all disappear. Also, there is a corruption of the spirit due to genetic modification, where the spirit of a person is not quite right because its positive karma, or the spiritual blueprint, has been influenced along with the instructions of how to grow and develop and how to be in touch with the spirit; that is a more severe problem. This will also disappear in time.

"Genetic modification of plants created similar problems for plants as it did for humans, according to heavenly beings. Some plants did not shed the genetic changes as quickly as humans and animals, so there are still many plants all over the world that have modified genes from Atlantis. According to the heavenly beings, wheat is one of the modified plants, which most of the people all over the world eat. Those who eat wheat suffer from its lack of spirit. It does not contribute all that it should for people who eat it. Wherever people eat genetically modified grains and foods, spiritual damage is done to people who consume it.

"There are only a few genetic modifications from Atlantis that are still being carried on in humans and animals. They shook off the genetic modifications easier. Plants did not get rid of genetic modifications as easily. So many of the foods we eat still have this lack of spirit or lack of fulfillment of the karmic destiny. This affects people's spirituality drastically, because eating food does not just satisfy the body; it also satisfies the soul. The frustration of the spirit because of lack of spiritual satisfaction leads to the continual attempt to eat more and more, which leads to addictions, and this leads to overweight problems. With the food that has not been genetically modified, you get the full effect of spirit, the satisfaction of the soul. With the hunger that comes from eating the food that has come from genetically modified plants, people are left with spiritual hunger, more and more.

Heavenly beings, through my hypnotized patients, claim that some of the addictions that are caused due to the use of certain plants, such as plants which produce alcohol, tobacco, opiates, marijuana, cocaine, heroin, LSD, etc., are the plants which were genetically modified and remain modified. You get the physical effect but lack spiritual satisfaction from them. This leads a person to use more and more without satisfaction, leading the person to become addicted to these drugs. The Atlanteans modified these plants to get an intense effect.

Originally, God created these plants for medicinal purposes and they were used for these reasons effectively, according to the heavenly beings. Atlanteans genetically modified these plants for the "high" effects, to produce certain chemicals, which became out of balance. For example, originally, opium had a balance of compounds that produced the desired medicinal effect and strengthened the body. When Atlanteans genetically modified the opium plants, the addictive high effect was intensified, while the rest of the chemicals that were necessary for spiritual complements were either eliminated or reduced drastically. Now they have the chemical that has the "high" effect over-amplified and it does damage to the body because other chemicals that support the body and heal it are missing or are very little in concentration.

One of my patients under hypnosis recalled a past life in Atlantis when he did genetic modifications on different plants, increasing their addictive qualities as follows:

- *"I am a twenty-eight-year old male living in the city of Theron in the southern part of Atlantis. This is 47,520 BC. I am a research chemist. I am working with various plants and studying addictive qualities of the plants and a variety of drugs, such as cocaine, marijuana, heroin, PCP, barbiturates, etc. Another area I am researching is on different foods that have addictive qualities, such as chocolate, caffeine, etc. I am trying various combinations of sugar canes to make these foods more attractive.*

*"We are doing genetic modifications on different plants to achieve those results. I am successful with chocolate and with caffeine in coffee. We are working on a variety of beans and growing strains that are more and more addictive. We want to do it to control people by making them addicted to those substances and deadening their minds and keeping them slaves to the addiction. We keep them dull, dense, sleepier, and lazier. With stimulants like caffeine, we are able to make them work longer and produce more. Also, we entice them by using sweets and chocolates that are fancy and engaging, and basically keep people enslaved by making them addicted to sweets. I am also working on cocoa beans, and how they can be enriched and sweetened.*

*"We are doing genetic modifications in the plants and drugs, and refining the techniques that make more and more addictive products. We have horticultural labs that are part of this facility. We do genetic engineering and testing to see the impact on human subjects. My role was to design these particular crops by genetic engineering and then testing how effective they are. We perfected it and made it more and more addictive.*

*"I live in an apartment complex with my wife and children. My wife is also involved in similar research. She is a research chemist, primarily researching different compounds and how they can be added to the plants so that, when we work on genes, we can add those compounds. We both work in the same research facility.*

*"When I am forty-two, we are starting to get into other foods, such as doing genetic engineering of grains such as barley, corn, etc., and also on cows. We began to introduce mind-controlling chemicals into the foods, such as certain hormones and neurotransmitters. I worked more on the genetic side and tested a variety of compounds. Then we worked on how we can add genes to the DNA of plants, so that the plants themselves will end up producing these chemicals. We are doing this research to control the population so rulers do not have to worry about uprisings and revolts.*

*"In my fifties, I am invited to a conference as a professor emeritus, and am given an award for my work. They are also showing a movie about how effective the outcome of our research was. It is sickening me, realizing what I have done. They used these foods and drugs as a reward to pacify the people when they rebelled. These are very highly engineered foods and drugs that make them highly addicted, and they will do anything to get them. This made me very depressed and I began to drink alcohol.*

*"At the age of sixty-nine, I am sick with cirrhosis of the liver due to my drinking. My last thoughts are that I will not abuse people anymore. I must find a way to stop this. After my death, my spirit is still depressed and bent down. I am helped by two angels to heaven. After cleansing and healing, I go for life review.*

*"From heaven, I can see my life and implications of what I had done and have a deep sense of remorse for being involved in creating the technology that was used to control the society. I also see how I was controlled by the rulers through the device in my neck. I saw how I will have to suffer with similar symptoms I caused to others through my research. I am shown how the "Light devices" can be put into people to reduce the desire for addictive substances and overcome the problems.*

*"From heaven, I see that my problems of overeating, chemical dependence, addictions to sweets, and diabetes*

*came from that life. I also see that I had many karmic lives since that life, where I had to suffer with similar problems. There were three or four lives where I was a subject for drug, alcohol, and chocolate testing. I was also in a concentration camp in Germany, where they did medical experiments on me.*

*"When you, Dr. Modi, prayed to God and requested angels to realign, restore, and transform the DNA of all plants, animals, and humans who were genetically modified to the original pattern and put Light magnetic devices in the appetite center and in other addiction centers in the brain so people can control the addictions, I saw it happening."*

The advice given by heavenly beings is to get rid of these genetically modified plants and get the natural plants back. Then these drugs could be used for medicinal purposes and would not be as addictive as they are now. They would be spiritually uplifting and would physically help the body to accomplish both medical and spiritual purposes. Unfortunately, we have very few natural plants left on the Earth and are not even recognizable as such.

Obviously, this pattern is beginning to repeat now, in what the western world recognizes as Frankenfood; that is, genetically modified food. People are able to recognize instinctively that making those modifications leads to a lack of spirit in the food.

The Atlantean rulers wanted to control the genetic experiments, have political control, and have authority on the process of modifying genes and studying how the genes affected the body. They wanted further information on how genetic changes occurred and how they could control that process and what the results would be. There was a gradual control of rulers on the genetic experiments and they actually took over the whole process just before 50,000 BC.

The most bizarre genetic manipulations and transplant operations took place during the last few thousand years of

Atlantis. These were not medical experiments; they were for fun, as an amusement for the ruling classes. They transplanted the head of one animal onto another, putting animal heads on humans, human heads on animals. They were transplanting organs and limbs, not with any medical purpose in mind, not for any experimental knowledge, but just so they could laugh at what they did. The results were devastating. Some survived a few hours and provided amusement for the rulers.

Genetic experiments continued after 50,000 years, but gradually died down. Ruling class members also got sick, so they made sure that the medical group did not die out completely. The doctors may not bother to treat the peasants, but the rulers sure wanted to be treated themselves and prolong their lives.

### Neck Implants to Control People

When the tall, thin human-looking alien race four of group two arrived in Atlantis about 70,000 BC, they were really startled that the Atlanteans had figured out the crystal structure and the effects of different inclusions in a crystal, so that they could be used as massive solid state circuit control device. Each little crystal was individually grown to do a particular job, as a tiny little crystal had all the parts, all the electronics necessary, to be able to function as a fantastically huge computer. The parts in a crystal were the size of an atom. This really astonished the aliens, that the Atlanteans had this kind of sophistication in growing and understanding crystals. In the area of crystals, Atlanteans were more advanced than the aliens were. The aliens could also see that the rest of the Atlantean science and technology were far behind theirs.

According to my hypnotized patients, in Atlantis, the main crystal at the electrical power station transmitted the electromagnetic energy through a crystal in the homes. Then it would send it to the electronics sitting on an electronic box in the house that would broadcast signals throughout the house. Just like a radio station's broadcast, a certain frequency went to the master crystal for the radio station. The electrical vibrations were set up in it and the electromagnetic waves spread from it and contacted the other crystals in each of the homes that were attuned to it, which generated the electrical current in them, which was amplified and transmitted in each house.

In their studies of the human brain, Atlanteans found that certain parts of the brain worked at a certain frequency. By superimposing an electromagnetic field of the proper frequency focused on that area of the brain, they could change the messages that the brain was transmitting internally. By changing the message, they could control what the person thought and felt, such as controlling the person's moods, impressions, and what the person understood about themselves and their environment.

They implanted a tiny device in the back of the neck of babies shortly after they were born. It was a radio-amplifier transmitter that would receive a signal and then would broadcast that signal to the selected area of the brain. This tiny little device actually served as the control mechanism, modifying what went on in the human brain. Then the messages were sent to them all their lives, as the masters saw fit. People were controlled like robots and did not even know it. Their free will was snatched from them and it was one of the most hideous crimes committed against them.

In the crystal device, there was an electronic control circuit. The original implant was hard-wired; that is, wires were actually slid through the area of the brain that the rulers wanted to control. The rest of the wire would be insulated, but the part that would actually be exerting control by stimulating the brain would be bare so the current could flow. The original crystals were as big as a thumb, and made a big lump in the skin, plus all the wiring coupled with the damage it was causing. Toward the end, the control device that was inserted by a needle was much smaller and it literally inserted itself.

It was at this point that they made a refinement in the crystal-growing electronics. They got from the aliens the ability to build the circuit, so that the signal from that part of the circuit could be directed to the particular part of the brain, and the little crystal, which by this time had shrunk to an inch and a half to two inches long and the width of a pencil. It was simple to insert a needle at the back of the neck and to blow the crystal in with compressed air. The crystal, from there, was relocated in the parts of the brain where it was needed. It could get feedback and retransmit it back, so that there would be two-way communication between this brain and the main computer, and the computer could keep a very close watch on this brain.

My hypnotized patients say that as the crystal was being grown from scratch at a certain precise location, the electronic circuits were implanted in it. In this tiny little crystal, there were little components that could be scarcely detected. It had a fully functioning computer in it and it was constructed in three dimensions. So as you go from one end of the crystal to the other, and from side to side and front to back, there was a massive amount of computing power. They grew these crystals in mass scales and implanted them in the back of people's necks.

One section of the crystal would be a radio receiver that would receive signals over a broad spectrum, and separate the signals that would go to the part of the crystal it was designed to affect. So here was this huge radio signal coming into the crystal, broken into different components, each controlling something and each received by a particular part of the computer for processing.

So you have this brainwave frequency transmitter and a lot of little tunable antennas in it. Once the crystal was in place, these little tunable antennas located in the part of the brain, receiving signals and sending them out until the entire crystal was oriented. Each antenna and each little tiny dot on the surface or near the surface of the crystal was focused on a particular spot in the brain. Then the brainwave energy was broadcast from the main computer to the brain. The crystals had three main sections: first was the receiver, where the signal comes in from the outside, which was taken in by the receiver, broken up into its component parts and sent to all different parts of the crystal. Second was the computer, and third was the transmitter.

The rulers did not have implanted crystals. Their brain waves were picked up by the crystal outside. The programming messages they made were transmitted to the crystal outside on the device, but they did not wear it.

My hypnotized patients state that in a controlled population, people who were closer to the masters (the rulers), or those who had physical access to the masters, were very tightly controlled. One thing that they would not automatically think of was about a master who was trying to control another master. It did happen every now and then. It was a strange situation. All the masters recognized this possibility and each of them was fiercely independent, wanting to be their own slave owner. They got together to oppose and depose any master who took over another master. They self-regulated as a group so each could feel safe and protected.

### Psychology and Psychiatry

To influence and control people, what do you have to do? Do you do it by feeling their thoughts or obliterating their thoughts? Atlanteans were interested primarily in what change to make to control somebody. Atlantean rulers controlled people through electronics, psychology, genetics, and psychic ability. You have to have at least a tiny bit of psychic talent to be able to control anybody. They used people's psychology, meaning detecting somebody's wants and needs and used them as motivation.

### Propaganda Techniques

Atlanteans used propaganda techniques to control the flow of information. Controlling things by what was being broadcasted and influencing what was perceived gives you a real good handle on controlling information that you do not want people to know. They also used information to control people. Even the people in technology who were controlling the general masses were controlled by the higher-ups. In fact, the people in the technology class were the first ones the masters wanted to take over because they were their biggest fear. Technologists were the people who understood what was going on and why.

## Medical Experiments During the Dark Ages

Medical care went down during the Dark Ages because when you lose your trained medical doctors and you are not creating new ones, then medical care declines. Atlanteans had medical technology people who were not really doctors. The genetic modifications and medical transplants occurred just before the Dark Ages and were leading to the cultural downfall of Atlantis. They created mixed embryos and did the medical transplantation, where they transplanted animal heads on human bodies. They did genetic manipulation so that the next generation would have different characteristics. The first tentative step was taken about thirty thousand years before the collapse of Atlantean culture, about 50,000 BC. Before that, there were genetic experiments, but they were experiments. They were not programs set up on a regular basis.

## Experiments to Breed Superior Children

As described before, the rulers realized that the people in the ruling class were just as ordinary as the general masses except that they had more powers. So they began to open institutes to breed superior kids for the rulers. Following is an example where, in a past life, a patient was used for genetically breeding superior kids for the ruling class and how devastating it was for her, as she was treated like a farm animal.

- *"I am a ten-year-old girl living on a farm near the city of Z'Noir in central Atlantis, north of the mountains. My name is Lani and this is 64,200 BC. I have an older brother who is fourteen and a younger brother who is four. A man comes on a horse and tells my father that the ruler of the city is inviting some of the farm youngsters between eight and twelve years of age to come to the city to live and go to school for a period of time. He tells my parents that I was selected by the ruler for this purpose because I am at the right age. My parents decide to send me. My father takes me to the dormitory in the city.*

    *"I live with about twenty other girls in the dormitory. We learn about physical fitness, racing, lifting, music, painting, drawing, reading, writing, arithmetic, making pottery and decorating it. I am slim but strong, about average height, and have a light complexion. I am considered beautiful. I have been selected for a special program. I am told that it is on the basis of physical accomplishment and I am one of the best in the arts and in reading and writing, too. They talk to my parents and my parents give their permission. They also told my parents that I would not be able to come home for several years.*

    *"At the age of eleven, I am taken, along with a few other girls and boys, from this dormitory to another dormitory on the other side of the city. There, I go through all types of medical tests and exams. They stick me with needles and take bits and pieces of tissue from here and there. They do not tell me much about what they are doing. I am told that I am ideal for the program they have. I am the right size, height, and weight. I am one of the best and brightest and I do well in everything. They want to take little pieces from my mouth and nose and examine them.*

    *"One day, they tell me that I am qualified for a very special program. They take me to another place and I have a room in a big building. I am still eleven. At this place, they begin to give me shots but do not tell me why, and I am feeling scared and isolated. They lock my room*

*and there are bars on the windows and I am not allowed to get out. They continue to give me injections regularly and continue to scrape my cheeks and nose for tests from time to time. I don't like it here and I want to go home but I cannot.*

*"My body begins to change and grow rapidly. They keep on measuring and testing me. They seem to be interested in how much I am growing. Every day seems to be the same. The only schoolwork is from the books I was allowed to bring. There is nothing else to do. I cannot go out of the room, and do not get to see anybody except those people who give me shots and do the tests on me.*

*"Now I am twelve years old and I am taken to another place. This place is not as nice and not as comfortable. At times they unlock the doors and let everybody out, where we walk around and meet the other people who are there. Then when the bell rings, we go back to our own rooms and they lock the doors. I find out that they did the same things to everybody who is here that they did to me and that they were all the best in their schools.*

*"They continue to give me shots and I am growing and maturing prematurely and my body is almost adult size. I begin to have menstrual periods. At the age of thirteen, they tell me that it is time to have a child. I am just shocked. I know I am not married; how can I have a child? I am taken to another place in the same area and put in a room with a boy. Apparently we are genetically matched up. They tell me that both of us are very bright and good-looking. He also was given shots to grow faster. After being together for a while, I get pregnant, and when the baby is born, they take him away immediately to raise somewhere else. They tell us to make another baby. I feel angry, resentful, and unhappy. I feel cheated and feel a terrible loss.*

*"My partner and I figured out that they are trying to breed babies who will grow fast and be good-looking and intelligent. I have three children with the first boy. Then*

*I am put with another boy who is also good-looking and intelligent. I have a total of eight children with three different boys, almost one child every year, and all the babies were taken away right after their birth. I am very upset, resentful, unhappy, and feeling worn out.*

*"At the age of twenty-eight, I am depressed, upset, and feeling trapped. Life seems pointless and I want to get away. I want to go home and live like a normal person. They do not let anybody go home and talk about what happens here, because that will keep people from sending their children here and that will be negative publicity for them. I go to the roof of the building to escape, but I slip and fall and am hurt badly. They find me, take me inside, and poison me. I die promising myself that I will never be beautiful or intelligent again. I do not want to be that outstanding again.*

*"After my death, I am angry and I try influencing and attacking people. I find the director of the program and try to hit him but I cannot, so I enter his body. I try to influence him by demanding, insisting, talking to him as he sleeps, intruding in his dreams, and asking him to stop it because it is wrong. When I find out that his orders come from the rulers of many cities funneling money into this program, I want to go into the main ruler and influence him, but I feel stuck in this director's body and cannot come out. I try to relax, and then become aware that there are other spirits and that the Light exists. By concentrating on the spiritual world instead of upon this man and his physical world, I come out of his body. I feel the draw of the Light and do not feel so keen to go into the ruler. My mother shows up in the Light and takes me to heaven.*

*"I talk to a Light being about what happened to me, how I was imprisoned and how they took away my babies. When I am done talking, I feel better. Then I go for cleansing and then for my life review with a Light being, the god Talabian, the sun god, in whom I believed in Atlantis. As I review my life, I get this bad feeling in my stomach that I also felt*

*when they took me away from my parents. The Light being is saying that I need to pay attention to those feelings in my stomach as a warning sign. I lost everything: my parents, my children, my freedom, my dignity, and my life in the end. I need to learn the lesson of acceptance, that if you are powerless to change something then you should just accept it. Also to keep it from happening again.*

*"From heaven, I see many problems that came from that life to this life, such as weight problems, memory problems due to damage to my brain, high blood pressure, metabolism problems, stomach discomfort, throat irritation, and miscarriages due to damage to my uterus. I can see that they were injecting growth hormones in me to step up my growth and development. Part of their experiment was to see how much mass I could put on, as if they were raising people like farm cows.*

*"From heaven, I can see that this was a breeding program and they were trying to modify people so they can grow them faster, bigger, and brighter. Although these experiments were just beginning in Atlantis, it spread faster, and every seven or eight cities had a common research center and each of them was picking out the very best of the best and sending them to the research institute. This was going on for several hundred years before my life.*

*"I see that the ruling class was getting genetically superior children for themselves, which was one of the primary functions of the program. These genetically bred superior kids were taken into noble families to be married off to the other ruling families, thus improving the genes of the ruling class. Their kids would be half the genes, or actually two-thirds. They try not to take in too many of these kids at a time. As the rulers see it, it is farming the people, taking the very best of the crop and using them for a seed, as if the people belong to them."*

Another patient recalled many past lives when he was a physician doing different types of medical experiments in Atlantis:

- *"First life: I am a thirty-four-year-old male living in Ed-nos City in the north central part of Atlantis. This is about 44,260 BC. I am married and have three children. I am a surgeon working in an experimental building. I do a great deal of organ transplants to find if animal or other organs can be transplanted in a human whose organs are not functioning. We do experiments on normal humans from the working class. Some survive for a few hours, to a few days, to a few months. I have worked on several hundred people in my lifetime. I am doing kidney, stomach, lung, and liver transplant experiments. I also did a few brain parts and thyroid experiments.*

    *"I die of pneumonia at the age of sixty. When I review my life from heaven, I can see that the spirits of people on whom I did different experiments came into me after the death of their physical bodies because they were angry and revengeful, and all the symptoms they had become mine. I see many of my problems in the current life are coming from that life, such as joint problems, GI tract problems, and memory problems.*

    *"From heaven, I can see that at this time Atlantis and its people were under a strong demonic influence. We did not respect human life, and abused people in the name of research. Much of our emotional, mental, physical, and spiritual problems are coming from the negative lives in Atlantis.*

    *"From heaven, I can see that I had four more lifetimes when I was a physician and did different types of experiments on normal healthy humans.*

    *"Second life: I am a thirty-seven-year-old male living in a city called Zerbua in the south central part of Atlantis. I was trying to create stronger and more vibrant human beings by experimenting with different racial groups and mixing their genes. I crossbred different ethnic groups to create a stronger, brighter, bigger, healthier, more vibrant human being. From heaven, I see that my colleagues and I created human beings with different defects, such as humans with disfigured faces, blind, shorter arms, legs*

with one shorter than the other, feet with eight toes, etc., because of the genetic modifications. I also incorporated animal DNA into human embryos. The crossbreeding between humans and animals created humans with disfigured bodies, such as ape-like arms and legs with basically human-looking faces; facial features like an ape; a face that was normal but the body and limbs were shaped like a baboon; in some cases, there was a very short tail. Some of them died early, some lived through childhood, and others lived through adulthood.

"Third life: I was a thirty-nine-year-old female living in a city called Erb in south central Atlantis in 38,200 BC. I was doing experiments on heart transplants. I was part of a team in a lab constructing artificial hearts and testing them on healthy experimental people from the working class and also on criminals. We also tried to transplant ape hearts in humans. Most of these transplant subjects died in a few hours, to a few days or months. I died of heart failure when I was sixty-nine years old. From heaven, I see that many problems of my current life are coming from that life, such as high blood pressure, dizziness, nausea, lung problems, etc.

"Fourth life: I was a thirty-year-old male doctor living in a city in the north central part of Atlantis in 36,883 BC. I was assigned to work in an experimental center. I specialized in joints and did experiments on human joints to find ways to improve their function. I did a series of experiments on different joints. I interchanged human joints with animal joints. I tried various experimental treatments with heat and cold on human subjects. I died in an accident in a subway where a car derailed and we were violently thrown around. My neck was broken. I see many of my problems came from that life to the current life, such as arthritis in different joints, which is karmic, headaches and neck pain, and generalized aches and pains.

"Fifth life: I was a medical doctor. I did consulting work, where I advised doctors who were doing medical *experiments with surgical techniques. I also did research on formulating medicine that can be used to help patients who had surgery, because I had a strong chemistry background. Some of the experimental drugs formulated were tried on healthy experimental patients, and caused severe, long lasting problems. Some lost their minds, some went blind or deaf or lost hair, and some went into convulsions or comas and died, but these medicines also helped relieve pain and healed some people.*

*"I died of a heart attack at the age of seventy-five. From heaven, I see that many of my current life problems came from that life, such as joint problems and aches and pains."*

Another person recalled the following past life in Atlantis as a physician where he was doing senseless genetic modifications and transplant surgeries.

• *"My name is Eito Garzinni. I am twenty-eight years old and I live in the city of Beard in Atlantis in about 49,009 BC. The city is about one hundred miles from the coast on the south eastern side of the continent. I have light brown skin and hair. I live with my wife, two boys, and two girls. I was selected to become a physician because of my strengths in math, science, and general intelligence. It was my choice to become a doctor, but I was required to get approval from the rulers of the country.*

*"Houses and buildings are constructed of blocks of stone. Buildings are single and multistoried. They are attractive and well appointed. Roads are hard surfaced. I see crystal devices on all the buildings. These devices work like antennae. I live in a house. Inside the house, there is a television built into the wall. I am able to view movies, comedy, drama, action, etc. on the TV. Sometimes I view newscasts, which are controlled by the nobility. From time to time, the rulers come out to broadcast their messages to the people. There is a crystal in the living*

*room. It is used to receive and transmit messages to the neck implant.*

*"There are phones in my house. They are cordless. They work from crystals that transmit and receive. The house is luxurious. It is spacious, with four bedrooms, a nice balcony, and an area that is designed for servants' quarters. There are fine carpets on the floors and beautiful paintings and wall hangings on the walls. I have a radio and a computer that features many advanced science and math programs. The kitchen has a stove and refrigerator. All the appliances are powered by the sun through crystals. Each house has its own generator.*

*"I am paid well by the nobility. The payment is received on the first of each month. I pay my servants according to scale. They are people from the working class. They live several miles from our section of the city. They are one of four classes of people in Atlantis. The other three classes are: the nobility, the rulers; the wealthy class, high level professionals; and the street people, who are poor and homeless people from the working class. All classes live in separate sections of the city. The servants receive only a small fraction of what I am paid. They live in small, run-down houses. They own a few basic appliances but they are without TVs and computers.*

*"I work in a medical research complex with many other doctors. At the complex, we work on genetics and experimental surgery in an attempt to better the quality of life and to find ways to extend life. I have a specialty in genetic engineering. I work in a research laboratory and experiment on people from the county's working class population. Generally, I work with DNA and cell transplanting. I help to create hundreds of genetic babies.*

*"I am also experimenting in growing fuller heads of hair, finding ways to make healthier teeth and gums, studying how to improve or maintain normal vision for longer periods of time, discovering ways to correct hearing loss*

*and improve hearing, and analyzing blood and compar-*
*ing one blood type to another blood type.*

*"But my primary focus for eleven years has been work-*
*ing to make genetic babies. I work with human embryos.*
*I transplant human cells, animal cells, or combinations*
*of human and animal cells in them. A great percentage of*
*these experiments are unsuccessful. The three to five per-*
*cent of babies that survive are freakish looking humans.*

*"Some of them have extra fingers, seven to nine, or*
*a leg or an arm shorter than the other. Some have only*
*one eye. Many are visually and hearing impaired. Several*
*are mentally retarded. But the products of crossbreeding,*
*mixing animal and human cells, are extremely grotesque.*
*These babies grow up with ape-like heads and human*
*bodies, or with ape-like physiques and bizarre looking*
*human heads. Some babies take on the facial features of a*
*dog, a wolf, a goat, or even a bird. Some have birdlike feet*
*and hands. Some have three legs or three arms, and some*
*have no legs or arms.*

*"When I am thirty-nine, there is a shortage of surgeons*
*and an abundance of genetic engineering specialists. As*
*a result, I am moved out of genetics and into surgery. I*
*worked on attaching human and animal extremities to*
*humans. I worked on transplanting human and animal*
*organs, kidneys, lungs, colons, and livers, into humans.*
*I believe in what I am doing because I feel my contribu-*
*tions will advance our nation. And like most of the other*
*surgeons, I am also doing my share of installing implants*
*in people's necks.*

*"These implants in the neck are used as tracking de-*
*vices and mind control devices. By this time, almost ev-*
*eryone except the nobility has an implant. This tiny little*
*rectangular device looks like metal or hard plastic on the*
*outside. On the inside, it contains a small piece of cre-*
*ated crystal, which has a receiver and a transmitter. The*
*authorities send out messages from their computer cen-*
*ters to the receivers in the implants. Once received, the*

*message is transmitted to the individual's brain. The individual believes the messages he or she is receiving are his own thoughts. The messages are designed to strengthen the nobility's position while their controlled subjects do the dirty work.*

*"I become ill when I am forty-five. I have dizzy spells, stiffness in my arms and legs, and get tired very easily. At forty-seven, I start to have regular fainting spells. I collapsed in the lab and am ordered to have a full medical evaluation. My knuckles are enlarged and I have lung and heart problems. In addition, I have a little swelling in my brain. I have begun to take on the symptoms of all those I abused. I am admitted to the hospital with other regular sick people from my class. The nobility had their own hospitals and the working class had their own limited medical care facilities. I remain in the hospital for ten days and then I died in my sleep.*

*"My spirit leaves my body. I am in the dark and cannot find the Light. As a result, my spirit stayed on Earth for one hundred years because it was trapped inside a dark demon. During this time, I possessed nine people. I affected them by passing on the symptoms of those I had abused and who were trapped inside of me.*

*"I make the transition to the Light (heaven) from the last person I possessed. She is a nurse in my research lab. She always had doubts about the work we were doing because she had some psychic powers. She prayed for guidance on a regular basis, and her prayers bring the Light to my dark shell. I find the Light and ascend into heaven. When I review my life from heaven, I see how wrong it was to have the callus disregard for human life. I see how the darkness and negativity influenced the people of Atlantis.*

*"From heaven, I discovered that I had no spirituality. I did not have One God to which I could connect. I discovered that I created much negative karma in that life due to my negative actions. I recognized four people in that life who are in this life. Two were working class people*

*who I refused to treat when they were sick. In this life, they are two childhood friends who did not care for me. I amputated the fingers and toes of a woman in that life and replaced them with an ape's fingers and toes. I also attempted to substitute an animal's kidney in this woman. In this life, this woman is my sister-in-law who does not like me. The other person in that life was a female experimental patient. I transplanted animal DNA into her embryo. She miscarried and bled to death. In this life, the woman is my wife.*

*"From the Light (heaven), I see three other negative lives in which I was a physician in Atlantis doing different experiments."*

Some of my patients recalled the following past lives in Atlantis, when doctors did different hideous medical experiments on them, including transplants.

• *"I'm a seven-year-old male living in Atlantis. It is about 50,000 BC. I live with my mother and father and two older sisters in a small three-bedroom house. My father is a policeman and my mother takes care of us and the house. I have brown skin and hair. I am taken to a large multistoried medical clinic. This impressive structure is made of large stone blocks. Inside, people are hustling to complete their tasks. My parents are directed by a receptionist to take me down a hall and into a little examining room. A nurse comes in and takes my history from my parents. Then I am taken to a larger examining room. Attendants grab me and put me on a table and tie my hands and feet.*

*"I'm frightened! My sisters had previously told me that I might get hurt by the doctors. An attendant comes forward and sprays something on my neck to numb the area. Another liquid is applied to sterilize the area. A doctor and two others enter the room. The doctor makes a vertical cut of less than an inch at the base of my neck on the right side just above my shoulder blade. Then the doctor*

*and two assistants insert a small rectangular device in my neck. It looks something like a small domino, without the white dots. It looks like metal or hard plastic and it is almost black. They finish and one of the assistants sews up my neck and sprays the area to disinfect it. I am in a state of panic and crying.*

*"At age ten, my parents are notified and I am taken back to the clinic. Once there, I'm given a complete medical exam and sent home. I am brought back to the clinic one week later. Once again I'm strapped to a table and a liquid concoction, designed to make me grow faster, is pumped into my veins. I am in panic and very emotional. I feel a burning in my chest. After this procedure, I'm sent home. In about twelve hours, I have a severe allergic reaction to the liquid. There are red splotches on my face, chest, and neck. My face swells; my eyes bulge. I'm lightheaded and nauseous. My parents take me back to the clinic. The doctor gives me a pill and a shot in my arm muscle. In a few hours, all my symptoms are gone.*

*"A few months pass. I'm still ten, and I'm ordered back to the clinic. I'm anxious and upset. Once again I'm strapped to a table. A technician enters and applies a hot iron to my right arm just below the shoulder. Certain personnel at the clinic are studying burn therapy and I'm the experimental subject. I'm very upset and in a great deal of pain. This procedure continues for a few months, getting burned and being treated with different medications. I've discovered there are several groups of children on the burn therapy experiments, the purpose being to find the best way to treat people who have experienced burns.*

*"At sixteen, I have four back teeth removed. The purpose of this experiment is twofold: one, the doctors want to see if there is any way to grow teeth after the second teeth are removed, and two, the doctors are experimenting with the use of false teeth. My parents feel for me. When they were young, both had neck implants and both had some burn experiments on their arms and legs.*

"*In the meantime, my gums are not healing properly. The doctors can do no more to stop the infection in my gums. I'm sent home with a high fever. I'm fading away and dying. My last thoughts are that I don't like doctors and clinic people because they hurt me. I'm afraid of them. After the death of my body, I stay around for a couple of months to watch my family. I am angry with the doctors but I do not enter anyone.*

"*There are some psychic people in our village who pray for those of us who have been victims of experiments. As a result, their prayers send Light to me and I find the Light and ascend to heaven. After cleansing and resting, I review my life with four heavenly beings. From heaven, I see they took a vein from my leg and tried substituting an animal vein in its place. I see that when my father was younger, he had both arms broken and reset in a study that dealt with bones growing back together. He also had the small toe on his left foot amputated so that an animal toe could be attached. This experiment failed and he was without a small toe. My mother was used in experimental studies that involved tattoos. At the time, they were experimenting with ways to identify and classify people. She had a tattoo on her buttock. She was also used in burn therapy experiments. She had burn marks on both her arms.*

"*My oldest sister had an eardrum removed and another eardrum inserted. The experiment failed and she was deaf in one ear. My other sister had several amputations. She had two fingers removed. One finger was replaced with a human finger and the other with an animal finger. She had a kneecap removed and another human kneecap was inserted. Her appendix was removed as a test case to see if people could function without an appendix.*

"*There were four classes of people in Atlantis: the working class, the wealthy class (upper to middle class), the nobility (rulers and leaders), and the fourth class was made up of street people from the working class who were victims of medical experiments. They were poor and homeless people without means. Many were psychologically damaged as a result of the medical experiments.*

*"Schools were available in Atlantis at this time. Working class children attended school into their early teens. They received a basic education in reading, writing, arithmetic, and language. Near the end of their schooling, they would receive skill enhancement training. For example, certain youths would take courses in mechanics while others would take courses in carpentry. Working class children were not permitted any advanced education at this time, while wealthy class children became high-level professionals. Ruling class children could attend the university but most stay with their own class and receive private tutoring.*

*"The government was a central one, made up of the ruling class. Under the central government, officials were in charge of regions, cities etc. These officials were also members of the ruling class. People must be born into a ruling class family to be nobility. The ruling class, the wealthy class, and the working class all lived in separate sections of the city.*

*"From heaven, I see that the purpose of the implant in the neck was for identification and tracking of people. People were without much emotion. They accepted the society without questioning it. Thoughts of rebellion did not occur. People, in many ways, lived like they were in a concentration camp.*

*"I discovered two people who were in that life who are also in my present life. They were doctors in Atlantis and they abused me. They are doctors in my present life and they help me.*

*"The problems that came from that life to the current life are: fear, anxiety, and panic in the doctor's office, and fear, contempt, and anger toward authority. From heaven, I see that I lived three more lives in Atlantis which were responsible for my fear of doctors as follows:*

"Second life: I am a sixteen-year-old female. The doctors performed a sex change operation on me. They removed parts of my female organ and attached parts of the male organ. I died five days after the operation due to infection and loss of blood."

"Third life: In another life, I was a fifteen-year-old female who lived with my parents. In that life, I had several organs (kidney, stomach, liver) removed and replaced with animal organs. I died of infection."

"Fourth life: In yet another life, I was a one-year-old female taken from my family for the purpose of psychological experiments. I, along with many other children, was subjected to many psychological experiments. At certain intervals, from ages one to five, I was made to sleep on the floor of a cold steel cage. And at times I was tied down and water was allowed to drip on my forehead. These were experiments in aggressive behavior."

"From ages five to eleven, I was put on a series of different diets so that the authorities could find an "ideal" diet from both a psychological and physical perspective. From ages twelve to seventeen, I underwent several harsh experiments so that the doctors could study the breaking point of individuals. They put a device on my head that was used to measure brain waves and put me in a cage with wild animals, tigers and lions. While there was an invisible shield that protected me, I was unaware of it at the time of the experiment. They also tied me to the floor and let a razor-sharp pendulum come closer and closer to my neck and chest. Sometimes they would tie me to a wall and had an expert knife thrower throw knives at me. They brushed my skin and touched my hair as they flew by me. During these three experiments, I experienced high anxiety and full-blown panic.

"At age seventeen, they withheld food at intervals and then water at intervals. It was again an experiment on the breaking points of individuals. During this same year, *they put me out in the hot sunshine for hours to do physical labor. Water and breaks were withheld. At another time, they put me in a freezer for a long time without any clothing to test my psychological endurance. Once they put me and two others in a cage with only limited food and water to see how we would act and react when the food and water were served.*

*"They also applied elastic devices to my wrists, fingers, and ankles to test circulation and psychological reaction. Sometimes they made me stand on my tiptoes for hours. They attached a hot electrical wire to the floor where my heels would normally be in a regular standing position. When I came off my tiptoes, I would get an electric shock. At different times, I was hanged from the wrists, the ankles, and waist for many hours at a time. Frequently I was made to stand in attention position for several hours in the hot sun while bugs crawled over my body. Sometimes they forced me to stand on one leg for several hours and then on the other leg for several hours. At twenty-three, I was very depressed and psychologically damaged. One morning they called for me to get out of bed. I refused! I was on the top of a double bunk. They overturned the bunk. I fell, striking my head on the hard floor. I had a concussion and lapsed into a coma and died within twelve hours."*

- *"I am an unmarried twenty-two-year-old male, a street cleaner living alone in a small two-room apartment in Atlantis. I have a father and mother, two brothers, and one sister who live in another part of town. One day, the authorities broke into my place, tied me up, and took me to a medical experiment complex. I was placed in a cell with twenty-five to thirty other people. (I later discovered there were hundreds of people in this complex). We were there against our will, as guinea pigs for a variety of medical experiments. In the cell, I saw people who had had arms, legs, fingers, toes, hands, and ears removed. This was a very frightening experience.*

"Soon, I was taken to an operating room by a woman and two men. They informed me that I would be experimented on, but did not reveal the specifics. The operating room looked impressive, with many sophisticated looking machines, but I did not know their purpose. I saw doctors with white coats and white caps. They strapped me to an operating table, securing my hands and feet. An attendant gave me something to make me drowsy. I am afraid and want to get away but I cannot.

"After a time, I wake up in a recovery room. There are many others here and we are attended to by nurses. I discover that I have no left arm, no kneecaps, and was cut open around the stomach. I'm given some pain pills. I am depressed and afraid of what will happen to me next. I am anxious and afraid of dying.

"In a couple of weeks, I am taken for more experiments. I'm afraid! I think they are going to put other people's parts or animal parts on or in my body. I know that they have put animal organs in other people. They continued these experiments to try to find ways to extend lives. After my second operation, I wake up and find another person's left arm attached to me. Also, I have another person's kneecaps. Later I discover they have also exchanged one of my kidneys. I am becoming very ill because my body is rejecting the transplants. After a time, all my medicines stop working and I'm taken from the recovery room to a room where people are dying.

"Here, people are monitored and observed so the doctors can study the process of death. I see many people here. Some have had sex change operations; some have undergone animal organ transplants, while others have had animal limbs attached to them. People have had eyes, ears, and parts of brains and glands removed so that doctors can study them to see how this might affect aging.

"Those who are no longer useful are left to die without pain pills, food, or water. Many are gagged to reduce the groans and screams. A time comes when I no longer get *food and water. I'm in and out of consciousness as I feel myself fading away. I am angry hurt, and upset about the way I was treated. I want revenge. I begin to fade and my spirit leaves my body. I die from infection and loss of blood. I stay around to watch my physical body and other bodies being burned. I watch the experiments. There are many experiments all over Atlantis but I remain where my physical body was.*

*"I begin to enter doctors, nurses, and attendants, causing them to have the problems they gave to me. I remain on earth for about two hundred years.*

*"I'm inside a doctor, with thirty-eight others. The doctor is extremely ill. He is dying. I am able to go to heaven as a result of prayers from the doctor's family. As some Light flows into the doctor, my dark barrier is pierced and I realize that I'm a Light being. As I am being transformed, I see the Light and I see angels calling me to it. I take their hands and ascend into heaven. I am cleansed in a bath where all darkness is washed away and converted into Light. After resting, I sit with five spirit guides and review my life. I review the entire life but focus mainly on the important events.*

*"From heaven, I see that I was from the working class, where I grew up in a small cottage. The nobility approved of the medical experiments. Implants were inserted in the back of the neck in all classes, except for the nobility, at an early age. These implants served as identification devices.*

*"The problems that came from that life to the current life were, irrational fear of medical doctors, anxiety with resulting high blood pressure, and being critical and judgmental toward authority."*

## Heinous Crimes in Atlantis During the Dark Ages

My hypnotized patients claim that Atlanteans, until about 55,000 BC, lived in family units, generally a father, mother, and children, and had contact with their extended families. They dealt with their employers on a fairly even level, and people were prosperous and happy. As the balance of power shifted, the rich and powerful used their money to take over society. They used technological advances to control the population until it reached the point where little crystal devices were installed in the back of the neck in every newborn, to better control them. The rulers told the people that it was good for their health. Before that, there was gradual control, and by about 50,000 BC, there was the end of the old Atlantean culture and the beginning of the Dark Ages.

During the Dark Ages, there were shifts going on. More people were needed in the technology section, fewer people in agriculture, and fewer people in transportation. They had new energy sources. They had better power supplies for moving water freight. This was an increase in the living standard. Things were better than they used to be. Only it was not really better, because yesterday they were free and today they were not. In the earlier time of the controlling period, people were still fairly independent, and economics and political factors were being brought to bear on the people to insure their vote for the favorite candidate. This all changed later on.

Atlantean rulers during the Dark Ages also used economics as a control mechanism, making it almost impossible to survive in a culture without using money. They regulated the amount of money people could get. Generally, by regulating wage rates, sometimes by law and also by incentives, such as if you did this you would live a better life, but it was always an empty promise and things did not get better. Later, people were not paid for their work. They were just given the basic needs of shelter, food, and clothing. Essentially, what the ruling class did was reduce the working class to this level. So whatever profit was there, the masters got to keep it for themselves.

Heavenly beings, through my hypnotized patients, said that the Atlantean rulers committed several hideous crimes.

The first and foremost heinous crime was that the rulers interfered with the lives of the human beings and did not allow them to live out their own lives and achieve their destinies, which they had planned in heaven before being born. It is equivalent to murder when you force someone out of his or her life plan. It was the ultimate interference with a life plan and destroyed God's plan. The second disgraceful crime was interfering with the free will of another person. The third major reprehensible crime was modifying or changing how human beings acted in the life plan by interfering with the family units, by separating males from females and putting them in separate dorms and removing the concept of marriage, putting man and woman together to breed children, separating babies from the parents, and putting neck implants to control people's thoughts and brains. These were hideous crimes against the fundamental nature of the universe. Strictly speaking, these were the most heinous crimes ever committed in the universe.

### Interfering with the Family Unit

One of the heinous crimes was that they took away the concept of marriage. Men and women became breeding pairs. The rulers selected which man and which woman would become a pair and they were simply put together, literally without consent, without any involvement on their part. The ruling groups hoped to get certain desirable characteristics in the children born to these couples. When the rulers had as many children from a couple as they wanted, the couple was simply sent back to their respective dormitories, where they lived in a group with other people of the same sex. There was no pretense of a family structure or of togetherness.

The next heinous crime was that they took children away from the parents. Parents would raise the child till six months or one year of age, then the child would be removed and raised in a childcare facility, where they were often abused physically, mentally, and sexually. Children were placed in a facility that was their home, their school, and their training ground. The children were trained and conditioned for certain roles in adult life, such as menial labor, repetitive tasks, and whatever the rulers had in mind for this particular child. There was no free will on the part of the child and no choice was involved. There was very little creative education or training. They were educated in reading and writing, without any higher education. It got to the point that there was no information worth passing on, at least as far as the ruling class saw it. So education became much less important. Only a few of the children had higher education. Usually their parents were highly educated as doctors, scientists, and other professions, but their children did not know it.

### Putting Neck Implants in People

In their studies of the human brain, Atlanteans found that certain parts of the brain worked at a certain frequency. By superimposing an electromagnetic field of the proper frequency focused on that area of the brain, they could change the messages that the brain was transmitting internally. By changing the message, they could control people's thoughts and feelings, such as controlling the people's moods, impressions, and what they understood about themselves and their environment.

They implanted a tiny crystal device in the back of the neck of the babies shortly after they were born. It was a radio-amplifier transmitter and it would receive a signal and would broadcast that signal to the selected area of the brain. This tiny little device actually served as the control mechanism, modifying what went on in the human brain. Then messages were sent to them, all their lives, as the masters saw fit. People were controlled like robots and did not even know it. Their free will was snatched from them, and it was one of the most hideous crimes committed against them.

The masters usually chose the group of messages that would be transmitted to the people. Very seldom, an individual message was transmitted. Usually, these were all-pervasive messages that went to everyone who was controlled by that transmitter, unless it was necessary to single out a particular individual.

Each individual had a particular frequency assigned, and of course there would be two or three people in the country that had the same frequency, but they were not assigned the same transmitter. So they could send the message to one person, and anybody with the same frequency was too far away to pick up the message. The radio transmitters were crystal-based and the power and the signals were transmitted through the crystals.

Through these disgusting control devices, people lost their free will. They were incapable of exercising their free will because this control was forced on their psyche. They became robotic slaves. Their mind and body were totally controlled, but not the soul. If the mind was totally controlled, who would the soul tell? The soul may have the knowledge, but if it could not transmit it, then the knowledge did the soul no good. The soul is an independent being. It is not a part of the body. It and the body are separate entities. The soul can independently pray to God for help and some of the souls did pray to God, and as a result, usually the person's problems got better.

The control device was generally implanted in the back of the base of the neck any time from birth to six months of age, and the ordinary growth and development of the child was interfered with and thwarted. The experiences were scientifically planned to get what the masters wanted or needed for a particular child. If the child was to be trained as a technologist, then the experiences deferred from a child who was to be trained for a manual worker. In the childcare centers, the children were trained and conditioned rather than educated. They were conditioned to work at menial jobs.

### *Separating Males From Females – The Dorm System*

Another reprehensible crime was that the sexes were separated and were not permitted to grow up in normal interaction, according to my hypnotized patients. Men and women were put in different dormitories and then separated by subcategories. They put mechanical workers in one dormitory, electrical workers in another, psychics in another, artists in another dormitory, and on and on. Males and females did not know much about the other sex. They did not associate with each other at all. During adolescence, with emerging sexuality, the ruling class came up with a method of releasing sexual tension to keep a lid on the dormitories and prevent trouble. Their solution was to encourage homosexuality, and they grew up thinking that homosexuality was normal and that was how they were supposed to act.

In male dormitories, there were male caretakers, and vice-versa, except for male guards and other male workers having access to female dormitories, who sexually abused them. The program was established initially by psychologists and behavioral experts, according to what the rulers wanted. The children were put through programs for a particular age. If children showed exceptional maturity, they would be slowly pushed forward, and those who were immature were put a year behind.

The dormitories were totally enclosed and had fences across the yard. Kids did not go out to school or work. Everything that went on happened in that building with the enclosed area. They were totally isolated from the outside world.

People went through basic patterns, depending upon what was intended for their lives. They would go through certain conditioning experiences; that is, strength building or fine muscle coordination for certain types of work. There were some general patterns for everybody, and a specific pattern for each child. They were often trained for labor and menial work. Some were trained to repair machinery because they had to keep the machine running, but they were not trained to build new machinery. By age fifteen, boys and girls were ready to go to work and were moved to the adult dormitories.

## Choosing Male and Female as a Mating Pair

My hypnotized patents state that when a man and a woman were chosen to have children they were sent to the couple dormitories. Males and females had very little contact with each other until they were put together to produce children. The males and females literally had to be taught proper sexual behavior when they were put together as a mating pair. Their early experiences frequently made the union unsatisfactory because they were used to homosexual activities. Some even felt that the forced re-separation after the children were born was a beneficial thing. They did not have to stay with that man or with that woman anymore and could go back to their former way of life, thinking it was the normal way to live.

They continued with the work they were doing before and had to travel to the work. The couples generally ate in a cafeteria in their dormitories. A typical life for a couple consisted of getting up in the morning, getting ready, stopping at a feeding center, eating breakfast, and going to work, eating at the feeding center at work, finishing work, coming home, stopping at the feeding center on the way, and then the rest of the night at home. There were very few shared activities.

They had time-wasting entertainment, such as television of the Atlantean version, and radio. Their understanding of electromagnetics was very, very advanced. Any society that had learned to transmit electrical energy through the air, through space from one crystal to another, had all the technical understanding of establishing television and radio. Atlanteans were beyond that because they could actually communicate directly into the brain, operating through the crystals. Television was a very popular entertainment. In order to keep people quiet, you have to have something to keep people busy. They had radios, telephones, and what you could call an ultrasound, which could be directed and used in different ways as a scientific tool and as entertainment.

Following are some past lives recalled by my hypnotized patients during the Dark Ages in Atlantis:

- *"As I review my life from heaven, I can see that my parents were put together and were told to have children. As soon as I was born, they put a device in the back of my neck through a needle. They did not worry about putting it in the exact place because they did not need to. It sought out the part where it needed to go and adjusted itself. The antenna, the receiver, received signals no matter where the device was. The device was put in the back of the neck and the transmitter end actually searched though the brain and picked out the right spots.*

  *"I was taken from my parents when I was nine months old. My mother was kind of strange and tentative, as if she did not want to bond with me. Then I was taken by people who raised the children in a dormitory. I see my mother crying a lot. There were about thirty children in one room and one caretaker. They fed us well so we could grow up strong to do the work. They also gave us clothes to wear. If we cried, they would hit us. Until three years of age, we just lay around a lot and did not do much.*

  *"At the age of four, they moved us to a different dormitory, and then to another at the age of seven, and then every two years, they moved us to a different dormitory. People who took care of us just gave us food and did not pay any attention as to what happened to us. They did not care if we ate the food or not. From heaven, I see that they gave "shut up" shots to all the kids, especially to those who cried. They also used a place called a "squeezer" in the second dormitory when we were four. It had a front and a back wall and it squeezed us mechanically.*

"*They would leave us in there for hours like that and it was very painful. It made us scream. We felt helpless. We could not breathe and could not move. We felt desperate to move. The squeezer spaces were open on the top and walls had holes and the skin and flesh popped through the holes, which was even more painful. The older we got, the longer they kept us in there, but usually not for more than a day.*

"*They would hit us with sticks and twist our penis and balls, and it really hurt. Sometimes they would shock us with electricity. They would put connections between an arm and a leg and shock us. The worst was when they connected a nipple to the penis and then shocked us. That was really painful. The caretakers also abused us sexually whenever they wanted. They would bend us over and tie us down and then have sex with us. They put objects in our behinds. From heaven, as I look back, I see them molesting even the babies by putting their finger in their anus, or a man would put his penis in their mouth or anus.*

"*At four years of age, we learned to march together and follow orders. We learned colors and different signs and learned how to organize things. As we grew older, we had to learn difficult things and the directions got harder. We had to pick up heavy boxes and heavy bags and stack them, and then unstack them and put them somewhere else; just moving back and forth to practice. If we made a mistake, they would leave us outside without clothes and food and keep us hungry. As we were growing up, nobody showed any affection. There was no formal education, just learning words and pictures.*

"*The dormitories were long steel buildings maybe forty to fifty feet across and a couple of hundred yards long. They were divided into rooms. There was a sleeping section and restrooms. We slept on racks, like bunk beds. They were stacked one on top of the other. At the doorway, there was a cleaning section. We had to walk through it to get in or out, and the water just sprayed hard on you and you got all soapy. Then the soap was washed off and you were clean. There were walls on two sides, and the nozzles stuck down through the pipes. When you walk in, the water comes from the front, top, back, and the sides all at once. The top was not covered. When you got to the other side, hot air came and it dried your skin. Then you were outside.*

*"On the side was an eating area. We were given enough to eat because they wanted us to grow up to be strong to do hard labor. There were no windows. We hardly remembered our parents. When we looked at women, we wondered why they were so different. There were no schools and no formal education.*

*"At the age of ten or twelve, they would take us to a warehouse or a work place. It was better than being locked up in the dorms. At this age, boys in the dorms would have sex with each other and were also abused sexually by grown caretakers. In the next dorm, between the ages of twelve and fourteen, there was more sex between the kids and the caretakers and guards. They did not tie the boys anymore unless they had to. They would just tell them what they wanted and the boys had to do it.*

*"At the age of fourteen and sixteen years, we were sent to work in the warehouses. We had to carry sacks of food and load them in the vehicles, bring them in the warehouse to store them, and keep track of them. That is all we did, day after day. We did not get paid for our work, just food and shelter. Vehicles were like electric trucks, smaller than pickup trucks. They were actually pretty light. There was a place for the driver and there was a cart behind to haul the bags.*

*"They picked out males and females to pair up and have kids. I was never picked to have kids. I guess they did not want my genes. As I look back into that life from heaven, if we were not physically fit to do the job for any reason, we were killed, like I was because my back was becoming stiff and my legs and knees were hurting and I*

*could not carry much of a load. At the age of thirty-two, they moved us to another dormitory and started to check us for any problems, and if we could not do our work, they would get rid of us by killing us.*

*"From heaven, I can see that Atlantis and its people were completely controlled by the demon entities. People looked completely dark. All of Atlantis was totally black except for a few streaks of Light here and there. Practically everyone was controlled by Satan and his demons and appeared as gray or black. I see a huge black command center covering all of Atlantis, and black cords going to every person and every building, and the demons talking to people through those black cords.*

*"I see that we had no religious or spiritual knowledge. Once or twice a year, a preacher would come and talk to us. He would tell us that we have to behave and to be good, but said nothing about spirituality. Sometimes they would wear colored clothes and sometimes they would wear what they called "god" costumes, such as an alligator, bird, or other animal heads as a headdress."*

### Physical, Emotional, Mental, and Sexual Abuse

Other horrible acts had to do with how children were raised. They separated boys and girls and kept them in separate dormitories. They were routinely abused: physically, emotionally, mentally, and sexually by the caretakers and guards. When boys and girls reached puberty, the masters (rulers) were well aware that there were strong sexual urges. They did not change that in the human body. Both sexes were encouraged toward homosexuality and facilities were provided in the adolescent dormitories for this. This gave them a sexual release, and was done to diffuse the sexual urges in the population so that anger and frustration would not build up. By the time the breeding units were selected and paired, there were individuals in the breeding unit who actually found the other sex repugnant. They simply went through the experience to have the children.

People were also used as sex slaves for the masters and the ruling class, depending on the particular sexual desire of the master. They were pretty cruel. They had absolute power over the thoughts, feelings, and body of the slaves. They were simply there to be used in whatever way the master and other rulers desired. This also included priestly groups, because the upper religious priests were also part of the ruling class. There was nothing to hold them back because they had no laws. The population of Atlantis was living in miserable conditions, only sufficient to keep them alive.

Masters and other rulers would use conditioning through electronics so the person would seem madly in love with the masters. After using them as sex slaves, masters threw them back in the dormitories or killed them. There were alternative sexual practices by the rulers and their families, such as different types of sadistic sexual acts including sexual torture, whipping, beating, or whatever would cause pain.

Following are some of the past lives in Atlantis recalled by my patients in which they were brutally tortured by the members of the ruling class:

- *"I am a twenty-three-year-old female living in Kress City in the south central part of Atlantis. This is about 21,602 BC. I have dark tan skin and dark brown hair. I have been living in female dormitories with thirty-five other females. There are double bunk beds lined up on both sides, and there is a big central area through which we can walk. There are common bathrooms and showers. I work in a government office where I clean the offices. I am escorted out with many other workers and escorted back to the dorm. Other women who live in my dorm work in laundries, and some work in the kitchen as cooks in the dorm or outside. I also worked in the kitchen as a helper.*

  *"A lot of the females are sexually abused by the guards and government workers. I have been abused sexually by*

the guards. I am working ten to twelve hours a day, non-stop. When I come to the dorm, the male guards are always after me. I am tired. I just want to be left alone. I cannot take it anymore. One day I resist a guard's attempt to have sex with me, so he kicks me, slaps me, beats me with a stick, and kills me. My spirit after death stays around for a long time, for many years, because I am very angry. I possess the guards and all those people who abused me, going from one person to another.

"After about five hundred years, angels helped me to heaven because some people were praying to help the lost souls. In heaven, after cleansing and resting, I review my life with three higher beings. From heaven, I can see that my parents were selected to produce children. They did not know each other. They were living in separate dorms till they were ordered to live in an apartment and to have children. They had no choice. They did not care for or love each other. They lived together just to produce children because they were ordered to do so.

"From heaven, I see that I was brought to the dorm when I was about one year of age and I never saw my parents again. There were caretakers here who fed us, occasionally washed us, and took care of us. There were about fifty children in one large room, with rows of double and sometimes triple bunk beds. The caretakers did not care about us and were indifferent and unloving toward us.

"I lived in a series of dorms until I was twelve years old. The caretakers abused us physically, verbally, and sexually. They kept us clean and fed us well because they wanted us to grow up to be strong to do the work. They were not caring or affectionate. We were given basic elementary education only. Then we were trained to do different chores, such as cooking, cleaning, and washing clothes. If we did not do it right or did not behave, we were severely punished. Sometimes we were put into an isolation room, which was five feet by five feet, with no windows, and there was dead silence. Sometimes they *whipped us or shocked us by putting wires on our temples, genitals, and different places on the body, and then we would receive a burst of electricity that caused a sharp pain. Sometimes they used sexual abuse as a punishment, where they would insert a rod or stick in us or have sex with us, including anal and oral sex.*

*"I was not chosen to have children because I was sterile and I could not have any children because of the damage to my reproductive system due to the sexual abuse. I see that my general anxiety, irrational stress, and difficulty with authority in the current life came from that life in Atlantis. From heaven, I see that all of Atlantis and everybody there were totally dark and were completely taken over by demons because there were no prayers and no belief in One God. There were only a few streaks of Light here and there."*

- *"I am a twenty-five-year-old female living in Daries City in Atlantis, in a dorm with other women. It is about 21,650 BC. My job is to help clean the dorms. Sometimes I am taken out of the dorms to help clean the offices outside. One day while cleaning, I fell down and hurt my back so I could not work efficiently anymore. So I was taken out and put into another dorm with people who were sick and could not work anymore.*

  *"I am taken to a room and tortured by five members of the ruling class. They are wearing different animal costumes of a lion, a wolf, a cat, a bird, and a goat. They rape me repeatedly and beat me. They are torturing me like the animals they represent would do. The wolf is attacking by biting and scratching, the bird claws and pokes with its beak at my eyes, and the lion is ripping and tearing me. Then they tie me by my hands to a wall, hang me, and cut my throat and wrist veins and let me bleed to death. My spirit comes out and my body dies. I watch them taking my body to a meat-processing plant.*

*"From the heaven, during my review, I see many of my problems coming from that life to the present life, such as my lung problem, throat problem, eye problems, and muscle problems."*

- *"I am a thirty-five-year-old male. My name is Hamas. I live in Merfouse City in Atlantis. It is 22,000 BC. I live in a dormitory-barracks with a bunch of men. I work in a warehouse hauling food sacks. I have been doing this since I was twelve years old.*

  *"I am tied down on this table. I am naked. There are people torturing me. They are hitting me with thin whips. These people are wearing animal costumes of wolf, bear, and cat. There are five men and three women. Men are about five feet ten inches tall and about a hundred and sixty pounds. Most of them have darker hair, brown eyes, and a copper skin color. Women are about five feet four inches tall, and pretty. Each has a kind of a head thing on that looks like an animal head, like a wolf, bear, and cat, but the face is not covered. They are wearing fur robes, which are open in front. They are naked underneath.*

  *"They are laughing and joking. They are torturing me by hitting, pinching, and squeezing with their hands. They have sex with me, both men and women, and with each other. I cannot move or do anything because I am tied up. They stick things in my behind, they squeeze my balls, twist and pull on my penis. They cut me all over with knives and laugh at me. I am crying and screaming but they do not care.*

  *"They give me a shot that makes me fierce. I struggle hard to get loose and they laugh and laugh. Then they give me another shot that makes me have an erection and the women get on me and have sex with me. One woman bites me hard on the neck, shoulders, and chest, and like an animal, she is taking bites out of me. Their eyes are looking dark and glazed. Finally they hang me upside down by my feet and then they cut my throat. I can feel the blood*

*running over my face. They are whipping me as I am dying.*

*"I am feeling terrible pain everywhere. I did not do anything to deserve this. It is wrong. If I ever get a chance, I will kill them all. I am very sad that they are doing this to me and there is nothing I can do to stop them. I will never get trapped like this again. You have to explode to keep things in balance. These are horrible people.*

*"My soul pops out of the third chakra and my body dies. I do not feel dead. Those people are peeling my skin off. I cannot stand to watch what they are doing to my body. I feel very angry with these people. I go inside one woman and hurt her, but I do not like to be here. I want out. I yell in her ears all the time. I interfere with her in any way I can, with what she sees, hears, feels, and how she moves. I interfere with her hands and feet. I can hide something she sees or change the words she hears. All the pain I felt before the death of my body is transferred over to her and now she is feeling it. I am so glad that now she is feeling all that pain. I wish I could kill her. I concentrate on the pain I felt, then she feels it too. I see many other people who are inside her.*

*"After many years, I get repulsed and turned off from how she is torturing others. I can see through her eyes and I do not like it. I do not want to be here and hurt her, either. I feel repelled and am pushed out of her body. I look around and I see a bright white Light and it feels good and right. I feel myself drifting toward it. I seem to be passing through objects and places. As I go closer to the Light, there are some people I knew and they are inviting me in. They are dressed funny. They are not wearing work clothes like they used to, but are wearing a kind of white robe.*

*"As I am about to go into this Light, somebody yells at me and tells me that I can really hurt those people who hurt me. I think about it and decide that I do not really want to do it. So I keep going on into the Light (heaven).*

*I go to a table, and there is a man and a woman sitting at the table. They invite me to sit down and talk to them about how I died. I start to tell them all about it. I talk on and on for a long time. I talk loud and fast until all my feelings come out. Finally it feels like the well has dried out. Then they send me to a cleaning station.*

*"I have seen cleaning stations like this before while I was on Earth, in our dorms. You walk into one end of it and walk through to the other end and the water sprays at you from the front and back, from the sides and from the top. It sprays water, soap, water, and hot air, almost like a car wash. You just walk through and you come out clean. It is very much like we used in the barracks in Atlantis on Earth. They were called cleaning stations and we were supposed to stop there and get cleaned. After cleaning here in heaven, I feel different. I feel relaxed and more peaceful. I go to the next station. There are three wise men there who help me in reviewing my life.*

*"I understand from heaven that I needed to learn many lessons from that life, such as mercy, compassion, self care, and an unusual one, which is reaching beyond the limits, like when you are restricted, you have to reach out beyond limitations and keep improving.*

*"I see many people who were in that life in Atlantis are also here in my current life, including some friends and family members. I see from heaven that many of my problems came from that life to my current life. One of them is to keep quiet and not be heard for fear of being hurt.*

*"Then, when you, Dr. Modi, asked for cleansing for everybody who ever lived in Atlantis, and everything. I see a tornado of Light coming to the whole city, to all of Atlantis, and to all the people, lifting out all the dark entities, energies, and devices from everything and everybody. The angels destroyed the dark command centers and created a Light center there.*

*"I see that the devices in the neck caused some brain damage, attention deficit disorder, petit mal epilepsy,*

*feelings of being controlled, paranoia, aggression, schizo-*
*phrenia, disassociative disorder, feelings like somebody is*
*inserting thoughts or taking away thoughts from them in*
*that life and in the current life. I see that when the de-*
*vices were put into babies, they lost soul parts from that*
*area of the neck and were in the possession of demons. In*
*this lifetime, demons are putting dark devices in that place*
*through those soul parts. They look like black rods.*

*"As you, Dr. Modi, asked angels to remove them from*
*me and from everybody who had ever lived in Atlantis*
*and bring everybody's soul parts back and integrate them*
*with whom they belong, after cleansing and healing, I see*
*angels going everywhere and doing it. It is a massive un-*
*dertaking. It is like a wind blowing across and ripples of*
*changes occurring in everybody all over who ever had*
*a life in Atlantis. Almost every human being has lived in*
*Atlantis. I see people in mental hospitals feeling better but*
*confused because they do not understand what is happen-*
*ing to them."*

### Medical Care During the Dark Ages

As time went on, medical care became more and more primitive; not that they did not have medical technology, but during the slavery time, they did not bother to use any great
medical care of the replaceable work unit; that is, people.
The only ones who used great medical care were the rich and
the ruling classes, and even then, because of lack of practice
and experience and lack of development during this time,
medical care of the ultra rich and ruling classes suffered
also. Doctors did meaningless research on dorm people with
devastating outcomes for the research subjects. These doctors also had neck implants and were controlled by the rulers
about what to do and how to act.

- *"I am a male physician living in Atlantis in 25,000 BC.*
  *I am in charge of a female dormitory, where women are*

*treated as slaves and used to make babies. Men can go and have sex with them and the women do not have any say in it and do not have any say about their babies. I treat these women as things and feel no human connection to them. I do different experiments with them. I purposely deliver all the babies through cesarean section. Sometimes we will open the abdomen just to see how the baby is doing.*

*"At times, we will get embryos that have been genetically modified in different ways and implant them in women just to see what will happen. Sometimes we remove a gene or a chromosome from the cell just to see what will happen. I also do experiments to find out what will happen if we take out one tube and ovary.*

*"By the time I am sixty-five, I am depressed about what I am doing. I am taken to a different place and they use me as an experiment subject. They give me different hormones to see how they affect my testicles, my body, my hair growth, and my emotions. Then they cut my penis off. I feel depressed. I want to die. They put me in a dark, gloomy room and give me poison to drink. Initially I feel cold and tingly, and then my body freezes and my jaw feels locked. My last thoughts are, "I want it to end. Is there anything more? What will happen to me?'*

*"When I come out of my body, I feel resigned. I walk around and see more experiments being done on different people. Ultimately, I go to the ruler who is responsible for all this and watch him for a while. I have this sense that there is more than people being mean to each other. After a while, I am in a place where people are praying for the lost souls, and as a result, angels come and take me to heaven.*

*"From heaven, I see that I had lived many lifetimes in Atlantis, when different types of experiments were done to me, and also a life in Germany in a concentration camp as a karmic payback."*

## Life in the Countryside During the Dark Ages

The countryside of all the cities was comparatively better and had some Light coming through because the control of people was mostly inside the cities and did not reach into the periphery. The mountains were practically clear, but each city got darker and darker toward the center, where the rulers lived. The cities had become more and more isolated within themselves because that is where the ruler's radius of control was. As a result, the inside and outside of the city became more distinct. The rulers feared people living outside the city. They thought that something might come from outside the city and destroy them, because those outsiders were too far away from the controlling devices. Eventually, contact between the city and the outside drops off, except, in the end, they needed the outside people because inside they could not raise their own food. They could not make things on their own because they literally destroyed their own people; they also had to buy stuff from the outside. They were powerful but they had nothing. If they wanted something, they had to buy it from the outside and that encouraged sea trade.

The following past life was recalled by a hypnotized patient who lived on the countryside of Atlantis:

- *"I am a sixteen-year-old female living in a small village outside the city in a swampy coastal area southeast of the mountains in Atlantis. This is 31,582 BC. My name is Lorel and I am living with my parents and a younger sister and brother. I have black hair and olive skin. My family and I harvest the swamp, collecting healing and medicinal herbs. We take them into town and a dealer buys them. My mother makes medicine from the herbs and we sell the medicine for more than we can get for the raw herbs. The medicine has to be prepared just right; otherwise, it is not effective. After a while, I become very knowledgeable in recognizing different plants and distinguishing them from look-alike plants.*

*"I go into town to the government hall to sell the herbs with my father. In the basement, there are people who buy things, or they can go to the stores further into town, but the prices are pretty much the same. A man in the store offers my family and me a job. I also look for somebody who knows about the mountains and other herbs, because we do not know much about them. My father also gets into selling the medicine we make.*

*"One day, I go to the bigger city with my father. People there are strange and look like zombies. Their eyes are vacant. They look straight ahead and they ignore anything that gets in their way. It is a matter of not hearing, seeing, and not speaking to anybody. They just go on doing whatever they are doing and ignore everything else around them. This is a scary place and it is difficult to do business here. I cannot wait to get out of there and I fear that Atlantis is going to end pretty soon. I am quite shaken by what I saw. My father tells me this is the reason we moved to the swamp area, to get away from that kind of life. He took me there so I would understand how people live there. Of course he was taking a chance. These were the cities and towns that were totally controlled by the rulers. It seems that the only people who are free of control are those who live outside the big cities and towns. The further away from the cities, the better off they are, and the control devices do not reach that far.*

*"We find a lady who is knowledgeable about the mountain herbs and learn from her about them, while we teach her about the swamp herbs and their preparation techniques. I realize that, in time, the rulers will want to control our villages also. So we have to stay away from the cities and towns. The old medicine man who hired me already knew this and is happy that I also figured this out. He begins to teach me the rest of the business while my mom and the other woman are training my younger sister about herbs and their preparation. My brother is trying herb farming. We also find a man who knows about plants*

*on the plains, and we teach each other. The old man dies when I am twenty-seven and leaves his business to me.*

*"I set up a series of dummy shops so it looks like we have herb specialists from all over, because if the rulers suspected how much we were making, they would be after us. We have places in the swamps to live in case we have to hide and disappear for months.*

*"I meet a man in a nearby village who does touch and spiritual healing, and also thinks the way I do, and we get married. After a while, I get pregnant. It is a very disturbing time in Atlantis, so I am thinking of moving to Europe with my family. I go to Italy on a ship. I find colonies of Atlanteans who settled there thousands of years ago. I am learning about European plants. I give birth to my baby boy in Italy. After two years, I am determined to bring my family here, so I get on a ship that is going to Atlantis. I leave my son in Italy with the colonists because I want him to be away from Atlantis.*

*"When I return to Atlantis, everything seems strange. When I go to the medicine shops, there are strangers running them and our shelters are burned down. There are strangers living there and my family is gone. The ruler's men catch me. The ruler is upset that I made money and he did not profit from it. His men and the ruler tie me down and beat me. They break the bones in my hands and feet. They hook two wires carrying electricity and push them through my eyes to my brain and then shock me. There are about twenty men and women wearing costumes and masks as if they are having a party. The louder I scream, the louder they laugh. They stick things in my ears and puncture my eardrums. They are burning my hair, scalp, and face. They put holes through my nose and hang me with wires. They split my heel bones with a chisel. Then they split the long bones in my legs and arms and separate my joints. They shock me by attaching wires to my nipples and clitoris. After a while, they strangle and kill me. Then one of the men opens my chest and takes my heart out.*

*"My last thoughts are, "I hate these people. I wish I knew what happened to my family." After death, I am angry and I despise the stupidity of the rulers and the whole system. They destroyed their own lives and the lives of their people, and they cannot change that fact. They are stagnant, going backward, losing ground, and they cannot stop their backslide. I can look around and see the deterioration everywhere. There is no innovation, no progress, and no development. The rulers have ruined all that. They cannot understand how to make it better. Instead, they tortured me because I did well.*

*"I go after these people. I find that I cannot do anything to them. I follow the torturers and ruling class around. I try to find out what happened to my family. I go inside the ruler and try to influence him, then go into another and another. After several hundred years, I will myself out of the person I am in. I look around and I see the Light and I feel pulled into it and I am in heaven.*

*"In the receiving area or debriefing area, I see a man who asks me to talk about life. I tell him about how I feel bitter about being treated so badly because I was doing well and helping people. I also felt badly for not helping my family. Then I go for cleansing and then to my life review. During the review, I see five beings. Bathyous, the god of the swamps; Naxous, the god of the mountains; Erdos, the goddess of growing things; Leader, the god of wisdom and knowledge, and Garnish, the god of swamp creatures. I see Bathyous, the god of the swamps. He is saying he really appreciated how I honored him all my life even though I never did formal worship. I took good care of the swamp, respected it, and saw the beauty of it. Although I never worshiped formally, I did worship in my everyday life, with my respect for people, life, and plants.*

*"The one in the center is lizard-like. His name is Garnish. He is a swamp creature god. That is why he looks like a cross between an alligator and a lizard.*

*"Part of my mission was to revive spirituality in Atlantis, by using herbs that would stimulate the spiritual*

*centers in the brain so they could have spiritual experiences and understand and see more. The herbs activate the spiritual centers but they are not hallucinogenic. They are like mushrooms. The hope was that, by developing spiritually in the sparsely inhabited towns away from the cities, it might increase the spiritual fields and help the conditions in the cities. I succeeded in doing it.*

*"I was to organize people so that if the city tried to extend its domination, the people could fight it. If the city sent out soldiers, there would be resistance to them in one form or another. When I was planning to move my family to Europe, it was not a good choice. It would have been safer to organize a resistance to the city, and help everyone to see how evil the rulers in these cities were. I see that we could have ended up with pockets of free Atlanteans outside the cities.*

*"Every seaport was in a city. So we would not have had communication with the outside world, but we would have had communication everywhere else in free areas across Atlantis. It would have been like a free Atlantis, like little blisters around cities. I was establishing the trade in the outskirts of the cities, but the plan slipped. Re-establishing spirituality and establishing free Atlantis outside the cities would have been complete with trade routes, a communication system, and active resistance to the cities. It would have been remaking Atlantean culture outside the city. These were my group goals. We did not completely succeed.*

*"My personal spiritual goals were to intensify spiritual development and there were two parts to this. One was to activate spirituality through the spirit-inducing plants. The second one was to be fulfilled through spiritual practices by making the herb preparations, a sort of spiritual ritual with prayers, and make the process a form of worship that we would follow while preparing the herbs.*

*"My personal developmental goals were of improved wisdom by trying to remove the developmental blockages. As I go through my developmental stages from life to life,*

*there are blockages, and every blockage I overcome dimin-*
*ishes the rest, so finally they will be resolved completely. If*
*I do not succeed in a life, it does not get worse but it stays*
*the same. Every time I succeed in a lifetime, it becomes less*
*and less of a barrier to me until, finally, the quality is mine*
*forever, such as wisdom, understanding, and proper ap-*
*plication and action. The barrier will not always look the*
*same. To develop understanding and wisdom, and take the*
*proper course of action, we will have different qualities in*
*each life, but it is still the same barrier to overcome, and*
*every time we do, it is less of a problem in the next life. This*
*is true in the development of every soul.*

*"I see from heaven that my husband was a freedom*
*fighter. He was encouraging active resistance by the free ter-*
*ritories, getting a communication network, creating a trad-*
*ing network, and getting ideas around and developing op-*
*position and resistance to the cities. I got scared of his ideas.*
*I was two months pregnant and that changed my outlook. I*
*began to think of the safety of my family and me, rather than*
*the safety of the whole community. That is when I made the*
*wrong decision. I wanted to move to Europe to save my fam-*
*ily. He did not support my decision to go to Europe.*

*"After I went to Europe, my husband openly rallied the*
*people, arming the men and marching them around. This*
*got the ruler's attention and most of our townspeople were*
*killed, including my husband and family. From heaven, I*
*see that if I had stayed in Atlantis, I could have modified*
*him so that he would not have attracted so much attention.*
*As long as the rulers saw it as a harmless commercial and*
*spiritual venture, they would not have seen any harm in*
*it. But when he began to provide weapons to people and*
*organize them, it got threatening. Also, having a son in*
*his life would have discouraged him from being so violent*
*and he would have been more cautious.*

*"From heaven, I see that many of my problems came*
*from that life to the current life. They burned my hair,*
*scalp, face, and ears, leading to the thinning of my hair*

*and fluid in my scalp. They were sticking sharp objects through my ears and brain. This caused the disturbance of balance. They poked at my eyes with needles, which penetrated the brain, and then they gave electric shocks to the brain that caused the floating vision like mirages and headaches. It also caused the scarring of my eyes, which is part of the cataract formation, and also the black floaters in my left eye. They stuck a pincher through the base of my nose and hung my body with it, causing my sinuses and throat to fill with blood, and caused me sinus and throat problems today. They cut and split my bones and joints, which caused arthritis, muscle weakness, and aches and pains all over my body. They cut my abdomen and intestines, leading to gastrointestinal symptoms. They finally strangled and killed me, leading to throat problems and asthma. They also burned and cut my skin all over, causing the dry skin in my current life.*

*"After forgiving those who harmed me and bringing all my and other people's missing soul parts back from people, places, and darkness, and integrating them with us after cleansing and healing, there was a great deal of improvement in my symptoms."*

- *"I am an eighteen-year-old female living in a town outside a city in Atlantis. This is 33,462 BC. My name is Namini, after a goddess of the forest. Our home is in a village near a forest area. The cities are already isolated. We supply wood to the city. I live with my father, mother, my fiancée, my sister and her fiancée, and two younger brothers. We heard soldiers are coming, so we all hide. We do not know what they want. My fiancée and I are going to a dry, wooded area. The rest of my family is going deeper into the forest. My fiancée goes to the village after a few days to see what happened, but he never comes back. Later, I found out that they wanted young people because, in the cities, they are not producing enough children and the population is dropping.*

"The rest of my people go back to the village and live a regular life. I stay in the forest and withdraw from society. I pray there. My family thinks that I went crazy because I am praying and worshiping the goddess. My family brings food and other things for me from time to time. The village thinks my lifestyle is strange and obscene. In the forest I pray and do spiritual practices such as worship rituals and meditation, which are given to me by goddess Namini. I have visions of her off and on when she guides me about what to do.

"At the age of thirty-eight, I go to the village and talk to the people individually about how to pray and worship the goddess. It becomes a scandal and the people think I am talking dirty. I talk to some mothers with children and ask them to teach their children how to pray. They are unsure. They do not want their children to stand out and be different. I am trying to remake the Atlantean culture. I have more success with females than males. Some of the females even meet me in the forest and I show them the worship rituals. All of them are praying more and some of them are worshiping at home. At the age of fifty-two, I begin to go out to the other villages and talk to people in the fields. I am trying to start this culture with the young people. Sometimes I pray out loud with three or four people.

"I tried to start a worship culture to change Atlantis. I had a small success. In my native village, there are actually groups who get together in the forest and pray. There are not enough to make it a common activity. I also got some of the women from the neighboring villages to start praying. There was no success with the men at all. I am dying at the age of seventy-three of pneumonia. I die thinking that it was a difficult job. My spirit wanders around for a couple of days and then I see the goddess Namini, who takes me to heaven.

"In heaven, after cleansing, I go to the life review. There are three beings. One is Namini, the goddess of the woods; another is Borus, the god of wind, and the third is *a human soul. They are helping me review my life. From heaven, I see that I planned to establish some spirituality in the Atlantean culture. This was an impossible job. Even to get a few people to pray and do some spiritual practices was a big success. If they can keep up the prayers, there is a chance of it spreading. Since some women were also teaching their children to pray, as a result, there will be some men in the next generation who will tend to be spiritual.*

*"I was also supposed to start the worship of other gods and bring back the idea that they are all aspects of one true God and that we are just worshiping different aspects of Him. This just barely got started and was not fulfilled.*

*"The third goal I planned was to suffer a family loss to resolve some karma from a past life when I was responsible for breaking up families."*

### Psychics During the Dark Ages

There were also some spiritual healers and psychic people in Atlantis, but they did not tell others about it because most people did not believe in spirituality and psychic abilities. As described before, when Lamurians came to Atlantis about 80,000 BC, Atlanteans watched them communicating with people who were far away from them. They did not understand the psychic gifts of the Lamurians and did not want to spend time in spiritual development to develop those psychic gifts. They began to develop psychic skills through research and technology. Some of my patients described lives as a psychic in Atlantis. My patients recalled following past lives as a psychic in Atlantis during the Dark Ages:

- *"I am an eleven-year-old female, living with my mother and a twin brother in Atlantis. My mother has lung disease so we have to help her a lot. My twin brother and I have a special gift. Since the age of three, we know of events before they happen, and we can communicate with each other from a distance. Our mother told us not to talk to anybody about it because we can get into trouble. So we keep it secret. We do not know where our father is. We never saw him. We live in a hilly area where we have a nice house. Our grandfather is in a high position in government and he takes care of us financially. We live outside of a big city in the countryside.*

"One day when I am eleven years old, someone comes from the government who is like us. He recognizes us immediately. There are more people who are psychic here than any other place. There are waves of different colors around us, which he can see. We tried to hide it but we were not good at it. We are taken away to another school and the teacher could not stop it. My brother and I are separated, which is hard on each of us. Our mother was all alone and sick.

"In the new school, there are about fifty students of different ages. We are asked to say what is written on a paper without looking at it, to levitate things, to start fires with our mind, to tell what other people are thinking and what their intentions are, etc. If we do not do it, we are kept hungry or are beaten. As long as we do what we are told, we are fed and treated well. I think they are afraid we might get together and try to bring the government down.

"I am transferred to another school when I am fourteen years old. I am chosen to go to that school because I have pre-knowing. We are trained here to see auras, clear the chakras and energies, and to do vibrational healing, sound healing, remote viewing, etc. Every kid here has some type of gift. I can sense if people are sick and have the knowledge of what to do about it. I am very good with plants. By touching them, I can feel what they can be used for. I can feel if people have malicious intent and if they are lying or hiding things. In this school, kids are more energy-sensitive and I am, too. I do not like it because I had friends in the other school. I never saw my family,* *and the connection with my brother is getting weaker. They are doing different experiments on us. They are taking samples of our hair, fingernails, and blood about every six weeks and trying to find out why we are psychic. They put us in dangerous situations to see if we know that we are in danger.*

"*In this new school, they are actually giving us some training, such as how to be a medical intuitive and how to do remote healing, sound healing, and vibrational healing. Some of the people here look robotic. They have flat affect, and no emotions or expressions, as if they are programmed or brain dead. We are also taught about some fun things, such as dancing. I think they are planning to use me and some others for royal entertainment, maybe, or be a spy, and to be with somebody and read his or her mind. I like it here but I am still angry because I am not allowed to see my mother or brother. They said I could, but they never let me visit them.*

"*I want to see my mother because she is sick. I try to leave but I cannot. I am asking too many questions and rocking the boat a little bit. They do not want others to see this so they take me away by force to a hospital, where they do a hysterectomy and take my uterus out. I had no choice and no control of my life. I become deeply depressed and want to die. They gave me steroids so I can be sent to a farm to work.*

"*I am sent to a farm when I am eighteen years old. I stay there for a long time. As long as I do what they tell me, they are nice. Most women here have had hysterectomies. Seems like they are using ovaries to make some drugs. These women were bred and raised to work on the farm. It was decided by somebody else. They do not want them to be breeders. They do not want them to become pregnant.*

"*At the age of thirty-two, I am living in a hilly country. I am single. Never married. I live with other women of my age. There are bells and there are rules and schedules when to get up, eat, go to work, come back and go to eat and sleep. We live in a high-rise apartment where two women live in a room. I have this urge to be a mother and I want to be a mother. I feel it has been stolen from me. Even animals can have children, but I am not allowed to. I have a knowing. I knew they were going to do it, so I was trying to escape, but they caught me and did the operation on me. The same thing was done on all of us, and now, we are like a herd of cows or flock of sheep, and are not functioning well. Most are just apathetic. I pretend to be that way but I am not that way. We are isolated and are like a captive bunch of cows that have no free will. I have been living here since I was eighteen years old.*

*"I am very depressed because I had a female lover who died. I never saw my family and cannot have any children. There is no hope for me. I want to end it all. One day we all are taken to a festival at a time square. There is a big statue. I am planning to escape, although I know I am not going to because there are guards with guns with us. I do not care anymore. As I am walking away from the group, the guards try to shoot me but they miss and end up shooting the head of the statue, which exploded, and then they shoot me in my head. As I am dying, I am thinking, "I do not care, you have killed me but I am the one who won because I escaped."*

*"I am really angry at God for all the terrible things that happened to me. My spirit goes to see my mother. She is very sick. Then I go to see my brother, who is in a terrible place in a mental institution. They have done a lot of terrible experiments on him, many surgeries on his brain. He has gone insane as a way of coping. I cannot watch him suffering, so I leave. I go up to a foggy place. I am confused, numb, and tired. I do not know where I am. I am disappointed again. I think I am in purgatory. Nobody comes for me and I have no help. Nobody is there. I feel lost. I was going up and I do not know how I ended there. I am spacey and tired. I stay there for a long, long time.*

"*I see people walking back and forth. I go to a place where there is a book. I open the book. I do not understand anything. As I look around, the building looks like a library, but it is a dingy place. Here it does not look lighted like in heaven, but it is not a bad place either. I think it is a purgatory, and from here, I am sent into different people's bodies for a long time. Then I am in a person who is drowning and struggling to come up but drowns. I see a shaft of light come and we both go to heaven. It is all Light here and there are shiny beings everywhere. I see my mother and brother in heaven. I look all white. I am still confused. I do not understand why it took so long to go to heaven.*

"*I am sitting on a bench. There are two angels standing on each side of me. They put their arms together on each other's shoulders, and their feet are on each side of the bench and I am in the middle, sitting down. They are straddling the bench and they put their heads together, thus making a chamber, and there is a yellow Light coming in between the angels and then it is green, then orange, violet, pink, and then white. It looks like they are doing color therapy. When they put their heads together, they put their third eyes together, and that makes a chamber and then the Light comes through them and I can feel it like a warm heat wave going through me. I see black things coming out of me and changing into the Light. After this, I feel cleansed and not confused.*

"*Then I see a train station. I see my mother and brother there. We all look white and happy. Then we go into an elevator that has tubes that are made up of clear Light. It is beautiful and brighter and a happier place than before.*

"*As I am reviewing my life, I see different events of my life. I see that my grandfather had an incestual relationship with my mother and we were his children. I see that we influenced a lot of people who we were around. We made them stronger and we were good examples. There*

*was lot of pain and sadness. As I look at Atlantis, it ap-
pears very dark, especially the cities. Areas outside the
cities were not as dark, including my hometown.*

*"As I look back from heaven, I see that I learned how
to survive and how to hide my gifts, which I used in many
lifetimes. I learned that we have everything within us to
survive. We do not need anybody else to survive. I see that
people in Atlantis did not understand the psychic gifts.
The rulers or government wanted to make sure that people
did not use those gifts against them. The rulers were trying to find a way where several good psychics could bring
their Lights together into a laser and create a panoramic
movie. What I see is a panoramic movie all around. They
wanted all these different psychics to be running different
mental pictures, which the rulers could watch, on the television screen. They also wanted to take several psychics
and have them focus on one thing and either destroy or
enhance it so they could use it against the enemies.*

*"I see many problems coming from that life to my cur-
rent life for me, such as feelings of not fitting into the family but being desperate to maintain a connection, conflicts
with authority, blocking my psychic gifts for a long time,
depression, and apathy.*

*"I see some of the people who were there in that life
are also here in my current life. On Dr. Modi's request,
the angels located and brought all my and other people's
soul parts back from Satan, his demons, and from people,
places, and darkness, and integrated them with me and
others. I feel much better."*

• *"My name is Arjuna. I am wearing a white robe. I have
blonde hair and blue eyes. I have angels around me. I live
in Pagasas City, which is in the southwest part of Atlantis.
I am a priestess. I pray and meditate. I do healing rituals. We meet with the angels and we do spiritual work by
requesting them to do healing the way you, Dr. Modi, ask
angels to go out and heal people. In our meditations, we*

*contact the people who need healing, then we telepathically communicate with angels and request them to go and do the healing. This is what I do all day long. The priestesses I work with have similar beliefs. There are other groups of priestesses who have other purposes. I feel a strong sense of purpose for the work I do.*

*"I am older now. I am one of the high priestesses. I work with the archangels. There is a lot of darkness in Atlantis. That is why we do such intense spiritual work, because darkness is taking over. They are getting more control of people. People are becoming infatuated with technology. They are forgetting who they are. They are becoming greedy and controlling, especially the ruling class. I see dark beings controlling people and the country. People are killed by the lords or made into slaves. The lords are killing people who have a belief in God. I can tune into everything telepathically and know what is going on. We are feeling that dark forces are growing faster than we can stop them. We are becoming concerned that the continent will not survive. Things have gotten out of control. A lot of spiritual knowledge has been destroyed. They are fighting against each other for power. Nobody knows who to trust anymore.*

*"The dark forces have taken over for power. There are now fewer people who are in control of everybody. Many people have been put to death. Many people are imprisoned and most people are made slaves. We continue to pray, but even the spiritual priests and priestesses are becoming disillusioned and are turning away from spiritual work, which gives the dark forces more control. Even I am having doubts. I am feeling more and more alone. I meet with the angels but I am also beginning to get influenced by the darkness.*

*"They have captured most of the spiritual people and imprisoned us. They burn our eyes. They hate us. They do not understand the third eye or our psychic abilities. They think we have psychic vision through our eyes and that,*

*by blinding us, they will destroy our psychic vision. They tie us up and throw us in a prison. They sexually assault and rape us. I am being beaten and they mutilated my body. I am losing blood.*

*"I am dying. My last thoughts are, "God, how could you let it happen? How can I ever trust you again? I will never trust a man. It is painful to be a woman. I will be more private about what I do so I cannot be found. I want to stay out of the limelight. It is better to have a quiet life." After death, the angels take me to the Light. They are repairing my body and then I rest for a long time.*

*"I go to the review counsel. They explain that I did help to bring some Light to the planet. People needed to learn from this self-destruction that everything goes in cycles. There was a cycle of Light and now there is a cycle of darkness. I needed to learn lessons of keeping my faith in times of trials and darkness. Light is always there in the worst of times if we continue to pray and ask for guidance. Everybody has his or her own individual responsibility and nobody can change that. As I look back from heaven, Atlantis and everybody in it looks all dark. There are volcanoes erupting and black lava flowing all over, and there are flames.*

*"I see that many problems came from that life to this life, such as sadness, a tendency to be alone a lot, wavering of my faith, weakness in the reproductive area due to sexual abuse, PMS, difficulty in trusting men, eye problems, watering of the eyes, fear of speaking, and hair loss because they used to pull my hair."*

## Final Insult

It was in the spiritual nature where the insult was the greatest when the spiritual freedom of the human being was neglected and that was the crowning error of Atlantis. This was literally the unforgivable sin when rulers began to treat human beings as totally abject animals, as if the soul did not exist at all, and as if they were simply an animal and a tool to be used. This was the final insult, the denial of the spirituality of humans.

The final insult was a composite of different things, including parts from the previous flaws put in by the Atlantean rulers, such as, the break-up of the family, removal of the children from the parents, interfering with reproduction, and interfering with DNA, not just of humanity but of animals and plants, as it was done without the full knowledge of the effect, plus the medical experiments that were conducted, and the sexual abuse and perversion. For some humans, homosexuality is a normal condition, but for most humans, heterosexuality is the norm. When heterosexuality was thwarted and both male and females were pushed to be homosexual against their nature, it was a serious crime and an insult to humanity. This was the total denial of human free will by the rulers. These were all contrary to the spiritual nature of humankind and the nature of God. These were part of the preliminary insult and make a totally negative package. As a final insult, during the last several thousand years before the destruction of Atlantis, the rulers began to consider humans as animals. People were murdered, skinned, and the flesh was sliced up for meat.

One patient recalled a past life as a butcher in Atlantis during the Dark Ages:

- *"I am a guard in a dormitory. Masters noticed that I am really good at torturing people, so they kept moving me up to another job until it became my job to kill people. I am a butcher. My job is to slaughter people for food. The older people, thirty years and older, are not tasty to eat because their muscles are kind of hard, so sometimes I am ordered to kill tender young kids for food specifically for the rulers. There are two other people working with me. One of them is angry with me and hit me on the head, cut my throat, and killed me. He does not even have to hide my body. He just cut my throat to let the blood out so the meat will taste better, and then cut me into pieces for food.*

*"From heaven, I see many problems coming from that life to the current life. Killing all those people by cutting their throats, and my throat being cut before my death, gave me throat problems in the current life. My knee and back problems are also coming from that lifetime."*

## Rulers During the Dark Ages

The ruling class, as it became jaded and lost interest in living, developed interest in other things. In general, they followed negative pursuits and were more interested in things that provided them with a thrill or satisfaction of some sort. Right and wrong, God and spirit were nonsensical concepts to them. Sexual perversion abounded and there was no law but theirs, and they had no limits.

Each little bit, the ruling class descended and this was matched, or preceded, by the diminishing spirituality of the common people. This of course is referring to the time of gradual takeover of the ordinary people by the ruling class, around 50,000 BC. This made it possible for the ruling class to become less spiritual and to take over. Meanwhile, there was an increase in negative behavior as the ruling class lost spirituality. They gained in negativity by turning toward the dark. In their jaded condition, where they had no positive things to look forward to, they became more and more negative, more and more non-demanding of the Light, turning to the darkness for their spiritual factuality due to their dark behaviors.

The personification of evil was not something they did. They did not view evil as a force or a being. When they did observe evil in action, it was thought of as just a part of life. They did not see evil as a separate force but as a normal way to be. They never worshiped the personification of evil; they were not even aware of Satan and his demons, but they did worship their own power. In this case, the personification of power was evil. Now this is not always the case. Power can be positive and can be used for good. What made this negative was how they abused their power.

The rulers took the labor of the population and provided bare conditions, such as just enough food to stay alive, enough shelter to keep you healthy, and enough clothing. Other than that, the general population got nothing. As a result, the rulers felt very rich and powerful, overlooking that they could not get any richer. When the masters kept it all, there could be no increase, and because they did not see through it, the situation ended up leaving them frustrated and unsatisfied, creating more abuses.

There was an absolute control over society because rulers were afraid of losing control, and they were able to feel rich and powerful for a while. But with the structure of society, their wealth did not increase. Their desperate bid for wealth and power was their downfall. Unless you have people working and sharing, and the society developing and growing, the rulers could not create new wealth. The only way new wealth came to Atlantis was when somebody's ship pulled in. That way, when the wealth of Atlantis increased, it all ended up with the rich. Getting richer did make them happy, but they would have been incredibly wealthy if they did not interfere in people's lives. This way, they damaged their own dreams.

Part of the final insult was the very first use of the control device in the first person. Even the developmental work in the control device was part of the package of the insult, so the control device came at the very beginning. Then, as the people were controlled, each step added to the insult. They became more and more controlled, and the situation became more and more negative and had dark overtones to it. After many, many years, there was less and less respect for humanity. Thousands of years before the destruction of Atlantis, the ruling classes reached the point where they began to treat their subject population as farm animals and had an absolute lack of respect for their humanness. The population of Atlantis had been pretty static for a while, since the masters controlled reproduction. There was no food shortage; they kept it with the resources available, but due to strong Satanic influences, the masters developed the taste for human flesh and they would butcher people and slice them up for food.

They purposefully killed people to use their skin as leather and to devour portions of their bodies as if they were farm animals. The leather byproduct was just that, to begin with. Then it became fashionable among the ultra-wealthy to have decorated leather and to use it for special purposes, so you might cover a book with it and make special artwork on the leather. Then somebody got the idea, since they liked the artwork, that they could do artwork on living human beings. They would make an incision and put color on the incision, brand the skin, and then allow it to heal. After it was healed, they would kill the person, strip off the skin, and have the so-called beautiful artwork preserved. The rulers used human skin for book covers, furniture, as polishing cloths, as a decorative covering, etc. They tortured people before killing them, by barbequing or inserting air or water just below the skin all over the body just for fun, and also to take out the whole shell of skin intact and then cook and eat the body parts.

One of my patients recalled a past life in Atlantis as a ruler during the Dark Ages as follows:

- *"I am a ruler on the southeast coast of Atlantis. The name of the city I rule is Methlapp. I own the city. This is my fifth year as a ruler. It is 21,598 BC. My name is Samam and I am a ruler of the house of Giurf. I am the head of a major family in Atlantis. I rule this city and the surrounding territory. In some cities, the system is different and manufacturers rule. As a matter of fact, my house grew out of a trade guild; that is how we came to power.*

   *"My palace is one of the finest palaces in the world. It has over five hundred rooms. It is made of stone and bricks and was built as a fortress. My wives have separate living arrangements in the palace. We usually choose the wives from the ruling family. We have a picture box*

*(television), music box (radio), and other entertainment. Sometimes we watch and see what is going on in other palaces on a picture box. Mostly, we masters amuse each other by comparing, bragging, pretending, and just chattering back and forth on the picture box.*

*"Every city has at least one ruler. Larger cities have more than one ruler. In some of the northern cities of Atlantis, which are larger, there are many rulers. The old capitol of Atlantis has seventeen or eighteen rulers. The old capitol was called Witness City. It is near the northeast seacoast. Then there was a new capitol in the middle, after the two kingdoms of north and south Atlantis joined. The old capitol was in the Northern Kingdom to start with, and is a rich and powerful city. There, they have headquarters of different regions and others, and each has a ruler. We have political rulers, trade rulers, manufacturing rulers, shipping rulers, technological rulers, religious rulers, and every type of rulers. There are over three hundred large cities in Atlantis. Most of the cities are in the north and most of the population is in the north, and as a result, most of the ruling class is in the north.*

*"I have brownish skin, dark hair, and brown eyes. Other people have blonde, red, or dark hair and white, black, or brown complexions. We wear loose clothes and wear crystals as ornaments on rings, in necklaces, and in ears. Ladies put crystals in their hair, and on clothes and ornaments on their hands, fingers, ears, and nose.*

*"I have several wives. We get married by a minister. I have a total of twelve children, one of whom will be the ruler after me. He will not necessarily be the oldest one. He has to be the wisest; the one who is able to put his law into effect, and he has to be strong-minded. That is the most important part. Strength of mind is crucial.*

*"Every few days, I go to the control room, sit down, and turn on the computer. I put the detector on my head and I think the thoughts I need to think to project on my people, such as, "It is so wonderful to work hard, I have to*

*be productive, obedience is important, obedience is bliss-
ful and everyone works together for the master's glory."
These thoughts are then transmitted to the people and become their thoughts. The control room is dark. Here on
the table sits the device that I put on my head. There are
wires, which go from it to a box in the room, and when I
think the thoughts, I see patterns on the screen. It shows
as white on the black screen. How thick the lines are
and how high the patterns are indicates how strong the
thoughts are. There are technologists in the room running
the machinery. I talk to my advisors about any problems
they foresee. Sometimes we plan the next set of suggestions we will put in to the machine.*

*"From the control room, I can see any part of the city
on the screen and make sure everybody is doing their job.
Occasionally, if somebody does not do the job, they are
brutally punished. If we find out that somebody is sick and
cannot do the job, they are taken to the treatment facility,
where they are killed. They are replaceable. We cut them
up for food and eat them. They taste nice and sweet. It is
good-tasting meat. It also depends on the cut. We do not
eat any low-grade meat, such as a foot. I personally prefer
parts of the back, the thick muscles that do not work very
hard. They are generally nice and tender. Young children
also taste real good.*

*"We regulate the breeding process of animals (peo-
ple). We select which ones can breed together to get the
best children. It depends on what characteristics you
want, such as endurance, speed, strength, intelligence,
etc. We keep men and women in separate dorms. If you
put them together, they create trouble. We allow sex between the same gender because it diffuses them. It gives
them an outlet so they don't get all pent-up and violent.
Sometimes I use them as sex slaves and cause them
pain in one way or another and hurt them. I beat them,
squeeze them, have sex with them, torture them, and then
kill them.*

*"All the wealth is kept by the ruling class. The animals (people) do not have anything except food, clothes, and shelter. The goods are shipped overseas and we get all the wealth. I feel fulfilled and at the same time I don't. I feel hollow inside.*

*"We have doctors but they are not very effective. They might do some experiments between animals and humans. Sometimes I do that, too. Depending on how bored I am, I might put animal limbs on a person. I even switched heads on them. There is not much to it. You just match up important parts and sew them. Some of them live for a day or two, some die after a few hours. It is fun. I am just thinking how things changed over time. I do not think my technologists can make those machines because nobody is educated to do so anymore. Now I realize it is a drawback. Of course I do not want them to become too smart, either.*

*"I am doing leather work for a panel piece for a window on a woman's back. As I am tracing the design on her back with a knife, she is screaming and crying, which gives me more sense of pleasure. I am also carving a design for the front and back covers of a book on her. Then I will create some other artwork on her. After the cuts are made, I put color in them and rub it in. When it heals, it will make a big heavy scar and it will have color in it. It will be very pretty. This is a real artwork.*

*"My lady wants a new powder puff. I think I will use her breast for that. I design the circle and make the decorative pattern on the part that will be held. The woman is crying and screaming, which creates more excitement. I also make a brush handle from the skin on her thigh. I want a rough, pebbled surface so I can grip it nicely. I make the holes and put the powder colors in the holes and rub it up and it makes a nice raised scar. I use the rest of her body to practice. It takes days and days to do all this. After it heals, I work on it two or three times till it is just right. It can take one to two years. I picked her out from the dorm because she was cute and will make good*

*designs. She is eighteen years old. I also have sex with her whenever I choose.*

*"With the lady, we have two or three carving sessions. I have sex with her before, during, and after the carving sessions. When the carving is just right, we have a special party, which my wives, children, and others attend. I have sex with her one more time and then I cut her throat. We hang her upside down and drain the blood out, and she goes off to become food. They remove the skin for the leather process and cut her up for dinner tonight.*

*"I am dying of a heart attack at the age of sixty. My last thoughts are, "I had a fantastic life. I wish I could live longer." I have selected and trained my son Joseph to be a ruler. I kind of drifted out of my body. I don't feel dead. I am looking around the palace. Nobody seems to pay attention to me. It feels funny. After so many years of everybody running for me, now nobody is paying attention to me. Eventually, after many years, I get called by a Light being who takes me to heaven. There is a big room like one in my palace. There is a bathing chamber. As I bathe, lots of black stuff comes out. I step out and these slave girls dry me off and give me clean clothes to wear. I am feeling different. I do not feel like the ruler anymore.*

*"Then I am like in my counsel chamber with a desk. There are two men and a woman sitting there. They are telling me that they are going to help me review my life. This strikes me as very funny. Why do I need to review my life? I have to compare it with what I intended to do in that life? Oh, gee! I have a sinking feeling in my stomach, knowing what I have done. I had many opportunities to make a difference and I failed. I had many chances to improve and I did not. I have done too much damage to myself spiritually.*

*"I needed to learn many lessons from that life, such as compassion, mercy, love, etc., and I failed in everything. I see many people who were there in that life are also here in my current life.*

*"I see many problems that came from that life to the current life, such as the desire to hit people for sexual pleasure, and that sometimes the ability to see others' point of view is blocked off. Also, my stomach problems are coming from that life.*

*"As I look back in that life from heaven, I see that there was extreme darkness. I was almost like a devil's puppet. I was totally dark. As a matter of fact, all of Atlantis and everybody in it were filled with the demons at that time.*

*"When you, Dr. Modi, asked the soul parts that I lost in that life, and soul parts of all the people who ever lived in Atlantis, to be brought back from people, places, and hell, I see the soul parts of everybody and mine coming back to every part of the body from head to toe. They are coming from people I tortured and from the palace and hell."*

The percentage of the ruling class varied from time to time, but about 1 percent of the total population were rulers and their families. That means about 99 percent of the people were controlled. By the end, the intermediate and regional levels of the rulers and priests were abolished. When the rulers did not need anything, these people were removed from the political system.

### Priests During the Dark Ages

The only way to get into the ruling class without being born into it was through the religious structure and the technology class. Since the priests did not have a hereditary class, the leaders of the priestly class had to be selected. The priests of the various levels of the temples were selected by the hierarchy of the priests with the approval of the rulers, and moved into the ruling class. In priestly class, the upper hierarchy was the ruling class and was not controlled. During the Dark Ages, since everybody was controlled and lived in the dorms, there was no need for any temples in the city and the priests never preached or counseled people. They, like the rulers, were able to maintain a family unit with a royal lifestyle.

Their religious structure was rudimentary, nature based, and the Atlanteans did not know the real spiritual God. At the same time, in their nature-based worship, they ordinarily did not deal with the concept of evil. It was as if you do not know of God and you do not know of Satan and his demons. The fact that they did not discuss religion certainly limited their growth in spiritual understanding. It was as if each person had his or her own childish religion and it stayed that way. It did not develop adult sophistication or an adult's viewpoint. This made their religion very easy to live with.

During the end of Atlantis, the negative influences were very strong. The spirituality of the people was completely gone. The remainder of religion was simply a hollow echo. It really served no useful purpose, even for the rulers, but they were afraid to completely eliminate it. There were heads of different religions who were part of the ruling class, and they fought for the preservation of it. They had to preserve religion to preserve their line of succession. They had a situation where spirituality was an empty echo and a memory.

One of my patients under hypnosis recalled a life in Atlantis when he was the high priest during the Dark Ages.

- *"I am a forty-five-year-old male living in Cardi City in the south east of Atlantis. This is 22,013 BC. I am a high priest. I live in a section of the same palace where my city ruler resides. I am an important advisor to him. My main duties are assisting my ruler and the sub-rulers in people control. Even before my birth, there was a series of natural disasters such as earthquakes, fires, and floods. Some of these disasters have affected our city. All the common people live in dorms. Over time, some dorm people have broken free when affected by natural disasters, so we are concerned about keeping them in confinement. This is why all my time is used to assist the rulers.*

"*My daily routine consists of being an advisor/counselor to my ruler. I am up at seven a.m. on my working days. I make notes for about half an hour then I go to breakfast with my ruler, sub-rulers, priests, and others in the ruling class. We discuss our concerns about the natural disasters and we discuss ways of developing greater security from the masses in the dorms, because by now we have a concern for our safety. Almost everyone has an implant, including all the priests and technologists. As the high priest, I am the only one of nine priests who doesn't have an implant at this time.*

"*We know that the masses in the dorms have the potential to reach out and destroy us under the appropriate circumstances. We've had escapes before during natural disasters. One time it took over six months to kill and/or round up all of those who escaped. It has been decided that we need to put on more soldiers around the palace and we need to put on additional soldiers to tighten up security in all the dorms.*

"*After our meeting, I go to the computer room, where I assist other sub-rulers in closed circuit TV to tune in to all the dorms. I have a computer and other advanced technology in my room. So sometimes I work from my room.*

"*I don't go to a temple anymore because everyone is in confinement monitoring the dorms of the city. Our computers have the technology that allows us to do that. I do go out to the various dorms to talk to those in charge. We discuss their needs and problems. We talk about any new roles or policies that our leader wants to put in place. I do not talk to the general population anymore. I don't pray! I believe in the nature gods and I use the temple in the palace as an administrative office. We have no wedding ceremonies anymore.*

"*In the evenings when I am not on duty, I go to our torture parties. We have daily torture parties, held mostly at night for recreation, pleasure, and for a meat source. These parties have gone on all my life. They are held in our large assembly room in the palace. Tonight there are twenty-five attending. This includes my wife and me. We are wearing loose fitting trousers and tops; it is casual wear.*

*"Up on a stage, there are ten naked males and females in a cage. A male is selected and tied to two narrow boards. These boards have ropes attached to them and they go up through a series of pulleys high overhead. This screaming person is hoisted and slowly lowered down over a bed of sharp steel spikes. The spikes begin to penetrate his body. His screams of pain and anguish serve only to excite the crowd. Everyone is cheering, laughing, and yelling for more, more, more! The process is repeated with a female and another male. Each time it is done, the crowd gets more and more excited. These three bodies are butchered and cooked on the spot. Next a young male and a young female are selected. The male is castrated and hung upside down. The castration is done for "sport;" some believe that removing the testicles will help the flavor of the meat. The female is offered up to anyone who wishes to perform a sexual act with her. I don't, but I have many times in the past. After this, she too is hung upside down. These two have their veins opened up with a knife and they bleed to death.*

*"In the meantime, the crowd is getting higher and higher. A male is selected for the grand act of the evening. He is pulled up high overhead while he is upside down and hanging from a long rope. He is being swung back and forth like a human pendulum. As he screams out in fright, people yell and cheer and get more excited. He is being slowly lowered as he swings. A razor-sharp piece of steel with edges on both sides awaits him. He continues to be lowered until part of his head is sliced off. People cheer uncontrollably. I am really enjoying myself as I watch him being sliced to the base of his neck. Meanwhile, many in the crowd are so worked up that they are seeking releases in sexual orgies. Now all of us are involved in the orgy.*

*After the people are butchered and cooked, we have a big banquet and feast on their meat. After we eat, there is more drinking and more orgies. Finally, everyone is very drunk and they all find a place to go to sleep.*

*"When I am forty-six, our city experiences a major earthquake. It is around ten a.m. and the tremors are violent. Parts of the palace fall to the ground. Floors give away and many people fall to their death. People are confused as they try to run to safety. I am in full-blown panic. The floor where I stand is beginning to cave in and I fall to the floor below. I have cuts and bruises all over my body. I have blood and dirt mixed together on my arms and hands and other places that I can see. Heavy pieces of flooring fall on my legs and I cannot move. I see some dead bodies around me and I hear others moaning.*

*"I am upset and afraid. I am conscious, but I have a lot of pain in my legs and shoulders. I am trapped. I hear a cracking sound above me. It sounds like something is going to give away. I am frightened and alone. Finally, after thirty hours, the cracking sound bursts into an explosion releasing stones and heavy pillars down upon my head and body. I am killed instantly. Just prior to my being hit, my spirit leaves my body. I stay around Atlantis for several hundred years before going to the Light.*

*"From heaven, I can see how dark Atlantis and everyone was. Atlantis was a godless society and we were evil and were totally controlled by the demons. I can look at myself and see how I was filled with demons who were acting through me. I believed it was I who was doing the evil things, but it was really the demons. I see demons and the spirits of those we killed all around the party room. It was a very dark place.*

*"From heaven, I see some people in the current life who were also in that life. I see many problems that came from that life to this life, such as problems with right ankle (gout), pain in my shoulders, being blocked from the*

*Light, fear, anxiety, panic, dread of natural disasters, and sleeping disorders."*

### Technologists During the Dark Ages

The technological class developed through science. Primarily it began as agricultural science, biology, metallurgy, and crystal growing. Then from these came biology, genetics, chemistry, and physics. The development of science was different than that of our modern culture. The very basics of technology began with selecting the best grain to grow, which seed do you pick, breeding animals, irrigation, developing machines, etc. The technological people were in every branch of science.

Technologists were individuals to begin with. At the very beginning, they were simply interested in improving their regular jobs and would experiment and make new discoveries. Eventually they became proficient, and a group developed which did this as a living, working at developing technology and answering questions for others. This was the true beginning of the technology class. Atlantis developed a great deal and was very prosperous between 70,000 to 50,000 BC. Then the rulers developed loss of respect for the workers and humanity about 50,000 BC.

The top technology class was also part of the ruling class. They were not technologists anymore by the time of the Dark Ages. They could not build, could not replace, and could not develop anything new. Just like masters and other rulers, they maintained their family units, because they could not have a dynasty unless they had family; the upper level of the priestly and the technology groups also maintained the family units. These technologists at the high level were like business people rather than scientists because they did not have any knowledge of technology except how to repair the existing machines. The technologists who were protecting rulers were themselves controlled. Implants were put into them at the beginning of the

Dark Ages when they were babies; they had no choice. It was kind of like an alien kidnapping and the control device was inserted without knowledge and consent. Then when turned on, they were controlled.

Technology was taught to some on the basis of keeping the machinery running, but the creative developmental work died. When the different aspects of technology died, knowledge died, too, except for how to repair those machines. There was no additional inventive work. The current structures continued to be in place. For those in need of repair, new parts could be made and put in place, but the system did not advance any further.

They could not build, could not replace, and could not develop anything new. They did not do any new research and just knew how to repair what they had, but not how to create new ones. They lost creativity in their training. Nobody was doing any research or building anything. Research died completely. Technologists were only taught how to repair machines they already had. They were simply following the recipes by reading the directions and pushing the buttons. They did not really know why it worked anymore, and it would have been impossible for them to recreate it without any training. They were like business people rather than scientists during the Dark Ages, because they did not have any knowledge of technology.

One of my patients recalled the following past life in Atlantis during the Dark Ages as a technologist.

- *"I am a forty-nine-year-old male living in Beal City on the south west coast of Atlantis. My name is Beri and this is 22,591 BC. I grew up in the dorms. I've lived in four different dorms from five months of age until graduating from college at twenty-three. I was always assigned to a dorm that housed other boys selected for a career in technology.*

   *"I had twelve years of regular school and five years of college. While in college, I studied math, engineering,*

*science, and technology. As a matter of fact, technology was the only program offered by the college at this time. After college, my assignment placed me in a government building outside the dorm. While there, I work to keep the computers running smoothly and do some problem-solving. I don't do any research. No one does research by this time.*

*"My life has always been unstable. All of us live under a threat of natural disasters, such as earthquakes, fires, and floods. This is compounded by the controlled and cruel society in which we live. No one in Atlantis is free. Everyone has implants by now, except the ruler and his close family members.*

*"At the age of twenty-nine, I am being reassigned to the ruler's palace. I'm given a small house located on the palace compound. I live there with four other male technologists. There is a need for more technologists at the palace. In the past, I have demonstrated an outstanding aptitude for problem solving. This has a great deal to do with my new assignment.*

*"At the age of thirty-one, I am put together with a female technologist. This is an arranged union by our ruler. We keep house and live together as husband and wife; the other four male technologists are reassigned to other housing on the compound. We have a daughter when I'm thirty-two, and another daughter when I'm thirty-three. We are permitted to keep and raise them. I continue to do computer maintenance and problem solving.*

*"I've been made chief technologist at the age of forty-two. The ruler and sub-rulers have always found me highly capable. The current chief technologist is retiring and I am replacing him. My main job is administrative. I advise the ruler and coordinate all the technology in the city. My other responsibilities include updating computer memory and speed, adding new hardware and software when necessary, and helping the ruler with people control. In addition, I oversee the implant program to insure*

*that everyone has an implant. I have developed a new software program that allows for coordination of all of our databases. But for all purposes, we don't invent or research anymore. Our concerns are centered around natural disasters and people control.*

*"There is no freedom in our city or anywhere in Atlantis. Our ruler is a controlling and selfish individual. Everyone, especially the general population, is controlled right down to the last detail. Abuse is the norm of the day. During the day, I meet with underlings, both inside and outside the palace. I confer with officials in the government building outside the palace and with the chief administrators of the dorms. I also oversee those who are in charge of the implant program. I'm not diplomatic. I analyze a problem and tell someone how to fix it and expect it to be fixed immediately.*

*"I have two to three meetings with the ruler and his sub-rulers every day. I report on the problems and concerns of the city. I teach seminars concerning technical updates to our other technologists. I also help plan the school curriculum. At this time, we deal in technology schooling only. Plus, I directly oversee the seventeen technologists who work in the palace.*

*"In the evenings, we attend torture parties. They are held every night. Tonight, forty-five of us are attending a human barbecue party. There are three large hearths in our party room. Tonight, there are three naked people (two males and one female) awaiting their fate. The first male is stood up and our ruler drives a sharp steel rod through his ear, through his head, and it comes out the other ear. Others push a steel rod through the back of his ankles. A long steel shaft (perpendicular to the other rods) is attached to these two rods. The victim is attached to a device that holds him over the fire. Slaves on each end of the victim turn him continuously for over two hours.*

*"During this time, we are drinking and cheering. Orgies have begun to break out, as the people get more excited.*

*I'm feeling a rush of adrenaline as the excitement builds. The next two are tied in the same way and they are placed alive over the open fire, which at first barely singes their hair. As they scream in pain, people cheer more loudly and drink more heavily, and they are slowly lowered to the fire. More orgies occur until everyone (my wife included) ends up in a gigantic orgy.*

*"After a few hours, these three are barbecued and we have a banquet and feast on their meat. After the banquet, there is more drinking and more orgies. This party lasts until after sunrise, but very few are standing. I passed out between four and five a.m. and fell asleep. I woke up around noon and someone took me to my apartment.*

*"We have had several small earthquakes in the past that affected our dorms. After our largest escape, it took about a month to round up and kill those who escaped. At the age of fifty-three, we are experiencing a major earthquake. It is noon and we just sat down for lunch. The tremors are violent. Food and dishes fall from the table. Wall hangings tumble to the floor. Furnishings are crashing down around us. I'm in panic. We are running around trying to find a safe place, but there is nowhere to run. Suddenly I'm on the ground outside the palace. I was thrown through a window that was a few feet above the ground.*

*"I'm trembling in fear. I'm shaken up but not injured badly. The tremors continue! I hear people screaming and I see people fall to their death as sections of the palace are destroyed. I see fires blazing all around me. I am on the street, but I'm trapped by fire on all sides. Buildings are falling and the smoke is beginning to choke me. I'm in fear and panic. An object falls and strikes my shoulder. I scream as I'm knocked to the ground. I feel the fire starting to burn my feet and legs. My spirit leaves my body before I catch on fire. My spirit is in shock. I can see that people in the dorms get free. Those who are not free are set free by angry mobs. I see a lot of violence. Any government officials remaining are killed by the mobs. The*

*palace is totally destroyed by the earthquake. I see sick and dying people all over the city. I go to the Light after hundreds of years.*

"In reviewing the life in heaven, I can see that every-body, including me, was controlled by demons. There was no Light anywhere! There were demons and spirits of the dead everywhere, in the palace, the dorms, and in and around people. I also see that the demons moved some land masses in such a way that they became unsta-ble, eventually causing the land to shift and fall into the ocean. From heaven, I see that my parents also lived in the dorms. My father was a technologist and my mother was a research scientist in the technology class. My parents were "put together" to produce me, another technologist. Then I was taken away from them when I was five months old and was raised in a dorm.

"From heaven, I can see different problems that came from that life to the current life, such as difficulty in com-municating with the Light, difficulty in interacting with people, and allowing others to influence me instead of thinking for myself."*

### Brutal Torture During the Dark Ages

Following are some of the past lives during the Dark Ages in Atlantis recalled by my hypnotized patients, which give us glimpses of inhumane, brutal, and hideous tortures done to people during the Dark Ages.

One of my patients recalled the following life in Atlantis as a source of her weight problem.

- *"I am a seventeen-year-old female living in a female dor-mitory in the city of Nabith on the west coast, south of the mountains in Atlantis. My name is Lanhe and it is 30,029 BC. I am a seamstress. I sew clothes for the slaves. I am tied to a frame and the guards put a metal tube in my stomach and force-feed me. They are telling me that they*

were ordered to make me fat. I am kind of plump in spite
of the dorm food. The ruler thinks that if I can get plump
on that type of food, then they can fatten me up fast by
force-feeding me large amounts of food. He thinks that I
will taste better fattened up when I am cooked. They take
the tube out but they put it back in every three or four
hours. So I am getting large quantities of food four or five
times a day. The guards tell me that I am being fattened
up for slaughter because I am plump, but if I had been
fat, they would not want me. Sometimes they mix the food
with seasoning, trying to flavor the meat in me before it is
cooked after they butcher me. They also restrict my exercise so I cannot burn off the fat and build muscles. They
just want smooth fat muscles so it will be real tender and
tasty to eat. I get very fat in a short amount of time.

"After about five months of force-feeding, I get extremely fat. I am taken to the palace, where they take
my clothes off and tie me with my arms and legs spread.
There are several men and women from the ruling class.
There are some servants here to help. There are also several burners, cooking vessels, and a table full of knives.
They are talking about first taking the fat off me and rendering lard from it to turn it into cooking fat. I am just
horrified to death.

"They start on one side and cut away the skin and fat.
I am screaming but cannot move because I am still tied
down. They peel off a thick layer of yellow, smelly fat and
toss it to the servants who prepare the grease. Different
people are working on different parts of my body to cut
the fat off. After all the fat is peeled away, they have anal
and vaginal sex with me and also with each other. I cannot stand it. I want to die but cannot. I start drifting in my
mind. I seem to turn inward and separate my soul from my
body, as if putting a wall around myself. They cut my legs
at the knees and then in the middle of the thigh with a saw.
I pass out and my spirit is out of my body. They clamp my
arteries so I do not bleed to death. Then they cut open my

*abdomen and take out my intestines, stomach, liver, and
pancreas, and pop out my eyes. At this point, I die.*

*"My last thoughts are I want to be fat so they will not
want me, as the guards explained, and not be cut open
and eaten. I never want to feel this way again. The guards
told me I was chosen because I was plump but not fat. My
spirit is confused, dazed, and just wandering around. I am
not trying to possess or harm anyone, but I feel oblivious
to everything. I am just withdrawn, sort of like into myself,
just going around and not really in touch with anyone. I
am just wandering aimlessly and blindly, as if I am shut
off from everything. It was almost as if I were driven insane by the torture.*

*"After about twelve years, I am not as dazed and con-
fused. I see a being in a bright Light who takes me to
heaven. There are two women sitting in the reception area
because my experiences with the male guards and the rulers were so negative. I tell these women about what happened to me. It did not bother me that I was raised in the
dorm and had to work hard, because I did not know of
anything different. I told them how empty and emotionless
that life was. There were no connections with anybody,
not a single human being, male or female. The guards told
me that I was selected because I was plump, that if I had
been fatter, my muscles would have had too much fat in
them and would not taste good. By force-feeding me, they
hoped to give me a huge outer layer of fat but with little
fat in my muscles. Apparently it makes a difference. If I am
fat as I grow and remain fat for a long time, the fat gets
mixed into the muscles. If you are lean and then suddenly
get fat, it doesn't get incorporated into the muscles.*

*"I began to wish to be fat so they would not want me
and would not do this to me. I did not like it when they
force-fed me to get me fat so that they could slaughter
and eat me. Then I talked about being confused and lost
as a spirit and was unable to perceive the outside, as if
I was catatonic. It was as if I were in a void and had a*

*screening wall around me. From heaven, I see that the demons could not get to me because the wall looks like a white fog. When I came to the reception area in heaven, my body still did not have skin or fat. As I vented my feelings, I became whole.*

*"Then I was sent to a cleansing station where I cleansed myself in a pool, and all the excess fat disappeared and I was slim again. After that, I am sent for a life review, where I see Melson, a god of the coastal areas, who was worshiped in Atlantis. From heaven, I see that part of my purpose was to experience the feelings of helplessness I had inflicted on others in past lives.*

*"I see that I lost soul parts from every part of my body, and demons have them in hell. They are stuffing dark fat-like stuff through these soul parts and their connecting cords in my body, which is making me fat.*

*"I see that I planned to learn the need for compassion and empathy by experiencing the absolute lack of it from the torturers, and also to make up for a life in the past when I was hard-hearted and cared little for other people and animals and their feelings. Even doing this to animals sickens me. It is as bad as doing it to humans. To use animals for research, we must have respect and compassion for them. We cannot be cruel or callous, and if the animal suffers some pain, we need to do our best to alleviate it. If an animal gets burned, we shouldn't just leave it to be burned; we should protect it. We cover it or do whatever we can do.*

*"If the animal is cut up for research or dissected like in science class, we do what we can to anesthetize it and provide stitching and pain relief or whatever we can do. We have to have respect and compassion for animals, just as we do for people. From the heavenly point of view, sometimes the research is needed, but we must work with compassion and with respect toward the animals. The animal may not understand why it is being used this minute, but there was consent in heaven. If we treat the animal with cruelty and without compassion and respect, then*

*it becomes our karma that will have to be paid in future
lives. You can repay the karma by doing positive work or
by suffering the same ill.*

*"From heaven, I see many problems coming from that
life to the current life, such as my weight problem, back
pain, arthritis, aches and pain all over my body, and gastrointestinal problems. I also have throat pain due to the
metal feeding tubes and when they pulled my tongue out
and put nails in it so I could not scream so much.*

*"When you, Dr. Modi, asked the angels to remove all
the dark and negative fat that was pumped in me, it came
out as fragmented , dark gray fat. Then they cleansed
my whole body and brought back all my soul parts to my
whole body and also to the fat that I lost when it was cut
from my body, from people, places, and hell, and integrated with me after cleansing and healing them."*

- *"I am a twenty-seven-year-old female living in a female
dorm in Gaspon, a big city on the northeastern coast of
Atlantis. My name is Nailina and it is 21,386 BC. There
are no old people in the dormitories. They are not desired
in some ways. I was told to cohabit with a man to have
children. I had three children with that man but they were
taken from us after six to twelve months. I miss them.*

*"My job is to grow things. First I plant the seeds in
pots and then transfer them to fields. I've lived in the
dorms all my life except for the time I was asked to live
in another place with a man to have children. There are
hundreds of women living in this dorm. I live in a room
with twelve females. The room is long and narrow, with
beds stacked on both sides and a space in the middle to
walk around and sit. There are no electric lights anymore. We work when it gets light, so we can see what we
are doing, and plant until it is almost dark. Some women
are responsible for preparing food, cleaning different
places, and other jobs. We do the same thing day after
day. In the night, we have to be in our rooms and are*

*not allowed out. So we play games in the dark. We play sexual games with each other.*

*"I feel that my time is coming close because people are taken away and they never come back. There is a feast day coming up. It is the festival of Marduk, the god of ocean commerce. Our city is near the ocean, so this god is very important to us and the festival is celebrated for three days. A lot of people disappear on the feast day and never come back. Sometimes, all the people from a room disappear and never come back. I do not know what happens to them.*

*"Guards come and they are dragging all of us out of the room. We are gagged and bound and only our feet can move. They put us in tall cages in a long hallway. There is a partition between each cage. I am feeling terror. I do not know what is happening but I know it is not good. The next day they take me to a big room and it smells funny, like crusty blood. They strap me down on a slanted board, naked, with my arms and legs spread apart. There are two or three hundred people here, both male and female, and there is electric light. It is like a party. They are drinking. There is a lot of laughter. There are three girls on tables in this room down the hall.*

*"They are poking me with a knife and talking about preparing dinner. I realize they are talking about me. I am the dinner and they are going to eat me. I am terrified and shaking all over. It is very bizarre. They are tenderizing the meat in me by beating me all over the body with a device with a lot of streamers on the handle. There are lumps at the end of the streamers; they sting and hurt. I am screaming and crying, feeling powerless. They are laughing and joking and taking their clothes off. They are taking turns raping and beating me and also having sex with each other. They cut my skin all over so they can see the blood drip.*

*"They are talking about lady fingers, and one person grabs my finger with what looks like a pair of pliers and*

*pulls apart the finger joint and then cuts my finger off at the joint and does the same with all my fingers. An oven is wheeled in, and there is a charcoal fire. My fingers are laid on the tray and put in the oven on low heat. They are talking about how good lady fingers are. Similarly, they cut off my toes one by one. They are clamping the blood vessels so that I do not die of blood loss. The women are even crueler. They are putting pinchers on my nipples and crushing my breasts with devices and pushing tools with teeth into my vagina.*

*"Somebody has grabbed my hair and is pulling it. It comes out along with patches of scalp. It hurts like crazy. I am screaming and screaming but they do not care. They are talking about using my hair for decoration. They are cutting different parts of my body systematically and clamping the blood vessels so that I do not die. The pain is so excruciating that most of my soul comes out and only a small part is left in my body to sustain it.*

*"My spirit outside is like anesthetized and feels no pain. I am looking down and watching what they are doing to my body. They cut my legs into pieces up to my hips and then they begin to cut off my hands and my body dies. I am watching in horror. When I realize I am free, I try to attack them with my fists, but get nowhere. I cannot make them see me. I see black demon blobs all over the place. The people are also packed with these black demons. I scream in people's ears but they cannot hear me. I also see two unusual beings that do not look like humans. They are humanoids, short, stocky beings in the spirit form. They are just watching what is going on. I see two spirit people, who come to me and say they are my parents and they have come to take me to the Light (heaven) and I go with them.*

*"My parents take me to heaven. They take me to the reception room and there are two beings waiting for me. They are asking me to talk about my death. I tell them about being bound and helpless, raped, beaten, and cut*

*up, and how scared and panicky I felt. My throat hurts because of the screaming and my disgust with the people for what they did to me. Then I talk about how they took away my three children a few months after they were born. When I came in here, I was hysterical, screaming, yelling and crying and hurting all over, and as I expressed my rage about the brutality, I felt calmer and my body becomes whole.*

*"After cleansing, I am sent to another room. There are Isha, the cow goddess, Diti, a love goddess, and Marduc, the ocean god, who was worshiped when I was in Atlantis. I am furious at him. It was his feast day when I was tortured and killed. He has a human body but a fish face superimposed on his face. Marduk gently reminds me that the demons in the people who were torturing me, and also in the room, were influencing the people, not him. He is asking me to look back and see what I hoped to accomplish in the life. From heaven, I see that I planned to have healthy children as a woman and suffer their loss, even though they continue to live and were healthy. The purpose of this was to balance my actions in past lives when I broke up families. Being tortured and killed was also to make up for negative actions in many past lives when I tortured and killed others.*

*"I also see that during the review stage in heaven, I am also making the choice to carry these marks or symptoms of hair thinning, eye problems, aches and pains, and other symptoms in another lifetime. It is made in the review stage and then reaffirmed when planning for another life, when I chose to have it, and carry it through and keep it until I decide to terminate it. This is part of the mechanism for how this healing works. Marking down means passing it down or handing it down into future lives. I am making a decision to remember the pain in the body in a future life, which is the current life.*

*"In heaven, we also planned a group goal to attempt to start some spirituality in Atlantis, to cut through the*

*negative mist of darkness. Everything and everybody was taken over by the demons and very little Light was there. Since all the social structure and religious beliefs of Atlantis were gone, we planned in the Light (heaven) that we might be able to reintroduce spirituality because the old beliefs and taboos about discussing spirituality were broken.*

*"Another group plan was to develop spirituality through the culture of caring in the dormitories, and that was partially successful. When planting the seeds and plants and working with other girls, I started a culture of caring and helping each other. It was partially successful, and the lesbian relationships at night made it easier to connect and care for each other. My individual goal was to develop personal spirituality.*

*"The lessons I needed to learn were not to do physical damage to other people, and the symptoms I carried over to this life are there to remind me of the positive message of compassion, mercy, love, and caring behind it.*

*"There were many people who were there in that life that are also here in the current life. I also see that many problems came from that life to the current life, such as thinning hair, eye problems, gastrointestinal tract problems, and aches and pains. It was my choice to carry these symptoms over into the current life and now I can choose not to have them. I chose to have those symptoms to help me understand the mechanism that goes into reincarnation and karma."*

• *"I am a twenty-two-year-old female living in Naprox, a southwestern city in Atlantis. My name is Lumilla and this is 21,577 BC. I am living in a woman's dormitory with twelve other females. I had one child a couple of years ago. We were put together in another place and were told to have a child. After a year, our baby was taken away and we were put back in our respective dorms again. I never saw my child or that man again. I work in a factory close to the dormitory. We make shoe parts out of leather.*

*"One night several men came and gagged and bound all the women in my room and took us away. They put us in holding rooms that were soundproof so we could not communicate with each other. I am scared to death. I do not know what is happening. I have heard stories about people who disappeared and never came back. I do not know what happened to them. The next day I am taken into a big room to a platform where they strap my hands, stretching them up and out. I am standing with my feet spread.*

*"There are many men and women in the room drinking and laughing. A group of women come to me. They rip my clothes off and say they are going to enjoy torturing me. Several different women take turns brutally whipping me all over. The men are just watching. After they beat me viciously, the women have sex with the men, as if whipping me excited them sexually. Pretty soon they are having sex with people of the same and opposite sex, while others are still beating me and poking me with knives. I am crying and screaming with pain, but nobody cares. The more I scream, the more vicious they get.*

*"One of the women, who is a queen and whose birthday is being celebrated, puts tubes in my rectum and vagina and pumps in air with a hand pump. I feel stretched and swollen. Then she puts a thick needle in my belly button, not too deeply though, and pumps air just beneath the skin so they can easily take my skin off. My skin is stretching and getting loose. Then she puts the tubes in my breasts and upper and lower back and again pumps air in. Pretty soon I am all ballooned up and the woman screams to stop. She does not want any stretch marks on my skin because she wants to use it as leather later on. Now the men are coming and squeezing my ballooned up breasts to see how they feel. As I am crying and screaming with pain, they are laughing and making cruel remarks.*

*"Then the queen claims my skin. She takes a sharp knife and makes a cut around the front of my neck from*

*side to side. She then begins to cut right down the middle of the front of my body going through my chest, abdomen, though my pubic hair and straight down the inside of both legs. She cuts around the edge of both feet and between my toes and carefully separates the skin. Then she makes cuts on the inside of my arms and around my palms, in between my fingers and very carefully separates the skin to preserve its shape in the form of my body. I am screaming like crazy. Then she starts cutting in the center of the back of my neck and around the top of my head and begins to peel off my face and I am still screaming. They clamp off the bleeding blood vessels so I do not die. I am getting weak and cannot scream anymore. They separate all the skin from my body and take it away, but I am still alive.*

*"Then they begin to cut my body, part by part, starting with my legs, but my body is dead and the rest of me comes out. I realize that when they began to pump air through my rectum and intestines the pain was so intense that my spirit was forced out of my body and only a small part of my spirit remained inside to activate the body. Initially my spirit wanders around in shock. After I get stable, I realize that it is my body being tortured and I watch in horror. My eyes look dead, as if there is nobody inside my body even though it is still alive. I try to hit people but I cannot. After my body dies, the rest of my soul joins me. I am still trying to punch people, and then somehow I am inside a woman who is of low ranking nobility. I am prompting her to stab the queen, and she is tempted, but does not want to do it in front of everybody. I can see through her eyes that they are cutting my body apart. They are cooking and eating pieces.*

*"Several weeks later, I continue to influence the woman I am in. I get her to push another woman into the fire while they are preparing another victim to be barbecued alive. There is a wood fire with a brick and clay oven around it and there is a metal rod to fasten the person to, with a handle on the outside to turn it. They are getting the fire*

*hot so it will be ready to roast. I give her the idea to push another woman into the fire who is helping her prepare the fire, and she does it. The other royals accept it as an accident. I prompt the woman I am in and she kills two other lower ranking royals, one by throwing into a mechanical grinder and another by pushing her off a tower. Now people are suspicious of her.*

*"I can see through the eyes of the woman I am in, the different ways they torture and kill their victims. They tie a person to a rod and roast her over a fire. As the skin is cooking, it becomes crisp, and the victim screams and screams. They also use electric shock, cutting, twisting, whipping, skinning, scalping, sexual tortures, and twisting the body in ways it could not go. They have these torturing parties almost every day. The reason these lower royals are doing all the preparations themselves is because they do not trust their servants. They are afraid the servants might kill them.*

*"By now I am aware that I am not alone in this person. I am sensing a dark, malevolent presence. It just clicks in my thinking that what these dark evil beings are pushing these people to do is the same as what I am pushing her to do. It is as if the dark ones and I are cooperating, and if they are evil, then what am I? Could these dark and evil things also be in me? Why am I so angry and vengeful? I find that a very chilling thought. I do not want to do anything with these evil dark beings that could probably tear my soul apart. This pushes me into a lot of introspection.*

*"I look for any dark thing in me and find it. I do not have much religious inclination, so I use an Atlantean phrase, which is, "In the name of all that's holy," which is considered swearing because it talks about the spiritual in public. I am yelling at the demon in me, "In the name of all that's holy, get out of me," and it works. I am cursing at the demon and it is forced out of me and I am healed enough to be free. I manage to push myself out of the lady. I am not confused anymore and I can actually see clearly.*

*I see a woman I knew who liked me when I was a child who points to the Light and explains that is where I need to go. I still do not trust anybody. I tell her to go first then come back and then I will go with her. The closer I get to the Light, the more I feel love expanding in me and around me. I never felt this in Atlantis.*

"I am taken to a table where two Light beings invite me to talk to them about my life. One of them is introduced as the third king of Atlantis named Hegaman, who dates back to a time long ago when there was only one king for the whole continent. When we swore, we did not swear "by god" but "by King," since they were the most famous, powerful, and important people in Atlantis. I knew his name. People in Atlantis knew him as caring, fair, and respectable, and Atlanteans called on him to witness our oaths. Another king's name was Gunine, and he was also a central king of Atlantis long ago. He was very fair, kind, and caring.

"I tell them how horrible and humiliating it was to be tortured that way and how the demons came into me, and how I possessed that woman and influenced her to kill others. Also how I pushed the demon out and then willed myself out of her body. Then I tell them about all the misery I went through growing up in the dorm without any love or affection. I tell them how I worked for years and about being put with a man and forced to have a baby who was taken away at one year of age. I feel better after unloading all these feelings.

"After cleansing, I am sent to a room for life review. There are three people there. One of them is Nemotion, who was the first king of all of Atlantis. He was a central ruler who was fair and kind and people called on him for help. We used to hear stories in the dormitory about how great Atlantis used to be when they had a central king.

"From heaven, I see that one of my life's purposes was to interfere and disrupt how Atlantis operated. I did succeed to some extent in this by keeping the old memories *alive by telling old stories about how great Atlantis and its rulers were a long time ago, and repeating the stories of peace, prosperity, and freedom. Also at the end, my possessing the lower royalty member and motivating her to kill other royals caused suspicion and a split in the ruling class. I began the use of curses, which were in fact prayers, and I was responsible for reestablishing these curses. I created some new stories in the dorms that were true and inspirational. I see that my heavenly guides were providing these stories to me. I told stories of the central kings and rulers during the Golden Age of Atlantis who ruled for the good of the people and not what would make them more powerful. These kings showed up during my debriefing and also during my life review stage in heaven. I also chose to have demons in me due to pain and suffering and learn how to get rid of them and reject them on my own, which was a real challenge. These were my personal and group goals.*

*"As I look back from heaven, I see all of Atlantis completely black and the rulers packed with black and red demons, which were walking, talking, and acting through their bodies as a person's soul was controlled and pushed back. I literally see these demons in these people watching TV, having sex with each other, and plotting and planning to torture and kill people. It is like they were in charge of the body, and the soul of the person was covered by a demon and pushed back.*

*"Many of my current life problems came from that life, such as abdominal bloating, dry skin, arthritis, and aches and pains all over my body. After the forgiveness, the soul parts were brought back and integrated to complete the healing. I saw the soul parts coming back to all the parts of my body and being re-integrated.*

*"Anytime I tried to exercise in the past, I felt more swollen, as if somebody had pumped something in me. This comes partly from that life when air was pumped into me.*

"*I can see that the way the queen made a cut in the skin from the center of my head, face and front parts of my body, affected all my chakras, and the cut in the center of the back from the head down to the lower end of the spine affected the kundalini, and all the other cuts down the limbs affected the meridians, which are blocked in this life. This interferes with the energy flow supply to the body. There is also a dark overlay of the negative energy resulting from the memory of this vicious attack.*

"*From heaven, I can see that when the attack came in that life upon the body and upon the spirit, it was not just by the person holding the knife, but there was also a spiritual attack by the demons inhabiting the person's body, of the other demons that were inhabiting the bodies of the people in the room. It was a combined demonic attack. So, as each of the chakras was being physically injured, the demons in the people also attacked the spiritual bodies. This clogged the energy system of that body at that time and the spiritual memory of it is carried over so that from incarnation to incarnation it affected me moderately or not at all, depending upon my life plan. It is as if the demons had planted a booby trap so that in the current life, which is devoted to the spiritual and to God's work, these blocks in the energy system from that past life would lead to a concentrated demonic attack on the soul.*

"*When the demons attacked me through these people, not only my soul parts left from the physical body but also from each of the spiritual or non-physical bodies, too. So it is possible for the demons to launch an attack on any of the specific bodies, such as the physical, spiritual, etheric, or mental. This caused me some depression, and aches and pain and lethargy. My psychic and healing abilities were interfered with. I see that because of today's healing, I can use my fourth chakra to broadcast God's Light to people and hands to heal.*

*"From heaven, I see that there is a huge black Satan's command center in the space almost covering most of Atlantis. From this black command center, there are black cords going to every person and every building, and the demons in that command center are feeding different ideas to torture people and do other evil actions. The command center was blocking the Light from heaven, and since most people did not pray for help, very little Light was going to Atlantis and its people."*

## Role of Satan and His Demons in Atlantis

There were many things that caused extreme demonic influences all over Atlantis and led to the downfall of Atlantean culture and the ultimate destruction of Atlantis. Satan and his demons influenced, possessed, and totally controlled Atlantis and its people by influencing them in certain areas, such as: religion, technology and its use, motivating people to use drugs, and ultimately influencing rulers who lost respect for humanity and treated them as animals. Also they affected energy vortexes negatively and influenced people, leading to atomic explosions and the destruction of Atlantis.

According to heavenly beings, Satan had a special plan for Atlantis from the beginning and he succeeded in it. Here, we will look at the role of Satan and his demons as they influenced and created the attitudes of Atlanteans. In Atlantis, different factors made it more open to negative influences. One was lack of support for each other. They did not have the integrated bringing in of God's Light. Individuals could get Light, but there were no spiritual or religious groups to bring more Light in their areas. There was no mutual support within the group. There was no group that was serving as a channel for the Light to come in. One individual cannot bring as much Light as a group can.

Some of the reasons responsible for the downfall of Atlantis are as follows:

### *Religion and Demonic Influences*

As described before, starting way back when Atlantis was lightly populated and before there was any homogeneous mixing, there were people of all colors and races who came from Africa, Europe, Mediterranean, South, Central, and North America, and settled there. Over the years, they intermingled in Atlantis and spread. Although there were tendencies toward skin color, darker in the south and lighter in the north, still Atlantis had a pretty homogenous population. These people brought the elements of their religions with them, which Satan and his demons emphasized, such as the privacy of religion. Within the groups that came from Africa were those who believed there were rites to be conducted in secret and no one else should know what they are doing. Some religious rituals were only for two people and not for a congregation or a group of people. This tendency was emphasized to keep it private and to keep religious activities limited to only one person rather than in groups.

Among the brown people who came from South America, the oral tradition was very weak. Knowledge was passed on individually and as much by example as by describing or speaking. Satan also enforced that tendency. The settlers who came from Africa and those who came from South America had multiple gods. These tendencies were also encouraged by Satan, and different groups were motivated to amplify the role of one of the gods. So they had different primary gods from village to village as their people spread out in Atlantis.

On the west central coast of Atlantis, there were groups made up of North American Indians with red skin. They were worshipping elemental things such as rain, water, fire, and wind. They recognized the spirits in them. Here Satan introduced a personification of the non-material beings and tried to turn them into material beings and encouraged people to worship material beings rather than the spiritual being. They were also promoted to worship the animal spirits as if the animal spirits were superior to the human spirit. South and North American Indians also came together, but very slowly. They were very different in their looks and in religious beliefs. The primary reasons for the slow settlement of the North American Indians were that there were very few women and their numbers did not grow fast.

The settlers who arrived from the northwestern part of Europe also had belief in multiple gods when they arrived. Here also, Satan applied the tactics of different villages worshiping different gods so there would not be any central figure. These people had collective worship as well as private worship at home. With them, Satan enforced the idea of private worship at home and diminished the importance of worshipping in groups in public.

As these groups spread, Satan caused them to emphasize privacy in religion and lessened the importance of public and group worship, making sure that there were multiple primary gods and stressing different gods in different villages. He also personified spirits so that the spirit of the wolf was not the important thing, but the personification of the spirit, by creating a picture or statue of the animal, was the important thing.

As the people were spreading and more and more of Atlantis was being colonized, these tendencies were encouraged and the importance of group worship was diminished. The secrecy and the lack of public teaching were emphasized, and one-to-one instruction became important. Satan tried to apply modesty and social restrictions to religion, giving it the feeling that it was forbidden and was a taboo. People were embarrassed to discuss religion and spirituality in public.

Over hundreds of years, people of different races, of various colors and religions, began to run into each other and merge with each other, not always peacefully. There were disagreements and fights. The merging was occurring fastest in the south between brown and black people, then between red and brown Indians. The darker and white groups merged in the mountain range. Then white people went south and blacks and browns moved north as the merging occurred. Usually Satan works through racial and religious hatred, but he did not do that in Atlantis.

As the Atlanteans settled and there was a merger of all these religions, Satan emphasized different things, such as shame and embarrassment about discussing religion and spirituality in public and keeping it personal and private; minimal religious instructions; religious rituals were kept private; and stressing the belief in multiple gods with each city having a chief god.

Not only did the people from different parts of the world bring their own religion, each city and region of Atlantis had their local gods. So in the same coastal city with traders or settlers from the foreign lands, there were perhaps as many as four gods of the sea, all with their own characteristics and their own representative form. All in all, when they were combined, they would have a complete picture of what these gods of the sea would be like in all aspects. As settlers moved inland from area to area, they ran into other views of what the gods of the sea would be like. They had gods of the river, gods of the lake, gods of the rain, and gods of all the aspects of water. So they ended up with multitudes of gods representing one part of nature.

Atlantean gods were mostly nature gods and animal gods. Very seldom did people of Atlantis identify any aspect of human behavior or human understanding of divine person-ification. It seemed to be a very foreign concept to them. They did not see anything divine in the nature of man. They went outside of themselves in search for divinity, finding more divine in animals and nature than they did in humans. They had a low concept of the divine nature of humanity. It did not occur to them that any part of humanity had a divine character. Their eyes were turned outward from themselves. The essential human nature as they saw it was greedy, lust-ful, and deceitful; all in all, not inspiring a confidence in the human spirit.

Conversations about religion, philosophy, psychology, and spiritual discussions, became obscene and the scholars would back off from the topic. These topics were not a matter for discussion. This kept scholars from noticing any aspect of humanity that might be divine. The belief in multitudes of gods made it very easy for Satan to induce error in the thinking of the worshippers. Satan can start any group on a path of error and allow it to spread in all the religions that worshipped the deity of that aspect.

As always, Satan worked in many ways at the same time. The individuals believing in different gods were influenced to produce different aspects of their worship, which could spread around the whole continent. Satan also affected the priestly class, who were most responsible for religious education, rituals, and worship. They were influenced on a philosophical basis to change the direction of the religion, the content of the understanding of God, and to interfere with the relationship between God and men. The attack upon the priests was very damaging because it ended up influencing more people or the whole society quickly. In Atlantis, by controlling the priestly class, Satan changed the content of religion, changing the approach to worship and the intent of the priestly class, so that they became less mercy centered.

Another technique Satan used here was that he discouraged the religious orders and encouraged individual priests, so there was no central force for the worship of one particular god. The priest of the individual god at each city would not associate with the priest of the next city. There was no common ground, no mutual understanding, and even the priests were embarrassed to discuss religion. There were no central religious or spiritual authorities. A standard of conduct was not imposed by religion; instead, it was a civil thing done by the civil rulers. Some of the towns had elected officials, some had hereditary rulers, and some had officials appointed by virtue of merit. Satan had managed to make religion obscene and embarrassing. A single individual could bring some Light through individual practice, but not anywhere close to what a group of people could. A group of three is the smallest group you can use. The amount of Light enlarges exponentially with a group of three than when three people pray individually.

When the Lamurians came to Atlantis around 80,000 BC, Satan had a very hard time influencing them because of their intense spiritual nature, so he tried to block Atlanteans from understanding the spiritual concepts of Lamurians. Satan immediately created a wall between Lamurians and Atlanteans. In Lamuria, people had intense spirituality. They were doing many spiritual practices and had their minds turned toward God. It made it very difficult for Satan and his demons to get a foothold in Lamuria. Lamurians could see, sense, and recognize the demonic influences and totally rejected them. Atlantis was a different proposition all together. Demonic influence was there in Atlantis all along. This was definitely a culture that was influenced by the dark side from the beginning. Lamurians first came where the North American Indians settled, in the middle of the west coast of Atlantis. Atlanteans saw the Lamurians having psychic ability, which they did not understand, and they tried to duplicate it with technology.

The religions did not exert a strong positive influence worth mentioning on anybody until after the Lamurians came to Atlantis about 80,000 BC. Lamuria was probably the most uplifting thing that happened to Atlantis. They became the first positive influence for the Atlantean culture. There was always law and always an element of fairness till that time, but it was not the most stressed part of the culture. When Atlanteans came in contact with Lamurians, they detected that Lamurians had the spiritual nature and psychic abilities that the Atlanteans did not have, and they could see the potential value of it. So the Atlanteans decided to duplicate it through technology without developing spirituality first. This was a decision that was influenced by Satan and his demons.

Atlantis had the culture and the background to be able to develop, but religion did not hold them back or interfere with scientific development, because of religion's fragmented nature; that is, the worship different aspects of God. According to heavenly beings, there were places on earth where culture had enough ability but religion held down scientific achievement. This happened in Europe with Christianity, and also in some Moslem countries after the Golden Age, when religion served as a negative influence in science. They over-stressed spiritualism and neglected the physical world. There are always negative effects when things get out of balance.

### Technology and Demonic Influences

Satan also influenced alien race four, who came to Atlantis around 70,000 BC, and alien race five of group two, who came around 50,000 BC, to give different technology to Atlanteans that they were not ready for, and they were not ready to cope with the advancement that technology provided to their society. Satan gave Atlanteans the idea to use technology to control and dominate society, to use it uncritically without thinking about what effect it would have upon humanity. Atlanteans were growing crystals and studying their properties. They already had learned physics and chemistry. When the aliens came, they gave Atlanteans the technology to include impurities into the crystals so that the crystal would function in a different way. Atlanteans learned about electricity, optics, magnetism, the science of how light acts, how it changes speed from one medium to another and how it diffuses, and atomic theory through crystallography.

Atlantis advanced in technology much more than any other part of the world because, being an island, it was bounded all around and was self contained as compared to other parts of the world. Later, with the strong central government, there were people under one will, so there was a great deal of cooperation but no religious and moral restriction. The technology given by aliens was developed and later misused by the Atlanteans because of their lack of spirituality, morality, and respect for fellow human beings. They withdrew and became isolated from the world. They had communication via radios throughout the country so new information and technology would spread all over the continent.

### Genetic Modification and Demonic Influences

Satan also influenced Atlanteans to do genetic modifications on humans, animals, fishes, and plants, which obliterated their spiritual karmic imprints and the organism did not even know how to grow because its purpose and destiny was changed. This also allowed more demonic influences in everything.

Atlanteans did genetic modifications on fishes, different animals, and plants they would eat, by making animals bigger and fatter and plants more productive. Here is another heinous crime they did not understand. When they modified different plants, they changed the seed that was produced, and that seed was no longer in keeping with the karmic plan for this plant. Plants have karmic imprints, too. Everything has DNA, and when you make a modification in DNA, you change the plan. By making changes in the plant DNA, they changed the plan for that plant. The contact with the spirit that infuses the food with life, above and beyond the simple chemistry, is missing. It provides substance to the body, sustains the body, but does not sustain the spirit. You can eat this food to satisfy the body's hunger and still be spiritually hungry.

According to my hypnotized patients, at the beginning, there was a great improvement in people's lives due to genetic modifications, but there were drawbacks too. When we tamper with the DNA, we are not just tampering with the physical; we are also tampering with the spiritual. Positive and negative karmas are also imprinted on the DNA, so when we tamper directly with the DNA, we are also interfering with the spiritual part of the DNA. The Atlanteans did not conceive of this at all, and they had no understanding of this.

According to heavenly beings, in Atlantis when the genetic experiments began, there were a few people who were genetically modified. In the next few years, there were dozens, and in a hundred years, there were thousands of genetically modified humans, until it became like a factory process and roughly half the population had some genetic modifications. People were getting more and more out of touch with the spirit and less and less in touch with their karma.

### Rulers and Demonic Influences

Over the years, the influence of Satan became stronger and moved more directly into the governing people who affected the lives of all Atlanteans. The aliens, who were basically good, were also influenced by the demons who manipulated them to give technology to Atlanteans before they were ready. The seeds of destruction were being planted by Satan from the beginning of Atlantis, and the technology that would bring about the destruction was already coming into play.

In Atlantis, there was an essential selfishness in people to begin with. People had a basic underlying suspicion; that is, "I am suspicious of you; I need to feel secure." This was a fertile field for Satan and his demons. You can think in terms of some paranoia; that is, do not give others an advantage over you. I have mine and I do not care where you get yours as long as it is not mine. Selfishness was in every aspect of their lives.

At the end, Satan totally took over the ruling class that was the most influenced. It was those who were responsible for the final downfall of Atlantean culture and society. They were totally possessed and controlled by Satan and his demons. The misapplication of technology, loss of morality, suspicious nature, lack of prayers and spirituality, no understanding of the nature of humanity, and lack of respect for humanity made it possible to take humans down to animal food status, all under the direction of Satan and his demons.

They did not recognize the unity of God, did not realize that there is one supreme being, and did not pray. Instead, they looked at the different aspects of God as being separate gods.

## Demonic Command Centers

According to my hypnotized patients, because of the lack of spirituality, there were strong demonic influences turning Atlanteans into selfish, evil people. During the Dark Ages, all of Atlantis was covered with a huge black command center in the space, and from it, there were black cords going to every person and place. Demons were literally controlling them through those dark connections telling them what to do. There was very little Light coming from heaven because people did not pray and ask for help.

## Energy Vortexes and Demonic Influences

According to heavenly beings, Atlantis had many vortexes, which were the natural consequences of creation. Vortexes are formed by spiritual currents everywhere, as the natural consequences of matter through the spirit. Since the universe actually has spirit, manifestations of matter moving through spirit causes a movement of spiritual energy. Where conditions are right, spiritual energy can turn into a whirlwind. To begin with, the vortexes are of positive energy; that is, of the Light source. Those places where vortexes exist on Earth are called "power places," because powerful, positive Light energy floods in the vortexes and the surrounding areas.

Vortexes can be strengthened positively or negatively, depending upon the people living around them and their culture. If people are spiritual, more positive Light energy floods through the vortexes and their surroundings. If people are not spiritual, it decreases the positive qualities of the vortex. If negative influence is very strong, it actually turns the vortex into a negative force. It is a progressive thing, first by diminishing the positive value of the vortex until it is neutral, and then, if the negativity of people is even stronger, then that starts to turn the vortex to negative. We then develop a sort of equilibrium situation as the vortex is putting out its negative energy. When people get that negative energy, they become more negative, and when they become more negative, they feed the negativity back to the vortex. The vortex in turn enlarges and becomes more negative, and it puts out the strong negative energy to the people. So you have this mutual feeding of the system set up.

Vortexes normally are in mountainous areas, and spiritual energy flows more freely there.

My hypnotized patients, from the Akashic records, described that in Atlantis there were many vortexes. The big vortex was on the north side of the mountains, which was in the center of the continent. It was in the high plains area. There were more vortexes in the rough country, the high places in mountains, and two smaller vortexes in the high country south of the mountains. There were only two in the flat areas, one down in the southwestern tip of Atlantis, and one in the northeastern side, just above the big seacoast city.

According to my hypnotized patients, before people came to settle in Atlantis, all the vortexes were of positive Light energy. Later, as the people became less spiritual and more dark, they attracted more and more darkness to Atlantis and its vortexes, which in turn fed more negative energy to people, who in turn became very dark and negative and rejected the Light. As a result, the Light had to be retrieved from Atlantis because God does not interfere with people's free will. In time, Atlantis became totally dark, around 30,000 BC and its people were totally controlled by Satan and his demons.

## Drug Use and Demonic Influences

There was continual shipment of raw materials from Atlantean colonies to Atlantis. Also drugs such as opium, marijuana, cocaine, and other hallucinogenic drugs came to Atlantis from all over. Satan encouraged the use of drugs in the general population and also in the priestly and ruling class, thus opening them to demonic influences even more.

Atlanteans knew of opium, marijuana, and other hallucinogenic drugs. They already knew that drugs can alter consciousness. After they got the concept of spiritual and psychic experiences from observing the Lamurians, they realized that there were other benefits in the altered states of consciousness. They assumed, without practical experience, that the drug-induced trance was a religious state, identical or, at least, very similar to what the Lamurians had. So they began to use drugs that way, thinking they were experiencing spiritual and psychic experiences similar to the Lamurians.

They had this concept of a quick and easy way and it seemed to be very attractive to them to be spiritual without having to be spiritual. In Atlantis, spirituality was considered to be a waste of time and very silly. Rather than go through the developmental process of prayers, meditation, worship, etc., they tried to speed up the process and short-circuit it by using drugs, believing that they were experiencing the same thing as the Lamurians were.

Atlanteans did not realize that spiritual trances are vibration-raising, positive experiences, while the drug-induced trances lower a person's vibrations and are negative experiences. Drugs are something that actually slow vibration rates and result in an altered state, but not one that is beneficial. They certainly do not bring you closer to the Light or closer to the creator. Drug-induced states have a dampening effect. First, by lowering the vibration rate, they put people into a lower state of being and cut down on the flow of the higher vibrations from the Light. People are less easily influenced by the Light and more easily influenced by the demons. Drugs also weaken the protective electromagnetic energy fields around people, allowing the demons and other spirits to come in and control them.

During the Dark Ages, drug use for spiritual experiences was widespread among the ruling class which weakened their electromagnetic energy fields around them. This made it easier for demons to totally and completely possess them and make them violent, greedy, and have desire to control people for selfish reasons. This was another reason for the downfall of Atlantis and its ultimate destruction.

## Destruction of Atlantis

Heavenly beings, speaking through my hypnotized patients, say that Atlantis was always unstable and shifting, and as parts of it went under, new land was raised up. Atlantis changed shape dramatically over the years, even shifting a bit to the south and to the west. There were also three atomic explosions and shifting of the tectonic plates under the land. As they moved, the plates got pushed down and dipped into the water. This caused a lot of earthquakes and volcanoes as the material melted. This sinking of land was a gradual process. Many flood stories came out of this, including the story of the Noah's Ark. The geologic conditions and the alien interference disrupted the power supply, causing the back-up system to fail and allowing technologists in the palace to destroy the control mechanism so that the ordinary people could rise up.

### Geologic Conditions

The cataclysmic destruction began around 30,000 BC, when earthquakes and volcanic activities began to rock the continent. There were atomic explosions, leading to more disruptions. Initially, disasters were scarce. Then, generation after generation, they escalated more and more, and by 20,000 BC, most of Atlantis was under the waves with only small parts left. By 13,000 BC, it was all gone except a few mountain remnants here and there, where they exist now as small islands in the Atlantic Ocean.

The reason for the disappearance of Atlantis was a rapid shifting of the crust of the earth, which was displaced downward where it dropped. When the crust shifted and dropped, it was accompanied by many earthquakes and volcanic activities. The land dropped dramatically and new volcanoes erupted, both on the continent of Atlantis as well as around Atlantis. When that crust plate dropped, it drew a lot of water in and, as a result, the sea level went down and the shift in the sea level occurred. Some of the volcanoes have not been found because they have submerged. One big one that has been found has been considered to be a crater where an asteroid hit, but it was a giant volcano.

There were weaknesses in the landmass that gradually began to separate and pull apart. Disasters like earthquakes, fires, and floods disrupted the control system in some cities. Dorm people felt confusion and a rush of relief. They felt as if bondage was broken and then they felt freedom. Once they realized that for all their lives they were totally controlled like robots, they became furious. As they found out the rulers were responsible for controlling them, they rushed to the palaces like an angry and violent mob. They found and killed rulers and government officials and their family members. They were shocked to find human parts and were horrified to find that the rulers were eating humans. Many people died due to disasters, while others were killed by angry mobs. Those who could find a ship or a boat escaped to another country. Some died during the journey and others landed in other countries and settled there. Those who could not escape lived in almost empty cities until they died in another disaster.

### Atomic Explosions

The Atlanteans were using power sources to run their control devices and provide the energy to their cities. According to my hypnotized patients, they started out using natural means, such as sunlight, heat energy, ocean water, or the wind to create their electricity. They had nuclear sources, which they used without proper understanding and concern for those who worked around nuclear power, and without appreciation of the destructive power of nuclear energy. This also contributed to the destruction of Atlantis. During the Dark Ages, technologists became incompetent and nuclear reactors were tended improperly, with a lack of knowledge, lack of caring, and lack of forethought. As a result, there were nuclear explosions, and some of them shook the land, which broke the foundations of the land and contributed to the destruction.

My hypnotized patients say that in Atlantis there were three atomic power plants. The first power plant was toward the center and just south of the mountains on the plains. The second was among the mountains in the valley. Here, the city itself was on the fault line and the atomic pile was on one side of the fault line. Here, they did not have other sources of energy, such as wind power, water power, or sufficient sunlight. So atomic energy was brought into use. The third atomic power plant was in the southeast part of the continent, near the coast. Here, people were importing radioactive ore from South America. They had plenty of sunshine here but needed concentrated energy.

There were many radioactive accidents before the explosion. They were learning how to get energy from volcanic heat through the crystals and to convert it into electricity. This way they could use a more concentrated source of energy when energy from sunlight was diffuse. The Atlanteans were great at using very low amounts of electricity to perform a lot of work, but in this case, they needed a concentrated source of energy to power the crystals. This was in the time of the Dark Ages, around 30,000 BC, and they lacked technology, research, and inventions.

The scientists were concentrating on the radioactive elements to get heat energy to power the crystals. They used a combination of radioactive elements, which proved to be a very dangerous cocktail. It made the nuclear reactions very unstable and eventually led to atomic explosions. In addition, they did not have much knowledge of radioactivity and did not have a system to measure it. They learned of the destructive effects of the radioactive elements by seeing people get sick and die from prolonged exposure to them.

Without enough knowledge about geology, the scientists created an atomic pile that eventually exploded on the fault line. As a result, a tremendous amount of energy was released, leading to earthquakes and volcanoes all over the island continent. It was as if Atlantis had been lubricated, as if somebody had squeezed oil in the fault line, and in truth that was what happened. The water and gases were forced between the tectonic plates.

These atomic explosions were most destructive and opened magma channels. This allowed the flow of hot fluid under the earth and made it possible for the continent to slide easily. There was also nuclear fall-out, which caused some radiation damage. Some of the nuclear explosions happened before the revolt and resulted in great loss of life and earth changes.

By this time, nobody was sharing their technology, and everything was done in secret, even the experiments. This first explosion wiped out the entire technical staff and there was nobody left to issue a warning about building the piles too big. When people realized that it was dangerous to be around radioactive material, they piled it up in a large cave at the second atomic plant.

The first atomic explosions did the most damage to Atlantis and shook the entire continent. The fault lines were loosened by the earthquakes and, together with the volcanic activity, they hastened the destruction of the continent by pushing air, gases, and water into the fault lines and lubricating them. The continent broke apart more quickly and began to slide into the ocean.

The city Marduresh, the site of the second atomic power plant, was in a mining area. Their wealth was built on the mines. They had enough agriculture production to support the city, and they produced minerals and ores. This was one of the cities where they had democratically-elected officials,

including those in law enforcement. There were no hereditary rulers. After the first atomic explosion, most of this city
was destroyed because it was on the fault line. They eventually rebuilt it and resumed mining. The residents needed
a massive amount of electric power, so they created bigger
atomic piles, which later caused the second atomic explosion, causing more destruction.

The third atomic power plant was in a southern city that
served as a spiritual center in Atlantis. Its name was Ham-
rvsac. There were no mines and no radioactive material.
People imported radioactive materials from South America
because the ore from the central mines in Atlantis was very
expensive. This power plant also exploded at a later time,
thus explaining why the destruction of Atlantis happened so
rapidly, and how this was geologically possible.

The technologists at this time did not have the research
capacity and did not know how to measure radioactivity.
They knew it was there by its effects on people, but did not
know of the existence of the particles. They just knew that
if you put enough radioactive material together, you could
generate a lot of heat, which they could then use as an energy supply. People became sick with weight loss, hair loss,
cataract formation, gastrointestinal symptoms, ulcerations
in the mouth and gastrointestinal tract, and reproductive
problems, including sterility.

One of my patients who had many physical symptoms recalled a past life in Atlantis in a city in the center of Atlantis,
near the mountains. She was a technologist working in an
atomic power plant that caused her several physical problems, leading to her death.

- *"I am a twenty-four-year-old female living in a dormitory
  in a city called Gonesh, in a valley between the mountains in central Atlantis. My name is Uluwalla and this
  is 24,891 BC. I am a science graduate and a technologist working in an atomic power plant that is close to the
  dorm. The mines are near the power plant. People are*

*hauling the ore to a cave. I have been working here for about a year. We do not have much training or research anymore. We have a rudimentary test for measuring radioactivity. We found that radioactivity will destroy static electricity. Every now and then, we take a chunk from the piles to a separate area and do the test to see how long it takes to destroy the electricity. This gives us a measure of how strong the radioactivity is. We are still learning. I have to go to the pile often without any protective measure.*

*"I am losing weight fast, losing my hair, and my teeth are getting loose. I am developing cataracts in both eyes, having sores in my gums, mouth, and throat, having nausea and vomiting, and am unable to eat anything. I die feeling miserable.*

*"After death, I am very confused. I float around and I find myself in another place, out of Atlantis. I see people living in a family unit with their children. In Atlantis, we never lived in a family unit. I realize what I missed. I stay around a couple, sometimes entering the wife's body and then coming out of her, mostly seeking things I did not have in Atlantis, such as relationship, family, and children. I stay around them for about twenty years. Then I perceive the Light and go to it.*

*"After cleansing and healing, I go for the life review. In heaven, I realize that I planned to spread the word about the dangers of radioactive material in that life and in future lives. It was also a sort of a penance life, to balance my negative karmas from my past lives. I was one of those who served as an object lesson and taught them that they have to get the radioactive material away from people.*

*"From heaven, I see that many problems came from that life to my current life, such as revulsion for technology, eye problems, sores in my mouth, teeth problems, reproductive problems, bone and joint pain, and hair falling."*

- *"I am a twenty-year-old female living in Atlantis in a city
called Sampoon. It is 20,510 BC. I live in a dorm with
twenty-four other women who are all technologists. There
is a nuclear power plant about twenty-five miles away
from the city. People suspect that nuclear energy might
be leaking and affecting people in the city, so they built
a huge building with extremely thick concrete walls with
a dome-shaped structure. They are doing research, ex-
posing the building to nuclear energy and putting several plants, animals, and humans, who are slaves, in the
building. They are giving them certain foods exposed with
nuclear energy and then give shots of an antidote to see if
they live longer. They all look skinny and dehydrated, and
have patchy hair and scaly skin that is peeling off. They
cannot move. I do not like what they are doing to them. I
am working in an office that has big, old computers, and
our job is to make sure that all the data are collected from
the atmosphere.*

*"At the age of twenty-six, we are worried that the nu-
clear plant will explode. I am trying to give this secret
information to other people in the underground group,
and I give them supplies of the antidote that I stole. I am
afraid somebody will find out. I am realizing that these
people with the underground activity, who live in small
villages outside the main city, have more emotions than
all of us who live in the dorm in the main city. We function
almost like robots. I also find a list of elite people, such as
the rulers and other people in the government, who have
some underground shelters.*

*"The core of the nuclear power plant is getting very
hot and we are afraid that it might explode anytime. The
atmosphere is getting bad and there is not much time. Our
supervisors locked me and my five co-workers in the office so we cannot tell anybody what really is happening,
and they all went to the underground shelters. The nuclear power plant, which is about twenty-five miles away
from the city, explodes. It gets hot where I am. I take one*

*breath and it burns my insides. I feel extreme shock and pain, and all of us die instantly. A big Light comes and I see all six of us being pulled into it. We go through dark clouds, then clear sky, and then we are in heaven with baby angels.*

*"We all go to a room where a wise man with a white robe with gold trim is sitting. We are confused and do not know what happened to us. He is trying to explain what happened but we cannot understand him. He and the angels are healing us by putting the Light in us. We feel better and begin to remember what happened. I find myself on a table where several angels are healing me. They take dark devices from the base of my neck and brain, and all the demons, humans, and other spirits and dark energy come out of me. Then they are repairing my DNA and adding the Light in my spine and brain. They have a Light wand and are touching me with it to heal me. I feel happy and blissful. It seems like they are giving my spiritual and emotional self back to me.*

*"Then I am taken to another room where I review my life with three Light beings. I am seeing the movie of my life in my mind and they are seeing it, too. I see that I was born in a sterile environment and people put an implant in the base of my neck. Then they put another device in my brain to take away my emotions. Only the people in the main city had these devices in them, while people who lived in nearby villages do not have these implants because the ruler's central control system could not reach those villages. So they were normal emotionally, mentally, and intellectually. These are the people I was secretly giving information to so they could escape and survive. The Light beings are pointing out that I had some emotions and that is why I wanted to save those people. I see that some of the people to whom I gave the information and shots of antidote survived.*

*"From heaven, I see that it was a karmic life. I needed to learn that you do not have to do anything big. It takes*

*just a little bit of Light to impact a lot of people. Also, how people's lives can be destroyed without love and emotions and that technology without spirituality can be very destructive.*

*"As I look back from heaven, I see many problems came from that life to my current life, such as difficulty in making decisions and not liking computers or technology. They suck the energy out of me. I also do not like a structured environment. That is why I did not like college in the current life.*

*"I see from the Light (heaven) that the explosion of the nuclear power plant caused shifting of the tectonic plates and caused a lot of earthquakes in Atlantis. Part of the land went under the ocean, creating holes.*

*"I see many people who were there in that life are also here in my current life.*

*"When Dr. Modi requested the angels to bring all the soul parts of me and other people who were there and integrate them with whom they belong after cleansing and healing, I saw them doing it. I saw soul parts coming back to my immune system, neck, brain, heart, and to every part of my body and being.*

*"I also see a massive healing of the Atlantic Ocean and all the other water bodies throughout the earth and all the life forms in them."*

### Alien Intervention

The tall, thin human-like aliens of race four of group two regretted giving the technology to Atlanteans who misused it. So they helped in freeing the people by interfering with the power supply. They did not actively promote the destruction in any way. That is, they did not attack the land; they did not cause volcanoes or earthquakes or use weapons against the land. They simply caused interference with the electrical power source. They created the electromagnetic disturbance in the power conduction apparatus, and suddenly all electricity went off and the same thing happened to the back-up supply because they interfered with the main flow of electricity.

These aliens were living in their mountain bases in Atlantis and also on the spaceships. They focused beams of electromagnetic energy at the power supply, generating a huge current surge within the wires and effectively shut the current off. The aliens did this by beaming the electromagnetic energy from two directions at once, from the spaceship and from the mountains, because they had to have the correct line of sight initially to get that set up. That is why they first picked the city near the mountains. After practicing a few times, they got sophisticated enough that they did not need to have the line of sight. They could interfere with indirect beams, while the spaceship would have the direct beam hovering over the city. Together, they made the power surge that caused the power to die.

When the power supply died, the machines could no longer power the crystals that controlled the people, and all of a sudden, the whole population was free of control, including the technologists in the palace. One of the technologists who was in the palace immediately turned off the power-generating crystal so that it could not be restored. The technologists who were in the palace killed the guards and set out to destroy the mechanism. Shortly after that, a crowd of angry people arrived, broke into the rulers' compounds, and killed everybody in the palace. So the whole ruling class, and even the technologists, were also wiped out.

This was done very systematically by the aliens, causing power disruption in one city at a time, which allowed people to get away without extreme crowding and confusion. Part of aliens' concern was to free the cities close to the ocean first so that the docks would be opened and all those people could get out. Then a city further inland would be freed. Otherwise, they were afraid that the people who escaped from an inland city might be captured and they would not have any way to get off the island. The aliens freed many cities, one at a time, and were systematic about it so the people would have time to escape. There were waves after waves of people getting away. Many people went to the coast, boarded ships, and headed east to Europe, the Mediterranean, Africa, and Asia Minor. Some of them headed for Central, North, and South America, but most of them went east. As they settled into new lives, they totally rejected the memories of Atlantis, its technology, and the horror of it. Shortly thereafter, there were a series of earthquakes and large portions of Atlantis went under the water.

Alien race five of group two, who are short, stocky, and human-looking, also helped, but differently. They provided food to people who survived. They would put the food where people could find it. They also stocked the ships with food so that the people would have food and water for the ocean voyage. People often found warehouses full of food on the docks.

A series of cataclysmic events took place from about 22,000 BC to 20,000 BC, during which a major part of Atlantis was submerged in water and only few small highlands and mountains remained above water.

According to heavenly beings, people in Atlantis became so evil that it was literally a cleansing by God, even though God's hand did not reach out and push Atlantis under water. It was like removing that evil from the face of the Earth, as if God removed his sustaining power from the land and did not hold it up any more. If God had willed, he could have moved the tectonic plates and Atlantis would have gone on. So we can look at it from a spiritual point of view, or the physical means by which it was accomplished. These appeared to be two different things but they were not.

My patients recalled the following past lives during the end of Dark Ages when, due to the alien interference and earthquakes, control over the people was broken and dorm people got free. When they realized that rulers had controlled them all their lives, they became angry and hateful and killed everybody in the palace. Some boarded the ships and left, while some stayed in their abandoned city to live the rest of their lives.

- *"I am a thirty-seven-year-old male living in the city of Zarus, located in the northeast of Atlantis about thirty-five miles from the sea. My name is Mica and this is 20,841 BC. I am the son of a ruler. I live in a palace with many servants. I live well and experience many pleasures. I am in line to become the ruler after my father. I am arrogant, short-tempered, selfish, and self-centered. I can be this way because my father is the ruler. I have a wife, many mistresses, and four children. We have crystal devices on all of our buildings and crystal implants in all of our people except the very top-level rulers and their families. My father and I send our control messages through a microphone-like device that is part of our computer. These messages of control are transmitted to the crystal on top of our palace, and from there to all the crystals over the buildings in the city, which receive our messages and transmit them to all our subjects, who think of them as their own thoughts. That is why our control system is so successful.*

    *"Long before my birth, there were a series of earthquakes, fires, and floods. As a result, control of the people in the city has been disrupted numerous times. When I was fifteen, an earthquake destroyed part of the city. Control was disrupted and it took over a month to restore it. When I was thirty, a major earthquake was followed by fire and floods. As high as 20 percent of the people were free to roam about the city. It took over a year to restore control. As a result, we spent most of our human resources on extra security. We are under a lot of pressure to keep things in order.*

    *When I'm thirty-seven, I share the duties of ruler with my father. At this time, a major earthquake destroys most of the city. As a result, control was broken. I know that the end is near. I'm feeling anxious, upset, uneasy, tense, nervous, irritable, and have trouble sleeping. After nine days, the mob storms our palace, kills our guards, steals our treasures, and finds our hiding place.*

*"I am hiding with my wife and two of my children. I am trembling and shaking in full-blown panic. I hear loud voices and angry words. I hear people screaming. I see blood flowing down the halls. My two children and wife are grabbed and killed with axes and other tools. The angry men grab me and yell, "Get him! Get him! Kill him! Kill him!" They are wild eyed! They say I am responsible. I spit on one and he hits me with a board, breaking my nose and knocking out several teeth. Blood is gushing down my face.*

*"I am dragged from the hiding place to a central area. I am tied, and twenty-five or so march around me and torture me by striking me with different objects. I lose consciousness as they begin to stab me with knives. For a while, part of my soul stays in me while most of it leaves and rises above my body as they mutilate me after I am dead. Then they drag my dead body through the streets. My spirit watches and feels anger toward them. After a day of this, they build a huge fire and burn my body to ashes.*

*"I stay around for over three hundred years possessing different people. I watch the country continue to fall apart. Finally I go to the Light and I review my life. From heaven, I see that it was a dark life in a dark place. I can look inside myself and see that I was filled with demons. I can see how these demons had taken over my body. They stole my consciousness and became the functioning part of my body. They walked, talked, and functioned through my body. My mind, body, and soul were totally possessed and under their control.*

*"I can see the demonic influences in our daily lives. We tortured people in many different ways, such as mating human females with male animals; caging humans with wild cats; putting people in large vessels of water and*

*watching them drown; hanging people upside down and cutting a small vein and allowing them to slowly bleed to death; throwing knives at people for target practice; and hanging people by the neck and watching them twist until they died; etc. The heavenly beings allowed me to understand the wrongs of my arrogant, selfish, and self-centered attitude. I see how wrong it was to torture, slaughter, and kill other human beings for fun."*

From heaven, I can see different problems I brought from that life to the current life, such as feelings of anxiety and panic, a critical and judgmental attitude, lacking an emotional attachment to others, and living an isolated life with constant worry.

- *"I am a thirty-five-year-old male living in Dalor City, located in north central part of Atlantis. My name is Zeb and this is 18,250 BC. I am a physician's assistant, almost like a nurse. I grew up in different dorms since I was a baby. I never saw my parents. I lived in a dorm where kids were selected to go to school and become some type of a professional person. I went to a school located in the dorm compound for fifteen years and became a male nurse. It was decided for me by the higher government officials and the ruler. I did not have a choice. Most people in other dorms never go to school and are taught only the basics of reading, writing, and arithmetic in the dorms. I work in a clinic located in the dorm compound, where dorm people are treated. There are no hospitals for them anymore. Only the rulers and the government officials outside the dorm compound have access to hospitals.*

  *"I am living in a male dorm near the clinic with other professional people. One day, as we are working in the clinic, we feel intense and violent tremors and the whole building starts to shake and stuff is falling all over and we are thrown around. We are able to run out of the building and escape. We stay out for about thirty-six hours. We are*

*scared and panicky. Dorm buildings are destroyed. I am feeling something different, but I am not sure what. There is nobody telling us what to do. After a while, we realize that somehow our thoughts and feelings were controlled and we were functioning like zombies or robots. This realization is making everybody furious and we want to find out who is responsible for that.*

"All the dorm people are wandering around and no one is trying to tell us what to do. We are wondering what is going on. People break into the government offices and find the records, categories, and compiled lists of the dorms by location, and names of people listed alphabetically and by identification numbers. We find databases on the computer. We put everything together and come to the conclusion that the rulers are responsible.

"We find out that most of the palace was destroyed and parts of the palace where the control system was installed are completely gone. As a result, the whole control and communication system was disconnected throughout the city, freeing all the people. Everybody is extremely hateful and revengeful, and the whole crowd goes through the palace and kills anybody who is still alive. Then we burn the whole place.

"The crowd goes through the city and finds all the government officials and kills them. It takes several weeks for things to settle down. I am mostly wandering around in the city without any restrictions or control. I find a broken-down hotel and decide to live there. Many people are leaving the country by the ships that come every couple of weeks, and about forty people are able to leave at a time. There is a big line and thousands are waiting for their turn. I meet a woman and live with her and we have a little girl. Food and water are scarce and life is hard.

"After a couple of years, we decide to leave the country by ship. I am hired as a paramedic and my wife has computer training, so she can also be valuable. We are on the ship for twenty-five days and then there is a violent storm.

*There are heavy winds, a heavy downpour of rain, and the waves are knocking the ship up and down in the water. We are in a cabin being knocked around, leading to bruises and injuries. This goes on for eight hours. In the meantime, water is coming in the ship and we are in the water up to the waist and the seawater is going in our nose, lungs, and eyes, causing problems. Finally, after ten hours, the ship is cracking apart and separating, and we are dumped into the sea. I am scared and panicky and do not want to die. I want to go to a land of freedom. I am feeling a lot of burning, choking, and suffocation, and I die.*

*"My spirit comes out and is shocked that I do not feel dead. I stay earthbound for many years because I have no idea where to go, until two angels find me and take me to heaven. As I look back from the Light (heaven), I see many problems coming from that life to the current life, such as high blood pressure due to rupture of the blood vessels, lung problems, eye bulging and irritation, and skin problems due to salt water."*

- *"I am a twenty-nine-year-old female living in Rowe City, located in the south central coastal area. My name is Ritz and this is 20,211 BC. I live in the basement of an old broken-down high-rise apartment building. There have been and continue to be natural disasters, such as earthquakes, fires, and floods, all over the city. Life is very hard because food and water are scarce and it is difficult living under the threat of being destroyed by a natural disaster.*

*"I live with my common-law husband and two children. We live in freedom. The ruling control ended over seventy-five years ago, when natural disasters destroyed the control system and a large segment of the population of the city was killed. Even the rulers were killed, by the natural disasters or by mobs of angry Atlanteans who had been imprisoned in the dorms. My grandparents spent part of their lives in the dorms, but after control ended, they lived in freedom. My parents lived all their lives in freedom.*

*"I am a teacher and teach young children in a neighborhood school. I've had no formal training. However, my mother taught me a lot about teaching and I seem to have a natural gift to teach children. My two children are very sick with upper respiratory infections. They have very high fever and die within ten days of one another. I have a deep sadness inside my heart and I get the idea to leave this place for good.*

*"There is an opportunity to leave the country and we take advantage of it. We don't have much money or influence, but we work out an arrangement with the ship's captain. I will cook and do domestic work while traveling, and my husband, who is a gifted handyman, will help with the ship's maintenance. His skills are in demand and that is the main reason we are able to get this ship.*

*"We board the ship and head for Europe. This uneventful trip takes fifteen months and we sail to the coast of what is now Portugal. We leave the ship and go inland, living off the land for almost six months. We discover a few Atlanteans living in small camps. All are helpful, although somewhat reserved and mostly putting themselves first.*

*"I'm almost thirty-two when my husband suffers from appendicitis. I get the services of an Atlantean physician who operates in the field but without proper facilities. My husband dies in two days. Now I'm alone in the camp. It is a place with small shelters made from wood and rocks. Life is rough, but safer than it has been.*

*"At the age of thirty-five, I'm on a walk with other Atlanteans. We are picking fruit when, suddenly, I have a dizzy spell. I fall and strike my head on a sharp rock and become unconscious. I'm taken back to the camp but never regain consciousness. My spirit leaves my body in four days. I stay around for almost fifty years and then am helped by an angel to heaven.*

*"From heaven, I see this was a difficult life to live. It was emotionally draining and depressing. I lost my two*

*young children and a few years later lost my husband. I
lived in fear of natural disasters most of my life.*

*"I realize that my plan was to be born in Atlantis and
become a rescue worker for the people of Atlantis. I was
supposed to coordinate people, arranging for masses of
people to leave the continent of Atlantis. This was important because people could be removed from this dark and
unsafe place and go somewhere to lead a positive and productive life. My plan did not materialize. I became influenced early on as the fear of the natural disasters opened
me up to darkness.*

*"From heaven, I see that many of my problems came
from that life to the current life, such as irrational fears of
not finding peace and stability, hopelessness and helplessness, no motivation, lack of direction, and not following
through my career goals."*

## Problems Coming From Atlantis

According to heavenly beings, the problems coming from
Atlantis are divided into those that are physical and those that
are spiritual. When genetic modifications were made in the
brain, different chemicals were produced in different quantities, not always for the betterment of human beings. Most of
those genes have left the human race and the animals. The
problems we see now primarily come from the foods we eat
leading to physical and emotional problems, such as cramps,
bloating, diarrhea, allergic reactions and hives, weight gain,
sleepiness and lethargy after eating, being hungry, etc., and
dysfunction of the nervous system. Perhaps even a more
drastic problem is that the spiritual imprint on the DNA is
lacking. So the saying that the "spirit is willing, but the flesh
is weak" has a sort of basis in fact. Atlanteans did not realize or think of it when they made genetic modifications.
The selection process for picking the genes to go into the
reproductive cells is much more selective in animate beings
like humans and animals, in whom the variant genes drop

out very quickly. But with plants, the selection process for putting the DNA into the seeds is not as discriminating. That means we may never be able to get rid of these plants, not without identifying them and purposely eliminating them.

These genetic modifications are causing physical, emotional, mental, and spiritual problems. The spiritual problems are the real reason for mental illness, because lack of proper spirit can appear as mental illness. Those who are born normal and are more sensitive to the spirit-lacking foods that cause allergies when the person eats those plants and grains. Chemicals from the plants do not interact properly with the brain, causing different problems.

Devices in the neck caused some brain damage, attention deficit disorder, petit mal epilepsy, feelings of being controlled, paranoia, aggression, schizophrenia, dissociative disorder, feelings like somebody is inserting their thoughts or taking away thoughts from them in that life and in the current life. I see that when the devices were put into babies, they lost soul parts from that area of the neck and are in the possession of demons. In this lifetime, demons are putting dark devices in that place through those soul parts. They look like black rods. Through these dark devices, they are creating similar symptoms in people in the current life that they experienced in those lives.

# Time Line

|  |  |  |
|---|---|---|
|  | First human soul infused on Earth | 3 ½ million years ago |
| **First Alien Group** | | |
| (1) | Pharoni Vegans or Pleadians (Human-like) | 1 million years ago |
| (2) | Grays or Epsilon Eraidante (with round eyes) | 800,000 years ago |
| (3) | Sirians (like an insect or reptile or a praying mantis) | 770,000 years ago |
| **Second Alien Group** | | |
| (1) | Chikanse (bug- or insect-like) | 250,000 years ago |
| (2) | N-hante (reptilian or lizard-like) | 200,000 years ago |
| (3) | Kicks (in sounds and growls) | 150,000 years ago |
| (4) | Zipson or Capella (human-like – tall and slim - 6'6") | 70,000 years ago |
| (5) | Med-dac or Kubold (human-like – short and stocky - 4' to 5') | 50,000 years ago |
|  | Lamuria -Tribe transplanted | 200,000 years ago |
|  | Lamuria - Destroyed | 70,000 years ago |
|  | Atlantis began | 130,000 years ago |
|  | Atlantis flourished positively | 100,000 years ago |
|  | Lamurians contacted Atlanteans | 80,000 years ago |
|  | Golden Age in Atlantis | 70,000-50,000 years ago |
|  | Fall of Atlantean culture (slavery began) | 50,000 years ago |
|  | Atlantis dispersed and destroyed | 20,000 years ago |
|  | Stone Age | In 2 generations - 60 years |
|  | Ice Age began | 50,000 years ago |
|  | Ice Age peaked | 20,000 years ago |
|  | Ice Age declined | 10,000 years ago |

# AFTERTHOUGHTS

The scientific history of mankind is far longer than anyone has previously conceived. There will undoubtedly be negative reactions to these revelations. Many parallels exist between the olden times and the current times in which technological advances are making new and amazing inventions possible. Although the current picture of Atlantis is a place of great technology and a place of sweetness and Light, but in fact according to my patients there were extremely bad times in Atlantis which have been forgotten, primarily because humanity developed a collective amnesia-a total rejection of Atlantean culture and Atlantean technology.

Atlanteans had a much better understanding of the biochemical nature of the brain psychology. So as they worked with humanity, they were able to access parts of the brain which current psychiatric and psychological practice cannot compare. This was the basis for their control mechanism. They had a much finer understanding of the electronic nature of the brain, which enabled them to create the electronic circuits that would impress on the brain and put it under the control of the person who had the control device.

In general, the rulers of Atlantis did not broadcast specific commands to certain people. The general form of their control was to broadcast feelings of contentment, feelings that this is the way the world should be, feelings of wanting to do their best for their master, for their city, for their God. Then the rulers controlled those feelings and thoughts. They defined what was best for the city and the masters. This was a very effective control mechanism.

In current American culture people view the American flag with reverence. The flag does not represent cloth or different colors, but it does represent ideals and national purpose. If anyone defaces or desecrates the flag, they do not just damage a piece of cloth, which in fact that is all they are doing. It is seen by the population as devastation of the national purpose, as an expression of contempt for everything they hold dear. This can be seen as an example of controlling the population by giving them a symbol or a purpose which is outside of themselves. This is the type of control they practiced in Atlantis.

If we examine everyday life and religion as it is lived in this current culture, we can come up with numerous examples of implanted ideas which came from outside of a person that gives extraordinary significance and purpose in the lives of the people. In their own ways, they are a control mechanism. For example, the news is accepted by the population in our culture as being sacred. "The news will not lie to us," and it makes an ideal control mechanism for implanting ideas in people's heads.

In the current time technologically we are as advanced as Atlantis was during its peak time. Because of their lack of spirituality and selfishness Atlanteans ended up destroying the whole Atlantis. This is an important lesson for the whole humanity now that if we are not careful; we can end up destroying our country, the whole planet and even the whole solar system.

In Volume II of "An Amazing Human Journey," you will read about what happened after the dispersion from Atlantis and how things went downhill rapidly. How people underwent a complete revulsion and avoidance of technology, and in three or four generations, they completely forgot that the technology had ever existed. The great-grandparents did not speak of it. Once the technological decent began, people abandoned the cities and went back to the Stone Age. This was rapid, and humanity was literally reduced to wandering the Earth, living in caves. They lost agriculture, lost practically all their skills, and had to redevelop from scratch. It happened worldwide. In Volume II, you will also read what happened to humanity after Atlantis till now. How humans progressed very slowly spiritually and technologically over the years till God sent many spiritual teachers and masters to sprout spirituality on Earth. You will also read how many alien aces were inspired to give us different technologies over the years and also during the present time, how we all incarnate on other planets and why, and different reasons for the current abductions by aliens, and our future interactions with different alien races.

You will also read in Volume II that we humans are not alone in this journey. We have had many different types of beings working with us and helping us along the way, beings such as insects animals, plants and elementals like Undines - the water elementals, sylphs - the air elementals, salamanders – the fire elementals, and Earth. Also, beings like gnomes, mermaids, and fairies are working with us, even though most of us cannot see them. Insects, plants, and elementals bring a lot of Light to Earth because they live short lives. They have very little dark energy and they spread Light on Earth.

You will also read how astrology plays an important role in our journey and how intricately we are connected to the masters of our solar system and how thy help us with everything we do every day.

You will learn about the mysteries of different monuments and the power places on Earth, and the crop circles, and the important role they will play during the transition of Planet Earth and the human beings from the third dimension to the fifth dimension.

Review Requested:   If you loved this book, would you please provide a review at Amazon.com?